ADVANCED MANAGEMENT ACCOUNTING

ROBERT S. KAPLAN

Dean
Graduate School of Industrial Administration
Carnegie-Mellon University

 Prentice/Hall International, Inc.

Library of Congress Cataloging in Publication Data

KAPLAN, ROBERT S.
  Advanced management accounting.

  Bibliography
  Includes index.
  1. Managerial accounting. I. Title
HF5635.K15   658.1′511   81-21118
ISBN 0-13-011395-6   AACR2

Editorial/production supervision and interior design: Linda Mason
Manufacturing buyer: Ray Keating

To:
Ellen, Jennifer, and Dina

Printed in the United States of America
10 9 8 7 6 5 4

ISBN 0-13-011395-6

Prentice-Hall International, Inc., *London*
Prentice-Hall of Australia Pty. Limited, *Sydney*
Prentice-Hall of Canada, Ltd., *Toronto*
Prentice-Hall of India Private Limited, *New Delhi*
Prentice-Hall of Japan, Inc., *Tokyo*
Prentice-Hall of Southeast Asia Pte. Ltd., *Singapore*
Whitehall Books Limited, *Wellington, New Zealand*
Prentice-Hall, Inc., *Englewood Cliffs, New Jersey*

Prentice-Hall Series in Accounting
Charles T. Horngren, Editor

AUDITING: AN INTERGRATED APPROACH, 2/E
Arens/Loebbecke

FINANCIAL STATEMENT ANALYSIS
Foster

FINANCIAL ACCOUNTING: PRINCIPLES AND ISSUES, 2/E
Granof

INTRODUCTION TO FINANCIAL ACCOUNTING
Horngren

INTRODUCTION TO MANAGEMENT ACCOUNTING, 5/E
Horngren

COST ACCOUNTING: A MANAGERIAL EMPHASIS, 5/E
Horngren

**CPA PROBLEMS AND APPROACHES TO SOLUTIONS, 5/E
VOLUMES I & II**
Horngren/Leer

ADVANCED MANAGEMENT ACCOUNTING
Kaplan

DICTIONARY FOR ACCOUNTANTS, 6/E
Kohler

A NEW INTRODUCTION TO FINANCIAL ACCOUNTING, 2/E
May/Mueller/Williams

AUDITING PRINCIPLES, 5/E
Stettler

BUDGETING, 4/E
Welsch

Robert S. Kaplan is Dean of the Graduate School of Industrial Administration at Carnegie-Mellon University. He has been on the faculty of GSIA since 1968, becoming a tenured full professor in 1973. He received a B.S. and M.S. in Electrical Engineering from M.I.T. and a Ph.D in Operations Research from Cornell University. He has contributed more than forty articles in monographs and the leading professional journals in accounting and management science. He received the AICPA Accounting Literature Award in 1971. Dr. Kaplan is an active member of the American Accounting Association, serves as Consulting Editor for *The Accounting Review*, and *The Journal of Accounting and Economics*, and is on the editorial board of the *Journal of Accounting Research*. He has been a consultant to CPA firms and financial institutions on the application of statistical methods to auditing and financial analysis. Recent research interests have included mathematical models in accounting and auditing, empirical research on the uses of financial accounting information, and financial analysis of the Social Security System.

Dr. Kaplan serves on the Board of Directors of the Pittsburgh Branch of the Federal Reserve Bank of Cleveland, and on the Board of Directors of the Pittsburgh Chamber of Commerce. He is chairman of the AACSB Task Force on the Supply and Demand of Ph.D's for Business Schools.

CONTENTS

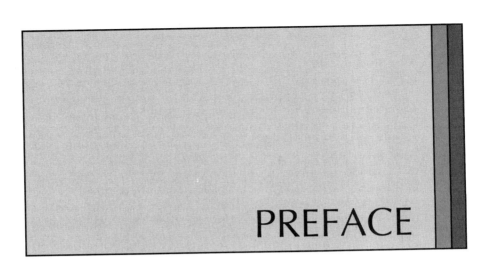

PREFACE

The purpose of this text is to teach students how to apply analytic reasoning and use formal models when designing and evaluating management accounting systems. Management accounting systems collect, classify, summarize, analyze, and report information that will assist managers in their decision making and control activities. Historically, management accounting has evolved from the need to assign costs to products for external financial reports. Introductory cost accounting textbooks initially emphasized these cost allocation issues but during the past twenty years, these texts have expanded their coverage to include the use of cost data for decisions and control within the firm. Thus, these texts now treat topics such as cost-volume-profit analysis, budgeting and planning, capital budgeting, and variance analysis of standard cost systems.

Research in management accounting has established that the underlying disciplines for the field include economics, operations research, statistics and behavioral science. Despite the introduction into the management accounting literature of the new ideas from these disciplines, most introductory cost accounting textbooks have modified their contents in only a minor way. For example, textbooks have introduced statistical analysis, decision theory, or operations research models only by adding chapters on these subjects at the end of the book. Students, therefore, have yet to be exposed to a systematic and in-depth analytic treatment of management accounting topics. This book closes the gap between management accounting research and practice.

The book assumes that students have previously taken an introductory cost accounting course that covered topics such as job order costing, full and direct costing, standard costing with flexible budgeting, variance analysis and budgeting. These topics are generally well treated in introductory courses and require little expansion in an advanced textbook. The focus in this book will be on the firm's planning and control decisions that require a more sophisticated approach than the rule-of-thumb procedures advocated for traditional cost accounting problems.

Students should also have taken courses in economics, statistics (including introductory probability theory), and management science. Management accounting topics provide a superb opportunity for students to apply techniques such as regression analysis, linear programming, and decision theory in actual managerial settings. The book serves as a synthesis for skills learned in quantitative courses by demonstrating their role in the important decisions of the firm. The use of this book in an advanced cost or managerial accounting course can be the capstone of the student's program, integrating and synthesizing discipline-based courses in the study of the firm's planning and control activities.

The cost accounting chapters (Chapters 1 to 12) are designed so that each topic is introduced by a simple numerical example. Assumptions and limitations of the example are then made explicit and extended by use of formal models and analytic procedures. In this way much of a chapter is still accessible to students even without all the analytic prerequisites.

The book opens in Chapter 1 with a historical perspective of management accounting starting from its origins in cost allocation for financial reporting purposes. Recent trends, 1) the decision-oriented approach, 2) the information-economics philosophy, and 3) the current research focus on management accounting in a multi-person setting, are identified and summarized. Extra emphasis is placed in this opening chapter on the information-economics paradigm so that instructors who want to build their course around this framework can introduce the key concepts early in the course. Instructors who wish to de-emphasize the information-economics approach can skip this material and pick it up later in Chapter 8. Since the information-economics approach requires previous training in decision theory, the approach selected may depend on the educational background of the students.

Chapter 2 reviews important cost concepts that arise constantly in decision and control models; fixed and variable costs, incremental and escapable costs, sunk costs, and opportunity costs. It also discusses procedures and problems when collecting cost data for analysis. Chapters 3 and 4 contain an extensive treatment of statistical analysis, primarily regression procedures, for understanding the variation of cost behavior. The goal of the statistical procedures is to identify the fixed, variable, and incremental costs of a given activity. The emphasis is on proper model formulation and interpretation rather than on the details of calculating regression coefficients or summary statistics of a regression. We assume that either students or the instructor will have access to a computer-based statistical package for performing the actual computations. Topics in these chapters include dealing with auto-correlation, multiple independent variables, collinearity, dummy variables, multiplicative and nonlinear relationships, and learning curve effects.

Chapters 5 and 6 study extensions to traditional cost-volume-profit analysis. Chapter 5, on deterministic extensions, treats nonlinear cost and revenue functions, multiple products, production and sales constraints, and multi-period C-V-P analysis. Chapter 6 introduces uncertainty into C-V-P analysis, characterizing the probability distribution of sales, obtaining estimates of probability distributions, multi-product C-V-P analysis under uncertainty, and decision theory approaches. These two chapters are more analytical than most in the book requiring background in linear programming, probability, and decision theory.

Chapter 7 provides a comprehensive survey on the role of cost data in pricing decisions. Many problems with the economist's deterministic rule of setting marginal revenue equal to marginal cost are discussed. The rationale is presented for full-cost pricing, target rate-of-return pricing, and incremental cost pricing. A brief section on strategic pricing for new products concludes the chapter.

Chapter 8 synthesizes the previous chapters, on cost data for product-related decisions, by developing the opportunity loss concept for measuring the effect on decisions of cost estimation errors. This chapter features the information-economics approach and uses, as an extended example, the estimation of cost parameters for standard inventory models. The chapter also includes an advanced topic, which may be omitted at the instructor's discretion, on measuring the opportunity losses caused by information delays.

Chapter 9 is an extension of traditional variance analysis to compute sales mix and sales volume variances. A decomposition approach to variance analysis is introduced for organizing systematically all the variances that can be computed when comparing actual to budgeted results.

Chapter 10 develops statistical models to aid the decision on when to investigate cost variances. Simple percentage rules-of-thumb are presented with extensions to statistical and decision theory models.

Chapters 11 and 12 provide decision and control perspectives to two topics in cost allocation; service department costs and joint/by-product costs. Both chapters open with intuitive explanations for allocating these costs. The consequences of alternative cost allocation procedures are illustrated with simple numerical examples. Chapter 11 contains an extended treatment of the simultaneous equation procedure for allocating the costs of interacting service departments. Chapter 12 develops a procedure, based on a nonlinear programming formulation of the firm's sales and production opportunities, to allocate joint costs in a way that is compatible with decisions on joint and by-products.

Chapters 13–17 focus on the management and control of decentralized operations. Chapter 13 discusses the benefits and costs of decentralization, and the role of performance measures to motivate and evaluate local managers. Chapter 14 treats the problems associated with measuring the profit of decentralized units with particular emphasis on the transfer pricing problem. The properties of market prices, marginal costs, fully allocated costs, and negotiated prices for pricing the internal transfer of goods between decentralized units are fully developed. Chapter 15 extends the analysis of divisional profit to include the value of investment in a division. The strengths and weaknesses of return-on-investment and residual income for evaluating investment center performance are presented, including issues of the appropriate depreciation method, effect of price level changes, and selection of assets to include in the investment base.

Chapter 16 introduces the vital role of management incentive contracts for understanding the critical decisions of managers. This chapter is an outgrowth of research and phenomena in the 1970s that highlight the challenges of devising a management compensation system to motivate goal congruence between the managers and the owners of the firm. Various compensation plans are analyzed in the context of an informal risk-sharing model between owners and managers.

The book concludes, in Chapter 17, with an introduction to the use of formal models for studying management accounting topics. This chapter requires a greater background in decision theory and utility theory than any of the previous chapters. It serves to illustrate contemporary research directions and analytic methods in management accounting. Topics addressed include optimal risk-sharing and incentive contracts, truth-inducing budgeting schemes, and information acquisition for resource allocation to decentralized units.

COURSE ORGANIZATION

The book can be used in a flexible manner. By spending up to one week on each chapter, the book can be used for a fifteen-week course. Each chapter contains a significant amount of new material that can be reviewed and discussed for at least one class session. Problems and cases at the end of each chapter can occupy the one or two more sessions available for each chapter. Instructors working under a quarter (10-week) system can choose to spend two sessions for most chapters (one session reviewing the textual material, the other to go over problems and cases).

Alternatively, instructors can choose to select from among the chapters and work more intensively on these. For example, a course concentrating on cost accounting topics would emphasize the first half of Chapter 1, Chapters 2 to 7, and Chapters 9 to 12. A course featuring the information economics approach, with applications to management control systems, could select Chapters 1 to 4, Chapters 8 and 10, and Chapters 13–17. At Carnegie-Mellon, graduate courses are taught in 7½-week mini-semesters and we have found it useful to split the advanced management accounting course into two parts; the first course emphasizes cost accounting topics and covers Chapters 1 to 12. The second course features management control topics and uses Chapters 13 to 17 plus supplements of outside readings and cases.

Each chapter contains problems and cases that require the student to apply the concepts of the chapter. Short problems require the student to apply procedures developed in the chapter on actual or simulated data. Cases, available for most chapters, involve the students in more unstructured situations, drawn from actual company experiences. With the cases, students must focus on the critical issues and propose recommended solutions. Both the problems and case material will provide challenging assignments to enhance the students' learning experiences. Enough material is provided for at least two problem and case sessions per chapter.

Instructors can use this text with supplementary books. Books of readings in management accounting are available so that students can have an opportunity to read the research articles that developed ideas featured in this text. Many reading books are available but Rappaport, Alfred (ed.), *Information for Decision Making, Third Edition* (Englewood Cliffs, N.J.: Prentice-Hall), 1982, contains readings specifically designed to supplement the material in this textbook.

Another good supplement is a book of cases. I have been fortunate to be able to draw cases from each of two excellent collections:

Shank, John, *Contemporary Managerial Accounting* (Englewood Cliffs, N.J.: Prentice-Hall), 1981.

Barrett, Edgar, and William Bruns, *Case Problems in Management Accounting and Control* (Homewood, Ill.: Irwin), 1981.

Both of these books contain many excellent cases that would be fine supplements in an advanced cost or management accounting course.

ACKNOWLEDGMENTS

Many people provided invaluable assistance to me. My colleague and mentor, Yuji Ijiri, read each chapter and provided extremely helpful criticism and suggestions. Anthony Atkinson provided feedback on all drafts of this book and, even more, generated an entirely new set of problems for me to use to illustrate the concepts developed in the book. I benefited from the insightful review of Charles Horngren who also provided encouragement for this project from its outset and direct help by allowing me to use selected problems from the fifth edition of his *Cost Accounting* text. Other colleagues to whom I am indebted for their review of chapters include Stanley Baiman (particularly the chapters on decentralization and management control), Katherine Schipper, and James Noel. The commissioned reviews of Ronald Hilton, Joanne Collins, Soliman Soliman, and Douglas Johnson assisted me in preparing the final draft of the manuscript. The reviews of Ron Hilton, W. Bruce Johnson, and Timothy Crichfield of the first draft of four key chapters helped to structure my thinking at an early stage of the project.

I am especially thankful for the people and organizations that allowed me to use their problem and case material. I have already mentioned the many new problems developed by Tony Atkinson specifically for this book. Over a period of several years, Rene Manes sent me problems he had developed to teach advanced cost accounting concepts. George Foster contributed cases he had developed and used at Stanford. John Shank allowed me to use cases from his casebook and Ed Barrett and Bill Bruns granted similar permission for cases from their collection. Cases and problem material were also contributed by Ed Deakin, Felix Kollaritsch, and Ron Hilton. I appreciate the permissions granted by the Harvard Business School for use of their copyrighted case material and by the Institute of Management Accounting for use of problems from the Certified Management Accounting examinations. All these contributions provided a valuable diversity of material that will enable students to test their knowledge of the ideas developed in each chapter.

My secretary and administrative assistant, Eleanor Riess, typed almost all of the chapters and helped keep this project organized over its four-year lifetime, tasks over and beyond her normally heavy workload as a dean's secretary. Joan Velar also provided typing assistance, particularly chapter revisions and problem material.

At Prentice-Hall, Ron Ledwith provided encouragment from the outset, and helped keep my enthusiasm high for successful completion of the book. Linda Mason handled production aspects of the book with dispatch and Elinor Paige maintained a constant flow of communication from Prentice-Hall to me.

Finally, I must acknowledge the patience and understanding of my wife Ellen and children, Jennifer and Dina, from whom I took time normally available for family activities to work on this project during the past four summers.

INTRODUCTION:
Past, Present, and Future of Management Accounting

Management accounting is a system that collects, classifies, summarizes, analyzes, and reports information that will assist managers in their decision-making and control activities. Unlike financial accounting, where the primary emphasis is on reporting to people outside the firm, management accounting focuses on internal planning and control activities. Therefore, management accounting requires the collection and analysis not only of financial or cost data, but also data such as prices, sales backlog, product demands on capacity resources, and measures of physical quantities and capacities.

Because the internal planning and control procedures are not constrained by external reporting requirements, the management accounting system can use data that are less objective and less verifiable. Greater use can be made of forecasts or estimates, and uncertainty can be explicitly treated. Also opportunity costs, based on transactions not undertaken or from a formal model of the decision process, play a central role in management accounting. Ultimately, the test of a management accounting system is whether it motivates and assists managers in fulfilling all their organizational objectives in a timely and efficient manner.

Management accounting is a relatively recent phenomenon, especially when compared to the long historical development of financial reporting for external parties such as owners, creditors, regulators, and tax authorities. Cost accounting was the first manifestation of the current management accounting system. Cost accounting was developed to fill a need generated by the financial reporting process. Costs had to be allocated so that product-related expenditures could be separated between cost of goods sold and inventory. The emphasis was on fully allocating all costs in an objective and unambiguous way. People debated over which allocation method was more "accurate" or more "fair," but few doubted that research could eventually establish the actual costs of a given product. Horngren [1975] refers to this period as the search for "true costs" or the *absolute-truth approach*.

During the 1950s and 1960s, accountants gradually discovered that product costs, which had been constructed for financial reporting purposes, were being taken seriously by operating executives. Executives were using the cost of a product, as computed by accountants, as if it were a unique unambiguous figure upon which decisions on product profitability, pricing, product mix, and management control could be based. With a greater realization of these internal uses of cost accounting data, accountants began devising cost accounting procedures that would be most relevant to particular decisions. Emphasis shifted from external to internal users of cost accounting data. One could now think of recording cost data for internal purposes in a manner different from that used for external purposes. For example, while fully absorbed cost was required for financial and tax reporting purposes, direct costing was advocated as more relevant for internal decision making and control.

As accountants sought cost accounting procedures that would be relevant for many different planning decisions and control actions, they realized that cost aggregations or allocations should vary as a function of the decisions being made with the cost data. No unique cost assignment was equally relevant for all decisions. This was the start of management accounting, which emphasizes cost allocation for internal decisions and control rather than for financial reporting. Horngren [1975] refers to this user-oriented or decision-model approach to cost accounting as the *conditional-truth approach*; that is, truth depends on how the cost assignment will be used. This approach will be featured throughout the book.

In the late 1960s and early 1970s, a third school of management accounting thought developed that attempted to subsume the two previous approaches into a broader conceptual framework.[1] This *information-economics approach* viewed a management accounting system as a particular type of information system. Recent developments in statistical decision theory and economics under uncertainty had shown that information is a commodity that can be purchased and sold much like other commodities.[2] As an economic commodity, it is not appropriate to talk about a "need" for information without regard to the cost of acquiring and producing it. With the information-economics approach, we attempt to measure the *demand* for information, a demand based on the value of the information, and the cost of supplying it, including the cost of accuracy and timeliness. Horn-

---

[1] Joel Demski and Gerald Feltham were the initiators and missionaries for this approach. The interested reader can trace the development in Feltham [1968], Feltham and Demski [1970], Demski [1980], Feltham [1972], and Demski-Feltham [1976].

[2] Information has some special properties that make it different from traditional commodities. Unlike bread, the consumption of information by one individual does not preclude other individuals from consuming (or using) the same quantity of information. Thus, information is what economists call a public good. The economics of public goods is more subtle and complex than the economics of private goods (such as bread or apples).

gren [1975] classifies this as the *costly-truth approach* to cost accounting.[3] The value of the information is derived from an explicit model of (1) the environment faced by the decision maker, (2) the actions available to the decision maker, (3) the possible outcomes as a function of the actual environment and actions taken, (4) the role and cost of the information system in signaling the state of the environment and the outcome of the decisions, and (5) the risk attitude or preferences of the decision maker.

It is difficult to quarrel with the basic idea behind the information-economics approach. It is conceptually correct; how can one disagree that we should attempt to place a value on an information system and compare this value to the cost of supplying the information system? To date, however, the formal treatment of the benefits and costs of an information system has not proven operationally useful in enabling us to develop improved cost accounting systems. We shall elaborate on this approach later in the chapter.

To bring our brief history of management accounting up to date, developments since 1975 have recognized that an information and reporting system has an effect on individuals. While the information-economics approach stresses the impact of an information system on the beliefs of decision makers (more precisely, it revises their probability distributions about events and states of nature), the newer approach recognizes that the mere act of measuring and reporting the actions of individuals will affect these actions. This approach was foreshadowed by Ijiri [1975], who stressed that an accounting system is not just another information system for the firm. Rather, an accounting system is unique in that it is a part of a system of *accountability*. Resources have been entrusted to a manager. The management accounting system records and reports on the sum total of all transactions with these resources and provides an evaluation or interpretation of the consequences of these transactions to the supplier of the resources.

This accountability concept is now being developed in a formal context in which the information system is determined endogenously as the result of the contracting activities between economic agents. In this paradigm, when one agent, say the owner or central management, hires another agent, such as the manager of a decentralized unit, to manage a set of resources, the employment contract includes not only a specification of the resources under control and a permissible set of actions but also a performance measure by which the hired agent will be evaluated. The performance measure must be based on variables observable to both agents and must be able to withstand the maximizing actions of the hired agent. Thus, a measure based on a management forecast may not be a good performance measure because it can be manipulated by the divisional manager, without obvious recourse by the owner or central management.

---

[3] Strictly speaking, this appellation is a misnomer, since the concept of "truth" never arises in the information-economics approach. Individuals may misrepresent their information if a benefit-cost analysis shows this to be optimal.

With this approach, information from the management accounting system provides the basis for determining and enforcing contracts among economic agents. Different information implies different contracts, different action choices, different allocations of rewards between agents, and different levels of efficiency. The objective for which information is generated, then, is not "truth" but economic efficiency in the contracts among managers or between managers and owners. That is, contracts are determined with a view to maintaining local incentives while diversifying some of the risk away from the local manager. This view of the accounting system as being derived from the act of contracting between economic agents has already enabled researchers to understand the use of budget-based contracts[4] and certain variance investigation models.[5] But this research is still at a preliminary stage. It has helped us to appreciate the critical role of accounting systems and observability in devising performance-management systems. It alerts us to ways in which the management system will affect the actions of managers. But it has not yet yielded dramatically new insights into the design of cost accounting systems. We provide an introduction to this literature in Chapter 17, and the theme of contracting between maximizing managers runs throughout the discussion on decentralization in Chapters 13 through 16.

In the remainder of this chapter we discuss the different approaches to management accounting in more depth and indicate the items that will be stressed in the text. Because the information-economics approach will not be pursued throughout the text, we will outline its fundamental concepts more fully than others in this chapter.

FULL-COST ALLOCATIONS

Historically, cost accounting procedures have emphasized methods for allocating costs to products and departments. Fixed costs have been divided by standard or actual activity measures to obtain a fixed cost per unit (even though this is virtually a contradiction in terms). Joint costs and other common costs have been allocated based on reasonable but still arbitrary measures.

In some circumstances, these full-cost allocations seem necessary. The Cost Accounting Standards Board developed rules governing the accumulation and allocation of costs for government contracts. Many of these contracts are based on the contractor's costs or are subject to renegotiation if contractor's profits (defined as revenues less "costs") are deemed excessive. The purpose of CASB

---

[4] See Harris-Raviv [1978] and Demski-Feltham [1978].

[5] See Baiman-Demski [1980] and Baiman [1979].

standards should not be to determine the "true costs" of the contracted goods and services, since this is an unattainable ideal. Rather, where actual monetary payments are affected by definitions of "cost," it will be important to have objective and well-defined procedures for accumulating costs. Otherwise there will be endless debate and litigation over what items are properly included in "costs." In this application, the resulting definitions of cost may neither be useful for decisions nor serve as a useful basis for evaluating and rewarding managers. The definitions are the consequence of a political process (in this case, a governmental committee that solicited outside opinions) and are agreed to by contracting parties to facilitate a commercial transaction.

Fully allocated costs are also important for regulated companies. Price-setting regulatory agencies require cost estimates to judge whether revenues are sufficient to earn an adequate rate of return after costs have been recovered. Problems of the allocation of joint and common costs are particularly important when a regulated company provides many different kinds of services. For example, American Telephone and Telegraph equipment is used for local calls, long distance calls, international calls, data transmissions, television and radio program transmission, private-line telephone and telegraph service, and outward and inward Wide Area Telecommunications Service (WATS), among others. AT&T has competition on some of these services and has a monopoly on others. Rate-setting commissions, principally the Federal Communications Commission, are now requiring AT&T to develop a fully distributed cost allocation system for each class of service. This involves allocating extensive fixed-asset costs in some manner to all classes of service using these assets. AT&T is also defending a variety of private and public antitrust cases by justifying pricing policies as a fair recovery of its costs. Such regulatory and judicial proceedings should provide a continued source of employment for cost accountants able to develop convincing or creative stories to justify one cost allocation system or another.

This book will not discuss allocation of costs for these external constituencies, since traditional cost allocation methods are well covered in introductory texts. There is also an empirical question, to which we do not have an answer, as to why companies continue to use fully allocated costs for internal decision and control purposes. Full costs apparently serve for managers as a better proxy for long-term opportunity costs than do the short-term variable costs that seem most relevant for our decision models. Perhaps our decision models under certainty are not sufficiently rich to capture the value of fully allocated costs for internal planning and control purposes. In this case, as research continues on the fourth generation of management accounting theory—that of optimal contracting between economic agents—we may gain further insights into why companies devote so much attention to fully allocated product and division costs. Once we learn why they are doing this, we will be in a better position to suggest improved methods for accomplishing the allocation. An interesting start in this direction has been provided by Zimmerman [1979].

In the past twenty years we have greatly increased our understanding of how cost data and, more broadly, how all data about a firm's assets, liabilities, and products can be used to assist management in its planning and control decisions. Numerous articles have been written applying management science, statistical analysis, and economic theory to these decisions.[6] These articles, however, have had relatively little impact on current practice. One possible explanation for the limited adoption of quantitative models in cost accounting applications is that these models are not addressing important problems; they would make little contribution to improved decision making and control within the firm. This may be true but an alternative explanation is that these models are not being adopted because they were not taught to current controllers and financial managers when they studied cost accounting.

Introductory cost accounting texts have concentrated on traditional issues—cost definitions, job order costing, budgeting (including capital budgeting), standard costs, variance analysis, cost allocation, direct and absorption costing. Analytic models are usually not stressed, and the most significant technique for improving planning and control decisions has been to develop the dichotomy between fixed and variable costs. More generally, incremental cost is the most advanced concept distinguishing these texts from those that could have been written twenty years ago.

The present text will show students the application of analytic techniques to important planning and control decisions of the firm. In this way, students may obtain a better appreciation for the relevance of analytic techniques for management accounting applications. The book, however, is not organized around a series of techniques, nor does it attempt to teach these techniques. We assume that students have learned analytic skills in their courses in operations research, probability, statistics, and economics. A management accounting course, even an advanced one, is hardly the place to learn the theory of mathematical programming or multiple regression. The book does provide a vehicle to learn *how* these techniques can be applied to interesting management accounting topics.

The key ideas in most chapters can be understood without extensive training in mathematics or statistics. On occasion, however, and as required to develop a particular point, quantitative material at the level of an introductory course in management science, microeconomics, or probability and statistics may be used. Thus, at various places the book will use statistics (hypothesis testing and multiple regression), probability theory (Bayes' rule and decision analysis), elementary differential and integral calculus, linear algebra, linear and nonlinear programming, and microeconomic analysis including an introduction to utility theory.

---

[6] Many articles with particular relevance to cost accounting issues are surveyed in Kaplan [1977].

When these techniques are introduced, the emphasis will not be on manual computation of ordinary least-squares estimates or simplex tableaus. Analysts usually have access to computer packages that compute regression coefficients or linear programming solutions. Although the text can be read and understood by a student who is unable to use a computer, access to statistical and management science computer programs will be of significant benefit in working the problems in several chapters.

Chapters 2 through 4 are concerned with classifying and estimating costs. The extremely important dichotomy between fixed and variable costs is fully discussed by introductory cost accounting texts. But how to obtain reasonable estimates of variable or incremental costs is not trivial. We focus here on techniques for obtaining good estimates of fixed and variable costs—or, more generally, incremental costs. Cost-volume-profit analysis leading to product-mix decisions is one of the firm's most important planning decisions. Chapters 5 and 6 discuss extensions of traditional C-V-P analysis to conditions of multiple products, production constraints, and uncertainty. Chapter 7, on pricing decisions, also contains an extensive analysis of an important planning decision.

Other planning decisions of the firm include capital-budgeting and inventory-management decisions. Capital-budgeting analysis is covered extensively in introductory management accounting texts and in introductory and advanced finance courses. This topic is therefore not repeated in this text. Inventory management is best learned in production or operations management courses. Issues in cost measurement for inventory decision models are discussed in Chapter 8 in the context of estimating the value of obtaining accurate cost estimates for these models.

Chapters 9 and 10 focus on extensions to standard cost analysis and control. Again, introductory texts contain excellent discussions of standard cost systems, flexible budgets, analysis of cost variances, and the overall budgeting process. We have little to add to most of these discussions and we do not repeat them. Chapter 9 does provide a more complete decomposition analysis of profit and cost variances, which facilitates ex post analysis of operating results. Chapter 10 develops statistical models to help in deciding when to investigate a cost variance—a topic lightly covered, at best, in introductory texts.

Chapters 11 and 12, on allocating service department costs and joint costs, treat these common cost allocation issues from a decision-oriented viewpoint. The emphasis is on developing costing procedures compatible with and helpful in the decision and control processes. Both chapters start with relatively simple economic analysis but go on to treat more complex situations, using management science techniques of matrix algebra and nonlinear programming.

Thus, much of the book—Chapters 2 through 7 and 9 through 12—develops traditional cost accounting topics in the context of particular decision models or control procedures. Relevant costing procedures are developed as a function of the uses of the data. Many of the decision or control models will require nonfinancial information, data that are not measured in dollars. These data include physical quantities, capacity of resources, product demands on resources, back-logged orders, and lost sales. The user decision-model approach also highlights the importance of the opportunity costs of transactions not undertaken. These opportunity costs may be needed for a model but would not be measured by a traditional transactions-based accounting system.

The user decision-model approach can be criticized by advocates of the information-economics approach for not fully incorporating the cost of providing the information to the various decision models or for not formally evaluating the benefit of alternative costing approaches for particular decisions. This criticism is formally correct, but we still believe that the user decision-model approach is a necessary step before the complete information-evaluation approach can be applied. We have to know what can be done before we can decide whether it is worth doing. Therefore, in reading through the decision- and control-model chapters, the reader must maintain an implicit awareness that all the proposed analyses must still be subject to a benefit-cost analysis, even informally, to insure that proposed analytic procedures are not so costly or so unreliable that the promised benefits in improved decision making and control are not dissipated. The philos-ophy behind the heavy focus on user decision models is that a period of imple-mentation and experimentation is required before we can evaluate their utility in a formal benefit-cost approach. Introducing formal information-economics con-cepts throughout the book would make the implementation of even relatively simple analytic models seem too imposing.

INFORMATION ECONOMICS

The essence of the information-economics approach can be illustrated with a simple example. A company is contemplating the introduction of a new product but is unsure about its production costs. If production costs are high (H), the company will lose $125,000 on the product. If production costs are low (L), the company will earn $150,000 on the product. Based on past experience, the man-ager estimates that the probability of low production costs is 0.6. Symbolically we write $Pr(L) = 1 - Pr(H) = 0.6$. An expected-value (EV) calculation reveals that if the company introduces the product, the expected gain is

$$EV = 0.6(150,000) + 0.4(-125,000) = \$40,000,$$

and if the manager and company are risk neutral, the new product will be introduced.[7]

Suppose that the company has the option of installing a special cost ac-counting system at a cost of $10,000. This system will measure the cost of similar

---

[7] The situation in which the manager (or the company) is risk averse can be formally modeled by assuming a concave utility function for wealth. This complication is developed in Problem 1-1 at the end of the chapter.

items now being produced in the factory and give a prediction about whether the new product is going to be low-cost or high-cost. Unfortunately, the prediction is not 100 percent accurate. The manager believes that if the low-cost state (L) will occur, the system will predict low cost (we will call this signal y_1) only 60 percent of the time. That is,

$$\Pr(y_1 \mid L) = 0.6.$$

Therefore, even when the low-cost state occurs, the system will signal high cost (y_2) with probability 0.4. The system predicts much better if the actual state will be high cost (H). In this case, an incorrect low-cost signal (y_1) occurs only with probability 0.1 and the correct high-cost signal (y_2) occurs with probability 0.9.

To summarize, the manager has the option of buying the information system with two signals (y_1 or y_2) at a cost of \$10,000, with the following characteristics:

$$\Pr(y_1 \mid L) = 0.6, \qquad \Pr(y_1 \mid H) = 0.1,$$

$$\Pr(y_2 \mid L) = 0.4, \qquad \Pr(y_2 \mid H) = 0.9.$$

Should the manager use this noisy information system [noisy because it does not provide perfect signals, such that $\Pr(y_1 \mid L) = 1$ and $\Pr(y_2 \mid H) = 1$]?

We analyze this situation using our knowledge of conditional probability and Bayes' rule. First, we compute the likelihood of obtaining each signal:

$$\Pr(y_1) = \Pr(y_1 \mid L)\Pr(L) + \Pr(y_1 \mid H)\Pr(H)$$

$$= (0.6)(0.6) + (0.1)(0.4)$$

$$= 0.4.$$

Similarly,

$$\Pr(y_2) = 0.6.$$

Then we compute the probability of low and high cost, given either signal:

$$\Pr(L \mid y_1) = \frac{\Pr(y_1 \mid L)\Pr(L)}{\Pr(y_1)} = \frac{0.36}{0.40} = 0.9; \qquad \Pr(H \mid y_1) = 0.1,$$

$$\Pr(L \mid y_2) = \frac{\Pr(y_2 \mid L)\Pr(L)}{\Pr(y_2)} = \frac{0.24}{0.60} = 0.4; \qquad \Pr(H \mid y_2) = 0.6,$$

and then the expected value of introducing the product given either signal:

$$\text{EV} \mid y_1 = 0.9(150{,}000) + 0.1(-125{,}000) = 122{,}500,$$

$$\text{EV} \mid y_2 = 0.4(150{,}000) + 0.6(-125{,}000) = -15{,}000.$$

Therefore, if we obtain signal y_1 we will not change our initial decision; we will introduce the new product with even more confidence than before. If we obtain signal y_2, however, we will not introduce the product because the expected value is now negative. In this case, the signal from our special cost accounting system has changed our decision. This characteristic is a necessary but not sufficient condition for an information system to be cost effective. We still need to verify that the value of the information system in improving our decisions exceeds the cost of providing the system.

Before installing the cost accounting system, our expected value was $40,000. If we install the system and introduce the product if we receive signal y_1 but do not introduce it if we receive signal y_2, our expected value, including the $10,000 cost of the system, is

$$EV = Pr(y_1) \cdot EV \mid y_1 + Pr(y_2) \cdot 0 - 10,000$$

$$= (0.4)(122,500) + (0.6)(0) - 10,000$$

$$= 49,000 - 10,000$$

$$= 39,000.$$

The net expected value has decreased and we would not install the cost accounting system, since its $10,000 cost exceeds the $9,000 increase in expected benefits from improved decision making.

Although this is an idealized, highly simplified example, it highlights the principal features of the information-economics approach. We describe the cost accounting system, not in terms of whether it is accurate, but in terms of the probability revision it induces on the decision maker. A priori, the decision maker has a 0.6 probability that the low-cost state (L) will occur. After the signal is received from the information system, this probability is revised either upward to 0.9 if y_1 occurs or downward to 0.4 if y_2 occurs. The signal, y_1 or y_2, increases the expected value of the decision, but in this case the improvement is not sufficient to pay for the cost of installing the system.

The system would be more valuable if it were more accurate. Suppose that for $10,000 we could obtain a perfect information system; one for which $Pr(y_1 \mid L) = 1$ and $Pr(y_2 \mid H) = 1$. Then the system would be worth installing, since our analysis would yield

$$Pr(y_1) = Pr(L) = 0.6 \quad \text{and} \quad Pr(y_2) = Pr(H) = 0.4.$$

Obviously, we would introduce the product if y_1 were received and not introduce if y_2 were received, so that

$$EV = Pr(y_1) \cdot 150,000 + Pr(y_2) \cdot 0 - 10,000$$

$$= 80,000,$$

and the decision maker is clearly much better off than before.

Another way of obtaining the same result is to observe that receiving signal y_1 does not change the decision to introduce and hence is not useful to the decision maker (though the increased certainty may help the decision maker sleep better at night). But receipt of signal y_2 causes a major change in the decision and enables the decision maker to avoid a loss of \$125,000. Thus, with a probability of 0.4 [equal to $Pr(y_2)$], the information system saves \$125,000, so there is an expected savings of 0.4(125,000) = \$50,000. After deducting the \$10,000 cost of the information system, the net improvement in expected value is \$40,000 (thereby increasing EV from 40,000 to 80,000).

The information-economics paradigm is intellectually pleasing, since it provides a conceptual framework for evaluating any information system in terms of the characteristics of its signals—how they will affect the beliefs, actions, and outcomes in a decision-making environment. We can obtain quantitative estimates on the value of improved accuracy as a function of the cost. The problems with using this approach, however, are also obvious. In order to play the information-economics game, even in the very simple situations, we need to know:

1. All possible signals from the system $(y_1, y_2, \ldots)$.
2. The a priori probability of receiving each of these signals [$Pr(y_1)$, $Pr(y_2), \ldots$].
3. The effects of each signal on the beliefs of the decision maker [for example, $Pr(y_1 \mid L)$, $Pr(y_2 \mid H), \ldots$].
4. The effects of each signal on the actions of the decision maker (a calculation using Bayes' rule plus a completely specified decision model including the payoff functions).
5. The cost of the information system (\$10,000 in our simple example, but, in general, a difficult number to estimate; there could be an initially heavy investment for developing and installing the system with a relatively low cost per signal once installed).
6. The risk attitude of the decision maker (we assumed a risk-neutral decision maker; most decision makers, however, have considerable risk aversion, requiring a specification of the decision maker's utility function).

Some students have observed that an information-economics philosophy applied to the information-economics approach would suggest that the exercise may not be worth the cost. Also, the choice of an accounting system based on the information-economics approach will, in general, be sensitive to the specification of the prior probabilities (item 2 above), a specification that is usually difficult and unverifiable.

Because of the complexity required for a formal treatment of the information-economics approach, this text has focused more on particular user decision models. Chapter 8, however, on the measurement of opportunity losses from inaccurate measurement of parameters, develops the framework for estimating the benefits of improved information on decision making. These benefits can be compared to the cost of obtaining more accurate information, and they provide upper bounds on how much should be invested in improved information systems as a function of the decisions that will be made with this information. Thus, Chapter 8 emphasizes the benefit-cost philosophy of evaluating information systems, which is the principal message we wish to obtain from the information-economics approach. The reader would do well to approach all the decision and control models presented in this text with such a benefit-cost philosophy in mind. Decision models and sophisticated control procedures are expensive to estimate, implement, and maintain. They should be used only in contexts where the benefits are expected to exceed their costs. Unfortunately, decision makers do not yet have techniques available with which to measure the costs or benefits of information for decision making, so that the benefit-cost calculation must be based on a subjective evaluation.

INFORMATION-EVALUATOR APPROACH

The simple information-economics approach, as illustrated by the example in the preceding section, does not capture the multiperson aspect of most settings in which cost accounting systems are found. One attempt to develop at least a two-person setting treated the cost accountant as an ''information evaluator,'' separate from the manager who makes the decision based on the cost accounting data.[8] In this paradigm, the decision maker is known to follow simplified decision rules, using the information made available by the accountant. The accountant is assumed to know how the decision maker makes a decision, what the globally optimal decision is (if only the accountant were allowed to make it!), and properties of various information systems. The accountant's job is to select, from among costly information systems, the one with the greatest net benefits. The benefits are obtained by selecting the information system that induces the decision maker to take actions that the accountant knows are best for the firm.[9]

The information-evaluator approach was attractive for several reasons. First, it saw the accountant as the omniscient individual in the firm, attempting to influence the operating manager to make better decisions. Accountants are typically accused of distorting cost and profit measures by their arcane procedures, thereby hindering optimal decision making. The egocentric features of the information-evaluator approach placed the accountant in a much more favorable position.

The second positive aspect of this approach was that it focused attention on the multiperson environment in which information systems must be developed, selected, and implemented. In general, individuals in the firm will have different beliefs and preferences, so that the selection of an ''optimal'' information system

---

[8] This approach was first formulated in Feltham-Demski [1970] and is illustrated in Demski [1980].

[9] This complicated story can be clarified by working through Problem 1-3 at the end of the chapter.

requires complex and subtle considerations not easily captured in simple single-person choice models. The attempt to develop an information-evaluator/decision-maker dichotomy highlighted the difficulty of obtaining analytic solutions to multiperson choice problems under uncertainty.

The information-evaluator approach ultimately fails, however, because the second agent in the model, the decision maker, has no useful role other than to be a foil for the information evaluator. Basically, the information evaluator has a complete representation of the firm's decision problem but does not have authority to take actions other than to select an information system. Actions are selected and carried out by a dummy decision maker who is manipulated by the information evaluator. This is not a stable solution. The optimal policy is to have the information evaluator select both the information system and the action, with the manager left to implement the selected course of action. Despite this central flaw, the information-evaluator approach provided a useful bridge to current research, in which all economic agents are assumed to be clever, maximizing types. In this research, the cost accounting or information system facilitates contractual agreements among the different economic agents.

OPTIMAL CONTRACTING AMONG ECONOMIC AGENTS

Recent developments in the theory of the firm and of economic equilibrium with private information (not all economic agents fully informed about all aspects of a choice situation under uncertainty) have led to new insights into the central role of information and observability in the devising of contracts among economic agents.[10] This approach is frequently referred to as the *principal-agent literature*. For example, the principal could be the set of owners (shareholders) and the agent the chief executive of the company, hired to run the company for the owners. Alternatively, the principal could be the central management group that hires divisional managers (the agents) to manage decentralized units. The problem is to devise both an incentive scheme and a supporting information system so that the agents are motivated to act in the best interests of the principal.

This problem of organizational design is not new. People have been writing and talking about decentralization and delegation of authority for many years.[11] Accountants have addressed some of the relevant themes in management control

---

[10] The literature in this area is growing rapidly. Early contributions include Arrow [1964], Jensen-Meckling [1976], and Harris-Raviv [1978]. An excellent survey by Jennergren [1980] provides extensive references to this literature.

[11] References to this literature include Simon and others [1954], March and Simon [1958], and Galbraith [1973]. A historical perspective is provided in Sloan [1963], especially chaps. 7, 8, 10, 22, and 23.

of decentralized operations.[12] These themes include budgeting, profit centers, and evaluation of divisional and managerial performance.

The contribution of the recent literature (see footnote 10) is its development of formal economic models from which optimal incentives and performance measures can be derived endogenously.[13] Thus, we now hope that we can obtain a deeper understanding of the fundamental forces leading to decentralization and the demand for management control systems. Cost accounting data are a vital part of management control systems, but the design of these systems introduces a broader set of issues than just relevant costs, opportunity costs, or standard costs.

Chapter 13 introduces the benefits and costs of decentralization and the role of performance measures. It attempts to present both the traditional viewpoint as well as the insights obtained from the formal economic analyses of the principal-agent model. Chapter 14 focuses on problems in measuring profit in a decentralized unit, with particular emphasis on the transfer-pricing problem. Chapter 15 extends the analysis of divisional profitability to control for the investment in a division. It contains extensive analyses of the strengths and weaknesses of the return-on-investment and residual-income performance measures for investment centers. Chapter 16 describes a variety of incentive contracts and bonus plans that have been used to motivate managerial performance. Thus Chapters 13 through 16 should provide a good introduction to the broader set of issues arising in establishing decentralized operations, and the control and reward systems necessary to motivate, monitor, and evaluate the performance of managers. Chapter 17 introduces the recently developed formal models for incentive contracting and performance evaluation under uncertainty. Also, we survey models for inducing truthful forecasts from managers of decentralized units. Perhaps the payoffs from current and future research will cause the formal models in Chapter 17 to become better integrated into earlier chapters of this (and other) texts.

SUMMARY

Management accounting does not exist as a coherent, unified field. Diverse approaches and philosophies have attempted to guide the design of management accounting systems. A fundamental conflict exists between the use of accounting data for decision purposes and its use for contractual relationships between economic entities or agents. Cost accounting concepts were first developed to aid in the accountability relationship between the firm and interested external parties, principally of owners and creditors. The cost accounting system was therefore

---

[12] See Solomons [1965] and Anthony and Dearden [1980].

[13] As in the information-economics approach, however, these models are highly abstract representations of actual management accounting systems. Therefore, the conclusions are not directly transferable to current operating systems.

subservient to the needs of financial reporting. More recently, external parties interested in cost accounting data have expanded to include tax authorities, regulatory agencies, the courts, and government contracting agencies. For these constituencies, it is important that cost accounting data be objective and verifiable, since these data will affect large financial transfers to and from the firm.

Cost accounting data are also needed for planning and control decisions within the firm. For these applications, the data may have to be tailor-made. Data other than costs, such as resource capacity and consumption, may be required for these decisions. The emphasis here is on decision enhancement rather than accountability to external parties. Thus, the data can be more subjective, involve greater use of forecasts, and require an explicit treatment of uncertainty. The logical conclusion of this philosophy is the information-economics approach, in which the value of internal accounting data is measured by the improvement in the decision maker's utility. The information-economics approach can subsume any decision situation as a special case, but the measurement and evaluation of a proposed information system requires an extensive (and costly) specification of the costs and properties of the proposed system.

A third use of internal accounting data is for accountability relationships within the firm. Frequently, the same information useful for planning and decision making will be used for evaluating the performance of the managers or decision makers. Unfortunately, the subjectivity required to get relevant data for decision making may make the same data inappropriate to use for control purposes. Once managers learn that information elicited for decision making will also be used for evaluation, there will be incentives to misrepresent or distort the requested information. Thus, there are fundamental conflicts between uses of accounting data for decision making and for control. The challenge for future research is to resolve these conflicts by developing measures that are useful for decision making but also suitable for establishing accountability relationships.

This book has two major parts. Chapter 2 through 12 will focus on specific decision-making and control uses of internal accounting data. Chapters 13 through 17 will develop the principal concepts in decentralization and accountability relationships.

PROBLEMS

1-1. Use of Risk-Averse Utility Functions

Consider the new product introduction illustrated in the section on the Information Economics Approach. Suppose that the current wealth of the firm is $500,000 and that the owner of the firm has a utility function for wealth (w) given by $u(w) = \log(w/100,000)$. Thus, if the new product is successful (state L occurs), the wealth will increase by $150,000 to a new total of $650,000 whereas if the high cost state

(H) occurs, the wealth will decrease to \$375,000. The manager wants to make a decision to maximize the expected utility of the owner. Thus, before considering whether to purchase the special information system, the manager will introduce the product if

$$0.6u(650,000) + 0.4u(375,000) > u(500,000).$$

1. Should the manager introduce the product?
2. At the cost of \$10,000, should the manager invest in the information system providing imperfect signals on whether L or H will occur?
3. What is the maximum amount the manager would be willing to pay for a perfect information system; one for which

$$\Pr(y_1 \mid L) = 1 \quad \text{and} \quad \Pr(y_2 \mid H) = 1?$$

1-2. Decision Models and Information Evaluation

A credit card company has a utility curve that may be represented by the function $u(x)$:

$$u(x) = \begin{cases} x & x \geq 0 \\ 2x & x \leq 0 \end{cases}.$$

Experience has shown that applicants are of two types:

Good Risks (s_1)
Bad Risks (s_2)

A good risk represents a certain *profit* to the company of \$150. A bad risk represents a certain *loss* of \$100. Past experience has shown that 70 percent of prospective applicants are good risks. The company must decide whether to issue (a_1) or refuse to issue (a_2) a card to an applicant.

1. What is the optimum decision for the company given only this information? What is the expected value of perfect information (the value of an information system that could discriminate perfectly between good risks and bad risks)? The company has access to a credit-checking agency. The agency investigates the applicant's references, and issues either a favorable report (y_1) or an unfavorable report (y_2) on the applicant. If the applicant is actually a good risk, the agency is 60 percent accurate; i.e., $\Pr(y_1 \mid s_1) = 0.6$. If the applicant is actually a bad risk, however, the agency is much more reliable; $\Pr(y_2 \mid s_2) = 0.9$. Because of the nature of the reference-checking procedure, the agency charges a fixed fee of \$10 per report. An additional fee of \$30 is charged if the report turns out to be favorable, since it takes much longer to verify a good risk than to eliminate a bad one.
2. Evaluate the services of the credit-checking agency. Should the company use the services of the agency?
3. What is the lower bound on $\Pr(y_1 \mid s_1)$ before the company would stop using the credit-checking agency? How much more would the company

be willing to pay the agency for a good report (y_1) if the agency could raise its evaluation of good credit risks to a 90 percent accuracy rate; i.e., $\Pr(y_1 \mid s_1) = 0.9$? (Assume all other parameters remain the same.)

1-3.   Information Evaluator and Decision Maker

The product manager of Xylium has a cost function represented by $\frac{1}{2}q^2 + 2q$ where q is the amount produced in a period. Xylium is sold in a perfectly competitive market (the amount sold does not affect the price) but with an uncertain selling price. Assume that the product manager is risk-neutral; output is determined to maximize expected profits.

1. Compute the optimal production quantity as a function of the expected price.

The manager is not sure of the current price of Xylium. He believes the current price could be either 10, 15, or 20, each with probability $\frac{1}{3}$. He also believes that the best estimate of the future price, for which the production decision is being taken, is the current price.

2. Based on these beliefs, how much Xylium will the manager produce?

The company's information evaluator has the same beliefs about the current market price as the product manager. She knows, however, that the future period price is a more complicated function of the current price. Her beliefs about the likelihood of the future period price are summarized below.

Current Price	Future Price 10	Future Price 15	Future Price 20
10	$\frac{1}{2}$	$\frac{1}{2}$	0
15	0	$\frac{1}{2}$	$\frac{1}{2}$
20	0	$\frac{1}{2}$	$\frac{1}{2}$

3. What is the information evaluator's belief about the expected future price? What would she compute as the optimal production quantity based on this expected future price? What is her belief about the expected profits given the actual production quantity determined by the product manager (see the answer to question 2).

The information evaluator can invest in an information system which will reveal the current market price to the product manager. The manager will use this information to determine the production schedule.

4. Compute the production amount (as determined by the product manager) as a function of the signal from the information system (use the answer to question 1). Compute the production cost for each of these production

quantities. Compute the expected revenue based on the information evaluator's beliefs about the future price. (These beliefs are based on the signal from the information system.) What are the expected profits, computed by the information evaluator, if the information system is acquired and the product manager makes his production decision based on the signal from the system?

5. How much should the information evaluator be willing to pay for this information system?

6. How much would the information evaluator be willing to pay for the information system if she could determine the production quantity?

1-4. Decision Analysis, Value of Sample Information and the Effect of Risk Aversion on Information Value (A. Atkinson)

John Greene has just finished his management studies and received a windfall gift of $5000 from a trust fund for successfully completing his education. Looking to leverage this modest sum into a larger amount, John is contemplating a "hot" commodities deal. He has been approached by a small syndicate that is being formed to short sell six-month soybean contracts. Specifically by selling these contracts short, the syndicate promises to deliver a specified number of bushels of soybeans six months in the future for a price to be determined at present. The syndicate gains if the price of soybeans falls during the next six months since it could then buy a contract from another seller at the lower price or else buy the soybeans in the spot market, store them and arrange for delivery at the promised date. If the price of soybeans rises during the next 6 months, the syndicate has to purchase soybeans at the higher price in order to satisfy the promised delivery, and could lose a lot of money.

Rather than being exposed to the full range of these outcomes, the syndicate simplifies the payoff structure to John by partitioning all the outcomes into two possible states—Success (S) and Failure (F). If the syndicate is Successful, John will receive $15,000. If the syndicate Fails, John loses his entire $5000 investment. John constructs the following payoff table to guide his decision process:

	State	
Action	*Success (S)*	*Failure (F)*
Invest (*I*)	$10,000	$−5,000
Pass (*P*)	0	0

John believes that the probability of success, Pr(*S*), is 0.6.

Before plunging ahead and risking his modest investment, John decides to consult with Adam Smith Sangrist, a professor he met at the university who follows the commodity market closely and has been developing a reputation as a good forecaster of weather trends and crop yields. John knows that if weather is favorable so that crop yields are high, the price of soybeans will drop and the syndicate will be successful. If the weather is poor, a bad harvest will occur, the price of soybeans will soar, and the syndicate will be a financial disaster.

A. S. Sangrist will issue one of three possible forecasts: Good crop, Fair crop, and Poor crop. John assesses Sangrist's forecasting ability by the following table of conditional probabilities:

Sangrist Forecast	State	
	Success (S)	Failure (F)
Good (G)	.6	.2
Fair (F)	.3	.3
Poor (P)	.1	.5

That is, if the syndicate is successful, Sangrist will predict a good harvest with probability 0.6. If the syndicate will be a failure, however, there is a small chance (0.2) that Sangrist will still be predicting a good crop. Also, Sangrist informs John Greene that his forecasts are not free. Because his services are increasingly in demand, he must charge a $300 fee for such a consultation. He might, however, consider a reduced fee for a former student so there is some room for negotiation.

Required:

1. Should John Greene invest in the syndicate? What is the maximum amount John should be willing to pay his former professor for a crop forecast? Assume that John is risk-neutral.
2. John is most unsure about his prior probability estimate of Success. How does the analysis change if his prior probability of success is as low as $\frac{1}{3}$ or as high as $\frac{2}{3}$?
3. All these uncertainty calculations are making John realize that he is more risk averse than he had previously believed. John now recognizes that his preferences are well described by a logarithmic (natural) utility function:

$$u(x) = \log(5,301 + x)$$

where x is the net payoff from the syndicate investment (either -5000 or $+10,000$) and 5301 is John's current wealth. Compute John's optimal action now, given his initial prior probability of $\Pr(S) = 0.6$. Is the information of Professor Sangrist worth more to John when he is risk averse, or risk neutral?

REFERENCES

ANTHONY, ROBERT N., and JOHN DEARDEN, *Management Control Systems: Text and Cases*, 4th ed. Homewood, Ill.: Irwin, 1980.

ARROW, KENNETH, "Control in Large Organizations," *Management Science* X (April 1964), 397–408.

BAIMAN, STANLEY, "Optimal Conditional Variance Investigation for a Class of Principal-Agent Problems," Carnegie-Mellon Working Paper, 1979.

————, and JOEL DEMSKI, "Variance Analysis Procedures as Motivational Devices," *Management Science* XXVI (August 1980), 840–48.

DEMSKI, JOEL, *Information Analysis* 2d ed. Reading, Mass.: Addison-Wesley, 1980.

————, and GERALD A. FELTHAM, *Cost Determination: A Conceptual Approach*. Ames: Iowa State University Press, 1976.

————, and ————, "Economic Incentives in Budgetary Control Systems," *The Accounting Review* III (April 1978), 336–59.

FELTHAM, GERALD A., "The Value of Information," *The Accounting Review* XLIII (October 1968), 684–96.

————, *Information Evaluation*, Studies in Accounting Research #5. Sarasota, Fla.: American Accounting Association, 1972.

————, and JOEL DEMSKI, "The Use of Models in Information Evaluation," *The Accounting Review* XLV (October 1970), 623–40.

GALBRAITH, JAY, *Designing Complex Organizations*. Reading, Mass.: Addison Wesley, 1973.

HARRIS, MILTON, and ARTUR RAVIV, "Some Results on Incentive Contracts with Applications to Education and Employment, Health Insurance and Law Enforcement," *American Economic Review* LXVIII (March 1978), 20–30.

HORNGREN, CHARLES T., "Management Accounting: Where Are We?" in *Management Accounting and Control*, Beyer Symposium. Madison: University of Wisconsin, 1975.

IJIRI, YUJI, *Theory of Accounting Measurement* Studies in Accounting Research #10. Sarasota, Fla.: American Accounting Association, 1975.

JENNERGEN, L. PETER, "On the Design of Incentives in Business Firms—A Survey of Some Research," *Management Science* XXVI (February 1980), 180–201.

JENSEN, MICHAEL, and WILLIAM H. MECKLING, "Theory of the Firm: Managerial Behavior, Agency Costs and Ownership Structure," *Journal of Financial Economics* III (October 1976), 305–60.

KAPLAN, ROBERT S., "Application of Quantitative Models in Managerial Accounting: A State of the Art Survey," in *Management Accounting—State of the Art*, Beyer Lecture Series. Madison: University of Wisconsin, 1977; reprinted in *The Accounting Journal* I (Winter 1977–1978), 218–42.

MARCH, JAMES A., and HERBERT A. SIMON, *Organizations*. New York: Wiley, 1959.

SIMON, HERBERT A., HAROLD GUETZKOW, GEORGE KOZMETSKY, and GORDON TYNDALL, *Centralization vs. Decentralization in Organizing the Controller's Department*. New York: Controllership Foundation, 1954.

SLOAN, ALFRED P., JR., *My Years With General Motors*. New York: Doubleday, 1964.

SOLOMONS, DAVID, *Divisional Performance: Measurement and Control*. Homewood, Ill.: Irwin, 1965.

ZIMMERMAN, JEROLD L., "The Costs and Benefits of Cost Allocations," *The Accounting Review* LIV (July 1979), 504–21.

COST BEHAVIOR PATTERNS

2

FIXED AND VARIABLE COSTS

In cost accounting, a central aim is to determine how costs are affected by variation in activity levels. The knowledge of how costs vary with either outputs or inputs is necessary for all planning and control decisions. The simplest and most useful classification of costs distinguishes between fixed and variable costs. Fixed costs are those costs that will be unaffected by variations in activity level in a given period. They are expected to be constant throughout the period, independent of the level of output produced or inputs used. Conversely, variable costs are those costs that are affected by the level of activity in a period. Although many refinements and extensions of this fixed and variable cost dichotomy are possible, the basic classification of all costs into these two components is extremely important and useful.

The definition of fixed and variable costs must always be made with respect to a specific time period. Over a sufficiently long period, ranging up to several years or even decades, all costs will be variable. During such a long period of time, equipment can become obsolete so that it no longer needs to be replaced, buildings and land can be sold, and even the top management of a division can be transferred or fired in response to declining demand. Thus over a long time period, a contraction in activity can be accompanied by a contraction in all categories of costs. Similarly, a large expansion of activity can eventually cause all cost components to increase. In contrast, for a sufficiently short time period—a day, an hour, or perhaps a minute—virtually all costs will be fixed. Material has already been acquired, utilities are turned on, and the firm is already committed to paying its workers for this short time period so that variations in activity will not be associated with corresponding cost variations. Within these two extremes of very long and very short time periods, our usual notions of fixed and variable costs will prove to be interesting and useful. Typically, the relevant time interval will correspond to a period during which relevant accounting data are collected. It could be a week, a month, three months (a quarterly period) or a year (representing an annual budgeting cycle).

Fixed costs can be thought of as capacity costs; they are associated with resources that provide the capability for a planned level of activities during a period. Within the category of fixed costs, we can distinguish between committed fixed costs and discretionary fixed costs.

Committed fixed costs are the costs of plant, equipment, and key personnel—examples include depreciation, rent, insurance, property taxes, and the salaries and fringe benefits of key management personnel. These costs arise from long-term planning, capital-budgeting, production, and marketing decisions of the firm and are unlikely to be reduced even during a major strike, severe material shortages, or a general period of slack activity or idleness.

Discretionary fixed costs arise from periodic (usually annual) decisions by top management. These include research and development, advertising, sales promotion, employee training programs, and the costs of legal, accounting, and personnel departments. These costs generally correspond to expenditures on intangibles or on staff departments. Such expenditures are in areas where the relationship between output and input is difficult to measure, and they bear little relationship to short-term variations in the activity levels of the firm.

Note that the notion of "fixed" in fixed costs does not mean that these costs cannot be reduced. Clearly the level of discretionary costs is determined each year and can even be cut within the year, with little short-term effect, should the firm encounter unexpectedly hard times. The adjective "fixed" in fixed costs implies only that these costs are not directly affected by variations in the firm's activity level.

Some fixed costs, such as supervision or equipment rental, may be fixed with respect to moderate variations in activity level but can be affected by large expansions or contractions of activity. For example, if demand for a product increases so that a second shift needs to be added, another supervisor will have to be hired. If the firm wishes to expand its productive capacity to meet increased demand, it may lease additional equipment and thereby increase its fixed costs. As output expands, an additional quality-control supervisor may be hired. Conversely, if output contracts, the company may reduce the number of shifts it is working and may return equipment it has previously been leasing. These jumps or reductions in the levels of fixed costs are examples of *Semifixed costs.*

Exhibit 2-1 illustrates the nature of a semifixed cost. If daily volume is expected to vary between 200 and 300 units, then quality control supervision will be a fixed cost. But if daily volume can be as low as 100 units or as high as 400 units, there will be major decrements or increments in this cost category. Examples of semifixed costs can be identified by detailed knowledge of the production process or by careful examination of past data.

Variable costs are those costs directly affected by variations in the level of activity. It is usually assumed that variable costs will vary linearly with the level of activity, as shown in Exhibit 2-2. In this case the amount of change in the

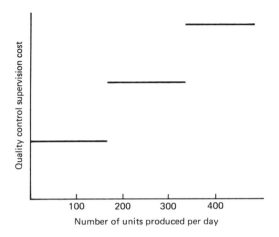

Exhibit 2-1   Semi-Fixed Cost: Quality Control Supervision

variable cost for each unit change in activity level is a constant, independent of the level of activity.

It is possible to have more complex forms of variable costs, such as piecewise linear or curvilinear. Exhibit 2-3a shows how the overtime premium makes labor cost a piecewise linear cost, and Exhibit 2-3b illustrates how the experience or learning-curve phenomenon causes the incremental cost per unit to decrease as cumulative output increases (the learning curve will be discussed in a subsequent chapter). In practice, the existence of nonlinear variable costs is best discovered by plotting and observing the data. One's first reaction will usually be to assume

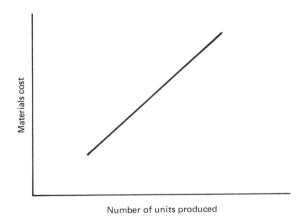

Exhibit 2-2   Linear Variable Cost: Materials

a linear relationship. Departures from strict linearity, such as those illustrated in Exhibits 2-3a and b, will be detected only by carefully examining systematic departures from the assumed linear fit.

Variable costs arise from a variety of relationships. *Direct variable costs,* the most familiar kind, reflect the direct relationship between the inputs of material and labor required to produce a unit of output. We know that each unit of output requires specified amounts of materials and labor, so that increases in output will cause materials and labor costs to increase proportionately. Direct variable costs will likely be strictly variable costs—costs that will decrease toward zero as output is reduced to zero. One rarely finds a significant fixed component in direct variable costs.

Indirect or overhead costs will also vary with output, though the relationship will not be as obvious as with direct costs. Indirect materials cost (scrap, lubrication, maintenance supplies), indirect labor cost (materials handlers, housekeeping, idle time), utilities, and many other overhead costs will vary with the level of activity. Unlike direct costs, these indirect or overhead costs may not vary strictly proportionately with activity levels; that is, they will likely have a fixed-cost component, representing standby capacity even if no output is being produced, and a variable-cost component that does vary with activity levels. The existence of such mixed costs (a mixture of fixed and variable costs) is detected by plotting the data on a graph and noting whether the linear approximation to the data has an intercept significantly different from zero.

A third category of variable costs are *discretionary variable costs*—costs that are usually fixed in nature but, because of management policy, are allowed to expand and contract with variation in activity levels. For example, some firms budget advertising and promotion expense as a fixed percentage of sales. Other such expense categories that may be budgeted proportional to activity levels are

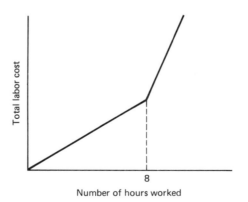

Exhibit 2-3a   Piecewise Linear Cost: Labor Cost

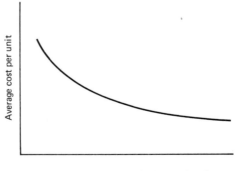

Exhibit 2-3b   Curvilinear Cost: Average Costs with Learning

maintenance, corporate donations, and contributions to employee welfare programs. Although some of these policies appear to have their direction of causality reversed (normally we invest in advertising and promotion to increase sales, rather than use increased sales to fund advertising and promotion expenditures; also, maintenance is best performed in low-demand periods when it is less likely to disrupt production schedules), the existence of such policies will cause some discretionary expenses to become a linear function of sales.

OTHER COST CONCEPTS

Besides the fixed and variable cost classification just described, a number of other cost characterizations are useful when we consider the role of costs in decision making.

Incremental costs represent the change in total cost caused by a change in the level of an activity. (Sometimes when considering a contraction in an activity, the negative incremental costs or cost savings are called escapable or avoidable costs.) Incremental costs can include not only variable costs but also semifixed costs if the decision involves large changes from current activity levels. Determining which costs are incremental for a particular decision requires a careful analysis of the decision. For example, when one is considering whether to attempt to expand sales of a particular product, the relevant incremental costs are the variable costs of production and the costs of additional promotion and advertising.

Sometimes the concept of incremental cost is tricky, such as when the variable costs are irrelevant to the decision and the incremental costs are the fixed costs. This seemingly paradoxical situation occurs in the deterministic inventory model leading to the *economic order quantity* (*EOQ*). In this model, total demand is assumed to be known. There is a fixed cost for placing an order (fixed in the sense that the cost is independent of the amount ordered) and a proportional holding cost for keeping an item in inventory. The problem is to determine how often to order and how much to order each time an order is placed. In this formulation of the inventory problem, the variable cost of acquiring the items for inventory is not relevant to the decision of how often to order, since, regardless of what inventory policy is chosen, all demand will be satisfied by acquiring a sufficient number of items. For the inventory decision, a relevant or incremental cost arises from the frequency with which the fixed cost of placing an order is incurred. Thus the variable cost is not important, but the fixed cost represents an incremental cost for the ordering decision.

In a capital-budgeting analysis of a machine-replacement decision, the incremental cost in the initial year is the cost of acquiring the new machine less investment tax benefits and the salvage or trade-in value of the old machine. In subsequent years, the incremental costs are the savings in operating costs (less tax effects) from using the new rather than the old machine.

Sunk costs are those costs unaffected by the choice from the present set of alternatives. Some managers mistakenly attempt to recover the costs of past decisions in their pricing or marketing decisions for new products and processes. Suppose for example, that an extensive research and development effort produces a new product. The decision to market the product depends only on the cost of new facilities to produce the product, its sales potential, and its costs of production. The amount already spent on R&D is irrelevant to the marketing decision; it has already been spent and the expenditure will be unaffected by whether the product is marketed or not. By now, it has become a sunk cost. Similarly, when one is pricing a product that is manufactured on equipment already acquired, the cost of the equipment is a sunk cost that should not affect the pricing decision. The relevant equipment cost is not its historical acquisition cost but its current market value—what the company could sell it for if it were not used to manufacture the product.

There is a danger in dismissing many costs as sunk without recognizing that they are still the responsibility of some manager. Someone authorized the R&D expenditure or the acquisition of equipment. Presumably these decisions were made in anticipation of successful products and were based upon forecasts of selling price, production costs, and market potential. But the time to be concerned with these factors is before the R&D expenditure is authorized or the equipment purchased. Once these expenditures have been made, the company must then make the best decision it can, given market conditions and its product library. The justification for authorizing the expenditures should be reviewed and evaluated in light of subsequent developments, but the actual pricing and marketing decisions should be made using the best currently available information. The R&D costs or the equipment acquisition costs are by then sunk costs irrelevant to this decision.

The *opportunity cost* of an asset is its value when it is used in its next-best alternative. Sometimes an asset will not be in immediate use—excess space in a warehouse, equipment not being used to capacity, cash not needed for immediate investment projects in the firm. One will be tempted to treat these assets as having zero cost associated with their use (since they are currently slack) and to use them for any project that has positive net benefits when use of the asset is assigned zero cost. But currently slack resources can be used in a variety of projects. Excess warehouse space can be used for many different products or deliberately kept empty to allow room for expansion of the current product line. If the warehouse space is treated as a free resource, it will fill to capacity quickly, so that future demands for space from normal product growth or new products will force the costly acquisition of new warehouse space. Similarly, introducing new products that use some of the spare capacity of currently idle equipment may eliminate the reserve for future growth in the current product line. The opportunity cost of using the equipment idle time is the cost of future expansion of equipment facilities when normal product growth causes the capacity of the existing machine to be exceeded.

With cash, the opportunity cost is more familiar. The use of cash always has an opportunity cost associated with it. It could be used to retire debt, re-purchase equity, pay dividends, or earn interest in credit markets. Therefore, projects requiring additional cash or working capital must earn at least as high a rate of return as could be obtained by reducing the capitalization of the firm, investing in the securities of other firms, or purchasing Treasury bills or the high-grade notes and obligations of other firms. The well-recognized practice of dis-counting future cash flows in a capital-budgeting analysis is simply a way of deciding whether the proposed project will yield a return in excess of the op-portunity cost (what could be earned in alternative investments) of the capital required to be invested in the project.

An opportunity cost that many people encounter arises when one is deciding whether to purchase a house or continue to rent. It is typical to compare the after-tax cash flows between these two alternatives (the monthly rent versus the monthly payment for mortgage repayment, interest on the mortgage, property taxes, and maintenance and upkeep), but it is easy to forget that the house pur-chase requires a down payment. The down payment is made with funds that otherwise could be placed in income-producing investments, so that an additional cost of home purchase is the unrecorded opportunity cost of foregone income from the down payment. Fortunately (for home owners), the rate of return on equity from home ownership during the past two decades has greatly exceeded the return available from more traditional investments, so that most purchasers who ignored this opportunity cost were not penalized for their omission.

Opportunity costs are particularly troublesome for accountants weaned on the transactions-based historical-cost system. Because opportunity costs arise from transactions not executed (they are either prospective or not undertaken), they rarely appear in a company's financial or cost accounting system. Yet they are extremely important for many decisions made by the firm. The opportunity cost of using capacity resources for production is rarely measured; likewise, the opportunity cost of investing funds in inventory or the cost of losing customer goodwill through frequent stockouts or slow deliveries is not typically measured in a firm's inventory reporting system. Opportunity costs become most obvious when a formal model is developed describing a firm's alternatives or options in a particular situation. Only with an explicit formal model can one be confident that a proposed course of action is not only adequate but superior to other op-portunities available to the firm, given its present configuration of financial, pro-duction, personnel, and marketing resources. Thus, it is important to consider opportunity costs when planning a transaction and to remember that they may not be immediately available or prominently featured in a firm's accounting sys-tem. Rather, one must make a careful, complete analysis of the firm's opportu-nities, which requires skill in modeling and optimization. These ideas will be stressed in subsequent chapters.

We illustrate these points with an example. The Connors Company manu-factures a basic chemical, Noxium, which can be sold directly or processed further into a more valuable chemical, Valmite. The Connors Company can sell all the Noxium that it produces at a price of $100 per ton. The Valmite market is more volatile, with prices ranging between $125 and $200 per ton. The Connors Company accounting system reports the following costs for Noxium and Valmite:

	Cost Per Ton	
	Noxium	*Valmite*
Raw materials	$50	
Direct labor	10	
Overhead	30	
Cost per ton	$90	$90
Processing cost:		
Additional materials		20
Direct labor		10
Overhead		15
Cost per ton		$135
Selling price	$100	$125–200

Further investigation reveals that the overhead cost per ton is obtained by dividing the total estimated overhead cost for the year by the total hours of available capacity. The overhead cost is allocated to products in proportion to processing time. Overhead costs, however, do not vary with the amount of production. Two hours are required to produce a ton of Noxium, and one additional hour is needed to process the finished Noxium into Valmite. Both products share the same production facilities, which can be used interchangeably to produce Noxium or Valmite.

The sales manager of the Connors Company argues that production and sale of Valmite should be discontinued whenever its selling price drops below $135 per ton, since otherwise the firm would be losing money on each ton sold. This reasoning is clearly fallacious, since, among other failings, it does not distinguish between the fixed and variable costs of production. The overhead costs charged to both Noxium and Valmite are fixed costs that will not change if production of Valmite is discontinued. On a variable-cost basis, Noxium costs $60 per ton to produce, so that its contribution margin (price less variable costs) per ton sold is $40. The $60 is also the variable cost of using Noxium as an input material for Valmite. Therefore the total variable cost of Valmite is the $60 Noxium cost plus the $30 materials and labor cost for additional processing. Even with a selling price as low as $135 per ton, Valmite shows a contribution margin per ton of $45. Thus, the initial analysis shows that by distinguishing between fixed and variable costs, we are not misled into thinking that the Connors Company is losing money on sales of Valmite.

But this is only the start of the complete analysis. For if Noxium can be sold outside the firm at a price of $100 per ton, every ton of Noxium that is used to produce Valmite costs the company not only the $60 variable cost but the $40 contribution margin that could otherwise be earned if it were sold. Therefore the cost of Noxium to produce Valmite is actually $100 (its opportunity cost in the best alternative of selling outside), not $60. With this refinement, the cost of producing Valmite is actually $130 (not $100), but it would still be a profitable product at a selling price of $135. In fact, at this stage, Valmite—at a price of $135 per ton—would appear to be more profitable than Noxium, since it can show a profit even after paying for the foregone contribution margin of Noxium. At the $125 price at the low end of the price range, Valmite does not cover its variable plus opportunity costs.

We now reach the final stage of the analysis, where we use the information that Noxium and Valmite share the same production facilities. Every hour used to produce a ton of Valmite consumes an hour that otherwise could be used to produce a half-ton of Noxium. Therefore the opportunity cost of producing a ton of Valmite is not only the $40 contribution margin from not selling a ton of Noxium but also the loss in production time that could otherwise be used to produce additional amounts of Noxium. If the price of Valmite is only $135, then each ton manufactured produces a contribution margin (after paying the opportunity cost of Noxium) of $5. But the one hour of time required to produce the ton of Valmite could have been used to produce a half-ton of Noxium, which would generate a contribution margin of $20 (0.5 · 40). Thus, after the opportunity cost of the scarce production facilities is recognized, a $135 selling price for Valmite makes it a less profitable product than Noxium. Only when the selling price reaches $150, where Valmite is generating a net contribution margin of $20 per hour of production time (the same as Noxium), are the two products equally profitable.

To summarize, the opportunity cost of producing a ton of Valmite is the $100 foregone by not selling the ton of Noxium required for Valmite plus the $20 in contribution margin lost by not producing a half-ton of Noxium during the hour that the production facilities are used to produce the ton of Valmite. Adding the direct materials and labor cost of $30 for Valmite to the $120 opportunity cost yields the $150 incremental cost (or foregone revenue) for producing Valmite rather than Noxium.

Notice that no traditional accounting system would generate the $120 opportunity cost for using Noxium to produce Valmite. We obtained this figure by analyzing alternative sales possibilities for Noxium (the $100 component) and alternative production possibilities (the $20 component) for producing Valmite. Relevant opportunity costs can be found only by considering alternative uses for the firm's resources. No analytic procedure can generate these alternatives; this is the role of analysts and management. Failure to consider alternative uses for the firm's resources could lead one to underestimate the opportunity cost of these resources and, consequently, to a less than optimal utilization.

Engineering Method

The most direct way to obtain cost estimates is by observing the physical process. An industrial engineering study of a repetitive process, which has a well-defined relationship between inputs and outputs, will yield standards for many of the variable costs incurred to produce a given level of output. The industrial engineering study will express standards in physical units—hours of labor of given skill classes, pounds of different input materials, minutes of machine time, number of supervisors—and these measurements can be transformed into costs by multiplying by the appropriate unit prices. An engineering study has the advantage of determining an ideal relationship between inputs and outputs rather than just measuring existing practice, which may not be the most efficient production process. Also, because physical-unit rather than dollar measures are obtained, the standards can easily be updated as inflation and relative price changes affect the unit prices of inputs.

The engineering method has the disadvantage of being expensive to implement. The value of highly accurate variable-cost information (relative to other estimates of these costs) will rarely be high enough to justify the expense of such a study solely for accounting purposes. If, however, the study is performed because it is believed that improvements in the production process will justify the cost of the study, then the accurate accounting information will be a useful byproduct.

A second disadvantage of an engineering study is that many indirect costs of a production process may not be directly observable. Indirect material and labor costs and the load on staff departments (such as personnel and accounting) may fluctuate with variations in the activity of a production process but be difficult to link by actual physical observation. For these indirect and overhead costs, careful analysis of historical data may more accurately determine causal relationships than an expensive engineering study.

A third limitation is that the engineering studies attempt to optimize the production process given the availability of equipment and the current prices of input factors such as material, labor, and energy. As the relative prices of the input factors change or alternative uses for the equipment develop or new technology emerges, it may become efficient to substitute among the input factors and change the production process. Alert production supervisors may intuitively respond to these environmental changes by substituting more of the lower-price factors for the now higher-price factors as long as they are not controlled too tightly by the engineering standards. Rapid changes in relative prices or technology may therefore distort the optimality of standards set under historic conditions. Changes in relative prices and technology, however, will also make the careful analysis of historical data less useful. When these changes are of sufficient magnitude, it may be worthwhile to restudy the production process and establish new production standards.

Preconditions for Historical Analysis of Cost Data

Careful analysis of historical data can be very helpful in estimating cost behavior patterns for repetitive production processes. As long as no major changes are made in the production process, past production experience can provide excellent guidance for understanding the variability of future costs with respect to changes in activity levels. Before embarking on such an analysis, however, a certain degree of care must be exercised to assure that the data are appropriate for the analysis.

Effects of Accounting Policies   First, we must choose the time-period for analysis. The time period will usually be dictated by the frequency of the internal reporting cycle. A month is a typical reporting period, since many accounts will be billed or accrued on a monthly basis. These include salaries, utilities, maintenance, and the costs of other service departments whose books are closed on a monthly basis. A problem can arise if most accounts are accrued on a monthly basis but hourly employees are paid weekly or biweekly. Unless the end of the month happens to coincide with one of these weekly or biweekly periods, labor cost will be accrued on a basis different from that of all the other accounts. It would not be a trivial task to convert a biweekly labor-expense account to a monthly one. The details will vary by company, but one should be aware of this potential problem of misalignment of accounting periods.

Another potential problem arises from delayed accruals or adjustments. Since a month or shorter period does not correspond to an external reporting period, less care may be taken in allocating costs to the proper month. But for estimating cost behavior patterns, an error in allocating costs to the proper month will weaken the relationship between cost and activity levels. A cost incurred in January but allocated to February because of a late billing will cause January's costs to be understated and February's to be overstated. A similar problem will occur if a detected error in one month's report is corrected by adjusting the next month's report rather than restating the initial month's total correctly. Such adjustments may be satisfactory for financial reporting, since they are performed within a quarterly reporting period, but they make the monthly figures less useful for analyzing cost behavior. Thus, when selecting an accounting period as the basis for an historical cost analysis, it is important to have good closings at the end of each period; accruals of all incurred costs (including the hourly or weekly labor payroll) should be estimated carefully, all relevant costs incurred during the period should be counted, and errors detected after the closing should be entered back into the period's results by restatement rather than handled as an adjustment to a subsequent time period. If the accounting period does not have good closings, any underlying relationship between costs and activity levels will be weakened.

It is interesting that the accrual accounting system, which receives some criticism for financial reporting purposes, is absolutely essential when we attempt to relate internal costs to activity levels. Without a well-functioning accrual accounting system, we could be in the position of correlating the firm's cash expenditures—rather than costs—with activity levels. For example, the cost of supplies or small amounts of inventory could be expensed as purchased rather than capitalized and expensed as used. Vacation pay, sick pay, or paid holidays could be charged to indirect labor expense as incurred rather than treated as part of the total annual labor cost. These fringe benefits are costs of doing business during the entire year and should be accrued, for cost accounting purposes, on an annual basis. Fluctuations in these indirect labor-expense components from month to month will bear little relation to fluctuations in activity levels. Thus, considerable thought and care should be taken at the beginning of any historical analysis of cost data to assure that the data have been produced from a well-functioning cost accrual system with a proper allocation of costs to the appropriate period. To the extent that this ideal is not met in practice, the analyst must recognize that estimated relationships will be weaker than they otherwise could be.

Data Properly Attributable to Costing Units   Many firms and nonprofit entities, such as hospitals and universities, have developed elaborate cost accounting systems, allocating all costs to revenue-producing departments or production cost centers. Before the cost behavior of a particular revenue or cost center is analyzed, the effects of costs incurred outside the center being studied should be removed. One does not need to perform sophisticated analysis of historical data to discover the simple and arbitrary rules frequently used to allocate fixed costs from outside a cost center to the cost center itself. Although such allocations may be deemed useful by the firm's management to inform local managers about all the costs that must be incurred to operate the firm, these costs usually bear no particular relation to fluctuations in the activity level of the cost center. Therefore, for cost estimation purposes, it is desirable to remove all such external cost allocations from a department's cost data.

In addition, the data and cost accounting system should be examined to assure that costs are assigned to the appropriate costing unit. We are attempting to measure the effects of activity variation in a given cost or revenue center. Counting costs incurred outside the center or not including all the costs incurred because of a center's activity level will reduce the explanatory power of the estimated relationship.

Selection of Appropriate Period: the Nonstationarity Problem   We have already discussed the importance of selecting a time period for which we can be assured of obtaining accurate data with reliable cost accruals. The time period should also be one that will generate some variability in activity levels. If too long a time period is selected, short-term fluctuations in activity levels may be smoothed (or averaged out). The greater the dispersion in the activity levels for the reporting periods in our historical analysis, the better able we will be to detect cost variability. If the activity levels in all our reporting periods are approximately the same, any variation in total cost among these periods will tell us only about the uncertainty in total cost for that given activity level and not about the variation in cost due to variation in activity level. Usually, however, the choice of the appropriate time period will be dictated by the accounting cycle used by the firm in order to be assured of obtaining reliable and valid data. Unless we are designing the accounting system *de novo,* we will be unlikely to influence the collection of accurate accrual data by a requirement that the time period be short enough to assure adequate fluctuation in activity levels. When a choice does exist in the selection of time period, a shorter time period (such as a week) may generate greater fluctuations in activity levels than a longer time period and hence yield a broader spread of data points for estimating fixed and variable costs.

A related consideration to the length of a time period is how many time periods to include in the historical-cost analysis. We are torn between two conflicting objectives. We would like to include as many observations as possible so that we can have more confidence in the validity of our estimated relationship. Having more observations will give us a greater range of cost and activity levels and more reliable estimates of cost behavior patterns. But as we increase the overall time period to obtain more cost observations, we become more vulnerable to problems of nonstationarity in the underlying relationship. Almost all historical analyses of cost data will treat each observation equally when estimating cost behavior patterns. An observation from 60 months ago will be given equal weight with an observation obtained one month ago. This procedure is fine if the technology of the production process has stayed constant for the last five years and if there has been no change in the absolute price level or in the relative price levels of the various input factors. But if there has been (1) significant technological change, (2) experience or learning in the production process, or (3) change in the prices of input factors, then observations from 48 or 60 months ago are not as descriptive of the cost of the current production process as the most recent set of observations.

The problem of technological change is the most severe. Whenever a significant change has occurred in the production process—new equipment, new materials, or reorganization in the production of output—the observations obtained before the change will not be helpful in describing the cost behavior of the process after the change. Rather than confound the analysis, it is probably best to discard observations that are not representative of the current production process. Unless we can estimate the effect of an abrupt change and control for it in the analysis, prechange observations may distort the estimation of the cost behavior pattern of the current process. Knowledge of when significant changes in the production process have occurred is therefore important in order to avoid the inclusion of nonrepresentative data in the analysis. Occasionally, if we are both careful and lucky, an analysis of historical cost patterns will reveal when an abrupt change in the production process occurred. This possibility will be discussed in the next chapter.

Nonstationarities introduced by a gradual but steady learning experience with a production process can be handled by explicitly modeling the exponential decrease in variable production costs that has been found to be typical of this learning. We will discuss techniques for estimating these learning effects in Chapter 4 when dealing with the general issue of nonlinear cost estimation. For our present purposes we should keep in mind that, after controlling for price-level effects, we can expect lower unit costs as the cumulative amount of production increases. Therefore, observations too far removed from the current time will tend to arise from a higher cost function than the one describing the present production process.

The third kind of nonstationarity, arising from general and specific price changes, will likely arise in almost all historical analyses of cost data. Even with an inflation rate of 6 percent per year (low by recent American standards), the price level of the most recent period will be 20 percent higher than the price level 36 months ago. In addition to (or even independent of) this overall change in the price level, there could be major shifts in the relative prices of all the input factors of the production process—especially labor, materials, and energy—so that present cost behavior will be very different from cost behavior of the production process 36 months ago. A period as short as twelve months could still see significant changes in the prices of the firm's input factors. There is no universal panacea to this problem but awareness, care, and thought can still be helpful to control for the effects of changing prices when analyzing historical cost patterns.

A highly desirable procedure is to obtain physical measures of the inputs used in the production process rather than the cost aggregates typically reported in a firm's accounting system. If we can obtain, for each accounting period, measures such as direct labor-hours, pounds of material consumed, machine-hours, kilowatt-hours of electricity, and indirect labor-hours, then our basic units of measurement will not be denominated in dollars and will, to a first approximation (assuming no substitution effects), be independent of price changes. Each category, such as direct labor-hours or pounds of input material, could be subdivided into important component classes representing different skill levels or material types. If we can obtain such estimates of the pattern of variation for physical measures of the inputs to the production process, then the current production cost function can be obtained by pricing each major component by its current average unit price. This procedure will be most helpful when we can also obtain physical measures of the output of the production process. This is likely when dealing with a continuous-process industry where we can measure tons of steel produced, barrels of oil refined, square feet of glass or paper manufactured, or gallons or pounds of chemical produced. It is also possible when producing homogeneous discrete units (number of widgets manufactured). It is less likely to be helpful if the output of the production process is heterogeneous (several hundred very different types of widgets), in which case no simple measure of output exists. For such heterogeneous production processes, the level of activity is usually approximated by a physical input measure, such as direct labor-hours or machine-hours, and these variables cannot serve as both the dependent and the independent variables. When possible, however, it is desirable to do the historical analysis using physical rather than dollar measures of the consumption of input resources. By focusing on physical rather than cost measures, we can circumvent the price-change problem.

Assuming that physical measures of consumed resources are unavailable or cannot be used, there are still some straightforward procedures to ameliorate the price-level problem. If the measure of activity is also denominated in dollars, then there could be a stable relationship between a cost component and activity level, even with changing prices. For example, indirect labor expense may be best explained (or predicted) by direct labor expense. If indirect labor expense is a constant percentage of direct labor expense (no fixed component), then we can use many months of historical data to estimate the constant indirect labor-expense percentage. In this case, we are hoping that changing prices affect both measures equally and therefore cancel out when one is measured as a ratio of the other.

A direct attack on the changing-price problem is to index past observations in an attempt to have all observations measured in the same dollar units. If nothing else were available, one could at least use the monthly Consumer Price Index (CPI) to have all observations measured in constant dollars of some arbitrary base year. Just to illustrate how such an indexing procedure would operate, suppose we had observations from calendar years 1977–1978 as shown in Table 2-1 (only every third observation is displayed). Even during this two-year period, the general price level increased 13.9 percent from the first observation to the-

TABLE 2-1.   **Indexed Cost Data: Eight Months from 1977–1978**

Month	(1) Cost Reported (thousands)	(2) Consumer Price Index (1967 = 100)	(3) = 100 · (1)/(2) Adjusted Cost (1967 dollars)	(4) = (3) · 1.997 Adjusted Cost (October 1978 dollars)
January 1977	$210	175.3	119.8	239.2
April	215	179.6	119.7	239.0
July	240	182.6	131.4	262.4
October	245	184.5	132.8	265.2
January 1978	230	187.2	122.9	245.4
April	240	191.5	125.3	250.2
July	260	196.7	132.2	264.0
October	250	199.7	125.2	250.0

last. Column (1) lists the actual total cost reported from the department. Column (2) gives the CPI for each month measured relative to a base level of 100 for 1967. Column (3) deflates the cost data in (1) by the CPI in (2). The numbers in (3) are the actual costs measured in 1967 dollars. They are lower than the costs in column (1) because the 1967 dollar was worth considerably more than the 1977 and 1978 dollar. The numbers in (4) measure costs in units of the October 1978 dollar (the most recent observation).

When a time series is indexed, the data can be converted to either base-year dollars [1967 as shown in (3)] or current-period dollars [October 1978 as shown in (4)]. There is no substantive difference between the two conversions. The base-year dollar conversion, column (3), has the advantage that the cost data for a month never have to be restated once they have been converted to the base year. With the current-period conversion, column (4), the entire time series has to be updated each time a new cost report and CPI monthly index number are generated. The current-period dollar conversion has the advantage of expressing costs in contemporary dollar units that are now being used throughout the firm's accounting system. If the base-year dollar method is used, then a prediction of cost behavior is obtained in base-year dollars. The analyst should not forget to convert the prediction back to current dollars (by multiplying by the ratio of the current-period index to base-period index) before using the data for planning and control purposes.

The CPI was used to illustrate the indexing technique because it is readily available and familiar to many people. But the CPI measures the change in price of a market basket of goods and services purchased by a typical urban wage earner. The price changes measured in the CPI (including mortgage interest rates, medical care costs, and the cost of hamburger) may bear little relation to the specific price-level changes in material, labor, and energy faced by a particular firm. The United States government produces an enormous variety of specific indexes that will likely be much more relevant to the price changes of a firm's input factors than the CPI. The Producer Price Index reports on the price changes of thousands of commodities and commodity classes. Specific components of this index would be excellent candidates for deflating material costs. The Bureau of Labor Statistics produces monthly time series on changes in labor costs in hundreds of different industries. Some firms produce their own indexes of material and labor costs. When available, these could be used to adjust prior period costs.

The indexing procedure itself, as illustrated in Table 2-1, is extremely simple to implement, especially when using computers. A small investment at the outset of the historical data analysis to select an index appropriate to the cost category being analyzed could have a highly favorable benefit-cost ratio. A longer time series of data can then be used in the historical analysis with less fear of distortions caused by price-level problems. Performing an historical cost analysis without any price-level adjustments of cost data makes the implicit assumption of no price-level changes for the historical period examined. No indexing procedure is perfect, and limitations in the construction of index numbers have been extensively documented. But an intelligently chosen indexing procedure is bound to yield more comparable numbers than an assumption of no price changes at all.

Selection of Measure of Activity Level: The Independent Variable   The discussion until now has focused on obtaining valid, reliable, and comparable measures of cost. We must also select the measure (or measures) of a firm's activity level that we believe causes variation in the firm's costs. For a department producing a relatively homogeneous output—steel, paper, petroleum, check processing, hamburgers, nursing care, ton-miles of freight carried—a physical measure of output should be available and would be an excellent measure of the department's activity level. As with the cost data, we must assure that the measurements of the physical output are accurate and correspond to the exact time period for which the cost data are collected.

When a department produces a heterogeneous output so that counting physical units does not provide a meaningful measure of activity (for example, a food-processing plant producing ketchup, soup, and baby food; a paper-products company producing napkins, tissues, towels, and bags), then we must try to find indirect or summary measures of the firm's output. Usually we will select one or more measures of input activity as a surrogate of the firm's activity level. For a highly automated plant, total machine-hours may be a good measure of activity. For a labor-intensive process, direct labor-hours is a good measure of activity, though this makes the implicit assumption that all labor contributes equally to the output of the department. The use of a weighted measure such as direct labor expense weights the activity of skilled workers more heavily than that of less skilled or less productive workers and hence may be more representative of labor intensity during the period. Use of this dollar-denominated measure, however, introduces the price-level problem just discussed. For some departments, the amount or cost of materials consumed (barrels of oil refined, board-feet of logs processed, tons of steel fabricated) may provide a good summary measure of the department's activity level. The selection of good measures of activity is an art. The guiding principle is to select a measure that can be reliably obtained and is likely to exert a major influence on the cost category being examined.

Plotting the Data   After all the accounting problems with the data have been solved, the appropriate time interval selected, nonstationarities removed, and explanatory variables (activity measures) chosen, we finally reach the most important part of the data-analysis procedure. The cost data should be plotted against the activity measure (or measures) on a scatter diagram (see Exhibit 2-4). The scatter diagram provides many valuable insights. It can help one decide whether the activity measure selected does help to explain the variation in costs. Departures from linearity such as jumps in fixed costs or curvilinear segments can be detected by observing the scatter of points about a linear approximation. Outliers, such as the lower right-hand point in Exhibit 2-4, will become obvious. Such outliers need to be further analyzed to determine whether they are due to measurement errors or unusual nonrecurring conditions in a period. Outliers arising

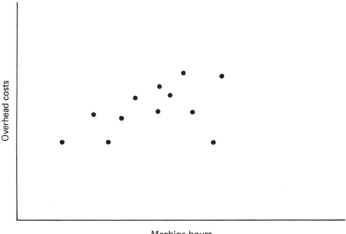

Exhibit 2-4   Scatter Diagram

from these causes should be excluded from the analysis (or the error should be corrected) because they are not representative of past or future cost behavior. If an outlier represents the variation that can occasionally occur, then it can remain in the analysis to demonstrate the inherent variability in cost behavior. Visual inspection of data on a scatter diagram leads to insights that cannot be obtained even by sophisticated analysis of tabular data. This step should not be skipped.

SUMMARY

The first step in analyzing cost behavior patterns is to identify which costs are affected by variations in activity levels and by decisions. The simplest and most important dichotomy distinguishes variable costs (those costs that are affected by the level of activity in a period) from fixed costs (those costs expected to be constant during the period, regardless of the level of output produced or inputs consumed). Within these two cost categories we can distinguish different types of fixed and variable costs. Some fixed costs are already committed by past decisions; others are discretionary, arising from the annual decisions of management for expenditures on intangibles (research and development, advertising, human resources, staff departments, and so on). Also, some costs may be fixed only for moderate variations in a firm's activity level. If output were to expand considerably, there could be jumps in fixed costs as extra shifts are worked, new machines added, or additional supervisors employed. Variable costs, although typically assumed to be linear, could also be piecewise linear (because of overtime) or curvilinear (because of learning-curve effects).

For decision purposes, incremental costs represent changes in total costs caused by changes induced by the decision. Sunk costs represent costs that will not change as a function of the decision or action taken. Opportunity costs value assets when used in alternative ways rather than based on historical cost or current (perhaps idle) usage.

Classifying costs is only the first step for using cost data for decision and control purposes. The next step is to obtain estimates of the magnitudes of these costs. Although engineering methods can yield estimates of desirable cost behavior between output produced and input resources (labor, material, overhead) used, these estimates are expensive to produce. Usually, cost estimates can be obtained from careful analysis of historical cost behavior. This requires the analyst to control for the effects of accounting policies, to attribute cost and output data to the relevant units, to select an appropriate time period for analysis, and to choose one or more measures of activity levels. The most severe problems arise from the nonstationarity of the historic data. The relation between cost behavior and activity levels may change because of changing price levels over time, technological change in the production process, and the effects of learning or experience gained by both workers and management with the production process. Plotting the cost data over time, after controlling for the effect of activity levels, should reveal any systematic nonstationarity in the cost-data time series.

PROBLEMS

2-1. Opportunity Costs

Verify the opportunity cost calculations in the chapter for Noxium and Valmite by assuming a finite amount of production time of 1000 hours per month. Compute the total profits for the Connors Company if the selling price of Valmite is:

1. $140
2. $150
3. $160

under the two extreme cases of

a. all Noxium produced is processed further to make Valmite,
and
b. all Noxium produced is sold at the $100 per ton price.

Compare your answers for these six cases with the predictions for profit maximizing, as a function of Valmite selling price, discussed in the chapter.

2-2. Opportunity Costs and Foregone Revenues (A. Atkinson)

Elmo Short manufactures pine tables which are distributed through a retail chain. Each table is sold for $100 and requires 2 hours of labour, 1 hour of saw time and $30 of materials. Due to shop size limitations, Elmo is limited to two carpenters who are paid $400 each for a forty-hour week. The variable cost of saw operation is $20 per hour.

Elmo received the following letter from Bart Slick, purchasing agent for Gross Furniture Limited.

> Dear Mr. Short:
>
> We are interested in purchasing your output of tables provided that an alteration can be made to the current model. This alteration would require 1 labor hour, $\frac{1}{2}$ hour of saw time, and $8 of materials. This will increase your costs by $28 per unit. Since your current mark-up over cost is $\frac{2}{3}$ we will pay $100 + 28 + 28(\frac{2}{3}) = \$140$ for the new table. We feel that this will provide you with reasonable profit on your operations.
>
> Sincerely,
>
> Bart Slick

Elmo Short has asked you to verify Slick's calculations and to draft a response to the proposal.

2-3. Cost Concepts in a Decision Process: Sunk Costs and Opportunity Costs

Pete Sanders has just received his management degree and is considering operating a small business. As part of a course in Design and Entrepreneurship, he has prepared a business plan for a new company, Coastal Oceanographics, to undertake oceanographic surveys, feasibility studies and consulting services. Before returning to business school Pete had worked for the Navy's Oceanographic Office, traveling around the world while mapping and charting underwater formations using sonar. He enjoyed this type of life and looked forward to running his own business while cruising about the ocean. In preparation for starting his business, he had already purchased $15,000 worth of equipment—sonar, echo sounders, and precise navigation equipment. His business plan showed the following pro forma annual income statement for each of the next three years:

Revenues:	$56,000
Material Costs	5,000
Wages for Boathands	20,000
Amortization of Equipment Purchases (3 year life)	5,000
Net Income	$26,000

While preparing to start this business, Pete receives an offer from an oil exploration firm to work on one of its exploration ships. This also seems like an attractive job, and the proposed salary of $28,000 is higher than the projected income of his new business. Pete is reluctant to accept the new offer because he already has invested $15,000 in equipment that would bring him only $8,000 if he were to resell it. Also he invested a lot of time during his studies preparing the business plan for Coastal Oceanographics. This course represented one eighth of his studies during the year, a year that cost him over $10,000 in tuition, books, room and board expenditures.

Required:

1. Which option maximizes the short term benefit to Pete Sanders. Provide supporting data using the concepts of sunk and opportunity costs.
2. If Pete decides to form and operate Coastal Oceanographics, what is the minimum value that he places on being an entrepreneur?

2-4. Incremental Analysis (CMA)

National Industries is a diversified corporation with separate and distinct operating divisions. Each division's performance is evaluated on the basis of total dollar profits and return on division investment.

The WindAir Division manufactures and sells air conditioner units. The coming year's budgeted income statement, based upon a sales volume of 15,000 units, appears below.

WindAir Division
Budgeted Income Statement
For the 1979–80 Fiscal Year

	Per Unit	Total (000 omitted)
Sales revenue	$400	$6,000
Manufacturing costs		
Compressor	$ 70	$1,050
Other raw materials	37	555
Direct labor	30	450
Variable overhead	45	675
Fixed overhead	32	480
Total manufacturing costs	$214	$3,210
Gross margin	$186	$2,790
Operating expenses		
Variable selling	$ 18	$ 270
Fixed selling	19	285
Fixed administrative	38	570
Total operating expenses	$ 75	$1,125
Net income before taxes	$111	$1,665

WindAir's division manager believes that sales can be increased if the unit selling price of the air conditioners is reduced. A market research study, conducted by an independent firm at the request of the manager, indicates that a 5 percent reduction in the selling price ($20) would increase sales volume 16 percent or 2,400 units. WindAir has sufficient production capacity to manage this increased volume with no increase in fixed costs.

At the present time WindAir uses a compressor in its units which is purchased from an outside supplier at a cost of $70 per compressor. The division manager of WindAir has approached the manager of the Compressor Division regarding the sale of a compressor unit to WindAir. The Compressor Division currently manufactures and sells a unit exclusively to outside firms which is similar to the unit used by WindAir. The specifications of the WindAir compressor are slightly different and would reduce the Compressor Division's raw material cost by $1.50 per unit. In addition, the Compressor Division would not incur any variable selling costs in the units sold to WindAir. The manager of WindAir wants all of the compressors used to come from one supplier and has offered to pay $50 for each compressor unit.

The Compressor Division has the capacity to produce 75,000 units. The coming year's budgeted income statement for the Compressor Division, shown below, is based upon a sales volume of 64,000 units without considering WindAir's proposal.

Compressor Division
Budgeted Income Statement
For the 1979–80 Fiscal Year

	Per Unit	*Total (000 omitted)*
Sales revenue	$100	$6,400
Manufacturing costs		
Raw materials	$ 12	$ 768
Direct labor	8	512
Variable overhead	10	640
Fixed overhead	11	704
Total manufacturing costs	$ 41	$2,624
Gross margin	$ 59	$3,776
Operating expenses		
Variable selling	$ 6	$ 384
Fixed selling	4	256
Fixed administrative	7	448
Total operating expenses	$ 17	$1,088
Net income before taxes	$ 42	$2,688

Required: (Each part should be considered independently)

1. Should WindAir Division institute the 5 percent price reduction on its air conditioner units even if it cannot acquire the compressors internally for $50 each?

2. Assume WindAir needs 17,400 units. Should the Compressor Division be willing to supply the compressor units for $50 each?

3. Assume WindAir needs 17,400 units. Would it be in the best interest of National Industries for the Compressor Division to supply the compressor units at $50 each to the WindAir Division?

2-5. Incremental Profit Analysis (CMA)

Helene's, a high-fashion women's dress manufacturer, is planning to market a new cocktail dress for the coming season. Helene's supplies retailers in the east and mid-Atlantic states.

Four yards of material are required to lay out the dress pattern. Some material remains after cutting which can be sold as remnants.

The leftover material could also be used to manufacture a matching cape and handbag. However, if the leftover material is to be used for the cape and handbag, more care will be required in the cutting which will increase the cutting costs.

The company expected to sell 1,250 dresses if no matching cape or handbag were available. Helene's market research reveals that dress sales will be 20 percent higher if a matching cape and handbag are available. The market research indicates that the cape and/or handbag will not be sold individually but only as accessories with the dress. The various combinations of dresses, capes, and handbags which are expected to be sold by retailers are as follows.

	Percent of total
Complete set of dress, cape, and handbag	70%
Dress and cape	6
Dress and handbag	15
Dress only	9
Total	100%

The material used in the dress costs $12.50 a yard, or $50.00 for each dress. The cost of cutting the dress, if the cape and handbag are not manufactured, is estimated at $20.00 a dress. The resulting remnants can be sold for $5.00 for each dress that is cut out. If the cape and handbag are to be manufactured, the cutting costs will be increased by $9.00 per dress. There will be no salable remnants if the capes and handbags are manufactured in the quantities estimated.

The selling prices and the costs to complete the three items once they are cut are presented below.

	Selling price per unit	Unit cost to complete (excludes cost of material and cutting operation)
Dress	$200.00	$80.00
Cape	27.50	19.50
Handbag	9.50	6.50

Required:

1. Calculate Helene's incremental profit or loss from manufacturing the capes and handbags in conjunction with the dresses.
2. Identify any non-quantitative factors which could influence Helene's management in its decision to manufacture the capes and handbags which match the dress.

2-6. Accepting a Special Order (CMA)

Auer Company had received an order for a piece of special machinery from Jay Company. Just as Auer Company completed the machine, Jay Company declared bankruptcy, defaulted on the order, and forefeited the 10 percent deposit paid on the selling price of $72,500.

Auer's manufacturing manager identified the costs already incurred in the production of the special machinery for Jay as follows:

Direct materials used		$16,600
Direct labor incurred		21,400
Overhead applied:		
Manufacturing:		
Variable	$10,700	
Fixed	5,350	16,050
Fixed selling and administrative		5,405
Total cost		$59,455

Another company, Kaytell Corporation, would be interested in buying the special machinery if it is reworked to Kaytell's specifications. Auer offered to sell the reworked special machinery to Kaytell as a special order for a net price of $68,400. Kaytell has agreed to pay the net price when it takes delivery in two months. The additional identifiable costs to rework the machinery to the specifications of Kaytell are as follows:

Direct materials	$ 6,200
Direct labor	4,200
	$10,400

A second alternative available to Auer is to convert the special machinery to the standard model. The standard model lists for $62,500. The additional identifiable costs to convert the special machinery to the standard model are:

Direct materials	$2,850
Direct labor	3,300
	$6,150

A third alternative for the Auer Company is to sell, as a special order, the machine as is (e.g., without modification) for a net price of $52,000. However, the potential buyer of the unmodified machine does not want it for sixty days. The buyer offers a $7,000 down-payment with final payment upon delivery.

The following additional information is available regarding Auer's operations:

Sales commission rate on sales of standard models is 2 percent while the sales commission rate on special orders is 3 percent. All sales commissions are calculated on net sales price (i.e., list price less cash discount, if any).

Normal credit terms for sales of standard models are 2/10, net/30. Customers take the discounts except in rare instances. Credit terms for special orders are negotiated with the customer.

The application rates for manufacturing overhead and the fixed selling and administrative costs are as follows:

Manufacturing
    Variable   50 percent of direct labor cost
    Fixed   25 percent of direct labor cost
Selling and administrative
    Fixed   10 percent of the total of direct
                                                        material, direct labor and
                                                        manufacturing overhead costs

Normal time required for rework is one month

A surcharge of 5 percent of the sales price is placed on all customer requests for minor modifications of standard models.

Auer normally sells a sufficient number of standard models for the company to operate at a volume in excess of the breakeven point.

Auer does not consider the time value of money in analyses of special orders and projects whenever the time period is less than one year because the effect is not significant.

Required:

1. Determine the dollar contribution each of the three alternatives will add to the Auer Company's before-tax profits.
2. If Kaytell makes Auer a counter offer, what is the lowest price Auer Company should accept for the reworked machinery from Kaytell? Explain your answer.
3. Discuss the influence fixed factory overhead cost should have on the sales prices quoted by Auer Company for special orders when:
    a. a firm is operating at or below the breakeven point.
    b. a firm's special orders constitute efficient utilization of unused capacity above the breakeven volume.

2-7. Effects of Price-Level Shifts on Statistical Analysis of Cost Behavior

Indirect Labor Expense (*ILE*) for the Parker Company is a simple linear function of Direct Labor Hours (*DLH*). At the start of 1979, this relationship is given by:

$$ILE = \beta_0 + \beta_1 DLH$$

with $\beta_0 = 200$ and $\beta_1 = 8$. Six months of operation occurred with these parameters. At the start of the seventh month, all cost categories in the Parker Company increased by 10 percent. Six more months of operation occurred at this price level and at the start of Month 13, another 10 percent across the board increase in all costs occurred. The Parker Company operated at this price level for six more months. Data for

Direct Labor Hours and Indirect Labor Expense for these eighteen months are given below.

Month	DLH (000)	ILE (000)	Month	DLH (000)	ILE (000)
1	20	$360	10	29	$475.2
2	25	400	11	27	457.6
3	22	376	12	25	440.0
4	23	384	13	28	513.0
5	20	360	14	32	551.8
6	19	352	15	35	580.8
7	24	431.2	16	34	571.1
8	28	466.4	17	30	532.4
9	26	448.8	18	36	590.5

Required:

1. Plot the data. Verify that the specified linear relationship holds within each six month period. What values do β_0 and β_1 have during Months 7–12 and Months 13–18?

2. Fit a straight-line (visually or by using a regression routine) to all 18 data points. What values of β_0 and β_1 do you obtain?

3. Perform a price level adjustment to the data and re-estimate β_0 and β_1 using all 18 data points. Assuming no cost increases for Month 19, what is your prediction for Indirect Labor Expense if there were 33(000) Direct Labor Hours in Month 19?

4. Interpret your results. What causes the difference in the linear relationship estimated in Step 2 and Step 3?

2-8. Graphical Analysis and Price-Level Increases of Historical Cost Data (A. Atkinson)

Kanata Manufacturing reports the following monthly data for variable manufacturing overhead in the last two years.

Month	Units Produced	Direct Labor Hours	Variable Overhead
1	20000	39373	384420
2	19000	39444	406433
3	24000	49036	500818
4	17000	32170	332572
5	25000	49174	513408
6	23000	43700	443361
7	21000	39117	408268
8	24000	52662	579595
9	26000	47710	516268
10	27000	49890	535322

Month	Units Produced	Direct Labor Hours	Variable Overhead
11	29000	56428	628611
12	24000	52593	590060
13	20000	40790	447812
14	19000	37554	424349
15	24000	48735	549967
16	27000	54295	622822
17	29000	58047	674509
18	31000	58854	690004
19	33000	69883	837694
20	28000	53278	638954
21	26000	51869	636651
22	27000	55902	692125
23	24000	50809	654152
24	25000	51042	635756

Ralph Smart, factory accountant, has been studying this data for the purpose of developing a predictive equation for variable overhead.

Required:

1. Use a scatter diagram to investigate the pattern of variable overhead cost behavior.
2. Ralph has concluded that the purchase price of overhead items has been increasing at the rate of 1 percent per month for the last two years. How would this new information affect your response to Question 1?

2-9. Relevant Time Period for Statistical Analysis of Cost Data (CMA Adapted)

The Alma Plant manufactures the industrial product line of CJS Industries. Plant management wants to be able to get a good, yet quick, estimate of the manufacturing overhead costs which can be expected to be incurred each month. The easiest and simplest method to accomplish this task appears to be to develop a flexible budget formula for the manufacturing overhead costs.

The plant's accounting staff suggested that simple linear regression be used to determine the cost behavior pattern of the overhead costs. The regression data can provide the basis for the flexible budget formula. Sufficient evidence is available to conclude that manufacturing overhead costs vary with direct labor hours. The actual direct labor hours and the corresponding manufacturing overhead costs for each month of the last three years were used in the linear regression analysis.

The three-year period contained various occurrences not uncommon to many businesses. During the first year, production was severely curtailed during two months due to wildcat strikes. In the second year production was reduced in one month because of material shortages, and materially increased (overtime scheduled) during two months to meet the units required for a one-time sales order. At the end of the second year, employee benefits were raised significantly as the result of a labor agreement. Production during the third year was not affected by any special circumstances.

Various members of Alma's accounting staff raised some issues regarding the historical data collected for the regression analysis. These issues were as follows.

1. Some members of the accounting staff believed that the use of data from all 36 months would provide a more accurate portrayal of the cost behavior. While they recognized that any of the monthly data could include efficiencies and inefficiencies, they believed these efficiencies/inefficiencies would tend to balance out over a longer period of time.

2. Other members of the accounting staff suggested that only those months which were considered normal should be used so that the regression would not be distorted.

3. Still other members felt that only the most recent 12 months should be used because they were the most current.

4. Some members questioned whether historical data should be used at all to form the basis for a flexible budget formula.

The accounting department ran two regression analyses of the data—one using the data from all 36 months and the other using only the data from the last 12 months. The information derived from the two linear regressions is shown below.

Least Squares Regression Analyses

36 Month Regression[a]	
$OH_t = \$123{,}810 + \$1.60$ DLH$_t$; $R^2 = .32$	
(1.64)	
12 Month Regression[a]	
$OH_t = \$109{,}020 + \$3.00$ DLH$_t$; $R^2 = .48$	
(3.01)	

[a] t-statistic is in parentheses below estimated variable cost coefficient

Required:

1. Which of the two results (12 months versus 36 months) would you use as a basis for the flexible budget formula?

2. How would the four specific issues raised by the members of Alma's accounting staff influence your willingness to use the results of the statistical analyses as the basis for the flexible budget formula? Explain your answer.

TABLE 1. Spending Analysis (000)

| | | Month | | | Year-to-Date | |
| | | Variance from Plan[a] | | | Variance from Plan[a] | |
Department	Actual	$	%	Actual	$	%
Professional/Care-Total	$1142	30	3	$6320	200	3
Anesthesiology	60	—	—	300	20	7
Blood Bank	40	(10)	(20)	200	(34)	(20)
Laboratory	175	(15)	(8)	825	(50)	(6)
Nursing Service	250	30	14	1310	90	7
Radiology-Diagnostic	120	10	9	590	74	14
⋮	⋮			⋮		
Services-Total	415	(80)	(16)	1600	(30)	(2)
Dietary	120	(15)	(11)	485	12	2
Housekeeping	75	3	4	330	30	10
Maintenance	160	(65)	(68)	530	(80)	(18)
⋮	⋮			⋮		
Overhead-Total	220	(8)	(4)	1120	12	1
Business Office	52	(3)	(5)	248	(20)	(7)
Depreciation	60	—	—	300	—	—
⋮	⋮			⋮		

[a] Favorable variance in parentheses.

2-10. Conditions for Statistical Estimation of Relationships from Historic Data*

Bob Nalpak has just been hired as a consultant to a large local hospital. His mission is to devise improved planning and control procedures that will aid the hospital administrator in managing the organization. Bob believes that improving the cost accounting and reporting system will provide a good project, yielding benefits that can be realized quickly and thereby establishing credibility with the hospital administrator.

At present, the hospital accounting system produces a monthly report on the cost of each department, patient unit, and service center in the hospital. This report (excerpts are shown above in Table 1) displays actual costs and the variance from budget for each month and year-to-date.

At present, the administrator reads this report each month and, if costs are too high, he sends a memorandum to the offending department requesting an explanation.

Nalpak felt that the basic idea of monthly reporting and follow up seemed sensible, but could be improved by controlling for variations in the amount of service

---

* This example is adapted from Robert S. Kaplan, "Management Accounting in Hospitals: A Case Study," in J. L. Livingstone and S. C. Gunn, *Accounting for Social Goals* (Harper & Row, 1974) 131–148.

delivered each month by a given department. It was possible that a higher than budgeted cost in a department could have occurred because it performed a larger number of procedures or processed a larger number of patients, or, in general, had a higher level of activity than had been expected that month. To the extent that incremental increases in volume lead to increased costs, the department would likely exceed its budget. Conversely, for months in which there was a lower level of service provided than was anticipated when the budget was prepared, departments should be expected to be *under* their budgeted costs. In these cases, Nalpak reasoned that the administrator should not be satisfied with actual costs just equalling budgeted costs.

Nalpak collected a monthly volume or units-of-service index for as many departments as he could (number of tests performed, hours of anesthesia, etc.) For those departments where no volume index was available, the number of patient days was used as a surrogate measure of activity. Nalpak then estimated a regression model for each major department or cost center:

$$C_{it} = a_i + b_i V_{it} + \epsilon_{it}$$

where C_{it} = Actual Cost in Department i in Month t
         V_{it} = Volume or Units-of-Service Index for Department i in Month t
         ϵ_{it} = Error Term
         a_i, b_i = Fixed and Variable Cost Coefficients for Department i

These regressions were estimated on the most recent 12 months of data from each major department.

Nalpak was greatly chagrined by the results. The variable cost coefficients, b_i, were mostly insignificant and frequently of the wrong sign. The explanatory power of the regressions was low and there was a high degree of serial correlation in the residuals. It appeared as if costs were just increasing over time and that there was no relation between costs and activity levels.

Before reporting these inconclusive results to the administrator, Nalpak decided to investigate further. He concentrated on one department, Radiology-Diagnostic, and examined the monthly reports from this department in as much detail as he could uncover. Excerpts and summaries from this discovery process appear below in Tables 2 and 3.

Required:

Explain why Bob Nalpak had trouble fitting his regression model to the monthly data from the hospital. Be specific in identifying as many causes as you can for the poor explanatory power of the regressions. What adjustments would you recommend be made that could improve the use of a regression model for this application?

TABLE 2.

Department:	Reported Units of Service Index
Radiology— Diagnostic	Running average of the number of procedures performed each month for the prior 12 months.

Month	Actual number of Radiology-Diagnostic procedures performed (not reported outside the department)
July 1979	4019
August	5805
September	5385
October	4558
November	5885
December	4613
January 1980	5926
February	6146
March	10791
April	8563
May	6874
June	6974
	75539

TABLE 3. Radiology—Diagnostic

Month	Salaries (total)	Films and Chemicals	Purchased Services	Equipment and Instruments
July 1979	$ 94,000	$26,800	$4,480	$ 160
August	104,600	21,000	2,900	7,300
September	100,600	20,400	2,800	580
October	103,000	19,400	640	12,540
November	103,000	59,000	4,600	380
December	114,000	16,400	3,800	1,070
January 1980	114,000	16,000	4,400	720
February	96,000	77,000	5,000	580
March	107,400	13,200	6,900	3,850
April	107,000	20,800	25,500	1,000
May	143,200	73,000	6,500	2,700
June	143,400	22,400	44,600	8,900

REFERENCES

HORNGREN, CHARLES T., "Choosing Accounting Practices for Reporting to Management," *NAA Bulletin* XLIV (September 1962), 3–15.

KAPLAN, ROBERT S., "Management Accounting in Hospitals: A Case Study," in J. L. Livingstone and S. Gunn, *Accounting for Social Goals: Budgeting and Analysis of Non-Market Projects.* New York: Harper & Row, 1974.

"Separating and Using Costs as Fixed and Variable," *NAA Bulletin* XLI (June 1960).

SHILLINGLAW, GORDON, "The Concept of Attributable Cost," *Journal of Accounting Research* I (Spring 1963), 73–85.

ESTIMATING COST BEHAVIOR

3

ACCOUNT CLASSIFICATION

In Chapter 2 we discussed the careful collection and preparation of data for analysis of historical costs. The objective of such analysis is to obtain estimates of the fixed and variable costs of the firm. The simplest and fastest technique for obtaining first estimates of these costs is by direct analysis of each component of cost. We use our knowledge of each component to make a preliminary estimate of whether it is likely to be fixed or variable. For instance, direct materials and labor will usually be variable, leaving just the overhead costs to be classified.

Consider the monthly overhead budget for the machining department of the Garner Company given in Table 3-1. Supervision is most likely a fixed cost within a normal range of activity. Indirect labor, including material handlers and idle time, probably has variable components. Without knowing the budget or actual costs at a level of activity other than 14,000 machine-hours, we cannot estimate fixed and variable components. Therefore, we initially classify indirect labor as a variable cost and estimate a variable cost per machine-hour of $2,400/14,000 = $0.17. Alternatively, we can make an arbitrary judgment as to the proportion that is fixed and the proportion that is variable. For example, we can assume that half of the costs in this category are fixed and half are variable, in which case the fixed-cost component is $1,200 per month and the variable cost is $0.086 per machine-hour ($1,200/14,000). For now, we will assume it is completely variable at $0.17/machine-hour. Supplies costs are probably variable and equal to $0.05/machine-hour. Payroll taxes, being directly proportional to labor expense, will also be variable (though if indirect labor expense has some fixed costs, the payroll taxes associated with these costs will also be a fixed expense). Assuming payroll taxes are all variable, we get an estimate of $0.12/machine-hour. Overtime premiums will be variable and equal to $0.016/machine-hour, whereas depreciation will be fixed.

Miscellaneous factory overhead includes charges for building depreciation,

55

TABLE 3-1. **Budgeted Overhead Costs at 14,000 Machine-Hours—Garner Company**

Account	Budgeted Overhead Cost
Supervision	$1,900
Indirect labor	2,400
Supplies	700
Payroll taxes	1,680
Overtime premiums	220
Depreciation	800
Miscellaneous factory overhead	3,000
Total	$10,700

insurance, utilities, and janitorial and maintenance expenses. Clearly, some of these are fixed, while others (utilities, housekeeping, and maintenance) could have variable components. Further investigation reveals that the factory overhead charge is based on the total cost of these items throughout the factory and allocated proportional to the square feet of space occupied by each department. Therefore, to a first approximation—neglecting the minor effect on total utility and maintenance cost caused by activity changes in the machining department—we can consider the factory overhead to be a fixed cost. Summing up these components yields the classification in Table 3-2. This account classification yields a flexible budget for the department of:

Monthly overhead costs $= \$5,700 + \$0.357 \cdot$ machine-hours.

Obviously this method is easy to implement. Its limitations are:

1. It depends heavily upon our classification of an account as fixed or variable. If indirect labor expense is actually entirely a fixed

TABLE 3-2. **Fixed and Variable Costs**

Account	Fixed Cost	Variable Cost	Variable Cost Machine-Hour
Supervision	$1,900		
Indirect labor		$2,400	$0.171
Supplies		700	0.05
Payroll taxes		1,680	0.12
Overtime premiums		220	0.016
Depreciation	800		
Miscellaneous factory overhead	3,000		
Total	$5,700	$5,000	$0.357

expense, the flexible budget should be $8,100 + $0.186 · machine-hours, which represents almost a 50 percent reduction in the estimated variable-overhead coefficient.

2. It relies on only a single observation at a single activity level to determine the cost equation. We have no evidence on the cost fluctuation even at the assumed level of 14,000 machine-hours and obviously none on costs at levels other than 14,000 machine-hours.

3. It gives us no insight as to whether some costs are partially fixed and partially variable (mixed costs). If indirect labor expense were actually half fixed and half variable, the flexible budget would become $6,900 + 0.271 · machine-hours, producing a 25 percent reduction in the variable-overhead cost coefficient.

The first two objections can be overcome if we have estimates of costs at more than one activity level. Suppose that the Garner Company has prepared overhead budgets at four different activity levels, as shown in Table 3-3. We see that supplies is a completely variable cost at $0.05/machine-hour. Also, depreciation and factory overhead are completely fixed costs. Supervision is a semifixed cost that increases by $300 when machine-hours exceed a level somewhere between 14,000 and 16,000. Indirect labor expense is a mixed cost with a fixed component of $1,000 and a variable component of $0.10/machine-hour. Payroll taxes are all variable with a slope of $0.12/machine-hour. Overtime premium is curvilinear, increasing at a more rapid rate as the activity level increases. Thus, by having budgeted or actual costs at different activity levels, we obtain better indications as to the nature of the cost behavior for each account category.

The account-classification method still does not provide evidence on the underlying variability or uncertainty in the cost process from one observation to another. Typically, only the most recent set of observations may be used to estimate fixed and variable costs. It is a simple and inexpensive method to use, but it does require that the analyst make a number of arbitrary judgments. A

TABLE 3-3. Budgeted Overhead Costs

	Volume (machine-hours)			
	10,000	*12,000*	*14,000*	*16,000*
Supervision	$1,900	$1,900	$1,900	$2,200
Indirect labor	2,000	2,200	2,400	2,600
Supplies	500	600	700	800
Payroll taxes	1,210	1,430	1,680	1,930
Overtime premiums	50	70	220	400
Depreciation	800	800	800	800
Factory overhead	3,000	3,000	3,000	3,000
Total	$9,460	$10,000	$10,700	$11,730

deeper understanding of the actual pattern of cost behavior can be obtained by a statistical analysis of historic data.

STATISTICAL ANALYSIS OF COST BEHAVIOR

We now embark on a serious exploration of the use of statistical techniques for analyzing cost variation. We will start with the fifteen months of data of overhead costs from a cost center of the Robinson Company shown in Table 3-4. The first step should always be to plot the data to see whether there is a relationship between the variable of interest, overhead cost, and the proposed explanatory variable, direct labor-hours. To conform with statistical terminology, we will refer to the variable we are interested in explaining (overhead costs) as the *dependent variable*. Variables such as direct labor-hours used to predict the variation in a dependent variable will be called *independent variables*.

Exhibit 3-1 provides the scatter diagram of overhead cost and direct labor-hours. Inspection reveals a definite relationship between the two variables without strong suggestions of nonlinearities. It seems reasonable to proceed to estimate a linear relationship between these two variables.

The *high-low method* provides a quick but highly approximate procedure for fitting a straight line through these points. The method is aptly named, since it consists of connecting the highest point (1,290, 30,200) to the lowest point (740, 20,800) with a straight line. We estimate the straight line using the well-known equation of a straight line we learned in high school:

TABLE 3-4.   **Robinson Company Overhead Cost**

Month	Overhead Cost	Direct Labor-Hours
1	25,200	840
2	24,800	830
3	20,800	740
4	27,500	1,130
5	23,300	770
6	26,900	910
7	24,800	950
8	26,100	1,170
9	29,100	1,160
10	27,300	1,030
11	27,600	1,200
12	21,100	780
13	21,700	750
14	30,200	1,290
15	27,300	1,060

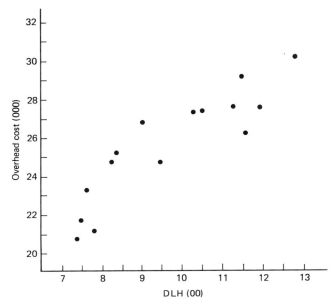

Exhibit 3-1   Scatter Diagram: Overhead Cost Versus Direct Labor-Hours

$$y = mx + b, \tag{3-1}$$

where m is the slope of the line and b is the y intercept (where $x = 0$). We estimate m and b by

$$m = \frac{y_2 - y_1}{x_2 - x_1} = \frac{30{,}200 - 20{,}800}{1{,}290 - 740} = \frac{9{,}400}{550} = 17.1$$

and

$$b = y - mx = 30{,}200 - 17.1\,(1{,}290) = 8{,}150.$$

The high-low method came to popularity before the ready availability of inexpensive electronic calculators and time-shared computers, which now make it easy to obtain regression estimates of intercepts and slopes. The advantage of the high-low method is its simplicity. Its disadvantage is that it uses only the two extreme observations to fit the data. If you connect the two extreme points in Exhibit 3-1, you will see that of the remaining thirteen observations, ten are above the line and only three are below it. Therefore this line is not representative of all the data points. By relying on just the two extreme points, the high-low method uses observations that may represent abnormal rather than typical operating conditions. There is also some ambiguity in the method. If the observation with the lowest x value is not also the one with the lowest y value, there is not a unique low point. A similar ambiguity could arise when attempting to identify the high point.

An alternative method is to draw a line in by moving a straight edge (preferably a transparent one) amidst the data until you are satisfied that you have a line that seems to fit the data adequately. This visual method is also easy to perform but it requires an additional step to estimate the slope and intercept parameters after the line is drawn. Obviously it is subjective, and different analysts may fit quite different straight lines to the data. Neither the high-low nor the visual method provides any insights about the statistical properties of the data or the estimated straight line produced by the method.

ORDINARY LEAST-SQUARES REGRESSION

Regression analysis assumes a linear relationship between the dependent and independent variables. It makes explicit assumptions about the distribution of the error term—the term that represents departures from the assumed linear relationship. With regression analysis, we obtain (1) an estimated fit to the data (usually linear but not necessarily) and (2) procedures for estimating the confidence we have in the fitted relationship, and (3) confidence intervals for the predictions from the fitted model. Recent advances in calculators and computers make the computational aspects of regression analysis almost trivial, so the technique is now accessible to all interested analysts. The danger is that an analyst may use it unthinkingly, unaware of its assumptions, opportunities, and limitations.

Our discussion of regression analysis can only survey the principal ideas and critical issues. Greater confidence in the proper use of regression analysis must be obtained from entire courses devoted to linear models or econometrics and from supervised experience with the procedure.

For the data in Table 3-4, we let

$$y_t = \text{overhead cost in month } t,$$

$$x_t = \text{direct labor hours in month } t,$$

and assume a simple linear model:

$$y_t = \beta_0 + \beta_1 x_t + \epsilon_t. \tag{3-2}$$

The coefficients β_0 and β_1 are unknown parameters, and ϵ_t is an error term representing the effects of omitted and transitory random factors in month t that also affect overhead costs. It would be rare for all the observations on costs and activity levels to have an exact linear relationship. The error term, ϵ_t, attempts to capture the departures from strict linearity (such as unusual efficiencies or inefficiencies in a month, and factors other than direct labor-hours affecting overhead costs).

In the linear relationship, β_0 represents the fixed overhead in the Robinson Company's cost center. We do not literally mean that we would expect the overhead cost to equal β_0 were the activity level (x_t) to be reduced to zero. We see from Table 3-4 or Exhibit 3-1 that we have observations for the independent variable only in the range of 740 to 1,290 direct labor-hours (DLH). We have no evidence of how costs would behave were DLH to be well outside this range (such as 0). Therefore, our interpretation of β_0 should be consistent with the available evidence; β_0 represents the level of fixed costs when DLH is in the range of 740 to 1,290 DLH.

The parameter β_1 is the variable component of overhead costs in this region. If DLH increases by one hour, we expect overhead costs to increase by β_1 dollars. The linear relationship implies that if DLH increases by 100 hours, expected overhead costs will increase by $100\beta_1$ dollars.

Typically, β_0 and β_1 are estimated by an *ordinary least-squares* (*OLS*) regression routine to minimize the sum of the squares of the vertical distances from each observation point to the estimated line. That is, estimates b_0 and b_1 are obtained that minimize the quantity

$$\sum_t (y_t - b_0 - b_1 x_t)^2.$$

Using calculus, one can show that

$$b_1 = \frac{\sum (x_t - \bar{x})(y_t - \bar{y})}{\sum (x_t - \bar{x})^2} \qquad (3\text{-}3)$$

and

$$b_0 = \bar{y} - b_1 \bar{x}, \qquad (3\text{-}4)$$

where $\bar{x} = \sum x_t / n$, the mean of the independent variable,

$\bar{y} = \sum y_t / n$, the mean of the dependent variable,

n = number of observations.

(For the data in Table 3-4, $n = 15$.) Note that the definition of b_0 forces the regression line to pass through the mean $(\bar{x}, \bar{y})$ of the observations. The quantities b_0 and b_1 (and initially all other regression statistics) are usually obtained from computerized packages, so that we do not have to compute them manually using the above equations.

For the Robinson Company data in Table 3-4, we obtain the estimates

$$b_0 = 12{,}290, \qquad b_1 = 13.6,$$

which are quite different from the values obtained by the high-low method. In Exhibit 3-2 we plot the estimated regression line in the scatter diagram.

Table 3-5 tabulates the actual overhead cost, y_t, the predicted overhead cost, $\hat{y}_t = b_0 + b_1 x_t$, and the error from the regression, $e_t = y_t - \hat{y}_t$.

A frequently used measure of how well the linear relationship explains the variation in the dependent variable (overhead costs) is the *coefficient of determination* or R^2. With data on only the dependent variable (overhead cost), all we would observe would be the variation in overhead cost over the fifteen-month period. The variance of this cost, also called the *total sum of squares (SST)*, is given by

$$SST = \frac{\sum_t (y_t - \bar{y})^2}{n} = 7,597,600. \qquad (3\text{-}5)$$

Without observing any other variables, we would have to conclude that overhead cost was highly variable from month to month, ranging from a low of $20,800 in month 3 to a high of $30,200 in month 14. Most of this variation, however, can be explained by the dependence of overhead cost on activity levels (as measured by DLH) and the variation in DLH from month to month. If there had been less variation in DLH, there would have been less variation in overhead cost. We can measure how much of the variation in overhead cost is explained by the variation in DLH by computing the explained or regression *mean sum of squares (SSR)* as

$$SSR = \frac{\sum (\hat{y}_t - \bar{y})^2}{n}, \qquad (3\text{-}6)$$

where $\hat{y}_t = b_0 + b_1 x_t$, the predicted overhead cost for each month from the fitted regression line. For our data, SSR = 6,036,500. Therefore, of the total variance in the dependent variable of 7,597,600, the regression equation explained a total

TABLE 3-5. **Summary of Regression Predictions**

Month	y_t	$\hat{y}_t = 12{,}290 + 13.6 \cdot x_t$	$e_t = y_t - \hat{y}_t$
1	25,200	23,752	1,448
2	24,800	23,615	1,185
3	20,800	22,387	−1,587
4	27,500	27,709	−209
5	23,300	22,796	504
6	26,900	24,707	2,193
7	24,800	25,253	−453
8	26,100	28,254	−2,154
9	29,100	28,118	982
10	27,300	26,334	956
11	27,600	28,664	−1,064
12	21,100	22,933	−1,833
13	21,700	22,524	−824
14	30,200	29,892	308
15	27,300	26,753	547
Mean	25,580	25,580	0
Mean sum of squares	7,597,600	6,036,500	1,561,100
Standard deviation	2,853	2,543	1,293

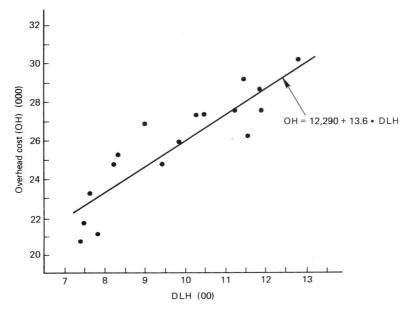

Exhibit 3-2   Regression Line

of 6,036,500. The ratio of these two quantities, the percentage of explained variation, SSR/SST, is called the coefficient of determination or R^2:

$$R^2 = \frac{\text{SSR}}{\text{SST}} = \frac{6{,}036{,}500}{7{,}597{,}600} = 0.79. \tag{3-7}$$

Thus 79 percent of the variation in departmental overhead costs is explained by the linear relation between overhead and DLH. Only 21 percent is due to random or omitted factors. The R^2 of a regression is a convenient measure of the goodness of fit of the regression. Values of R^2 above 0.5 or 0.7 indicate a reasonably good fit; above 0.9, the regression is explaining almost all the variation in the dependent variable. If R^2 is below 0.1, we are explaining little of the variation in the dependent variable.

We can get an estimate of the variance of the error term, ϵ_t, by computing the mean sum of squares of the residuals (SSE = sum of squared errors). The residual or error of the tth observation is displayed in Table 3-5. The variance of the residuals, or SSE, is computed as

$$\text{SSE} = \frac{\sum e_t^2}{n} = \sum (y_t - b_0 - b_1 x_t)^2. \tag{3-8}$$

For our data, SSE = 1,561,100. Note that

$$\text{SST} = \text{SSR} + \text{SSE}, \tag{3-9}$$

so that an alternative definition of R^2 is

$$R^2 = 1 - \frac{\text{SSE}}{\text{SST}} \, . \tag{3-10}$$

From Table 3-5, we see that the mean of the predicted values, $\sum \hat{y}_t/n$, equals the mean of the actual values ($\bar{y} = 25{,}580$) and that the mean residual ($\sum e_t/n$) is zero. This is not an accident. It is a consequence of the definition of the constant term b_0 in the regression, which forces the regression line through the mean ($\bar{x}$, $\bar{y}$) of the independent and dependent variables. Whenever a constant term is included in the regression, the mean of the residuals should always sum to zero (except for an insignificant rounding error). This is a good check on the precision of your computer program, for if the residuals do not have a zero mean, the regression routine is not operating properly.

An important characterization of the fitted relationship is the standard error of the regression, s_e:

$$s_e = \sqrt{\frac{\sum e_t^2}{n - 2}} \, . \tag{3-11}$$

We divide by $n - 2$ rather than by n because two parameters, b_0 and b_1, have been estimated from the data. (Convince yourself that with only two observations, the regression line would fit the two observations perfectly so that there would be no errors—e_1 and e_2 would both equal 0.) For our data,

$$s_e = \sqrt{\text{SSE} \cdot \frac{n}{n - 2}} = 1{,}342;$$

this quantity represents the magnitude of errors encountered about the estimated regression line. From Table 3-5, we can see that ten of the fifteen observations are within one standard error (s_e) of the regression line and none of the observations is more than 1.65 standard errors from the prediction of the regression equation.

STATISTICAL INFERENCE IN REGRESSION

Until now we have not made explicit assumptions about the distribution of the error term. By assuming that the error term has a normal distribution, we can use classical normal distribution theory to infer the distributions of the coefficient estimates, the regression line, and forecasts from the regression line. In particular, we assume

$$\epsilon_t \sim N(0, \sigma^2);$$

that is, we assume that each error term is normally distributed with zero mean and constant variance σ^2. This assumption implies that the distribution of the error term is independent of the magnitude of the independent variables (this property is called *homoscedasticity*)—that is, large values of x_t are not associated with large errors. Also, we assume that error terms from different observations are independent of each other: $E(\epsilon_t \epsilon_s) = 0$ for $t \neq s$. The independence assumption implies that the deviation of one point from the regression line is unrelated to the deviation of any other point. This independence assumption is most likely to be violated with time-series data when the errors in successive observations may be correlated. We will discuss this problem, called autocorrelation, later in the chapter.

If the error terms, ϵ_t, are normally distributed, then it can be shown that the regression estimates, b_0 and b_1, are themselves random variables drawn from a normal distribution. Formally,

$$b_1 \sim N(\beta_1, \sigma_{b_1});$$

that is, b_1 is normally distributed with a mean equal to the true (but unobservable) parameter, β_1. The true standard deviation is also unobservable but its sample estimate, s_{b_1}, is given by

$$s_{b_1} = \frac{s_e}{\sqrt{\sum_t (x_t - \bar{x})^2}}, \tag{3-12}$$

where s_e is the standard error of the regression, defined earlier. The measure s_{b_1} is the amount of sampling error in the coefficient b_1, the average dispersion we expect b_1 to be from its true (but unknown) value β_1. With the data in Table 3-4, we find that $\sum_t (x_t - \bar{x})^2 = 486{,}360$, so that

$$s_{b_1} = \frac{s_e}{\sqrt{486{,}360}} = \frac{1{,}342}{697.4} = 1.92.$$

Therefore the estimated coefficient of $b_1 = 13.64$ has a standard error of 1.92.

If we wish to test whether the variable overhead coefficient, β_1, is statistically significant, we test the hypothesis that β_1 equals 0; in other words, we test whether b_1 could have come from a distribution with zero mean. We form the t ratio

$$\frac{b_1}{s_{b_1}} = \frac{13.64}{1.92} = 7.1.$$

This statistic has a t ratio with $n - 2 = 13$ degrees of freedom, not a normal distribution, because we are using an estimate of the standard deviation, s_{b_1}, rather than the true standard deviation. The probability of obtaining a t ratio as large as 7 by chance (when the true value is zero) is miniscule, and we can be confident that there is a significant variable-overhead cost component—that $b_1 > 0$. A standard rule of thumb is to believe that a regression coefficient is significantly different from zero if its t ratio exceeds 2, roughly a 0.05 significance level.

For profit planning, we will be interested in knowing more than whether the coefficient b_1 is different from zero. In order to compute the variable cost of production we need an estimate of the actual value of the variable-cost coefficient, β_1. Our best estimate is the regression coefficient, $b_1 = 13.64$, but the standard error enables us to compute reasonable upper and lower bounds for the variable-cost coefficient. Typically we compute a 95 percent confidence interval about the estimated value. For a normally distributed estimate, the 95 percent confidence interval is obtained by multiplying the standard error by ± 1.96 (the 2.5 and 97.5 percent fractiles of the cumulative normal distribution, leaving 2.5 percent of the area in each extreme tail).

Since we are using an estimate of the standard deviation, the coefficient estimate actually has a t distribution. With 13 degrees of freedom, the appropriate factor (from a table of the t distribution) is 2.16, so that the 95 percent confidence interval for the variable-overhead cost coefficient is

$$b_1 \pm 2.16 \cdot s_{b_1} = 13.64 \pm 2.16 \cdot 1.92$$

$$= 13.64 \pm 4.15 \text{ or } (9.49, 17.79).$$

This is a fairly wide interval. We could obtain smaller intervals by choosing a lower degree of confidence or by trying to get a better regression fit so that the standard error of the coefficient would be reduced.

Most analysts interpret the confidence interval in a way that is not precisely correct. It is often said, erroneously, that the probability is 0.95 that the true value of the variable-cost coefficient, β_1, is between 9.49 and 17.79. The correct statement is that 95 percent of the confidence intervals constructed in this manner will contain the true value. For any particular confidence interval, such as (9.49, 17.79), the true value is either in the interval or it is not. The probability is either 1 or 0 that the true value is within the confidence interval.

For many regression applications, an analyst would not be interested in testing the significance of the fixed-cost coefficient, b_0, since it has been chosen mainly to position the regression line to pass through the mean of the independent and dependent variables $(\bar{x}, \bar{y})$. For cost estimation, however, we are interested in whether there is a significant fixed-cost component. If not, we could treat the entire account as a completely variable cost. The standard error of the fixed-cost component, s_{b_0}, is defined as

$$s_{b_0} = s_e \left\{ \frac{\sum x_t^2}{n[\sum (x_t - \bar{x})^2]} \right\}^{1/2}$$

$$= \sqrt{\frac{\sum x_t^2}{n}} \, s_{b_1} \qquad (3\text{-}13)$$

$$= 1{,}906.$$

The t ratio for the fixed-cost coefficient is, therefore,

$$\frac{b_0}{s_{b_0}} = \frac{12{,}290}{1{,}906} = 6.45,$$

and it is clear that the overhead cost does have a significant fixed-cost component. If the fixed-cost coefficient proved to have a low t ratio, say 1.5 or less, we could reestimate the model assuming that the overhead-cost category was completely variable within the range of the data used to estimate the relationship. In this case, the regression would be estimated with no fixed component ($b_0 = 0$), and

$$b_1 = \frac{\sum x_t y_t}{\sum x_t^2} \tag{3-14}$$

would be the ordinary least-squares estimate of the variable cost.[1]

PREDICTING FROM A REGRESSION
EQUATION

In the preceding section we obtained estimates of the variable cost coefficient b_1 and its likely range of variation. These estimates are helpful in product planning and cost-volume-profit analysis to determine the variable-cost components of a product, particularly the variable-overhead cost. The regression equation is also useful in cost control to develop a flexible budget for a department. For cost control purposes we are less interested in the particular value of b_1 than in the predicted value of overhead cost in a period. For example, suppose that in month 16 the overhead cost in the Robinson Company's cost center is $24,000 and the DLH worked equals 800. Is this observation consistent with the preceding fifteen months used to estimate the regression line?

As a first step, we should check that the observation is within the range of observations used to estimate the linear relationship. Our data can only support predictions for values of the independent variable that are in the limited range of the historical data. We really have no evidence about how costs will behave outside the range of our experience. In this case, the historical data show values of DLH between 740 and 1,290, so that the new observation is within the range of data used to estimate the regression line.

The next step is to obtain the prediction from the regression line as

$$y_f = b_0 + b_1 \cdot 800 = 12{,}290 + 13.6 \cdot 800 = 23{,}170.$$

The error is $24{,}000 - 23{,}170 = 830$. Is this an unusually large error or is it of a magnitude we would expect, given the precision of the regression line?

---

[1] Not all computerized regression packages can estimate a linear relationship with no constant term. Some packages automatically insert a constant for every regression.

There are two sources of error in obtaining a forecast from a regression line. The first is the standard error of observations about the estimated regression line (see equation (3-11)), the quantity we defined as $s_e = 1,342$. The second source arises from the uncertainty in the regression line itself—how much variation there could be in the slope and intercept of the line. Combining these two sources of error, we obtain the standard error of a forecast, s_f, for a new observation (one not used to estimate the regression line) as

$$s_f = s_e \sqrt{1 + \frac{1}{n} + \frac{(x_f - \bar{x})^2}{\sum (x_t - \bar{x})^2}} \tag{3-15}$$

where x_f is the value of the independent variable for the forecast observation. Notice that this standard error of forecast is minimized when $x_f = \bar{x}$, the mean of the independent variables used to estimate the relationship, and increases as the distance between the new observation and the mean value increases. This occurs because the regression line must always go through the mean of the independent and dependent variables; we are most sure about the height of the line at this point. As we move away from this mean value, small changes in the slope of the line will cause greater uncertainty in the height of the line. Hence, the standard error of the regression line increases as the independent variable takes on values far from the mean, $\bar{x}$.

For our example, $\sum (x_t - \bar{x})^2 = 486,360$, and $x_f - \bar{x} = 800 - 974 = -174$. Therefore,

$$s_f = 1,342 \left[1 + \frac{1}{15} + \frac{(-174)^2}{486,360} \right]^{1/2} = 1,342(1.0625)$$

$$= 1,426.$$

The forecast error is 830, which is 0.58 standard errors ($0.58 = 830/1,426$) from the expected value, certainly within the range of dispersion we would expect given the historical spread of observations about the regression line.

Knowing the standard error of the forecast from a regression line is helpful in deciding whether a given observation is statistically significant. If an overhead standard has been established using regression analysis, we can report the significance level of any accounting variance from the standard. In this case, the deviation of $830 is only 0.58 standard errors from the regression line, which is not statistically significant. If the cost had been, say, $26,500, when DLH equaled 800, the prediction error would have been $26,500 - 23,170 = 3,330$, which is 2.34 standard errors from the expected value:

$$\frac{y - y_f}{s_f} = \frac{3,330}{1,426} = 2.34.$$

The probability of a deviation this large, from a t distribution with 13 degrees of freedom, is well below 0.05. Therefore, the chances are less than 1 in 20 that an overhead cost of $26,500, when DLH equaled 800, is consistent with the fifteen observations used to establish the overhead standard.

When overhead or other standards are established from statistical analysis of historical cost data, these standards do not necessarily represent efficient or optimal performance. Rather they represent the level of performance or cost behavior experienced in the past. They can signal whether current performance has deteriorated (or improved) from previous experience but cannot signal, by themselves, whether past performance represented a reasonable level of efficiency. That would require a more detailed study of the cost center or the process. If the standard error of the regression line is too high, however, this could signal a lack of control in the cost center. High standard errors (or low R^2) are the result of large unexplained fluctuations in the cost center. Thus, if the analyst, when modeling the cost behavior in a cost center, observes a poor fit to the historical data, he or she may conclude that the cost center is not operating in a state of statistical control—that too many large fluctuations have occurred that cannot be explained by variations in the cost center's activity levels. This situation may signal the need for a careful examination of the operating procedures in an attempt to reduce the erratic cost behavior in the cost center. Thus investigation decisions may be triggered either by shifts in the mean of the distribution (observations more than 2 standard errors from the expected value) or by a too dispersed distribution in the historical data.

One final observation on the use of regression models for predictions: do not expect the explanatory power of the model in the prediction period to be nearly as good as that encountered in the estimation period. Even if we obtained an excellent linear fit on the historical data, say with an R^2 above 0.9, we would be unlikely to explain 90 percent of the variation in the dependent variable (cost) in the future. Recall that the R^2 of a regression indicates the percentage of variation of a dependent variable, *as measured from the mean of the dependent variable,* that is explained by variation in the independent variable. An R^2 near zero suggests that the best explanation of the historical data is random fluctuation about the historic mean of the dependent variable. When attempting to predict future values of the dependent variable, however, we will not know the mean of these future observations. If the mean of future values of the dependent variable differs significantly from the mean of the predicted values, the regression model is bound to predict much less accurately than we might have expected. After the fact, we might have done better using the mean value of these new observations (had we known it) than we did using the predictions from our historically based regression models. Thus, the uncertainty in the mean of future values of the dependent variable will reduce the explained variation of these future observations. There is not much one can do about this problem other than to be aware of its existence and to avoid expecting superb fits to future observations even when the R^2 of the estimated regression has been near 1.

An important assumption for the simple linear regression model is the independence of errors across observations; formally, we assume that $E(e_s, e_t) = 0$ for $s \neq t$. In many time-series models this assumption is violated because of the correlation of errors in successive observations. This correlation occurs when a positive error tends to be followed by another positive error and a negative error tends to be followed by another negative error. Autocorrelation is especially likely to occur when time-series data have not been adjusted for the nonstationarities caused by factors we discussed at the end of Chapter 2: price-level changes, technological changes, and other changes, over time, in the process being studied. As noted earlier, we should attempt to modify the data directly to account for known changes in the process before performing a statistical analysis.

Even after we have attempted to adjust historical data, autocorrelation may still exist. Techniques are available to compensate for the effects of autocorrelation. For example, consider the sequence of data in Table 3-6, which came from a different cost center in the Robinson Company. These data are plotted in Exhibit 3-3. The simple linear regression of overhead cost versus DLH is

$$y_t = 6{,}935 + 16.23 \cdot x_t,$$
$$(1{,}870) \quad (1.96)$$

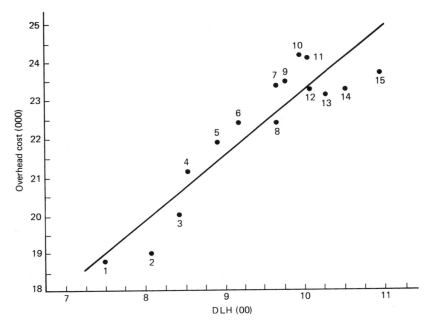

Exhibit 3-3 Scatter Diagram and Regression Line

Month	Overhead Cost	Direct Labor-Hours (DLH)
1	19,000	750
2	19,000	810
3	20,000	840
4	21,200	860
5	21,800	890
6	22,400	920
7	23,400	970
8	22,400	970
9	23,500	980
10	24,200	1,000
11	24,100	1,010
12	23,300	1,010
13	23,200	1,030
14	23,300	1,060
15	23,700	1,100

TABLE 3-6. **Overhead Cost and Direct Labor-Hours**

where the standard errors of the coefficients are shown in parentheses below the coefficients. The R^2 of the regression line is 0.84. The line is plotted on the scatter diagram in Exhibit 3-3. While the fit—as measured by highly significant coefficients (the t ratio of the variable-cost coefficient is 8.3) and high R^2—seems quite good, a visual inspection of the scatter diagram (Exhibit 3-3) or a sequential plot of the residuals (Exhibit 3-4) reveals a high dependence among successive residuals. We see a sequence of negative residuals at the beginning and end of the

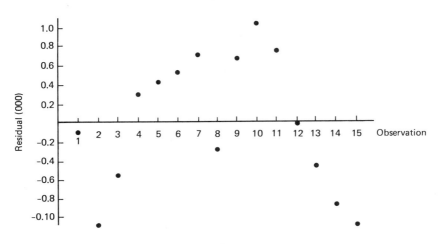

Exhibit 3-4   Residuals from Regression

time series and, with only one exception, all positive residuals in the middle of the series.

Most regression packages compute the *Durbin-Watson statistic* (*DW*), a summary measure of the amount of serial correlation in the residuals. With uncorrelated errors, the Durbin-Watson statistic takes on values near 2. If the errors are highly positively correlated, DW will be less than 1 and can be near 0. (Negatively correlated errors, less frequently encountered, yield values of DW above 3, with an upper limit of 4.) While exact values for testing the significance of the DW statistic are not readily available, a good rule of thumb is to be concerned if the DW statistic is near or below 1 (for negatively correlated errors, the corresponding value is 3). For the above regression, the DW statistic equals 0.75, indicating significant autocorrelation.

If the errors are autocorrelated, the ordinary regression procedure still produces good estimates of the regression coefficients but the estimated standard error of the regression underestimates the true variance about the linear relationship. Also, the standard errors of the coefficients tend to be underestimated, so that the coefficients appear to be more significant than they really are (for example, the t ratio of 8.3 for b_1 in the above regression is too high; the statistical significance of this coefficient is not this strong).

One solution to an autocorrelation problem is to search for additional variables that might explain the systematic deviations from the simple linear relationship. This requires the use of multiple linear regression, a topic discussed in the next chapter. A simple procedure is to adjust the data in an attempt to remove the autocorrelation from the residuals. We estimate the first-order autocorrelation coefficient of the residuals, r, from

$$r = \frac{\sum\limits_{t=2}^{n} e_t e_{t-1}}{\left(\sum\limits_{t=2}^{n} e_t^2 \sum\limits_{t=1}^{n-1} e_t^2\right)^{1/2}}. \tag{3-16}$$

This coefficient can also be estimated from the Durbin-Watson statistic as

$$r \approx \frac{2 - DW}{2}. \tag{3-17}$$

For our data in Table 3-6, $r = 0.59$.

We adjust the independent and dependent variables to remove the autocorrelation by computing

$$x_t^* = x_t - r x_{t-1},$$

$$y_t^* = y_t - r y_{t-1},$$

TABLE 3-7. **Adjusted Data**

Month	Overhead Cost*	Direct Labor-Hours (DLH)*
2	7,788	367
3	8,788	362
4	9,398	364
5	9,290	383
6	9,536	395
7	10,182	427
8	8,591	398
9	10,282	408
10	10,332	422
11	9,819	420
12	9,078	414
13	9,450	434
14	9,609	452
15	9,950	474

for $t = 2, 3, \ldots, n$.[2] Note that we lose one observation from the time series with this adjustment procedure. With our data, the adjusted independent and dependent variables are shown in Table 3-7. The regression on the adjusted data yields

$$y_t^* = 4,276 + 12.63x_t^*, \qquad R^2 = 0.35.$$
$$(2,036) \quad (4.97)$$

Note that the estimate of the variable cost coefficient has not changed dramatically (it has dropped from 16.2 to 12.6) but its estimated standard error has increased by a factor of 2.5. Also the R^2 of the regression has dropped from 0.84 to 0.35. Thus, by removing the high autocorrelation in the residuals, the standard errors of both the regression and the regression coefficients have increased. The DW statistic for the regression on the revised data is 1.49, suggesting that we have not removed all the autocorrelation from the data. But a statistic as high as 1.49 can be tolerated without further adjustment.

Of course, this adjustment introduces complications to a cost accounting system. When predicting overhead costs in month t, the predicted value, $\hat{y}_t$, must now be obtained from

$$\hat{y}_t = b_0 + b_1 x_t + r(y_{t-1} - b_1 x_{t-1})$$

---

[2] This process is a more generalized version of the simplest procedure for adjusting highly autocorrelated data. Many analysts would reestimate a highly autocorrelated data series in first-difference form; that is, assume $r = 1$ and estimate the relationship:
$$(y_t - y_{t-1}) = b_0 + b_1(x_t - x_{t-1}).$$

to account for the effect of prediction errors from the previous month on the expected costs in the current month. If we performed the regression to obtain an estimate of the variable-overhead cost coefficient, β_1, for product-planning analysis, it is disconcerting to have this component vary from month to month based on prediction errors in the preceding months. Therefore for cost accounting purposes, if significant autocorrelation is encountered, it may be better for the analyst to attempt to determine the source of the correlated errors by a more detailed examination of the data and the production process, rather than attempting to adjust the data as we have demonstrated above.

One source of autocorrelation in accounting data is the speed of adjustment to changes in activity level. As output expands, managers may resort to short-term expedients—deferring maintenance, working men and machines overtime—to enhance short-term productivity. Eventually, the managers adjust to the higher level of activity by hiring more workers and acquiring more equipment. Were output to drop from this point, the new workers would not be fired immediately nor the new machinery sold, so that average costs would be higher for a while. Thus, delays in adjusting the production process to fluctuations in activity levels can cause autocorrelation in the cost data. It would be better to model this process directly rather than use the somewhat ad hoc time-series adjustment process we performed.

SUMMARY

In this chapter we introduced a variety of techniques for estimating the fixed and variable components of total costs. The simplest procedure classifies each account as being either fixed or variable. But this procedure depends heavily upon the accuracy of the account-classification process and, unless observations are available at different activity levels, does not properly classify accounts that are partially fixed and partially variable. Also, no estimate is provided about the range of uncertainty in the estimates of fixed- and variable-cost components.

Ordinary least-squares regression analysis can be used to provide statistical estimates of fixed and variable costs based on data from previous periods. Besides obtaining these coefficient estimates, the regression analysis provides estimates of the standard deviation of the coefficient estimates. These estimated standard deviations can be used to test whether the coefficients (fixed or variable) are significantly different from zero. If the fixed-cost coefficient (β_0) is not statistically significant, the account can be classified as completely variable; if the variable-cost coefficient (β_1) is not statistically significant, the account can be considered a fixed cost. The estimated standard deviation of the coefficients can also be used to obtain a confidence interval on how large or small the variable-cost coefficient could be. This interval would be useful in sensitivity analysis for cost and profit planning. A third use of the estimated standard deviations is to forecast the range of costs that would be expected for a given activity level in a future period. A cost report outside this range would suggest a departure from historical performance and could signal an investigation to determine the cause of the unusual departure from standard.

Perhaps the largest problem when estimating fixed and variable costs from a historic time series of data is to eliminate the effects of nonstationarities. Procedures to adjust the data for known nonstationarities (caused by changing prices, changing technology, or any change in a procedure or process) can eliminate the most obvious causes of autocorrelated errors. Remaining autocorrelation may be controlled for by estimating the model in first-difference form, using the estimated autocorrelation coefficient to weight successive observations. The use of dummy variables, as discussed in the next chapter, provides still another procedure for dealing with autocorrelated data.

PROBLEMS

3-1. Cost Analysis by Account Classification (CMA, adapted)

The Tastee-Treat Company prepares, packages, and distributes six frozen vegetables in two different size containers. The different vegetables and different sizes are prepared in large batches. The company employs an actual-cost job-order costing system. Manufacturing overhead is assigned to batches by a predetermined rate on the basis of direct labor hours. The manufacturing overhead costs incurred by the company last year are presented below:

Direct Labor Hours worked

(000)	2,160

Manufacturing Overhead Costs

($000)

Indirect Labor	$ 8,640
Employee Benefits	3,240
Supplies	2,160
Power	1,728
Heat and Light	552
Supervision	2,625
Depreciation	7,930
Property Taxes and Insurance	3,005
	$29,880

The company expects to operate at a 2,300 (000) DLH level of activity this year.

1. Estimate manufacturing overhead for this year. You can prepare a (1) low, (2) median, and (3) high estimate depending on your assumptions on the amount of fixed and variable expense in each account.
2. For each of your three estimates compute the average rate used to allocate overhead costs to products and the flexible budget.
3. How can you attempt to obtain better estimates of the fixed and variable cost components for manufacturing overhead? Why would improved estimates be useful to Tastee-Treat?

3-2. Choice of Independent Variable

The Oliver Company wants to develop a flexible budget to predict how overhead costs vary with activity levels. It is unsure whether to choose direct labor hours (DLH) or units produced, as the best measure of activity for the firm. Monthly data for the preceding twelve months appear below:

Month	DLH	Units	Overhead
1	1250	111	$29,900
2	1497	132	34,600
3	1184	121	28,900
4	1499	147	34,300
5	1356	154	32,400
6	1300	125	31,200
7	1222	122	28,700
8	1259	131	29,400
9	1109	120	27,000
10	1435	144	33,400
11	1121	112	27,700
12	1433	145	34,100

Required:

Determine which measure, DLH or Units, should be used for the flexible budget and obtain the flexible budget for the firm's overhead costs.

3-3. Analysis of Natural Gas Usage

The Wheeling Corporation is concerned with its rapidly increasing utilities expense. Due to the much higher prices that it now pays for natural gas, it wants to be sure that energy conservation is practiced at all its plants. As part of this effort, the company is monitoring gas usage at each of its plants on a weekly basis. From this data-collection effort, the company will attempt to develop a standard for current usage. The standard will also provide a benchmark from which the benefits from future energy conservation efforts can be evaluated.

Since most of the company's natural gas consumption is for heating plants, the controller believes that gas usage should be proportional to the number of degree days each week. A degree day is the difference between 68°F and the average daily temperature. The readings from the first ten weeks of data collection appear below:

Week	Degree Days	MCF of Natural Gas
1	173	4310
2	228	3855
3	245	4340
4	306	5670
5	284	5200
6	328	5340
7	360	5600
8	314	5235
9	273	5650
10	265	4515

Required:

1. Examine the data to determine whether a linearity assumption between natural gas consumption and degree days seems warranted. Are any observations obviously outliers?

2. Obtain OLS estimates of the fixed and variable components of natural gas usage as a function of degree days per week. Comment on the goodness of fit of the model.

3. Is the model affected by deletion of outliers—observations with unusually large residuals?

4. What factors contribute to the unexplained variation in weekly natural gas usage?

5. Why did the Wheeling Corporation use MCF of natural gas (a physical measure) rather than natural gas expense each week, since the company is obviously more interested in controlling the *cost* of natural gas than the *usage* of natural gas?

6. In Week 11, there were 290 degree days. Obtain a prediction of MCF of natural gas consumed in Week 11 and a 95 percent confidence interval for this estimate.

3-4. Statistical Analysis of Cost Data

The Anderson Company operates a chain of retail stores. It is attempting to evaluate the efficiency of the various stores by measuring how total store expense (excluding merchandise costs) varies with the number of employees. During the most recent month, it collected data from all twenty of its stores:

Store	Number of Employees	Store Expense (000)	Store	Number of Employees	Store Expense (000)
1	53	$45	11	54	$59
2	36	43	12	73	77
3	88	89	13	65	56
4	84	79	14	29	28
5	86	84	15	52	51
6	64	66	16	22	27
7	45	49	17	76	76
8	48	48	18	32	34
9	39	43	19	51	60
10	67	76	20	37	32

Required:

1. Estimate the fixed costs per store and the variable costs per employee using the High-Low method.
2. Using the Ordinary Least Squares criterion, estimate the fixed and variable cost components from a regression program.
3. What is the standard error of the regression? What is the explanatory power of the regression as estimated by the coefficient of determination (R^2)?
4. Evaluate the statistical significance of the estimated coefficients.
5. Suppose that a new store opens with forty employees. Obtain the 95 percent confidence interval for the expected expense for this store.
6. Show how the standard error of the forecast of store expense for new stores varies with the number of employees. Consider:
   a. 55 employees
   b. 75 employees
   c. 90 employees

3-5. Model Selection and Predictive Ability

The Monongahela Corporation is attempting to model the relationship between Cost of Goods Sold and Sales. Data for 1979 through 1981 were analyzed, but unfortunately, the regression analysis gave differing results depending upon the time period used for estimation. Regression summaries appear below:

Time Period	Number of Observations	Intercept	Slope[a]	$\overline{R^2}$
1979–81	36	4950 (1.40)	0.77 (16.1)	0.88
1980–81	24	−700 (0.30)	0.85 (23.9)	0.96
1981	12	17,800 (2.07)	0.62 (5.6)	0.73

[a] (t-statistics appear in parentheses below the estimated coefficients.)

Data for the first four months of 1982 showed:

	Sales	Cost of Goods Sold
January	$78,800	$68,500
February	76,300	66,900
March	94,200	77,500
April	79,400	66,300

Required:

How can these data be used to help the Monongahela Corporation select among the three models?

3-6. Time Series Analysis of Overhead Costs

The Watson Company is trying to obtain an improved estimate of its variable overhead cost. For the past two years, it has collected accurate monthly data on direct labor hours (DLH) worked and overhead costs:

Month	DLH	Overhead Costs	Month	DLH	Overhead Costs
1	904	$20,810	13	824	$22,700
2	972	21,890	14	876	24,590
3	864	20,660	15	1,152	29,120
4	836	21,050	16	1,080	27,870
5	1,060	24,070	17	956	26,210
6	1,148	25,300	18	1,004	26,750
7	832	21,820	19	868	24,800
8	1,044	25,470	20	1,192	31,590
9	1,096	26,500	21	1,024	28,530
10	1,004	25,250	22	956	27,200
11	1,076	26,270	23	1,084	30,380
12	960	25,240	24	1,060	29,140

Required:

1. Analyze the relationship between Overhead Costs and DLH. Obtain estimates of fixed and variable cost components and comment on the quality of the explained relationship.

2. As part of the Watson Company's detailed analysis of overhead costs, it has developed a price index of labor, material, utilities, and other components of overhead costs. This index provides an aggregate measure of how the unit prices of the components of overhead have increased over time. The index was started two years ago, and the firm now has the following time series for the index.

Month	Overhead Cost Index	Month	Overhead Cost Index
1	100	13	115
2	100	14	115
3	102	15	116
4	103	16	117
5	104	17	119
6	106	18	120
7	108	19	120
8	108	20	123
9	107	21	123
10	110	22	124
11	113	23	126
12	114	24	126

Show how this index can be used to improve the estimated relationship between DLH and Overhead Costs.

3. While you have been conducting all this analysis of historic data, one month of the current year has already gone by. A total of 1,010 DLH were worked and Overhead Costs equaled $29,800. The overhead cost index for the most recent month has not yet been computed. Is this most recent observation consistent with the historic relationship between Overhead Costs and DLH?

3-7. Time Series Analysis of Macro-Economic Data: Autocorrelation and Inflation Adjustments

The planning department of the National Motor Company is building a model to predict total automobile sales each quarter. Previous research has revealed that automobile sales are highly correlated with the Personal Consumer Expenditure (PCE) component of the national income accounts. The department has not been able to accurately forecast the quarterly PCE series, but it has been much more successful in predicting a more aggregate measure of economic activity, the Gross National Product (GNP). It seems plausible that there should be an approximate linear relationship between PCE and GNP each quarter.

The department has collected four years worth of statistics on these two accounts:

Quarter	GNP	PCE
1/77	1839.1	1163.9
2/77	1893.9	1186.2
3/77	1950.4	1217.4
4/77	1988.6	1254.5
1/78	2032.4	1278.3
2/78	2129.6	1330.1
3/78	2190.5	1369.9
4/78	2271.9	1416.6
1/79	2340.6	1454.1

Quarter	GNP	PCE
2/79	2374.6	1478.0
3/79	2444.1	1529.1
4/79	2496.3	1582.3
1/80	2571.7	1631.0
2/80	2564.8	1626.8
3/80	2637.3	1682.2
4/80	2730.6	1751.0

Required:

1. Perform a simple linear regression of PCE v. GNP and interpret the results.

2. Is auto-correlation a problem with the simple linear model? If so, re-estimate the model with a procedure that attempts to reduce auto-correlation in the residuals.

3. The analyst knows that 1977–1980 was a time when government spending grew rapidly, and that the 50 percent increase in both GNP and PCE over the four-year period contains a considerable component of inflation. Inflation adjusted data for GNP and PCE (both measured in 1972 dollars) are also available from the national income accounts:

Quarter	GNP, Constant (1972) Dollars	PCE, Constant (1972) Dollars
1/77	$1345.9	$851.9
2/77	1363.4	856.0
3/77	1385.8	866.4
4/77	1391.5	881.3
1/78	1402.3	884.1
2/78	1432.8	900.6
3/78	1446.7	911.2
4/78	1465.8	923.4
1/79	1479.9	925.5
2/79	1473.4	922.8
3/79	1488.2	933.4
4/79	1490.6	941.6
1/80	1501.9	943.4
2/80	1463.3	919.3
3/80	1471.9	930.8
4/80	1485.6	946.8

Estimate the PCE versus GNP relationship using these inflation-adjusted data. Compare this estimated relationship with the relationship estimated on nominal (unadjusted) data, attempting to explain any differences between the estimated models.

4. The nominal GNP in the first quarter of 1981 was $2853.0 (nominal) and $1516.4 (constant $1972). Give your best prediction for the level of nominal PCE in the first quarter of 1981.

REFERENCES

Articles

BENSTON, GEORGE, "Multiple Regression Analysis of Cost Behavior," *The Accounting Review* XLI (October 1966), 657–72.

JENSEN, ROBERT, "Multiple Regression Models for Cost Control—Assumptions and Limitations," *The Accounting Review* XLII (April 1967), 265–72.

KAPLAN, ROBERT S., "Analysis and Control of Nurse Staffing," *Health Services Research* X (Fall 1975), 278–96.

MANSFIELD, EDWIN, and HAROLD H. WEIN, "A Regression Control Chart for Costs," *Applied Statistics* VII (March 1958), 48–57.

OLIVER, F. R., "A Cross-Section Study of Marginal Cost," *Applied Statistics* XI (June 1962), 69–78.

Books

PINDYCK, R. S., and O. L. RUBINFELD, *Econometric Models and Economic Forecasts*. New York: McGraw-Hill, 1976.

SPURR, WILLIAM A., and CHARLES P. BONNI, *Statistical Analysis for Business Decisions*, rev. ed. New York: Irwin, 1973.

WONNACOTT, RONALD J., and THOMAS H. WONNACOTT, *Econometrics*. New York: Wiley, 1979.

MULTIPLE AND NONLINEAR REGRESSION

4

COST BEHAVIOR—AN EXTENDED ANALYSIS

In Chapter 3 we explained the variation of the dependent variable, overhead cost, by a single independent variable, such as direct labor-hours. When only graphical techniques, such as the high-low and visual methods, were available to estimate fixed and variable components, the analyst was restricted to using one independent variable. Also, in most traditional explanations of flexible budgeting, only a single variable is used to measure activity levels. But we live in a complex world, and it is certainly possible that overhead cost or almost any interesting dependent variable in which we are interested can depend on more than one independent variable. Regression analysis enables us to estimate the effects and statistical significance of many independent variables. This opportunity, however, must be tempered by the warning that the analyst must still exercise thought and caution before adding independent variables in an extensive search to obtain a good fit to the historical data.

We start this discussion of multiple regression (referring to multiple independent variables) by reconsidering the cost behavior of the Robinson Company cost center (Table 3-4). We present the data again in Table 4-1, along with additional data on machine-hours worked and pounds of material used in this cost center. Ideally we would like to plot the overhead cost against all three possible independent variables, but four-dimensional graph paper is both expensive and difficult to work with. To get a rough idea as to whether there is a relationship, we can plot overhead cost against each independent variable (see Exhibit 4-1 as well as Exhibit 3-1). Although there is considerable scatter in the plots, overhead cost does seem to vary with machine-hours (MH) and pounds of material (MATL), though neither fit is as strong as that between overhead cost and direct labor-hours (DLH). In order to assess whether additional explanatory power of the variation in overhead cost is obtained by including more independent variables, we will eventually estimate the multiple linear regression model:

$$y_t = \beta_0 + \beta_1 x_{1t} + \beta_2 x_{2t} + \beta_3 x_{3t} + \epsilon_t, \qquad (4\text{-}1)$$

where x_{1t} = direct labor-hours (DLH)

$\quad\quad x_{2t}$ = machine-hours (MH),

$\quad\quad x_{3t}$ = pounds of material (MATL).

The β_i's are linear coefficients that measure the change in the dependent variable, overhead cost, associated with a unit change in each independent variable, while *holding all other independent variables constant*. By writing the model in the above form, we are assuming that the effect of a unit increase in machine-hours on overhead cost is independent of the level of the other independent variables and the current level of machine-hours. Formally, β_i can be thought of as a partial derivative:

$$\beta_i = \frac{\partial y_t}{\partial x_{it}}. \qquad (4\text{-}2)$$

Later in the chapter we will consider nonlinear regression models where the effect of a unit change in an independent variable is a function of the current level of that independent variable and the levels of the other independent variables.

The β_i's are estimated, as before, to minimize the sum of the vertical deviations of the actual observations from the regression line (strictly speaking, a regression plane, the multidimensional counterpart of a line). The actual formulas for the regression coefficients are complicated, requiring the use of matrix algebra, and are not important for us, since virtually no one estimates the coefficients of a multiple linear regression manually. Many computer programs exist that compute the regression coefficients, b_i, the standard errors of the coefficients, s_{b_i}, the explanatory power of the regression, R^2, the standard error of the regression,

TABLE 4-1.   Robinson Company Overhead Cost

Month	Overhead Cost	Direct Labor-Hours	Machine-Hours	Pounds of Material
1	25,200	840	740	400
2	24,800	830	1,020	430
3	20,800	740	880	400
4	27,500	1,130	990	580
5	23,300	770	930	400
6	26,900	910	1,090	420
7	24,800	950	760	490
8	26,100	1,170	1,020	620
9	29,100	1,160	1,220	540
10	27,300	1,030	1,070	480
11	27,600	1,200	1,010	650
12	21,100	780	620	430
13	21,700	750	710	350
14	30,200	1,290	1,330	650
15	27,300	1,060	1,110	570

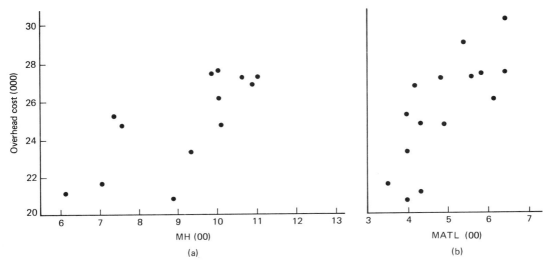

Exhibit 4-1   Overhead Cost, (a) Machine-Hours and (b) Material.

s_e, and the Durbin-Watson statistic, DW. These statistics have exactly the same interpretation and use as in the simple linear regression case.

Recall that the simple linear regression of overhead cost versus DLH (in Chapter 3) yielded

$$OH_t = 12{,}290 + 13.6DLH_t, \qquad R^2 = 0.79, \quad s_e = 1{,}342,$$
$$\quad (6.4) \qquad (7.1)$$

where the figures in parentheses are the t statistics of the coefficients (the ratio of the coefficient to its standard error), which measure the statistical significance of the coefficient. When we add machine-hours (MH) to the regression model, we obtain

$$OH_t = 11{,}058 + 9.2DLH_t + 5.8MH_t, \qquad R^2 = 0.87, \quad s_e = 1{,}122.$$
$$\quad (6.6) \qquad (3.9) \qquad (2.6)$$

The explanatory power (R^2) of the regression has increased from 0.79 to 0.87, and the standard error of the regression has decreased from 1,342 to 1,122. The coefficient of the new variable, machine-hours, has a t ratio of 2.6, well beyond the customary level of 2.0 used to determine statistical significance.[1] Notice that

---

[1] More formally, we should conduct a one-sided test that the coefficient is not greater than zero. The test is one-sided because we certainly do not expect overhead to decrease with an increase in the machine-hours used. With fifteen observations and estimating three coefficients, the coefficient has a t distribution with 12 degrees of freedom. From Table B in the Appendix we see that the probability of obtaining a t ratio with 12 degrees of freedom as high as 2.6 is only about 0.01 if the true coefficient equals zero. This low probability constitutes a high degree of statistical significance for the coefficient.

the coefficient of direct labor-hours has decreased from 13.6 to 9.2. This occurred because machine-hours is correlated with DLH and is also important in explaining the variation in overhead cost (if DLH were uncorrelated with MH, the coefficient of DLH would not have changed when MH was added to the regression). Therefore when DLH appeared in the regression by itself, its estimated coefficient reflected not only the direct effect of DLH but also the indirect effect, through its correlation with MH, a variable that had been omitted from the simple regression model.

The multiple regression model can be used to estimate the variable overhead cost of a product produced in this cost center. In this application the variable-overhead cost would be estimated as \$9.20 per DLH used and \$5.80 per MH used. Thus a product requiring 2 DLH and 1.5 MH would have an estimated variable-overhead cost of

$$2 \cdot 9.20 + 1.5 \cdot 5.80 = \$27.10/\text{unit}.$$

If we are interested in predicting the overhead cost for the cost center in a new month, we substitute the number of direct labor-hours and machine-hours used in that month into the regression equation. As with the simple linear regression model, we can also obtain the standard error of the forecast, so that the statistical significance of the deviation of the actual observation from the flexible budget can be evaluated. Unfortunately, many regression programs do not provide this forecasted standard error, so that it may have to be programmed (or computed) separately if the analyst needs it.[2]

---

[2] The formula for the standard error of the forecast is best presented using matrix notation. Assume we have n observations on k independent variables $(x_1, x_2, \ldots, x_k)$ where the constant term is denoted by $x_0 \equiv 1$. Let x_{ij} be the jth observation on the ith independent variable, and y_j be the jth observation on the dependent variable $(i = 0, \ldots, k; j = 1, \ldots, n)$. Define $\mathbf{x}$ as the matrix of independent variables and $\mathbf{y}$ as the matrix of dependent variables.

$$\mathbf{x} = \begin{bmatrix} 1 & x_{11} & x_{21} & \cdots & x_{k1} \\ 1 & x_{12} & \cdots & & x_{k2} \\ 1 & x_{1n} & \cdots & & x_{kn} \end{bmatrix}, \qquad \mathbf{y} = \begin{bmatrix} y_1 \\ \vdots \\ y_n \end{bmatrix}$$

The OLS coefficients, b, are obtained from

$$\mathbf{b} = (\mathbf{x}'\ \mathbf{x})^{-1}\mathbf{x}'\mathbf{y}.$$

The estimated variance of the forecast error at a new observation $z = (z_1, \ldots, z_k)'$ is given by

$$s_z^2 = s_e^2 z'(\mathbf{x}'\ \mathbf{x})^{-1}z$$

and the estimate of the variance of the total forecast error at the new observation z is

$$s_f^2 = s_e^2 + s_z^2.$$

The standard error of forecast can then be computed as

$$s_f = \sqrt{s_f^2} = s_e \sqrt{1 + z'(\mathbf{x}'\ \mathbf{x})^{-1}z}.$$

The critical step is obtaining the inverse matrix $(\mathbf{x}'\ \mathbf{x})^{-1}$, which is not printed out in many regression routines. The matrix $(\mathbf{x}'\ \mathbf{x})$ is the matrix of cross products. For two independent variables and a constant it can be written as

$$(\mathbf{x}'\ \mathbf{x}) = \begin{bmatrix} n & \sum x_{1j} & \sum x_{2j} \\ \sum x_{1j} & \sum x_{1j}^2 & \sum x_{1j}x_{2j} \\ \sum x_{2j} & \sum x_{1j}x_{2j} & \sum x_{2j}^2 \end{bmatrix}.$$

If necessary, this matrix and its inverse can be computed with a separate computer program.

EXPLANATORY POWER OF A MULTIPLE REGRESSION

Analysts are sometimes tempted to keep adding independent variables in a multiple regression in a misguided attempt to maximize the explanatory power of the regression. This tendency is reinforced because the apparent explanatory power of the regression, as measured by R^2, always increases when more independent variables are added. By discarding variables whose estimated coefficients have t statistics less than 1.5 or 2.0, we can avoid cluttering up the regression with insignificant variables. Another technique to limit the number of independent variables is to compute an adjusted coefficient of determination, $\overline{R^2}$, which is a function of the number of independent variables.

Recall our definitions:

$$SST = \frac{\sum (y_t - \bar{y})^2}{n},$$

$$SSE = \frac{\sum e_t^2}{n}, \qquad \text{where } e_t = y_t - \hat{y}_t = y_t - b_0 - \sum b_i x_{it}.$$

We computed the (unadjusted) coefficient of determination as

$$R^2 = 1 - \frac{SSE}{SST} = 1 - \frac{\sum e_t^2}{\sum (y_t - \bar{y})^2}. \qquad (4\text{-}3)$$

The adjusted coefficient of determination, $\overline{R^2}$, is computed as

$$\overline{R^2} = 1 - \frac{\dfrac{\sum e_t^2}{n - k - 1}}{\dfrac{\sum (y_t - \bar{y})^2}{n - 1}} = 1 - \frac{\dfrac{SSE}{n - k - 1}}{\dfrac{SST}{n - 1}} \qquad (4\text{-}4)$$

As the number of independent variables, k, is increased, the sum of squared errors in the numerator of the second term is divided by a smaller number, so that unless the error sum of squares is reduced by the additional independent variables, $\overline{R^2}$ may decrease. Table 4-2 shows the adjusted and unadjusted R^2 for the data in Table 4-1. By focusing on the adjusted coefficient of determination, $\overline{R^2}$, we reduce the temptation to drive R^2 arbitrarily close to 1 by adding independent variables to the regression.

TABLE 4-2. **Unadjusted and Adjusted Coefficients of Determination**

Independent variables	R^2	$\overline{R^2}$
Constant, DLH	0.79	0.77
Constant, DLH, MH	0.87	0.85

Finally, the analyst should use only those independent variables that he believes will actually be helpful in explaining or predicting variation in the dependent variable. If too many extraneous independent variables are tested, eventually a few may be found whose correlation with the dependent variable is spurious—that is, occurring by chance in the specific sample used.

COLLINEARITY

Another problem arises in multiple linear regression if two or more of the independent variables are highly correlated with each other. When this occurs, the highly correlated independent variables fluctuate together, and it is very difficult to obtain reliable estimates about the effect on the dependent variable of varying each independent variable by itself. When two or more variables are highly correlated, the coefficient estimates of these variables can be unreliable and the standard errors of the coefficients are increased, sometimes dramatically. It is a good idea to always compute the matrix of correlation coefficients when multiple independent variables are used in a regression. When two variables have a correlation of 0.9 or above, it is unlikely that reliable estimates of the separate coefficients will be obtained. Collinearity may also be suspected if the regression equation has a high explanatory power (R^2) but the coefficients have low t statistics or the sign of a coefficient is opposite from what was expected. In such cases the standard errors of the coefficients could be high because of the high correlation among the independent variables. One solution is to drop one of the correlated independent variables from the regression so that more reliable coefficient estimates can be obtained for the remaining variables.

With the data in Table 4-1, the correlation coefficient between DLH and MH is 0.73. This is fairly high but not fatal correlation. There is enough independent variation between the two variables to obtain reliable coefficient estimates. But the correlation does help to explain why the t ratio on DLH dropped from 7.1 in the simple linear regression, when it was the only independent variable (besides the constant), to 3.9 in the multiple regression, when MH was included. The collinearity between DLH and MH caused the standard error of the coefficient estimate to increase, thereby reducing the t ratio in the new regression.

When we run the regression with three independent variables, DLH, MH, and MATL, a severe collinearity problem becomes obvious. The correlation matrix for these three independent variables is

	DLH	*MH*	*MATL*
DLH	1.0		
MH	0.734	1.000	
MATL	0.953	0.629	1.000

The correlation between DLH and MATL is extremely high (greater than 0.95)

suggesting that it is very unlikely we will be able to get reliable estimates for the DLH and MATL coefficients. The regression, with all three independent variables, is

$$OH_t = 11,304 + 22.0DLH_t + 4.0MH_t - 22.3MATL_t, \quad R^2 = 0.92, \quad \overline{R^2} = 0.90.$$
$$\quad\quad (8.2) \quad\quad (4.1) \quad\quad (2.1) \quad\quad (-2.6)$$

We see that the coefficient on DLH has more than doubled and the coefficient of MATL is negative. (The MH coefficient has dropped some, from 5.8 to 4.0; it is less affected by the addition of the MATL variable because of its lower correlation with this new variable.) Even though the explanatory power of the regression has increased significantly, we should be very suspicious of the output from this regression. The negative sign on MATL is contrary to our prior beliefs. It is hard to understand why, after holding DLH and MH constant, overhead cost should *decrease* as we process more pounds of material. Also the large change in the DLH coefficient should alert us to a problem. In this situation, it would be preferable to accept a regression with lower explanatory power (using only DLH and MH as explanatory variables) rather than to draw conclusions from a regression with counterintuitive results and erratic coefficient estimates. This is a good example of why it is not always preferable to select a regression on the basis of having obtained the highest R^2.[3]

The collinearity problem is most severe when we are trying to obtain accurate coefficient estimates for product planning, pricing, and a cost-volume-profit analysis. If we are mainly interested in using the regression equation to predict cost behavior in a period (that is, as a flexible budget), then we are not concerned with the individual coefficient estimates. The standard error of the regression and of the forecasts from the regression are not affected by collinearity among subsets of the independent variables. Therefore, if the analyst feels that the correlated variables are all necessary for predicting overall costs, they can remain in the regression equation.

MODEL PREDICTIONS

A good procedure for evaluating alternative specifications of a regression equation is to compare the predictions of the alternative models on data not used to estimate the regression coefficients. Such data can be obtained by arbitrarily excluding observations from the historical analysis. In addition, there is usually a time lapse between the collection of the original data and the computation of the final set

---

[3] The overhead-cost data in Table 4-1 were generated from a model:
$$OH_t = 10,000 + 10DLH_t + 6MH_t + \epsilon_t,$$
where $\epsilon_t \sim N(0, 1,000)$. Thus in this case we do know the *truth* and that the apparent statistical significance of MATL is spurious. Note that the coefficient estimates in the two-variable regression (9.2DLH and 5.8MH) are less than half a standard error from their true values of 10 and 6.

of regression estimates, so that a few more new observations can be collected to test alternative specifications. Predictions from alternative models can be compared by computing the *root-mean-squared error* (*RMS*) of actual from predicted results:

$$\text{RMS} = \sqrt{\frac{\sum (y_t - \hat{y}_t)^2}{T}}, \tag{4-5}$$

where $\hat{y}_t$ is the prediction from a regression model, and the summation is over the T time periods used to test the model. By testing the derived model in time periods not used in the estimation phase, we can obtain more evidence on the accuracy of the proposed model. Also, if after the historical analysis we are still unsure about which of several models to choose as the best representation of the process, we can rank the competing models on the basis of the RMS error in a test or holdout sample of observations to determine which has the best predictive power.

DUMMY VARIABLES

The independent variables we have been using to explain the variation in the dependent variable (cost) have been continuous variables—variables that can take on a continuum of values. Occasionally an important explanatory variable may be discrete or categorical. For example, in estimating utilities expense, the heating-expense category will increase during the winter months. To control for this effect, a dummy variable can be included in the regression model. This variable will have a value equal to 1 during the winter months and 0 during all the other months. The coefficient of this variable will then estimate the increased cost during the winter months (when the variable is defined to be 1) relative to all other months.

A dummy variable can also be useful to control for jumps or shifts in fixed costs. Supervision or manning levels may have been increased, or increased charges due to new machines or expansion of floor space may have been imposed during the estimation period. This situation is well illustrated by the data shown in Table 4.3. A simple linear regression of overhead cost (OH) versus direct labor hours (DLH) yields

$$\text{OH}_t = 16{,}056 + 5.13\text{DLH}_t, \qquad \overline{R^2} = 0.16, \quad \text{DW} = 0.97.$$
$$(5.46) \quad (1.77)$$

The explanatory power of this regression is very low, the coefficient of DLH is barely statistically significant (using a one-sided test at the 5 percent level), and the Durbin-Watson statistic indicates a high degree of autocorrelation. A plot of residuals versus time (see Exhibit 4-2) shows that the first six observations have negative residuals while five of the next six have positive residuals. This evidence

TABLE 4-3. Nonstationary Overhead Costs

Month	Overhead Cost	Direct Labor-Hours
1	20,070	930
2	20,780	1,090
3	20,890	1,010
4	21,350	1,080
5	20,320	1,120
6	20,440	1,010
7	20,780	890
8	23,750	1,190
9	21,100	850
10	22,450	990
11	20,540	900
12	22,350	1,060

suggests that around the end of month 6 there was an increase in fixed costs. To test this hypothesis, we define a dummy variable, JUMP, where

$$\text{JUMP}_t = \begin{cases} 0, & \text{if } t = 1, 2, \ldots, 6, \\ 1, & \text{if } t = 7, 8, \ldots, 12. \end{cases}$$

Rerunning the regression with the dummy variable leads to the following output:

$$\text{OH}_t = 12{,}679 + 7.66\text{DLH}_t + 1{,}646\text{JUMP}_t, \quad \overline{R^2} = 0.77, \quad DW = 2.4.$$
$$\qquad\quad (7.55) \quad (4.78) \qquad (5.20)$$

The explanatory power of the regression is now quite good, and both the variable coefficient and the dummy variable coefficient are highly significant. Also, by controlling for the jump in fixed costs, we have eliminated the autocorrelation problem caused by the nonstationary costs. If we wished to predict costs beyond period 12, we would add the coefficients of the intercept and the dummy variable together to obtain OH $= 14{,}325 + 7.66$DLH.

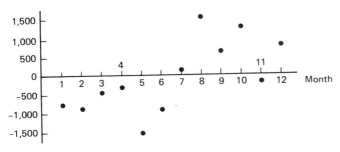

Exhibit 4-2 Residuals from Overhead Costs versus DLH Regression.

In another example, perhaps fixed costs increased more gradually because of a steady increase in the price level. In this situation we could assume a linear increase in costs by defining a variable indexed by the month:

$$OH_t = \beta_0 + \beta_1 DLH_t + \beta_2 t,$$

where the coefficient β_2 will measure the assumed linear increase in fixed costs each period.[4]

Dummy variables also arise when estimating a cross-sectional cost relationship. Suppose we had a company with a large number of retail chains around the country and we wished to estimate variable selling expense as a function of the gross sales of each store. Initially, we might estimate a simple model using the observations in the same period for each store, i:

$$\text{selling expense}_i = \beta_0 + \beta_1 \cdot \text{sales}_i.$$

A more careful study would reveal that wages and expenses are highly variable across the country. Northeastern urban stores may have higher hourly wages than rural southwestern stores. If so, the estimated relationship would not have strong explanatory power. In order to control for this variation, we could split the stores into mutually exclusive (and collectively exhaustive) categories in which stores that were considered reasonably homogeneous were grouped together within a category. A 0-1 dummy variable could then be defined for each category:

$$D_1 = \begin{cases} 1, & \text{if northeast,} \\ 0, & \text{elsewhere;} \end{cases} \qquad D_2 = \begin{cases} 1, & \text{if southwest, etc.,} \\ 0, & \text{elsewhere;} \end{cases}$$

or

$$S_1 = \begin{cases} 1, & \text{if urban store,} \\ 0, & \text{elsewhere;} \end{cases} \qquad S_2 = \begin{cases} 1, & \text{if suburban store,} \\ 0, & \text{elsewhere;} \end{cases}$$

$$S_3 = \begin{cases} 1, & \text{if rural store,} \\ 0, & \text{elsewhere.} \end{cases}$$

The coefficients of these dummy variables will measure the shift in fixed costs associated with having a store in a particular region.

When splitting observations into these mutually exclusive categories, we must remember to either omit one category from the regression or else estimate the relationship without the constant term. Otherwise, we will have a severe problem, since the independent variables will be perfectly collinear. For suppose we classify stores into three categories, as above, urban, suburban, and rural, where each store is in one (and only one) of the three categories. The constant term, X_0, is always defined equal to 1, so that for each observation, i, we have the following identity:

$$X_{0i} = S_{1i} + S_{2i} + S_{3i}.$$

[4] Strictly speaking, a variable such as t, taking on integer values, would be classified as a discrete independent variable rather than a dummy variable, whose only possible values are 0 and 1.

With this perfect collinearity, we will be unable to obtain regression estimates [because the matrix of cross products, $(x'\,x)$, is not invertible; see footnote 2]. To avoid this problem, it is simplest to omit one category, say rural, and estimate coefficients for just the constant and the remaining categories. We then interpret the coefficient of the categorical dummy variables as the increase (or decrease) in fixed cost relative to the omitted category; that is, the coefficient of S_1 would represent the increase in fixed costs of an urban store relative to a rural store.

Dummy variables are aptly named, since sometimes we use these categorical variables when we have not thought enough about a better way of measuring the relevant effect. It is preferable to attempt to identify what factor in a category leads to a shift in costs. For utilities expense, instead of defining a dummy variable for each season of the year, we might use the continuous variable of median monthly temperature. Then if we had an unusually warm or cold month, the regression model would be better able to explain the effect on heating expense. In the cross-sectional retail store example, we could use median wage levels in each region, a continuous variable available from the Bureau of Labor Statistics, rather than a dummy variable for each region. Again, such a variable would do better in tracking costs if there were relative shifts in wages among the various regions in the future. Dummy variables are best used when we do not believe that the dependent variable will vary linearly with the independent variable. For example, once the outside temperature gets above 65°F (18°C), further increases in temperature will not reduce heating bills. Therefore the underlying relationship is not linear over the range of variation of the independent variable. In such cases we can define separate dummy variables for subsets of the independent variable and not impose a linearity assumption.

MULTIPLICATIVE MODEL FOR NONLINEAR COST FUNCTIONS

All the cost models we have been developing have been linear and additive in the independent variables. Thus, the effect on the dependent variable of a change in an independent variable has been independent of the level of all the independent variables. This is a convenient assumption, and even where the underlying relationship is nonlinear, the linear model is a reasonable approximation for small variation in the independent variables. But the analyst should be prepared to estimate nonlinear models when they seem appropriate.

The easiest nonlinear model to estimate is the multiplicative model:

$$Y_t = \beta_0 X_{it}^{\beta_1} X_{2t}^{\beta_2} \cdots X_{kt}^{\beta_k} \tag{4-6}$$

With this model, the effect of a change in any independent variable, say X_{it}, is a function of all the other independent variables. Mathematically,

$$\frac{\partial Y_t}{\partial X_{it}} = \beta_i \beta_0 X_0 X_{1t}^{\beta_1} \cdots X_{it}^{\beta_i - 1} \cdots X_{kt}^{\beta_k} = \frac{\beta_i}{X_{it}}\, Y_t. \tag{4-7}$$

Solving this equation for β_i yields

$$\beta_i = \frac{\dfrac{\partial Y_t}{\partial X_{it}}}{\dfrac{Y_t}{X_{it}}} = \frac{\dfrac{\partial Y_t}{Y_t}}{\dfrac{\partial X_{it}}{X_{it}}}, \tag{4-8}$$

which students of economics will recall is the definition of an elasticity, the percentage change in the dependent variable caused by a given percentage change in an independent variable. The multiplicative model is therefore consistent with a model of constant elasticity for all independent variables. The elasticity constant for each independent variable is given by the regression coefficient β_i.

The multiplicative model is most useful when the dependent variable is naturally written as the product of independent variables. For example, total labor expense is the product of total labor hours and the average wage rate. Interest expense is the product of loans outstanding and the interest rate. It would be a mistake to estimate either of these relationships as additive in the independent variables, since the cost category is a function of the product, not the sum, of the independent variables. In both cases we would expect the exponential coefficients, β_i, of the independent variables to be close to 1.

The multiplicative model is estimated using standard OLS routines by taking the logarithm of the left- and right-hand side of the equation:

$$\log Y_t = \log \beta_0 + \beta_1 \log X_{it} + \cdots + \beta_k \log X_{kt}. \tag{4-9}$$

This relationship is now linear in the logarithms of the independent variables. Therefore, we first compute the logarithm of the independent and dependent variables and enter these "logged" values into a standard regression program. The estimated coefficients of the logged variables are the constant elasticities, β_i, in the multiplicative model.

An interesting application of the multiplicative model to estimating cost functions is described in Longbrake [1973]. With a sample of data on nearly 1,000 commercial banks, he estimated total costs as a function of the banks' many different activities and characteristics. Because of the complexity of a bank's operations and the expectation that the cost for any particular service will depend on current activity levels, Longbrake decided that a multiplicative model would provide a better explanation of the variation in operating cost among banks than a linear additive model. He estimated the log model with twelve independent variables:

X_1 = average number of accounts per office,
X_2 = average dollar size of a demand deposit account,
X_3 = average number of debits per account,
X_4 = average number of deposits per account,
X_5 = average number of non-home-bank checks (transit checks) deposited per account,

X_6 = average number of official checks issued per account,

X_7 = average number of checks cashed per account,

X_8 = average number of transit checks cashed per account,

X_9 = number of offices operated by the bank,

X_{10} = ratio of number of regular checking accounts to the sum of regular and special accounts,

X_{11} = average annual wage rate per employee,

X_{12} = ratio of dollar volume of demand deposits to sum of demand and time deposits.

The R^2 of the regression was about 0.93 and yielded the following coefficient estimates:

i	β_i	t_{β_i}
1	0.950	74.8
2	0.390	15.9
3	0.0470	1.7
4	0.140	4.1
5	0.0740	5.9
6	0.0580	5.3
7	0.0180	1.7
8	-0.0046	0.4
9	1.020	110.3
10	-0.063	2.5
11	0.43	9.2
12	0.011	0.4

From these results, we see that size (X_1 and X_9) is highly significant in explaining bank operating costs. The coefficients near unity of these two variables indicate that a 1 percent increase in the number of accounts per office or the number of offices per bank causes about a 1 percent increase in the total operating cost of a bank. The negative coefficient of X_{10} shows that if a regular account is substituted for a special account, costs will decrease. The coefficient of 0.43 for X_{11} indicates that increasing wage rates by 10 percent leads to a 4.3 percent increase in total costs.

When a cost function is estimated in multiplicative (or log-linear) form, the traditional dichotomy between fixed and variable costs is no longer clear. A relevant consideration is still incremental costs associated with a change in activity levels, but these incremental costs are now a function of the current or proposed activity levels. Analysis and interpretation are therefore more difficult with the multiplicative model. The interested reader should refer to the Longbrake article for an extensive discussion of these issues.

Before leaving this discussion of the multiplicative model, we need to discuss one point that occasionally confuses even experienced analysts. We have indicated that alternative models are frequently compared on the basis of explained variation in the dependent variable, as measured by the R^2 of a regression. With multiple independent variables, and lacking a theory to suggest whether the linear or the logarithmic form of the model is more appropriate, an analyst may estimate both forms of the model and choose the one with the highest R^2. This is an incorrect comparison. The R^2 of the linear model is the percentage of variation of the dependent variable, Y, explained by the linear model, whereas the R^2 of the logarithmic regression is the percentage of variation of log Y explained. The two measures are not comparable, since they are measuring the percentage of variation explained of two different variables, Y and log Y.

To compare the explanatory power of the two forms of the model, compute the antilog of the predictions from the log model, compare these predictions with actual values of the dependent variable, and compute the unexplained sum of squares to obtain an R^2 comparable to that computed for the linear model. Algebraically, we would have for each observation from the log model:

$$\log \hat{Y}_t = b_0 + \sum b_i \log X_{it}. \tag{4-10}$$

Compute $\hat{Y}_t = \exp (\log \hat{Y}_t)$ and obtain the unexplained sum of squares (SSE):

$$\text{SSE} = \sum (Y_t - \hat{Y}_t)^2. \tag{4-11}$$

Then compute the equivalent linear R^2 as

$$R^2 = 1 - \frac{\sum (Y_t - \hat{Y}_t)^2}{\sum (Y_t - \bar{Y})^2}. \tag{4-12}$$

This computation would have to be programmed as a separate subroutine, since it is not likely that any standard computerized regression package would have this capability.

OTHER NONLINEAR TRANSFORMATIONS

Another form of nonlinearity arises when the cost behavior is not linearly related to a single independent variable. We have been assuming a simple relationship of the form

$$Y = \beta_0 + \beta_1 X.$$

But the cost may vary in a nonlinear fashion with changes in the independent variable—what the economist calls economies or diseconomies of scale. In this case we could estimate a quadratic cost function

$$Y = \beta_0 + \beta_1 X + \beta_2 X^2$$

or a cubic cost function

$$Y = \beta_0 + \beta_1 X + \beta_2 X^2 + \beta_3 X^3.$$

These models allow for some curvature in the cost function to control for nonlinear effects. We can easily estimate them by computing and entering the square or the cube of the independent variable as separate independent variables. (These variables may have to be scaled to ensure that the numbers are not so large that they introduce rounding error into the computerized package.) In practice, strong evidence of nonlinearities is not often found in the time periods (biweekly or monthly) studied by accountants. Also, even the quadratic form may be hard to estimate, since, unless there is considerable variation in the independent variables, the variables X and X^2 will be highly collinear.

It is also possible to use other functional forms of the independent variable such as that obtained by taking the logarithm or the square root of the variable:

$$Y = \beta_0 + \beta_1 \log X \quad \text{or} \quad Y = \beta_0 + \beta_1 \sqrt{X}.$$

Occasionally this may be done to reduce the dispersion of the independent variable and obtain better properties of the residuals—for example, to avoid violating our assumption of homoscedasticity (see Chapter 3), which requires that the magnitude of errors be uncorrelated with the magnitude of the independent variable.[5] But unless there is some theory to suggest why costs should vary with the log or square root of an independent variable, such transformations are ad hoc and could be difficult to explain or justify to one's superiors.

One transformation that could be helpful in explaining increases in variable costs over time is

$$Y_t = \beta_1 X_t e^{rt},$$

in which the variable-cost coefficient is assumed to increase exponentially over time (constant percentage increase each period). We estimate this model in log form:

$$\log Y_t = \log (\beta_1 X_t) + rt = \log \beta_1 + \log X_t + rt,$$

in which the constant term would be the log of the variable-cost coefficient in the base period ($t = 0$), the coefficient of the activity level ($\log X_t$) should be equal to 1 (if our model is correct), and the coefficient of the time variable would give the estimated (constant) percentage increase in cost per period.

LEARNING CURVES AND NONLINEAR COSTS

The learning-curve phenomenon is another important cause of nonlinear costs. The learning curve was first observed in the aircraft industry, where the number

---

[5] The condition in which large errors are associated with large values of the independent variable is called *heteroscedasticity*. (Here the name of the disease may seem worse than the disease itself.) Attempts to cure heteroscedasticity are complex and usually make little difference in the coefficient estimates. Hence this problem is not discussed further here.

of direct labor-hours needed to produce a unit of output continually declined as more units were produced. Subsequently, this concept was extended to other activities, as it was found that the cost of doing most tasks of a repetitive nature decreased as experience at doing these tasks accumulated. This general concept of an ''experience curve'' is now being applied to the study of cost behavior of marketing efforts, new plant startups, and the output from highly automated equipment. Most experience curves, estimated on actual processes, indicate that costs decline 20 to 30 percent each time accumulated experience doubles. Factors that lead to this long-run decline in costs include:

1. *Labor efficiency*—learning by doing and by repetition; also, more effective maintenance and supervisory activities.
2. *New processes and improved methods*—improved production technology, industrial engineering studies.
3. *Product redesign*—reduction of costly or unnecessary features.
4. *Product standardization*—reduction of changeovers and setups; increased repetition.
5. *Scale effects*—economies of scale, since capacity costs increase slower than capacity.

These continuous declines in costs do not occur automatically but can be anticipated if management and labor make conscious efforts to reduce costs. Also,

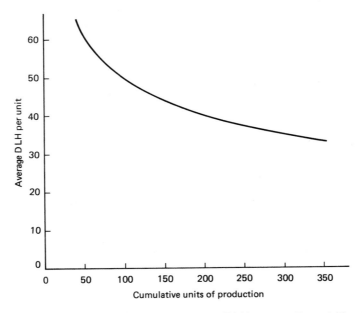

Exhibit 4-3 Learning Curve: Average DLH versus Cumulative Output.

the effect should be measured net of inflation, which can offset much or all of the savings achieved by the learning curve if costs are measured in nominal dollars. Therefore, the direct measurement should be made on the basis either of physical units (direct labor-hours or machine-hours) or of costs expressed in constant dollars so that changes in general prices are removed.

The learning-curve phenomenon is well represented by the following equation:

$$y = ax^{-b} \tag{4-13}$$

where y = average number of direct labor-hours per unit,
   a = number of direct labor-hours for the first unit,
   x = cumulative number of units produced,
   b = index of learning rate ($0 < b < 1$).

This equation indicates that average cost (or DLH) per unit declines exponentially with cumulative output (see Exhibit 4-3). Whereas in our previous models x represented the number of units produced each period, the independent variable, x, in the above equation represents cumulative output since these units were first produced. Another way of representing the learning curve is to compute total labor-hours, L:

$$L = y \cdot x = ax^{(1-b)}. \tag{4-14}$$

This relation is graphed in Exhibit 4-4 where we see how total labor-hours increase

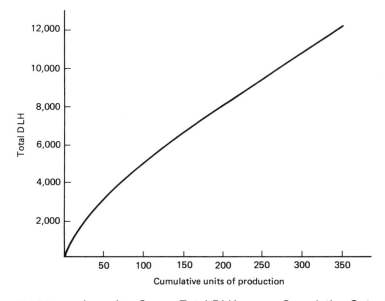

Exhibit 4-4 Learning Curve: Total DLH versus Cumulative Output.

at a decreasing rate as cumulative output expands. Thus the learning curve provides an explanation for economies of scale in production.

A third representation of the learning curve can be obtained by differentiating the total-labor-hour function to obtain the *marginal direct labor-hour* (*MDLH*):

$$\text{MDLH}(x) = \frac{d}{dx} L(x) = a(1 - b)x^{-b}. \qquad (4\text{-}15)$$

The marginal labor-hour function has the same exponent, b, as the average labor-hour function. Thus, the learning curve implies that both average and marginal labor-hours decrease at the learning rate, b.

For example, an 80 percent learning curve is commonly found in industry. On an average-DLH basis, the 80 percent learning curve implies that each time output is doubled from the previous total, the average DLH per unit of *total* production decreases to 80 percent of its previous average. With the marginal-DLH interpretation, the number of DLH for the last item produced, which doubles output from its previous level, is only 80 percent of the DLH of the item produced before we started to double output.

These concepts can be made more precise by an algebraic representation where we show how the learning-rate parameter, b, can be derived for an 80 percent learning curve ($b = 0.3219$). Using the average-DLH equation, we have by definition that at two different points of production (x_1, y_1) and (x_2, y_2)

$$y_1 = ax_1^{-b} \quad \text{and} \quad y_2 = ax_2^{-b}.$$

Taking logarithms of both sides yields

$$\log y_1 = \log a - b \log x_1,$$

$$\log y_2 = \log a - b \log x_2.$$

Subtracting the second equation from the first and solving for b:

$$b = \frac{\log \dfrac{y_1}{y_2}}{\log \dfrac{x_2}{x_1}} . \qquad (4\text{-}16)$$

The 80 percent learning curve claims that when $x_2 = 2x_1$, average cost, y_2, is 80 percent of y_1 so that

$$b_{80\%} = \frac{\log \dfrac{y_1}{0.8y_1}}{\log \dfrac{2x_1}{x_1}} = \frac{\log 1.25}{\log 2} = 0.3219. \qquad (4\text{-}17)$$

We get further insight by considering a specific example. Suppose the Milner Aerospace Company has been producing a guidance system and knows that the average labor-hours per unit follows a learning curve. To date it has produced 150 units and these units required a total of 60,000 direct labor hours. For the first 50 units a total of 28,500 DLH were required. The Milner Company is evaluating a bid to produce 100 additional units and is interested in knowing the incremental DLH required for this new order.

Initially, we must compute the parameters of the Milner Company's learning curve. We know two points on the curve. When $x_1 = 50$, $y_1 = 28,500/50 = 570$, and when $x_2 = 150$, $y_2 = 60,000/150 = 400$. Therefore we can use the preceding algebraic development to obtain

$$b = \frac{\log \dfrac{570}{400}}{\log \dfrac{150}{50}} = 0.322 \quad \text{(an 80 percent learning curve)}.$$

Substituting back, we find

$$\log a = \log 570 + 0.322 \log 50 = 7.6068,$$

$$a = 2012.$$

With $a = 2012$ and $b = 0.322$, the average number of DLH after 250 units are produced is

$$y = 2012(250)^{-0.322} = 340.$$

Therefore the total DLH to produce 250 units is $250(340) = 85,000$. Since 60,000 DLH were used to produce the first 150 units, the incremental DLH to produce the next 100 units equals: $85,000 - 60,000 = 25,000$ DLH. Notice that this batch of 100 units requires only 250 DLH per unit, whereas the first 50 units required an average of 570 DLH per unit. Therefore, an 80 percent learning curve produces dramatic drops in unit labor costs. This point is clearly demonstrated in Table 4-4, where we display for each batch of 50 units the cumulative total DLH, the average DLH for that cumulative output, and the marginal DLH (MDLH) to produce the last unit in each batch of 50 units. Notice that both average and marginal DLH are following an 80 percent learning curve: $y_{200} = 0.8y_{100} = 0.64y_{50}$ and $MDLH_{200} = 0.8MDLH_{100} = 0.64MDLH_{50}$.

TABLE 4-4. **Total, Average, and Incremental Costs for 50-Unit Batches**

Cumulative Output (x)	Total DLH	Average DLH for Cumulative Output (y)	Marginal DLH for last item in each batch $[a(1 - b)x^{-b}]$
50	28,500	570	387
100	45,600	456	310
150	60,000	400	272
200	72,900	365	248
250	85,000	340	231

Clearly, companies whose products are susceptible to learning-curve effects can price lower, counting on the increased business to move them even further along the learning curve and making it difficult for competitors to dislodge them from a leading market position. For the Milner Company, its historical experience with the first 150 units yielded an average of 400 DLH per unit. By exploiting the learning curve, it can count on an average of only 250 DLH per unit for the next 100 units it produces. Moreover, if it wins this order, it can expect the following order to have even lower marginal costs.

ESTIMATING LEARNING CURVES

The value of keeping learning-curve effects in mind is well illustrated by the following example. Suppose a company starts producing a new product and it keeps track of its monthly output and direct labor-hours for the first twelve months of production. These data are presented in Table 4-5. A new cost analyst is asked to estimate the average DLH to produce each unit and, remembering his introductory cost accounting and statistics courses, he decides to run a linear regression on the twelve observations. He is disappointed by the output from his regression program:

$$\text{DLH}_t = 226 + 0.916 \cdot \text{OUTPUT}_t, \quad R^2 = 0.05, \quad \overline{R^2} = -0.04, \quad \text{DW} = 0.57.$$
$$\phantom{\text{DLH}_t = }(0.35)\ (0.75)$$

Nothing seems to have worked well; both coefficients have t ratios less than 1, the adjusted R^2 is less than 0, and the Durbin-Watson statistic indicates that the data are highly autocorrelated. In fact, the residuals are ranked perfectly with

TABLE 4-5. **Monthly Output and Direct Labor-Hours for New Product**

Month	Output	Monthly DLH
1	570	1,400
2	410	710
3	550	840
4	420	580
5	510	660
6	530	660
7	540	640
8	500	570
9	540	600
10	580	620
11	560	590
12	590	610

TABLE 4-6. Cumulative Output and Average Direct Labor-Hours for New Product: Actual and Logged Values

(1) Month (t)	(2) Cumulative Output (x_t)	(3) Cumulative DLH (z_t)	(4) Average DLH Per Unit ($y_t = z_t/x_t$)	(5) Log Cumulative Output (log x_t)	(6) Log Average DLH (log y_t)
1	570	1,400	2.456	6.346	0.8986
2	980	2,110	2.153	6.888	0.7669
3	1,530	2,950	1.928	7.333	0.6565
4	1,950	3,530	1.810	7.576	0.5935
5	2,460	4,190	1.703	7.808	0.5325
6	2,990	4,850	1.622	8.003	0.4837
7	3,530	5,490	1.555	8.169	0.4416
8	4,030	6,060	1.504	8.302	0.4079
9	4,570	6,660	1.457	8.427	0.3766
10	5,150	7,280	1.414	8.547	0.3461
11	5,710	7,870	1.378	8.650	0.3208
12	6,300	8,480	1.346	8.748	0.2972

the first residual being the largest positive and successively decreasing until the last residual is the largest negative one.

Someone reminds the chagrined analyst that new products usually have a break-in period in which average costs decline exponentially. After learning about the learning curve, the analyst transforms the data in Table 4-5 into a format suitable for estimating the parameters of a learning curve, as shown in Table 4-6. The regression of the logged values of average DLH per unit [column (6)] versus logged cumulative output [column (5)] yields a perfect fit:

$$\log y_t = 2.5 - 0.252 \log x_t, \qquad R^2 = 1.0.$$

Thus, data that could not be explained at all with a simple linear regression of monthly DLH versus monthly output could be perfectly explained by a learning curve

$$y_t = ax_t^{-b}$$

with log a = 2.5 [a = exp (2.5) = 12.2] and b = 0.252. The value of b equal to 0.252 corresponds to an 84 percent learning curve.

The message, obviously, is to be sensitive to learning-curve effects when estimating the costs of new products and processes. For established products and processes the learning-curve effect is less important, since the ratio of monthly or annual production to cumulative production to date will be low so that the effect may be barely noticeable. Also, if data on total production and direct labor-hours (or other input or cost measure) have not been kept since the start of production, we will not know cumulative production and cumulative DLH and hence will be unable to estimate the learning-curve parameters as we did above.

In principle, if we knew total output to date, but not total costs or DLH, we could still estimate the learning curve by using the marginal rather than the average DLH learning curve. But in order to use the marginal learning curve, we would need to accumulate DLH or costs on an individual unit basis (or batch of homogeneous units, such as every 50 units). The monthly data given in Table 4-5 would not be adequate for this purpose because the monthly fluctuations in production prevent us from estimating marginal DLH per unit.

Suppose, instead, that we knew that production up to the start of the year totaled 4,000 units and that during the year the DLH to produce each of the next batch of 400 units were as given in Table 4-7. While the data are not completely monotonic, there clearly is a tendency for decreasing DLH as cumulative production increases. We can attempt to estimate a learning curve based on the marginal-cost function:

$$z_t = a(1 - b)x_t^{-b},$$

$$\log z_t = \log[a(1 - b)] - b \log x_t,$$

but we must be careful in our definition of x_t. Since we are measuring incremental costs based on 400-unit batches, the variable x_t is measured in the number of 400-unit batches produced to date. Thus, for the first observation (where cumulative production equals 4,400), x_t equals 11 (obtained from 4,400/400 = 11). For the second observation, x_t equals 12, and for the ninth or last observation (where cumulative production is 7,600), x_t equals 19. Running the regression with the logarithm of the nine new observations [(11,462), (12,447), . . . , (19,390)] yields

$$\log z_t = 6.878 - 0.313 \log x_t, \qquad \overline{R}^2 = 0.94.$$
$$(91.8) \quad (11.3)$$

TABLE 4-7.   **Output and Direct Labor-Hours, by 400 Unit Batches**

Observation	Cumulative Production	DLH to Produce Most Recent 400 Units (z_t)
Start of year	4,000	?
1	4,400	462
2	4,800	447
3	5,200	428
4	5,600	422
5	6,000	423
6	6,400	406
7	6,800	407
8	7,200	385
9	7,600	390

Thus, we have an excellent fit to a learning curve with $b = 0.313$ and

$$\log [a(1 - b)] = 6.878,$$

$$a(1 - b) = 971,$$

$$a = \frac{971}{0.687} = 1,413.$$

If we wish to predict the DLH of the next batch of 400 units (which would bring cumulative production to 8,000 units), we substitute into

$$z = a(1 - b)x^{-b}$$

$$= 971 \, (20)^{-0.313}$$

$$= 380,$$

where $x = 20$ is used because it will be the twentieth batch of 400 units produced.

In summary, the learning curve is estimated easily if we have data on cumulative production and cumulative costs (or DLH) from the start of the process. If we do not have data on costs before the start of our analysis, we can still estimate the parameters of the learning curve if (1) we know cumulative production to the start of analysis, and (2) data on future production are accumulated for batch runs of equal size. If either (1) or (2) is not satisfied, regression estimation of the learning-curve parameters will be much more difficult and the analyst will probably rely on approximate and visual techniques for estimating the learning curve.

SUMMARY

Multiple regression analysis is an extremely valuable tool for cost estimation, but it has many pitfalls for the inexperienced or untrained user. The analyst must decide how many and which independent variables to include in the regression analysis. Also, the choice between a linear and a nonlinear model must be made.

To supplement a simple linear regression, additional independent variables can be added to determine whether they increase the explanatory power of the statistical analysis. Ideally, these additional variables should be chosen because the analyst has some reason to believe they could be useful in explaining the variation of the dependent variable. Merely adding independent variables in the hope of eventually finding a few that seem to correlate with the dependent variable during the estimation time period is not recommended. If the independent variables are selected thoughtfully, then conventional statistical procedures, such as the t ratios of the coefficients and the increase or decrease in the adjusted R^2, can be helpful in obtaining a parsimonious model to explain and predict cost variation patterns. An additional check on the estimation procedure is to test the final model on a new set of data, not previously used to estimate the model. Either reestimating the model on this new set of data or comparing the predictions of the model relative to some simpler or alternative model (for example, using the RMS criterion) would provide further evidence on the model's validity. Also, the analyst should be suspicious of any variable whose coefficient has a sign different from that expected, even though it appears to be statistically significant. Similarly, the analyst should question any coefficient whose magnitude seems unreasonable. Naturally, this requires that the analyst have as much knowledge of the process being modeled as can be conveniently obtained. Regression analysis is not a substitute for thought or judgment. Rather, it is a way of enhancing and supplementing the analyst's knowledge about factors that he believes help explain the variation in cost behavior observed over time or across similar organizational units.

A common pitfall when adding independent variables, particularly in a time-series regression, is collinearity among a subset of the variables. Many variables move together over time, so that the statistical analysis cannot determine the unique effect of any one of them. The first check on collinearity is to examine the correlation matrix of independent variables, recognizing that it will be difficult to expect reliable individual coefficient estimates for variables with simple correlations in excess of 0.9. Other symptoms of collinearity in a multiple regression include (1) unusually large coefficients, (2) coefficients with unexpected signs, and (3) a model with high explanatory power but whose coefficients have relatively low t statistics. When two (or more) variables are highly collinear, and one wants to have a reliable estimate of the coefficient of at least one of them (say, to get a good variable-cost estimate), choose only one of the correlated variables to include in the final model. It would be best to choose that variable based on prior knowledge of the process, but alternative procedures include selecting that variable with the highest zero-order correlation with the dependent variable or the one that yields the best predictions in a holdout or test sample.

Dummy (0-1) variables are useful when there is a shift in the constant (fixed-cost) term between time periods or among regions. It is preferable, when possible, to model the variation over time or among regions by a continuous variable rather than a dummy variable, but the simple 0-1 variable frequently provides a simple structure to improve the fit of the model. Dummy variables are most useful when either no continuous variable is available to model the desired effect or the variation in the dependent variable is not linear over the range of variation of the independent variable.

The additive linear model assumes that the effect on the dependent variable of a change in any independent variable is independent of the *level* of that independent variable *and* the level of all the other independent variables in the regression model. This assumption provides a good first approximation and may actually be representative of many processes. But if the assumption is not valid, the analyst may prefer to estimate a nonlinear model of cost behavior. The multiplicative model permits the incremental effect of a change in an independent variable on a dependent variable to be a function of the level of all the independent variables in the model. It is easy to estimate, since the multiplicative model becomes additive in the log of the independent variables. The interpretation of the model is also simple, since the coefficients of the multiplicative model represent elasticities—the percentage change in the dependent variable caused by a given percentage change in the independent variable.

A specific form of nonlinearity in cost behavior occurs when the learning or experience curve is operative, especially for new products and new processes. In this case, the variable cost per unit declines with the total number of units produced. Assuming a linear cost function in this situation would yield a poor fit to the data and highly autocorrelated residuals, since costs would be underestimated in the early part of the sample and overestimated in the latter part. Greatly improved fits can be obtained by assuming the specific exponential cost decline associated with the learning curve and estimating the relationship between cumulative or average costs and cumulative output at various points in time.

PROBLEMS

4-1. MP Manufacturing (A): Estimating Fixed and Variable Costs*

In January 1983, managers of the MP Manufacturing Company were reviewing their profit plans for the coming year. During 1982, MP had enjoyed an unusually good year and was working close to capacity. A condensed income statement for 1982 appears below:

Sales		$10,816,800
Materials	$4,262,100	
Direct Labor	1,118,100	
Factory Overhead	2,815,200	
Selling & Admin.	1,620,900	9,816,300
Operating Income		$ 1,000,500

These results were better than had been expected but MP's management was not convinced that demand would remain at present levels and hence had not planned any increase in plant capacity. MP's equipment was specialized and made to order; over a year's lead-time was necessary on all plant additions. MP produces three products. While sales fluctuate from month to month, a typical month's sales mix is:

10,000 units of Product A at $60.	$600,000
4,000 units of Product B at $30.	120,000
2,000 units of Product C at $90.	180,000
Gross Revenues	$900,000

* This problem is adapted from Bayview Manufacturing Company in the Report of the Committee on the Measurement Methods Content of the Accounting Curriculum, Supplement to Volume XLVI of the *Accounting Review*, 1971; pp. 231–236.

Management has ordered a profit analysis for each product and has available the following information:

	A	B	C
Material	$21.00	$11.25	$49.80
Direct Labor	6.00	3.00	10.50
Factory overhead	15.00	7.50	26.25
Selling and administrative	9.00	4.50	13.50
Total Costs	$51.00	$26.25	$100.05
Selling Price	60.00	30.00	90.00
Operating Income Per Unit	9.00	3.75	($10.05)

Factory overhead has been applied on the basis of direct labor costs at a rate of 250 percent; and management asserts that approximately 25 percent of the overhead is variable and does vary with labor costs. Selling and administrative costs have been allocated on the basis of sales at the rate of 15 percent; approximately 50 percent of this is variable and does vary with sales in dollars. All of the labor and material expense is considered to be variable.

Tables 1 and 2 contain 1982 cost data that you are able to obtain from the accounting system.

Required:

1. Analyze the profitability of the three products, based on
   a. management's assertions of the cost structure of Products A, B, and C
   b. your analysis of the cost data in Tables 1 and 2.
2. Compare your two analyses in Questions 1(a) and 1(b) to each other and to the product profit analysis prepared by the company.

TABLE 1.

	Direct Labor Expense (Monthly)			Overhead Expense (Monthly)		
Department	1	2	Total	1	2	Total
Month 1	$42,600	$49,800	$92,400	$101,100	$133,500	$234,600
2	45,300	51,300	96,600	101,400	134,400	235,800
3	43,500	50,400	93,900	101,400	134,700	236,100
4	42,900	50,700	93,600	101,100	133,800	234,900
5	42,600	50,400	93,000	101,100	132,300	233,400
6	43,200	51,000	94,200	100,200	133,800	234,000
7	43,800	50,400	94,200	100,800	134,400	235,200
8	40,500	47,400	87,900	99,900	131,700	231,600
9	40,200	46,200	86,400	99,900	130,200	230,100
10	43,800	51,000	94,800	101,700	135,300	237,000
11	44,400	52,500	96,900	100,800	136,200	237,000
12	43,800	50,400	94,200	100,800	134,700	235,500
Total	$516,600	$601,500	$1,118,100	$1,210,200	$1,605,000	$2,815,200

TABLE 2.

		Sales Revenue			Selling and Administrative Expenses
Product	A	B	C	Total	
Month 1	$636,300	$132,300	$169,200	$937,800	$137,100
2	605,400	123,600	180,000	909,000	135,600
3	600,000	109,200	183,000	892,200	133,800
4	580,500	132,300	186,000	898,800	135,900
5	586,800	131,100	190,200	908,100	136,500
6	596,700	119,700	188,700	905,100	135,000
7	546,900	130,800	173,700	851,400	131,400
8	615,600	122,700	174,000	912,300	137,100
9	627,000	106,200	184,200	917,400	135,900
10	625,800	115,800	195,300	936,900	137,400
11	560,700	113,400	162,000	836,100	129,900
12	617,100	117,900	176,700	911,700	135,300
Total	$7,198,800	$1,455,000	$2,163,000	$10,816,800	$1,620,900

4-2. Predicting How Costs Will Vary

The Gardner Corporation is developing a model to explain and predict overhead costs. It produces only one product-line so that a simple count of the number of units produced each month may be a good measure of activity. Alternatively, the direct labor hours recorded each month can also serve as a good activity measure for the firm. The company has collected data on these variables for the past eighteen months:

Month	Overhead Cost	Production (units)	Direct Labor Hours	Absolute Change in Production
1	$24,200	463	2,490	37
2	24,500	487	2,250	24
3	23,500	483	2,460	4
4	25,600	527	2,610	44
5	25,900	548	2,710	21
6	26,400	563	2,790	15
7	25,600	528	2,530	35
8	25,600	547	2,560	19
9	26,400	556	2,990	9
10	26,900	594	3,240	38
11	27,000	570	2,870	24
12	26,500	578	3,110	8
13	27,500	602	3,210	24
14	28,300	630	3,090	28
15	28,700	660	3,570	30
16	31,000	707	3,320	47
17	30,500	711	3,780	4
18	30,000	681	3,170	30

1. Determine whether production units, or Direct Labor Hours, or both provide the best explanation of monthly variation in overhead costs.

2. The foreman, hearing of the attempt to explain overhead costs, pointed out that a certain amount of inefficiency, such as idle time or overtime occurred when production changed from month-to-month. This inefficiency arose from the need to adjust personnel and schedules to the new level of production. Therefore, he expects higher than expected overhead costs anytime there is a change in production levels. Test this idea using the data provided.

3. In the most recent month, Gardner produced 650 units, using 3,200 DLH. What is your best estimate for the level of overhead costs for the month?

4-3. Effect of Omitted Variables

Carol Frank, the manager of the Assembly Division of the Charleston Steel Company, has been approached by a customer for a special order. The customer wants to have some steel fabricated into a unit of the customer's design. At present, there is slack capacity in the Assembly Division, but Carol believes that the customer's proposal will not enable her to make any money on the project. The customer will supply the raw material and needs only the labor and machine-time capabilities of the Assembly Division. He has offered to pay $150 for each unit fabricated in the division. Carol estimates that the job will require 15 direct labor hours and 2 machine hours. Based on a previous cost analysis study, direct labor hours was found to be the single best predictor of total incremental costs (labor and overhead) in the division. The current flexible budget shows incremental costs are $10/DLH.

Carol is about to turn down the proposal since, at best, she breaks even on incremental costs and the offer would make no contribution to overhead costs. Before calling up the customer, however, she asks her assistant to update the cost analysis study to see whether the $10/DLH figure is accurate. The following data on total costs, direct labor hours, and machine hours for the most recent 12 periods are collected:

Period	Total Costs	Direct Labor Hours	Machine Hours
1	$63,100	4,300	3,110
2	50,500	2,890	3,020
3	60,700	4,230	2,970
4	54,600	3,600	2,830
5	43,800	2,460	2,450
6	52,400	3,330	2,720
7	58,300	3,890	2,770
8	57,600	3,790	3,010
9	51,900	3,720	2,120
10	66,960	4,600	3,360
11	57,000	3,440	2,900
12	43,600	2,740	1,940

1. Determine whether the $10/DLH incremental cost estimate is consistent with these data by performing a regression of Total Costs versus Direct Labor Hours.
2. Carol Frank's assistant notices that machine hours are usually more than 60 to 70 percent of direct labor hours for jobs in the Assembly Division. The current proposal, however, requires only 2 machine hours per 15 direct labor hours. To determine the simultaneous effect of machine hours and direct labor hours, perform a multiple regression of total costs versus both these variables.
3. What is your recommendation to Carol Frank based on your cost analysis in Questions 1 and 2? Why does the inclusion of a second variable (machine hours) in a regression change the estimated coefficient for the first variable (direct labor hours)?

4-4. Nonstationarities in Time Series Data

University Hospital is conducting a study to determine the amount of Registered Nursing Hours (RN Hours) required to staff its medical and surgical patient units. The hospital administrator, Dan Branchler, has found it difficult to recruit enough nurses, and wants to be sure that the nurses he does employ are being used effectively. At first, he was going to do a study on nursing costs versus patient days, but decided that such a study would confound the rising salaries of nurses with the variation in number of hours spent by nurses at the patient units. Therefore, he would use actual RN Hours as the dependent variable for his regression analysis. He hoped to compute the fixed and variable components of RN Hours as a function of patient days. Then he could develop a flexible budget for RN Hours for planning and control purposes.

Dan and his assistant collected data for the most recent 15 months:

Month	Patient Days	RN Hours
1	2,970	12,690
2	2,860	12,370
3	2,470	11,590
4	2,640	11,760
5	2,880	12,480
6	2,550	12,040
7	2,870	12,910
8	2,490	10,920
9	2,770	12,060
10	2,790	12,630
11	2,420	12,340
12	2,660	13,370
13	2,820	13,490
14	2,490	12,700
15	2,640	13,840

Dan obtained the following OLS estimates:

$$\text{RN Hours} = 7985 + 1.67 \cdot \text{PAT DAYS} \qquad \overline{R^2} = .091$$
$$\qquad\qquad (2.75)\quad (1.55)$$

$$DW = .61$$

He is chagrined when he obtains this result. The variable coefficient is not statistically significant at the 5 percent level, the $\overline{R^2}$ is low, and the Durbin-Watson statistic shows high autocorrelation in the residuals. Dan is frustrated with this effort and turns over the project to his assistant, Andrea Carney, who has more experience and ability in performing quantitative studies.

Andrea's first thought when she looks at the regression output was to examine the residuals (actually it was her second thought; her first thought occurred when her boss had thrown all the regression output on her desk and told her to make some sense out of the numbers). Andrea hoped that observing the residuals might reveal the cause of the high autocorrelation. She plotted each residual and obtained the following pattern:

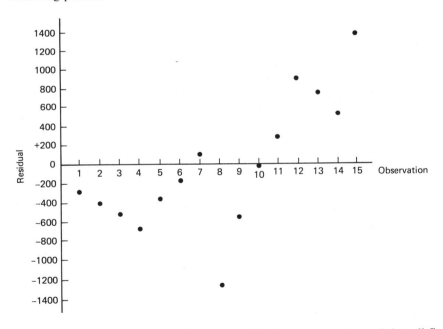

Andrea noticed that nine of the first ten residuals were negative and that all five of the last five residuals were highly positive, with magnitudes between +300 and +1435. It certainly looked as if extra nurses were added to the staff starting about Month 10 or 11.

Andrea did some further checking around the hospital and learned that nurse staffing levels had increased about Month 11 because of an extensive recruiting and hiring effort between Months 9 and 11. Andrea decided that the statistical analysis could be saved if she could incorporate this staffing shift into her analysis. She thought of the following possibilities:

1. Add a dummy variable equal to 1 for Months 11–15 and 0 elsewhere. In effect, this would assume the extra nurses contributed to an increase in the fixed component of nursing hours.
2. Estimate a separate variable coefficient, of nursing hours per patient day, for each sub-period (Months 1–10, Months 11–15). This could be accomplished by defining one variable equal to actual patient days for Months 1–10, and equal to 0 for Months 11–15. Define a second variable equal to 0 for Months 1–10 and equal to actual patient days for Months 11–15. With this formulation, the additional nursing staff would be assumed to increase the variable component of nursing hours.
3. Add a linear time trend (a variable that equals t for the observation in month t) and estimate the average linear increase in fixed costs over the 15-month time period.

Required:

Help Andrea Carney out by performing these regressions (plus any others you believe are appropriate). Analyze your findings and report your conclusions to Andrea. Provide an estimate of the number of nursing hours required in Month 16 when there were 3,000 patient days in the hospital.

4-5. Multiple Regression and Dummy Variables

The Franklin Furniture Company operates a fleet of trucks to deliver its merchandise. In the past few years, the company had purchased some diesel trucks because it had heard that these trucks were more economical to run. The manager of the truck fleet, however, has been reviewing the repair and maintenance bills for the trucks and has found that the diesel trucks seem to be more expensive to repair and maintain than the regular gasoline-powered trucks. He has collected the 1981 repair and maintenance (R&M) expense for each of the 14 trucks in the fleet, as well as the age and the number of miles driven for each truck:

Truck	Maintenance and Repair Expense	Mileage Driven (Thousands of miles)	Age in years (0 is new truck)	Power Type (D = diesel, G = gasoline)
1	$1,220	32.2	0	D
2	1,550	34.8	1	D
3	1,350	26.7	1	D
4	1,350	24.8	2	D
5	1,450	28.2	2	D
6	1,480	27.5	2	D
7	1,300	30.6	0	G
8	1,310	29.4	0	G
9	1,350	31.4	0	G
10	1,360	28.3	1	G
11	1,400	29.0	1	G
12	1,310	26.2	1	G
13	1,500	27.1	2	G
14	1,460	25.8	2	G

Indeed the 6 diesel trucks averaged $1400 in R&M expense whereas the 8 gasoline-powered trucks averaged only $1374 in that expense. The manager was also surprised to find that he found no apparent relationship when he plotted R&M expense versus mileage driven on a scatter diagram. Except for the high expense observation for Truck 2, there seemed to be a negative correlation between R&M Expense and Mileage. In previous years, there had always been a clear positive correlation between R&M expense and miles driven. The fleet manager is disappointed that the diesel trucks have not produced the expected savings in repair and maintenance expense and is puzzled by the breakdown in the relationship between R&M expense and mileage driven.

Required:

Do you agree with the manager's analysis? How would you analyze the above data to determine the effects on repair and maintenance expense of diesel v. gasoline powered engines and mileage driven?

4-6. Including Nonlinear Effects

The cost analyst of the Heller Manufacturing Corporation wished to explain the monthly variation in average manufacturing cost for the company's main product. In addition to the effect of labor and material costs, which were reasonably stable from month to month, the analyst believed that manufacturing costs were influenced by the level of operation of the factory. She felt that unit manufacturing costs declined as the firm worked closer to the capacity of the plant.

She prepared an index of labor and material costs for the past twenty months. Raw material costs have fluctuated in a narrow range and while labor rates had increased, they had been offset by improved procedures, resulting in stable unit labor costs during this period. The production rate had undergone much wider fluctuations as demand was volatile during this period and the company watched its inventory position closely.

Month	Average Manufacturing Cost per Unit	Index Material and Labor Costs	Production as Percentage of Capacity	Month	Average Manufacturing Cost per Unit	Index Material and Labor Costs	Production as Percentage of Capacity
1	$8.75	99.0	70	11	$6.96	100.3	84
2	6.56	99.5	85	12	7.65	99.7	78
3	7.16	101.5	84	13	6.22	100.6	94
4	7.83	101.5	78	14	9.77	99.4	66
5	8.36	100.0	72	15	7.97	101.1	76
6	7.57	100.4	79	16	5.72	101.5	92
7	8.13	101.2	75	17	7.63	99.1	75
8	8.33	102.3	76	18	7.92	99.2	74
9	6.23	102.8	92	19	7.76	102.6	80
10	7.99	100.0	77	20	5.94	101.0	92

Required:

1. Perform the multiple regression

$$Y = \beta_0 + \beta_1 X_1 + \beta_2 X_2$$

   where Y = Average manufacturing cost per unit
   X_1 = Index of material and labor cost
   X_2 = Production level as a percentage of capacity

   Interpret the coefficient estimates. Do average costs decrease as production levels increase?

2. Plot the residuals against X_2 to detect evidence of a curvilinear relationship.

3. In order to test for a curvilinear relationship, estimate the model:

$$Y = \beta_0 + \beta_1 X_1 + \beta_2 X_2 + \beta_3 (X_2)^2$$

   Is the estimated coefficient for the nonlinear term statistically significant? Interpret the type of cost behavior implied by the nonlinear model.

4. During Month 21, the material and labor index is expected to equal 102.5 and the plant will operate at 90 percent of capacity. What average manufacturing cost is predicted by the two models?

4-7. Comparison of Linear and Nonlinear Models

Henry Murphy, the marketing analyst for Gotham Motors, wants to understand the critical factors affecting automobile sales in his region. At present there are four other automobile dealerships in the city selling the same cars as Gotham Motors. The dealers all provide the same quality of service but differ in their price and advertising strategies. While Henry believes that price and advertising are important for influencing consumers, it is also true that many automobile buyers prefer to purchase from a dealer nearby so that the car can be serviced conveniently.

It would usually be impossible to find out the price, advertising, and number of cars sold of competing dealerships but a recent court case between another dealer in the city and the automobile manufacturer provided an interesting source of data for Henry. During the course of the trial, a witness for the manufacturer presented data on dealer profitability in the city which included data on car sales, average new car margin over dealer cost, and dealer advertising:

Dealer	Average Margin	Advertising	Total Sales
1	$300	$15,000	333
2	260	20,000	337
3	340	9,000	454
4	280	12,000	229
5	290	30,000	370

At first glance, the high sales of Dealer 3 seemed surprising, but Henry recalled that Dealer 3 was located in the most heavily-populated section of the city. He decided that a spatial model would give better insights into the pattern of new car sales. Henry subdivided the city into five contiguous regions representing the primary marketing area for each dealer (see below):

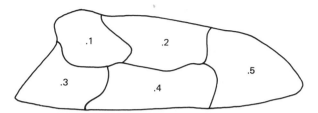

He then estimated the distance between each pair of dealers and the average distance that a purchaser within each dealer's region would have to travel to reach that dealer. This led to a matrix of distance, D_{ij}, representing the average distance a customer in region i would have to travel to reach dealer j:

			j		
D_{ij}	1	2	3	4	5
1	2	5	4	7	12
2	5	2.8	8	6	9
i 3	4	8	1.4	5	18
4	7	6	5	3	6
5	12	9	18	6	2.2

From census tract data, Henry estimated the population in each of the five regions:

Region	Population
1	20,000
2	16,000
3	30,000
4	25,000
5	10,000

Finally, by a tedious analysis of the zip codes of the purchasers of each automobile, Henry was able to estimate the number of cars sold by Dealer i in each region j:

Sales of Dealer i in Region j

				Region			
		1	2	3	4	5	Total
	1	193	27	89	17	7	333
	2	69	180	24	52	12	337
Dealer	3	58	16	325	54	1	454
	4	15	38	39	118	19	229
	5	16	14	8	54	278	370
	Total	351	275	485	295	317	1723

These data seemed reasonable since sales of a dealer were highest in its own region and were lowest in regions most distant from the dealership. Nevertheless because of the joint influence of price, advertising, distance and population on the amount and distribution of car sales, Henry believed that only a multiple regression analysis could sort out the contributions of these different factors. Henry decided to estimate the following model:

$$S_{ij} = \beta_0 + \beta_1 \cdot Price_i + \beta_2 \cdot Adv_i + \beta_3 \cdot Pop_j + \beta_4 \cdot D_{ij}$$

where S_{ij} = Sales of dealer i in region j.

Required:

1. Perform this regression; analyze and interpret the results.

2. Henry is disappointed in the results from his linear regression model. Only a minor amount of the variation in the dependent variable, S_{ij}, is explained by the model and at least one of the coefficient estimates has a sign different from what Henry had expected (which one(s)?). Henry reasons that perhaps the relationship is not well specified by a linear model. The effects of the price and advertising of Dealer 5 on a customer in Region 3, who is 18 miles away, is likely to be different from the effects on a customer in Region 4 or 5 who is much closer. Because of the possibility of such interaction effects, Henry decides to try a model for which the effect of variation in any single variable depends on the level of all the variables in the model. He estimates:

$$S_{ij} = \beta_0(Price_i)^{\beta_1} (Adv_i)^{\beta_2} (Pop_j)^{\beta_3} (Dist_{ij})^{\beta_4}$$

by taking the logarithm of the dependent and independent variables and estimating the coefficients using his standard OLS package.

Perform this regression for the multiplicative form of the model. Analyze and interpret the results.

3. Which model explains more of the variation in the sales of Dealer i to Region j? (Optional)

4. What assumptions are being implicitly made about the distribution of dealer sales by both the additive or multiplicative model that limit the usefulness of the model as a means for predicting the number of cars sold by a dealer?

4-8.   Learning Curve Analysis (R. Manes)

National Avionics has just completed the assembly of 50 meteorological balloons made for the Geodetic Survey specially equipped to measure atmospheric weather conditions in the Arctic. The company is now being asked to submit an estimate on costs of an additional 40 units. Its management has noted that the direct labor hours on each unit seem to be declining. For the first 20 units produced, the average hours were 420. For the assembly of the 50 units, however, the average hours per unit dropped to 325.

1. Using these two points, estimate the parameters of National's learning curve for assembly of meteorological balloons.
2. Using these values, calculate the total hours required to assemble 90 units.
3. Suppose incremental costs (labor plus variable overhead costs) are $12.00 per direct labor hour. What would be the incremental assembly costs for a new order of 40 units.
4. Assume that National Avionics discovers it has additional data on the first 50 units it produced:

Cumulative Units Produced	Average Labor Hours	Total Labor Hours
15	450	6,750
20	420	8,400
25	390	9,750
40	350	14,000
50	325	16,250

Using regression analysis on these data, estimate the parameters of the learning curve. What is the revised forecast of the incremental assembly costs for the new order of 40 units?

5. National Avionics wins its order for the next 40 units and, in addition, produces another 10 units for another customer. Its cumulative experience with producing these 100 balloons shows 28,000 total direct labor hours or an average of 280 DLH per balloon. Is this consistent with the learning curve you estimated? If not, suggest an explanation for the deviation.

4-9. Estimating and Using Learning Curve Effects*

The Sunnyvale Camera Company has just finished producing its first order of 1000 units of a new camera. Sunnyvale has been approached by a large department-store chain to produce a special order of these cameras that will be marketed under a private label and hence, will not compete with the cameras marketed under Sunnyvale's brand name. Sunnyvale must choose between two offers from the department store:

1. Sell 500 units at a wholesale price of $6.40 each, or
2. Sell 1000 units at a wholesale price of $6.18 each.

Sunnyvale experienced overtime problems with its initial run of 1,000 units, due to delays in shipments of materials. The supplier states it has now solved the problem and guarantees Sunnyvale it can promptly provide the materials for either

---

* This problem is adapted (with permission) from the Berkeley Camera Company case, written by George Foster (#S-A-126, Stanford University).

the extra 500 or 1,000 units. The supplier quotes $5.10 per unit for 500 units and $5.00 per unit for 1,000 units. Sunnyvale negotiates with its labor union a $7.20 per hour wage rate for the period covering the expected duration of either the 500 or 1,000 unit contract.

Part A

Sunnyvale hires Hobie Leland Jr. to help it to decide which offer, if either, should be accepted. Hobie determines that the two costs to consider are materials costs and labor costs—no incremental overhead costs will be incurred on either of the special orders. His major concern is predicting labor costs, as the supplier has provided written guarantees on the $5.10/500-unit and $5.00/1,000-unit order quotations. Hobie is provided with production statistics covering the initial run of 1,000 units—see Table 1. He initially decides to use ordinary least squares regression (OLS).

TABLE 1.   Production Statistics for Sunnyvale

Cumulative Units Produced X_i	Cumulative Labor Cost C_i	Cumulative Direct Labor Hours Y_i
100	$ 444	74
200	654	109
300	835	138
400	1,035	170
500	1,152	188
600	1,328	215
700	1,464	236
800	1,562	250
900	1,737	275
1,000	1,877	295

Required:

1. Plot C_i against X_i. Estimate

$$C_i = \beta_0 + \beta_1 X_i$$

using OLS. Comment on the specification of the model.

2. Using the model above, should Sunnyvale accept either the 500-unit or 1,000-unit special order?

Part B

Hobie then notes an interesting feature of the data in Table 1—to produce 100 units required 74 labor hours; whereas to produce 1,000 units, required only 295 labor hours. He has an instant flashback to his MBA days. He remembers his accounting instructor discussing the learning curve notion in the airframe industry and suspects a similar phenomena may be going on at Sunnyvale. He calculates a new variable Z_i (average labor hours required to produce i units).

Required:

1. Plot Z_i against X_i. Is there evidence of a learning effect?
2. Estimate

$$Z_i = a \cdot X_i^{-l}$$

   using OLS where—
   a = number of labor hours for the first unit, and
   l = a measure of the "learning" improvement.
   Comment on the specification of the model.
3. Alternatively, estimate

$$Y_i = b \cdot X_i^{(1-l)}$$

   to determine whether the learning parameter, l, is the same in both specifications of the learning curve.
4. Predict the direct labor hours required to produce the extra 500 and the extra 1,000 units. Which option will Hobie recommend if he assumes the learning curve phenomenon will continue to be operative for the special order?
5. While on assignment with Sunnyvale, Hobie picks up a *Harvard Business Review* and reads the following in an article on learning curves in the motor vehicle industry:

> "While there must be a theoretical limit to the amount by which costs can ultimately be reduced, a manufacturer reaches the practical limit first. However, the practical limit is not reached because he has exhausted his means of cutting costs; it is rather determined by the market's demand for product change, the rate of technological innovation in the industry, and competitors' ability to use product performance as the basis for competing."
> [HBR, Sept–Oct 1974, p. 118]

   What factors should Sunnyvale consider in deciding if it will reach the "practical limit" to its learning curve before it has "exhausted its means of cutting costs?" Should Hobie be overly concerned with the above comment in his present assignment?

Part C

Sunnyvale decides to accept the 1000-unit alternative. After completion of the contract, Sunnyvale's accountant prepares the following report:

Revenue from Contract	$6,180
Less Materials Costs	5,000
Less Labor Costs	1,385
Loss on Contract	$ 205

The President of Sunnyvale is far from happy. He calls you in to examine what went wrong on the contract and provides you with production statistics covering the contract shown in Table 2.

Required:

1. Present a report to the President about "what went wrong" on the contract.
2. What recommendations would you make on the procedures Sunnyvale should adopt when analyzing the profitability of similar special orders in the future?

TABLE 2. Production Statistics for Sunnyvale

Cumulative Units Produced X_i	Cumulative Labor Cost C_i	Cumulative Direct Labor Hours Y_i
1,200	$2,107	327
1,400	2,330	358
1,600	2,585	393
1,800	2,922	439
2,000	3,262	485

4-10. Estimating Accounts Receivable Balances

The Carlyle Corporation wishes to obtain a model to explain and predict its Accounts Receivable balance each month. Such a model would be very helpful in determining when the balance in this account differs significantly from its historical relationship to sales so that changes in credit policy or in customer payment schedules can be detected rapidly. Also, the model would help to predict future account balances, as a function of estimated sales. These predictions would greatly enhance the ability of the company to forecast cash and working capital requirements during the year.

Monthly data for the 1980 and 1981 on Sales and Accounts Receivable appear below:

| | 1980 | | 1981 | |
Month	Sales	Accounts Receivable	Sales	Accounts Receivable
January	$88,300	$148,800	$77,600	$108,700
February	74,600	152,200	73,700	114,200
March	73,000	142,300	87,400	121,200
April	66,900	117,400	78,500	113,400
May	60,300	102,700	78,000	131,900
June	62,300	85,000	79,200	116,500
July	47,700	70,100	66,100	105,400
August	52,000	73,400	74,200	111,900
September	64,800	83,800	78,200	112,600
October	70,400	89,500	81,600	115,900
November	64,600	96,800	77,500	117,100
December	67,000	94,000	77,200	111,000

Since Accounts Receivable may be a function of not only the current month's sales, but also of the sales in preceding months, the sales data for the last few months in 1979 were also obtained:

	Sales	Accounts Receivable
October, 1979	$94,200	$140,000
November	83,200	138,900
December	70,100	132,500

Required:

1. Estimate and test a model explaining the level of Accounts Receivable for the 24 months, January 1980—December 1981, as a function of current and, perhaps, past monthly sales.

2. An alternative procedure to estimating the level of Accounts Receivable each month would be to estimate the amount of Collections each month. It might prove easier to predict the level of a flow variable, such as Collections (COL) rather than a stock variable, Accounts Receivable (AR). The Collections each month can be estimated from the accounting identity:

$$COL_t = Sales_t + AR_{t-1} - AR_t.$$

Estimate a model of Collections for the 24 month period as a function of current and, perhaps, lagged monthly sales.

3. Which model explains more of the month-to-month variation in the level of Accounts Receivable from January 1980 to December 1981? Does either model outperform a naive model:

$$AR_t = AR_{t-1}?$$

4. Data for the first four months in 1982 have recently become available:

	Sales	Accounts Receivable
January, 1982	$78,800	$112,000
February	76,300	110,000
March	94,200	134,000
April	79,400	123,300

Compare the performance of the three models (AR as a function of Sales, Collections as a function of Sales, and $AR_t = AR_{t-1}$) in predicting the level of Accounts Receivable during the first four months of 1982.

4-11. Comprehensive Problem on Multiple Regression* (G. Foster)

Cost Estimation in the U.S. Brewing Industry

Hobie Leland, Jr. has just completed his MBA and accepts a job with the Pabst Brewing Company in Milwaukee, Wisconsin. His initial assignment is to estimate the cost-volume relationship of Pabst vis-a-vis several other of its competitors in the U.S. brewing industry. He first makes an analysis of the internal records of Pabst and discovers that since 1962 Pabst has been a single line of business company. Prior to 1962, it also owned a soft-drink company (Hoffman Beverage Company) and the accounting records did not separately report the costs associated with the brewing and soft-drink operations. Hobie decides to base his analysis on the 1962 to 1980 period and collects the data in Table 1. Parts A to C of this case cover issues Hobie faces in choosing an appropriate model with which to estimate the cost-volume relationship of Pabst. Parts D to F cover issues faced when comparing the estimated relationship for Pabst with that of other firms in the U.S. brewing industry.

Part A

1. What problems might occur in using the data in Table 1 to estimate the cost-volume relationship at Pabst?
2. Estimate the following linear relationship between cost of sales (C_t) and barrels of beer sold (V_t) over the 1962 to 1980 period using (a) the high-low method, and (b) the ordinary least squares (OLS) regression method:

$$C_t = \alpha + \beta \cdot V_t$$

3. Evaluate the results in A2.
4. Why might the OLS method yield more efficient estimates of the cost-volume relationship for Pabst than does the high-low method?

---

* © 1981 by the Board of Trustees of the Leland Stanford Junior University. (Reproduced with permission).

TABLE 1. **Pabst Brewing Company: 1962–1980**

Year	Cost of Sales[1] ($000,000's)	Barrels Sold (000,000's)	Wholesale Price[2] Index of Beer
1962	166.943	5.844	.533
1963	184.981	6.672	.533
1964	206.666	7.444	.535
1965	229.200	8.219	.536
1966	252.122	9.047	.540
1967	285.380	10.123	.552
1968	313.070	10.910	.557
1969[3]	305.044	10.225	.570
1970	324.391	10.517	.596
1971	367.779	11.797	.611
1972	395.559	12.600	.612
1973	431.398	13.128	.623
1974	530.769	14.297	.719
1975	630.160	15.669	.759
1976	696.039	17.037	.769
1977	688.045	16.003	.794
1978	720.258	15.367	.848
1979[4]	765.303	15.115	.933
1980	832.018	15.091	1.000

Notes to Table 1

1 The level of detail in Pabst's Annual Report for the "Costs of Sales" item has increased since 1962. The 1980 Annual Report broke this item into three components:

Cost of Goods Sold	$607.526
Federal Excise Taxes	$133.539
Marketing, General and Adminstrative Expenses	$ 90.953
	$832.018

2 The Wholesale Price Index of Beer is Index 0261–01 (Malt Beverages) in the Bureau of Labor's Wholesale Price Index. Prior to 1967, the Index was labelled 1441 (Malt Beverages). Index 0261–01 has 1967 as the base year ($=100$); the index is rescaled to make 1980 the base year.
3 On June 30, 1958 Pabst acquired the Blatz Brewing Company. On September 2, 1969, under a court-ordered divestiture Pabst sold the Blatz brands to G. Heileman Brewing Company, Inc. In the 1968 fiscal year, sales of Blatz brands totaled 1.854 million barrels.
4 On April 2, 1979 Pabst acquired the Blitz-Weinhard Company, a Portland based brewer. The results of operations of Blitz are included since the date of acquisition. The 1978 sales of Blitz were approximately $41.9 million.

Part B

One problem in using time series data to estimate cost-volume relationships arises from inflation. One technique proposed to handle this problem is to deflate the dependent variable by a price index (P_t). The "Wholesale Price Index of Beer" over the 1962 to 1980 period is presented in Table 1, above.

1. Estimate the following linear relationship using the OLS regression method:

$$\frac{C_t}{P_t} = \alpha + \beta \cdot V_t$$

Evaluate the results.

2. What problems might arise in using the "Wholesale Price Index of Beer" in this context? How would you gain evidence on the severity of these problems?

Part C

Hobie then remembered a warning from his MBA days—serial correlation in the residuals is frequently encountered in regressions using time series data.

1. What is serial correlation in the residuals of a regression model?
2. Why might it arise when using time-series data?
3. Why is it a problem? What are its consequences?
4. How would you detect it?
5. A common approach to serial correlation of the residuals is to estimate the model in the first differences of the variables, rather than in the levels of the variables:

$$\left(\frac{C_t}{P_t} - \frac{C_{t-1}}{P_{t-1}}\right) = \alpha + \beta(V_t - V_{t-1})$$

Estimate this relationship for Pabst using OLS. Is serial correlation in the residuals less of a problem than with the model estimated in B1?

Part D

Hobie decides that the best specified model for Pabst uses first differences for the dependent and independent variables with the dependent variable being Cost of Sales in Year t deflated by the Wholesale Price Index of Beer in Year t. He now collects data from the published Annual Reports of several other brewing companies. See Table 2, page 126.

1. What problems might occur in using the data in Table 2 to estimate the comparable cost-volume relationship for each of Pabst's competitors?
2. Use OLS to estimate the following cost-volume relationship for each of Pabst's competitors in Table 2:

$$\left(\frac{C_t}{P_t} - \frac{C_{t-1}}{P_{t-1}}\right) = \alpha + \beta(V_t - V_{t-1})$$

3. What inferences do you draw from the results in C5 and D2?

TABLE 2.   Other U.S. Brewing Companies: 1962–1980

Year	Anheuser Busch Cost of Sales ($000,000's)	Anheuser Busch Barrels Sold (000,000's)	Olympia Brewing Cost of Sales ($000,000's)	Olympia Brewing Barrels Sold (000,000's)	Jos. Schlitz Cost of Sales ($000,000's)	Jos. Schlitz Barrels Sold (000,000's)	Wholesale Price Index of Beer
1962	392.752	9.035	59.617	1.742	236.650	6.869	.533
1963	416.025	9.397	60.336	1.776	269.476	7.833	.533
1964	452.979	10.370	72.715	2.168	284.894	8.258	.535
1965	504.351	11.841	82.849	2.461	295.250	8.607	.536
1966	569.967	13.575	90.941	2.678	326.238	9.467	.540
1967	662.433	15.535	97.464	2.867	356.145	10.382	.552
1968	759.554	18.393	106.711	3.075	398.089	11.904	.557
1969	780.340	18.712	118.942	3.375	479.278	13.709	.570
1970	915.527	22.202	120.088	3.379	527.530	15.129	.596
1971	1038.996	24.309	112.549	3.094	594.473	16.708	.611
1972	1128.319	26.522	122.354	3.330	686.034	18.906	.612
1973	1321.302	29.887	134.867	3.637	782.975	21.343	.623
1974	1673.241	34.097	178.426	4.301	922.335	22.661	.719
1975	1861.545	35.196	256.494	5.574[2]	1046.954	23.279	.759
1976	1624.704	29.051[1]	342.104	7.163[3]	1102.017	24.162	.769
1977	2046.453	36.640	342.341	6.831	1073.224	22.130	.794
1978	2479.349	41.610	359.100	6.662	1047.224	19.580	.848
1979	3016.654	46.210	354.638	6.029	1050.281	16.804	.933
1980	3509.500	50.200	388.542	6.091	997.658	14.954	1.000

Notes to Table 2

1. The 1976 Annual Report of Anheuser Busch noted that "the decline in beer sales volume was the result of a three month work stoppage." (p. 4).
2. On March 1, 1975, Olympia acquired the brewery operations of Theodore Hamm Company. The 1975 results reported by Olympia include the 1975 results of Hamm's from the date of acquisition. In 1974, Hamm's had sales of $105.314 million. Included in the acquisition was a brewing facility in St. Paul, Minnesota.
3. Effective December 29, 1976, Olympia acquired the net assets of Lone Star Brewing Company. The 1976 results reported by Olympia include the results of Lone Star for the January 1, 1976, to December 31, 1976, period. In 1975 and 1976 the total net sales of Lone Star Brewing Company were $61.332 million and $53.068 million respectively. Included in the acquisition was a brewing facility in San Antonio, Texas. Also included in the acquisition was a truck leasing operation. The net sales of the truck leasing operation were $11.275 million in 1975 and $12.686 million in 1976.

TABLE 3. U.S. Brewing Industry: 1980

Firms	Fiscal Year	Cost of Total Sales ($000,000's)	Barrels Sold (000,000's)	Total # of Employees[1]	# of Brewing Plants	Ratio of Beer Sales ($) to Total Sales(s)[2]	Total Sales ($000,000's)[3]
Anheuser–Busch Companies	12/31	3509.500	50.200	18,040	10	.92	3822.400
Jos. Schlitz Brewing	12/31	997.658	14.954	6,100	6	> .90	1027.743
Adolph Coors Company	12/31	923.608	13.779	9,650	1	.87	1021.198
G. Heileman Brewing	12/31	771.293	13.270	5,600	10	.88	840.784
Olympia Brewing	12/31	388.542	6.091	2,164	3	.92	391.974
F & M Schaefer	12/31	204.898	3.572	1,342	1	1.00	209.075
Genesee Brewing	4/30	165.476	3.604	932	1	1.00	177.245
Falstaff Brewing	12/31	96.061	1.600	594	3	1.00	95.574
Pittsburgh Brewing	10/31	48.786	.993	416	1	1.00	49.804

Notes to Table 3

1. Three of the five companies having non-beer activities provide in their 1980 10K a breakdown of the number of employees in each activity:

   Coors: "The Company has approximately 9,650 employees. Of those, approximately 1,100 employees work full-time in construction and engineering and approximately 2,100 work for the Company's six subsidiaries which produce ceramic products." (p. 6).

   Heileman: "The Company has approximately 5,600 employees of which 3,650 are employed in brewing operations, 1600 are employed in baking operations and 350 are employed in other areas" (p. 4).

   Olympia: "The number of persons employed on December 31, 1980 was 2,164 of whom 374 were engaged in the leasing business" (p. 6).

2. The ratio of beer sales to total sales is computed with the numerator being before the deduction of excise taxes on beer.

3. Total sales of Pabst in 1980 were $853.441. Table 3 excludes the second largest U.S. brewing company, Miller Brewing Company, which is a fully owned subsidiary of Philip Morris. Beer sales of Miller Brewing in 1980 were $2,542.300 million (34.300 million barrels). Table 3 also excludes privately held companies, e.g., Stroh Brewing Company and General Brewing Company.

127

Part E

Hobie decides to show his new employer just how thorough an employee they have hired. He now uses a cross-sectional approach to cost-volume estimation. He collects the data in Table 3 from the 1980 Annual Reports and 10K's of the publicly listed U.S. brewing companies.

1. What problems might occur in using the cross-sectional data in Table 3 on page 127 to estimate cost-volume relationships?
2. Using ordinary least squares, estimate the following linear relationship:

$$C_i = \alpha + \beta_1 V_i + \beta_2 E_i$$

where C_i is the 1980 cost of sales of company i, V_i is the 1980 barrels of beer sold by company i, and E_i is the number of employees of company i in 1980.

Part F

Hobie now has second thoughts about the multiple regression model in Part E. He remembers that a common problem with cross-sectional data is multicollinearity and decides to use a more parsimonious model to estimate the industry cost-volume relationship.

1. What is multi-collinearity?
2. Why might multi-collinearity arise between the independent variables?
3. Why is it a problem? What are its consequences?
4. How would you detect it?
5. Using ordinary least squares estimate the following linear relationship:

$$C_i = \alpha + \beta V_i$$

What inferences do you draw from the results in C5 and F5?

REFERENCES

Supplemental Reference

LONGBRAKE, WILLIAM A., "Statistical Cost Analysis," *Applied Statistics* XI (June 1962) 69–78.

Learning-Curve References

ABERNATHY, W. J., and K. WAYNE, "Limits of the Learning Curve," *Harvard Business Review,* September–October 1974, pp. 109–119.

BUMP, EDWIN A., "Effects of Learning on Cost Projections," *Management Accounting,* May 1974.

CONLEY, PAT, "Experience Curves as a Planning Tool," *IEEE Spectrum,* June 1970.

NANDA, RAVINDER, and GEORGE L. ADLER, *Learning Curves: Theory and Application, Work Measurement & Methods Engineering Series No. 6.* Norcross, Ga.: American Institute of Industrial Engineers, 1977.

"Note on the Use of Experience Curves in Competitive Decision Making," ICCH Case #9-175-174.

DETERMINISTIC EXTENSIONS OF C-V-P ANALYSIS

5

USES OF C-V-P ANALYSIS

Many managerial decisions for product planning and control require a careful analysis of the behavior of costs and profits as a function of the expected volume of sales. In the short run, the costs and prices of a firm's products will, in general, be determined. The principal uncertainty therefore is not the cost or price of a product but the quantity that will be sold. Thus, the short-run profitability of a product line will be most sensitive to the volume of sales. Cost-volume-profit (C-V-P) analysis highlights the effect of changes in volume on the profitability of a single product. Many assumptions are usually made to facilitate the C-V-P analysis, most of which can be relaxed to approximate more realistic or complex situations. In this chapter we will consider a variety of extensions of the deterministic C-V-P model. The model is deterministic in that all cost and revenue functions, no matter how complex, are assumed to be known for certain. In the next chapter we will relax the deterministic assumption to treat C-V-P analysis under conditions of uncertainty.

THE SIMPLE MODEL

We start by considering a single product, generically referred to as a widget. Traditional analysis assumes that the selling price of the widget is given and independent of the amount of widgets we wish to sell. Thus we assume a fixed price, p, for each widget we sell. The cost behavior for producing widgets consists of a fixed cost, a, associated with providing the capability to produce widgets and a unit variable cost, b, for each widget produced. The fixed cost, a, includes all those costs associated with producing widgets that will not vary with the amount of widgets produced. Such costs include depreciation on machinery and buildings used in the production of widgets, the cost of utilities to heat and light areas where widgets are produced, and the salary of the plant superintendent. The cost of minimal levels of promotion, advertising, and inventory can also be considered to be fixed, independent of the volume of widgets produced and sold. Occasionally an accountant or a manager computes a fixed cost per unit by dividing the total fixed cost by the expected number or maximum number of units to be produced. There is virtually no justification for such a computation. It is a contradiction in terms. By their very nature, fixed costs are independent of the number of units produced, so that it makes no sense to talk about a fixed cost per unit. Indeed a principal contribution of C-V-P analysis is to highlight the differences between fixed and variable costs and to illustrate the volume of sales necessary in order to cover fixed costs and achieve a targeted profit level.

The unit variable cost per unit, b, includes direct material, variable labor, and variable overhead. In the simple model we assume that the unit cost, b, is a constant no matter how many units are produced. That is, each extra widget produced costs the firm an additional $\$b$. With these assumptions, the total cost of producing some number, x, of widgets, which we denote by $TC(x)$, is given by

$$TC(x) = a + bx.$$

[Note that taking the derivative of the total-cost function with respect to output, x, yields

$$\frac{dTC(x)}{dx} = b,$$

which corresponds to our assumption that the marginal cost of producing an extra unit of output is a constant (b).]

For purposes of this analysis, we assume that the amount produced equals the amount sold. Having production different from sales would require treatment of a multiperiod inventory problem, which would unnecessarily complicate the analysis.

The profit from selling x widgets will be denoted $\pi(x)$. If we sell x widgets, we will receive px in revenues and will incur $a + bx$ in costs to produce this number of widgets. Therefore,

$$\pi(x) = px - (a + bx) \qquad (5\text{-}1)$$
$$= (p - b)x - a.$$

The quantity $p - b$, price minus variable costs, is called the *contribution margin* for each widget. For a numerical example, assume that

$$p = \$10 \text{ per unit},$$

$$b = \$4 \text{ per unit},$$

$$a = \$12,000.$$

Then $\pi = (10 - 4)x - 12,000 = 6x - 12,000$. The contribution margin is $\$6$ per

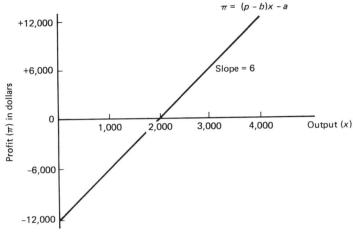

Exhibit 5-1   Cost-Volume-Profit Chart

widget, the amount realized from each widget produced and sold to cover fixed overhead and contribute to profit.

Equation (5-1) is frequently illustrated graphically in a cost-volume-profit chart in which profit, π, is plotted on the vertical axis and output, x, is plotted on the horizontal axis. Exhibit 5-1 is a C-V-P chart for our numerical example.

BREAKEVEN QUANTITY

A quantity of particular interest is the level of output at which the company breaks even (earns zero profits) from producing widgets. With our algebraic representation, the breakeven output is the quantity x_{BE}, which yields zero profits ($\pi = 0$) in equation (5-1):

$$0 = (p - b)x_{BE} - a$$

or

$$x_{BE} = \frac{a}{p - b} \qquad (5\text{-}2)$$

From equation (5-2) we see that the breakeven output level equals the ratio of fixed costs to contribution margin. With our numerical example,

$$x_{BE} = \frac{12,000}{6} = 2,000 \text{ widgets.}$$

Equation (5-2) shows us that the breakeven volume increases if either fixed costs (a) or variable costs (b) increase, and decreases if the price per unit increases.

There is nothing particularly significant about just breaking even. Apparently, though, many managers consider a $2,000 increase in profits that transforms a $1,000 loss to a $1,000 gain much more valuable than a $2,000 increase that raises profits from an $8,000 profit to $10,000. Even though the firm has $2,000 more cash in both instances, the $2,000 increment in the first case enables the manager to avoid the stigma of showing a loss and hence is considered more significant.

Perhaps the significance of the breakeven volume is that it provides a useful summary statistic of the three parameters, price, variable costs and fixed costs, in the C-V-P equation. It gives managers a simple number by which to judge whether a given level of activity in a product line will be profitable. In the public sector, for example, most municipal transit systems operate at a loss and require subsidies from the local or federal government. Occasionally the amount of loss or subsidy is expressed as a dollar amount per rider (based, say, on the number of riders the preceding year). Thus we hear that the municipal bus line lost say, $0.64 per rider. This conjures up the vision of buses avoiding losses by riding around town with doors closed, never accepting passengers, since each person who got on would cost the bus $0.64. The average-loss-per-rider figure implies also that losses could be reduced if we raised prices by $0.64 per ride, a computation which ignores the reduction in the number of riders who would use the bus were the price to be increased (see Exhibit 5-2). The dialog might be improved if, instead of computing the average loss per rider, the bus line managers determined the number of passengers at which the bus line would break even. This quantity could then be compared with the actual number of passengers.

More generally, we may be interested not just in breaking even but in achiev-

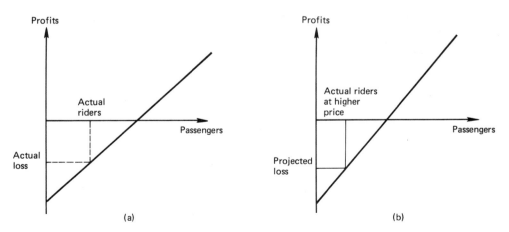

Exhibit 5-2   C-V-P Chart showing effect of price rise: (a) Current situation: "Loss per rider" equals Actual loss/Actual riders, (b) Projected loss increases if ridership falls significantly when prices are increased.

ing a targeted profit level for our product line of widgets. For example, we may desire to achieve a profit of π^* from selling widgets, a profit that provides an adequate rate of return on the capital we have invested in the widget product line. The level of output, x^*, that will enable us to achieve this targeted profit level can be obtained by rearranging equation (5-1) as

$$x^* = \frac{\pi^* + a}{p - b} .$$ (5-3)

Continuing our numerical example, if there is \$50,000 of capital invested in the widget production and distribution process and we desire a 15 percent before-tax rate of return on invested capital, our targeted profit level is \$7,500. Given the price and cost structure, we would need to produce and sell

$$x^* = \frac{7,500 + 12,000}{6} = 3,250 \text{ widgets}$$

in order to reach our \$7,500 profit level. [The reader should check by substituting back into equation (5-1) that for $x = 3,250$, the profit, π, does indeed equal \$7,500.]

DISCUSSION OF ASSUMPTIONS

The preceding analysis is useful in focusing attention on the distinction between fixed and variable costs and emphasizing the variation in profit with changes in output level. A necessary but usually suppressed assumption is that of the time period for which the C-V-P analysis is valid. Recall from our earlier discussion, on estimating fixed and variable cost components, that costs can be considered to be fixed and variable only with respect to a given period of time. For a sufficiently long planning horizon, most costs can be considered to be variable, while if our time period is short, most costs will be fixed. C-V-P analysis is best used to project the results of operations when little change is expected in the fixed resources or mode of production in the firm. We thus assume a given configuration of capital equipment and technology. Initially, we may consider that labor, material costs, overhead, and price will remain constant during the period for which C-V-P analysis will be performed. Given these parameters, we are interested in predicting the profitability of products at varying levels of volume. Extensive sensitivity analysis can then be performed to show the effects of changing the price, variable costs, and discretionary fixed costs, such as advertising, promotion, and distribution, on overall product profitability and breakeven volume.

The decision to change the production technology either by acquiring new equipment (this could have the effect of increasing the fixed costs, a, and decreasing the variable cost, b) or by selling some existing equipment is best handled by a formal capital-budgeting analysis rather than by tinkering with the C-V-P analysis. Of course, given a change in the production technology, C-V-P analysis can still

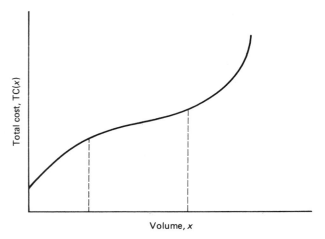

Exhibit 5-3 Nonlinear Cost Curve

be performed to project the profitability of future operations and determine the sensitivity of future profits to variations in volume, price, and variable and fixed costs.[1] But the guiding principle is to select a time period for analysis and determine the price and the fixed and unit variable costs for that time period.

A second set of assumptions leading to the C-V-P equation is the linearity in the model: price (p), fixed cost (a), and unit variable cost (b) are all assumed to be constant at any volume of production. These linearity assumptions facilitate the analysis but are not necessary for analyzing the variation of costs and profits with volume. In general, one could allow for a price that depends on the quantity to be sold:

$$p = f(x).$$

The function $f(x)$ corresponds to the inverse of the economists' demand curve [$x = f^{-1}(p)$; that is, the quantity sold is a function of the price]. Similarly, the cost of production, TC(x), could be a nonlinear function of output with varying marginal costs and jumps in fixed costs when output exceeds certain limits. With these more general revenue and cost functions, it is still possible to obtain a C-V-P equation linking profits with output:

$$\pi = xf(x) - TC(x). \tag{5-4}$$

As a specific example, economists often consider firms to have a total-cost curve as shown in Exhibit 5-3. Such a cost function has fixed costs even at zero

---

[1] In fact, such a sensitivity analysis is probably the most common procedure for recognizing uncertainty in parameter estimates. That is, profits are forecasted under varying assumptions of costs, prices, and volumes. Chapters 6 and 8 provide an explicit and formal treatment of uncertainty in a C-V-P analysis.

volume. As output expands, marginal cost (the slope of the total-cost curve) decreases initially because of learning effects and improvements in efficiency as a company's fixed resources and labor force are used at planned levels of operations. There is a midrange of operations in which the total cost increases about linearly with volume. This is the region where our simple C-V-P model is most appropriate, with the approximately constant slope of the cost curve equaling the unit variable cost, b. As output expands beyond the upper limit of this linear midrange, marginal cost per unit starts to increase because of second-shift operations, increased use of overtime, and use of less efficient machinery and labor.

The cost curve in Exhibit 5-3 can be approximated algebraically by a cubic function:

$$TC(x) = a + bx + cx^2 + dx^3. \tag{5-5}$$

The marginal-cost function, $MC(x)$, is obtained by computing the derivative of the total-cost function:

$$MC(x) = \frac{d}{dx} TC(x) = b + 2cx + 3dx^2.$$

If the marginal cost is to decline at low levels of output, c must be less than 0. For the marginal cost to increase as output gets very large, d must be greater than zero. The fixed cost, a, and the linear cost, b, must also be greater than zero to obtain a curve of the form shown in Exhibit 5-3. A final consideration is that c^2 must be less than $3bd$ in order for the cost curve to increase monotonically.

For a simple nonlinear revenue function, we can assume that the demand for widgets is a linear function of price:

$$x = e + fp$$

with $f < 0$ to obtain the property that sales decrease as price is increased. The total-revenue function, $TR(x)$, is then given by

$$TR(x) = xp = \frac{x(x - e)}{f},$$

a quadratic function. The total-revenue and total-cost functions are displayed in Exhibit 5-4. From Exhibit 5-4 we see that there are two breakeven volumes, corresponding to the output levels where the total-revenue and total-cost curves intersect. Analytically, these breakeven points are the solutions to the equation

$$TR(x) = TC(x)$$

or

$$\frac{x^2 - ex}{f} = a + bx + cx^2 + dx^3.$$

Of more interest is the volume at which total profits are maximized. From eco-

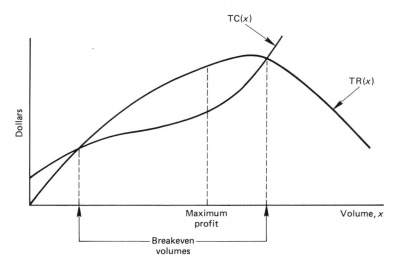

Exhibit 5-4   Nonlinear Revenue and Cost Functions

nomic theory (and from elementary calculus) we know that profits are maximized when marginal revenue equals marginal cost:

$$MR(x) = MC(x)$$

or

$$b + 2cx + 3dx^2 = \frac{2x - e}{f}.$$

As a specific numeric example, assume

$$TC(x) = 200 + 15x - 2x^2 + 0.2x^3$$

and

$$TR(x) = 100x - 4x^2.$$

(Note that the total-revenue curve corresponds to setting $f = -0.25$ and $e = 25$ so that the demand curve is given by $x = 25 - 0.25p$.) The breakeven volumes are the solution to the equation

$$200 + 15x - 2x^2 + 0.2x^3 = 100x - 4x^2$$

or

$$200 - 85x + 2x^2 + 0.2x^3 = 0.$$

By trial and error we obtain $x \simeq 2.55$ and $x \simeq 14.53$ as the two breakeven volumes. Therefore, the product will be profitable as long as output is greater than 2.55 and less than 14.53. Of course it would be foolish for the firm to ever sell more than 12.5 units, the point at which total revenues are maximized [$MR(x) = 100 - 8x = 0$ for $x = 12.5$]. Total revenues actually decrease for sales in excess of 12.5 units. The maximum profit is achieved when marginal revenue equals marginal cost:

$$MR(x) = 100 - 8x,$$

$$MC(x) = 15 - 4x + 0.6x^2,$$

$$MR(x) = MC(x), \quad \text{when } 0.6x^2 + 4x - 85 = 0.$$

Using the formula for finding the roots of a quadratic equation, the maximum profit is achieved for

$$x = \frac{-4 + \sqrt{16 + 4(0.6)(85)}}{1.2} = 9.03.$$

At this point, the marginal revenue of 27.78 equals marginal cost. The profit at this output level is 257.2.

Thus while nonlinear revenue and cost functions complicate the analysis, the basic and important idea behind C-V-P analysis—to examine the behavior of profits as a function of volume—is still highly relevant for managerial planning and decisions. The traditional assumptions of constant selling price and unit production cost are simplifying but not necessary assumptions for a C-V-P analysis.

MULTIPRODUCT C-V-P ANALYSIS

The C-V-P analysis is easily extended to handle the more realistic situation when a firm produces more than one product. In general, we consider a firm with n products. We use the subscript i to denote the ith product, $i = 1, \ldots, n$, and define

p_i = selling price for product i,

a_i = fixed cost for product i,

b_i = variable cost per unit for product i,

x_i = output of product i.

With our simplifying linearity assumptions, the basic profit equation is

$$\pi = \sum_i p_i x_i - \sum_i (a_i + b_i x_i)$$

$$= \sum_i (p_i - b_i)x_i - \sum_i a_i.$$

(5-6)

While the algebraic treatment of the multiproduct case is straightforward, as shown above, it is no longer possible to display the profit equation on a simple chart as in Exhibit 5-1. This occurs because profit now varies with many different output products—$x_1, x_2, \ldots, x_n$—rather than with the single product as before.

The C-V-P chart is so ingrained as a communications device, however, that artificial attempts have been made to display equation (5.6) on a graph. For example, one technique has been to assume that as output expands, all products are sold in the same proportion. With this approach we select one product, say product 1, as the numeraire or index of volume. The output of all other products is assumed to vary proportionally with the output of product 1. Algebraically, define a sequence of constants K_i that relate the sales of product i to the sales of product 1.

$$x_i = K_i x_1, \qquad i = 1, \ldots, n, \tag{5-7}$$

(Note that $K_1 \equiv 1$.) For example, with three products we might have a low sales output situation in which

$$x_1 = 10, \qquad x_2 = 20, \qquad x_3 = 30.$$

In this case $K_2 = 2$, $K_3 = 3$. If overall sales expand by 50 percent, the assumption of strictly proportional increase in sales implies that

$$x_1 = 15, \qquad x_2 = 30, \qquad x_3 = 45.$$

Given the sales-proportions constants, K_i, and equation (5-7), we can rewrite the multiproduct C-V-P equation (5-6) as

$$
\begin{aligned}
\pi &= \sum_i (p_i - b_i)x_i - \sum_i a_i \\
&= \sum_i (p_i - b_i)K_i x_1 - \sum_i a_i \\
&= x_1 \sum_i (p_i - b_i)K_i - \sum_i a_i.
\end{aligned}
\tag{5-8}
$$

The term $\sum_i (p_i - b_i)K_i$ can be interpreted as the contribution margin achieved by expanding sales of product 1 by one unit and having the sales of all other products expand proportionately (for example, product i would increase in sales by K_i units). Equation (5-8) can then be displayed on a simple C-V-P graph plotting profit, π, versus output as measured by x_1. The value of such an exercise is questionable, however, because of the highly restrictive assumption of strictly proportional sales increases, as represented in equation (5-7).

Maintaining the simplifying assumption of equation (5-7), one could solve for the breakeven level of sales for the numeraire product just as was done for the single-product case:

$$x_{1,BE} = \frac{\sum_i a_i}{\sum_i (p_i - b_i)K_i}, \tag{5-9}$$

or for the level of sales of product 1, x_1^*, that would achieve any targeted profit level π^*:

$$x_1^* = \frac{\pi^* + \sum_i a_i}{\sum_i (p_i - b_i)K_i}.$$ (5-10)

Such an exercise should be viewed, however, as only a crude approximation to the broad range of product mixes that yield zero profits or any targeted level of overall profits. A more general approach to computing product mixes, yielding a specified level of profits, uses the algebraic representation. If we are interested in determining product mixes that yield a specified profit level, π^*, we wish to find all the solutions to the equation

$$\sum_i (p_i - b_i)x_i - \sum_i a_i = \pi^*$$ (5-11)

with the additional constraint that we can not produce negative amounts of any product; that is,

$$x_i \geq 0, \qquad i = 1, \ldots, n.$$ (5-12)

There are an infinite number of solutions to equation (5-11) satisfying the nonnegativity constraints, (5-12). For example, one solution is

$$x_1 = \frac{\pi^* + \sum_i a_i}{p_1 - b_1}, \qquad x_2 = x_3 = \cdots = x_n = 0,$$ (5-13)

and a second solution is

$$x_1 = 0, \qquad x_2 = \frac{\pi^* + \sum_i a_i}{p_2 - b_2}, \qquad x_3 = x_4 = \cdots = x_n = 0.$$ (5-14)

Continuing in this manner, it is easy to see that we can generate n different solutions; each of these solutions would have $n - 1$ products at zero activity level and one product produced in sufficient quantity so that its total contribution margin would cover all the fixed costs plus the desired profit level. But in addition to these n different solutions, an infinite number of linear combinations of these n solutions would also yield the desired profit level. For example, denoting the solution given by equation (5-13) as $x^{(1)}$ and the solution given by equation (5-14) as $x^{(2)}$, then

$$\gamma x^{(1)} + (1 - \gamma)x^{(2)} \qquad \text{with } 0 \leq \gamma \leq 1$$

would also be a solution to equation (5-11). [This is easy to verify:

$$\frac{\gamma(p_1 - b_1)(\pi^* + \sum a_i)}{p_1 - b_1} + \frac{(1 - \gamma)(p_2 - b_2)(\pi^* + \sum a_i)}{p_2 - b_2}$$

$$= [\gamma + (1 - \gamma)](\pi^* + \sum a_i).]$$

In general, any convex combination of the n basic solutions

$$\sum_i \gamma_i x^{(i)}$$

with $\gamma_i \geq 0$ and $\sum \gamma_i = 1$ would also be a solution to equation (5-11). Thus it is easy to be overwhelmed by the infinite number of possibilities for achieving breakeven or targeted profit levels in the multiproduct environment.

EXAMPLE OF MULTIPRODUCT BREAKEVEN ANALYSIS

To illustrate these points, assume we have two products with the following price and cost characteristics:

Product Type	p_i	b_i	a_i
$i = 1$	10	4	12,000
$i = 2$	15	7	24,000

Taken individually, the breakeven volume for product 1 is $12,000/(10 - 4)$ or 2,000 units and the breakeven volume for product 2 is 3,000 units. Combining the contribution margin of both products yields the profit equation:

$$\pi = 6x_1 + 8x_2 - 36,000.$$

In order to break even, the output vector (x_1, x_2) must satisfy

$$6x_1 + 8x_2 = 36,000.$$

One possible solution (call it $x^{(1)}$) is $x_1 = 6,000$ $x_2 = 0$, while another solution, $x^{(2)}$, is $x_1 = 0$, $x_2 = 4,500$. In addition, all product mixes of the form $\gamma x^{(1)} + (1 - \gamma)x^{(2)}$ with $0 \leq \gamma \leq 1$ will also yield breakeven profits. For example, with $\gamma = \frac{2}{3}$ we have the solution:

$$\tfrac{2}{3}(6000, 0) + \tfrac{1}{3}(0, 4,500) = (4,000, 1,500).$$

Thus we can break even if $x_1 = 4,000$ and $x_2 = 1,500$. By allowing γ to vary continuously between 0 and 1 we can obtain an infinite number of product-mix possibilities yielding zero profits. This relationship can be visualized by graphing the profit equation as shown in Exhibit 5-5. For each targeted profit level, π^*, all points on the line

$$6x_1 + 8x_2 = 36,000 + \pi^*$$

will indicate combinations of x_1 and x_2 that will yield an overall profit of π^*. Exhibit 5-5 displays the lines for breakeven profits ($\pi^* = 0$) and for profits equal to $6,000. Naturally such a graphical representation is only possible when considering two products.

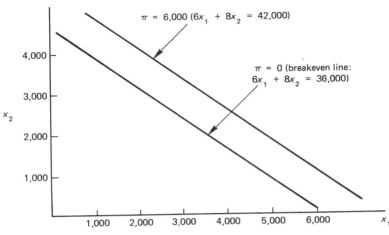

$\pi = 6,000 \ (6x_1 + 8x_2 = 42,000)$

$\pi = 0$ (breakeven line: $6x_1 + 8x_2 = 36,000$)

Exhibit 5-5   The Profit Equation

MULTIPLE-PRODUCT C-V-P ANALYSIS WITH PRODUCTION CONSTRAINTS

One considerable benefit of attempting a C-V-P analysis in a multiproduct environment is to focus attention on products with high contribution margins, $p_i - b_i$. Managers and salesmen can direct their efforts to increasing the output of high-contribution-margin products and thereby maximize the contribution margin to cover fixed costs and generate profits. Indeed, it could be desirable to base salesmens' commissions on the contribution margin of the products that they sell rather than on the traditional measure of gross revenues. Unfortunately, one should not always attempt to maximize the sales of high-contribution-margin products. Most firms have limits on how much of each product they can produce or sell. With such constraints, they may choose not to emphasize the sales of high-unit-contribution-margin products.

For simplicity, we will maintain our assumptions of a linear world and introduce constraining or capacity resources of the firm. We need to identify all the resources of the firm that could limit production. Such resources could include availability of machine time, transportation, particular types of labor including supervision, and raw materials.

A particularly simple and instructive situation arises when there is only one constraining resource. This can occur if the firm's products are all produced on a single machine and output is limited by hours available on this machine. Returning to our two-product example from the preceding section, assume that product 1 requires 3 hours of machine time per unit and that product 2 requires 6 hours of machine time per unit.

Product Type	Contribution Margin	Machine Hours Per Unit
1	6	3
2	8	6

Looking solely at contribution margin, product 2 appears to be the more profitable, generating $2 more contribution margin than product 1 for each extra unit produced and sold. Indeed, if there were no constraints on production or if current production levels were far from the maximum, the firm would do better to attempt to sell more of product 2 than product 1. But assume that a maximum of 24,000 hours of machine time are available. If we produce and sell only product 2, the best we can do is to produce 24,000/6 = 4,000 units of product 2 for a contribution of $32,000 toward fixed overhead and profit. But if we concentrated production and sales solely on product 1, we could produce 24,000/3 = 8,000 units, yielding a total contribution of $48,000.

At first glance, it may seem surprising that the product with the lowest contribution margin is the most profitable to produce. This seeming paradox is resolved once one realizes that in the presence of scarce production resources, the correct measure with which to rank product profitability is not contribution margin but contribution margin per unit required of the limiting resource. In our example, product 1 generates $2 contribution margin per machine-hour ($6 contribution margin/3 machine-hours) whereas product 2 generates only $1.33 contribution per machine-hour. Thus, if we are constrained by the number of machine-hours available, we will wish to maximize the production of products that have the highest contribution margin per machine-hour, in this case product 1.

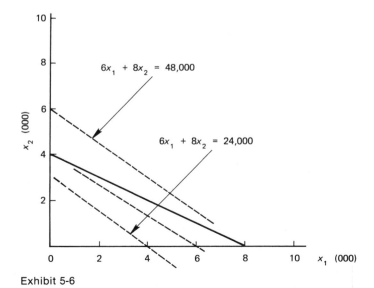

Exhibit 5-6

Assume now that we have m constraining resources and let j index the various resources ($j = 1, \ldots, m$). For each resource j, choose a unit for measuring the consumption of that resource (for example, machine-hours) and estimate the maximum amount of that resource available in the time period. Let c_j represent the maximum availability or capacity of each resource j. For each combination of resource j and product i we define r_{ij} as the amount of resource j used to produce one unit of product i. We again make a simplifying but reasonable linearity assumption that r_{ij} is a constant for each unit of product i we produce. That is, if 1 unit of product i uses up 4 units of resource j, then 5 units of product i use up 20 units of resource j, 50 units of product i use up 200 units of resource j, and so on. For many product-resource combinations, r_{ij} will equal 0, since resource j will not be required to produce the ith product.

If we attempt to produce the output vector ($x_1, x_2, \ldots, x_n$) (recall that x_i is the amount of output of product i; $i = 1, \ldots, n$), we will require the following amount of resource j:

$$r_{1j}x_1 + r_{2j}x_2 + \cdots + r_{nj}x_j, \qquad j = 1, \ldots, m.$$

Since c_j is the maximum amount of resource j available, any feasible production plan must satisfy

$$\sum_i r_{ij}x_i \le c_j$$

for each resource $j, j = 1, \ldots, m$.

For the moment, we can ignore the fixed costs, a_j, since maximizing contribution margin is identical to maximizing profits. In order to maximize the total contribution margin from all the firm's products, subject to its resource constraints, we must solve the following linear programming problem:

Maximize: $\sum_i (p_i - b_i)x_i$

Subject to: $\sum_i r_{ij}x_i \le c_j, \qquad j = 1, \ldots, m,$
$\qquad\qquad x_i \ge 0, \qquad i = 1, \ldots, n.$

Returning to our simple two-product, one-resource example, the linear programming representation is:

Maximize; $6x_1 + 8x_2$

Subject to: $3x_1 + 6x_2 \le 24{,}000,$
$\qquad\qquad x_1, x_2 \ge 0.$

The optimal solution is easily seen to be $x_1 = 8{,}000$, $x_2 = 0$ (see Exhibit 5-6). If there are many products but only one constraining resource, we obtain an excellent measure of product profitability by dividing the contribution margin by the amount of scarce resource consumed per unit. Algebraically, we solve:

Maximize: $(p_1 - b_1)x_1 + (p_2 - b_2)x_2 + \cdots + (p_n - b_n)x_n$

Subject to: $r_{11}x_1 + r_{21}x_2 + \cdots + r_{n1}x_n \leq c_1,$

$$x_i \geq 0.$$

Assuming no additional constraints, such as on maximum sales of each product, the solution to the program above is to produce only the product for which the ratio $(p_i - b_i)/r_{i1}$ is the largest. With only one scarce resource, the ratio of contribution margin per unit of scarce resource consumed $[(p_i - b_i)/r_i]$ provides an excellent ranking of profitability. Given any discretion in the mix of products that we can sell, we should try to sell relatively more of products that have the highest values of this ratio.

In general, there will be more than one resource constraining how much we can produce. For this more general situation, it is not possible to obtain a simple ranking of products by using the ratio of contribution margin per unit of scarce resource. We will get a different ranking of profitability for each scarce resource, and it will be unusual for the rankings across different resources to show much similarity. For example, we can expand our simple numerical example by assuming that only 12,000 hours of supervisory time is available and that both products require 2 hours of supervision time for each unit produced. For this resource, product 1 has $3 of contribution margin per hour of supervision used and product 2 has $4, thereby reversing the profitability rankings when only machine time was considered.

When there are multiple constraining resources, simple profitability rankings among products are no longer possible. We must revert to the general linear program in order to determine the optimal product mix.

Maximize: $6x_1 + 8x_2$

Subject to: $3x_1 + 6x_2 \leq 24,000,$
$2x_1 + 2x_2 \leq 12,000,$
$x_1, \quad x_2 \geq 0.$

The optimal solution to this program is $x_1 = 4,000$, $x_2 = 2,000$ for a total contribution margin of $40,000 (see Exhibit 5-7). Note that the addition of the supervision time constraint has reduced the maximum contribution margin from $48,000 to $40,000. Observe, also, that unlike the situation with only one constraining resource, the optimal solution is to produce some of both products. This is not an accident. If there are m constraining resources, the optimal solution will be (in the absence of a degenerate solution) to produce m different products.

In summary, extending the simple single-product C-V-P analysis to multiple products with multiple constraints on production leads naturally to a linear programming formulation of the product-mix problem. The linear programming approach highlights the concept that the most profitable products are those that have maximum contribution margin per unit of scarce resource consumed. While

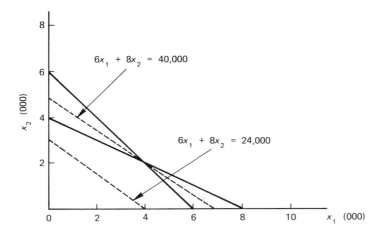

Exhibit 5-7

simple profitability rankings are not available if multiple constraining resources exist, the linear programming solution maximizes total contribution margin subject to the described constraints.

MULTIPLE PRODUCTS, MULTIPLE CONSTRAINTS, AND FIXED COSTS

The astute reader will have noticed the sudden disappearance of the fixed costs, a_i, from the discussion in the preceding section. There are a number of good reasons for ignoring fixed costs initially in a multiproduct setting. First, the allocation of fixed costs to products is usually quite arbitrary. Spreading a given amount of fixed cost, A, to the n products such that $\sum_i a_i = A$ may require many arbitrary decisions that reduce the meaningfulness of the final allocation vector $(a_1, a_2, \ldots, a_n)$. Second, if the total level of fixed costs, A, is independent of the product-mix decision [that is, independent of the output vector $(x_1, x_2, \ldots, x_n)$], the allocation of fixed costs to individual products is irrelevant to the profitability analysis. If, in the short run, the fixed costs of the firm are independent of the outputs produced, we need not be concerned with the allocation or even magnitude of the fixed costs when making our product-mix decision. Our goal must be to do the best we can, in the short run, with whatever capacity resources and sales opportunities we have available as we enter the planning period. Doing the best we can subject to production constraints and sales opportunities is well handled by the linear programming formulation presented in the preceding section.

In order for us to be interested in the fixed cost of a particular product, the fixed cost, a_i, must therefore be clearly *traceable* to the product and be *avoidable* were the product to be discontinued. This requires us to distinguish fixed costs that are *unavoidable* during a period from those fixed costs that are *avoidable,* should there be significant contractions in the level of activity of individual products.[2] We are interested in those fixed costs that do not vary with incremental volume changes but that could be avoided entirely were a product line to be shut down. Examples of such avoidable fixed costs could include supervisory costs, costs of maintaining an inventory and distribution system for a product, capital costs for producing a product line (leasing of equipment or the opportunity costs of selling special purpose machinery), and advertising and promotional expenditures.

If traceable and avoidable fixed costs do exist, then the linear programming analysis in the preceding section gives an incomplete representation of the problem. We might find ourselves producing small amounts of a product whose total contribution margin did not cover the fixed costs that could be avoided were we to shut down the product line entirely. We can incorporate escapable fixed costs into our analysis by using a more general but, unfortunately, more complex model called the *fixed-charge* problem.

Let a_i be the amount of fixed costs that can be avoided if product i is not produced at all (that is, when $x_i = 0$). Define a new variable z_i that we allow to only take on two values, 0 or 1. The variable z_i equals 0 only if $x_i = 0$ and equals 1 if $x_i > 0$. Thus, z_i is a simple integer variable that indicates whether product i is produced or not. With this integer or indicator variable, the firm's optimal product mix can be determined by solving:

$$\text{Maximize:} \quad \sum_i (p_i - b_i)x_i - \sum_i a_i z_i \tag{5-15}$$

$$\text{Subject to:} \quad \sum_i a_{ij}x_i \le b_j, \qquad j = 1, \ldots, m,$$
$$x_i \le z_i U, \qquad i = 1, \ldots, n,$$
$$x_i \ge 0,$$
$$z_i = 0, 1,$$

where the constant U, in the second set of constraints, is an arbitrary but very large number, well in excess of the maximum sales of any product. The constraint, $x_i \le z_i U$, assures that whenever $x_i > 0$ in a proposed solution, then the variable z_i must equal 1 and the escapable fixed cost, a_i, associated with positive production of product i will be subtracted from the objective function. If $x_i = 0$ in a proposed solution, then z_i can also equal 0, without violating the constraint, and the escapable fixed cost will not be subtracted from the objective function. The fixed-charge algorithm determines whether the contribution margin obtained

---

[2] The terms *inescapable* and *escapable* are frequently used synonymously with *unavoidable* and *avoidable*.

from production and sale of product i warrants incurring the fixed cost a_i (that is, whether $x_i > 0$ and $z_i = 1$ or $x_i = z_i = 0$).

While the fixed-charge representation may appear to be a straightforward extension to the linear programming formulation, the addition of the constraint

$$z_i = 0, 1 \qquad \text{for } i = 1, \ldots, n$$

makes the fixed-charge problem much more difficult to solve. The traditional simplex method and other linear programming algorithms cannot be used, since they cannot be modified simply to force a decision variable (z_i) to only take on integer values (0 or 1 in this case). The fixed-charge problem is a special case of a class of models called *mixed-integer programming problems*. The problems are mixed since they have both continuous variables (x_i) and integer or discrete variables (z_i). Special algorithms have been developed to solve fairly large-scale fixed-charge problems, but their solution still takes considerably longer than solution of the same-sized problem without the integer constraint. Unfortunately, one must probably solve the problem with the integer constraint, since rounding off a continuous solution from a linear programming algorithm (for example, if $z_i > 0.5$, let $z_i = 1$, but if $z_i < 0.5$, round to $z_i = 0$) is likely to give a solution far from the maximum obtainable.

We summarize the relevant issues of a multiproduct C-V-P analysis with escapable fixed costs by means of the following example:

The ABC company produces three products, A, B, and C. It produces product-line income statements on a full cost basis, and its projections for the next period show the following:

	A	B	C	Total
Units sold	400	300	500	1,200
Sales revenue	$4,000	$3,000	$2,000	$9,000
Cost of goods sold:				
Direct material	$1,200	$ 900	$1,000	$3,100
Direct labor	1,000	1,000	400	2,400
Factory overhead absorbed	400	400	200	1,000
Total	$2,600	$2,300	$1,600	$6,500
Gross margin	$1,400	700	400	$2,500
Selling Expenses:				
Commissions	$ 120	$ 90	$ 60	$ 270
Traceable fixed costs	200	60	60	320
Common fixed costs	480	360	240	1,080
Administrative expenses:				
Order processing	30	30	20	80
General administration	320	240	160	720
Total operating expense	$1,150	$ 780	$ 540	$2,470
Net income (loss) before tax	$ 250	$ (80)	$ (140)	30

Further examination yields the following analysis of factory overhead and fixed operating expenses:

	A	B	C
Factory overhead			
Variable (with direct labor cost)	$150	$200	$160
Fixed but escapable if product line shut down	150	100	20
Fixed and inescapable if product line shut down	100	100	20
Traceable fixed selling expense			
Escapable if shut down	180	60	60
Inescapable	20	0	0
Common fixed selling expense			
Escapable if shut down	200	210	200
Inescapable	280	150	40
General administrative expense			
Fixed but escapable if shut down	20	40	100
Fixed and inescapable	300	200	60

Also, sales commissions are paid at the rate of 3 percent of sales to the company's salesmen. Order-processing costs can be considered variable.

Based on the ABC company's full cost system, products B and C are unprofitable, suggesting that overall profits could be increased by dropping both products. But this computation avoids a careful analysis of the variable contribution margin and escapable fixed costs associated with each product.

The selling prices, p_i, for the three products are $10, $10, and $4, respectively. The variable costs for the three products are:

	A	B	C
Material	$1,200	$ 900	$1,000
Labor	1,000	1,000	400
Factory overhead	150	200	160
Sales commissions	120	90	60
Order processing	30	30	20
Total variable costs	$2,500	$2,220	$1,640
Variable cost per unit	$ 6.25	$ 7.40	$ 3.28
Contribution margin per unit	$ 3.75	$ 2.60	$ 0.72

The fixed costs associated with the three products are:

	A	B	C
Factory overhead	$ 250	$200	$ 40
Selling expenses	680	420	300
General administrative	320	240	160
Total fixed costs	$1,250	$860	$500

Our multiproduct C-V-P equation is:

$$\pi = 3.75x_A + 2.60x_B + 0.72x_C - (1{,}250 + 860 + 500).$$

With the projected sales of $x_A = 400$, $x_B = 300$, $x_C = 500$, we obtain

$$\pi = 1{,}500 + 780 + 360 - 2{,}610 = 30,$$

which agrees with the profit from the product-line income statement above. With this traditional C-V-P analysis, it appears that all three products are generating positive contribution margins for the company and hence should be retained if sales will be as projected.

Tracing all fixed costs to the individual products, we can compute the break-even volumes as the ratio of fixed costs to per-unit contribution margin:

$$x_{BE,A} = 1{,}250/3.75 = 333,$$

$$x_{BE,B} = 860/2.60 = 331.$$

$$x_{BE,C} = 500/0.72 = 694.$$

We see that the projected sales for both products B and C are below the breakeven volume, which explains why both products show losses on the product-line income statement. To achieve breakeven, product B must have 10 percent more sales, while product C must increase sales by almost 40 percent.

This analysis, however, is misleading, since a substantial part of the fixed costs associated with the products would not disappear were these products to be dropped from the firm's product line. A more meaningful product-line prof-itability analysis would use only the escapable fixed costs, since the excess of contribution margin over escapable costs helps to cover those (inescapable) costs that will be incurred regardless of the product-mix decision. The fixed costs must be separated into escapable and inescapable components as follows:

Product	Escapable Fixed Costs	Inescapable Fixed Costs	Total Fixed Costs
A	$550	$700	$1,250
B	410	450	860
C	380	120	500

We now see that shutting down product line B would lower the profits of the firm, since only $410 of the $860 fixed expenses traceable to B would be avoided if product B were discontinued. Since B generates $780 contribution margin based on projected sales, it contributes $780 - $410 = $370 to cover inescapable fixed overhead and profit contribution. Product C, on the other hand, is generating only $360 in contribution margin, which is less than the $380 of fixed costs that could be avoided were it to be purged from the product line. Thus, the more detailed analysis of product C's fixed costs suggests that strong consideration be given to dropping this product. Based on escapable fixed costs, product C's sales would have to increase to at least 380/0.72 = 528 units (a 5.6 percent increase from current levels) before it could break even by covering its traceable and escapable fixed costs.

So far we have analyzed the three products without regard to production constraints. Product A apears to be more profitable than B, since its contribution margin is $3.75 whereas B's is $2.60. Product A has higher escapable fixed costs than B ($550 to $410), but its much higher unit contribution margin enables it to break even at a volume of 147 units (550/3.75), whereas B's breakeven volume on escapable costs is 158 units (410/2.60). If we add the fact that sales of products A and B could be expanded on a one-for-one basis (we can increase the sales of A by x units by decreasing the sales of B by x units and vice versa), we would apparently want to promote the sales of A at the expense of B. But if we add a further complication, that A and B share a common machine on which A requires 3 hours of processing per unit whereas B only requires 2 hours per unit, the situation becomes quite different. For if the output of the firm has the machine working to capacity, A generates $3.75/3 = $1.25 contribution margin per machine-hour whereas B generates $2.60/2 = $1.30. Thus B becomes the more profitable product to promote. In the limit, if we could completely offset any loss in A's sales with increased sales of B, we would attempt to run A's sales down to zero, avoid $550 of escapable fixed costs, and produce and sell only B.

This example highlights the importance of carefully segregating both fixed from variable costs and escapable from unavoidable fixed costs, and determining when any production interdependencies exist among the various products being considered. Relatively simple algebra enables us to incorporate the effects of the fixed versus variable and escapable versus unavoidable cost dichotomies, but when production interdependencies exist, we must turn, at least conceptually, to a mathematical programming formulation of the problem. Such a formulation permits us to find the product mix that maximizes contribution margin less escapable fixed costs with a feasible production schedule.

MULTIPERIOD EXTENSION TO C-V-P ANALYSIS

The final extension to the simple C-V-P model will illustrate how breakeven analysis can be incorporated into a multiple-period capital-budgeting analysis.[3] In traditional capital-budgeting analysis, the cost of a new piece of equipment (or other investment in a long-lived asset) is compared to the discounted cash flows from that asset. If the discounted cash flows exceed the investment cost, the investment is considered worthwhile. Typically, the analysis is done using a single set of assumptions for future-period sales and cash flows. Multiperiod

---

[3] This extension was developed by Manes [1966].

breakeven analysis provides a more generalized framework for approaching the capital-investment decision.

Consider a firm contemplating the acquisition of a new piece of semiautomatic equipment for manufacturing widgets. Recall from our earlier example in this chapter that (1) widgets sell for $10 each, (2) the current variable cost of producing each widget is $4, and (3) the annual fixed costs are $12,000. If the new semiautomatic equipment is acquired, the variable cost of producing widgets will decline to $2 per widget but there will be an increase in the annual (fixed) cash outlays of $3,000 to a new total of $15,000 per year. The new equipment will cost $6,000 and has a useful life of four years (which is independent of annual production volume). The firm has a cost of capital of 10 percent and, for simplicity, we ignore the effects of taxes (though a problem at the end of the chapter will enable the reader to develop this particular extension).

Rather than make a specific assumption about the annual sales of widgets for analyzing the investment decision, we can demonstrate what level amount of annual sales is necessary in order for this investment to just break even—that is, generate enough annual profit to repay the initial capital cost and the required rate of return on this capital. First, consider the situation in which the firm is unable to produce widgets at all without the semiautomatic equipment (ignoring the possibility of producing normally at $4 per widget). Letting x represent the annual level of widget sales, we have the following equation for the profits (and cash flows) for each of the four years of the machine's life:

$$\pi = (p - b)x - a = (10 - 2)x - 15,000$$

$$= 8x - 15,000.$$

We make the simplifying assumption that this cash flow occurs at the end of each year, so that the present value of the four years of cash flows is given by

$$PV = (8x - 15,000)a_{\overline{0.10}|4},$$

where $a_{\overline{0.10}|4}$ is the annuity factor representing the present value, at an interest rate of 10 percent, of receiving $1 at the end of each of the next four years:[4]

$$a_{\overline{0.10}|4} = \left[\frac{1}{1.10} + \frac{1}{(1.10)^2} + \frac{1}{(1.10)^3} + \frac{1}{(1.10)^4}\right] = 3.17.$$

The C-V-P equation for the multiperiod investment opportunity computes

---

[4] More generally, the annuity factor $a_{\overline{r}|n}$ is the present value at an annual interest rate of r percent of receiving $1 at the end of each of the next n years:

$$a_{\overline{r}|n} = \sum_{i=1}^{n}\left[\frac{1}{(1 + r)^i}\right] = \frac{1 - (1 + r)^{-n}}{r}.$$

This factor is tabulated at the back of introductory cost accounting and capital-budgeting texts, and the function is available on many business calculators.

the net present value (NPV) of the project as the discounted annual cash flow less the initial investment of \$6,000 in the equipment:

$$\text{NPV} = (8x - 15{,}000)(3.17) - 6{,}000 \qquad (5\text{-}16)$$

or

$$\text{NPV} = 25.36x - 53{,}550.$$

The project just breaks even at an annual sales volume of

$$x_{BE} = \frac{53{,}550}{25.36} = 2{,}112 \text{ widgets.}$$

This figure of 2,112 widgets is a convenient summary of the investment project. Rather than just stating that the project has a positive net present value for sales at a particular volume, say 2,500 widgets, we give a more general representation by declaring that the project will at least pay for itself as long as annual sales exceed 2,112 units. We also have a multiperiod C-V-P equation (5-16) in which the effect of varying the discount rate or the life of the project can be determined by adjusting the annuity factor, $a_{\overline{r}|n}$. The general (before-tax) multiperiod C-V-P equation can be written as

$$\text{NPV} = [(p - b)x - a]a_{\overline{r}|n} - I, \qquad (5\text{-}17)$$

where I is the investment in the multiperiod asset. The project breaks even for sales in excess of

$$x_{BE} = \frac{a}{p - b} + \frac{I}{p - b} \cdot \frac{1}{a_{\overline{r}|n}}. \qquad (5\text{-}18)$$

The first term in equation (5-18) represents the single-period breakeven volume and the second term represents the higher volume required to pay for the capital investment in the new equipment.

This analysis has developed the multiperiod C-V-P equation (5-17) and break-even-volume equation (5-18) under the assumption that production is possible only if the new piece of equipment is acquired. This analysis, however, is not appropriate for our actual situation, in which we have a choice between manual production at \$4 per unit or semiautomatic production at \$2 per unit. In this case, we should find the volume of sales at which the cost of production for the two different methods is equal. We can ignore the revenue from the sales of widgets, since for any given sales volume the revenue will be identical regardless of which production process is used.

The annual costs of manual production are $4x + 12{,}000$. Therefore the net present value of the costs using manual production is

$$\text{NPV}_M = (4x + 12{,}000)a_{\overline{0.10}|4} = (4x + 12{,}000)3.17.$$

With the new machine the annual costs of production are $2x + 15{,}000$, so that the net present value of semiautomatic production costs, including the initial capital investment of \$6,000, is given by

$$\text{NPV}_{SA} = (2x + 15,000)a_{\overline{0.10}|4} + 6,000 = (2x + 15,000)3.17 + 6,000.$$

The production volume at which we are indifferent between manual and semiautomatic production occurs when $\text{NPV}_M = \text{NPV}_{SA}$, or when

$$(4x + 12,000)3.17 = (2x + 15,000)(3.17) + 6,000.$$

Simplifying this equation yields

$$2x = 3,000 + \frac{6,000}{3.17}. \tag{5-19}$$

The left-hand side of (5-19) represents the variable-cost savings of $2 per unit with the new machinery and the right-hand side represents the increase in fixed annual cash outlays of $3,000 plus the annual amount (6,000/3.17) required to pay for the new machine at the assumed interest rate of 10 percent. Solving (5-19) for x yields

$$x = 2,446$$

as the annual sales volume at which the semiautomatic form of production starts to produce lower net discounted costs of production than the manual production mode. This amount is somewhat higher than the previously calculated breakeven volume of 2,112 because the new form of production not only must pay for itself but must also have a high enough production volume so that the variable-cost savings over the current mode can offset the capital cost and the higher annual fixed costs.

SUMMARY

The cost-volume-profit approach highlights the importance of separating fixed from variable costs when analyzing product profitability. The simple single-product, linear, unconstrained, single-period C-V-P equation

$$\pi = (p - b)x - a$$

provides a convenient representation of the variation of profits as a function of volume, given the three parameters of price, variable cost per unit, and fixed costs. The breakeven volume

$$x_{BE} = \frac{a}{p - b}$$

is a simple summary of the effects of these three parameters, so that rather than talk about a virtually meaningless "fully absorbed" profit per unit, in which we unitize fixed costs by dividing them by an assumed volume of production, a manager can compute a production and sales volume at which contribution margin just covers the product's fixed costs.

   In this chapter we showed how the simple C-V-P analysis could be extended to more general situations. If demand sales volume is a function of price or if production costs are not linear with the amount produced, we can obtain a nonlinear C-V-P equation and compute a range of production (and sales) for which the product is profitable. More generally, in the nonlinear C-V-P analysis, we can compute an optimal sales volume at which the marginal revenue from the last unit sold just equals the marginal cost of producing this last item.

The single-product C-V-P equation can easily be generalized to represent the variation in profitability of multiple products:

$$\pi = \sum_i (p_i - b_i)x_i - \sum_i a_i,$$

though a graphical representation of this equation is no longer convenient. For the multiple-product situation, an infinite number of combinations of sales volumes will yield breakeven, or any given level of, profits.

When the multiple products share common and constraining production resources, we need to generalize our notions of product profitability. It is no longer possible to conclude that products with the highest contribution margins per unit are the most profitable. We now prefer to sell those products with the highest contribution margin per unit of constraining resource consumed in production. If there is more than one constraining resource, we must obtain the optimal product mix from solving a linear programming problem.

A further complication is introduced if some or all of the fixed costs associated with a product are avoidable were there to be zero production of that product. With no constraints on production, we can handle this situation by identifying those products whose contribution margins, at assumed sales volumes, exceed their avoidable fixed costs. In the more general situation where these products compete for scarce production resources, the optimal product mix can be obtained by solving a mixed-integer programming problem, called the fixed-charge problem.

The final generalization treated the C-V-P analysis in a multiperiod setting. We developed profitability equations to demonstrate the variation in the net present value of discounted cash flows as a function of the annual sales volume. These equations can be used to compute the annual breakeven sales volume required to cover not only annual fixed costs but also the capital costs of investments in new facilities and equipment.

PROBLEMS

5-1. Cost-Volume-Profit Analysis (C. Horngren)*

The income statement of the Hall Company appears below. Commissions are based on sales dollars; all other variable expenses vary in terms of units sold.

* Problem prepared by Charles Horngren for *Cost Accounting* 5th edition (Prentice-Hall, 1982); reproduced with permission.

The factory has a capacity of 150,000 units per year. The results for 1981 have been disappointing. Top management is sifting a number of possible ways to make operations profitable in 1982.

Required: **(Consider each situation independently.)**

1. The sales manager is torn between two courses of action.
   a. He has studied the market potential and believes that a 15 percent slash in price would fill the plant to capacity.
   b. He wants to increase prices by 25 percent, to increase advertising by $150,000, and to boost commissions to 10 percent of sales. Under these circumstances, he thinks that unit volume will increase by 50 percent.

   Prepare the budgeted income statements, using a contribution margin format (Sales Variable Expenses, Fixed Expenses) and two columns. What would be the new net income or loss under each alternative? Assume that there are no changes in fixed costs other than advertising.

HALL COMPANY
Income Statement
For the Year Ended December 31, 1981

Sales (90,000 units @ $4.00)			$360,000
Cost of goods sold:			
Direct materials		$90,000	
Direct labor		90,000	
Factory overhead:			
Variable	$18,000		
Fixed	80,000	98,000	278,000
Gross margin			$ 82,000
Selling expenses:			
Variable:			
Sales commissions*	$18,000		
Shipping	3,600	$21,600	
Fixed:			
Advertising, salaries, etc.		40,000	$61,600
Administrative expenses:			
Variable	$ 4,500		
Fixed	20,400	24,900	86,000
Net loss			$(4,500)

* Based on sales dollars, not physical units.

2. The president does not want to tinker with the price. How much may advertising be increased to bring production and sales up to 130,000 units and still earn a target profit of 5 percent of sales?

3. A mail-order firm is willing to buy 60,000 units of product "if the price is right." Assume that the present market of 90,000 units at $4 each will not be disturbed. Hall Company will not pay any sales commission. The

mail-order firm will pick up the units directly at the Hall factory. However, Hall must refund $24,000 of the total sales price as a promotional and advertising allowance for the mail-order firm. In addition, special packaging will increase manufacturing costs on these 60,000 units by 10¢ per unit. At what unit price must the mail-order chain business be quoted for Hall to break even on total operations in 1982?

4.   The president suspects that a fancy new package will aid consumer sales and ultimately Hall's sales. Present packaging costs per unit are all variable and consist of 5¢ direct materials and 4¢ direct labor; new packaging costs will be 30¢ and 13¢, respectively. Assuming no other changes in cost behavior, how many units must be sold to earn a net profit of $20,000?

5-2.   C-V-P Analysis for Airline Fare Pricing* (Edward Deakin)

Trans Western Airlines is considering a proposal to initiate air service between Phoenix, Arizona and Las Vegas, Nevada. The route would be designed primarily to serve the recreation and tourist travelers that frequently travel between the two cities. By offering low cost tourist fares, the airlines hopes to persuade persons who now travel by other modes of transportation to switch and fly Trans Western on this route.

In addition, the airline expects to attract business travelers during the hours of 7 a.m. to 6 p.m. on Mondays through Fridays. The fare price schedule or tariff would be designed to charge a higher fare during business-travel hours so that tourist demand would be reduced during those hours. The company believes that a business fare of $75 one way during business hours and a fare of $40 for all other hours would result in the passenger load being equal during business-travel and tourist-travel hours.

To operate the route, the airline would need two 120 passenger jet aircraft. The aircraft would be leased at an annual cost of $3,800,000 each. Other fixed costs for ground services would amount to $1,500,000 per year.

Operation of each aircraft requires a flight crew whose salaries are based primarily on the hours of flying time. The costs of the flight crew are approximately $400 per hour of flying time.

Fuel costs are also a function of flying time. These costs are estimated at $500 per hour of flying time. Flying time between Phoenix and Las Vegas is estimated at 45 minutes each way.

The costs associated with processing each passenger amount to $3. This includes ticket processing, agent commissions, and variable costs of baggage handling. Food and beverage services cost $7.80 per passenger and will be offered at no charge on flights during business hours. The cost of this service on non-business hour flights are expected to be recovered through the charges levied for alcoholic beverages.

---

* Copyright 1982 by CIPT Co. Reproduced with permission.

Required:

1. If five business flights and three tourist flights are offered each way every weekday, and ten tourist flights are offered each way every Saturday and Sunday, what is the average number of passengers that must be carried on each flight to break even?

2. What is the break even load factor or percentage of available seats occupied on a route?

3. If Trans Western Airlines operates the Phoenix-Las Vegas route, its aircraft on that route will be idle between midnight and 6 a.m. The airline is considering offering a "Red Die" special, which would leave Phoenix daily at midnight and return by 6 a.m. The marketing division estimates that if the fare were no more than $20, at least 60 new passengers could be attracted to each "Red Die" flight. Operating costs would be at the same rate for this flight, but advertising costs of $1,225 per week would be required for promotion of the service. No food or beverage costs would be borne by the company. Management wishes to know the minimum fare that would be required to break even on the "Red Die" special assuming the marketing division's passenger estimates are correct.

5-3. *Multiple Product C-V-P Analysis* (CMA, adapted)

Hewtex Electronics manufactures two products, tape recorders and electronic calculators, and sells them nationally to wholesalers and retailers. The Hewtex management is very pleased with the company's performance for the current fiscal year. Projected sales through December 31, 1982 indicate that 70,000 tape recorders and 140,000 electronic calculators will be sold this year. The projected earnings statement, which appears below, shows that Hewtex will exceed its earnings goal of 9 percent on sales after taxes.

The tape recorder business has been fairly stable for the last few years, and the company does not intend to change the tape recorder price. However, the competition among manufacturers of electronic calculators has been increasing. Hewtex's calculators have been very popular with consumers. In order to sustain this interest in their calculators and to meet the price reductions expected from competitors, management has decided to reduce the wholesale price of its calculator from $22.50 to $20.00 per unit effective January 1, 1983. At the same time the company plans to spend an additional $57,000 on advertising during fiscal year 1983. As a consequence of these actions, management estimates that 80 percent of its total revenue will be derived from calculator sales as compared to 75 percent in 1982. As in prior years, the sales mix is assumed to be the same at all volume levels.

The total fixed overhead costs will not change in 1983, nor will the variable overhead cost rates (applied on a direct labor hour base). However, the cost of materials and direct labor is expected to change. The cost of solid state electronic components will be cheaper in 1983. Hewtex estimates that material costs will drop 10 percent for the tape recorders and 20 percent for the calculators in 1983. However, direct labor costs for both products will increase 10 percent in the coming year.

1. How many tape recorder and electronic calculator units did Hewtex Electronics have to sell in 1982 to break even?
2. What volume of sales is required if Hewtex Electronics is to earn a profit in 1983 equal to 9 percent on sales after taxes?
3. Derive the equation describing the level of profits in 1983 as a function of the number of tape recorders and electronic calculators sold. Plot the breakeven line and the line representing a profit of 9 percent of sales after taxes.

HEWTEX ELECTRONICS
Projected Earnings Statement
For the Year Ended December 31, 1982

	Tape Recorders		Electronic Calculators		Total
	Total Amount (000 omitted)	Per Unit	Total Amount (000 omitted)	Per Unit	(000 omitted)
Sales	$1,050	$15.00	$3,150	$22.50	$4,200.0
Production costs:					
Materials	$ 280	$ 4.00	$ 630	$ 4.50	$ 910.0
Direct labor	140	2.00	420	3.00	560.0
Variable overhead	140	2.00	280	2.00	420.0
Fixed overhead	70	1.00	210	1.50	280.0
Total production costs	$ 630	$ 9.00	$1,540	$11.00	$2,170.0
Gross margin	$ 420	$ 6.00	$1,610	$11.50	$2,030.0
Fixed selling and administrative					1,040.0
Net income before income taxes					990.0
Income taxes (55%)					544.5
Net income					$ 445.5

5-4. *Nonlinear Cost Structure and Breakeven Analysis*

Frank Alexander was President of the Mason Company, a small producer of valves in a highly competitive market. A recent drop in the price of the valves has caused him great concern, since the price was now below the Mason Company's standard cost. Standard cost was determined from operating at 80 percent of the maximum capacity of 10,000 valves per month. Alexander did not normally operate above this level (of 8,000 valves per month) since the higher production required overtime work that significantly increased variable costs.

The fixed costs of the Mason Company were $40,000 per month and variable costs were $15 per valve for production levels up to 8,000 valves per month. Consequently the standard cost of the valve was set at a $20, based on operating at the desired level of 80 percent of capacity. Normally the price of the valve ranged from $21 to $23 allowing a small but adequate return on the Mason Company's modest investment in machinery and facilities.

For production above the standard volume, unit variable costs for the additional units increased by:

15 percent above the normal variable cost for volume between 80 and 85 percent of capacity;

20 percent above the normal variable cost for volume between 85 and 90 percent of capacity;

30 percent above the normal variable cost for volume between 90 and 100 percent of capacity.

Recently, the price of the valves had dropped about 10 percent to $19 per valve. Mr. Alexander felt he was now in a no-win situation since he was losing money on every valve he was selling. While he saw some opportunities for increasing his sales volume above the current level of 8,000 units per month, he felt this would only make matters worse, since he felt he was losing money at current volumes and the variable costs on the additional units produced would be even higher.

Required:

1. Comment on Frank Alexander's analysis of the price-cost squeeze in which he now finds himself. At what point would you recommend that he actually turn down orders at $19 per valve.

2. Assuming the price returns to its previous level of $21, at what volumes would the Mason Company operate profitably?

5-5. Nonlinear Cost and Revenue Analysis (Joanne Collins)

Edith Wharton, a graduate of an Eastern business school has decided to establish a business school to compete with Alma Mater. She is planning for an institution that will handle from 1,000 to 5,000 students.

Based on a survey conducted by one of her associates, she believes the following demand curve is relevant for her enterprise:

Tuition/Student/Year	Demand (Students)
$10,000	1000
9,000	2000
8,000	3000
7,000	4000
6,000	5000

Her fixed costs (for facilities and administrative expenses) are expected to be $8,000,000 per year up to an enrollment of 3,000 students. Above 3,000 students, additional facilities must be provided and fixed costs will double.

Her variable costs per student include the cost of instructors and instructional supplies. Assume she wishes a student/faculty ratio of 10:1 for an enrollment of 3,000 students and that instructors are paid an average of $30,000 per year. Supply costs per student are $1000. Finally, assume variable costs will decline by $1.00 per student for each additional student enrolled (beyond 3,000 students) and conversely will increase $1.00 per student for each reduction in the number of students below 3,000 students.

Required:

At what tuition does the school break-even? What tuition maximizes operating income?

5-6. Choosing a Product Mix* (C. Horngren)

Brian Jones has just received a university degree in management. He has taken the position of assistant to the president of a fairly small company in South Africa that manufactures tungsten carbide drill steels for the gold-mining industry.

Two types of drill steels are manufactured. One has a steel rod of $\frac{3}{4}$-inch diameter and the other a diameter of 1 inch. The manufacturing takes place in three departments. In the tip-fabricating department, tungsten carbide tips are manufactured from powdered wolfram. In the steel-forging department, the steel rods are slotted and prepared for the insertion of the tips. The assembly department puts the tips and steel rods together in a brazing process.

Each department has severe capacity limits. The first constraint prohibits further capital expenditure because of a very weak liquid position arising from the past losses; the second is the labor situation in South Africa, which makes the hiring of more labor or the working of overtime virtually impossible. The capacity of each department is as follows:

Tip fabricating (Dept. A)	240,000 hours
Steel forging (Dept. B)	180,000 hours
Assembly (Dept. C)	180,000 hours

The treasurer has just completed the budget for the forthcoming year. Because of the renewed confidence in gold, the company is expected to produce at full capacity.

The treasurer has produced the following profit analysis of the two products, on which a major production decision was based:

	$\frac{3}{4}"$	$1"$
Selling price	$5.00	$6.00
Direct materials		
Tungsten carbide	$ .75	$1.00
Steel	1.45	2.05
	$2.20	$3.05

---

* Problem prepared by Charles Horngren for *Cost Accounting* 5th edition (Prentice-Hall, 1982); reproduced with permission.

	$\frac{3}{4}''$	$1''$
Direct labor		
Department A	$ .60	$ .30
Department B	.20	.30
Department C	.20	.15
	$1.00	$ .75
Prime costs (from above)	$3.20	$3.80
Factory overhead	.80	.60
Selling and administration	.50	.60
Total costs	$4.50	$5.00
Profit	$ .50	$1.00

The market survey performed by the sales manager showed that the company could sell as many of either type of rod as it could produce. However, the sales manager urged that the needs of three of the big gold mines must be satisfied in full, even though this meant producing a large number of the $\frac{3}{4}$-inch rods that had only half the profit of the 1-inch rods. The quantities required by these three gold mines amounted to 270,000 $\frac{3}{4}$-inch rods and 540,000 1-inch rods.

As the 1-inch rods have twice the profit of the $\frac{3}{4}$-inch rods, the treasurer suggested that the remaining capacity be used to produce two 1-inch rods for every $\frac{3}{4}$-inch rod. This would mean producing an additional 135,000 $\frac{3}{4}$-inch rods and 270,000 1-inch rods. Department B would then be working at full capacity and would be the constraint on any further production.

The treasurer then produced the following budgeted income statement for the forthcoming year. Sales are expected to occur evenly throughout the year.

	$\frac{3}{4}''$	$1''$
Sales (in units)	405,000	810,000
Sales (in dollars)	$2,025,000	$4,860,000
Direct materials	891,000	2,470,500
Direct labor	405,000	607,500
Factory overhead	324,000	486,000
Selling and administration	202,500	486,000
Total costs	$1,822,500	$4,050,000
Profit	$ 202,500	$ 810,000

Jones, as his first assignment, is asked by the president to comment on the budgeted income statement. Specifically, the president feels that capacity might be better utilized with a different sales mix. He wants to know just how much it is costing the company in lost profits by supplying the full needs of the three big gold-mining customers. He feels it might be more profitable to produce only the 1-inch rods.

Jones gathers the following additional information before making his recommendations:

Wolfram is purchased at $10 per kilogram (1,000 grams). The $\frac{3}{4}$-inch tips use an average of 75 grams and the 1-inch tips 100 grams. The special alloy steel costs $2,000 per 2,000 pounds. The $\frac{3}{4}$-inch rods use 1.45 pounds and the 1-inch rods 2.05 pounds.

Direct-labor costs per hour follow:

Department A	$2.40
Department B	1.80
Department C	1.50

Tip fabricating (Department A) is a skilled process. The smaller tips require twice as much detailed work. Owing to the nature of the work, most of the labor is considered fixed because it would be difficult to replace. Approximately 200,000 hours per annum in Department A are considered fixed. In the steel-forging process, the bigger rods require more time because of the handling difficulties. In the assembly department, the smaller rods again take more time because of the intricacies of the operations. However, this is not skilled work.

Factory overhead in the budgeted income statement is considered 50 percent fixed. It has been allocated to the products on the basis of direct labor.

Fixed selling and administrative expenses have been allocated on the basis of the number of units sold. Variable selling expenses are predicted to be 10¢ per unit sold of either size.

Required:

If you were Jones, what would be your recommendations to the president?

5-7. MP Manufacturing (B): Choosing an Optimal Production Mix*

The sales department of MP Manufacturing has been asked to prepare estimates of what it could sell each month. These estimates have been confirmed by the firm's consulting economist and by top management. They are as follows:

A	13,000 units
B	5,000 units
C	5,000 units

Production of these quantities was immediately recognized as being impossible. Estimated cost data for the three products, each of which requires activity of both departments, were based on the following production rates:

	Product		
	A	**B**	**C**
Department 1	2 per hour	4 per hour	3 per hour
Department 2	4 per hour	8 per hour	4/3 per hour

Practical capacity in Department 1 is 6,700 hours and in Department 2, 6,300 hours,

_____

* This problem is a continuation of MP Manufacturing (A); Problem 4-1 which should be worked prior to or at the same time as MP Manufacturing (B).

and the industrial engineering department has concluded that this cannot be increased without the purchase of additional equipment. Thus, while last year Department 1 operated at 99 percent of its capacity and Department 2 at 71 percent of capacity, the maximum sales would require operating both Department 1 and 2 at more than 100 percent capacity.

These solutions to the limited production problem have been rejected: (1) subcontracting the production out to other firms is considered to be unprofitable because of problems of maintaining quality, (2) operating a second shift is impossible because of shortage of labor, (3) operating overtime would create problems because a large number of employees are "moon-lighting" and would therefore refuse to work more than the normal 40 hour week. Price increases have also been rejected; although they would result in higher profits this year, the longrun competitive position of the firm would be weakened resulting in lower profits in the future.

The treasurer then suggested that Product C has been carried at a loss too long, and that now was the time to eliminate it from the product line. If all facilities are used to produce A and B, profits would be increased.

The sales manager objected to this solution because of the need to carry a full line. In addition, he maintains that there is a group of customers who have provided and will continue to provide a solid base for the firm's activities and these customers' needs must be met. He provided a list of these customers and their estimated purchases (in units) which total as follows:

A	8,000
B	3,200
C	1,200

It was impossible to verify these contentions, but they appeared to be reasonable and they served to narrow the bounds of the problem so that the president concurred.

The treasurer reluctantly acquiesced, but maintained that the remaining capacity should be used to produce A and B. Because A produced 2.4 times as much profit as B, he suggested that the production of A (in excess of the 8,000 minimum set by the sales manager) be 2.4 times that of B (in excess of the 3,200 minimum set by the sales manager).

The production manager made some quick calculations and said that this would result in budgeted production and sales of:

A	10,483
B	4,234
C	1,200

The treasurer then made a calculation of what profits would be as follows:

A	10,483 at $9.00	$94,347
B	4,234 at $3.75	15,878
C	1,200 at − 10.05	(12,060)
		$122,285

As this would represent an increase of 17 percent of average monthly profits in 1983, there was a general feeling of self-satisfaction. Before final approval was given, however, the president said that he would like to have his new assistant check over the figures. Somewhat piqued, the treasurer agreed and at that point the group adjourned.

The next day the above information was submitted to you as your first assignment on your new job as the president's assistant.

Required:

Prepare an analysis showing the president what he should do.

5-8.   Calumet Steel: Product Profitability at Production Capacity.*
(John Shank)

In December of 1977, Robert Baxter organized a meeting of his staff to discuss specific product policy decisions for Calumet Steel's production of galvanized products in 1978. Baxter was president of Calumet Steel, a division of one of the nation's largest steel manufacturers, Pohasset Steel. He was fully responsible for the profit performance of Calumet, a modern, nonintegrated, cold-finishing mill.

Reports from corporate headquarters and regional sales representatives indicated that 1978 would be a year of substantial industry sales for galvanized products. If accurate, this forecast meant that Calumet's galvanizing equipment would be operating at 100 percent capacity for the year. Calumet, normally supplied with hot strip steel by its sister divisions, converted strip steel into three basic product lines: cold-rolled, tin plate (for cans), and galvanized products. Galvanized products accounted for about 30 percent of annual production tonnage and were generally considered to be the division's most profitable items.

Faced with a capacity-constrained situation in the galvanizing area for 1978, Bob Baxter was anxious to formulate a product strategy that would maximize the profits generated by this product group. He also hoped that by drawing together various department managers for the December strategy meeting, he could get them to expand their inputs into a long-term strategy with wider application for improving the return on invested capital at Calumet.

The Meeting

ROBERT BAXTER: *President*

Gentlemen, I've called you together to consider our strategy for 1978 for our galvanized business. Market forecasts indicate that we should be operating our galvanizing equipment at full capacity for the year. Since galvanized products are our most profitable ones, a good strategy here is essential for improving our overall division profitability. If we're going to be capacity-constrained in this area, it will

---

* This case was prepared by Ms. Cynthia Kerr and Professor John K. Shank as the basis for class discussion rather than to illustrate either effective or ineffective handling of an administrative situation. All numbers in the case have been disguised to protect confidential data. However, relationships among the numbers that are relevant to the issues in the case have not been distorted. Reproduced with permission.

be critical for us to get as much profit as we can from this part of our operations. This involves identifying our most profitable galvanized items and assigning marketing and production priorities to these products. First, we need to get agreement on the criteria that we should be using to measure profitability. This may be the most difficult part of the planning job. We need to establish guidelines for this that are consistent with our divisional profit objectives. Our criteria can then be applied to strategy planning for situations with less favorable market conditions.

HUGH CRUMAY: Sales

We couldn't ask for more favorable conditions in 1978, Robert. If we're going to capitalize on this situation, we should be loading our order book with requests for the top-profit item, light-gauge coil products. Of the four galvanized product areas, this is our obvious profit winner [see Table 1]. We make over $100 gross profit per ton on these items and $89 net profit per ton—about $25 more than the profit per ton of the heavy-gauge coil product. Our light-gauge sheet products are profitable, too, but the demand for sheet products has always been low in comparison to coil products. I think we should bank on light-gauge coil business to maximize our profits during the coming year.

DAN SULLIVAN: Production

Wait a minute, Hugh, I've got to question your definition of a profit winner. If we're facing an operating capacity constraint in the galvanized area, then I think the logical thing to do is maximize the volume of tons we convert into galvanized steel. If we give production priority to light-gauge products, we're just further complicating the capacity problem. We would essentially be tying up a critical production unit with material that takes 50 percent longer to process [see Table 2]. I just can't believe that this is an optimal solution for us; even though, as you indicate, this is what our profit reports show.

BILL MOWERY: Financial Planning

I think you've got a good point, Dan. I think that's one issue Bob is trying to get us to resolve this morning. It seems to me that we have to be thinking about maximizing our return on the galvanizing equipment. To do this, we do not necessarily want to maximize tons produced or profit dollars per ton. We need to stress profit per unit of our scarce resource. If hours available on the galvanizing lines is constraining our capacity, we need to act to maximize our profit dollars relative to this variable.

GEOFFERY BITTNER: Production Control

You know, Bill, I agree with your logic, but I'm not sure the galvanizing lines are really the major constraint we should be considering here. The cyclicity of demand for galvanized steel only creates a galvanizing capacity problem for us about 25 percent of the time. Our pickle line, on the other hand, runs at full capacity 90 percent of the time. In fact, when demand for cold-finished steel is high, we have to purchase prepickled steel to meet the volume of orders that our finishing mills can support.

SAM KAUFMAN: Metallurgy

If you're arguing that the pickle line is the major bottleneck to be considered, Geof, that leads us back to supporting profit per ton as the most meaningful profit measure

TABLE 1. Calumet Steel Galvanized Product Profile

Product Description	Product A[a] (.019 × 42-in.; G-60 light-gauge coil)	Product B[a] (.019 × 42-in. × 60-in.; G-60 light-gauge sheet)	Product C[b] (.040 × 42-in.; G-60 heavy-gauge coil)	Product D[b] (.040 × 42-in. × 60-in.; G-60 heavy-gauge sheet)
Revenue/Ton	$500	$507	$443	$450
Material Cost/Ton	338	342	327	331
Cost Above/Ton[c]	56	62	31	36
Gross Profit/Ton	106	103	85	83
Selling, General, and Administrative; Mill Overhead; and Depreciation/Ton[d]	17	18	16	17
Net Profit/Ton	89	85	69	66
1977 Monthly Average Tons Produced	18,000 tons	2,500 tons	10,300 tons	2,000 tons
Potential Sales/Month[e]	24,500 tons	12,000 tons	29,000 tons	10,000 tons
Markets Served and Share of Produced Tons:	Steel Converters 38% Steel Service Centers 27% Building Products 25% Duct Products 10%	Steel Service Centers 90% Dust Products 8% Farming Products 2%	Farming Products 36% Appliance 24% Automotive 20% Steel Service Centers 20%	Steel Service Centers 50% Automotive 35% Appliance 15%

[a] Processed through the 48-in. galvanized line.
[b] Processed through the 72-in. galvanized line.
[c] Cost above/ton is the standard cost above basic steel and zinc material required to produce a ton of steel.
[d] SG&A and mill overhead are absorbed on the basis of total production conversion cost (i.e., cost above and material cost/ton).
[e] Estimated competitive discount allowances necessary for attaining these sales levels (includes competitive price allowance, freight equalization, and potential customer claims costs) are as follows: product A, $9/ton; product B, $12/ton; product C, $24/ton; and product D, $18/ton.

TABLE 2. Calumet Steel

| Equipment | Capital Cost (Million $) | | Standard Equipment Hours Required to Produce a Finished Ton of Galvanized Steel | | | |
	Original Cost 1961	Replacement Cost 1977	Product A	Product B	Product C	Product D
Pickle Line	9.8	28.9	0.0051	0.0052	0.0048	0.0049
Cold Reduction Mill	35.2	92.5	0.0102	0.0104	0.0048	0.0049
48″ Galvanize Line	10.0*	30.1*	0.0508	0.0586	0.0335	0.0399
72″ Galvanize Line	16.1*	29.0*	0.0380	0.0420	0.0191	0.0239

Pickle Line: This unit prepares hot strip steel for the Cold Reduction Mill by cleaning rust, scale and other oxide contaminants from the surface and sidetrimming the steel to fit order specifications.

Cold Reduction Mill: This unit reduces the gauge of the incoming pickled steel and imparts a special surface finish and temper to the reduced product.

Galvanize Line: This unit cleans, anneals and applies a zinc coating to the cold reduced steel, converting it into galvanized product.

* Shearing equipment included in Capital Cost:
    Original Cost $2.5MM
    Replacement Cost $4.5MM

for the division. From the operating standards for the four product areas at the pickle line (Table 2), you can see that there is little difference between them. Since we pickle a hot band before it is cold-reduced to any given gauge, the per ton versus per hour argument disappears. All the bands are the same thickness when we pickle them. This means that we can go back to the per ton measure as the profitability determinant. The catch to this argument, in my view, is Hugh's point that profit per ton doesn't mean much if we can't sell the tons. In other words, we have to recognize the individual limitations of demand for the four product areas and incorporate these into our analysis if we hope to maximize our return.

TOM LEE: Cost Accounting

You're right, Sam, but there is another problem here which we haven't considered yet. We have to focus on the costs that are relevant in determining specific profitability figures. I don't think we should consider the fixed costs that are included in the profit per ton figures. The allocations for the fixed costs are pretty arbitrary and, besides, those costs don't really change as product mix changes anyway.

BILL MOWERY: Financial Planning

But, Tom, I have always had the impression that in a capacity-constrained situation, full costing is considered to be the most relevant determinant of profit. After all, if prices don't cover fixed costs when we're operating at maximum capacity, they never will.

HUGH CRUMAY: Sales

We're not talking about price cutting, Bill. As I see it, we are looking for profitability criteria with the most general applicability. We are capacity-constrained in our galvanized area at the present time, but demand won't always be this great. We've got to devise a way of comparing the relative profitability of our products that is not conditional on static market conditions.

TOM LEE: Cost Accounting

I still think the problem with the full cost figures is that if we determine product profitability on that basis, we are tying ourselves too closely to the fixed-cost-allocation structure of our cost system. Our fixed costs are normally allocated to individual products on the basis of a specific monthly level of operations [see Table 3]. If, during a specific month, we do not operate at this level, we generate volume variances. As a result, the standard product costs generated by the system often do not reflect the actual cost of producing a given product during this period. I think we should avoid this confusion of allocated fixed costs and deal strictly with variable costs and contribution margins in our product profitability comparisons.

HUGH CRUMAY: Sales

Tom, do you mean we should be ignoring fixed costs? I have always been a believer that we can't really measure the profitability of any product without considering all the costs associated with its production and with its delivery, for that matter. In fact, instead of excluding some of the reported costs, we ought to be adding on some

TABLE 3. **48-Inch Galvanized Line Monthly Production Cost Center Budget**[ab]

Expense Item	Fixed Cost	Variable Cost	Total Cost
Direct Labor	$ —	$ 47,892	$ 47,892
Repair and Maintenance	46,700	553	47,253
Extraordinary Maintenance	4,510	—	4,410
Utilities	67,210	92,100	159,310
Roll Shop	815	2,456	3,271
Supplies	365	—	365
Chemicals[c]	—	8,596	8,596
Department General	117,400	—	117,400
Total	$237,000	$151,597	$388,597

[a] This table illustrates how the "cost above" per ton figures are generated for one particular cost center. The data here are carried forward to Table 4.
[b] Costs are based on 614 monthly budgeted equipment hours. Maximum monthly equipment hours available are 695. This budget is used to determine the "cost above" portion of standard cost associated with the 48-in. galvanize line.
[c] This is a variable material cost/surface area processed that is converted by the mill operating standards into a variable cost/equipment hour.

you don't include. It has always bothered me that your cost system ignores the impact of freight equalization and competitive discounts that we incur in filling specific customer orders. These extra costs are not reflected in the standard cost figures, but probably average $5 per ton for light-gauge products and $10 per ton for heavy-gauge galvanized items.

SAM KAUFMAN: *Metallurgy*

I agree, Hugh, and another item like that is the additional impact of claims costs on the profitability of our galvanized products. The automotive markets we serve with our heavy-gauge items persistently file defective material claims averaging $5-6 per ton. Plus, they're always returning products to us which we have trouble reapplying to other orders. With these kinds of intangible costs associated with heavy-gauge products, I find it difficult to consider them at all profitable relative to our light-gauge products.

DAN SULLIVAN: *Production*

Sam, don't be too hasty with your conclusions. I think that if we are searching for a long-term galvanized product strategy, heavy-gauge material may be the answer. My guys really like to run the heavy gauges. Also, part of the profit differential in Tom's accounting reports is because of our somewhat arbitrary decision to run heavy gauges on the more expensive 72-inch line. If we reversed it and costed out the heavy-gauge products on the 48-inch line and the light gauges on the 72-inch line, the figures in Tom's report would change a lot. The only real difference there is our choice of where we normally run the product. Also, we serve a much more concentrated market with the heavy coil products; a market that is characterized by relatively constant volume, a few predictable customers, consistent quality standards, and good steady growth.

HUGH CRUMAY: Sales

Sam, I hate to disagree with you, but if you are attempting to characterize the markets we serve with our heavy-gauge products, you're glossing over some of their biggest drawbacks from a sales point of view. Take the automotive market, for instance. This is really our least profitable galvanized market. Short-term, it may represent guaranteed volume, but the economic cyclicity of the auto industry creates real headaches for us in the long run. The material engineering changes they have been making during the 1970s to conform to federal EPA regulations and to reduce their own manufacturing costs have not made them the most predictable customers, either. I think they will be an even less desirable market for our galvanized business in the future.

GEOFFERY BITTNER: Production Control

I agree, Hugh, especially if we can't allay the chronic quality problems, we run into with the order mix we accept from the auto manufacturers. Most automotive items are either for exposed or unexposed applications. Calumet accepts such a high percentage of critical exposed items that we end up producing more distressed material than prime product to fill these orders. Sam hit the nail right on the head that it is a full-time job for more than one person in production control to keep track of this unacceptable material and apply it to other galvanized orders with less critical quality specifications. Any rework that we perform on this dispositioned steel incurs additional yield and processing costs on which we certainly lose money. I can't say that I feel comfortable considering the farm product manufacturers as one of our more profitable markets, either. Grain bin manufacturers represent a large portion of the heavy-gauge coil market. Their sales have been growing a steady 4 percent for the past few years, and they have become a more stable and sophisticated group of manufacturers. But the seasonality of their business isn't compatible with that of our other customers. Also, the critical delivery performance they require is just about beyond the capabilities of our operations.

ROBERT BAXTER: President

I seem to recall, also, that this is the most competitive, heavily discounted galvanized market we serve at the present time. What about the market characteristics for light-gauge galvanized products, Hugh? Do you really feel these are the most profitable markets for the division to penetrate?

HUGH CRUMAY: Sales

This is difficult to judge, Bob. I think that in the long run, the building and duct product markets will be extremely profitable for Calumet. Both are vulnerable to the cyclicity of the construction industry and the national economy, however. In spite of this element of risk, the dispersed customer base of the market and the excellent relations that we are establishing with some of these manufacturers have convinced me of the markets' future potential.

DAN SULLIVAN: Production

Are we scheming about galvanized products 5 years down the road, or are we formalizing a product strategy for next year? I am of the opinion that our efforts should be concentrated on 1978 and the market forecast for that period alone. If you take care of the short-term problems, the long run will take care of itself. To me, the profitability of catering to the light-gauge galvanized markets in 1978 is very suspect.

ROBERT BAXTER: *President*

Let me interrupt, Dan, and try to tie together what we have discussed so far. I think we have surfaced some significant issues regarding profit criteria for the division, but we need to resolve these before we can begin to formulate any specific product strategies. First, the profit per ton or profit per equipment hour issue needs to be settled with respect to our galvanized products. If equipment hours are chosen as the critical measure, then a decision has to be reached about which equipment really represents the most serious bottleneck for our operation. Next, we need to agree on whether a share of the fixed costs should be included with the variable costs in determining product profitability, and whether we should try to go outside the standard cost system to associate claims costs and discounts with individual products. I'm also bothered by the fact that the profitability measure for a product is influenced by the choice of which galvanizing line we run it on. I'm not sure how to handle the arbitrariness of that. Finally, we need to worry about the investment differentials across the products. In the long run, return on investment is what we're after rather than just profits. After quantifying all of these problems, we still face the task of incorporating the intangible marketing issues into our profitability analysis. Let's break this up now and get back together next week after Tom [Tom Lee, Cost Accounting] has had a chance to get us more specific data to help clarify the points of contention.

Required:

1. In order to gain a better understanding of Calumet's "cost above" concept [see Table 4] and the comparability of products A through D, compute the costs associated with processing each product through either the 48-inch or 72-inch galvanize lines. From these calculations, evaluate the relative profit impact if the heavy-gauge products were switched to the 48-inch line and the light-gauge products to the 72-inch line.

2. Complete Table 5, the product profitability matrix. The point is relative ranking across four product groups for a given profit criterion. Note that logic may enable you to avoid some of the calculations. (Which cell entries are known by logic to dominate which other cells?)

3. On the basis of information discussed during the initial planning session and the answers to the previous questions, what measures of profitability do you feel are most relevant to Calumet's operation under what specific conditions? Do you feel that one of the four product groups is more profitable than the other three?

4. Formulate a 1978 galvanized product strategy for Calumet using your own profitability criteria. Be specific about ranking the four products and outlining individual marketing/production plans for each.

5. How could the cost accounting and/or the internal reporting system(s) be improved to better highlight the viewpoint about product profitability which you feel is more appropriate?

TABLE 4. **Processing Cost Above Material Per Equipment Hour**

Equipment	Total Fixed Cost	Total Variable Cost[a]	Equipment Hours Available	1977 Equipment Hours Budgeted	Cost/Available Hour			Cost/Budgeted Hour		
					Fixed	Variable[a]	Total	Fixed	Variable[a]	Total
Pickle Line	$573,100/month	$ 120/hr	695	695	$825	$ 120	$ 945	$825	$ 120	$ 945
Cold-Reduction Mill	$438,500/month	$1,080/hr	695	483	$631	$1,080	$1,711	$908	$1,080	$1,988
48-Inch Galvanized Line	$237,000/month	$ 245/hr	695	614	$341	$ 245	$ 586	$386	$ 245	$ 631
72-Inch Galvanized Line	$332,200/month	$ 408/hr	695	678	$478	$ 408	$ 886	$490	$ 408	$ 898

[a] Most variable costs included in cost above are expressed in terms of dollars/equipment hour. Sulfuric acid used at the pickle line is a critical variable cost of this production unit expressed separately in terms of dollars/ton produced. The magnitude of this cost is $2.20/ton produced.

TABLE 5. Product Profitability Matrix

Profit Measure	48-Inch Galvanize Processing				72-Inch Galvanize Processing			
	Product A	Product B	Product C	Product D	Product A	Product B	Product C	Product D
Fully Absorbed Profit/Ton	$ 89	$ 85					$ 69	$ 66
Profit Contribution/Ton	$139	$137					$100	$101
Profit Contribution/Galvanizing Equipment Hour								
Profit Contribution/Pickling Equipment Hour								
Fully Absorbed Profit/ Galvanized Equipment Hour								
Fully Absorbed Profit/Pickling Equipment Hour								
Profit Contribution/Ton Allowing for Discounts, Claims, etc.								
Profit Contribution/Galvanizing Equipment Hours, Allowing for Discounts, Claims, etc.								
Return on Investment (%)								

California Products Corporation: Analyze Product Profitability with Machine Constraints and Fixed and Variable Costs (F. Kollaritsch)

History

The California Products Corporation was started in 1955 by several members of the Black family. From 1955 to 1960, Product "I" was the only product produced, and, although profits were not high, they were sufficient to satisfy the family stockholders.

During 1960, the management of the California Products Corporation, mostly members of the Black family, decided to change from absorption costing to direct costing (variable costing) upon the advice of a consulting firm. Product "J" was started into the production line in 1960 and Product "K" was started in 1964.

Since 1960, the company had losses or very small profits. The Profit and Loss Statement for 1965, (see Table 1), shows that the company "broke even" during that year. At the board meeting, held shortly after the financial statements for 1965 were released, optimism was voiced concerning the future profit prospects of the company. The reasons given for this optimism were as follows:

1. Products "J" and "K", it was believed, have overcome starting-up troubles and have finally found acceptance by the public.
2. Products "J" and "K" are both high contribution margin products. (See Table 4.)
3. During 1965 some overtime had been incurred, which it is claimed, cut into profits. It was anticipated that this would not be repeated next year.
4. The sales force had finally become convinced of the necessity of pushing Product "K" because of its high contribution margin.

The Profit and Loss Statement for the year 1966 (see Table 2) was anything but encouraging to the management of the California Products Corporation. The company sustained a loss during this year, and paradoxically had a considerable backlog of unfilled orders. The overtime was not eliminated, although the overall production in units of output decreased by 50,000 units. (See Table 5.)

The board meeting which followed the release of the 1966 financial statements was unfriendly and everyone accused everyone else of inability. Without producing any evidence, the vice president in charge of sales accused the production people of gross inefficiency. Evidence was, however, introduced which indicated that sales had to be turned down because production could not supply the goods within the normal delivery time.

The vice president in charge of production accused the sales people of pushing the wrong product. He pointed out that all the troubles started with the introduction of Product "J" and Product "K." He also accused the vice president in charge of finances of "trickery" and stated that the contribution margin (see Table 4) was nothing except "fancy data" which would mislead everyone.

This meeting resulted in ill feelings among the various functional staff managers. The chairman of the board finally obtained their consent to call in a consulting firm to investigate what had happened and to suggest possible means of making the firm profitable.

An investigation into the variable expenses, shown in Table 3, revealed them to be correct, and to include a charge for normally expected overtime. The prices for the products had not been changed for several years and there was no expectation that a price change was feasible in the next few years.

An investigation into the $800,000 fixed expenses, shown in Table 1 and Table 2, showed that $430,000 was a joint fixed cost and that $370,000 was a separable fixed cost attributable to the company's products as follows:

Product "I"	$ 60,000
Product "J"	200,000
Product "K"	110,000
	$370,000

An analysis of the joint fixed costs of $430,000 showed them to be made up of:

Manufacturing Expenses	$ 40,000
Selling & Administrative Expenses	70,000
Depreciation:	
Machine "A"	100,000
Machine "B"	20,000
Machine "C"	200,000
	$430,000

Regardless of the above classification, the full amount of $800,000 was fixed costs and had been properly classified by the company. Information gathered concerning the production process disclosed that each product had to be worked on by each of the three machines and that each of the three products required different machine times on the various machines. (The average production capacity of the machines is given in Table 6.)

It was estimated that each machine was operated about 1750 to 1800 hrs. during a normal year (practical capacity), which takes into consideration maintenance, repairs, resetting, etc. The maximum operational time one could expect from each of these machines during a given year without overtaxing them and incurring unreasonably high additional expenses was 1900 hrs. to 2000 hrs.

TABLE 1. California Products Corporation Profit and Loss Statement Year 1965

	Product "I"	*Product "J"*	*Product "K"*	*Total*
Sales	$1,479,000	$1,320,000	$284,000	$3,083,000
Variable Costs	1,131,000	960,000	192,000	2,283,000
Contribution Margin	$ 348,000	$ 360,000	$ 92,000	$ 800,000
Fixed Expenses				800,000
Net Profit				$ –0–

TABLE 2. California Products Corporation Profit and Loss Statement Year 1966

	Product "I"	Product "J"	Product "K"	Total
Sales	$1,224,000	$1,056,000	$568,000	$2,848,000
Variable Costs	936,000	768,000	384,000	2,088,000
Contribution Margin	$ 288,000	$ 288,000	$184,000	$ 760,000
Fixed Expenses				800,000
Net Loss				$ (40,000)

TABLE 3. California Products Corporation Variable Product Costs

	Product "I"	Product "J"	Product "K"	Total
Materials	$2.00	$3.00	$2.50	$7.50
Labor[a]	1.00	1.20	1.00	3.20
Indirect Manufacturing Expenses	.30	.40	.30	1.00
Selling & Administrative Expenses	.60	.20	1.00	1.80
Total	$3.90	$4.80	$4.80	$13.50

[a] Includes reasonable allowance for normal overtime.

TABLE 4. California Products Corporation Contribution Margins

	Product "I"	Product "J"	Product "K"	Total
Sales Price	$5.10	$6.60	$7.10	$18.80
Variable Costs	3.90	4.80	4.80	13.50
	$1.20	$1.80	$2.30	$ 5.30

TABLE 5. California Products Corporation Products Sold (in Units)

	1965	1966
Product "I"	290,000	240,000
Product "J"	200,000	160,000
Product "K"	40,000	80,000
Total	530,000	480,000

TABLE 6. California Products Corporation Average Product Output Capacity per Machine Hour[a] (in Units)

	Product "I"	Product "J"	Product "K"
Machine "A"	312	260	130
Machine "B"	364	208	156
Machine "C"	520	312	104

[a] Each machine could work at any given time on one product, only.

Analyze the data of the California Products Corporation given above and summarize your findings in a report to the board of directors of this corporation, addressing your remarks specifically to the questions of overtime, production deficiencies and inefficiencies, the product sales mix, the cost method, the loss during 1966, and the profit potentials of the various products. You might wish to prepare an initial analysis assuming that none of the fixed costs are escapable even were there to be zero production of one or more products. Then you can determine whether your proposed solution remains optimal if the separable fixed costs for products I, J, and K are escapable if there is no production of one or more of these products.

5-10. Cost of Capital and CVP Analysis of Mutually Exclusive Projects (R. Manes)

Machine A costs $8,000 has a 4-year life and no salvage value. It yields output which sells at $25 per unit and costs $15 per unit in variable costs of production so that its contribution margin is $10.

Machine B costs $12,000, also has a 4-year life and no salvage value. Its output is identical to that of Machine A, also sells at $25 per unit but has a contribution margin of $13 per unit.

Required:

1. Ignoring out-of-pocket fixed costs per period, taxes, inflation and growth and making no allowance for the cost of capital, what is the cross-over point with respect to acquisition of Machine A or B; that is obtain the volume at which one machine becomes preferable to the other?
2. What is this point for a 12 percent discount rate?
3. Which machine should the company acquire if it contemplates per period sales of 375 units?

5-11. Review of Multi-Period Breakeven Analysis and Extensions for Taxes, Depreciation, and Inflation (R. Manes)

A company is contemplating the purchase of fully automatic machinery for producing widgets. The price of a widget is $10, the variable cost with the new machinery is $1.25 per widget, and the fixed annual cash operating cash outlays are $16,000. The machinery costs $15,000 and has a useful life of 4 years, independent of production volume. The firm has a cost of capital of 10 percent.

Required:

1. Compute the annual breakeven volume, ignoring capital costs.
2. Compute the annual breakeven volume including the cost of the machinery and the 10 percent cost of capital.

3. Compute the annual breakeven volume, including capital costs, relative to the current alternative of producing widgets manually at a cost of $4 per widget and with annual fixed cash outlays of $12,000 per year.

4. Repeat parts (a), (b), and (c) when the firm pays income taxes at a 40 percent rate, and uses straight-line depreciation for the machinery. Assume that the after-tax cost of capital is also 10 percent.

5. (More complicated version) Ignore the option of producing widgets manually. What is the annual breakeven volume if there is a 5 percent annual inflation (affecting both prices and costs); the company uses sum-of-the-years digits depreciation, and the company now requires 15 percent after tax cost of capital (a higher discount rate to compensate for the expected inflation during the next four years)?

REFERENCES

CHARNES, A., W. W. COOPER, and Y. IJIRI, "Breakeven Budgeting and Programming to Goals," *Journal of Accounting Research,* I (Spring 1963), 16–41.

DOPUCH, NICHOLAS, "Mathematical Programming and Accounting Approaches to Incremental Cost Analysis," *The Accounting Review* XXXVII (October 1963), 745–53.

GOGGANS, TRAVIS P., "Breakeven Analysis with Curvilinear Functions," *The Accounting Review* XL (October 1965), 867–71.

GROVES, ROGER, RENE MANES, and ROBERT SORENSEN, "The Application of the Hirsch-Dantzig 'Fixed Charge' Algorithm to Profit Planning: A Formal Statement of Product Profitability Analysis," *The Accounting Review* XLV (July 1970), 481–89.

IJIRI, YUJI, *Management Goals and Accounting for Control.* Chicago: Rand McNally, 1965.

————, F. K. LEVY, and R. C. LYON, "A Linear Programming Model for Budgeting and Financial Planning." *Journal of Accounting Research* I (Autumn 1963), 198–212.

JAEDICKE, ROBERT K., "Improving Breakeven Analysis by Linear Programming Techniques," *NAA Bulletin* XLII (March 1961), 5–12.

MANES, RENE, "A New Dimension to Breakeven Analysis," *Journal of Accounting Research* IV (Spring 1966), 87–100.

COST-VOLUME-PROFIT ANALYSIS UNDER UNCERTAINTY

USES OF UNCERTAINTY MODELS

The discussion of C-V-P analysis in Chapter 5 did not explicitly recognize uncertainty in any of the variables. Profits were computed assuming different volume of sales or different product mixes. The deterministic C-V-P model is helpful for profit planning, preparation of flexible budgets, and ex post analysis of operating results. But without a formal model of uncertainty in sales, price, or cost parameters, we cannot obtain information such as the probability of achieving a targeted profit level or the expected opportunity loss from following a given course of action. In Chapter 6 we will explore the opportunities for introducing probabilistic elements into the traditional C-V-P analysis. We will primarily emphasize the uncertainty introduced by an uncertain sales forecast. In Chapter 8 we will study the effects introduced by uncertain cost estimates.

We start with our basic single-product C-V-P equation:

$$\pi = (p - b)x - a. \tag{6-1}$$

To see why formal models of uncertainty are helpful, let us consider an example. A firm is attempting to choose between producing either of two alternative products. Assume that both products have the same contribution margin per unit ($4), the same increment in annual fixed costs ($400,000), and require similar amounts of processing facilities. Both products will have the same break-even volume (100,000 units) and for any level of sales will yield the same profit contribution. If sales (x) are uncertain, both products will have the same level of expected profits as long as the expected sales $E(x)$ for each product are equal. Even under these highly similar and restrictive conditions, the firm may not be indifferent between the two products. Consider the probability of sales for the two products given in Table 6-1.

TABLE 6-1. **Probability Distribution of Sales for Products 1 and 2**

Units Sold	Probability Distribution, Product 1	Probability Distribution, Product 2
50,000	0.1	0.2
75,000	0.2	0.3
100,000	0.3	0.2
125,000	0.3	0.1
150,000	0.1	0.1
225,000	0	0.1

The expected sales for product 1,

$$0.1(50K) + 0.2(75K) + 0.3(100K) + 0.3(125K) + 0.1(150K) = 102.5K,$$

equals the expected sales for product 2,

$$0.2(50K) + 0.3(75K) + 0.2(100K) + 0.1(125K + 150K + 225K) = 102.5K.$$

But even though both products have the same expected sales and hence the same expected profits (of $2,500), the firm is unlikely to be indifferent between them. Product 2 will be viewed as riskier, since the probability is 0.5 that sales will be less than or equal to 75,000 units compared to a probability of 0.3 for product 1. Product 2 has probability 0.7 of being just at breakeven sales or below, whereas product 1 has probability 0.6 of this event. Product 2 has a higher variance and a higher probability of loss than product 1, but both have the same expected profits. Given risk aversion on the part of decision makers, the firm will prefer product 1.

In general, a manager can choose between two risky investments by obtaining his utility function for cash returns and selecting the project that maximizes expected utility. This approach is conceptually correct but difficult to implement in practice. In this section, therefore, we will simply characterize the probability distribution of returns and leave it to the manager to apply his own risk attitude toward the different probability distributions when selecting a course of action.

PROBABILITY DISTRIBUTION OF SALES

The analysis in this chapter requires only one additional characterization of sales beyond those in the deterministic case. The additional information needed is the probability distribution for sales. We can supply this by specifying the cumulative distribution function for sales or by estimating the parameters such as the mean and variance for a particular type of probability distribution (such as the normal). Once the probability distribution function has been so specified, then the procedures described in this section enable the analyst to compute expected profits, the probability of attaining any given level of profitability (including just breaking even at zero profits), expected opportunity losses, and the production decision that maximizes expected profits when all production must occur before actual sales are known. Therefore, a wide range of computations can be performed to characterize profits under uncertainty, once the sales probability distribution has been specified.

For ease in exposition it is convenient to explore the situation when the sales variable, x, is normally distributed. All the analyses we will demonstrate under the assumption of a normal distribution we can also do, albeit with more complexity, using any specified distribution for sales. Thus the use of the normal distribution is a simplifying but not necessary assumption for C-V-P analysis under uncertainty.

For example, in order for the normal distribution to be a reasonable characterization of the sales distribution, the mean must be at least three to five times the standard deviation so that there is virtually no probability of negative sales. For situations where this assumption is not valid, one should use a probability distribution (such as the lognormal, uniform, gamma, or beta) that is bounded below by zero. While these distributions are perhaps less familiar to analysts, it is still straightforward to compute probabilities from any of them. We will discuss techniques for eliciting estimates of the sales probability distribution later in this chapter.

Let $F_N(\cdot)$ be the cumulative distribution for a standard (zero mean, unit standard deviation) normally distributed random variable. We will denote random variables by capital letters (X) and the particular realizations on outcomes of the random variables by small letters (x). Thus if Z is a standard normal variable, by definition we have

$$\Pr(Z \le z) = F_N(z)$$

If X is a normally distributed random variable with mean μ and standard deviation σ [denoted $X \sim N(\mu, \sigma)$], we know that

$$\Pr(X \le x) = \Pr\left(\frac{X - \mu}{\sigma} \le \frac{x - \mu}{\sigma}\right) = F_N\left(\frac{x - \mu}{\sigma}\right). \tag{6-2}$$

If sales, X, is a normally distributed random variable (with mean μ and standard deviation σ) and if price, variable cost, and fixed cost are known constants, then we know, from the fact that linear combinations of normal random variables are themselves normal random variables, that profit, π, is also a normally distributed random variable. The mean or expected profit is given by

$$E(\pi) = E[(p - b)X - a] = (p - b)E(X) - a$$
$$= (p - b)\mu - a. \tag{6-3}$$

Similarly, the standard deviation of profit, $\sigma(\pi)$, is given by

$$\sigma(\pi) = (p - b)\sigma. \tag{6-4}$$

Thus, $\pi \sim N[(p - b)\mu - a, (p - b)\sigma]$. Given this information on the distribution of π, we can compute the probability of at least breaking even:

$$\text{Pr(breakeven)} = \text{Pr}(\pi > 0) = 1 - \text{Pr}(\pi \le 0)$$

$$= 1 - \text{Pr}\left\{\frac{\pi - [(p - b)\mu - a]}{(p - b)\sigma} \le -\frac{(p - b)\mu - a}{(p - b)\sigma}\right\}$$

$$= 1 - F_N\left(\frac{\dfrac{a}{p - b} - \mu}{\sigma}\right). \tag{6-5}$$

SIMPLE EXAMPLE OF PROBABILITY OF BREAKEVEN

As a simple example, suppose that $X \sim N(102,500, 20,000)$ and that $p = 12$, $b = 8$, and $a = 400,000$. The expected profit, $E(\pi)$, is \$10,000 and the standard deviation of profit, $\sigma(\pi)$, is \$80,000. Also

$$\frac{\dfrac{a}{p - b} - \mu}{\sigma} = \frac{\dfrac{400,000}{4} - 102,500}{20,000}$$

$$= \frac{-2,500}{20,000}$$

$$= -0.125.$$

The figure of -0.125 can be obtained from an alternative computation. Since $\pi \sim N(10,000, 80,000)$, the probability of at least breaking even equals the probability that π is not less than \$10,000 below its mean value of \$10,000. This distance of \$10,000 is $\frac{1}{8}$ or 0.125 of a standard deviation below the mean, hence the -0.125 figure. The probability of at least breaking even is

$$\text{Pr(Breakeven)} = 1 - F_N(-0.125)$$

$$= 1 - [1 - F_N(0.125)]$$

$$= F_N(0.125)$$

$$= 0.55,$$

where the algebraic manipulation arises from properties of the normal distribution function, and the value of $F_N(0.125)$ is obtained by interpolation from any standard table of the normal distribution function. Thus, given the distribution of sales and the cost and price parameters, the probability is 0.55 that the sales of the product will exceed the breakeven level of \$100,000.

It is straightforward to extend this analysis to compute the probability of achieving (or failing to achieve) any specified profit level. For example, if we wish to compute the probability that profits will be at least π^*,

$$\Pr(\pi > \pi^*) = 1 - \Pr(\pi \leq \pi^*)$$

$$= 1 - F_N\left(\frac{\dfrac{\pi^* + a}{p - b} - \mu}{\sigma}\right) \tag{6-6}$$

With our numerical example, the probability that profits will exceed $40,000 is

$$\Pr(\pi > 40,000) = 1 - F_N\left(\frac{\dfrac{440,000}{4} - 102,500}{20,000}\right)$$

$$= 1 - F_N\left(\frac{7,500}{20,000}\right)$$

$$= 1 - F_N(0.375)$$

$$= 0.35.$$

While this product has a better than even chance of breaking even and more than one chance in three of making a profit in excess of $40,000, it still may be considered too risky. The probability of losing $10,000 or more is

$$\Pr(\pi \leq -10,000) = F_N\left(\frac{\dfrac{390,000}{4} - 102,500}{20,000}\right)$$

$$= F_N(-0.25)$$

$$= 0.40.$$

Thus, while the deterministic analysis shows that the expected sales will exceed the breakeven level, the explicit analysis of the uncertainty in sales reveals that the probability is 0.45 that the product will not reach breakeven sales and there is a 0.40 probability that losses of $10,000 or more will be realized.

OBTAINING PARAMETER ESTIMATES
FOR A NORMAL DISTRIBUTION

Once the cost analyst has the probability distribution for sales, the computations to obtain the expected profit, the probability of breakeven, and the probabilities of achieving losses or gains of various magnitudes are relatively straightforward, as shown above. When attempting to apply these techniques in actual situations, however, the analyst will soon discover that probability distributions for interesting and real-world random variables are not lying around on the shop floor, imbedded in accounting records, or even stored in the most sophisticated computerized data base. It is easy for an instructor to illustrate the techniques by saying, "Assume that X is normally distributed with mean 102,500 and standard deviation 20,000." The newly trained analyst, however, is unlikely to know the mean or standard deviation of sales, or even whether the normal distribution is an appropriate representation of the probability distribution of sales. Thus, more important than the knowledge of how to compute expected values and cumulative probabilities is the ability to obtain the probability distribution when confronted with a decision problem under uncertainty.

Some guidance can be provided on how to construct the probability distribution for a continuous random variable such as sales. Let us refer to this random variable of interest as the Unknown Quantity, denoted UQ. A particularly simple situation occurs if the analyst is willing to accept the restriction that the UQ is normally distributed. If the normal distribution seems appropriate (there are ways of testing for this), then we need estimate only two parameters—the measure of central tendency or location (in this case the mean, median and mode are the same) and the measure of dispersion (the standard deviation). If historical data for the UQ exist and the process is believed to be stationary, so that we have confidence that future values will be drawn from the same distribution as the past, then we can use results from classical statistics to estimate the mean and standard deviation of the normal distribution for the UQ. For example, if we have past observations $y_1, y_2, \ldots, y_n$ of the UQ, we can estimate the mean of the distribution as

$$\hat{\mu} = \frac{\sum_i y_i}{n} \tag{6-6}$$

and the standard deviation as

$$\hat{\sigma} = \left[\frac{\sum_i (y_i - \bar{y})^2}{n - 1} \right]^{1/2} \tag{6-7}$$

If relevant historical data do not exist, or if we have only two or three past observations on the UQ, the above classical statistical estimates will not be useful for the analyst. In this case the analyst must rely on subjective probability estimates, either his own or those he can elicit from the experienced manager and decision maker. If we can remain satisfied that the normal distribution is a reasonable approximation to the distribution of the UQ, we can first try to identify the mean of the distribution. We should be able to obtain this estimate by asking for the most likely value or the value for which the actual value of the UQ is equally likely to be above or below. (Here we are exploiting the unique property of the normal distribution that the mean, median, and mode are the same quantity.)

When eliciting this quantity from an expert, such as a sales manager, we could ask her whether she is happy accepting an even-money bet that the UQ will be below this value. If she accepts too quickly, ask her whether she is willing to take the other side of the bet, that the UQ will be above this value. After a few iterations we should be able to obtain a quantity such that the expert is indifferent between betting that the actual value will be above or below this estimate.

We can continue with this hypothetical betting exercise to obtain an estimate of the standard deviation. There are two approaches we can try. First we can try to determine the 25th and 75th percentile points. To do this we ask our expert to consider all the values below the median and try to find the point, call it Q_1, such that the UQ is equally as likely to be from 0 to Q_1 as between Q_1 and the median (we'll call the median Q_2 from now on). Again, we adjust Q_1 up or down until the expert is indifferent between choosing the interval $[0, Q_1]$ and $[Q_1, Q_2]$, given that the UQ is going to be below the median. We obtain Q_3 in a similar manner by considering values of the UQ above the median and adjusting Q_3 until the two intervals $[Q_2, Q_3]$ and $[Q_3, \infty]$ have about the same probability of containing the UQ.

At this stage, we have two internal consistency checks we should perform. First, if $Q_2 - Q_1$ does not approximately equal $Q_3 - Q_2$, we have violated our prior assumption of normality, which requires a symmetric probability distribution. If we cannot resolve this discrepancy, we must reject the normal distribution as a good representation of the probability distribution of the UQ and estimate a more general probability distribution. The second consistency check is to see whether our expert is indifferent between an even money bet that the UQ will be between Q_1 and Q_3 or that it will be outside this range ($[0, Q_1]$ or $[Q_3, \infty]$). If Q_1 and Q_3 do represent the 25th and 75th percentile points, the UQ is equally as likely to be between Q_1 and Q_3 as to be below Q_1, or above Q_3. If the values in the interval $[Q_1, Q_3]$ do not seem to contain half the probability, Q_1 and Q_3 should be adjusted until we are indifferent about which side of a 50-50 bet we would accept that the UQ will be between Q_1 and Q_3.

Assuming that we obtain estimates of Q_1 and Q_3 and that they are symmetrically placed on either side of the median, Q_2, so that the normality assumption is maintainable, we can estimate the standard deviation of our assumed normal distribution. The 75th percentile of the normal distribution is 0.675 standard deviations above the mean. (By symmetry the 25th percentile is 0.675 standard deviations below the mean.) Thus,

$$Q_3 - Q_2 = 0.675\sigma$$

or, for an estimate of the standard deviation,

$$\hat{\sigma} = \frac{Q_3 - Q_2}{0.675} . \tag{6-8}$$

An alternative estimating procedure for σ exploits the specific properties of the normal distribution. From a table of the cumulative normal distribution, we learn that the probability is 0.68 that the UQ will be within one standard deviation of the mean:

$$Pr(\mu - \sigma < UQ \leq \mu + \sigma) = 0.68.$$

Therefore the odds are about 2 to 1 that the UQ will be within 1σ of the mean. Our expert can try to determine a quantity, $\hat{\sigma}$, such that she is willing to give 2-to-1 odds that the UQ will be within $\pm\hat{\sigma}$ of the mean. That is, she should be indifferent between being betting \$1 to win \$2 that the UQ will be more than $\hat{\sigma}$ from the mean, and betting \$2 to win \$1 that the UQ will be within $\hat{\sigma}$ of the mean.

Naturally, we can try to estimate $\hat{\sigma}$ by both methods (estimating the quartiles and estimating $\hat{\sigma}$ directly) and hope that the two estimates come close to agreement. If not, we have to identify the source of the inconsistency, which may require us to abandon our normality assumption. Given consistent estimates of μ and σ, we can conduct other betting-type experiments, using our assumed normal distribution to verify that we are happy with its implications. For example, since 95 percent of the probability in a normal distribution is within 2σ of the mean, we should be willing to offer 19-to-1 odds that the UQ will fall in the range $[\hat{\mu} - 2\hat{\sigma}, \hat{\mu} + 2\hat{\sigma}]$ or to accept 19-to-1 odds that the UQ will fall outside this range.

ESTIMATING NON-NORMAL DISTRIBUTIONS

If the normal distribution is not a good representation of our subjective feelings about the distribution of possible outcomes of the UQ, we can try to estimate an arbitrary probability distribution. It turns out to be more convenient to estimate the cumulative distribution function than to estimate the more familiar probability mass function (for discrete variables) or density function (for continuous variables). Again we can start with the situation in which historical data are available.

Assume that we have sales data for our product from twelve previous periods and we are reasonably satisfied that the sales for the next period should come from the same distribution that generated these twelve observations. (Implicitly we must also assume that each of these twelve observations came from the same distribution, too.) Suppose that the sales (in thousands) for the previous twelve periods are given below:

Period	1	2	3	4	5	6	7	8	9	10	11	12
Sales	118	96	99	95	107	131	78	97	92	108	86	100

The mean of these twelve observations is about 100.6. To fit a probability distribution to these observations, we compute for every possible value of demand the historical relative frequency of demand for that value or less, as shown in Table 6-2. We can plot the data in Table 6-2 as shown in Exhibit 6-1. The dots

TABLE 6-2. Historical Cumulative Relative Frequency of Sales

Demand, x	0–77	78–85	86–91	92–94	95	96	97–98	99	100–106	107	100–117	118–130	131–∞
Percent of Periods with Demand ≤ x	0	$8\frac{1}{3}$	$16\frac{2}{3}$	25	$33\frac{1}{3}$	$41\frac{2}{3}$	50	$58\frac{1}{3}$	$66\frac{2}{3}$	75	$83\frac{1}{3}$	$91\frac{2}{3}$	100

on Exhibit 6-1 correspond to the historical cumulative frequency data in Table 6-2. The analyst can draw a smooth curve through these dots, as shown in Exhibit 6-1. This smoothed curve should serve as a good approximation to the cumulative probability distribution for sales. From the curve, one could compute the probability of sales being above, below, or between any specified values.

If an analytic representation of the approximate cdf of Exhibit 6-1 is desired, one could fit a high-degree polynominal (a fourth- or fifth-degree polynomial should be accurate enough) using numerical analysis programs. For a numerical

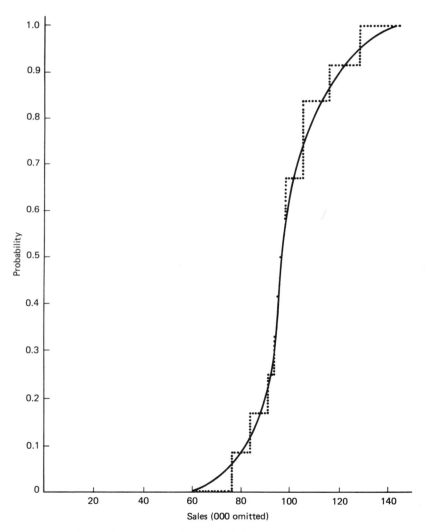

Exhibit 6-1   Cumulative Probability of Sales

analysis, one specifies a number of pairs of observations corresponding to a probability level and a sales figure—for example,

$$(0, 63), (0.1, 84), (0.2, 91), (0.3, 94.5), \ldots, (0.9, 122), (1.0, 140),$$

and attempt to find coefficients $a_0, a_1, \ldots, a_4$ such that the function

$$F(x) = a_0 + a_1x + a_2x^2 + a_3x^3 + a_4x^4$$

provides the best possible fit to the observation pairs. Such curve-fitting routines are available in many mathematical computing packages.

The cdf obtained in this manner will be most reasonable in the area where we have the most data. In our example this would be for sales between 90 and 110. The analyst must decide on the appropriate lower and upper sales limits for the bottom and top of the curve, since it is unlikely, with only twelve observations, that we will have seen the lowest or the highest possible sales figures. Thus, expert judgment will be most helpful for estimating the shape and location of the curve for cumulative probabilities less than 0.10 and greater than 0.90.

The final situation to consider is that in which historical data are not available, and we do not want to assume that a normal distribution is a reasonable approximation, so that we need to obtain the subjective judgment of an expert about the probability distribution. In this case, we use the iterative questioning and hypothetical betting procedure that we described to estimate the parameters of a normal distribution. We first estimate the median; we try to find a point, Q_2, such that the expert is willing to accept or offer an even-money bet that the sales or unknown quantity (UQ) will be below Q_2. Once we are happy with the choice of Q_2, we estimate the 25th and 75th percentiles (Q_1 and Q_3) as described previously. The only difference is that we don't require Q_1 and Q_3 to be located symmetrically about the median; $(Q_2 - Q_1)$ need not equal $(Q_3 - Q_2)$. Besides these three points we will need some estimates of the extreme values of the distribution. One possibility is to estimate the minimum and maximum values of the UQ. We could label the minimum value of the UQ as the 0 or 0.01 cumulative probability point and its maximum value as the 0.99 or 1.0 cumulative probability point. Since such extreme values may be difficult to identify, it is helpful to try to estimate the 10th and 90th percentile points, too. For the 10th percentile, we are interested in that value such that there is only 1 chance in 10 of obtaining a value of the UQ that low or lower. Equivalently, we should be willing to offer 9-to-1 odds that the UQ will be higher than this value. A third way of verifying this figure is to offer the expert the following bets:

Bet 1:   Prize is won if a red ball is drawn from an urn containing one red and nine white balls.

Bet 2:   Prize is won if actual value of UQ is less than estimated 10th percentile.

At the point when these two bets seem about equally valuable, the estimate can be considered satisfactory. After obtaining estimates of sales for cumulative probability levels of 0.01, 0.10, 0.25, 0.75, 0.90, and 0.99, we can plot these seven points on a graph, similar to Exhibit 6-1, and draw a smooth curve through these points. For an algebraic representation, we can fit a polynomial function through the estimated points using a numerical analysis algorithm.

These techniques represent only a basic background of how to obtain probability distributions for a UQ. More detailed procedures with illustrative examples are available in the literature.[1] But the described techniques should serve to indicate that, in general, it is possible to obtain probability distributions for a UQ and hence to conduct a formal probabilistic analysis based on this probability distribution. Naturally, knowledge of the degree of subjectivity in obtaining the underlying probability distribution should temper the analyst's enthusiasm for reporting probabilities of events to four significant digits.

MULTIPRODUCT C-V-P ANALYSIS UNDER UNCERTAINTY

It is relatively straightforward to extend the single-product C-V-P analysis under uncertainty to the multiproduct case. The analysis is greatly simplified if we can assume that the sales of all products follow a multivariate normal distribution. To perform even this analysis, however, we will need to know not only the mean and standard deviation of the distribution for each product but also the correlation in sales between all pairs of products. Having just struggled through a discussion of how to estimate the mean and standard deviation of the distribution of sales for a single product, one must be cautious about advocating a procedure extending such procedures to n products and, in addition, estimating $n(n - 1)/2$ correlation coefficients. Such estimation problems are rarely confronted by researchers who advocate the use of multivariate distributions theory for C-V-P analysis. Let us assume, though, for presentation purposes, that based on historical records and statistical analysis, the means, standard deviations, and covariances of the n-product multivariate normal sales distribution can be estimated.

Let X_i be the sales of product i, $i = 1, \ldots, n$. By assumption X_i is normally distributed. Let μ_i be the expected sales of product i and σ_i be the standard deviation. Thus, $X_i \sim N(\mu_i, \sigma_i)$, $i = 1, \ldots, n$.

In addition to the marginal sales distributions for the n products, we need to know the covariance of sales between each pair of products. We define

$$\text{Cov}(X_i X_j) \equiv E(X_i - \mu_i)(X_j - \mu_j) \tag{6-9}$$

$$\equiv \sigma_{ij},$$

---

[1] An excellent survey of these procedures is given in Spetzler and Von Holstein [1975]; see also Winkler [1967].

where $\sigma_{ii} = \sigma_i^2$, the variance of sales of product i,

$\quad\sigma_{ij} = \sigma_i\sigma_j\rho_{ij}$,

$\quad\rho_{ij} =$ the correlation coefficient between the sales of product i and product j.

By definition, $\rho_{ij} = \rho_{ji}$. The correlation coefficient, ρ_{ij}, is a number between -1 and $+1$. The value of $+1$ indicates perfect positive correlation between the two variables, 0 indicates statistical independence, and -1 indicates perfect negative correlation. In general, products in similar lines will have positive correlation coefficients as long as they are not substitutes for each other. When overall demand for steel increases, it is likely that each particular steel product group will have increased sales.

We let $p_i - b_i$ represent the profit contribution for product i. The profit random variable is therefore

$$\pi = \sum (p_i - b_i)X_i - \sum a_i. \tag{6-10}$$

Since, by assumption, $X_1, \ldots, X_n$ have a joint multivariate normal distribution, any linear combination of the X_i's will also have a normal distribution. In particular, π has a univariate normal distribution with parameters

$$E(\pi) = \sum_i (p_i - b_i)\mu_i - \sum_i a_i \tag{6-11}$$

and

$$\begin{aligned}
\text{Var}\,(\pi) &= E(\pi^2) - (E\pi)^2 \\
&= \sum_i \sum_j (p_i - b_i)\sigma_{ij}(p_j - b_j) \tag{6-12} \\
&= \sum_i (p_i - b_i)^2\sigma_i^2 + 2\sum_{i \neq j}\sum (p_i - b_i)(p_j - b_j)\sigma_i\sigma_j\rho_{ij}.
\end{aligned}$$

EXAMPLE OF MULTIPRODUCT C-V-P ANALYSIS UNDER UNCERTAINTY

We can illustrate the role of such algebraic manipulations through a simple numerical example. Consider a company presently marketing a single product with the following characteristics:

$$(p_1 - b_1) = 4,$$

$$a_1 = 400,000,$$

$$X_1 \sim N(110,000, 10,000).$$

From these figures, we readily determine that

$$\pi \sim N(40{,}000, 40{,}000).$$

Expected profit is \$40,000 and, since the expected profit is one standard deviation above zero, the probability is 0.84 that the product will at least break even. The company is considering adding to its product line a second product that will take some sales from the first product because it is a lower-price substitute. The second product has the following characteristics:

$$(p_2 - b_2) = 3,$$

$$a_2 = 50{,}000,$$

$$X_2 \sim N(50{,}000, 5{,}000),$$

but if it is marketed, the sales distribution of product 1 will shift downward to

$$X_1 \sim N(85{,}000, 8{,}000).$$

(Product 2 cannot be marketed without product 1. The relatively small fixed expenses associated with introducing product 2 arise from sharing existing production facilities of product 1.)

With the two products being marketed together,

$$E(\pi) = (p_1 - b_1)E(X_1) + (p_2 - b_2)E(X_2) - (a_1 + a_2)$$

$$= 4(85{,}000) + 3(50{,}000) - (400{,}000 + 50{,}000)$$

$$= 40{,}000.$$

Thus, introduction of the second product does not change the expected profit for the firm.

$$\text{Var}(\pi) = (p_1 - b_1)^2 \text{ Var}(X_1) + (p_2 - b_2)^2 \text{ Var}(X_2)$$

$$+ 2(p_1 - b_1)(p_2 - b_2) \text{ Cov}(X_1, X_2)$$

$$= (16)(8{,}000)^2 + 9(5{,}000)^2 + 2(4)(3)\sigma_1\sigma_2\rho_{12}$$

$$= (12.49)10^8 + (9.6)10^8\rho_{12}.$$

Therefore, the standard deviation of π, $\sigma(\pi)$, is given by

$$\sigma(\pi) = \sqrt{12.49 + 9.6\rho_{12}} \cdot 10^4.$$

If sales of the two products are perfectly correlated, $\rho_{12} = 1$ and

$$\sigma(\pi) = \sqrt{22.09} \cdot 10^4 = 47{,}000.$$

In this case, the mean of the profit distribution has remained the same but the standard deviation has increased so that there is no benefit from adding the second product to the line. In general, adding products whose sales are highly correlated with existing products (ρ_{ij} near $+1$), does little to reduce overall risk. Because of the reduction in sales to the more profitable product in this case, the risk actually increases.

If sales of the two products are independent, $\rho_{12} = 0$ and

$$\sigma(\pi) = \sqrt{12.49} \cdot 10^4 = 35,000,$$

and the overall risk has decreased. The largest acceptable value of ρ_{12} can be obtained by solving for the value for which the standard deviation in the one-product and two-product situations are equal:

$$\sqrt{12.49 + 9.6\rho_{12}} = 4,$$

or

$$\rho_{12} = \frac{16 - 12.49}{9.6} = 0.37.$$

In general, given values for contribution margins ($p_i - b_i$), fixed costs (a_i), product mean sales (μ_i), standard deviations of sales (σ_i), and correlation coefficients between product sales (ρ_{ij}), it is a straightforward exercise to obtain the univariate normal distribution for profits, π. Of the above parameters the correlation coefficients, ρ_{ij}, will be the most difficult to obtain, but unfortunately they are critical, as the above example indicates, in determining the standard deviation or risk of the profit distribution. Ideally, we prefer products with negative correlations so that the overall variance of profit will be reduced. Realistically, we will usually have products with positive correlations, and the best we can hope is to obtain relatively independent products with correlations near zero. By adding products with positive expected profit and correlations near zero, the ratio of standard deviation of overall profit to expected profit will decrease, thereby reducing overall risk to the firm.

UNCERTAINTY IN PRICE AND COST PARAMETERS

The discussion so far has only considered uncertainty in the quantity of sales, x, in the basic C-V-P equation. In general, there may be uncertainty in the selling price and the fixed and variable cost parameters, too. In this case, the profit random variable would be defined as

$$\pi = (P - B)X - A,$$

where the capital letters indicate that each variable is a random variable. This situation is much different from the situation in which sales, X, is the only uncertain quantity. For even if we make the simplifying assumption that $P - B$ and X can be modeled with a joint normal distribution, it is not true that π will be normally distributed. Sums of normally distributed random variables are normally distributed, but products of normal distributions are not normal. Thus, the distribution of π will be much more complex than the distribution of its component parts P, B, X, or A. Numerous articles have been written obtaining approximations to the distribution of π under these circumstances. A further complication arises because economic theory suggests that sales, price, and costs are not independent of each other. Therefore, besides having to be concerned with the complexity of the distribution of π, under the simplifying assumption that P, B, S, and A are assumed to be independent, one must realistically recognize that these various random variables are statistically interdependent.

One simplifying distributional assumption occurs if fixed costs are assumed known for certain and the variables $P - B$ and X are lognormally distributed. Since the product of lognormally distributed random variables is also lognormally distributed, we can in this situation know the distribution of π. But this is a restrictive distributional assumption, and one must still be concerned about modeling the interdependencies among variable cost, price, and sales.

For a more satisfying approach, the interdependencies are modeled directly by allowing price to be a linear function of output:

$$p = g - hx.$$

We can assume that output, x, is fixed but that g and h are random parameters, so that price is a random function of output. Alternatively, we can assume that management fixes price, p, and the firm sells a random amount of output x at this price. Under either approach, we can solve for the expected profit-maximizing output or price and obtain the distribution of profits, given this maximizing choice. These approaches are discussed and illustrated in Constantinides, Ijiri, and Leitch [1981].

DECISION-THEORY APPROACH TO C-V-P UNDER UNCERTAINTY

Our previous analysis in this chapter has been descriptive. We have modeled uncertainty in the underlying variables and attempted to obtain the probability distribution of profit. The analysis, however, has not been directed toward making specific decisions or specifically incorporating the formal model of uncertainty into an actual decision context. By studying the C-V-P analysis under uncertainty in the context of a formal decision problem, we can obtain some real insights into the value of a formal representation of the uncertainty in sales.

We consider our initial problem of a single product with known price and costs but uncertain demand. Recall our numerical example in which $p = 12$, $b = 8$, $a = 400,000$, and $X \sim N(102,500, 20,000)$. The expected profit from marketing this product is $10,000 and the probability of at least breaking even is 0.55. Suppose the manager is an expected-value decision maker who will market the product if the expected profit exceeds zero. In this case, the product will be marketed even with the relatively high (0.45) probability of not breaking even.

We can, however, extend the analysis to obtain further insights on whether to produce or not produce this product. With uncertain sales we have to be careful in specifying the production decision. For illustrative purposes, we will make the simplifying assumption that if we decide to produce the product, we are able to adjust the production schedule so that production exactly equals sales. This avoids transforming the problem from its current two-action form (produce or don't produce) to a more complex version in which the action is a continuous variable (the optimal amount to produce given an uncertain sales forecast). Technically, we will be solving what is called the "Wait-and-See" problem in which, once we enter the market, we learn sales and then produce. The more complex problem, which we discuss briefly later, is the "Here-and-Now" problem, in which we must choose a production amount first and then observe sales. This latter situation is well known in the decision theory literature as the "Newsboy Problem."

With the Wait-and-See approach, we can compute the opportunity loss associated with the act of marketing the product. The opportunity loss is the difference between the reward under the best possible action the manager could have taken, given the outcome or realization of the random variable, and the reward from the action that the manager actually did take. In this example, if sales exceed 100,000 units, the product will have covered its fixed costs and made a profit. Therefore, following our decision rule of marketing a product if its expected profit is positive, there is no opportunity loss if sales turn out to exceed 100,000 units. Under these circumstances, we took the best action possible and we have no regret about our decision. Though we would prefer higher sales to lower sales, by assumption the amount of sales is random and beyond our control. Our only decision is whether or not to market the product, and as long as sales exceeded 100,000 units we took the best possible action.

The situation is quite different if sales are less than 100,000 units. In this case we have lost money by marketing the product and have suffered an opportunity loss. This opportunity loss is measured against our alternative action, that of not marketing the product, which is the optimal action (ex post) if sales are less than 100,000 units. Formally, our profit (we will call a loss a negative profit) from marketing the product when sales are less than 100,000 units is given by

$$\pi = 4x - 400,000, \qquad x < 100,000.$$

The opportunity loss is the difference between this actual loss and the minimum loss (or maximum reward) from following the optimal action when sales are less than 100,000 units. In this case the optimal action is to not market the product, which results in a minimum loss of 0. (In general, there could be an actual loss associated with abandoning or discontinuing a product line. We have not included such a cost in our simple model.) The opportunity loss when sales are less than 100,000 is, therefore, the difference between minimum loss of 0 and the actual loss of $4x - 400,000$.

We can summarize this analysis by defining the opportunity-loss function:

$$\text{OL} = \begin{cases} 400{,}000 - 4x, & x \le 100{,}000, \\ 0, & x > 100{,}000. \end{cases}$$

EXPECTED OPPORTUNITY LOSS

We can proceed to compute the expected opportunity loss (EOL) by integrating the opportunity-loss function with respect to the normal density function of sales. Graphically this is represented in Exhibit 6-2. To obtain the expected opportunity loss, the OL function is multiplied (point by point) by the height of a normal density function with mean 102,500 and standard deviation 20,000 and summed over all values of sales (x):

$$\text{EOL} = \int_{-\infty}^{100{,}000} [400{,}000 - 4x] f_N(x \mid 102{,}500, 20{,}000)\, dx$$

$$+ \int_{100{,}000}^{\infty} [0] f_N(x \mid 102{,}500, 20{,}000)\, dx,$$

where

$$f_N(x \mid \mu, \sigma) = \frac{1}{\sqrt{2\pi}\,\sigma} \exp\left[-\frac{(x - \mu)^2}{2\sigma^2} \right]$$

is the density function for a normally distributed random variable with mean μ and standard deviation σ. By making the substitution

$$z = \frac{x - 102{,}500}{20{,}000}$$

to obtain a standardized normal deviate (mean = 0 and standard deviation = 1) we can rewrite the EOL as

$$\text{EOL} = -80{,}000 \int_{-\infty}^{-0.125} (z + 0.125) f_N(z \mid 0, 1)\, dz.$$

The function

$$L_N(D) = -\int_{-\infty}^{D} (z - D) f_N(z \mid 0, 1)\, dz, \tag{6-13}$$

called the *normal loss integral*, shows up frequently when one is computing expected losses in two-action problems with linear loss functions and normal probability distributions. Through some algebraic manipulation we can rewrite this integral as

$$L_N(D) = D F_N(D) + f_N(D), \tag{6-14}$$

where $F_N(\cdot)$ is the cumulative distribution function and $f_N(\cdot)$ is the probability

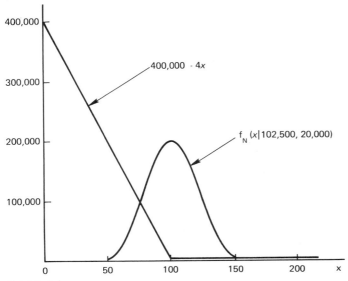

Exhibit 6-2

density function of a standardized random variable. For convenience, the function $L_N(D)$ has been tabulated (see Appendix Table C). For our example, $D = -0.125$. To use the table, we always look up the entry corresponding to the absolute value of D. For $D = 0.125$, we interpolate in Appendix Table C to obtain $L_N(0.125) = 0.34$. Thus the expected opportunity loss in our problem is

$$\text{EOL} = 80{,}000 L_N(0.125) = \$27{,}200.$$

We can obtain this result directly by defining

$$d = \text{absolute value of the slope of the opportunity-loss line}$$

$$= 4 \qquad (\text{since OL} = 400{,}000 - 4x \text{ for } x \leq 100{,}000)$$

and

$$D = \left| \frac{x_{BE} - \mu}{\sigma} \right| = \left| \frac{100{,}000 - 102{,}500}{20{,}000} \right| = 0.125.$$

Then the expected opportunity loss is

$$\text{EOL} = d\sigma L_N(D). \tag{6-15}$$

(Notice that $d\sigma = 80{,}000$, the term in front of the integral defining the EOL in the numerical example above.)

The expected opportunity loss is a function of three quantities:

$d =$ the slope of the opportunity-loss function. This slope equals $p - b$, the contribution margin associated with sales of each unit. Higher contribution margins per unit correspond to higher expected opportunity losses, since a given sales deviation will have a greater effect on profits.

σ = the standard deviation of the sales distribution. With a higher dispersion for sales, we have a greater probability for a low sales outcome and, therefore, for an opportunity loss to occur.

D = the distance, in standard deviation units, of the breakeven point from the mean of the sales distribution. As the breakeven point gets closer to the mean of the sales distribution, D gets smaller, and the possibility of an opportunity loss (actual sales below breakeven) increases.

EXPECTED VALUE OF PERFECT INFORMATION

The expected opportunity loss also represents the *expected value of perfect information (EVPI)*. The EVPI is the maximum amount we should be willing to pay for someone or some experiment that would reveal the true sales figure to us. We are willing to pay so much for this information because of the small margin of expected profit over breakeven and the large standard deviation of our sales estimate. We should recognize, however, that with probability 0.55, our source of perfect information will tell us that the true demand exceeds the breakeven volume of 100,000 units. This information may be reassuring and help us to sleep better at night, but it will not change our decision, since, in the absence of receiving this information, we would have marketed the product anyway. The information is useful only if it would change our decision, and this occurs with probability 0.45 when the true demand is revealed to be below the breakeven volume. The expected loss when demand is below breakeven is $27,200, and this is the maximum we should be willing to pay to avoid the possibility of a loss. Intuitively the EOL is a convenient summary of the downside risk for marketing the product.

EXPECTED VALUE OF SAMPLE INFORMATION

The EVPI of $27,200 is the most we would be willing to pay for perfect information. Market-test experiments and consumer surveys will provide good but not perfect information about demand. We might then ask how much we would be willing to pay for such imperfect information about demand. We can answer this question if we have an estimate of the standard deviation of the sales distribution after receiving the imperfect sample information. Such an estimate will be available if the information is obtained by a well-defined sampling process from the sales distribution. For example, we could survey individual retail outlets at random to determine how much of the product they are prepared to order. By use of statistical decision theory, we can predict the variance of the distribution after the sampling process. Details can be found in textbook chapters on decision-theory approaches to sampling from a normal distribution.[2]

As a specific example of how such information can be used, assume that after a survey of potential purchasers of our product, the standard deviation of the sales distribution will be halved from its initial value of 20,000 to 10,000. How much should we be willing to pay for such a survey? Before taking the survey, our best estimate of what the expected sales will be after the survey is still 102,500 units. Therefore we anticipate that after the survey, the sales distribution will be normal with mean 102,500 and standard deviation 10,000. To obtain the expected value of sample information (EVSI) we first need to compute the reduction in variance due to the sample,

$$S_*^2 = (20,000)^2 - (10,000)^2 = (3)10^8,$$

and compute the square root of this quantity:

$$S_* = 17,300.$$

Then

$$\text{EVSI} = dS_*L_N \left| \frac{X_{BE} - \mu}{S_*} \right| \tag{6-16}$$
$$= (4)(17,300)L_N(0.1445) = (69,200)(0.331) = \$22,900.$$

Hence we would be willing to pay up to \$22,900 for a survey that reduced the standard deviation of the sales estimate from the prior value of 20,000 to the posterior value of 10,000. This 50 percent reduction of standard deviation reduces considerably the chances of incurring large losses on the product. Before the survey, a low sales estimate, 2σ below the mean, would be $102,500 - 40,000 = 62,500$ units, resulting in a loss of \$150,000. After the survey, the comparable sales estimate, 2σ below the mean, would be 82,500 units, which results in a much smaller loss of \$70,000. This computation suggests why there is such a significant reduction in expected opportunity loss from the 50 percent reduction in standard deviation.

In general, if σ is large relative to the difference between the breakeven volume and expected sales, we would be willing to pay more for sample information. In this case, there is a reasonably high probability that the additional information will change our decision and, therefore, enable us to avoid a loss situation. If the ratio $(x_{BE} - \mu)/\sigma$ is high, then $L_N(D)$ will be low, so that the expected value of information will also be low. This occurs because we are unlikely to get a sample outcome that will cause us to change our decision.

---

[2] For example, "Decision Making and Sampling: The Normal Distribution," chap. 14 in W. A. Spurr and C. P. Bonini, *Statistical Analysis for Business Decisions*, rev. ed. (Homewood, Ill.: Richard D. Irwin, 1973); "Decision Theory," chap. 9 in R. L. Winkler and W. L. Hays, *Statistics*, 2d ed. (New York: Holt, Rinehart and Winston, 1975); and chaps. 20–21 in R. Schlaifer, *Introduction to Statistics for Business Decisions* (New York: McGraw-Hill, 1961).

The entire previous analysis was developed under the assumption that once the decision was made to produce the product, we could adjust production to exactly equal sales. This greatly simplified the analysis, since we did not have to worry about the effects of producing more or less than actual sales. If we must choose a production amount before we know sales (because of long lead times in production and delivery), we have to be concerned about balancing the costs of underproduction against the costs of overproduction. This problem is frequently called the Newsboy Problem (how many papers to order each day with uncertain daily demand for newspapers) or the Christmas tree problem. The problem is characterized by a product with essentially no value after the one time period in the analysis.

We can compute the optimal order quantity by an intuitive marginal-revenue, marginal-cost calculation that should be much simpler to follow than the formal approach, requiring differential and integral calculus, that is usually used to derive the optimal production decision (as, for example, in Shih [1979]). At the optimal order quantity, call it x^*, the expected revenue from producing one more unit should just equal the variable cost of producing this last unit. The expected revenue from the last unit produced equals the probability that this unit is sold multiplied by the selling price:

$$\Pr(X \geq x^*) \cdot p + \Pr(X < x^*) \cdot 0.$$

(If demand, X, is below x^*, the last item produced is not sold and hence yields zero revenue.) The quantity x^* is optimal if the expected revenue from producing the x^* unit just equals the variable cost of producing this last item.[3] Therefore x^* is the solution of

$$\Pr(X \geq x^*) \cdot p = b. \tag{6-17}$$

If the last item produced is less than x^*, the expected revenue will exceed the variable cost, while if the last item produced is larger than x^*, the expected revenue will be less than the expected price (since its probability of sale will be less than b/p).

We can rewrite the above equation as

$$[1 - \Pr(X < x^*)] \cdot p = b$$

or

$$\Pr(X < x^*) = \frac{p - b}{p}. \tag{6-18}$$

---

[3] For a discrete distribution, where precise equality of expected revenue and cost does not occur, x^* is defined as the largest quantity for which the expected revenue from the last item produced exceeds the variable cost.

Therefore, we can obtain the optimal production quantity by finding that point, x^*, for which the probability of sales below x^* just equals the ratio of contribution margin to price.

We illustrate this computation for our simple numerical example. The ratio of contribution margin to price is 1/3 [since $(p - b)/p = (12 - 8)/12$]. We need to find that quantity on the normal distribution of sales for which the probability is 1/3 that sales are less than this quantity. Referring to a table of the normal distribution, we find that one-third of the area occurs up to 0.43 standard deviations below the mean.[4] Our sales distribution has a mean of 102,500 and a standard deviation of 20,000, so that the optimal production quantity is computed as:

$$102,500 - 0.43(20,000) = 93,900 \text{ units.}$$

Thus, when production must occur before sales are revealed, and there is no salvage value for units produced but not sold, the production quantity that maximizes expected contribution margin is $x^* = 93,900$ units. At this production level the expected contribution margin is $375,600, which is below our fixed-cost level of $400,000.

At this stage, we can decide to not produce if all or most of the $400,000 fixed costs are escapable, since the expected contribution margin at the optimum production level is only $375,600. Of course, we have ignored the possibility that unsold units might still have a positive salvage value or could be sold in some future period. This possibility is explored in a problem at the end of this chapter. The message, however, from the analyses of both the Wait-and-See problem and the Here-and-Now (newsboy) problem is that obtaining the probability distribution for sales and profits is only the start of possible analyses, not the ultimate objective.

SUMMARY

We have explored the opportunities for C-V-P analysis when uncertainty exists in the demand for our product and we are able to specify a probability distribution for demand. Once the probability or cumulative distribution function for sales is known, we can easily obtain the probability distribution for profits and can compute quantities such as expected profits and the probability of achieving any targeted profit level (including breakeven). Knowing the covariance structure among multiple products, we can obtain a similar profit probability distribution for the multiproduct case.

A decision-theory approach enables us to provide additional characterizations of the production decision under uncertainty. If production can be adjusted to match actual sales (the Wait-and-See problem), we can compute the expected opportunity loss from marketing or not marketing the product. This expected opportunity loss also equals the expected value of perfect information, the max-

---

[4] See Appendix Table A.

imum amount we would be willing to pay for a perfect forecast of sales. We can, in addition, quantify the value of obtaining additional, but not perfect, information that will enable us to narrow the dispersion of the sales probability distribution. When the production decision must be made before actual sales are known (the Here-and-Now or newsboy problem), we can compute the optimal production quantity to maximize expected contribution margin. This optimal quantity corresponds to a critical fractile of the cumulative probability distribution function for sales, determined by the ratio of contribution margin to price.

PROBLEMS

6-1. Calculating Expected Profits and Probabilities (R. Manes)

The R & J Company is establishing a production line for Product Y. Fixed costs will be $120,000 per period. The selling price will be $1,250 and variable costs $500 per unit. The R & J sales manager expects sales to be 200 units per period but there is a 50/50 chance that sales will be between 175 and 225 units. Assume a normal distribution for the amount sold each period:

Required:

1. What is the expected profit and the standard deviation of the profit.
2. What is the probability of at least breaking even?
3. What is the probability of making at least a $15,000 profit?
4. What is the probability of a loss of $5,000 or more?

6-2. Using the Binomial Distribution for Calculating Profit Probabilities (R. Manes)

The VLSI Company makes high-density semiconductor components for the electronic industry. The production process involves a complex etching and baking process from which the yield of good units, that successfully pass a stringent quality control process, is only 65 percent. The 35 percent of units which fail are scrapped with no salvage value. Good units sell for $15 each. The variable costs for each unit started through the production process is $6 each. VLSI typically runs a batch of 20 units each through the etching and baking process. The fixed cost of each batch (electricity, set-up, etc.) is $40 per batch.

Required:

1. What is the expected profit and standard deviation of profit for a batch of 20?
2. How many successful units in a batch must emerge if VLSI will at least breakeven on the process?

3. What is the probability of breaking even?
4. What is the probability of achieving a profit of at least $50 per batch?

6-3. Uncertain Production of High and Low Quality Items (R. Manes)

Farian Associates makes high quality tubes for microwave applications. These tubes emerge from a common production process and are then tested for performance accuracy. Twenty (20) percent of the tubes are typically very accurate and are goldbanded; the other 80 percent are silverbanded.

Goldbanded tubes sell for $50 each; silverbanded tubes sell for $10 each. Each month 1,000 tubes are manufactured. Fixed costs are $6,000 per month and variable costs are $10 per tube.

Required:

1. What is the expected monthly profit?
2. How many goldbanded tubes must be produced to breakeven?
3. Estimate the mean and standard deviation of gold and silverbanded tubes?
4. What is the probability that Farian will not breakeven after a month of production?

6-4. Estimating a Subjective Probability Distribution

Choose an event with a numerical outcome in the future, of which you have some knowledge, and attempt to construct a cumulative probability distribution function (cdf) for this event. Stock market trading provides an excellent repetitive source of such events though sports fans might wish to estimate the number of runs scored in the major leagues in a week or the number of points scored by professional football teams each weekend (and Monday night).

For example, you could estimate a cdf for:

a. The change in the Dow Jones closing average each week.
b. The number of shares traded on the New York Stock Exchange in a day, or a week.
c. The number of shares traded for a popular stock such as AT&T, IBM, or Exxon.

Over a period of several weeks, you can record the sequence of actual outcomes for your event and see how closely the histogram of these events approximates the cdf you specified at the outset of the exercise.

6-5. Estimating a Sales Distribution from Monthly Data

The Furness Company is considering whether to retain production and sales of one of its mature products. In recent years, sales have been erratic and the company now believes it is losing money by continuing to market the product. The product has a selling price of $8 per unit and its variable costs are $4.50 per unit. Fixed costs associated with producing and distributing the product are $190,000 per month. These costs would be escapable were the product to be discontinued.

The Assistant Controller of Furness has been reviewing the sales figures from the past 12 months:

Month	Unit Sales	Month	Unit Sales
1	51,600	7	60,900
2	44,400	8	27,900
3	45,900	9	57,800
4	51,300	10	59,400
5	57,500	11	57,500
6	55,400	12	41,200

He learns that the sales distribution for next year will be about the same as that shown above. He decides to model the erratic monthly sales as coming from a normal distribution.

Required:

1. Using the above data, estimate the parameters of the normal distribution characterizing monthly unit sales.
2. Compute the breakeven point for the product.
3. What is the expected *annual* profit and the standard deviation of this profit? Should Furness continue to market this product?
4. What is the expected value of perfect information about monthly sales?
5. Suppose instead of assuming a normal distribution, the assistant controller decides to fit an arbitrary cumulative distribution function through the 12 monthly observations. Using the procedure outlined in the chapter (see Exhibit 6-1), fit a cumulative distribution function for these 12 observations. From this graph, estimate the probability of breaking even and compare your answer to that obtained when the normal distribution was assumed.

6-6. *Estimating a Sales Distribution from a Limited Sample*

The market research department of the Bevacqua Company has just completed a test market study of its new product, Bertil. It introduced the product in 100 stores and noted the average sales per store each month over a several month period.

During the test market, the average monthly sales per store was 56 units and the standard deviation of the monthly sales across the stores was 36 units.

Required:

1. Using this information, estimate the expected total monthly sales in full distribution through Bevacqua's 100,000 retail outlets and the standard deviation of this total monthly sales. Calculate a 95 percent confidence interval for total monthly sales.

2. What is the probability that monthly sales:
    a. will exceed 6,000,000 units?
    b. will be less than 4,800,000 units?

6-7. Choosing Between Two Machines When Annual Sales Are Uncertain

The Banaszak Company is attempting to choose a machine it wishes to rent for production of a new product. The material and variable overhead costs (not including machine-related costs) for the product are $1.50 per unit and the selling price will be $6.00 per unit.

Machine A rents for $100,000 per year and the labor and variable operating costs when using this machine will be $2.50 per unit. Machine B rents for $190,000 per year but its labor and variable operating costs would be only $1.75 per unit.

The choice between these two machines would be easy if the sales manager of Banaszak could produce a certain forecast for annual sales. Unfortunately, because this is a new product, the sales manager can do no better than to provide a subjective probability estimate of sales. He is willing to state that his beliefs are well represented by a normal probability distribution with a mean of 110,000 units. He feels that sales are equally likely to be between 100,000 and 120,000 units as to be outside this interval.

Required:

1. Which machine should the company rent?
2. Using this machine, what is the probability that the company will
    a. earn at least a $100,000 annual profit from introducing this new product?
    b. at least breakeven?
3. At what sales level is the company indifferent between renting either machine?
4. What is the expected value of perfect information in this situation?

6-8. Pricing and Uncertain Demand

Tina Beasley, the sales manager of the Greenwood Company, is attempting to determine the price of a new product. She is debating between two prices: either $25 or $30 per unit. Tina believes that at the $25 price, demand will be between 8,000 and 12,000 units for the year with any value between these two limits being equally likely. At the higher $30 price, Tina is less sure about the product's demand. She believes it could be as low as 4,000 units or as high as 10,000 units for the year, again with all points within this range being considered equally likely. The incremental fixed costs of the product are $75,000 and the variable cost of production is $15 per unit.

Required:

1. Compute the expected profit for the two prices. Which price leads to the highest expected profit?

2. Compute the probability of breaking even with each price. Which price leads to a higher probability of breakeven?
3. Which price would you recommend that Tina Beasley select?

6-9. Stochastic C-V-P Analysis with a Linear Demand Function*

The Ijiri Company is concerned with the production and pricing of a product that has uncertain demand and cost. Robert George, the controller, believes that the uncertain demand can be characterized by a linear demand equation with stochastic parameters:

$$\tilde{p} = \tilde{g} - hx$$

where $\tilde{g}$ is a normally distributed parameter,
        h is a known constant
        $\tilde{p}$ is a random price determined by the random variable $\tilde{g}$, and
        x is the sales volume.

The cost function $C(x)$ is also random and linear:

$$\tilde{C}(x) = \tilde{a} + bx;$$

that is the variable cost per unit, b, is known but the fixed cost is a random variable.

Mr. George wishes to select an output level, x, to maximize expected profits in the presence of the uncertainty about costs and price.

Required:

1. Show that the profit function can be written as:

$$\tilde{\pi}(x) = -\tilde{a} + \tilde{m}x - hx^2$$

where $\tilde{m} = \tilde{g} - b$.
2. Compute the value of x that maximizes expected profits, and the maximum expected profit level.
3. The actual values and distribution of the parameters for the Ijiri Company's product is given below:

		Estimate	
Parameter		*Mean*	*Standard Deviation*
$\tilde{a}$		\$10,000/month	\$2500
b		\$15/unit	0
$\tilde{g}$		\$30	6
h		\$.001/unit	0
$\tilde{m} = \tilde{g} - b$		\$15/unit	6

Compute the expected profit and standard deviation of profit at a monthly

---

* This example is adapted from George Constantinides, Yuji Ijiri, and Robert Leitch, "Stochastic Cost-Volume-Profit Analysis with a Linear Demand Function," *Decision Science* (June 1981).

output and sales volume of (a) 5,000, (b) 7,500, and (c) 10,000. Which output level maximizes expected profits?

4. For each of the three output levels, compute the probability that profits will exceed:
   (a) $-50,000$
   (b) 0 (Breakeven)
   (c) $50,000
   (d) $100,000
   Which output level should Robert George select?

6-10. Stochastic Multiproduct C-V-P Analysis*

The Simjohn Company has one main product line (Product 1) but is considering the addition of two new products (Products 2 and 3). Despite the newness of Products 2 and 3, they are expected to have the same expected sales as Product 1. Also their costs and prices are identical. The only difference is that because they are new products, Products 2 and 3 have higher variances. This information is summarized in the following table:

Product	Expected Sales (Units)	Standard Deviation of Sales (Units)	Contribution Margin Per Unit	Fixed Expense (000)
1	5,000	200	$1,250	$5,800
2	5,000	400	1,250	5,800
3	5,000	600	1,250	5,800

Sales for the three products are jointly normally distributed with the following (identical) correlation coefficients between each pair of products:

$$\rho_{12} = \rho_{13} = \rho_{23} = .7$$

Required:

1. Compute the expected profit and the standard deviation of profit for:
   a. Product 1 alone
   b. Product 1 and Product 2
   c. Product 1 and Product 3
   d. Product 1, 2, and 3
2. Using the profit distributions computed in Question 1 calculate, for each of the four cases,
   a. the probability of breakeven ($\Pr\{\pi \geq 0\}$)
   b. $\Pr\{\pi > \$500,000\}$
   c. $\Pr\{\pi > \$1,000,000\}$
   d. $\Pr\{\pi < \$-150,000\}$
   e. $\Pr\{\pi < \$-300,000\}$

---

* This problem is adapted from G. L. Johnson and S. S. Simik, II "Multiproduct C-V-P Analysis under Uncertainty," *Journal of Accounting Research* IX (Autumn 1971) 278–96.

3. Which of the four product combinations seems most desirable?
4. Repeat Steps 1–3 when $\rho_{12} = \rho_{13} = -.7$ and $\rho_{23} = .7$; that is Products 2 and 3 are negatively correlated with the existing product line but positively correlated with each other.
5. Is it preferable to have positively or negatively correlated products? Be specific by referring to your calculations in Parts 2 and 4.

6-11. Probabilities and Profit Analysis (CMA, adapted)

Racell Corporation is a food manufacturer which produces several different kinds of cereals. Krinkles, one of Racell's cereals, is packaged and sold in a 500 gram box. The filling equipment used to fill the boxes cannot be set precisely enough to guarantee that each box will contain exactly 500 grams. The volume by weight of cereal put in the boxes is normally distributed with a standard deviation of 12 grams. The filling equipment can be adjusted to vary the mean fill, but the standard deviation is constant. Management has specified that the filling equipment be set so that no more than three boxes out of 100 have less than 500 grams. If a box does contain less than 500 grams, the box is emptied and the contents are reentered into the filling process.

The manufacturer of the filling equipment being used by Racell has informed the company that an attachment is available which can improve the performance of the filling operation. The manufacturer estimates that the standard deviation of the filling operation for Krinkles can be reduced to 8 grams. The attachment would have to be replaced after 150,000 boxes were filled and would cost $1,500.

Racell sells 900,000 boxes of Krinkles annually. Krinkles are sold on the retail market for $1.35 a box; the wholesale price is $1.10 a box. The standard variable production cost is $.75 to produce 500 grams.

Required:

1. Calculate the mean fill setting required for Racell Corporation's filling equipment in order to meet the specifications set by management assuming the new attachment is not added.
2. Should Racell Corporation acquire the attachment which would reduce the standard deviation of the filling process from 12 to 8 grams? Support your decision with appropriate calculations.

6-12. Analyzing a New Product Introduction and the Value of Information

The Harris Company is considering the introduction of a new type of package for an instant dessert. The variable cost of the new package is identical to the old one, but there is a one-time fixed cost of $270,000 to modify the machinery to produce the new package. Management believes that the package will promote sales in the short run but is not certain exactly what the magnitude of the effect will be. The most likely guess is a sales increase of 2,000,000 units but there is one chance in six that the increase could be as low as 1,250,000 units and one chance in six that sales could increase by more than 2,750,000 units. There is only one chance in twenty that the sales increase would be less than 500,000 or greater than 3,500,000 units. The contribution margin is $.12 on each package of dessert sold.

Required:

1. What is the breakeven level of sales?
2. Analyze this decision including factors such as the probability of breaking even and the expected value of perfect information about the increase in sales.
3. Suppose a market survey could be taken that would reduce the range of uncertainty by 50 percent; that is, after the survey the width of the interval containing ⅔ of the probability would be 750,000 units instead of the current width of 1,500,000 units. What is the maximum amount the Harris Company should be willing to pay for such a survey?

6-13. *Probability of Breakeven and the Expected Value of Perfect Information*

The Lacy Company was deciding whether to increase its dealer allowances in an effort to give a short term boost to sales. One plan called for an expenditure of $250,000 in dealer rebates and local promotions. The sales increase from this program was expected to be about $2,000,000 and there was a ⅔ probability that the sales increase would be between $1.6 and $2.4 million. The probability was only about one chance in twenty that the sales increase would be outside the $1.2 to $2.8 million range. The contribution margin on the Lacy Company's products averaged 15 percent of sales revenue.

Required:

1. What is the breakeven level of sales increases required to repay the rebate and promotion program? What is the probability that the company will at least breakeven from this sales promotion?
2. Assuming that the Lacy Company is about to go ahead with its dealer allowance and promotion program, what is the maximum amount it should be willing to pay for a clairvoyant who guarantees to be able to predict the sales increase exactly?

6-14. *Newsboy Problem*

Ralph Smart is moonlighting on the weekend by selling, on a streetcorner, the early edition of the Sunday newspaper on Saturday night. Demand is generally good as many people wish to get an early start on house, car and furniture sales the next day and don't mind missing the more current news (especially the Saturday evening sports results) that is not available until the next morning's edition is printed. Even though demand is good, it is highly variable from week-to-week depending upon the weather and the amount of people traveling by Ralph's streetcorner that night. Ralph estimates that he is equally likely to sell any number between 50 and 100 papers in one night. The papers cost him $.40 each and their retail price is $.75. Ralph discards any papers unsold by midnight and goes home to sleep.

Required:

1. How many papers should Ralph order each Saturday to maximize his expected profit? What is the expected profit from following this policy?
2. Suppose that Ralph can make a deal to sell to a local newsstand for $.25 each any papers he has not yet sold by midnight. How does this change Ralph's optimal ordering policy and his expected Saturday night profit? (Hint: Try to derive the critical fractile with a salvage cost of s per unit. Note that with a salvage cost, the expected revenue when x units are ordered is:

$$p \cdot \Pr(X \geq x) + s \cdot \Pr(X < x).)$$

6-15. Optimal Production for One Period Horizon

The Fuqua Textile Company produces fabric for high-fashion designer clothing. This market segment is high margin but high risk since there is great uncertainty about whether a particular color or fabric will be popular. Even if a fabric is very successful in one year, it may be worthless the following year, since fashions change each year. The business is such that after initial consultations with designers and buyers, Fuqua must make a single production run of a particular fabric and hope that most or all of it will be sold during the relatively short buying season.

John Frenchy, the Production Manager for Fuqua, agonizes each year over this production decision. Some years he sells his production quantity very easily and wishes he had produced more. Other years, he is almost up to his eyeballs in unsold fabric that eventually has to be scrapped. This year he would like to use a more systematic procedure for deciding how much fabric to produce.

A new fabric style, Lavender Lace, looks to be a popular item this fall. John's best guess is that he could sell 5,000 yards of this fabric but it could be as low as 2,000 or as high as 8,000 yards. The odds are about 50/50 that demand will be between 4000 and 6000 yards. The price per yard is $8 and this does not affect the total demand since the material cost is a relatively low fraction of the final cost of the clothing. The buyers, however, will not pay more than $8/yard for the fabric because of the availability of alternative suppliers.

The variable cost to produce Lavender Lace is $2.50 per yard. Fixed costs to establish the Lavender Lace production run are $10,000.

Required:

1. Assuming that John Frenchy's sales estimates could be modeled by a normal probability distribution, what is the optimal production run for Lavender Lace?
2. What is the probability that Fuqua will at least breakeven if this production decision is implemented?

3. Is the optimal production quantity sensitive to the normality assumption? Fit a piecewise linear distribution function through the five fractiles specified by John Frenchy and compute the optimal production quantity from this distribution function.

Fractile	0	.25	.50	.75	1.0
Sales (Yards)	2000	4000	5000	6000	8000

6-16. Computing Optimal Production Under Uncertainty*

The Davison Press, Inc.

In early June 1961, the general manager of the Davison Press, Mr. Frank Davison, called in his sales manager, Mr. Leroy Jervis, to discuss a production order soon to be sent to the firm's printing department for the next year's winter specialty line of diaries and calendars. It was Davison's policy to process in one lot an entire season's supply of each item of the line, since the selling season was so brief that it was impossible to foresee running out of any item before it was too late to produce a second batch without jeopardizing the company's ability to meet other commitments. Each spring, the sales manager prepared sales forecasts for all the items of the following winter's specialty line, taking into account the quantity of the same and similar merchandise sold in previous years by Davison and its competitors, the number and the volume of business of the retailers expected to be carrying the Davison line in December, and the general economic outlook. Mr. Davison's ordinary practice had been to go over Mr. Jervis' estimates with him, make revisions by agreement, and then produce a quantity equal to the forecast sales of each item.

Background

The Davison Press had been founded in 1921 in Cleveland as a small printing job shop, selling mainly to local small businesses. Letterheads, cards, price lists, and catalogs were produced to meet orders solicited by salesmen who visited nearby firms. During the next several years, Davison did an increasing trade in special-purpose forms designed in collaboration with large manufacturers to meet their special control and record-keeping needs. Acqusition of modern, high-speed machinery in the late twenties made possible the speedy and inexpensive handling of a large volume of relatively small individual orders. Setup costs (which ordinarily account for more than half the production cost of such orders) were tightly controlled. Ambitious advertising brought in customers throughout the Midwest and revenue increased to several hundred thousand dollars per year, although competitive conditions held profit margins very low.

After barely surviving the Depression under the burden of debts contracted in

* Copyright © 1963 by the President and Fellows of Harvard College. Reproduced by permission. This case was prepared by Andrew S. Kahr under the supervision of Robert O. Schlaifer.

the purchase of the new equipment, Davison in the middle thirties sought a line of business that would tie its fortunes less tightly to the ups and downs of the business cycle, and this led to the firm's entry into the retail stationery field. Sample books were compiled and taken by salesmen to variety, drug, and department stores within a few hundred miles of Cleveland. Customers could order personalized letter paper and envelopes, making their own choice of design and paper stock and buying as few as 60 sheets. This division of the business became increasingly profitable just before and during World War II. It involved little selling cost or effort on the part of Davison, demanding only the accurate and efficient handling of orders.

After the war, attention was given to the marked seasonal character of the business. At that time, only a trickle of orders came in during the four summer months, and most of those orders were small ones. It was under these circumstances that the winter specialty line was marketed for the first time in 1951 by direct selling to the outlets that had been handling the sale of stationery. The line, originally consisting of two diaries and two appointment books, was a quick success. By 1960, sales of the line had grown to nearly $250,000 per year and were yielding a net profit of about $70,000.

Sales of the company's other lines, however, had also grown very rapidly during the decade of the 1950s. Distribution area and sales volume expanded in each succeeding year, and by 1960 Davison was marketing its goods throughout the eastern half of the country. Total sales of the firm that year were over $3,100,000, yielding a net profit of about $410,000, and the seasonal pattern in sales had virtually disappeared. In fact, overtime operation of most of the company's facilities had been necessary through a great part of 1960. Although a move to larger quarters was planned, it seemed clear that overtime operation would be called for continuously until early 1962; it was estimated that about 20% of all direct labor hours worked during the remainder of 1961 would be performed on overtime. Mr. Davison did not believe that he would have to actually refuse any orders or that the effort to obtain them should be slackened, but he did believe that it was important to estimate sales closely enough to avoid any serious overruns, since the loss arising from the printing of one diary or appointment book too many would be far greater than the profit which would be forfeited if one too few were printed to satisfy demand.

Jervis' Record and Recommendation

In the summer of 1958 the whole winter specialty line had been redesigned and Mr. Jervis had been hired as sales manager, with responsibility for all lines except the custom-designed business forms. During the past three years, the items in the winter specialty line had been as follows: No. 1 was a large (8 × 11), handsomely laid out diary, with simulated leather cover, selling at retail for about $7.50; No. 2 was a smaller (5 × 8) diary and daily appointment book, of somewhat less sumptuous appearance, retailing at around $3; No. 3 was a weekly memorandum book, with spaces for notations relating to each hour (9 through 4) and each day of the week, which sold for $1.75; and Nos. 4 and 5 were pocket diaries, one bound in leatheroid and the other in paper, selling for $1 and $0.65, respectively. Mr Davison felt that uniformity and continuity were better buying incentives than novelty, and the 1962 line was to differ from its predecessors only to the extent necessary to accord with the change in the calendar. In general, Mr. Davison was quite satisfied with the rate of growth of winter specialty sales; the greatest potential for future growth, he felt, was in other directions, but winter specialty production would keep the expanded facilities fully employed, and on high margin goods at that.

As regards sales forecasts, Mr. Davison felt that Mr. Jervis' record in predicting sales of the winter specialty line (Table 1) was amazingly good, much better than that of his predecessor and much better than Jervis' own record in predicting sales of stationery. But even though he was impressed with the small percentage error in Jervis' predictions, Mr. Davison had noticed that the predictions were frequently on the high side, where errors were more expensive; and he wondered whether the sales forecast should not be revised downward in determining the number of units to be ordered into production. His reasoning was that "producing a lot too few is no worse than producing a few too many."

Mr. Jervis disagreed strongly with this view. He pointed out that when a store or consumer wanted to buy an item and could not do so, bad will was likely to be created that would endure and make future selling more difficult. In the first place, he said, someone who bought a diary this year was far more likely to buy one next year than someone who did not; hence, failure to make a sale should be considered to entail a far greater loss than the forfeited profit on one diary. Furthermore, a store owner who was disappointed or annoyed by the situation might stop pushing the line or might even refuse to handle it at all. Therefore, Jervis concluded, it was actually *worse* rather than better to produce too little rather than too much. Because of the marked dissimilarity of the prices and uses of the various items in the line, it was unlikely that a person wishing to buy one of them would be willing to take another instead; he would buy a competitor's product or none at all.

Mr. Davison acknowledged that Jervis had made out a good case for a generous production order, but he argued that at least as good a case could be made out on the other side. For instance, many of those who bought diaries and appointment books used them only during the earliest months of the year and then neglected them, and such people could not be considered as likely sales prospects in the

TABLE 1. **The Davison Press, Inc. Winter Specialty Sales and Forecasts**
(Hundreds of units)

	No. 1	No. 2	No. 3	No. 4	No. 5
1959 estimate	82	199	388	174	585
Actual to 11/15	68	134	218	130	413
Actual total	82*	189	301	174*	584
1960 estimate	128	316	564	261	915
Actual to 11/15	88	236	370	162	673
Actual total	123	316*	552	225	915*
1961 estimate	136	320	589	273	972
Actual to 11/15	92	294	369	191	627
Actual total	134	320*	539	273*	892
1962 estimate	176	435	770	360	1,175

* Sales limited by stockout.

following year. It might even be claimed that if such a person had *wanted* to buy an item in 1962, he would buy one in 1963 only if he had *not* actually bought one in 1962; in these cases, no money except possibly a small amount of interest would be lost as a result of the undersupply. In addition, regular users of Davison products would almost surely buy their new books soon after these appeared on the market, from the first shipment their retailers received from Davison; and even when Davison did run out of stock, this never prevented filling the retailer's *initial* orders, virtually all of which were received before November 15.

As to the matter of goodwill, Davison said that the primary objective of the Press was not to increase the respect or affection it received from customers; this was a pleasant incident, not to be confused with practical, dollar-and-cents considerations. If goodwill implied potential for future profits, it should be considered; but if it referred to a state of mind not closely connected with willingness to buy, it should be ignored. In this instance, his judgment was that Jervis' case was overstated. Davison had enjoyed good relations with most of its present outlets over a period of some years, and most of them handled the lucrative stationery sales the year round. They would regard an inability to fill orders at the tag end of the season as entirely understandable and forgivable. After all, they were themselves conservative in the stocking policy, preferring as a rule to run out and have to reorder rather than have to scrap surplus or sell it at a loss. For a retailer to hide the diaries behind the counter next year would be stupidly self-destructive; the retailer had more to lose by this than Davison. The retailer's profits from the Davison line were sufficient, even if lower than they might be, to dissuade him from trying to switch to a competitor, and in any case there was no reason to think that either of Davison's chief competitors in the field of diaries and appointment books was superior to Davison as regards out-of-stocks. On balance, Mr. Davison felt that while the total loss resulting from insufficient stock was perhaps a little greater than the foregone immediate profit, the difference was almost certainly negligible. He was satisfied to treat it as zero; and if this proved wrong, to learn from the experience. This seemed better than to assume the contrary and never be able to check the validity of the assumption. Damage done would not be permanent, especially on the retailer level, where it could be excused if necessary as a single year's aberration rather than the result of any change of policy. And since overtime was being incurred this year but would probably not be needed next year, the present seemed an unusually good time to try the experiment of producing below Jervis' sales forecast.

Jervis did not contest further the matter of "goodwill" losses, but he reacted quite strongly to Davison's mention of costs. "It's no wonder these diaries look expensive when the boys down in accounting are finished with us; we're charged for everything from the watchman's salary to the paint on the back of the fence. It's ridiculous; they could be printed in gold ink for the costs that they've got on the books. When are we going to get a fair deal on this? And another thing, why is our work charged at the overtime rate just because the company was making business forms before it got into the diary business? Davison Press makes a much higher profit margin per press hour on diaries than it does on forms and catalogs; if we had to choose between making diaries and making forms, we would certainly choose diaries. It's the *forms* that should be charged the overtime rate. The only real expense in producing more diaries is material and labor; but instead of recognizing this, accounting is even charging diaries with depreciation on the presses that are going to be sold for scrap when we move next year. And anyway, even if the costs *were* figured right, I don't understand this business of producing some number other than the number we expect to sell. Just because one kind of mistake is cheaper than another, why commit one of the cheaper mistakes on purpose?''

What Are the Costs?

Before trying to make up his own mind about Jervis' last question, Mr. Davison decided to clear up the cost question, and with this in view he asked Mr. Herman Lewis, his chief accountant and assistant treasurer, to prepare a detailed cost breakdown for each item of the winter specialty line, showing how much it would cost per unit to produce a lot of the size recommended by Jervis for each item. The next day, Mr. Lewis came to Mr. Davison's office with the information requested of him (Table 2). Mr. Davison raised the questions brought up by Mr. Jervis the previous day, with particular emphasis on the matter of overtime charges and undue overhead allocations, and Mr. Lewis vigorously defended his department's methods and results.

In the first place, he said, every penny of expense incurred by Davison had to be attributed or allocated to some product. "The reason why there is a back fence to be painted and a janitor to be paid is that we are making and selling printed pieces of paper of one kind or another. These costs wouldn't exist if we weren't here doing printing, and they are just as much a part of the total cost of the work we do as electricity and labor are. They appear on our income statement, and unless the prices we set and the revenue we receive takes account of them, we will be operating in the red and going broke. Nobody is smart enough to know what part of some of these overhead charges should be viewed as being due to production of business forms, which to stationery, and so forth, and I don't pretend that we can calculate the precise cost of each piece of paper that we sell. But the total amounts we allocate come from an overhead budget that has been very carefully prepared, and the formulas we use in allocating these amounts are consistent, reasonable, and fair. The manufacturing overhead we incur in the plant is divided among our products in proportion to direct-labor hours because the reason we have a plant is so that direct labor can be performed. Executive salaries and general office expenses are charged in proportion to what it costs us to make the products, the same as we would do if we bought the products outside, except, of course, that any expense that we can trace directly to a particular line, like the salaries of the stationery salesmen, is charged to that line. As to depreciation of buildings and equipment, it appears on our income statement as a cost and it *is* a cost, just the same as the ink we use up is a cost, whether we buy it in the same period we use it or not. Our method of cost accounting is entirely modern and accepted. Naturally, we'd all like to see the costs as low as possible; I don't blame Jervis for that. But he should see the effects beyond his own department. If we report a lower cost for one of his babies, we'll have to pile it onto someone else's, and he'll complain the same way that Jervis does now. I can't see that there's a suggestion here for a better *system* than the present one—just one fellow trying to get an advantage over someone else.

Mr. Lewis felt less certain about the proper handling of the overtime charges.

TABLE 2. The Davison Press, Inc. Estimated Costs for 1962 Winter Specialty Production (Dollars per 100)

Row	Account	No. 1	No. 2	No. 3	No. 4	No. 5
1	Setup labor	4.38	1.34	0.69	0.31	0.31
2	Pressroom labor	5.03	1.97	1.01	0.79	0.79
3	Total direct labor	9.41	3.31	1.70	1.10	1.10
4	Supervisory labor	3.51	1.23	0.63	0.41	0.41
5	Overtime premium	6.46	2.27	1.16	0.76	0.76
6	Payroll taxes, etc.	2.33	0.82	0.42	0.27	0.27
7	Setup materials and plates	12.14	4.08	2.13	0.82	0.82
8	Pressroom materials and stock	25.33	13.40	4.35	2.11	2.11
9	Power	0.78	0.64	0.61	0.42	0.42
10	Press maintenance	0.47	0.19	0.11	0.09	0.09
11	Press depreciation	2.46	0.98	0.51	0.40	0.40
12	Other plant overhead	27.67	9.73	5.00	3.23	3.23
13	Binding, fixed charge	3.41	1.15	0.65	1.11	0.08
14	Binding, per 100 units bound	81.17	29.94	20.25	12.63	3.23
15	Total manufactured cost	175.14	67.74	37.52	23.25	12.92
16	Winter specialty S and A	40.81	15.78	8.74	5.44	3.01
17	General overhead	128.20	49.59	27.46	17.09	9.46
18	Total cost	344.15	133.11	73.72	45.78	25.39
19	Price to dealers	485.00	187.50	105.00	65.00	37.50

NOTES

Row

1, 7   Total cost divided by estimated units produced.
4   37.3% row of 3.
5   50.0% of rows 3 and 4.
6   12.0% of rows 3, 4, and 5.
11   Straight-line depreciation allocated to products by press hours.
12   294% of row 3; includes insurance and property taxes.
13, 14   Binding done by outside contractor who charges a fixed amount for each style plus an amount proportional to number of units produced.
16   23.3% of row 15.
17   73.2% of row 15.

Historically, of course, the winter specialty line had been taken on mainly to keep the presses running during the slack season; business forms were the bread-and-butter line. Hence, on those few occasions prior to 1961 when overtime had been necessary during the summer, its cost had been charged to winter specialties. It was true that diary sheets and appointment-book pages were produced steadily throughout the working day (during both regular and overtime hours), whereas business-form orders, which often could be run off in only a couple of hours of press time, might be printed at any time, regular or not. The plant usually ran with a reduced work force after the regular closing time; in particular, the setup men almost never worked overtime. It would be possible to calculate costs on the basis of actual press-hour charges (orders run wholly or partly after 5:30 being charged at time and a half); or the costs could be averaged out and the average rate charged to all lines alike whether run on overtime or not. Basically, Mr. Lewis felt that this was a policy question that should be settled by Mr. Davison rather than by himself.

REFERENCES

CONSTANTINIDES, GEORGE, YUJI IJIRI, and R. A. LEITCH, "Stochastic Cost-Volume-Profit Analysis and a Linear Demand Function," *Decision Sciences,* June 1981.

FERRARA, WILLIAM L., JACK C. HAYYA, and DAVID A. NACHMAN, "Normalcy of Profit in the Jaedicke-Robichek Model," *The Accounting Review* XLII (July 1967), 516–25.

HILLIARD, JIMMY E., and ROBERT A. LEITCH, "Cost-Volume-Profit Analysis Under Uncertainty: A Log Normal Approach, *The Accounting Review* L (January 1975), 69–80; also, "A Reply," *The Accounting Review* LI (January 1976), 168–71.

JAEDICKE, ROBERT K., and ALEXANDER A. ROBICHEK, "Cost-Volume-Profit Analysis Under Conditions of Uncertainty," *The Accounting Review* XXXIX (October 1964), 917–26.

JOHNSON, GLENN L., and S. STEPHEN SIMIK, "Multiproduct C-V-P Analysis under Uncertainty," *Journal of Accounting Research* IX (Autumn 1971), 278–86.

LAU, AMY HING-LING, and HON-SHIANG LAU, "CVP Analysis under Uncertainty—A Log Normal Approach: A Comment," *The Accounting Review* XLI (January 1976), 163–67.

LIAO, MAWSEN, "Model Sampling: A Stochastic Cost-Volume-Profit Analysis," *The Accounting Review* L (October 1975), 780–90.

SHIH, WEI, "A General Decision Model for Cost-Volume-Profit Analysis Under Uncertainty," *The Accounting Review* LIV (October 1979), 687–706.

Estimating Probability Distributions

HAMPTON, J. M., P. G. MOORE, and H. THOMAS, "Subjective Probability and its Measurement," *Journal of the Royal Statistical Society,* Ser. A, CXXXVI (1973), 21–42.

SPETZLER, C. S., and C.-A. S. STAEL VON HOLSTEIN, "Probability Encoding in Decision Analysis, *Management Science* XXII (November 1975), 340–58.

WINKLER, R. L., "The Assessment of Prior Distribution in Bayesian Analysis," *Journal of the American Statistical Association* LXII (September 1967), 776–800.

COST ANALYSIS AND PRICING DECISIONS

7

Product pricing policies are among the most important and most difficult decisions made by managers. These decisions will affect the firm's scale of operation, its product mix, and its long-run profitability. While standard economic theory suggests a simple answer to price determination, the complexity and uncertainty inherent in the markets of most firms make the economic maxim of equating marginal revenue with marginal cost only an extremely rough guide to pricing policy.

Extensive discussions on pricing policy can be found in textbooks on managerial or business economics and marketing, so that a complete discussion of this subject can scarcely be justified in an accounting textbook. But since pricing recommendations usually require estimates of cost behavior, it is important for us to consider the role of costs in determining prices. In this chapter we will first discuss traditional economic models of pricing decisions and next analyze the common practice of cost-plus pricing. We then consider a synthesis of these two views, in which price is set to achieve a targeted return on investment. The chapter will conclude with some strategic and still controversial views on pricing behavior.

ECONOMIC PROFIT-MAXIMIZING PRICING

If the firm is selling a standard commodity, actively traded in commodity markets, then the firm will almost surely be a "price taker," accepting the price given in the marketplace. In this situation the firm may need to determine its scale of operation, its production technology, or whether to be in this market at all, but it will not have to worry about how to set price. This function will be efficiently carried out in the marketplace.

Usually, however, a firm has some flexibility in its pricing decisions and has the option of trading off higher prices against lower output. The firm's objective is to determine the combination of price and output that maximizes total contribution margin. Normally this is achieved by equating marginal revenue with marginal cost. But if the cost or demand functions are discontinuous, a more detailed analysis is required. We illustrate this point with the following example.

The Bruce Company has been selling its only product at a price of $2 each. Recent increases in costs have caused the managers to contemplate a price increase, but they decide first to analyze the relevant factors. The manager of the market research department has been studying the prices and the quantities sold of this and related products and has tentatively formulated a schedule of price and demand:

Price Per Unit	Monthly Unit Sales
$2.00	100,000
2.05	90,000
2.10	80,000
2.15	70,000
2.20	60,000
2.25	50,000

The manager points out that this schedule can be represented as a demand curve:

$$p = \$2.50 - 0.005x,$$

where x is monthly sales (in thousands). The firm's controller has prepared the following schedule showing how current costs vary with the level of monthly output.

	Operating Costs	
Monthly Output (Units)	Fixed Cost	Variable Cost of Last Unit Produced
$\leq$ 50,000	$20,000	$1.20
50,001– 60,000	22,000	1.25
60,001– 70,000	25,000	1.30
70,001– 80,000	30,000	1.40
80,001– 90,000	30,000	1.45
90,001–100,000	40,000	1.50

The fixed-cost increases are caused by increases in supervisors, added shifts, and increased maintenance as output expands. The variable-cost increases are caused by shift premiums, increased overtime, and use of less skilled labor and less efficient machinery. While the price seems well above variable cost in the relevant range, the appropriate evaluation is to compare the incremental revenue from selling additional units with the incremental cost of producing them. The marginal revenue is obtained by differentiating the total-revenue function:

$$MR = \frac{d}{dx} TR = \frac{d}{dx} (2.50 - 0.005x)x = 2.50 - 0.01x.$$

The marginal-cost function is more complicated because of the jumps introduced by the semifixed costs.

Because of the semifixed costs in this problem, the traditional optimizing rule of equating marginal revenue with marginal cost is not a good one to follow. The optimality of setting marginal revenue equal to marginal cost occurs when the two cost functions are well behaved—marginal revenue should be declining and marginal cost increasing, with both functions being continuous. In this case, the marginal revenue function (MR = 2.50 − 0.01x) has these properties but the marginal-cost function is discontinuous owing to the jumps in fixed costs. Therefore, the optimum price-output combination is most easily obtained by tabulating the incremental revenues and incremental costs associated with 10,000-unit increases in volume. It is likely, but not necessary, that the optimum output will be at a point just before an increase in fixed costs occurs. It will still be necessary to verify that the marginal revenue at this point exceeds the variable costs. The computation of incremental revenues and costs is presented below.

Monthly Output (Units)	Total Revenues	Incremental Revenues	Incremental Costs	Net Contribution Margin
50,000	$112,500	$112,500	$80,000	$32,500
60,000	132,000	19,500	14,500	5,000
70,000	150,500	18,500	16,000	2,500
80,000	168,000	17,500	19,000	− 1,500
90,000	184,500	16,500	14,500	2,000
100,000	200,000	15,500	25,000	− 9,500

The fixed-cost increments make this a tricky computation. Proceeding mechanically, one could see the negative incremental contribution of $1,500, because of the fixed-cost increase when expanding output from 70,000 to 80,000 units, and conclude that the optimum output was at 70,000 units. But once output reaches 70,000 units, there are no further jumps in fixed costs until the 90,000-unit level is reached. Expanding output from 80,000 to 90,000 units produces a positive incremental contribution margin of $2,000, which more than covers the $1,500 loss incurred when going from 70,000 to 80,000 units. Also, the marginal revenue at an output level of 90,000 units is

$$MR = 2.50 − 0.01(90) = \$1.60,$$

which exceeds the variable cost of $1.45. Therefore, profits are maximized for the Bruce Company at an output level of 90,000, which is achieved by a price of

$$p = 2.50 − 0.005(90) = \$2.05.$$

This is only a small increase from the previous price of $2 and is optimal despite what may have happened to costs recently. Probably the price was too high previously and the firm was selling fewer items than was desirable.

The computation to obtain the price-output combination that maximizes net contribution margin is not difficult even when there are discontinuities in the revenue or cost functions. With no discontinuities, the marginal-revenue, marginal-cost equality is even simpler to compute. Why then is this method of pricing not observed more often in practice? The difficulties can be grouped into two categories. First, it is generally not easy to estimate the demand curve for a firm's products. Second, the appropriate marginal-cost curve can rarely be obtained from the firm's accounting records and can be computed only after considerable analysis, judgment, and, finally, even arbitrary allocations. We discuss each set of problems in turn.

The simple economist's model of demand and price is valuable because it focuses managers' attention on the external environment in which products must be sold. It forces the managers to think not just about what it will cost to manufacture a product but also about what consumers may be willing to pay for the product. In practice, however, actual demand curves for products are not readily available. Techniques for estimating them have been developed and have been applied by skilled practitioners for some standard products such as agricultural commodities, automobiles, housing, and alcoholic beverages. These techniques, or at least their published versions, have been applied mostly to industry data rather than used to estimate the demand curves for a particular company. The techniques require a fair amount of econometric modeling skill to insure that all relevant variables are included in the analysis and that nonstationarities and simultaneous-equation considerations are controlled for in the analysis. Certainly, for major categories of a firm's products (such as automobiles for General Motors, cigarettes for Philip Morris), it would be possible and even reasonable to attempt to estimate demand relationships. But for firms with thousands of different individual products, involving complementarity and substitutability relationships, we cannot expect to have demand curves for each product.

In addition, when constructing a demand curve at the firm rather than industry level, one would need to model the reaction of competitors to price changes by a single firm. Since the present state of oligopoly theory is not one of the proudest achievements of the economics profession, these competitive reactions are not easily anticipated or modeled. Even at the industry level, competitive reactions by producers of substitute products could upset the calculations of demand forecasts if major price changes were to be implemented. Further complications arise because price is only one factor that contributes to a purchase decision. Considerations such as advertising and promotion, distribution, service, delivery, and credit terms differ among firms and over time, so that studies looking solely at price will see only a portion of all the factors that contribute to a product's sales. None of these difficulties is insuperable. It is possible to perform a defensible study to estimate the demand for a firm's products. But the study could be complex and costly. Therefore, we should not be surprised if many firms choose to make pricing decisions without having constructed demand curves for most of their products.

The second consideration reducing the applicability of the marginal-revenue, marginal-cost paradigm is the difficulty of constructing the appropriate marginal-cost curve. When performing cost-volume-profit analyses, we focused on short-term considerations. We assumed that the capacity resources of the firm were given, and we would consider accepting any order whose price covered short-term variable costs (plus increments in fixed costs). This short-term policy, how-ever, is not viable for the firm's main product lines. In order for a product to be profitable over the long run it must cover not only its short-term variable costs but also

1. The costs of the capacity resources required for this product.
2. The increased overhead costs, both factory and general adminis-trative, that accompany increases in the activity level of the firm.
3. The cost of capital, including fixed resources and working capital, associated with the product.

Factor 1, the costs of capacity resources, is usually calculated by accountants as the depreciation on the fixed assets used in the manufacture of the product. But the depreciation schedule derived for financial reporting purposes is unlikely to be a good estimate of the decline in value of the assets through use or the passage of time. While economists are usually not very precise about their notion of depreciation, measurements on decline in value would be considered more relevant than allocations of historical costs. Other difficulties with measuring the use of fixed assets or any capacity resources (including supervision) arise from joint production. Many capacity resources are used to produce a variety of dif-ferent products, including intermediate products that are processed further into different final products. The allocation of capacity costs to the diversity of prod-ucts that use these resources can be difficult and, in some instances, essentially arbitrary. A final consideration is that the use of the capacity resources of the firm will preclude the production of other products on these resources, so that there is an opportunity cost associated with the production of the existing product line. Thus, measurement of factor 1 poses challenging problems for estimating economic depreciation, allocating joint costs, and measuring opportunity costs.

Normally, fixed factory overhead and general administrative costs (factor 2) are not considered relevant to product-mix and pricing decisions. Over extended periods of time, however, these costs will be influenced by the level of activity in the firm. Thus, these costs are part of the long-run cost of production. It will be difficult to get precise measurements of how "fixed" overhead costs vary in the long run with the output level of the firm, but some estimate needs to be made so that pricing decisions can be made for the firm's principal products that include these costs as part of the firm's long-run marginal-cost function.

The return on capital in factor 3 is called a profit by accountants but is considered a cost by economists—a cost also to be included in the long-run marginal-cost function. The cost of capital is applied both to the fixed or long-term assets used in the production process and to the investment in net working capital (accounts receivable plus inventory less accounts payable) required for the product. This capital cost is the opportunity cost of the invested capital for the product, and it must also be covered by the firm's pricing decisions.

In summary, the long-run marginal-cost function is not obtained by simple reference to a historic-cost transactions-based cost accounting system. It requires, in addition to short-term variable costs, estimates of the cost of capacity resources, the long-run incremental cost of service and staff departments to support a given level of output, and the cost of invested capital in the product's production, distribution, and sales functions. Despite the seductive simplicity of a rule that directs managers to price their products so that marginal revenues and marginal costs are equal, we now see that neither of these critical functions is obtained without considerable thought, effort, and subjective judgments.

FULL-COST PRICING

Full-cost pricing evolves naturally from standard cost systems which, in addition to specifying standard amounts of material and labor for each product, also compute an overhead burden rate. The overhead burden rate is set so that at standard or anticipated volumes, overhead costs are fully allocated to the firm's products. The existence of these standard costs apparently provides evidence to managers that the firm knows *the* cost of producing each of its products. Thus, it becomes convenient to add an allowance for general, selling, and administrative expenses to each product and specify an additional markup over all these costs to arrive at a price that covers all costs and provides a satisfactory profit percentage. Firms have elaborate schemes for constructing these full-cost prices, and considerable variation will exist among firms. We will give a simple example that indicates the essential structure of a full-cost pricing scheme.

The Wallace Company produces a variety of machine-tooled products. Some are standard and are sold to a set of regular customers. Throughout the year, though, opportunities arise to bid for new jobs or special orders, some of which may turn out to represent sources of long-term business. The Wallace Company has two principal operating units: a fabrication department and an assembly department. In addition it has a sales staff and the normal central staff functions of purchasing, personnel, controller, and so on. At the end of the year a budget is prepared for the upcoming year, projecting actual volumes and costs. Such a budget is presented below:

Fabrication		Assembly	
Materials	$100,000	Materials	$ 10,000
Labor costs	150,000	Labor costs	100,000
Variable overhead	50,000	Variable overhead	80,000
Fixed costs	100,000	Fixed costs	120,000
Total costs	$400,000	Total costs	$310,000
Estimated machine-hours	20,000	Estimated labor-hours	10,000

General, selling, and administrative costs $270,000

The Wallace Company attempts to follow a full-cost pricing scheme based on the amount of work performed in the Fabrication and Assembly departments. Since materials costs vary widely across different products, the company separates them from the accumulated costs based on machine-hours in Fabrication and labor-hours in Assembly. General, selling, and administrative expenses (GS&A) are allocated based on costs (excluding materials) accumulated in the two production departments. Thus, GS&A costs are proportional to a measure of value added in the firm (machine processing and labor input), not total costs. The specific formula is obtained from the following rules:

1. Labor, variable overhead, and fixed costs in the Fabrication Department total $300,000 or $15/estimated machine-hour.
2. Labor, variable overhead, and fixed costs in the Assembly Department total $300,000 or $30/estimated labor-hour.
3. GS&A expenses total $270,000 or 45 percent of the nonmaterial costs ($600,000) in the two production departments.
4. Shipping expenses and material costs are added to the processing and overhead expenses.
5. A profit margin of 20 percent over costs (the historical percentage) is added to total costs.
6. An additional 4 percent is added to cover the selling commission and the cash discount for prompt payment.

Suppose the Wallace Company receives an order for 1,000 units of a product that it estimates will have the following characteristics:

Materials cost	$3.15 per unit
Machine-hours in fabrication	0.80 hours/unit
Labor-hours in assembly	0.60 hours/unit
Shipping expenses	0.40 per unit

The price for this order will be obtained from a sequential computation:

Fabrication, 1,000 units @ 0.80 hours/unit · $15/hour	$12,000
Assembly, 1,000 units @ 0.60 hours/unit · $30/hour	18,000
Total processing costs:	$30,000
GS&A, 0.45 · processing costs	13,500
Materials costs, 1,000 units @ $3.15/unit	3,150
Shipping costs, 1,000 units @ 0.40/unit	400
Total costs	$47,050
Profit margin, 20% of total costs	9,410
Net selling price	$56,460
Commission and discount, 4% of selling price	2,258
Quoted price	$58,718

For this 1,000-unit order, the Wallace Company would quote a price of $58,718 or $58.72 per unit.

ADVANTAGES AND DISADVANTAGES OF FULL COST PRICING

Some of the advantages of a cost-plus pricing scheme should be obvious from this example. Once the departmental budgets have been established, the rate for processing in each department and for allocating GS&A expenses is easily obtained. As new orders are received or as prices are to be adjusted for existing products, it is a simple computation to compute the full costs based on the input requirements of each product. Thus the pricing computation can be handled as a straightforward and mechanical calculation without requiring the attention of top management. If this pricing policy does end up with the company's facilities being used at planned activity levels (20,000 machine-hours in Fabrication and 10,000 labor-hours in Assembly), the fixed costs should be fully absorbed into product costs and the company should achieve its targeted pretax profit goal of 20 percent above incurred costs.

Some of the disadvantages of the cost-plus pricing scheme should also be obvious. There is no consideration given to what a competitive market price might be for this product. It is fine to attempt to fully allocate all costs to each product and always obtain a 20 percent profit markup over and above all costs, but the final price may be considerably above (or below) what competitors are offering. If the full cost-plus pricing rule causes the firm to lose business to competitors, its facilities may not be utilized at planned activity levels and fixed overhead will be underabsorbed. The variable costs to the firm are $200,000 in Fabrication or $10 per machine-hour and $180,000 in Assembly or $18 per labor-hour. Therefore the incremental costs for the 1,000-unit order could be as low as $22,350:

Fabrication, 800 hours @ $10	$ 8,000
Assembly, 600 hours @ $18	10,800
Materials	3,150
Shipping	400
Total Incremental Costs	$22,350

These figures should be increased slightly because of variable GS&A expenses and the selling commission and discount, but even with out-of-pocket costs between $25,000 and $30,000, the offered price of $58,700 generates a substantial contribution margin to fixed overhead and profit. Competing firms, with similar resources and with some idle capacity, could offer substantially lower prices for such an order.

Thus, a full-cost pricing scheme makes the firm vulnerable to competitors with idle capacity who can quote prices on a contribution-margin basis. Should a full-cost pricing firm lose business to price-cutting competitors, it can find itself in a situation where all products are sold at prices above "cost" yet it loses money because fixed costs are underabsorbed at the lower volume. Conversely, at a time when demand is heavy, the firm may be able to earn a profit margin in excess of its historical percentage. A mechanical markup rule will prevent the firm from earning the maximum attainable profits, especially on products where it has a unique technological advantage.

Cost-plus pricing is also not sensitive to capacity bottlenecks within production departments. Products may differ in their requirements for equipment, skilled labor, supervision, or other resources that might be in short supply. A sensible pricing scheme would generate higher markups or cost-recovery percentages for products that use more of a department's scarce resources and lower markups for products that are using otherwise available or surplus resources. Applying uniform percentages for overhead and GS&A cost recovery and for profit contribution does not distinguish among the scarce-resource demands of alternative products. The mechanical pricing rule may cause the firm to reach capacity too soon because of a few critical bottlenecks in its production process while other forms of productive capacity are far from fully utilized. In principle, as planned use of a resource approaches capacity, the products making heavy use of this resource should be priced higher than normal to reflect the opportunity cost of filling the resource to capacity.

Another problem with full-cost pricing is to determine the profit percentage used to mark up costs. The Bruce Company used a 20 percent figure, which might have been satisfactory based on historical experience, but there is no economic theory to suggest what an appropriate percentage should be. There is no particular reason why firms are entitled to earn 20 percent, 50 percent, or 5 percent over costs. Supermarkets and food processing companies do well with very low profit margins on sales, and retail jewelry stores earn quite high percentages on sales without attracting an excessive number of competitors. The relevant consideration is what return the firm is earning on its assets; inadequate returns will make it difficult to attract new investment capital, returns well above a risk-adjusted cost of capital will attract competitors who will eventually lower the rate of return available in the industry. A danger, therefore, of cost-plus pricing is having pricing decisions driven from cost-recovery markups rather than from return-on-investment (ROI) considerations. Cost-plus pricing will be compatible with ROI pricing only if it happens that there is a high correlation between assets employed and costs incurred.

FULL COST PRICING: AN EVALUATION

Given these problems with full-cost pricing, why has this method lasted so long in common practice? There are many reasons for its popularity. We have already mentioned one: the method is simple and easy to use. It does not involve the extensive studies and calculations required to compute marginal-revenue and marginal-cost curves. With most firms facing thousands of pricing decisions, it is just too costly to analyze price-cost-volume relationships for individual products. Second, there may be too much uncertainty about the correct price-output decisions. The firm's managers may not be able to obtain probability distributions and risk attitudes toward its product line, hence they resort to simplified decision rules to suppress or absorb the uncertainty. Third, cost-plus pricing provides stability to pricing decisions. Especially if overhead is absorbed on a standard rather than projected actual level of output, prices will not fluctuate rapidly with demand changes. It is not clear what desirable attributes stable rather than fluctuating prices have, but some managers apparently wish to have a pricing policy that is not erratic. A fourth consideration is that cost-plus pricing may lead to relatively stable prices in oligopolistic industries that otherwise might be susceptible to short-term price cutting that reduces prices below long-run marginal cost. If all companies in an oligopoly use a cost-plus pricing formula, then the pricing structure in the industry will be stable even during periods of declining demand. At a time when all firms in the industry face similar cost increases due to industry labor negotiations or material price increases, firms will attempt to implement similar price increases even with no communication or collusion among the firms.

Cost-plus pricing also provides a defensible basis for price increases. At a time when there is great concern about inflation, it seems unpopular for firms to justify price increases as a mechanism for rationing the excess demand created by stimulative governmental fiscal and monetary policies. In an attempt to limit the price increases caused by these policies, governmental agencies scrutinize the pricing policies of many firms in large industries so that these firms are almost regulated utilities. In this environment, a cost-based defense seems important to obtain government and media understanding for higher prices.

In fact, few firms probably follow the rigid full-cost pricing policy we described for the Bruce Company. In a study of pricing practices in small firms, Haynes [1964] discovered that full-cost pricing was the exception rather than the rule. While many firms compute full costs for their products, the profit markups vary by individual product or by type of product. The markups also vary over time in response to changes in economic conditions. Full costs seem to serve as reference points to simplify the hundreds or thousands of pricing decisions that the firm would otherwise have to make on an individual basis. Once obtained, these reference prices are adjusted to reflect competitive and market conditions.

INCREMENTAL COSTS

At a minimum, firms should know the incremental costs of their products so that they can be sure prices are covering out-of-pocket costs. Incremental costs also provide necessary guidance for assessing the desirability of accepting special orders that will use available capacity and not affect the pricing structure of other products. These points are covered extensively in chapters on cost-volume-profit analysis in this and in introductory cost accounting textbooks. As a reminder, the incremental costs of a product include short-term variable costs (material, labor, and variable overhead) plus escapable or avoidable fixed costs—those fixed costs that would not be incurred were a product or product line to be eliminated.

Managers may be uncomfortable with delegating pricing decisions based on incremental costs. The concern is that sales personnel or product managers will attempt to build volume by setting prices only slightly above incremental costs. The firm will then cover incremental costs on all products but lack sufficient margin to provide adequate coverage of fixed costs, GS&A expenses, and profits. Carried to an extreme, the caricature is a firm making money on each of its products but showing losses on a companywide basis. Therefore, incremental costs should be computed to set a floor for pricing decisions and to provide relevant information on the acceptability of special orders. For the long run, the firm will need to price its products to cover its fixed overhead costs and provide an adequate return on invested capital.

TARGET ROI PRICING

Pricing to achieve a specified return on invested capital is a goal attempted by many large corporations (see Lanzilotti [1958]). For a single-product firm, invested capital can be measured by owners' equity plus interest-bearing debt, allowing for a portion of current assets to be financed by non-interest-bearing current liabilities. More typically, investment would be measured by the fixed assets plus the net working capital used for a product line. Fixed costs are allocated to the product on the basis of a standard volume, say 70 to 80 percent of capacity, and a normal product mix. The full costs, fixed plus variable, are then marked up so that at the standard volume of sales, the pretax profit margin is a targeted percentage of investment. This target percentage is specified high enough to provide an adequate risk-adjusted rate of return on investment but not so high that it invites new competitors or antitrust actions.

Consider the Donaldson Company, which is about to market a new chemical. The fixed investment in new buildings and equipment for the product is $3 million. Net working capital required for the product is estimated to be $1.50 per pound sold each month. The normal volume anticipated is 200,000 lb/month. The monthly production costs are $200,000 plus $2/lb (up to a maximum production of 250,000 lb/month. General, selling, and administrative costs are expected to increase by $80,000/month once the new chemical starts into active production and sales. The Donaldson Company aims for a pretax ROI of 20 percent in its pricing policy.

The computations of the price to achieve the targeted ROI proceed as follows:

Fixed costs	$280,000 per month
Standard volume	200,000 lb
Fixed costs/lb	$1.40
Variable costs/lb	$2.00
Total costs/lb	$3.40

Invested capital, $3,000,000 + $1.50(200,000)	$3,300,000
ROI	20%
Total profit margin	$660,000
Profit margin/lb	$3.30
Price: Total costs + profit, $3.40 + $3.30	$6.70

In this case, the cost of invested capital ($3.30/lb) is comparable to the full cost of production of $3.40/lb, an indication that the new chemical is a highly capital-intensive product.

PROPERTIES OF ROI PRICING

Target ROI pricing is intuitively appealing, since it relates price not only to the short-term costs of production (fixed and variable) but also to the capital investment required for production and distribution of the product. With cost-plus pricing, the percentage markup over costs is usually arbitrary and unrelated to the use of the firm's assets (unless the assets employed are proportional to costs). The target ROI approach generates a markup over costs that is proportional to the investment dedicated to the product line.

As a second feature, the company achieves stability in its pricing formula by relating its fixed costs and investment to a standard volume. If prices were based on anticipated actual annual volume, the company would find itself using a perverse pricing policy. In a high-demand year, the fixed costs and cost of invested capital would be spread over a large number of units and price would be lowered. Conversely, in a low-demand year, the target price would have to be raised. Such a policy would be contrary to a sensible approach to pricing with cyclical demand. It seems better to base price on an expected long-term utilization of capacity, earning above-average ROI's in high-demand years that help to counter the lower ROI's that will be earned in low-demand years.

The target ROI approach also provides a defensible price, permitting the company to cover its costs and earn a competitive return on its invested capital. It provides guidance to an industry price leader wishing to obtain a "fair" return— not so high that it encourages new entrants into the industry or attracts the attention of entrepreneurial anti-trust attorneys, but not so low that the firm could be accused of predatory pricing by making competition difficult.

Despite these attractive features, ROI pricing has some notable disadvantages. The ROI formula gives an impression of automating a decision that should command considerable judgment and evaluation. The managers of a firm may come to feel that they are entitled to the price derived from the ROI formula and not look closely at the nature of competition. A rigid adherence to the target ROI price can make a company complacent and unresponsive to the actions of competitors, both domestic and foreign. A price with too high a targeted return may encourage these competitors to invest heavily in new capacity. Once installed, the new capacity may put future profit margins under extreme pressure.

A second disadvantage is that the pricing formula uses only internal company data. Considerations of demand elasticity are suppressed. In practice, managers may compute a price to achieve a targeted ROI at a specified volume and then determine whether that volume can be achieved at the computed price. Thus, the target ROI price would be viewed as a first approximation to a reasonable price, with adjustments made about this price to exploit the nature of demand and competition for the product. But target ROI pricing does encourage internal rather than external determinants of price.

Both these disadvantages seem to have become more noticeable in recent years. *Business Week* (December 12, 1977) featured a story on the increasing tendency for large companies to cut prices in order to hold market share. Larger companies are now less willing to maintain a "price umbrella" under which many of their smaller and less efficient domestic companies can maintain adequate rates of returns. Also smaller companies are more willing to attempt price competition with market leaders rather than follow attempted price increases by these leaders. The increased volatility of the domestic economy and increased competition from foreign competitors have created the climate for these more aggressive pricing policies. As one top executive remarked: "We were fat, dumb and happy back in the 1960s but now most companies have been so badly burned that it will be a long time before they commit themselves to a long-run pricing strategy." Companies are becoming much more flexible and selective in their product pricing policies. They are able to implement a product-by-product pricing strategy because the widespread implementation of computerized cost accounting systems provides the capability for almost continuous monitoring and tracking of the labor, material, and energy costs for each product. Also, there is increasing acceptance of the value of building market share through aggressive pricing policies in order to lower unit production costs, a topic we will discuss shortly.

ASSET VALUATION FOR ROI PRICING

Accounting policies provide additional complications to the use of target ROI pricing policies; in fact, all cost-based policies are affected by accounting conventions. A significant component of the fixed costs is depreciation, the allocation of the costs of the fixed assets to their useful productive lives. During inflationary periods the cost of replacing a company's fixed assets will rise continuously (unless the industry is fortunate enough to be enjoying substantial technological advances). If prices are determined from historical costs, the firm may believe it is earning an adequate return on its assets but discover that, at current prices, it is unable to justify new investments. The managers of such a firm are being victimized by the *money illusion,* treating dollar expenditures in all years as being equivalent. This money illusion causes the numerator in the ROI calculation, the return or income, to be overstated because of the use of historical-cost depreciation. Similarly, the measurement of investment in the denominator of the ROI ratio is understated because the assets are recorded at their historical costs. Thus, inflation causes the ROI to be biased upward. Better guidance for a long-term pricing policy is achieved by using price-level-adjusted or replacement costs for depreciation and valuation of assets. When a company is earning an adequate return based on replacement costs, it can be more confident that the existing price structure will justify future investment.

Some commentators argue that firms should not price products based on replacement costs. Rather they should wait until the assets are replaced before raising prices (Anthony [1976]). This view ignores the actions of competitors. A firm with recently acquired high-priced productive assets will not likely have the cooperation of its competitors to permit it to raise prices to recover these higher asset costs. Only if all the leading firms are replacing their assets at the same time may prices rise abruptly to cover the now realized higher costs of production. This case excluded, a more stable pattern of investment and prices will be achieved when prices are adjusted frequently to cover the replacement cost of assets used in the production process.

For some products, of course, the availability of substitutes or lower-cost competitors will prevent the firm from pricing on a replacement-cost basis. But as long as these products are currently earning an adequate return on the opportunity cost of the existing assets, the firm should retain them. The firm would then be treating these products as "cash cows," products that are generating cash flows that can be reinvested in other product lines but that will not themselves receive new investment to expand or even maintain capacity as the existing assets deteriorate and become obsolescent. As an accounting point, the opportunity cost of the existing assets should be measured not by their historical cost but by either their salvage value or their highest value in alternative uses.

As usually implemented, the ROI pricing formula uses a broad definition of investment, summing together all the assets associated with a major product line. Looking in more detail at the capacity resources of the firm, it is likely that a few resources are used much more heavily than others. Also, individual products will differ in their use of these scarce resources. Therefore, it seems reasonable to attempt to recover a greater profit contribution from those products making heavy demands on the scarce resources and permit a lower target return on those products produced on the surplus resources, those not currently being used near capacity. Such a strategy would require that the firm know and continuously monitor the resource needs of each product and the available capacity of each resource. This strategy greatly expands the informational needs for pricing purposes, but it may be feasible to implement with the greatly decreased prices for distributed and interactive computing facilities.

COST-BASED PRICING: A SUMMARY

We have explored the use of cost data to assist in the pricing decision. Clearly, this is a very complex problem, and no mechanical pricing rule can guarantee that sales of a product will be sufficiently high to cover the fixed expenses and also earn an adequate return on investment. The aura of precision and defensibility engendered by a full-cost-plus or target ROI pricing formula should not lead the firm to ignore the nature of demand by customers or the actions of present and potential competitors. Nevertheless, we can understand the attraction of a cost-based pricing strategy as a means of simplifying the myriad of pricing decisions continually faced by the firm's managers. One way of rationalizing a cost-based pricing strategy is to recognize it as a means for implementing the firm's overall strategy, particularly once a master budget has been determined. In formulating a master budget, the firm makes assumptions about near-term objectives it wishes to achieve, such as growth in earnings, target market shares by product lines, new-product introductions, and short-term ROI. Price is one of the tactics available to the firm as it attempts to achieve a satisfactory trade-off among these frequently competing objectives. From the master budget, the managers can determine the overall profit goals, the planned product mix, and the anticipated level of production. These can then be used to develop a pricing formula based on three components.

First, the price must cover the incremental costs of production. For products that are expected to remain as a permanent part of the firm's product line, the incremental costs include not only short-term variable costs but also the replacement costs of the fixed assets. The incremental costs will also include the portion of factory and corporate overhead that, over the long run, varies with the level of activity in the firm. Some products may not be able to be priced to cover the replacement costs of their assets. At a minimum, these products must cover the costs that would be avoided were the production of the product to cease entirely. These avoidable costs include the market value of assets now being used in the production process.

The second component is the opportunity cost of producing the product. Products requiring resources that are in short supply in the firm should have a higher cost markup than products that use currently surplus resources. Therefore, cost markups can vary by product, depending on the demands they make on a firm's scarce resources. It is not sufficient that products be profitable on the basis of incremental or avoidable costs. They must be more profitable than other products that the firm could produce on the same resources.

Finally, the third component is the cost of invested capital to produce and distribute the product. This component may correspond to the profit margin for the product, but it seems better to obtain a profit margin from investment considerations rather than from a somewhat arbitrary percentage markup over full costs. Having obtained a price that covers incremental (or avoidable) costs, opportunity costs, and capital costs, the firm must still be flexible in adjusting this price to be responsive to the nature of demand and competition. At present, we can provide little guidance on these subjective but necessary responses. The cost-based price serves as a convenient reference point to be supplemented by incremental changes suggested by managerial judgment.

STRATEGIC PRICING FOR NEW PRODUCTS

The cost-based pricing formulas we have discussed in this chapter are typically applied to established products for which the firm has acquired considerable experience in production and sales. When the firm is introducing a new product, it may enjoy a short-term monopoly position if the product is successful. This permits a wider degree of discretion in its pricing policies. At one extreme, the firm can follow a policy called *vintage pricing,* in which a high price is set initially to exploit the inelasticity of demand for a unique product. The firm may hope to earn substantial revenues in the first few years of the new product's life that will pay back its R&D expenses and the investment in productive facilities. A high initial price also provides some protection against unexpected startup costs or increases in production costs. Over time, as competitors develop similar products or perhaps newer products that are substitutes, the firm will start to lower its price to meet these competitive forces. A price reduction will also encourage new uses, which can extend the life cycle of a mature product.

Vintage pricing is an example of a general form of monopoly pricing called *price discrimination.* The objective in price discrimination is to charge high prices in markets where demand is relatively inelastic (for example, a new product with almost no competition from similar or substitute products) and low prices in markets that are highly price elastic (for example, where there are many competing products). Price discrimination on an international scale occurs when a company that is shielded from foreign competition by import restrictions (quotas, high tariffs) can sell much of its output domestically at a high price and sell the remainder in the foreign or export market at the low price necessary to be competitive with other international manufacturers.

Price discrimination is an effective short-term profit-maximizing policy because it enables the firm to exploit the demand curve for its product. Rather than charge a single price to all its customers, the firm can work its way down the demand curve by charging a high price to the customers for whom the product is especially valuable and a low price to those for whom it is less valuable. For this policy to succeed, the different classes of customers must be separated from each other so that the "low-price" customers don't go into competition with the firm by offering to resell the product to the "high-price" customers. If the firm is selling a service or if the difference in price of a product is caused by the presence or absence of a distribution service (prepaid freight, warehousing, liberal credit terms), the firm need be less concerned with competition from its "low-price" customers.

Despite or perhaps because of the profit-augmenting potential of price discrimination, firms in the United States are proscribed by the Robinson-Patman Act from charging different prices to competing customers for the same product. Any price differentials across customers must be justified by cost differentials, usually the incremental costs of distributing to or servicing the different customers. The Robinson-Patman Act has benefited some (mainly accountants, economists, and professors who have been called upon to cost-justify alleged price differentials in numerous court cases) and has served to limit some of the more obvious forms of price discrimination. Vintage pricing, however, is a form of price discrimination that does not violate the law, since the sales of the same product are made at different times in the product's life cycle rather than at the same time to different customers. Therefore it remains a potential pricing strategy for new products.

The profitability of a vintage-pricing strategy is limited by the incomplete information about the marketplace that managers typically have. In practice, the demand elasticity for the product at different prices and at different times will not be known very precisely. Therefore, the firm may find it difficult to time its price decreases to coincide with an increasing price elasticity in the marketplace.

More importantly, vintage pricing may be precisely the wrong strategy if the product is vulnerable to competition from other producers. A high initial price will encourage competitors to invest in new facilities and enter the market in order to obtain the high profits apparently available. Strategically, the firm may decide it is more important to limit competition in the long run rather than extract high profits in the product introduction period. The use of an initially low price to discourage entry by competitors is even more important if the product is subject to the learning- or experience-curve phenomenon, which we discussed at the end of Chapter 4. With an experience-curve effect, it will pay the firm introducing a new product to build volume rapidly so that it can be much further down its cost curve than any of its potential competitors. The introducing firm may gain a cost advantage that can never be profitably overcome by a potential competitor. The leading advocate of this aggressive pricing strategy has been very explicit about its goal: "The basic objective in pricing a new product should be to prevent competitors from gaining experience and market share before the new product has achieved major volume." (Henderson [1979, p. 161]).

An initial low price has two beneficial effects. First, with any price elasticity for the product, it permits volume to increase rapidly, thereby compressing the time required to obtain a given reduction in unit costs. Second, it discourages or delays entry by competitors, so that the innovating firm can achieve a high market share that can be defended and even expanded with the cost advantage enjoyed over its competitors.

The problem with implementing this pricing strategy is that the optimal initial price may be below unit costs. Unit costs are high at the introduction stage because of low volume relative to capacity and startup costs. Initial costs may appear to be even higher if the firm allocates already spent R&D costs and promotional expenditures to the new product. Thus, the managers of the firm must have faith that the uncertain long-run benefits from an experience-curve pricing strategy will overcome the obvious and certain near-term costs of a low initial selling price. In effect, the firm must treat the rapid accumulation of volume and experience as an investment decision. It must sacrifice short-term benefits to obtain the long-term profits available from having the dominant market position for a product for which it is the low-cost producer. If the firm adopts this new-product pricing strategy, it would seem to create a demand for cost accounting data to track and verify that unit costs (as measured in constant dollars) are indeed decreasing as expected. This requires that cost and production data be collected on a cumulative basis so that the estimation techniques discussed in Chapter 4 can be applied.

SUMMARY

Pricing decisions are among the most complex that managers make. Managers must balance short- and long-run considerations in their pricing policies. Over the long run, prices must cover all costs and generate an adequate return on investment. These considerations, however, may lead the firm to adopt fairly rigid pricing strategies that leave it vulnerable to aggressive competitors in the short run and could prevent it from ever reaching the "long run." Cost data can provide guides to pricing decisions but should not deter managers from adjusting prices to expand demand or respond to competitive pressures. Conceptually, a product's price should cover incremental (or avoidable) costs plus opportunity costs plus a return on invested capital. Implementing this policy, however, requires subjective judgments about cost behavior and an extensive data-collection and information-processing system. For strategic purposes, an aggressive pricing policy may be used to build market share and obtain production experience that will lower unit costs relative to those of competitors. If this strategy is followed, the initial profit margins will be well below normal levels. As costs decline with the increased volume experienced from an expanded market share, the firm will realize substantial profits that will repay the profits foregone in the early stage of this pricing strategy.

PROBLEMS

7-1. Pricing in an Imperfect Market (CMA)

Stac Industries is a multi-product company with several manufacturing plants. The Clinton Plant manufactures and distributes two household cleaning and polishing compounds—regular and heavy duty—under the Cleen-Brite label. The forecasted operating results for the first six months of 1980 when 100,000 cases of each compound are expected to be manufactured and sold are presented in the following statement.

Cleen-Brite Compounds—Clinton Plant
Forecasted Results of Operations
For the Six-month Period Ending June 30, 1980
($000 omitted)

	Regular	Heavy Duty	Total
Sales	$2,000	$3,000	$5,000
Cost of sales	1,600	1,900	3,500
Gross profit	$ 400	$1,100	$1,500
Selling and administrative expenses			
Variable	$ 400	$ 700	$1,100
Fixed*	240	360	600
Total selling and administrative expenses	$ 640	$1,060	$1,700
Income (loss) before taxes	$ (240)	$ 40	$ (200)

* The fixed selling and administrative expenses are allocated between the two products on the basis of dollar sales volume on the internal reports.

The regular compound sold for $20 a case and the heavy duty sold for $30 a case during the first six months of 1980. The manufacturing costs by case of product are presented in the schedule at the top of the next column. Each product is manufactured on a separate production line. Annual normal manufacturing capacity is 200,000 cases of each product. However, the plant is capable of producing 250,000 cases of regular compound and 350,000 cases of heavy duty compound annually.

	Cost per Case	
	Regular	Heavy Duty
Raw materials	$ 7.00	$ 8.00
Direct labor	4.00	4.00
Variable manufacturing overhead	1.00	2.00
Fixed manufacturing overhead†	4.00	5.00
Total manufacturing cost	$16.00	$19.00
Variable selling and administrative costs	$ 4.00	$ 7.00

† Depreciation charges are 50% of the fixed manufacturing overhead of each line.

The schedule below reflects the consensus of top management regarding the price/volume alternatives for the Cleen-Brite products for the last six months of 1980. These are essentially the same alternatives management had during the first six months of 1980.

Regular Compound		Heavy Duty Compound	
Alternative Prices (per case)	Sales Volume (in cases)	Alternative Prices (per case)	Sales Volume (in cases)
$18	120,000	$25	175,000
20	100,000	27	140,000
21	90,000	30	100,000
22	80,000	32	55,000
23	50,000	35	35,000

Top management believes the loss for the first six months reflects a tight profit margin caused by intense competition. Management also believes that many companies will be forced out of this market by next year and profits should improve.

Required: (Each question should be considered independently)

1. What unit selling price should Stac Industries select for each of the Cleen-Brite compounds (regular and heavy duty) for the remaining six months of 1980?

2. Assume the optimum price/volume alternatives for the last six months were a selling price of $23 and volume level of 50,000 cases for the regular compound and a selling price of $35 and volume of 35,000 cases for the heavy duty compound. Should Stac Industries consider closing down its operations until 1981 in order to minimize its losses?

7-2. Pricing a new Product with Nonlinear Opportunity Costs (A. Atkinson)

Ralph Smart, the owner of the Blackburn Garage, is considering the possibility of becoming a *Silencer Muffler* franchise.

Ralph's garage operations consist of eight gasoline pumps and six service bays (areas). Each service bay is dedicated to a specific area of auto repair. These areas are: (a) tune ups, (b) lubrication and oil change, (c) wheel alignment, (d) brake repair, (e) major engine overhaul, and (f) transmission repair.

When a customer brings an automobile in for repair, the job is costed by referencing the "blue book" for repairs. This gives the average cost for the job in the general geographical vicinity of Ralph's garage. Because of the competitive nature of the auto repair business and the quality of work at Blackburn Garage, Ralph's customers have found this "standard cost" approach to pricing very acceptable.

For internal control purposes, Ralph uses a job order costing system to accumulate costs by each job. Parts are charged at cost. Labor and overhead are charged to each job at a rate of $36 per mechanic hour. This rate is comprised of: (a) a labor cost of $15 per hour, (b) variable overhead cost of $5 per labor hour and

(c) a normalized charge of $16 per hour to allocate fixed costs. The normalized fixed overhead rate is computed as follows:

$$\text{Overhead rate} = \frac{\text{Fixed overhead assigned to repair operators}}{\text{Anticipated labor hours}}$$

Ralph estimates the following "profits" for a *typical job* in each of the six service areas:

	Tune Ups	Lube and Oil	Wheel Alignment	Brake Repair	Engine Repair	Trans Repair
Blue Book Price	$54	$15	$30	$79	$500	$380
Parts Cost	12	4	3	16	172	200
Allocated Cost (@ $36 per DLH)	36	9	27	54	288	144
Profit per job	$ 6	$ 2	$ 6	$ 9	$ 40	$ 36

Blackburn currently employs six mechanics who may work a maximum of 36 hours per week and 48 weeks per year. Because of space limitations no more than six mechanics may be employed.

The muffler franchise would work as follows. The customer would be charged for the muffler at cost plus an installation charge. The muffler cost is $25 and it is expected that, on average, installation time will be 30 minutes. The variable overhead rate for this work will be the same as for other garage work.

Because of facility requirements, mufflers can only be installed in the bays used for tune ups, lubrication and oil, or transmission repair. In each of these bays, muffler work may be interchanged with the normal work in that bay. Only one mechanic may work in one service bay at a time.

Suppose that demands at the current price for repair hours in tune up (TU), lubrication and oil (LO) and transmission repair (TR) are 1,900, 1,500, and 1,600 hours respectively and that prices must be the same to all muffler customers. The *Silencer Company* also requires that any franchisee must give the muffler customer priority service. Any franchisee failing to do this is terminated. The practical consequence of this is that demand must be met if facilities exist.

In each of the following questions, unless otherwise indicated, assume that the mechanics are paid hourly on the basis of actual hours worked.

Required:

1. What is the minimum price for mufflers if the demand for mufflers in units per year is:
   a.   500
   b.   1,000
   c.   5,000
   d.   8,000
   e.   12,000
   Explain these price differences using the notion of opportunity cost.

2. Recompute the five prices in Question 1 under the assumption that mechanics are paid an hourly salary irrespective of hours worked.

7-3. *Price Justifications with Wage and Price Guidelines* (CMA)

Berco Company manufactures and wholesales hardware supplies. One of its product lines is composed of drill bit sets and router bit sets. The company employs a calendar year for reporting purposes.

The company is subject to voluntary wage and price guidelines. Berco's management is attempting to determine how much latitude it has for wage and price increases in the drill/router bit product-line and still be in compliance with the voluntary guidelines.

Certain key dates and time periods are specified in the guidelines and are defined below.

Base Quarter. Last complete fiscal quarter prior to October 2, 1979. For Berco Company this quarter runs from July 1, 1979 through September 30, 1979.

Program Year. 12-month period immediately following the base quarter. The program year for Berco extends from October 1, 1979 through September 30, 1980.

Base Period. Two-year period measured from the end of the last calendar or complete fiscal quarter of 1976 through the corresponding quarter of 1978. The base period for Berco extends from December 31, 1976 through December 31, 1978.

Base Year. The 12-month period prior to the program year or October 1, 1978 through September 30, 1979 for Berco Company.

The guidelines specify standards for wages and prices but the standards for each are not interrelated. The price standard is really a deceleration standard, i.e., the rate of the price increase allowed in the program year must be less than the price increase instituted in the base period. The standards with which Berco must comply are defined as follows.

Wage Standard. Increases in the hourly wage rate in the program year cannot be more than 7 percent of the average hourly pay rate in effect in the base quarter (July 1-September 30, 1979).

Price Standard. The rate of price increase for a product line in the program year must be the lesser of (1) one-half of one percent (.5 percent) less than the average rate of price increase for a product line for the base period stated as an annual percentage, or (2) no more than 9.5 percent annually.

The regulations which accompany the standards define the average rate of price increase for a product line for the base period as the weighted average of the price increase rates of each individual product line during the base period (12/31/76-12/31/78), stated as an annual rate. The regulations specify that the average rate is to be calculated as follows. The price increase rate for the base period of each individual product in the line is to be weighted by the ratio of actual sales revenue of each individual product in the line to the actual total sales revenue of the product line as measured at the beginning of the base period. The weighted average price increase rates for the base period for all products in the product line are summed and then divided by two (base period is a two-year period) to get the average annual rate of price increase for a product line for the base period.

Once the allowable rate of price increase for a product line for the base period is determined (i.e., the amount calculated above less .5 percent or the maximum of

9.5 percent), the rate of price increase is shared among all products in the line according to the ratio of actual sales revenue of each individual product in the line to the total sales revenue of the product line as measured at the end of the base quarter (September 30, 1979).

Historical data on wages and prices for the drill/router bit product-line are given in the following schedule.

| | | Price Data | | | | | | Wage Data | |
| | Drill Bit Sets | | | Router Bit Sets | | | | | |
Quarter Ending	Unit Price	Units Sold (in millions)	Revenue (in millions)	Unit Price	Units Sold (in millions)	Revenue (in millions)	Total Revenue (in millions)	Labor Hours (in millions)	Labor Costs (in millions)
12/31/76	$3.00	5.00	$15.00	$12.00	3.75	$45.00	$60.0	2.20	$16.50
12/31/78	3.75	5.80	21.75	13.80	4.25	58.65	80.4	2.40	21.12
9/30/79	4.20	6.00	25.20	15.00	4.32	64.80	90.0	2.60	23.92

Required:

1. Calculate the maximum hourly wage rate Berco Company can have in the drill/router bit product-line in the program year and still be in compliance with the wage standard of the voluntary wage and price guidelines.

2. Calculate the maximum rate of price increase Berco Company is allowed in the drill/router bit product-line in the program year and still be in compliance with the price standard of the voluntary wage and price guidelines.

3. Assume that Berco Company is allowed the maximum rate of price increase of 9.5 percent for its drill/router bit product-line. Further, Berco Company plans to increase the price of its router bit sets to $16.20 during the program year. Calculate the maximum price the company can charge for the drill bit sets in the program year and still be in compliance with the price standard of the voluntary guidelines.

4. The voluntary wage and price guidelines exclude the following product groups from compliance with the price standard:
   a. Commodities traded in open exchange markets.
   b. Exported goods and services.
   c. New products introduced during or after base year.
   d. Custom or one-time products.
   e. Products delivered during the program year under a contract signed prior to the start of the program year.
   f. Products exchanged in other than arms-length transactions, e.g., intracompany sales.

   For any three of these product groups, discuss why the product group was probably excluded from the guidelines.

7-4. Price Leadership in an Oligopoly*

General Motors Corporation

In an article in the *NACA Bulletin*, January 1, 1927, Albert Bradley described the pricing policy of General Motors Corporation. At that time, Mr. Bradley was general assistant treasurer; subsequently, he became vice-president, executive vice-president, and chairman of the board. There is reason to believe that current policy is substantially the same as that described in the 1927 statement. The following description consists principally of excerpts from Mr. Bradley's article.

General Policy

Return on investment is the basis of the General Motors policy in regard to the pricing of product. The fundamental consideration is the average return over a protracted period of time, not the specific rate of return over any particular year or short period of time. This long-term rate of return on investment represents the official viewpoint as to the highest average rate of return that can be expected consistent with a healthy growth of the business, and may be referred to as the economic return attainable. The adjudged necessary rate of return on capital will vary as between separate lines of industry as a result of differences in their economic situations; and within each industry there will be important differences in return on capital resulting primarily from the relatively greater efficiency of certain producers.

The fundamental policy in regard to pricing product and expansion of the business also necessitates an official viewpoint as to the normal average rate of plant operation. This relationship between assumed normal average rate of operation and practical annual capacity is known as standard volume.

The fundamental price policy is completely expressed in the conception of standard volume and economic return attainable. For example, if it is the accepted policy that standard volume represents 80 percent of practical annual capacity, and that an average of 20 percent per annum must be earned on the operating capital, it becomes possible to determine the standard price of a product—that is, that price which with plants operating at 80 percent of capacity will produce an annual return of 20 percent on the investment.

Standard Volume

Costs of production and distribution per unit of product vary with fluctuation in volume because of the fixed or nonvariable nature of some of the expense items. Productive materials and productive labor may be considered costs which are 100 percent variable, since within reasonable limits the aggregate varies directly with volume, and the cost per unit of product therefore remains uniform.

Among the items classified as manufacturing expense or burden there exist varying degrees of fluctuation with volume, owing to their greater or lesser degree

---

* This case was prepared from published material.

of variability. Among the absolutely fixed items are such expenses as depreciation and taxes, which may be referred to as 100 percent fixed, since within the limits of plant capacity the aggregate will not change, but the amount per unit of product will vary in inverse ratio to the output.

Another group of items may be classified as 100 percent variable, such as inspection and material handling; the amount per unit of product is unaffected by volume. Between the classes of 100 percent fixed and 100 percent variable is a large group of expense items that are partially variable, such as light, heat, power, and salaries.

In General Motors Corporation, standard burden rates are developed for each burden center, so that there will be included in costs a reasonable average allowance for manufacturing expense. In order to establish this rate, it is first necessary to obtain an expression of the estimated normal average rate of plant operation.

Rate of plant operation is affected by such factors as general business conditions, extent of seasonal fluctuation in sales likely within years of large volume, policy with respect to seasonal accumulation of finished and/or semifinished product for the purpose of leveling the production curve, necessity or desirability of maintaining excess plant capacity for emergency use, and many others. Each of these factors should be carefully considered by a manufacturer in the determination of size of a new plant to be constructed, and before making additions to existing plants, in order that there may be a logical relationship between assumed normal average rate of plant operation and practical annual capacity. The percentage accepted by General Motors Corporation as its policy in regard to the relationship between assumed normal rate of plant operation and practical annual capacity is referred to as standard volume.

Having determined the degree of variability of manufacturing expense, the established total expense at the standard volume rate of operations can be estimated. A *standard burden rate* is then developed which represents the proper absorption of burden in costs at standard volume. In periods of low volume, the unabsorbed manufacturing expense is charged directly against profits as unabsorbed burden, while in periods of high volume, the overabsorbed manufacturing expense is credited to profits, as overabsorbed burden.

Return on Investment

Factory costs and commercial expenses for the most part represent outlays by the manufacturer during the accounting period. An exception is depreciation of capital assets which have a greater length of life than the accounting period. To allow for this element of cost, there is included an allowance for depreciation in the burden rates used in compiling costs. Before an enterprise can be considered successful and worthy of continuation or expansion, however, still another element of cost must be reckoned with. This is the cost of capital, including an allowance for profit.

Thus, the calculation of standard prices of products necessitates the establishment of standards of capital requirement as well as expense factors, representative of the normal average operating condition. The standard for capital employed in fixed assets is expressed as a percentage of factory cost, and the standards for working capital are expressed in part as a percentage of sales, and in part as a percentage of factory cost.

The calculation of the standard allowance for fixed investment is illustrated by the following example.

Investment in plant and other fixed assets	$15,000,000
Practical annual capacity	50,000 units
Standard volume, percent of practical annual capacity	80 %
Standard volume equivalent (50,000 × 80%)	40,000 units
Factory cost per unit at standard volume	$1,000
Annual factory cost of production at standard volume (40,000 × $1,000)	$40,000,000
Standard factor for fixed investment (ratio of investment to annual factory cost of production; $15,000,000 ÷ $40,000,000)	0.375

The amount tied up in working capital items should be directly proportional to the volume of business. For example, raw materials on hand should be in direct proportion to the manufacturing requirements—so many days' supply of this material, so many days' supply of that material, and so on—depending on the condition and location of sources of supply, transportation conditions, etc. Work in process should be in direct proportion to the requirements of finished production, since it is dependent on the length of time required for the material to pass from the raw to the finished state, and the amount of labor and other charges to be absorbed in the process. Finished product should be in direct proportion to sales requirements. Accounts receivable should be in direct proportion to sales, being dependent on terms of payment and efficiency of collections.

The Standard Price

These elements are combined to construct the standard price as shown in Table 1. Note that the economic return attainable (20 percent in the illustration) and the standard volume (80 percent in the illustration) are long-run figures and are rarely changed;[1] the other elements of the price are based on current estimates.

Differences Among Products

Responsibility for investment must be considered in calculating the standard price of each product as well as in calculating the overall price for all products, since products with identical accounting costs may be responsible for investments that vary greatly. In the illustration given below, a uniform standard selling price of $1,250 was determined. Let us now suppose that this organization makes and sells two Products, A and B, with equal manufacturing costs of $1,000 per unit and equal working capital requirements, and that 20,000 units of each product are produced.

---

[1] A Brookings Institution Survey reported that the principal pricing goal of General Motors Corporation in the 1950's was 20 percent on investment after taxes. See Lanzillotti, "Pricing Objectives in Large Companies," *American Economic Review*, December, 1958.

However, an analysis of fixed investment indicates that $10 million is applicable to Product A, while only $5 million of fixed investment is applicable to Product B. Each product must earn 20 percent on its investment in order to satisfy the standard condition. Table 2 illustrates the determination of the standard price for Product A and Product B.

From this analysis of investment, it becomes apparent that product A, which has the heavier fixed investment, should sell for $1,278, while Product B should sell for only $1,222, in order to produce a return of 20 percent on the investment. Were both products sold for the composite average standard price of $1,250, then Product A would not be bearing its share of the investment burden, while Product B would be correspondingly overpriced.

Differences in working capital requirements as between different products may also be important due to differences in manufacturing methods, sales terms, merchandising policies, etc. The inventory turnover rate of one line of products sold by a division of General Motors Corporation may be six times a year, while inventory applicable to another line of products is turned over thirty times a year. In the second case, the inventory investment required per dollar cost of sales is only one-fifth of that required in the case of the product with the slower turnover. Just as there are differences in capital requirements as between different classes of product, so may the standard requirements for the same class of product require modification from

TABLE 1. Illustration of Method of Determination of Standard Price

	In Relation to	Turnover Per year	Ratio to Sales Annual Basis	Ratio to Factory Cost Annual Basis
Cash	Sales	20 times	0.050	—
Drafts and accounts receivable	Sales	10 times	0.100	—
Raw material and work in process	Factory cost	6 times	—	0.16⅔
Finished product	Factory cost	12 times	—	0.08⅓
Gross working capital			0.150	0.250
Fixed investment			—	0.375
Total investment			0.150	0.625
Economic return attainable, 20%			—	—
Multiplying the investment ratio by this, the necessary net profit margin is arrived at			0.030	0.125
Standard allowance for commercial expenses, 7%			0.070	—
Gross margin over factory cost			0.100	0.125
			a	b

$$\text{Selling price, as a ratio to factory cost} = \frac{1 + b}{1 - a} = \frac{1 + 0.125}{1 - 0.100} = 1.250$$

If standard cost   = $1,000
Then standard price = $1,000 × 1.250   = $1,250

TABLE 2. Variances in Standard Price Due to Variances in Rate of Capital Turnover

	Product A		Product B		Total Product (A plus B)	
	Ratio to Sales Annual Basis	Ratio to Factory Cost Annual Basis	Ratio to Sales Annual Basis	Ratio to Factory Cost Annual Basis	Ratio to Sales Annual Basis	Ratio to Factory Cost Annual Basis
Gross working capital	0.150	0.250	0.150	0.250	0.150	0.250
Fixed investment	—	0.500	—	0.250	—	0.375
Total investment	0.150	0.750	0.150	0.500	0.150	0.625
Economic return attainable, 20%	—	—	—	—	—	—
Multiplying the investment ratio by this, the necessary net profit margin is arrived at	0.030	0.150	0.030	0.100	0.030	0.125
Standard allowance for commercial expenses, 7%	0.070	—	0.070	—	0.070	—
Gross margin over factory cost	0.100	0.150	0.100	0.100	0.100	0.125
	a	b	a	b	a	b
Selling price, as a ratio to Factory cost $\left.\begin{array}{c} \\ \\ \end{array}\right\} = \dfrac{1+b}{1-a}$	$\dfrac{1.+0.150}{1.-0.100} = 1.278$		$\dfrac{1.+0.100}{1.-0.100} = 1.222$		$\dfrac{1.+0.125}{1.-0.100} = 1.250$	
If standard cost equals	$1,000		$1,000		$1,000	
Then standard price equals	$1,278		$1,222		$1,250	

248

time to time due to permanent changes in manufacturing processes, in location of sources of supply, more efficient scheduling and handling of materials, etc.

The importance of this improvement to the buyer of General Motors products may be appreciated from the following example. The total inventory investment for the 12 months ended September 30, 1926, would have averaged $182,490,000 if the turnover rate of 1923 (the best performance prior to 1925) had not been bettered, or an excess of $74,367,000 over the actual average investment. In other words, General Motors would have been compelled to charge $14,873,000 more for its products during this 12-month period than was actually charged if prices had been established to yield, say, 20 percent on the operating capital required.

Conclusion

The analysis as to the degree of variability of manufacturing and commercial expenses with increases or decreases in volume of output, and the establishment of "standards" for the various investment items, makes it possible not only to develop "Standard Prices," but also to forecast, with much greater accuracy than otherwise would be possible, the capital requirements, profits, and return on capital at the different rates of operation, which may result from seasonal conditions or from changes in the general business situation. Moreover, whenever it is necessary to calculate in advance the final effect on net profits of proposed increases or decreases in price, with their resulting changes in volume of output, consideration of the real economics of the situation is facilitated by the availability of reliable basic data.

It should be emphasized that the basic pricing policy stated in terms of the economic return attainable is a policy, and it does not absolutely dictate the specific price. At times, the actual price may be above, and at other times below, the standard price. The standard price calculation affords a means not only of interpreting actual or proposed prices in relation to the established policy, but at the same time affords a practical demonstration as to whether the policy itself is sound. If the prevailing price of product is found to be at variance with the standard price other than to the extent due to temporary causes, it follows that prices should be adjusted; or else, in the event of conditions being such that prices cannot be brought into line with the standard price, the conclusion is necessarily drawn that the terms of the expressed policy must be modified.[2]

Required:

1. An article in the *Wall Street Journal*, December 10, 1957, gave estimates of cost figures in "an imaginary car-making division in the Ford-Chevrolet-Plymouth field." Most of the data given below are derived from that article. Using these data, compute the standard price. Working capital ratios are not given; assume that they are the same as those in Table 1.

Investment in plant and other fixed assets $600,000,000
Required return on investment ....30% before income taxes
Practical annual capacity 1,250,000

---

[2] This paragraph is taken from an article by Donaldson Brown, then vice-president, finance, General Motors Corporation, in *Management and Administration*, March, 1924.

Standard volume—assume		80%
Factory cost per unit:		
Outside purchases of parts		$ 500*
Parts manufactured inside		600*
Assembly labor		75
Burden		125
Total		$1,300

* Each of these items includes $50 of labor costs.

"Commercial cost," corresponding to the 7 percent in Table 1, is added as a dollar amount, and includes the following:

Inbound and outbound freight	$ 85
Tooling and engineering	50
Sales and advertising	50
Administrative and miscellaneous	50
Warranty (repairs within guarantee)	15
Total	$250

Therefore, the 7 percent commercial allowance in Table 1 should be eliminated, and in its place $250 should be added to the price as computed from the formula.

2. What would happen to profits and return on investment before taxes in a year in which volume was only 60 percent of capacity? What would happen in a year in which volume was 100 percent of capacity? Assume that nonvariable costs included in the $1,550 unit cost above are $350 million; i.e., variable costs are $1,550 − $350 = $1,200. In both situations, assume that cars were sold at the standard price established in Question 1, since the standard price is not changed to reflect annual changes in volume.

3. In the 1975 model year, General Motors gave cash rebates of as high as $300 per car off the list price. In 1972 and 1973 prices had been restricted by price control legislation, which required that selling prices could be increased only if costs had increased. Selling prices thereafter were not controlled, although there was always the possibility that price controls could be reimposed. In 1975, demand for automobiles was sharply lower than in 1974, partly because of a general recession and partly because of concerns about high gasoline prices. Does the cash rebate indicate that General Motors adopted a new pricing policy in 1975, or is it consistent with the policy described in the case?

7-5. *Price Leadership in an Oligopoly**

Atherton Company

Early in January, 1975, the sales manager and the controller of the Atherton Company met for the purpose of preparing a joint pricing recommendation for Item 345. After the president approved their recommendation, the price would be announced in letters to retail customers. In accordance with company and industry practice, announced prices were adhered to for the year unless radical changes in market conditions occurred.

The Atherton Company was the largest company in its segment of the textile industry; its 1974 sales had exceeded $12 million. Company salespersons were on a straight salary basis, and each salesperson sold the full line. Most of Atherton's competitors were small. Usually they waited for the Atherton Company to announce prices before mailing out their own price lists.

Item 345, an expensive yet competitive fabric, was the sole product of a department whose facilities could not be utilized on other items in the product line. In January 1973, the Atherton Company had raised its price from $3 to $4 a yard. This had been done to bring the profit per yard on Item 345 up to that of other products in the line. Although the company was in a strong position financially, it would require considerable capital in the next few years to finance a recently approved long-term modernization and expansion program. The 1973 pricing decision had been one of several changes advocated by the directors in an attempt to strengthen the company's working capital position so as to insure that adequate funds would be available for this program.

Competitors of the Atherton Company had held their prices on products similar to Item 345 at $3 during 1973 and 1974. The industry and Atherton Company volume for Item 345 for the years 1969–74, as estimated by the sales manager, is shown in Table 1. As shown by this exhibit, the Atherton Company had lost a significant portion of its former market position. In the sales manager's opinion, a reasonable forecast of industry volume for 1975 was 700,000 yards. He was certain that the company could sell 25 percent of the 1975 industry total if it adopted the $3 price. He feared a further volume decline if it did not meet the competitive price. As many consumers were convinced of the superiority of the Atherton product, the sales manager reasoned that sales of Item 345 would probably not fall below 75,000 yards, even at a $4 price.

During the pricing discussions, the controller and sales manager had considered two other aspects of the problem. The controller was concerned about the possibility that competitors would reduce their prices below $3 if the Atherton Company announced a $3 price for Item 345. The sales manager was confident that competitors would not go below $3 because they all had higher costs and several of them were

TABLE 1.   Item 345, Prices and Production, 1969–74

| | Volume of Production (yards) | | Price | |
Year	Industry Total	Atherton	Charged by Most Competitors	Atherton Company
1969	610,000	213,000	$4.00	$4.00
1970	575,000	200,000	4.00	4.00
1971	430,000	150,000	3.00	3.00
1972	475,000	165,000	3.00	3.00
1973	500,000	150,000	3.00	4.00
1974	625,000	125,000	3.00	4.00

TABLE 2. **Estimated Cost Per Yard of Item 345 at Various Volumes of Production**

	75,000	100,000	125,000	150,000	175,000	200,000
Direct labor	$ .800	$ .780	$ .760	$ .740	$ .760	$ .800
Material	.400	.400	.400	.400	.400	.400
Material spoilage	.040	.040	.038	.038	.038	.040
Department expense:						
Direct*	.120	.112	.100	.100	.100	.100
Indirect†	.800	.600	.480	.400	.343	.300
General overhead‡	.240	.234	.228	.222	.228	.240
Factory cost	$2.400	$2.166	$2.006	$1.900	$1.869	$1.880
Selling and administrative expenses§	1.560	1.408	1.304	1.236	1.215	1.222
Total Cost	$3.960	$3.574	$3.310	$3.136	$3.084	$3.102

* Indirect labor, supplies, repairs, power, etc.
† Depreciation, supervision, etc.
‡ 30 percent of direct labor.
§ 65 percent of factory cost.

in tight financial straits. He believed that action taken on Item 345 would not have any substantial repercussions on other items in the line.

The controller prepared estimated costs of Item 345 at various volumes of production (Table 2). These estimated costs reflected current labor and material costs. They were based on past experience except for the estimates of 75,000 and 100,000 yards. The company had produced more than 100,000 yards in each of the last ten years, and earlier experience was not applicable because of equipment changes and increases in labor productivity.

Required:

1. How, if at all, did the company's financial condition relate to the pricing decision?
2. Should $3 or $4 have been recommended? (Assume no intermediate prices are being considered.)
3. What information not in the case would you like to have in making this pricing decision? (Do not let the lack of information prevent your answering Question 2!)

7-6. Aggressive Pricing of a New Product*

Federal Express, within eight years, has become the Number 1 company in the overnight cargo delivery market. Its 1980 sales of $580 Million edged it ahead of Emery Air Freight (1980 sales of $553 Million), the perennial market leader. The Courier subsidiary of Purolator ranks Number 3 ($391 Million), it handles more than

---

* This problem is adapted from "Federal Express Dives into Air Mail," *FORTUNE* (June 5, 1981) pp. 106–108.

twice as many packages as Federal but ships most of them short distances by truck. Airborne ranks fourth in the industry with sales of $287 Million.

Federal achieved this remarkable growth because it adopted a dramatically different strategy from its competitors. Emery and Airborne collected freight of any size and shipped it by commercial carriers, eliminating almost all capital investment requirements—no airplanes, hangars, or high priced pilots. Federal decided to concentrate solely on the high-profit business of moving small packages fast. Fred Smith, the 36 year-old Chairman and founder of Federal, purchased a fleet of planes, and based them in Memphis. Memphis is near the center of business shipping in the U.S. and has excellent weather for uninterrupted flying conditions. Packages in feeder cities are loaded onto Federal's planes each afternoon and flown to Memphis. There, they are sorted in the late night and early morning hours and reloaded onto outbound planes. Federal can now deliver 99 percent of its packages overnight.

Initially, capital expenditures were very high and profits were depressed. But since 1976, when Federal first became profitable, earnings have grown at a 76 percent annual compounded rate and the stock has gone up more than 10 fold. Federal's competitors are now scrambling to catch up to Federal but it is a difficult task since they lag far behind the quantity and quality of the aircraft and ground facilities. Federal is now the industry's low-cost operator and competitors have trouble matching its costs. Federal uses local college students to work at the Memphis hub. They receive a modest hourly wage but have their tuition paid in full. Their short term employment (four years or less) and the generous fringe benefit package have enabled Federal to not have a single employee represented by a union. Thus its total labor costs are lower than those of any of its more unionized competitors.

Recently, the small-package market has been showing signs of saturation. Federal is now investigating a new product: under a 1979 change in Postal Service Regulations, private delivery is allowed for "extremely urgent" mail. Federal test marketed overnight letters in Memphis, Pittsburgh, and Cincinnati and these showed the feasibility of and demand for guaranteed overnight delivery of letters. Federal has decided to price this new service very aggressively. The $9.50 price is less than half the price of the next-largest envelope, the two-pound Courier-Pak selling for $21. The two-ounce letter will generate much more revenue per pound but weight is only an important cost factor for aircraft transportation, a segment representing about one-third of total costs. The expense of delivery and sorting is nearly the same for the letter as for the Courier-Pak.

"The overnight letter won't even be profitable for *us* for the first year," says Smith. "I can't see anybody making it profitable without our low unit costs—which nobody has." Competitors are thus facing a difficult situation. Either they can enter the overnight letter market but lose money because of Federal's low pricing strategy, or they can stay out of this market entirely, thereby conceding the entire letter market to Federal along with the packages that may be shipped by the same customers using the overnight letter service.

Required:

1. Why, given that Federal Express is Number 1 in its industry, does it introduce a product at a money losing price?
2. Compare Federal's pricing strategy with the traditional view of short term

monopoly pricing in which the dominant firm determines its price to max-imize short term profits (i.e., by setting marginal revenue equal to marginal cost).

3. Federal Express is contemplating helping out its largest non-commercial rival—the U.S. Postal Service—by allowing it to use Federal's mail sorting hubs and aircraft during slack conditions. Why would Federal consider allowing access for the U.S. Postal Service to its highly efficient operations?

7-7. Competitive Bidding with Experience Curve Effects (A. Mitchell, adapted)

The Henderson Company is bidding on a recently developed component for a truck-ing manufacturer. Last year it produced 20,000 units for the manufacturer, winning the first bid of 10,000 units at a price of $22 per unit and the second bid of 10,000 units at a price of $15.40 per unit. An initial bid for 15,000 units at $19.25 per unit was also let to one of Henderson's competitors, the Braxton Corporation. This represented Braxton's first production of this component. Recently, Braxton outbid Henderson for a 5,000 unit order by quoting a price of $13.50 per unit, beating Henderson's bid by almost $.50 per unit.

Henderson quotes prices based on a 10 percent markup over anticipated costs and it believes that Braxton follows a similar practice. Nevertheless, Henderson is suspicious that Braxton may be shaving prices in an attempt to build volume and move out along an experience curve so that it will become a lower cost producer than Henderson.

A new contract for 15,000 units is now coming up for bid and the President of Henderson Company wants to be sure that his bid is competitive. He recognizes that if he loses this contract, he will be at a cost disadvantage relative to Braxton on all future bidding. On the other hand, he would hate to bid so low on a contract that he will lose money on it were he to be the successful bidder.

Required:

What bid do you recommend that Henderson submit? Provide an analysis that justifies this bid. You may assume, for simplicity, that there are no price changes (past, current, or future) affecting the cost structure of Henderson or Braxton.

7-8. Contribution Margin Pricing

Lewis Redi-Mix (A)*

Lewis Redi-Mix is a supplier of ready-mixed concrete located in metropolitan Cleve-land, Ohio. At the end of 1958 the company was completing its twentieth consecutive year of operation.

---

* Reproduced by permission from Touche, Ross and Co.

Bob Lewis founded the company in the late thirties and served as its president and maintained controlling interest of the outstanding capital stock. In the early fifties, Lewis Redi-Mix became the largest supplier of ready-mixed concrete serving the metropolitan Cleveland area. Mr. Lewis took great pride in maintaining a large and modern fleet of delivery mixer-trucks. He employed a sizable staff of drivers, yard workers, and garage personnel, and always seemed to have the capability to meet the sudden, unscheduled needs of contractors. A radio-controlled dispatching operation made it possible for office personnel to keep close track of delivery operations at all times. Company advertising emphasized the quality and service features of Lewis Redi-Mix.

In 1957, Lewis Redi-Mix experienced a financial loss for the first time in its history. The loss for the year 1958 was even greater. The nationwide economic recession of 1957–1958 played havoc with the construction industry. Suppliers of building materials such as ready-mixed concrete no longer found themselves in a seller's market.

Bob Lewis was quite disturbed by developments within the ready-mixed concrete business. A number of smaller suppliers entered the Cleveland market area during the building boom of the early fifties. With the building boom on a downhill skid, there was significant excess capacity in the ready-mixed concrete industry. Many of the smaller firms were resorting to price-cutting tactics in order to survive. Lewis Redi-Mix was fortunate to have been in a healthy working-capital condition when the recession began. Lewis had hoped that the construction lag would be short-lived. The company continued to stress the quality and service image of Lewis Redi-Mix without resorting to price cuts. The even greater financial loss of 1958 and discouraging forecasts of little or no upturn in building activity for 1959 was forcing Mr. Lewis to reexamine the entire operation of his business.

Late in 1958, he had attended a conference on managerial accounting techniques for decision-making purposes. One of the points frequently made at the conference was the need to analyze and segregate expenses by their variable and fixed components. The conference had stressed a concept called "profit contribution." Mr. Lewis was particularly interested in the application of the profit-contribution concept to pricing and volume decisions. Upon his return to the company, Lewis discussed the conference proceedings with his chief accountant. They decided to seek the assistance of a management consultant well qualified in the area of

TABLE 1. **LEWIS REDI-MIX (A) Historical Sales Data**

Year	Sales (cubic yards)	Sales	Profits	Market Share (%)
1952	424,000	$5,520,000	$130,000	26
1953	455,000	5,910,000	240,000	25
1954	440,000	5,730,000	190,000	25
1955	515,000	6,690,000	450,000	23
1956	467,000	6,070,000	270,000	20
1957	375,000	4,870,000	(50,000)	17
1958	348,000	4,530,000	(140,000)	15

TABLE 2. **LEWIS REDI-MIX (A) Original Budget for the Year 1959 Full-Costing System**

Sales (Cubic Yards)		377,000
Sales		$4,901,000
Less Cost of Goods Sold		
Raw Materials	$2,488,200	
Delivery Expense	801,440	
Truck Repair, Maintenance, and Garbage Expense	280,540	
Yard Operation Expense	242,320	
Depreciation	248,000	
Heat, Light, and Power	112,800	
Rent	120,000	
Total Cost of Goods Sold		4,293,300
Gross Margin		$ 607,700
Less Selling and Administrative Expenses		
Salaries–Sales and Administrative Personnel	$ 149,800	
Wages–Clerical Personnel	86,400	
Insurance	43,200	
Licenses	55,200	
Telephone	15,400	
Associations	7,200	
Legal and Professional Expenses	16,800	
Office Supplies and Postage	4,800	
Automobile Expense	14,400	
Guard Services	4,800	
Social Security Taxes	32,400	
Employees' Welfare Fund	32,400	
Employees' Pension Fund	21,600	
Life Insurance Premium	600	
Provision for Bad Debts	7,200	
Advertising	30,000	
Total Selling and Administrative Expense		522,200
		$ 85,500
Less Other Expenses		
Taxes	$ 78,000	
Repairs and Improvements—Building and Property	48,000	
Total Other Expense		126,000
Net Profit or (Loss)		$ (40,500)

profitability accounting to assist in converting the full costing system of Lewis Redi-Mix to a system incorporating the concepts of profit contribution.

Table 1 shows the sales, profits, and market share of Lewis Redi-Mix for 1952–1958. The consultant was particularly concerned that the market share had been declining. To him, this indicated that Lewis was suffering losses not solely due to economic conditions affecting the construction industry.

A look at the company's advertising for 1957 and 1958 revealed the same messages used during the preceding years of prosperity:

"Lewis *Quality* Concrete"

"Top-quality ingredients"
"Delivered promptly"
"Personal service"
"Don't gamble with bargain mixes"
"Lewis provides the best concrete on earth"

Bob Lewis summed up his company's marketing approach and competition as follows: "In the years of the seller's market that ended in 1956 we had all the business that we could get cement for. We waited for business to come to us. Then the concrete industry became depressed from coast to coast. It is now characterized by tough competitive practices, excess capacity, low selling prices, and lack of profit. We thought it would be temporary and wanted to maintain our image of high quality and good service. While we waited, our volume fell sharply. Our competitors cut prices and ran over us, through us, and around us. We're in a dilemma and seeking a way out.

"We aren't waiting any longer for conditions to change. We'll take prices the way they are, meet them, and learn how to make a profit at lower price levels."

Mr. Lewis then proceeded to outline the jobs he wanted done by the consultant. Among them was an analysis of cost-reduction possibilities and methods of improving efficiency. But prior to the beginning of these tasks, Mr. Lewis wanted the accounting system revised on a profitability accounting basis. He felt it imperative to begin pricing on the basis of profit contribution as quickly as possible.

Table 2 is the original budget for the year 1959 prepared by the chief accountant

TABLE 3. LEWIS REDI-MIX (A) Variable-Cost Data

Raw Materials Cost per Cubic Yard

	Cement Sack Content				
Type of Aggregate	3	3½	4	4½	5
Large Buckshot	$5.60	$6.00	$6.40	$6.80	$7.20
Small Buckshot	5.80	6.20	6.60	7.00	7.40
Fine Buckshot	6.00	6.40	6.80	7.20	7.60

The four-sack, small-buckshot mixture with a raw materials cost of $6.60 per cubic yard represents the most frequent or average order.

Other Variable Costs

Truck Drivers' Wages and Compensation	$.01815 per minute per cubic yard
Garage Workers' Wages and Compensation	.0227 per mile per cubic yard
Yard Workers' Wages and Compensation	.36 per cubic yard
Dispatching Personnel Wages and Compensation	.20 per cubic yard
Gas, Oil, and Grease	.00326 per minute per cubic yard
Tires	.0053 per mile per cubic yard

The average delivery round trip is 15 miles and takes 90 minutes.

under the company's full-cost accounting system. Based upon business forecasts and contracts for future orders already signed, sales volume was projected at 377,000 cubic yards. Mr. Lewis explained that this volume projection had been made assuming that the company would again maintain a fixed price level during 1959. For the past several years, Lewis had been selling his concrete at $13.00 a cubic yard.

TABLE 4.   LEWIS REDI-MIX (A) Revised Budget for the Year 1959 Profitability Accounting System

Sales (Cubic Yards)		377,000
Sales		$4,901,000
Less Variable Costs		
Raw Materials	$2,488,200	
Truck Drivers' Wages and Compensation	614,510	
Garage Workers' Wages and Compensation	128,180	
Yard Workers' Wages and Compensation	135,720	
Dispatching Personnel Wages and Compensation	75,400	
Gas, Oil, and Grease	109,330	
Tires	30,160	
Total Variable Cost		3,581,500
Profit Contribution		$1,319,500
Less Standby Costs		
Salaries–Sales, Administrative, and Supervisory Personnel	$ 214,000	
Wages–Clerical and Yard Personnel	172,800	
Depreciation	248,000	
Taxes	78,000	
Insurance	43,200	
Heat, Light, and Power	112,800	
Licenses	55,200	
Rent	120,000	
Telephone	15,400	
Associations	7,200	
Legal and Professional Expenses	16,800	
Office Supplies and Postage	4,800	
Automobile Expense	14,400	
Guard Services	4,800	
Social Security Taxes	10,800	
Employees' Welfare Fund	10,800	
Employees' Pension Fund	7,200	
Life Insurance Premium	600	
Provision for Bad Debts	7,200	
Total Standby Expenses	$1,144,000	
Less Programmed Costs		
Repairs and Improvements–Building and Property	$ 48,000	
Repairs and Modernization–Equipment	72,000	
Tire-Rotation Replacement Program	30,000	
Yard and Garage Supplies	36,000	
Advertising	30,000	
Total Programmed Expenses	$ 216,000	
Total Standby and Programmed Costs		1,360,000
Net Profit or (Loss)		$ (40,500)

TABLE 5. **LEWIS REDI-MIX (A) Quarterly Budget for the Year 1959 Profitability Accounting System**

	1st Quarter (Jan.-Mar.)	2nd Quarter (Apr.-June)	3rd Quarter (July-Sept.)	4th Quarter (Oct.-Dec.)	Total
Sales (Cubic Yards)	45,000	120,000	140,000	72,000	377,000
Sales	$ 585,000	$1,560,000	$1,820,000	$936,000	$4,901,000
Less Variable Costs	427,500	1,140,000	1,330,000	684,000	3,581,500
Profit Contribution	$ 157,500	$ 420,000	$ 490,000	$252,000	$1,319,500
Less Standby and Programmed Costs	340,000	340,000	340,000	340,000	1,360,000
Net Profit or (Loss)	$(182,500)	$ 80,000	$ 150,000	$ (88,000)	$ (40,500)

The consultant's first objective was to take the original budget shown in Table 2 and separate the variable costs from the fixed costs. With the help of the company's chief accountant, variable-cost data as shown in Table 3 was established.

The only components other than water entering into the concrete mix were cement and aggregate (often referred to as "buckshot"). Depending upon the contractor's requirements, the concrete could be mixed with one of three sizes of "buckshot" and appropriate quantities of cement. The cost variations for each possible mixture are summarized in Table 3. Other variable costs are also shown. The consultant discovered that some costs varied not only by the cubic yard, but by the number of miles the delivery site was from the plant and the number of minutes a round-trip delivery cycle required.

For budgeting purposes, the consultant wished to use a standard cost figure to project anticipated variable costs. He decided that a four-sack, small-buckshot mixture requiring a 15-mile round-trip delivery of 90 minutes best represented the average cubic yard sold.

The consultant then prepared a revised budget for 1959 based upon the projected sales level of 377,000 cubic yards. The revised budget shown in Table 4 separates the variable and fixed costs, and shows a profit contribution of $1,319,500 and a net loss of $40,500. The net loss projected under the new profitability accounting system was the same as that projected under the old full-costing system.

After the new accounting system was established, the consultant turned his attention toward application of the system for pricing and volume decisions.

"Understanding the relationship between the demand for ready mixed concrete and the price that can be most profitably charged for that concrete is of utmost importance in your business," the consultant explained to Mr. Lewis. "Establishing that relationship is not an easy or precise matter, however, and can only be an approximation of ever-changing demand-price relationships. As you are well aware, your business is quite seasonal. High sales volumes are typical of spring and summer months and low sales volumes typical of winter months. An analysis of previous year's records shows that your business actually has different demand characteristics each quarter. If the projected 1959 volume of 377,000 cubic yards is broken down quarter by quarter (Table 5), these seasonal effects upon profit contribution can be seen.

TABLE 6. LEWIS REDI-MIX (A) Historical Relationship of Booked Yards to Yards Actually Delivered in Future Months (As of January 1)

	Yards Booked on Jan. 1 as a Percent of Yards Actually Delivered in the Month
January	90
February	85
March	75
April	60
May	50
June	40
July	20
August	10
September	—
October	—
November	—
December	—

"In addition, we have found that there is a correlation between advanced bookings and sales. The correlation of booked yards to yards delivered in future months as of January 1 is shown in Table 6. Although we did not analyze data for all months of the year, it seems likely that such a correlation could be found for each month. This information would be of great value in establishing prices for future delivery, as it would give a good estimate of capacity utilization. This is another vital factor in pricing.

"To simplify your pricing procedures when bidding on various jobs, we suggest that you use a pricing form similar to Table 7. After the variable cost per yard is determined, the price at which you think you can get the job is determined and the profit contribution calculated. The pricing decision is then made based on whether you want the job at that profit contribution."

TABLE 7. LEWIS REDI-MIX (A) Job Pricing Form Variable Costs Per Cubic Yard

Raw materials: (_____ Aggregate _____ Cement Sack)	$ _____
Drivers' wages, etc.: _____ minutes @ $.01815	_____
Garage workers' wages, etc.: _____ miles @ $.0227	_____
Yard workers' wages, etc.:	.36
Dispatching personnel wages, etc.:	.20
Gas, oil, and grease: _____ minutes @ $.00326	_____
Tires: _____ miles @ $.0053	_____
Total variable cost per cubic yard	$ _____
Add probable profit contribution per cubic yard	_____
Bid price per cubic yard	$ _____
Total yards _____ × bid price $_____ = Total Bid Price	$ _____

1. The consultant used a standard variable cost of $9.50 for the average cubic yard sold for budgeting purposes. Show how the $9.50 figure was derived, based upon variable cost data in Table 3.

2. Lewis is to submit a bid to the ABC Construction Company for 10,000 cubic yards of large-buckshot, five-sack cement to be delivered in February 1959. The delivery point is 4 miles away from the plant and a complete round trip should require 40 minutes. What should be the total bid price if a $2.50 per yard profit contribution is considered appropriate at that time?

3. Describe a general pricing objective which applies to the company and any other company which bid prices. What are the practical problems involved in achieving this objective?

4. Suppose Mr. Lewis had told you that his primary objective was to maximize total revenue. Would you agree that this was an appropriate objective?

5. Suppose the company desired to set prices by a percentage mark-on to cost to yield a target profit. Do you think this would work?

6. How would you determine the variable cost rates in Table 3 for the elements of "other variable costs"?

REFERENCES

ANTHONY, ROBERT N., "A Case for Historical Costs," *Harvard Business Review* 54 (November–December 1976), 69–79.

BAUMOL, WILLIAM J., *Economic Theory and Operations Analysis,* 3d ed. Englewood Cliffs, N.J.: Prentice-Hall, 1971.

BAXTER, W. T., and A. R. OXENFELDT, "Costing and Pricing: The Cost Accountant versus The Economist," *Business Horizons* IV (Winter 1961), pp. 77–90.

COLBERG, MARSHALL, DASCOMB FORBUSH, and GILBERT WHITAKER, JR., *Business Economics: Principles and Cases,* 5th ed. Homewood, Ill.: Irwin, 1975.

HAYNES, W. WARREN, "Pricing Practices in Small Firms," *Southern Economic Journal* XXX (April 1964), 315–24.

HENDERSON, BRUCE D., *On Corporate Strategy.* Cambridge, Mass.: Abt Books, 1979.

LANZILOTTI, ROBERT F., "Pricing Objectives in Large Companies," *American Economic Review* XLVIII (December 1958), 921–40.

SILBERSTON, AUBREY, "Surveys of Applied Economics: Price Behavior of Firms," *The Economic Journal* LXXX (September 1970), 511–75.

OPPORTUNITY LOSSES:
Effects
of Estimation Errors and
Cost Changes

SIGNIFICANCE OF COST-MEASUREMENT ERRORS

Earlier chapters have discussed techniques for estimating costs and using cost estimates for product planning and profitability analysis. The uncertainty in cost estimates, however, that results from even careful estimation procedures was not formally acknowledged in the C-V-P or pricing analysis. We used estimates of fixed and variable costs as if they were known for certain. What is the consequence of treating these uncertain estimates as if they were known constants? An answer to this question requires us to be explicit about how the cost estimates are used in actual decision and control procedures. The simplified answer is that if decisions are unaffected by variations in the cost estimates, then there are no adverse consequences to cost-measurement errors. The consequences of an inaccurate cost estimate can be assessed only in terms of changes in outcomes, in the context of specific decision or control uses of the inaccurate estimate.

Differences between expected and actual costs can also arise from shifts in wage rates, material prices, labor or material usages, overhead costs, or process changes. If such shifts are either temporary or correctable, they can be dealt with in the context of investigating cost variances, the subject of Chapter 10. But should the cost shifts be permanent and irreversible, so that new standard costs will be established, then decisions made on the basis of the previous standards need to be reevaluated.

The subject of this chapter is the consequence of using cost estimates that differ from actual costs. The differences occur because of either (1) uncertainty in cost estimates arrived at from analysis of historical data, or (2) irreversible shifts in cost behavior. The objective is to obtain quantifiable estimates of the degree of loss associated with using inaccurate cost data for planning and control decisions. For many models, the loss caused even by fairly large cost errors will be relatively minor, indicating that for those models it is not vital to obtain highly precise cost estimates. The principal message from this chapter will be to establish a framework by which the analyst can assess the sensitivity of decisions and outcomes to uncertain or inaccurate cost estimates.

OPTIMAL PRICE-OUTPUT DECISIONS

We can illustrate all the relevant features of the assessment of opportunity loss by a simple price-output decision. Consider a firm producing a single product that has a demand curve given by

$$x = 500 - p,$$

where $x =$ amount produced and sold of the product,
$p =$ price of the product.

The cost function of the product is estimated to be quadratic in the amount produced:

$$TC(x) = 1,000 + 100x + x^2.$$

The objective of the firm is to maximize profit, total revenue less total cost, which can be achieved by setting marginal revenue equal to marginal cost. The total-revenue function, $TR(x)$, is obtained by multiplying price times quantity:

$$TR(x) = x \cdot p(x) = x(500 - x) = 500x - x^2.$$

The marginal-revenue function, $MR(x)$, is now easily computed:

$$MR(x) = \frac{d}{dx} TR(x) = 500 - 2x.$$

The marginal-cost function, $MC(x)$, is computed similarly:

$$MC(x) = \frac{d}{dx} TC(x) = 100 + 2x.$$

The optimal output, x^*, is the solution to

$$MR(x) = MC(x) \quad \text{or} \quad 500 - 2x = 100 + 2x,$$

yielding $x^* = 100$, which is sold at a price of \$400 per unit. At this point, total profits, π, equal

$$\pi = TR(100) - TC(100) = 40,000 - 21,000 = 19,000.$$

Thus at the start of the period the firm plans production of 100 units at a total cost of \$21,000 and expects profits to be \$19,000.

Suppose, however, that the linear cost coefficient in the total-cost function is actually 180, not 100. This difference could be caused either by the firm's misestimating its cost function or by a shift in the cost function at the start of the period that was not detected (or at least not reacted to) by management. With this change in the cost function, the actual cost for producing the 100 units is

$$1,000 + 180(100) + (100)^2 = \$29,000,$$

and actual profits for the period are only $11,000 (the demand curve has not shifted, so that the 100 units can still be sold at $400 each). With a traditional evaluation system, the firm will compute an unfavorable total cost (and profit) variance of $8,000. Thus, at first glance, the error in estimating costs seems to have cost the firm $8,000 in foregone profits.

But if the firm's cost function is actually given by

$$1,000 + 180x + x^2.$$

there is no way that the firm could actually have achieved a profit of $19,000. The unfavorable change in the linear cost parameter has made the firm worse off, and its response to this change is limited. The best it could have done was to have computed a new output-price combination where marginal revenue equaled revised marginal cost:

$$500 - 2x = 180 + 2x$$

or $x^* = 80$ and price $(p) = \$420$ per unit. At this new output, total profits would have equaled:

$$\pi = TR(80) - TC(80) = \$33,600 - \$21,800 = \$11,800.$$

Thus, the unfavorable shift in the cost parameter caused the maximum attainable profits to decrease from $19,000 to $11,800. This decrease, under the assumptions of the situation, is not controllable by the firm. The loss associated with not knowing the true cost parameter is caused by producing too much output (100 instead of 80), which caused the firm to have a profit of $11,000 when the maximum attainable was $11,800. The $800 difference between the maximum attainable profit of $11,800 and the actual profit of $11,000 is called the *opportunity loss*. It is the loss caused by misestimating the linear cost parameter. The difference of $7,200 between the a priori expected profits of $19,000 and the maximum attainable profits of $11,800 is called a *forecasting variance*; it is the unavoidable loss caused by the linear cost parameter's being 180 rather than 100. In this case, the 80 percent error in the linear cost parameter caused an opportunity loss of only $800, which is less than 7 percent of the maximum attainable profit. Thus for this decision, large variations in the linear cost parameter produce relatively minor opportunity losses.

If the firm were cash constrained and expected a net profit of $19,000 but only received $11,000, the $8,000 shortfall might have repercussions on other decisions and actions of the firm. But we can analyze these in a similar fashion— identifying what decisions were made assuming $19,000 of cash would be available, computing the best decisions that could have been made if it were known that only $11,800 (the maximum) or $11,000 (the actual) cash were available, and obtaining the opportunity loss caused by not knowing the actual amount of cash that was going to be received.

EXPECTED OPPORTUNITY LOSSES

Knowing that an opportunity loss is associated with misestimating a cost parameter, it would be helpful to have an advance idea about the loss caused by estimation errors. This advance knowledge provides guidance about the seriousness of estimation errors and how much we should be willing to pay to obtain more accurate estimates. In order to obtain the a priori estimates of opportunity losses, we need to consider the possible values that the cost parameter can assume and the opportunity losses associated with each possible value. We have already considered the case in which the cost parameter could be 180 when we thought it was going to be 100. The opportunity loss associated with this case was $800.

Suppose that we believe that the linear cost parameter, which we will denote by c, could take on only three possible values, 60, 100, and 180, with the following probabilities:[1]

Cost Parameter, c	Probability
60	0.2
100	0.7
180	0.1

The expected value of c, $E(c)$, is 100, $[E(c) = 0.2(60) + 0.7(100) + 0.1(180)]$, and the firm, wishing to maximize expected profits, uses this value in setting output and price. If c turns out to be 60, rather than 100, the ex post optimal decision is to have produced 110 units and sold them at a price of $390 each for a net profit of $23,200. The actual decision of producing 100 units and selling them for $400 each would have generated a profit of $23,000 (the reader should verify these computations by working through the revenue and cost functions with $c = 60$). Therefore, the opportunity loss associated with believing that $c = 100$ when, in fact, it equaled 60 is $200.

We can now compute the expected opportunity loss (EOL) from Table 8-1:

$$EOL = 0.2(200) + 0.7(0) + 0.1(800) = \$120.$$

The EOL of $120 represents the maximum we should be willing to pay to obtain precise information about c. It is the expected value of perfect information (EVPI). Since it is unlikely that perfect information would be obtained even with extensive analysis and investigation, an analyst who is paid about $100 a day should not

---

[1] This is a highly simplified and unrealistic situation, but the analysis is straightforward and sets the stage for a more realistic situation to be treated next.

TABLE 8-1. Computation of Expected Opportunity Loss

c	Opportunity Loss	Probability	Expected Opportunity Loss
60	200	0.2	40
100	0	0.7	0
180	800	0.1	80

spend more than a day attempting to obtain a more precise probability distribution than the one given above.

A three-point probability distribution like that analyzed above is unlikely to arise in practice, but it helped us to develop the methodology for computing expected opportunity losses. In general, the cost parameter could take on any of a continuum of values. For any particular value of c, the ex post optimum value of output is obtained by equating marginal revenue with marginal cost:

$$500 - 2x^* = c + 2x^*$$

or

$$x^*(c) = \frac{500 - c}{4}.$$

The optimum profit, given a particular value of c, $\pi^*(c)$, is computed as

$$\pi^*(c) = TR[x^*(c)] - TC[x^*(c)]$$
$$= 500x^*(c) - x^*(c)^2 - [1,000 + cx^*(c) + x^*(c)^2]$$
$$= \frac{(500 - c)^2}{8} - 1,000.$$

Assume that the expected value of c equals 100, so that the a priori optimal production plan to maximize expected profits is $x = 100$. The actual profit associated with producing $x = 100$ when the cost parameter is c is

$$40,000 - [1,000 + 100c + (100)^2] = 29,000 - 100c.$$

Therefore the opportunity loss as a function of the actual value of c [OL(c)] is

$$OL(c) = \pi^*(c) - (29,000 - 100c)$$
$$= \left[\frac{(500 - c)^2}{8} - 30,000 + 100c \right]$$
$$= \frac{(100 - c)^2}{8}.$$

(The reader can verify that this formula is consistent with the computations we did before for $c = 60$, 100, and 180.) The expected opportunity loss is therefore

$$\text{EOL} = E\left[\frac{(100 - c)^2}{8}\right].$$

But since, by assumption $E(c) = 100$, we can rewrite this expression as

$$\text{EOL} = \frac{E[c - E(c)]^2}{8} = \frac{\text{Var}(c)}{8}.$$

As a specific example, suppose the parameter c was estimated from a regression on historical data in which the coefficient was 100 and its standard error was 40 (yielding a significant t ratio of 2.5). The expected value of c is therefore 100, as we stipulated, and the variance of c is $(40)^2 = 1,600$. The EOL associated with using the cost estimate with this degree of uncertainty is

$$\text{EOL} = \frac{\text{Var}(c)}{8} = \frac{1,600}{8} = 200.$$

Thus, even with a probability distribution on c yielding a 95 percent confidence interval including, roughly, the range of values from 20 to 180, the consequences of using our best guess of this parameter $[E(c) = 100]$ are quite minor; there is an expected opportunity loss of only about 1 percent of expected profits of $19,000. Our extended analysis has established that we should not be overly concerned with the uncertainty in the cost estimate, c, within the context of the specific decision model in which this cost parameter will be used.

Besides establishing the framework for assessing the consequences of estimation errors or of shifts in the cost structure of a production process, we have developed a method for decomposing the profit variance caused by the differences between actual and expected costs. That part of the variance that is due to the change in the parameter estimate (for example, a shift in c from 100 to 180) is called a *forecasting variance* and is considered noncontrollable by the production manager. It is caused by a noncontrollable shift in one or more parameters of the model.

The other variance component, called the *opportunity-cost variance,* is associated with not adjusting the output decision given that a change in the cost parameter has occurred; for example, given that c has changed from 100 to 180, x^* should change from 100 to 80. The opportunity-cost variance represents the difference between what the firm could have done, given the actual realization of cost parameters, and what it actually did do based on its prior knowledge and plans. The opportunity-cost variance is caused by not reacting quickly enough to changes in the environment. For many decision models—and certainly for the marginal-revenue, marginal-cost decision used as an example—the opportunity-cost variance is relatively small even with large forecasting errors, since the payoff function is not highly sensitive to the decision variable.

Inventory decision models provide an additional illustration for determining the consequences of cost estimation errors on operating performance. Inventory models are covered extensively in production and operations research courses, so we will deal here only with the simplest version of an inventory model, the *economic order quantity (EOQ)* with known (deterministic) demand. The cost parameters required to compute the EOQ are exactly the same as those required to solve more complex inventory models, so that, for cost accounting purposes, the relevant features of inventory decisions are well captured by the simple EOQ model.

The assumptions for this model are:

1. Known constant demand, D, over a specified period of time (such as a year).
2. Order or purchase cost, C_o, incurred each time an order is placed.
3. Holding or storage cost per unit, C_h, the cost of holding items in inventory.
4. Stockout or shortage costs per unit, C_s, the cost of having to backlog demand because of inadequate supply.
5. Constant acquisition price for each unit of inventory.
6. Instantaneous delivery.

With these assumptions, the demand for holding inventory arises from the *transactions motive*, the desire to balance off the fixed cost of placing each order, C_o, against the holding cost, C_h, of keeping items in inventory. If C_o were 0, orders could be placed continuously to respond to the demand pattern. If C_h were 0, one huge order could be placed to meet demand for all future periods. With both C_o and C_h greater than 0, we hold inventory to balance off these two costs.

If demand, D, were uncertain, the firm would hold inventory to balance off the stockout costs, C_s, when demand is higher than expected in a period. This is called the *precautionary motive*. Because of the precautionary motive, the firm would hold inventory even if C_o were zero when faced with an uncertain demand pattern. If the acquisition prices of the items we were stocking for inventory were expected to fluctuate, the firm would hold inventory to protect itself against future increases in price, the *speculative motive*. Also, if there were quantity discounts, the firm would hold some inventory to take advantage of these cost savings. For our purposes, we can ignore the complicating features of inventory models that give rise to holding inventory because of precautionary and speculative motives, or for quantity discounts, and concentrate solely on the transactions motive.

Computing the EOQ

The mathematics of the economic order quantity are relatively simple and straightforward. Assume initially that no backlogging of demand is possible (or, equivalently, that $C_s = \infty$). We are searching for the optimal value of q, the amount to be ordered each time an order is placed. If an amount q is ordered each time our inventory supply drops to zero (we can wait this long because of assumption 6, instantaneous delivery), the average inventory level over the course of the time period is $q/2$. Since the inventory holding cost is C_h per unit, the total holding cost over the period is $C_h q/2$. With the total demand for the period equal to D, and if q units are ordered each time an order is placed, then we must place D/q orders during this time period. Thus the total ordering costs during the period are DC_o/q. The actual acquisition cost of the D items we will eventually purchase is not relevant to the decision, since this cost must eventually be incurred under any inventory ordering rule, given our implicit assumption that we will satisfy all demand. Thus the variable cost of inventory is not an incremental cost for this decision (recall our discussion in Chapter 2 of this point). The per-unit cost of acquired items will, however, show up as a component of the holding cost, C_h.

The EOQ model determines q to minimize the total holding and ordering costs of operating the inventory system:

$$\text{TC} = \frac{C_h q}{2} + \frac{DC_o}{q}. \tag{8-1}$$

Using differential calculus[2] to obtain a minimum of this function with respect to q yields

$$q^* = \sqrt{\frac{2C_o D}{C_h}} \tag{8-2}$$

as the optimal order quantity. Also, by substitition, we obtain the minimum total cost as

$$\text{TC}^* = \sqrt{2C_o D C_h}. \tag{8-3}$$

The development of the model with backorders permitted is more complex. Rather than work through the details, which again add little to our knowledge of cost accounting, we present the formulas without derivation:

$$q^* = \sqrt{\frac{2C_o D}{C_h}} \sqrt{\frac{C_s + C_h}{C_s}} \tag{8-4}$$

and

$$\text{TC}^* = \sqrt{2C_o D C_h} \sqrt{\frac{C_s}{C_s + C_h}}. \tag{8-5}$$

---

[2] $(d/dq)\text{TC} = (C_h/2) - (DC_o/q^2) = 0$, so that $q^2 = 2C_o D/C_h$.

Notice that if the shortage cost is infinite, these formulas reduce to those derived in the no-backlogging case, as we should expect. Allowing for backlogging reduces the minimum total cost by the factor

$$\left[\frac{C_s}{C_s + C_h} \right]^{1/2}$$

and increases the optimal order amount by the reciprocal of this factor.

Estimating Cost Parameters

The EOQ formulas are simple to use and implement, once we know the relevant parameters. Estimating these parameters, however, is a difficult task, since most components of the costs cannot be obtained by a simple examination of the firm's accounting records. Therefore, a considerable degree of uncertainty will exist in the cost parameters. Before determining the effects of this uncertainty on the operation of the inventory system, we discuss the relevant issues in obtaining even rough estimates of these parameters.

The *ordering cost*, C_o, is the fixed cost each time an order is placed. The cost is called "fixed" because it is independent of the amount of units ordered. Components in C_o include the cost of forms for purchasing and receiving, the clerical processing of orders and payments, and the fixed costs of receiving and inspecting items and placing them in storage. These costs will be hard to determine, because persons involved in placing or receiving orders and handling payments will also be performing many other functions during the course of a day. The time spent in each activity can be roughly estimated to give a crude approximation of costs. For a more formal approach, a multiple regression study could be performed, where the number and size of orders of different types could be included as independent variables to explain clerical costs (recall Longbrake's study of bank cost functions, described in Chapter 4, where he derived estimates of the cost of processing checks of different types).

A primary component of the per-unit *holding* or *storage cost*, C_h, is the opportunity cost of funds tied up in inventory. Funds that have been paid to acquire inventory are not available for repaying loans, investing in marketable securities, or other uses of funds. Therefore, the cost of holding inventory includes a cost of capital that is multiplied by the acquisition cost (including delivery charges) of each item in inventory. We see now that the acquisition price of inventory enters the EOQ decision through its effect on the holding-cost parameter. Other components of the variable per-unit holding cost are insurance and personal property taxes on the inventory, obsolescence, deterioration, breakage, and variable storage or warehousing costs. The fixed costs of a warehouse are not part of C_h, since these costs will not vary with the amount or timing of the inventory order.

Stockout costs, C_s, are perhaps the most difficult to estimate. They include customer notification, filling and expediting of special orders, and the loss of customer goodwill caused by not being able to satisfy demand immediately. The estimate of the cost of loss of goodwill could also include an estimate of future sales lost.

Many of the cost components of C_o, C_h, and C_s are difficult to obtain because of aggregation problems. The costs may be recorded but included in broader cost categories so that the particular part relevant to the inventory decision cannot be easily isolated. Other components are not even recorded in the firm's accounting system, since they represent opportunity costs—foregone returns from transactions not undertaken. Examples of components not specifically recorded are the cost-of-capital component of holding costs and the loss-of-customer-goodwill component of stockout costs. Therefore, we expect that the cost estimates used to compute the EOQ will be more uncertain than most cost inputs to decision models. If the EOQ model is to be used, we are interested in determining the sensitivity of the model to estimation errors in the cost parameters.

Opportunity Losses in the EOQ

Let us now compute the opportunity losses associated with cost estimation errors in the context of a specific example. Consider the Alexander Company, which uses 7,200 units per year of a particular item in its production process. The fixed cost to place an order is \$36, the units cost \$10 each, and the holding cost is computed as 15 percent of the unit cost (this includes the opportunity cost of funds, insurance, and property taxes). With no backlogging of demand, the optimal order quantity is

$$q^* = \sqrt{\frac{2C_oD}{C_h}} = \sqrt{\frac{2(36)(7,200)}{0.15(10)}} = \sqrt{345,600} \approx 588.$$

Each order represents about one-twelfth of annual demand, so that the firm will be ordering items every month. The minimum incremental cost of operating the inventory system is

$$TC^* = \sqrt{2C_oDC_h} = \sqrt{777,600} = \$882/year.$$

Suppose now that we could have up to a 50 percent error in estimating either the ordering cost or the holding cost. How would these errors affect the operation of our inventory rule? We start the analysis by allowing the true ordering cost to be 50 percent higher: $C_o = 54$, not 36. Following the policy we have just computed, assuming that $C_o = 36$, we obtain an incremental cost of

$$TC = \frac{C_hq}{2} + \frac{DC_o}{q} = \frac{(1.5)(588)}{2} + \frac{(7,200)(54)}{588} = \$1,102.$$

With $C_o = 54$, the optimal policy would have been

$$q^* = \sqrt{\frac{2(54)(7,200)}{1.5}} = 720 \text{ units}$$

at a minimum cost of

$$TC^* = \sqrt{2(54)(7,200)(1.5)} = \$1,080.$$

By following the policy based on the erroneous estimate of C_o (a 50 percent error), we incur incremental costs of \$22 per year over the optimal policy—an increase of only 2 percent. The forecasting variance would be \$1,080 $-$ \$882 = \$198, but the opportunity-cost variance—the cost of following the suboptimal policy because of parameter estimation error—is only \$22. The reader can verify that a 50 percent error in the other direction ($C_o = 18$) causes an opportunity loss of \$37 from the minimum obtainable cost of \$624.

With a 50 percent error in storage costs, the parameter C_h could be as high as 2.25 or as low as 0.75. At the lower figure, the actual cost of operating the system would be

$$TC = \frac{(0.75)(588)}{2} + \frac{7,200(36)}{588} = \$661,$$

whereas the optimal policy and minimum total cost would be

$$q^* = \sqrt{\frac{2(36)(7,200)}{0.75}} = 831 \text{ units}$$

and

$$TC^* = \sqrt{2(36)(7,200)(0.75)} = \$624.$$

The opportunity loss caused by estimating the holding costs too high is \$37 or about 6 percent of the minimum obtainable. An error in the opposite direction, causing C_h to be 2.25, would result in the identical \$22 opportunity loss computed when C_o was actually \$54 rather than \$36.

We can compute the opportunity loss directly by using the formula:

$$\frac{TC}{TC^*} = \frac{1}{2}\left(\frac{q^*}{q} + \frac{q}{q^*}\right), \tag{8-6}$$

where q^* is the optimal order quantity based on the true values of the model parameters and q is the order quantity computed, and implemented, with the misestimated values. From this formula we can compute the opportunity loss as a percentage of the minimal total cost:

$$\frac{TC - TC^*}{TC^*} = \frac{1}{2}\frac{(q - q^*)^2}{qq^*}. \tag{8-7}$$

To illustrate this computation, we consider the case in which C_o and C_h are simultaneously in error. The worst case occurs when one parameter is too high while the other is too low. (Why? Try working out the situation when both parameters are higher than expected: $C_o = 54$, $C_h = 2.25$.) With $C_o = 54$ and $C_h = 0.75$, the optimal policy yields

$$q^* = \sqrt{\frac{2(54)(7,200)}{0.75}} = 1,018,$$

$$TC^* = \sqrt{2(54)(7,200)(0.75)} = \$764.$$

Therefore,

$$\frac{TC - TC^*}{TC^*} = \frac{1}{2}\frac{(588 - 1,018)^2}{(588)(1,018)} = 0.15$$

and

$$\text{opportunity loss} = (0.15)(764) = 118.$$

Even in this worst-case situation the opportunity loss is \$118 or only 15 percent of the minimum achievable cost. These computations show that even large errors in estimating the cost parameters for the EOQ model cause only minor opportunity losses when operating the inventory system. The EOQ model is quite insensitive to the effects of large estimation errors.

We have ignored the possibility of having the Alexander Company run short of this item during each inventory cycle. Suppose that the shortage cost of not having this item available is \$18 per unit; this cost is caused by having to rearrange production schedules during the time when this item is not in stock. We can now compute a different opportunity cost—the cost not of misestimating a parameter but of using an overly simplified model (no backlogging) when in fact the firm did have the option of running out of this item periodically. With $C_s = 18$, the optimal policy is to order

$$q^* = 588 \sqrt{\frac{C_s + C_h}{C_s}} = 588 \sqrt{\frac{18 + 1.5}{18}} = 615,$$

and the minimum total cost is now

$$TC^* = 883 \sqrt{\frac{18}{18 + 1.5}} = \$847.$$

Allowing for backlogging at an annual cost of \$18 per unit reduces the minimum incremental cost from \$882 to \$847. This is an opportunity loss of \$35 or 4 percent caused by misspecifying the model. (We could also interpret the misspecification as being caused by initially treating C_s as extremely high and ignoring the option to backlog demand when, in fact, C_s was only \$18 so that some backlogging is optimal.)

When computing opportunity losses for the two models considered in this chapter—the marginal-revenue, marginal-cost decision and the EOQ inventory model—we assumed that the change in the cost parameter could have been known at the start of the period and that the manager could have changed the operating decision at that time. Recall that the opportunity-cost variance was computed assuming that the ex post optimal plan, given the change in cost parameter, could have been implemented for the entire period. In practice, of course, the change in a cost parameter would not occur or be noticed immediately. Sometime during the course of the period, an alert manager would notice the changed conditions and attempt to respond accordingly by altering the decision (assuming that the cost of the change, including computational efforts, was justified by avoiding the opportunity loss that would otherwise occur). The accounting system can be structured, at some cost, to provide rapid information or feedback about the values of key parameters in a decision model. It is therefore interesting to explore a technique for calculating the value of timely information—information that arrives early enough during a period so that the operating decision can be changed. This technique will provide an operational measure of the timeliness of information.

We illustrate the value of the information-timing computation in the context of a simple production-smoothing example. The production-smoothing problem is characterized by a firm, with a nonlinear cost function, that is producing an item to meet an externally determined demand. With perfect information, the firm would attempt to schedule production evenly during the period to avoid operating at high-marginal-cost portions of its cost curve. But precise information about demand is not known initially, so the firm must start production based on its best estimate of demand and modify production at the point when true actual demand is revealed. This model differs from the two previously considered in the chapter, since it is driven by uncertainty in a demand parameter rather than a cost parameter. But the method is general and can be applied to uncertain cost parameters, too. Also, we could just as easily have introduced parameter uncertainty in the demand function in our first example or in the total demand, D, for the period in the EOQ model. When working with production decision models, the analyst needs to be concerned about the quality of information for both cost and demand parameters.

Specifically, we assume that the firm has a daily cost function given by

$$TC(x) = a + bx + cx^2, \qquad a, b, c > 0,$$

where x is the amount produced each day. This is a generalization of the linear

---

[3] This material is derived from Ijiri and Itami [1973]. It assumes knowledge of constrained nonlinear maximization using Lagrange multipliers.

cost functions we usually consider to allow for increasing marginal cost (since $c > 0$) as production increases. An important characteristic of such a quadratic (or, more generally, convex) cost function is that minimum total cost is achieved by scheduling production to be the same amount each day.

Algebraically we can easily demonstrate this property. Suppose we have to produce a total amount X over n days. Let x_i be the amount produced on day i, $i = 1, 2, \ldots, n$. We wish to minimize total production costs over the n days,

$$na + b \sum_{i=1}^{n} x_i + c \sum_{i=1}^{n} x_i^2,$$

subject to the constraint that the total production over the n days must sum to X:

$$\sum_i x_i = X.$$

We obtain the minimum-cost solution by forming the Lagrangian:

$$L = na + b \sum x_i + c \sum x_i^2 - \lambda(\sum x_i - X),$$

and setting the derivative of L with respect to each decision variable, x_i, and λ equal to 0.

$$\frac{\partial L}{\partial x_i} = b + 2cx_i - \lambda = 0, \qquad i = 1, \ldots, n,$$

$$\frac{\partial L}{\partial \lambda} = \sum x_i - X = 0.$$

The solution is for each x_i to equal a constant:

$$x_i = \frac{\lambda - b}{2c}, \qquad i = 1, \ldots, n,$$

and $(\lambda - b)/2c$ must equal X/n in order to satisfy the total demand constraint.[4]

We can now introduce the timing aspect of demand information. Assume that there are n operating days in the period. The amount produced each day is stored in inventory (no deterioration, obsolescence, or pilferage) until the end of the month, when the entire period's production is shipped to the customer in a single delivery. The demand for the period is not known for certain until i days of production have been completed. Therefore, during the first i days, the firm must schedule production based on a forecast for total demand. Since we have

---

[4] The Lagrange multiplier λ is the shadow price representing the cost of producing the last item:

$$\lambda = b + 2c \frac{X}{n}.$$

The last item incurs the variable cost, b, plus the incremental quadratic cost ($2c$) of producing this last item uniformly over the period (X/n per day).

already demonstrated that it is optimal to have level production, we know that the firm will produce a constant amount in each of the first i days and another constant amount in the remaining $n - i$ days after the actual demand is revealed. Letting x represent the daily level production in each of the first i days and y the daily production amount in the remaining $n - i$ days, the total production cost for the n days is

$$i(a + bx + cx^2) + (n - i)(a + by + cy^2).$$

Let $D = nd$ be the total demand for the period (revealed after i days), where d is the equivalent daily production (the ex post optimum). After D is revealed, the firm must produce $D - ix$ items in the remaining $n - i$ days. For simplicity we will assume that either x is chosen small enough or i is early enough that $D - ix$ is not negative. Then the amount, y, to be produced in each of the remaining $n - i$ days is

$$y = \frac{D - ix}{n - i} = \frac{nd - ix}{n - i}.$$

We define $W(i, x, d)$ to be the cost of the policy of producing x for the first i days when the equivalent daily production turns out to be d:

$$W(i, x, d) = i(a + bx + cx^2) + (n - i)\left[a + b\left(\frac{nd - ix}{n - i}\right) + c\left(\frac{nd - ix}{n - i}\right)^2\right].$$

The minimum total cost, the ex post optimum, would have been to have produced d each day. This is represented by $W(i, d, d)$:

$$W(i, d, d) = n(a + bd + cd^2).$$

Therefore, the opportunity loss associated with not having the actual demand, $D = nd$, revealed until after i days have passed, $OL(i, x, d)$, is

$$OL(i, x, d) = W(i, x, d) - W(i, d, d)$$

$$= icx^2 + c\frac{(nd - ix)^2}{n - i} - ncd^2$$

$$= \frac{i}{n - i}nc(x - d)^2.$$

The opportunity loss is zero if we happen to have fortuitously chosen our initial production rate, x, to be equal to the equivalent daily demand, d. The loss increases more than proportionally with the information delay, i. (Formally, OL is a convex increasing function of i). Thus, we have derived a law of increasing marginal loss caused by information delay.

If d is a random variable with mean μ and standard deviation σ, the expected opportunity loss is computed as

$$EOL = \frac{i}{n - i}ncE(x - d)^2,$$

and this quantity is minimized by choosing $x = E(d)$, since

$$\frac{d}{dx} \text{EOL} = \frac{inc}{n - i} 2E(x - d) = 0.$$

With $x = \mu$, the minimum expected opportunity loss is

$$\text{EOL}^* = \frac{inc}{n - i} E(d - \mu)^2 = \frac{inc}{n - i} \sigma^2.$$

Thus, the expected opportunity loss is proportional to the variance of the demand distribution (analogous to a result we obtained in our marginal-cost, marginal-revenue model where EOL was found to be proportional to the variance of the distribution of the linear cost parameter) and is a convex increasing function of information delay.

Analysis of Operating Performance

In the marginal-revenue, marginal-cost and the EOQ inventory decision models, we decomposed the total variance between actual results and the ex post optimum into a forecasting variance and an opportunity-cost variance. We can obtain a similar variance analysis in the information-timing model. The analysis is more meaningful in this case because we can explicitly control for the timing of the receipt of information by the manager. At this point, the initial plan can be revised based on the more accurate forecast of demand. In the two previous models the opportunity-cost variance was computed as if the manager had access to information on the new cost estimate at the start of the period, an assumption that is not reasonable for evaluating the manager's performance.

For our information-timing model, the quantity $W(i, x, d)$ represents a realistic ex post standard for the manager to have achieved. It is the cost of following the initial policy of producing x units each day and adjusting optimally to the new demand information, that total demand D is equal to nd, which is revealed after i days. The ex ante standard, assuming that no further demand information would be revealed during the period, is the cost of producing x each day for the n days in the period. This quantity can be represented by $W(0, x, x)$:

$$W(0, x, x) = n(a + bx + cx^2).$$

Given that total demand, D, turned out to be equal to nd, the best we could have done was to have produced d from the start of the period. Thus, the quantity $W(0, d, d) = n(a + bd + cd^2)$ represents the ex post optimum. With these definitions, we can now compute the different variances.

Suppose that actual production costs during the period were W^o. Since the ex ante standard was $W(0, x, x)$, the total variance is given by $W^o - W(0, x, x)$, and we can decompose this variance as follows:

$$\text{Total variance} = W^o - W(0, x, x)$$
$$= [W^o - W(i, x, d)] + [W(i, x, d) - W(0, d, d)]$$
$$+ [W(0, d, d) - W(0, x, x)]$$
$$= \text{AV} + \text{FEV} + \text{UV}. \tag{8-8}$$

The *adaptation variance,* AV, is the difference between actual costs and the minimum achievable, given that demand, d, was disclosed at day i. AV is analogous to the traditional spending variance, since it represents factors controllable by the manager of the production department. It eliminates the effects of random, controllable environmental factors (the actual demand) and it controls for the time when the manager should have received the demand information. It focuses the manager's attention on adapting quickly to changes in the environment of the firm.

The *forecast error variance,* FEV $= W(i, x, d) - W(0, d, d)$, is the cost caused by not knowing demand for certain at the start of the period. It is always nonnegative (unfavorable) and represents the cost of the forecast error, since it is the difference between the minimum achievable cost (given that demand d is not revealed until after i days have passed) and what could have been achieved had we known actual demand at the start of the period. In the previous models we included the FEV as a component of the opportunity-cost variance [opportunity-cost variance $= W^o - W(0, d, d)$]. In this model we do not hold the manager responsible for adapting to changes before the information becomes available. Hence FEV is identified as a separate, noncontrollable variance.

The *uncertainty variance,* UV $= W(0, d, d) - W(0, x, x)$, is caused by the random variation in parameter values. It is identical to what we called the forecasting variance in the previous two models. The UV is the difference between the minimum ex post and the minimum ex ante production cost. It is caused solely by the difference between the actual realization of a random variable and its prior expectation. In a traditional flexible budgeting context, the UV is the variance caused by actual volume's being different from expected or standard volume. The UV can be positive or negative, depending on the realization of the demand parameter.

By decomposing the total variance into these three components, we obtain a variance (AV) controllable by the manager, given the timing and cost parameters of the problem, a variance (FEV) due to the delay in receiving information about the actual value of demand in the period, and a variance (UV) due to the inherent uncertainty in the model. We are able to focus attention on having the manager respond quickly and accurately to perceived changes in the environment, and we do not hold the manager responsible for uncontrollable delays in receiving accurate information or for the realizations of random variables that differ from prior expectations.

MONITORING DECISION-MODEL PARAMETERS

This chapter has developed a framework to assess the consequences of inaccurate cost estimates and of delays in receiving accurate cost and demand information. Without this framework, we would be unable to determine how much to invest in more accurate or more timely information. It should be clear that the demand for accurate and timely cost data arises from the specific uses to be made of this information. Thus, we must analyze the demand for cost information by being explicit and formal about the decisions that will be made using these data.

The use of formal decision models to evaluate the quality of cost data raises other interesting considerations. Historically, firms have accumulated data on actual transactions to support their financial reporting systems. As formal decision models are increasingly used to aid decision making within firms, a demand is created for the accumulation and monitoring of data not involving actual transactions. In the EOQ inventory model, the important cost parameters could not be obtained from a traditional transactions-based cost accounting system. The relevant data either were collected on too aggregate a basis or arose from opportunity costs. When a decision model is first implemented, special studies will therefore have to be made to estimate the relevant cost, demand, capacity, and technology parameters. But because many of these parameters are not measured periodically as part of the firm's financial or cost accounting system, it is all too easy for the parameter estimates derived in such special studies not to be monitored or reestimated periodically. Over time, the opportunity losses caused by making decisions using outdated and inaccurate parameter estimates could be considerable. Therefore, procedures to monitor the assumptions and parameter estimates for a firm's decision models may need to be established. Of course, such procedures should not be more costly than the benefits expected, or the opportunity losses avoided, by having more accurate cost estimates.

To illustrate the importance of these remarks, consider the use of linear programming in the product-mix decision. In order to set up and solve such a model we need estimates of

p_i　　the price of product i,

b_i　　the variable cost of product i,

c_j　　the capacity of resource j,

r_{ij}　　the amount of resource j used to produce one unit of product i.

The b_i's can be derived from the cost accounting system using procedures discussed in Chapters 2, 3, and 4. The remaining parameters are not cost based and will likely not be collected on a regular basis, especially the capacity and resource requirement parameters. Therefore, if there are significant changes in these parameters, the decisions made using the old parameter estimates may cause significant opportunity losses. At some point, and probably on a regular basis (which could be annual or biannual), it will probably pay to "audit" the firm's decision models to update and validate all the relevant model parameters.

As a further extension, the opportunity-cost and adaptability variances introduced in this chapter require that parameter estimates be obtained even for products that were not produced in the optimal schedule. The ex ante optimum was generated with the initial set of parameter estimates. When evaluating this decision based on ex post or realized data, we need to obtain price and variable-cost estimates on the products we chose not to produce as well as those that were actually made. For there could have been major changes in the prices or variable costs of previously excluded products that would have made these products much more desirable to produce had these changes been anticipated. Therefore, the use of a formal model for decision making creates a demand for continued measurement of opportunities not taken in order to evaluate properly the consequences of actions actually taken. This is a striking departure from the information generated in a traditional transactions-based cost accounting system. It would be unusual to find such a system collecting cost data for products not being manufactured.

SUMMARY

Formal decision models are necessary to evaluate the consequences of inaccurate and delayed cost data. Using formal models also creates a demand for monitoring and revision of cost, demand, and technology parameters that are used in the decision models. Finally, since the decision models may select only a subset among the set of all possible actions available to a firm, the characteristics of actions not taken should still be monitored to determine when conditions may have changed enough so that the original decisions should be reevaluated. These tasks are novel, and the detailed estimates and modeling required may be difficult to perform in complex dynamic settings. The management accountant, however, should have the basic concepts of opportunity loss and its measurement firmly in mind when evaluating the accuracy requirements of cost data and when assisting in the implementation or evaluation of decision models used by the firm.

PROBLEMS

8-1. Opportunity Loss when Actual Production Unequal to Planned Production

Consider the firm with the cost and revenue functions given in the first part of the chapter:

$$TC(x) = 1000 + 100x + x^2$$

$$TR(x) = 500x - x^2$$

Recall that the optimal plan was to produce 100 units, sell them for $400 each and obtain maximum profits of $19,000. Suppose that because of material shortages, the firm can only produce 80 units which it sells for its established price of $400 each.

Required:

> Compute the actual profits in this situation and explain the difference between your computed figure and the budgeted figure of $19,000 in terms of the forecasting variance and the opportunity cost variance.

8-2. Production Plan and Expected Opportunity Losses (A. Atkinson)

Sackville Foundry manufactures a standard line of quality castings used in automobile assembly. These castings are purchased by Giant Motors at a price of $100 each (F.O.B.). There is virtually unlimited demand for these castings but production is limited by foundry size and labor availability.

Each casting requires 5 labor hours (at $10 per hour) of labor, $11 of materials, and 2 machine hours. Labor is hired or discharged as required, but due to supply limitations a maximum of 3600 hours are available each month. Machine availability is 1500 hours per month. Machine and factory overhead (which includes a return on invested capital) is $6,000 per month if the machines are not operated and rises linearly to $28,500 when machines are operated at capacity. Factory overhead is applied at a rate of $19 per machine hour which assumes that the machines are operated at capacity. At present, however, the firm is more limited by its labor supply as it produces only 720 units per month.

The firm's income statement is as follows:

		Total		Unit	
Sales (720 × $100)		$72,000		$100	
Cost					
Labor (720 × 5 × 10)	$36,000		$50		
Materials (720 × 11)	7,920		11		
Overhead (720 × 2 × 19)	27,360	$71,280	38	99	
Net Income		$ 720		$ 1	

Dick Chessman, a wealthy local entrepreneur has approached the firm with a proposition for a new product. The product would require 1 machine hour, 2 labor hours, and $5 of materials cost.

Dick will receive $5 sales commission per unit sold. The problem is that the market price is uncertain. The following probability mass function defines price:

Price	Probability
50	.2
49	.5
48	.3

The factory accountant, Max Well, has prepared the following report for the new product:

Expected Price		48.9
Cost		
Commission (1 × 5)	$ 5	
Labor (2 × 10)	20	
Materials (1 × 5)	5	
Overhead (1 × 19)	19	49
Expected Net Income (Loss)		(0.1)

On the basis of this report, Max recommended that Dick's offer be rejected. The company makes decisions on an expected monetary value basis.

Required:

1. Prepare a report indicating whether you agree or disagree with Max.
2. What is the expected opportunity loss associated with the optimal decision?

8-3. *Ex-Post Analysis of a Product Mix Production System* (R. Hilton, adapted)

Complex Company has two producing departments, denoted $P1$ and $P2$. The company has two products, A and B, each of which must pass through both $P1$ and $P2$. Following are estimates of the variable costs of production to be incurred in departments $P1$ and $P2$ during the year 1983:

	Product A	Product B
Variable Costs Incurred in $P1$		
Direct Material	$1.00	$ 2.00
Direct Labor (labor rate $1/hour)	2.00	4.00
Variable Overhead	4.00	6.00
Total Variable Cost in $P1$	$7.00	$12.00
Variable Costs Incurred in $P2$		
Direct Material	$6.00	$3.00
Direct Labor (@ $1/hour)	1.00	1.00
Variable Overhead	2.00	2.00
Total Variable Cost in $P2$	$9.00	$6.00

The fixed costs traceable to *P*1 are $1,000 and to *P*2 are $2,000. There are no selling or administrative costs.

Complex Company uses one type of labor in both *P*1 and *P*2. The supply of this labor for the year 1983 is 3,000 hours.

Complex can sell all of its output of Product A at $20 per unit and its total output of B at $23 per unit.

Required:

1. Calculate the budgeted (ex ante) contribution margins for Products A and B during 1983.

2. Formulate the firm's ex ante production problem and obtain the optimal solution.

3. Actual results for 1983 revealed the following:
   a. Production and sales of A were 300 units.
   b. Production and sales of B were 180 units.
   c. The average price of Product A turned out to be $21 per unit.
   d. The direct material costs in department *P*1 were $3 per unit for both Products A and Products B.
   e. Because of a strike, the supply of labor for *P*1 and *P*2 was only 1800 hours instead of the predicted level of 3000 hours.
   f. All other cost and price predictions for 1983 were accurate.
   g. Of all the changes between budgeted and actual costs, only the increase in A's direct material cost could have been affected by the Plant Supervisor's actions.

   Analyze the operations of Complex Company during 1983 using the forecasting and opportunity cost variance approach.

8-4. *Opportunity Costs in a Product Mix Problem* (R. Hilton, adapted)

The Ives Company is currently preparing its budget for 1983. The company has two producing departments and two products. Product A requires labor and material in both departments; Product B is produced *entirely* by Department 2. The following information is available:

Department 1

	1980	1981	1982
Units of product A processed	200	400	300
Direct labor cost	$400	$800	$650
Direct Material X cost	100	200	150
Overhead traceable to Department 1	300	500	400
Total production costs	$800	$1500	$1200

Direct Material X is the only material applied to Product A in Department 1. There is an unlimited supply of Material X available.

Department 2

Direct Material Y:	Standard price per lb.: $2.00
	Standard quantity of Material Y
Product A	0.4 lb.
Product B	0.6 lb.
Direct Material Z:	Standard price per lb.: $5.00
	Standard quantity of Material Z
Product A	0.3 lb.
Product B	0.3 lb.
Direct Labor:	Standard price per hr.: $4.00
	Standard quantity of labor
Product A	0.5
Product B	0.4

The laborers in each department work only in their own departments. There is an unlimited supply of both types of labor.

Raw materials Y and Z are in short supply. It is estimated that only 5000 pounds of Y and 4000 pounds of Z will be available.

The Ives Company uses the high-low method over the prior three years to budget labor, material, and overhead costs in Department 1. The company uses linear regression to estimate Department 2 overhead, and the following equation has been estimated for 1983:

$$\text{Overhead cost in Department 2} = .5\text{DL\$} + \$1000$$

DL\$ denotes direct labor dollars in Department 2. Department 2 variable overhead is budgeted to Products A and B in proportion to budgeted direct labor dollars.

The R^2 for the equation is 0.9 and the t-value for the coefficient of DL\$ is 3.92.

Variable selling costs are $3.50 per unit for Product A, and $2 per unit for Product B. Product A sells for $20 and Product B for $15. Ives Company is a price taker (i.e., cannot affect prices by its actions). Fixed selling and administrative costs are $2,000. Ives Company sells all of its output.

Required:

1. What are the estimated unit contribution margins for Products A and B?

2. Ives Company uses linear programming for its planning model. Formulate and solve the Ives Company's production planning problem. Interpret the solution.

3. Based on the LP, what is the budgeted total contribution margin and budgeted total profit?

4. During the period, Ives noted several changes in the usage of materials and labor when compared to the standards.

   a. Because of new federal safety standards imposed on Product A, 0.4 lb. of raw material Z was required for each unit of A. This allowed usage of raw material Y to be reduced to 0.3 lbs. per unit of A.

   b. A new production technique allowed Product B to be produced with only 0.5 lbs. of raw material Y per unit of B.

   c. Union negotiations resulted in the direct labor rate increasing to $4.50 per hour in Department 2.

   d. Scheduling problems resulted in each unit of Product A using 0.6 hours of direct labor.

   e. No other discrepancies existed between observed and ex-ante predictions of parameters, and Ives maintained its faith in the regression estimate of Department 2 overhead costs.

   f. Actual production was 10,000 units of Product A.

   What are the ex-post budgeted contribution margins for Products A and B?

5. Which parameter changes represent forecasting errors, and which ones represent implementation (avoidable) errors?

6. Formulate and solve Ives Company's ex-post LP production plan. What is the ex-post budgeted total contribution margin?

7. What is the forecasting variance?

8. What is the opportunity cost variance?

8-5. MP Manufacturing (C) (Continuation of Problems 4-1 and 5-7)

The managers of MP are uncertain about some of the predictions they made in arriving at their production plans for 1983 (see MP(B)—Problem 5-7). You are to analyze the cost of the following possible prediction errors if they were to occur and if the production plans were based on the analysis done in MP(B). The errors in each section are to be analyzed separately. You should assume, however, that any production rate changes systematically affect the respective product's labor cost.

1. The selling price of Product A may actually be $54 instead of the predicted magnitude of $60.
2. The material cost of producing Product B may actually be $9.75 instead of the predicted magnitude of $11.25.
3. The production rate in Department 1 for Product C may actually be 4 per hour instead of the predicted magnitude of 3 per hour.
4. Major repairs to the machinery in Department 2 may reduce its capacity to 6,000 hours.

If the planned production is infeasible, MP's production staff usually cuts back the production of Product C (since that showed the smallest profit. With management's full cost profit analysis, see MP(A)—Problem 4-1) subject to the restriction that the production of any product must be sufficient to satisfy the demands of the customers whose needs must be met.

8-6. Inventory Ordering Rules: Discounts and Opportunity Costs

1. Roger Smith is operating an inventory ordering management system for a standard part used extensively in the production of the firm's products. Roger knows that the demand for the unit is predictable at 20,000 units per year. The unit costs $12 each but Roger can obtain a discount of 5 percent if he orders in batches of at least 1000 units.

   It is difficult for Roger to estimate the fixed cost of placing an order but he has the following best estimates associated with processing and receiving an order:

Preparing and processing the order:	$ 5
Receiving and inspecting the order	15
Paying for the order	10
	$30

   The variable costs of holding inventory include:

   > Insurance and taxes on inventory: 6 percent of average inventory value per year
   >
   > Cost of capital invested in inventory: 14 percent
   >
   > Breakage, spoilage, and deterioration: 2 percent of average annual inventory.

   What is the optimal quantity for Roger Smith to order each time he wishes to place an order?

2. Roger is also monitoring the purchase of another part. The demand for this part is 4,000 units per year and each unit costs $5 (no quantity discounts are available). Assuming the fixed cost to place an order and holding costs are the same as in Part 1, what is the optimal order quantity? What is the minimal incremental cost of operating the inventory system for this part?

3. Roger is most unsure about his estimate of the cost of placing each order (C_o). What is the opportunity loss associated with following the policy computed in (2) for one year when the ordering cost could be as low as $15 per order (a 50 percent reduction) or as high as $60 per order placed (a 100 percent increase)?

4. Roger believes that the probability that the ordering cost (C_o) equals $30 is 0.5. The probability that the ordering cost is as low as $15 is 0.3, and as high as $60 is 0.2. What is Roger's annual expected opportunity loss (EOL) from following the policy computed in (2)? What is the EOL as a percentage of the minimum inventory operating cost computed in (2)?

5. Roger is now concerned that both his estimates of the ordering cost (C_o) as well as the variable costs of holding inventory could be either too high or too low. Which combination(s) of errors (see below) will cause the highest opportunity loss assuming that Roger will follow the policy based on his initial estimates as computed in (2)? No computation is required but provide a brief justification for your answer:

Ordering Cost

		Too Low	Correct	Too High
Holding Cost	Too Low			
	Correct			
	Too High			

6. After operating the inventory system for this part for a year according to the policy computed in (2), Roger discovers that the cost of not having the part available when needed is $10 for each unit backlogged during the year (eventually all the demand for this part is satisfied). What was the opportunity loss associated with Roger's not allowing for backlogging of this part during the year?

7. Ignoring (6), suppose that Roger is approached at the beginning of the year and is offered his entire year's supply of the part at a 5 percent discount; that is, Roger can buy 4000 units at a cost of $19,000 ($4.75 per unit) saving $1000 in purchase costs for the year. The vendor will deliver all the units immediately and place them directly in the warehouse so that the only additional expenses are $15 to process and pay for the order. Should Roger accept this offer?

8. Roger decides to accept the vendor's offer of the one-time delivery of the annual supply at a 5 percent discount. A standard cost system is used to evaluate Roger's performance as a purchasing manager. Compute the material price variance for the year for this part. Comment on the appropriateness of a standard cost system for monitoring performance in this setting. Can you suggest an alternative scheme for evaluating Roger's performance as a purchasing manager?

8-7. Inventory Problem with Finite Production Rate (R. Manes)

A firm produces its own units in batches of size Q at a rate of P per day. Set-up costs per batch are C_o. The demand rate is d units per day with a total demand of D units per period. The length of the run will be Q/P, i.e., the batch amount to be produced in one run divided by the production rate. Maximum inventory (assuming a zero beginning inventory at the start of each run) will be equal to $(P - d)Q/P$ and average inventory will be $(P - d) \cdot Q/2P$. Using C_h to represent holding cost per unit over time t, the total cost of this production and inventory process, depicted in Exhibit 1, is:

$$\text{TC} = \frac{D}{Q} \cdot C_o + (P - d)\frac{Q}{2P} \cdot C_h$$

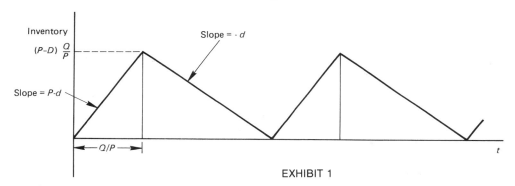

EXHIBIT 1

Assume that:

d $=$ 10 units per day
P $=$ 30 units per day
C_o $=$ \$500 per set-up
C_h $=$ \$8 per unit per time period
D $=$ 300 units per time period

Required:

1. Calculate Q^*, the optimal production batch size. Also, what is the length of time required to complete the production of this batch size?
2. What is the total incremental cost of operating this inventory system for one time period?
3. Suppose that the production manager finds a way to increase the production rate to 40 units per day but that the old batch size Q^* remains the same.
   a. What is the new incremental cost of operating the inventory system.
   b. What is the opportunity cost of using the old optimum batch size Q^*, with the new production rate quantity?
   c. Why do total inventory costs increase when there has been an improvement in the production process?

8-8. Relevant Inventory Costs and Opportunity Costs (A. Atkinson)

Matawa Coats produces two types of arctic coats: Adventurer and Explorer. Derek Acroyd, the company accountant, has recently provided the following data regarding these products.

	Adventurer		Explorer	
Price		$120		$160
Cost				
Direct Materials	40		45.50	
Direct Labor	30		50	
Variable Overhead	12		20	
Selling Commission	12		18	
Fixed Manufacturing	8		10	
Fixed Selling and Admin	8	110	10	153.50
Profit Per Coat		$ 10		$ 6.50

Each Adventurer coat requires 3 seamstress hours and an Explorer coat requires 5 hours. There are 200 seamstresses employed in the factory and each works 2,000 hours per year.

A maximum of 100,000 Explorer coats and 60,000 Adventurer coats may be sold per year. In addition, the company has a contract to deliver 30,000 parkas to the military. Each of these parkas requires 4 seamstress hours, and $40 of materials. In addition, fixed manufacturing costs of $7 and fixed selling and administrative costs of $7 are allocated to each parka.

The parkas require special set up because of their design. It takes one hour to switch over from regular production of coats to production of parkas and one hour to switch back. Each one hour switch requires the services of 50 seamstresses who prepare the set up while the others remain on production. All production runs of parkas require 5 hours of planning by the factory planner.

All labor in the factory is paid hourly at the rate of $10 per hour. A recent study concluded that factory overhead is $500,000 per year plus $4 per labor hour.

The parkas will be put into Smith's Storage which will charge the company $4 per coat per year. The cost for putting a parka into the warehouse is $12.80 a unit. Units will be withdrawn uniformly through the year for delivery to the military. A $2 per parka charge will be incurred for withdrawal and shipment. The company's required return on funds invested is 20 percent.

Required:

1. What is the economic batch size (EOQ) for production of parkas?

2. Suppose that the company can store a maximum of 1,000 parkas. The company's only alternative is to rent a warehouse for $15,000 per year. If the warehouse is rented, the only cost difference is the $15,000 rent and the $4 storage cost avoided. Which alternative is preferred? The maximum capacity of the rented warehouse is 3,000 units.

3. (Ignore the storage constraint in Question 2). Suppose that the maximum demand for Adventurer coats turns out to be 200,000. The company has implemented the optimal plan computed by you in answering Question 1. What is the cost of prediction error (opportunity loss) of this misestimate?

8-9. *Value of Timing of Information When Producing for Unknown Demand* (Y. Ijiri)

Pittsburgh Printing Shop of Sports Printing Company specializes in printing programs for Pittsburgh Steelers' home games. Since the Shop has only a small press, printing for a Sunday game is spread over the preceding six days, Monday through Saturday. Production volumes for Monday through Friday are determined based on estimated sales. On Friday night a sales agency at the Three Rivers Stadium, the sole distributor of the programs, places a non-cancelable order for the program for the following Sunday game. The production volume for Saturday is then adjusted to meet the order. If the order quantity is less than what had been produced by Friday, the surplus copies are disposed of at some cost. The contract stipulates that the order must be satisfied even when the cost of meeting the order may be expensive due to crash work on Saturday. The agency pays the shop $.80 a copy.

James Cartwright, General Manager of Pittsburgh Shop, says his past experience with daily operating cost may be summarized by a quadratic cost function: $a + bx + cx^2$.

The above daily operating cost includes all costs of operating the shop with the exception of headquarters overhead that is allocated to the shop as a fixed monthly charge. This function also fits well for negative production (i.e. disposal) volumes: When production volume is negative, the cost function shows daily operating cost net of any recovery from disposal of surplus copies.

Cartwright's experience with the demand is such that he believes the number of copies ordered s (in thousands of copies) is uniformly distributed in the range $12 \le s \le 24$.

Since Cartwright must often perform expensive crash work on Saturday to meet the order, he is negotiating with the agency to see whether they can give the shop a non-cancelable order on Wednesday night, instead of Friday night, so that the shop has three operating days to adjust the production volume and meet the order. The agency is willing to do so if Cartwright can offer a discount on the price per copy.

Suppose that actual demand is revealed after k days, $k = 1, 2, \ldots, 5$ (Initially $k = 5$ in this example). Also, x is measured in thousands of copies. Cartwright decides to follow a policy of level production on each day to meet demand. That is, he will produce an amount x for each of the first k days and an amount $(s - kx)/(6 - k)$ for each of the remaining $(6 - k)$ days after the true demand is revealed.

Required:

1. Is this policy optimal?
2. Cartwright decides to choose x to minimize the following expected incremental cost function:

$$w(x) = \text{expected weekly cost due to quadratic cost}$$
$$\text{component following the above policy}$$

$$= kcx^2 + (6 - k)E\left[c\left(\frac{s - kx}{6 - k}\right)^2\right]$$

Why does this function represent the expected weekly cost due to the quadratic cost component? Would you agree with Cartwright that the value of x that minimizes $w(x)$ minimizes overall expected costs?

Show how Cartwright obtains the following expression for the expected weekly cost when following the above policy:

$$w(x) = kcx^2 + \frac{c}{6 - k}[336 - 36kx + k^2x^2]$$

3. a.   What is the maximum amount that Cartwright should offer to learn total demand, s, after 3 days rather than current practice which reveals total demand after 5 days?

b.   Assuming the Stadium Authority prefers a discount per copy rather than a lump sum payment, what is the maximum discount Cartwright should offer to learn demand after 3 days rather than after 5 days?

4.   Cartwright has reviewed his past records and feels that past experience with daily operating cost may be summarized as follows:

Daily Production Volume (thousands of copies)	x	1	2	3	4
Daily Operating Cost		$600	$1000	$1600	$2400

Compute the values of the cost function parameters and give a numerical answer to the question in 3a and 3b above.

5.   Headquarters is considering a change in the method of overhead allocation from the present fixed monthly charge to one of the following three methods:

as a percent of total production cost,

as a percent of sales, or

as a perfect of profit.

The rate will be adjusted so that the total overhead charge will remain the same as before on the average.

a.   Without recalculating the maximum amount of discount that Cartwright can offer, logically deduce the impact upon the discount of adopting each of the three alternative methods of overhead allocation.

b.   From the headquarter's standpoint, which of the four methods, including the existing method of a fixed charge, is best in inducing desirable actions by shop managers, assuming that they attempt to maximize profit of the shop?

c.   From the shop-managers' standpoint, which method results in a profit figure that is considered to be most "fair"?

8-10. *Value of Information in a Stochastic Cost-Volume-Profit Setting* (R. Hilton)*

The Gem Chemical Company, produces a single industrial chemical compound with the trade name Lenroc. The company is currently faced with its production quantity

---

* This problem is based on the article, Ronald W. Hilton, "The Determinants of Cost Information Value: An Illustrative Analysis," *Journal of Accounting Research* (Autumn 1979) 411–35.

decision for the coming production period. The market for Lenroc is perfectly competitive with a unit sales price of r. Gem Chemical Company faces the following total cost function for production of Lenroc:

$$\text{Total cost} = Ta \left(\frac{x}{T}\right)^2 + Tb \left(\frac{x}{T}\right) + Tc$$

$$= a \frac{x^2}{T} + bx + Tc$$

where $a, b, c, T, x \geq 0$

T is the length of the production period during which the quantity, x, is produced. Thus x/T is the production rate. a, b, and c are parameters of the total cost function. Note that c represents the fixed cost for each of the time units in which T is measured. Thus Tc is total fixed cost for the production period of length T. b represents unit variable cost, where "variable" means costs which vary proportionately with output. a is the "quadratic cost" parameter which determines the rate at which marginal cost increases.

Required:

1. Let $T = 1$ and graph the total cost function, total revenue function, and profit function. All costs are cash costs. What is the optimal production level? Treat the decision as a short-run, one-period problem.

2. Suppose Gem can costlessly alter its production rate at some point during the period. Denote the beginning of the period by Time 0, the end by Time 1, and the point when the production rate can be altered as Time t, $0 \leq t \leq 1$. What is the optimal production rate during each of the two production subperiods, $(0, t)$ and $(t, 1)$?

3. Suppose Gem knows r, a, and b, but is uncertain about fixed cost, c. Gem may employ an information system which provides information about c. The report will be received at Time t. What is the value of the fixed cost reporting system? Denote the system by h_t^c. Assume risk neutrality.

4. Now suppose that Gem knows r, a, and c, but unit variable cost, b, is uncertain. The management of the company does not believe, however, that unit variable cost could exceed the unit price, r. A unit variable cost reporting system is available which would provide imperfect information about b. The report would be received at Time t. Recall that Gem is able to alter its production rate at Time t. What is the value of the unit variable cost reporting system? Denote the system by h_t^b. (Your answer will be an algebraic expression.)

5. What are the determinants of the value of the unit variable cost reporting system, h_t^b? Describe their effect on the value of h_t^b.

6. What expression would you use to describe the accuracy of information system, h_t^b? What about its timeliness?

7. Suppose h_t^b provides perfect unit variable cost information. What is the value of the system?

8. Suppose h_t^b provides an imperfect unit variable cost report with an accuracy as a function of time as follows:

$$E_y[\text{var}(b \mid y)] = (1 - t)\,\text{var}(b)$$

The left hand side of the expression is the prior expectation of the posterior variance of unit variable cost given a signal, y, from the reporting system, h_t^b.

Describe the tradeoff between accuracy and timeliness for this information system.

9. What is the optimal report time?

10. Suppose the relationship between accuracy and timeliness is given by the following:

$$E_y[\text{var}(b \mid y)] = (1 - t^k)\,\text{var}(b), \quad k < 1$$

What is the value of the system? What is the optimal information time?

11. How could some of the concepts in this exercise be intuitively explained in terms of economics? (Hint: Recall that the producer seeks to equate marginal cost with marginal revenue in determining production output.)

REFERENCES

CUSHING, BARRY, "Some Observations on Demski's Ex Post Accounting System," *The Accounting Review* XLIII (October 1968), 668–71.

DEMSKI, JOEL, "An Accounting System Structured on a Linear Programming Model," *The Accounting Review* XLII (October 1967), 701–12.

————, "Analyzing the Effectiveness of the Traditional Cost Variance Model," *Management Accounting* XLVIII (October 1967), 9–19.

————, "Some Observations on Demski's Ex Post Accounting System: A Reply," *The Accounting Review* XLIII (October 1968), 672–74.

————, "Decision-Performance Control," *The Accounting Review* XLIV (October 1969), 669–79.

DOPUCH, NICHOLAS, JACOB BIRNBERG, and JOEL DEMSKI, "An Extension of Standard Cost Variance Analysis," *The Accounting Review* XLII (July 1967), 526–36.

IJIRI, YUJI, and HIROYUKI ITAMI, "Quadratic Cost Volume Relationship and Timing of Demand Information," *The Accounting Review* XLVIII (October 1973), 724–37.

ITAMI, HIROYUKI, *Adaptive Behavior: Management Control and Information Analysis* Studies in Accounting Research No. 15. Sarasota, Fla.: American Accounting Association, 1977.

STARR, MARTIN, "Inventory Management," chap. 12 in *System Management of Operations*. Englewood Cliffs, N.J.: Prentice Hall, 1971.

VARIANCES FOR SALES, PROFIT, AND COST ANALYSIS

9

SALES AND PROFIT ANALYSIS

Traditional variance analysis focuses on the production processes for manufactured goods. But the same techniques of identifying quantity and price variances can be useful for explaining deviations of actual from planned contribution margin when analyzing the sales performance of products. For a single product the analysis is straightforward. Define:

x_i = budgeted quantity of sales for product i.

m_i = budgeted contribution margin per unit (selling price less variable cost) for product i. Recalling the notation of Chapters 5 and 6, we define $m_i = p_i - b_i$.

$x_i m_i$ = budgeted contribution margin from sales of product i.

After the results for the period are known, we can compute the difference between actual and budgeted amounts. Define Δx_i as the difference between actual and budgeted sales of product i (measured in units) and Δm_i as the difference between actual and budgeted contribution margin per unit of product i. With these definitions, we have that:

$$x_i + \Delta x_i = \text{actual quantity sold of product } i,$$

$$m_i + \Delta m_i = \text{actual contribution margin per unit of product } i,$$

$$(x_i + \Delta x_i)(m_i + \Delta m_i) = \text{actual contribution margin from sales of product } i,$$

Total Variance = Actual − Budgeted contribution margin for product i

$$= (x_i + \Delta x_i)(m_i + \Delta m_i) - x_i m_i$$

$$= (x_i + \Delta x_i)\, \Delta m_i + \Delta x_i m_i,$$

where the first term, $(x_i + \Delta x_i)\Delta m_i$, is the contribution-margin variance, analogous to a price variance, and the second term $\Delta x_i m_i$ is a quantity or sales-activity variance. The contribution-margin variance shows the effect of the change in contribution margin measured at actual sales (as in traditional variance analysis, the common or joint variance $\Delta x_i \Delta m_i$ is arbitrarily assigned to the price or contribution-margin variance). The sales-activity variance shows the effect of the change in unit sales measured at the standard contribution margin.

As the analysis moves from a single-product to a multiple-product case, additional considerations arise. For simplicity, we assume a company with two models, regular and deluxe (labeled 1 and 2) of a product. The budgeted monthly sales and contribution margins of the two models are given below.

x_1	4,000	x_2	1,000
m_1	$8	m_2	$15
$x_1 m_1$	$32,000	$x_2 m_2$	$15,000

Aggregating across the two models, total sales of this product $(x_1 + x_2)$ equal 5,000 units and total revenues equal $47,000, so that the average contribution margin per unit equals $47,000/5,000 = $9.40. Suppose that for the month the actual sales are 4,400 units for model 1 ($\Delta x_1 = 400$) and 700 units for model 2 ($\Delta x_2 = -300$). Actual contribution margins are as budgeted. The total contribution margin is $4,400(8) + 700(15) = $45,700$, yielding an unfavorable total variance of $1,300. Even though more units were sold than anticipated (5,100 rather than the budgeted 5,000), and the contribution margin of each unit is exactly as predicted ($8 for model 1 and $15 for model 2), the total contribution margin for this product line is below expectations. The reason, of course, is that the increase in number of units sold is due to selling many more of the low-margin item (model 1) but fewer of the high-margin item (model 2). The sum of the activity variances for the two items,

$$\sum_i (\Delta x_i)m_i = 400(8) + (-300)(15) = -\$1,300,$$

yields the unfavorable variance. But reporting an unfavorable sales-activity variance of $-\$1,300$ does not reveal whether it is caused by a decrease in the total number of units sold (a sales-volume variance) or by an unfavorable mix of products (the actual situation in this case).

To remedy this ambiguity, the sales-activity variance, $\sum \Delta x_i m_i$, can be split into a sales-volume variance (holding the mix constant) and a sales-mix variance. There are many ways of splitting the sales-activity variance into two components, but the method presented below has some intuitively desirable properties that make it at least as good a method as any that have been proposed in the literature. We define a budgeted average contribution margin per unit, m^*:

$$m^* = \frac{\sum_i x_i m_i}{\sum x_i}. \tag{9-1}$$

In our example, $m^* = [(4,000)(8) + (1,000)(15)]/(4,000 + 1,000) = \$9.40$. The quantity m^* represents what the average unit contribution margin would be if all products were sold in proportion to the planned product mix. With this definition, we can compute the sales-volume variance as

$$\text{Sales-Volume Variance} = \sum_i (\Delta x_i)m^*. \qquad (9\text{-}2)$$

This variance will be positive if and only if the total number of units sold exceeds the budgeted amount.

The mix variance is defined as

$$\text{Sales-Mix Variance} = \sum_i (\Delta x_i)(m_i - m^*). \qquad (9\text{-}3)$$

The sales-mix variance is made positive (favorable) by either (1) selling more ($\Delta x_i > 0$) of higher-than-average-contribution-margin products ($m_i > m^*$), or (2) selling less ($\Delta x_i < 0$) of lower-than-average-contribution-margin products ($m_i < m^*$). Conversely the mix variance is driven negative by selling more of low-contribution-margin products ($\Delta x_i > 0$ and $m_i < m^*$) and selling less of high-contribution-margin products ($\Delta x_i < 0$ and $m_i > m^*$). It is easy to verify that the sum of the sales-volume variance and the sales-mix variance equals the sales-activity variance of $\sum (\Delta x_i)m_i$.

In our numerical example,

$$\text{Sales-Volume Variance} = 400(9.40) - 300(9.40) = \$940,$$

a favorable variance, since actual units sold exceeded budgeted sales.

$$\text{Sales-Mix Variance} = 400(8 - 9.40) - 300(15 - 9.40) = -(560 + 1,680)$$
$$= -\$2,240.$$

In this case the mix variance for each model is negative, since we sold more of the low-margin item (model 1) and less of the high-margin item (model 2). As guaranteed, the sum of the two new variances equals the sales-activity variance ($\$940 - \$2,240 = -\$1,300$). The advantage of separating the sales-activity variance into two components is to distinguish that portion of the variance due to selling a different total number of units from the portion due to changing the budgeted mix of products. It focuses attention on the important point that increasing total physical units of sales may not be as desirable as promoting the sales of high-margin items, even at the expense of losing some unit sales.

PRODUCTION-MIX AND YIELD VARIANCES

A similar analysis can be performed for the mix of input materials used in a production process. If there is some substitutability among the input materials, management can vary the mix of materials to affect the yield of the production process. Such substitution could occur in response to changes in material prices. Or perhaps the substitution was unintended and due to lax supervision. The computation of a mix and yield variance (the yield variance is analogous to what we called the sales-volume variance when analyzing the sales of the multiproduct firm) provides preliminary guidance on the consequences of variations from standard of the input mix.

As a simple example, consider the manufacture of a chemical, Kopane, produced by mixing two materials, labeled 1 and 2. In order to produce 1 lb of Kopane, we need to mix 1 lb of material 1 and 0.5 lb of material 2 (some waste occurs in the mixing process). Material 1 costs $1/lb and material 2 costs $0.70/ lb. Thus, the standard material cost for Kopane is $1.35/lb (1 × $1.00 + 0.5 × $0.70).

In January, the actual production of Kopane is 5,000 lb. Based on our standard cost system, we have the following standard quantities and prices of raw materials to produce this output:

x_1	5,000	x_2	2,500
p_1	$1.00	p_2	$0.70
$x_1 p_1$	$5,000	$x_2 p_2$	$1,750

The actual purchases and uses of raw materials 1 and 2 for January were:

$x_1 + \Delta x_1$	4,500	$x_2 + \Delta x_2$	3,500
$p_1 + \Delta p_1$	$0.90	$p_2 + \Delta p_2$	$0.75
Total cost of Material 1	$4,050	Total cost of Material 2	$2,625

The actual total cost of $6,675 (= 4,050 + 2,625) is slightly below the standard cost of $6,750. There is a favorable variance of $75. This variance can initially be decomposed into:

Price Variance: $\sum_i (x_i + \Delta x_i) \Delta p_i = 4,500 (-0.10) + 3,500(0.05)$

$$= -\$275 \quad \text{(favorable)}$$

and

Quantity Variance: $\sum_i (\Delta x_i) p_i \qquad = -500(1.00) + 1,000(0.70)$

$$= \$200 \quad \text{(unfavorable)}.$$

(Note that the signs of the variances are reversed for production variances, since using more materials at higher prices is unfavorable. When analyzing sales, selling more at higher prices is favorable. These conventions are arbitrary, but one *should* know when a particular variance is favorable or unfavorable.)

As before, the quantity variance can be decomposed further. First, compute the average price of raw materials per pound of input:

$$p^* = \frac{\sum x_i p_i}{\sum x_i} = \frac{5,000(\$1.00) + 2,500(\$0.70)}{7,500} = \$0.90.$$

Then

$$\text{Yield Variance} = \sum (\Delta x_i) p^*$$

$$= (-500)(0.90) + 1,000(0.90)$$

$$= \$450 \quad \text{(unfavorable)}.$$

The yield variance is unfavorable, since the total input (8,000 lb) exceeded the standard amount (7,500 lb) for the 5,000 lb of Kopane produced.

$$\text{Mix Variance} = \sum \Delta x_i (p_i - p^*)$$

$$= -500(1.00 - 0.90) + 1,000(0.70 - 0.90)$$

$$= -\$250 \quad \text{(favorable)}$$

The mix variance is favorable for each input material, since less is used of the higher-price material and more is used of the lower-price material.

Thus, the preliminary evaluation of the favorable variance of $75 finds a favorable price variance of $275 due to a 10 percent drop in the more expensive and more heavily used raw material 1, only partially offset by an increase in price of the less expensive and less heavily used raw material 2. The favorable price variance is offset by a decrease in yield, since total input exceeded the standard to produce the actual output, but a favorable mix variance helped to reduce the unfavorable yield variance.

The manager of the Kopane process could argue that he tried to shift the production process so that more of the low-cost material could be substituted for the high-cost material. Whether the extra usage of 1,000 pounds of material 2 can be explained by the 500 fewer pounds used of material 1 requires more knowledge of the production process and the degree of substitutability between the two materials than the problem statement gives us. If the manager did attempt such a substitution, he chose an unfortunate month, since the price of the high-priced material dropped while that of the low-priced material increased. A more detailed and formal analysis of these variances requires the use of an explicit production and decision model for the Kopane process, such as was illustrated in Chapter 8. For our purposes here, the decomposition of the total $75 January production variance of Kopane into price, yield, and mix variances does serve to highlight the details of, and focus attention on, different aspects of the production process that have different degrees of controllability and responsibility.

A DECOMPOSITION APPROACH
TO VARIANCE ANALYSIS[1]

Variance analysis by now may appear to the student as an arbitrary collection of ad hoc computations. While there is some truth to this view, an integrating framework can be developed to help organize the many variances that are computed from each period's financial reports. The motivation behind all variance analysis is to provide insight as to why actual performance differed from that budgeted or expected. No variance, by itself, gives definitive evidence as to the cause of unexpected increases or decreases in profits and costs. But a variance analysis isolates the many factors that eventually lead to differences between actual and expected operating results. Accounting variances provide a point of departure for more probing questions and investigations. They help to focus attention on those aspects of operations for which differences between actual and expected results had the largest impact on profits.

The aim, then, of variance analysis is to facilitate the judging of actual performance against a standard of management expectations. These expectations are established by a budget, profit plan, and standard cost system. Variance analysis is a valuable technique for implementing "management by exception"— allowing managers to lightly review activities that are proceeding essentially as planned and to allocate their scarce time to those areas where investigation or intervention will likely yield the greatest benefits.

A methodology for implementing an integrated variance analysis will be presented by means of a simple example. The method is not unique, nor is it in any sense optimal. Rather, it is just a systematic way of sequentially computing variances in greater levels of detail to obtain finer and more detailed explanations for the differences between what actually happened and what was expected to happen. Naturally, if the expectations are unrealistic and inaccurate, there will be little value to this exercise. The procedure is most useful when differences from expected performance are a genuine surprise rather than a confirmation that management is incapable of formulating realistic expectations.

Example: Omar Carpet Company

The Omar Carpet Company makes three grades of carpeting. Each year it prepares an annual budget, forecasting sales, expenses, and net income. The sales volume for the annual budget is determined by estimating the total market volume for indoor-outdoor carpet, then applying the company's prior-year market share, adjusted for planned changes due to company programs for the coming year. The volume is apportioned among the three grades based upon the prior year's product

---

[1] This material is adapted from Shank and Churchill [1977].

mix, again adjusted for planned changes due to company programs for the coming year.

Given below are the company's budget for 1982 and the results of operations for 1982. Industry volume was estimated for budgeting purposes at 40,000 rolls. Actual industry volume for 1982 was 38,000 rolls.

EXHIBIT 9-1. Budgeted and Actual Performance: Omar Carpet Company

	BUDGET			
	Grade 1	Grade 2	Grade 3	Total
Sales, units (rolls)	1,000	1,000	2,000	4,000
Sales, dollars (000 omitted)	$1,000	$2,000	$3,000	$6,000
Variable expense	700	1,600	2,300	4,600
Variable margin	$ 300	$ 400	$ 700	$1,400
Traceable fixed expense	200	200	300	700
Traceable margin	$ 100	$ 200	$ 400	$ 700
Selling and administrative expense				$ 250
Net income				$ 450

	ACTUAL			
	Grade 1	Grade 2	Grade 3	Total
Sales, units (rolls)	800	1,000	2,100	3,900
Sales, dollars (000 omitted)	$ 810	$2,000	$3,000	$5,810
Variable expense	560	1,610	2,320	4,490
Variable margin	$ 250	$ 390	$ 680	$1,320
Traceable fixed expense	210	220	315	745
Traceable margin	$ 40	$ 170	$ 365	$ 575
Selling and administrative expense				$ 275
Net income				$ 300

The net income of the Omar Company is one-third below the budgeted level. What caused this decline in profitability?

Level 0   The crudest form of a profit variance analysis displays the following information:

Actual profits	$300	
Expected profits	450	
Profit variance	$150	Unfavorable

This initial level of analysis indicates that actual profits are $150 (or one-third) less than expected profits.

Level 1   At the next level of analysis, we expand the variance report to display a comparison between actual and expected levels of performance for each major line item in the income statement. One possible presentation is:

	Actual	Expected	Variance	
Revenues	$5,810	$6,000	$190	Unfavorable
Variable expenses	4,490	4,600	110	Favorable
Contribution margin	$1,320	$1,400	$ 80	Unfavorable
Period expenses	1,020	950	70	Unfavorable
Net income	$ 300	$ 450	$150	Unfavorable

Here we see an unfavorable variance in revenues only partially offset by a decline in variable expenses. In general, revenue and variable-expense variances should be of opposite signs. Higher revenues, caused by higher unit sales, imply higher production costs. Conversely, when sales decline, production and hence variable expense will also tend to decline. We also see in the above presentation that fixed or period expenses were $70 above budgeted levels. This increase in fixed costs contributes almost 50 percent to the profit decline of $150.

Level 2 At the next level of analysis, we isolate the effects due to changes in the level of business activity from the effects due to changes in costs, prices, and operating efficiencies. The key computation at this level is to obtain the flexible budget. The flexible budget indicates what the expected profits would have been given perfect foresight about the actual sales volume and sales mix. For the Omar Company, we obtain the following flexible budget at actual sales volume:

Flexible Budget

	Sales (Rolls)	Contribution Margin Per Roll	Contribution Margin
Grade 1	800	$0.30	$ 240
Grade 2	1,000	0.40	400
Grade 3	2,100	0.35	735
Contribution margin			$1,375
Period expenses			950
Net income			$ 425

The $425 figure represents the budgeted net income given the actual level and mix of sales. From this figure we compute the two Level 2 variances:

Sales-Activity Variance			*Cost/Price/Efficiency Variance*		
Flexible budget	$425		Actual net income	$300	
Budgeted net income	450		Flexible budget	425	
Variance	$ 25	Unfavorable	Variance	$125	Unfavorable

The sales-activity variance of $25 represents the decline in profits caused by a change in actual units and mix of sales from the budgeted levels. It assumes that all prices and costs were exactly as budgeted. The cost/price/efficiency variance of $125 indicates the effects of unanticipated changes in unit selling prices and expenses given the actual level of sales. From the Level 1 analysis, we computed a contribution-margin variance of $80 (unfavorable). From the Level 2 analysis, we see that only $25 of this $80 variance is caused by an unfavorable shift in the level and mix of sales activity. The remaining $55 is caused by unfavorable price or variable-cost realizations. These points will be explored in greater detail as we move to subsequent levels of analysis.

In summary, the Level 2 analysis decomposes differences between actual and expected results into two components: (1) a sales-activity variance, representing differences caused solely by not anticipating the actual level and mix of sales, and (2) a cost/price/efficiency variance, representing differences between expected profits at the actual sales volumes and the actual profits realized at these volumes. Since we are controlling for the actual sales volume, this variance is caused solely by changes in unit prices, variable costs, and fixed expenses.

Level 3   Each of the two Level 2 variances can be analyzed in finer detail. We start with the sales-activity variance of $25 (Unfavorable), which we split into a sales-volume variance and a sales-mix variance. These are the two variances we introduced earlier in this chapter. Recall that we first compute the weighted margin, m^*:

$$m^* = \frac{\sum x_i m_i}{\sum x_1} = \frac{\$300 + 400 + 700}{4{,}000} = \$0.35.$$

The sales-volume variance, indicating the change in expected contribution margin caused solely by changes in the physical units of sales (holding mix constant), is computed as

$$\begin{aligned}
\text{Sales-Volume Variance} &= \sum (\Delta x_i) m^* \\
&= (-200 + 0 + 100)(0.35) \\
&= -\$35 \quad \text{(Unfavorable)}.
\end{aligned}$$

The sales-mix variance, indicating the change in expected contribution margin caused solely by changes in the different proportions of products sold, is

$$\begin{aligned}
\text{Sales-Mix Variance} &= \sum_i (\Delta x_i)(m_i - m^*) \\
&= -200(0.30 - 0.35) + 0(0.40 - 0.35) + 100(0.35 - 0.35) \\
&= \$10 \quad \text{(Favorable)}.
\end{aligned}$$

Thus, of the $25 unfavorable sales-activity variance, we lost $35 because of declining unit sales but gained $10 because the largest decline in sales occurred in the low-margin grade 1 product line.

The cost/price/efficiency variance of $125 (Unfavorable) is decomposed into a sales-price variance and a set of cost variances. The sales-price variance is easily computed as

$$\text{Sales-Price Variance} = \text{Actual Revenues} - \left(\begin{array}{c}\text{Budgeted Revenues at}\\\text{Actual Sales Levels}\end{array}\right)$$

$$= (810 - 800) + (2{,}000 - 2{,}000) + (3{,}000 - 3{,}150)$$

$$= -\$140 \quad \text{(Unfavorable)}.$$

Alternatively, we can define this variance algebraically as

$$\text{Sales-Price Variance} = \sum (x_i + \Delta x_i)(\Delta p_i)$$

where Δp_i represents the difference between actual unit selling prices and budgeted selling prices.

We can define, analogously, a variable-cost variance as

$$\text{Variable-Cost Variance} = \text{Actual Variable Costs}$$

$$- \left(\begin{array}{c}\text{Budgeted Variable Costs}\\\text{at Actual Sales Levels}\end{array}\right)$$

$$= (560 - 560) + (1{,}610 - 1{,}600) + (2{,}320 - 2{,}415)$$

$$= -\$85 \quad \text{(Favorable)}.$$

If more detail had been provided, the favorable variable-cost variance of $85 could be split into its constituent parts of labor, material, and variable overhead.

A third variance in this split is due to unexpected changes in fixed or period expenses:

$$\text{Period Cost Variances} = \text{Actual Fixed Costs} - \text{Expected Fixed Costs}$$

$$= 1{,}020 - 950$$

$$= \$70 \quad \text{(Unfavorable)}.$$

This variance can be subdivided between traceable fixed expenses (45, Unfavorable) and selling and administrative expenses ($25, Unfavorable).

The $140 unfavorable sales-price variance less the $85 favorable variable-cost variance yields $55 of the $80 unfavorable contribution-margin variance (see Level 1). The other $25 of this variance was previously identified (Level 2) as due to changes in sales activity. Thus we now see that the unfavorable $80 contribution-margin variance was the sum of many partially offsetting factors as summarized below:

Sales-volume variance	$ 35	U
Sales-mix variance	10	F
Sales-price variance	140	U
Variable-cost variance	85	F
Contribution-margin variance	$ 80	U

At first glance it may have appeared that the decline in profits was caused by the decline in unit sales. In fact, further analysis revealed that the largest unexpected component arose from a decline in selling prices only partially offset by the operating efficiencies indicated by a favorable variable-cost variance. Obviously, none of these factors is decisive by itself. Perhaps the favorable variable-cost variance was caused by a decline in the price of an important raw material—a decline common to all firms in the industry, passed through to customers via lower average selling prices. But the finer breakdown into volume, mix, price, and cost variances provides insights about where to start looking when attempting to explain significant differences between actual and budgeted profits.

Level 4   Each of the Level 3 variances can be decomposed further. The sales-volume variance can be separated into a component due to changes in overall industry sales and a component due to changes in the company's market share of overall industry sales. The budgeted data indicate that industry sales are projected at 40,000 rolls of carpet and the Omar Company expects to have a 10 percent market share, or 4,000 rolls. For the year, industry sales were down to 38,000 rolls but the Omar Company sold 3,900 rolls, thereby achieving a market share slightly above 10 percent (actually 10.26 percent). We can formalize these results by decomposing the $35 unfavorable sales-volume variance into

Market-Size Variance = (Actual Total Market − Expected Total Market) ·
(Expected Market Share) · (Expected Contribution
Margin per Unit at Standard Mix)

$$= (38,000 - 40,000)(0.10)(0.35)$$

$$= -\$70 \quad \text{(Unfavorable)}$$

and

Market-Share Variance = (Actual Market Share − Expected Market Share) ·
(Actual Market Volume) · (Expected Contribution
Margin per Unit at Standard Mix)

$$= \left(\frac{3,900}{38,000} - 0.10\right)(38,000)(0.35)$$

$$= \$35 \quad \text{(Favorable)}$$

Thus, the small increase in market share offset 50 percent of the loss in expected profits caused by the decline (of 5 percent) in total industry sales.

The $10 favorable sales-mix variance can be broken down by individual product. The variance for product i is given by $(\Delta x_i)(m_i - m^*)$:

Sales-mix variance, Grade 1: $-200(0.30 - 0.35) = \$10$ F
Sales-mix variance, Grade 2: $0(0.40 - 0.35) = 0$
Sales-mix variance, Grade 3: $+100(0.35 - 0.35) = 0$

For this example, the sales-mix variance is caused solely by the reduction in sales of grade 1.

The sales-price variance can similarly be decomposed by product line:

$$(x_i + \Delta x_i) \cdot (\Delta p_i)$$

Sales-price variance, Grade 1:	$800 \cdot (1.0125 - 1.00)$	=	$10 F
Sales-price variance, Grade 2:	$1,000 \cdot (0)$	=	0
Sales-price variance, Grade 3:	$2,100 \cdot (1.4286 - 1.50)$	=	−150 U
Total Sales-price variance			−$140 U

Here we see that the unfavorable sales-price variance was caused by a 5 percent drop in the average selling price of grade 3 carpeting.

The favorable variable-cost variance of $85 could also be split by product line:

Variable-cost variance, Grade 1:	$800(0.70 - 0.70)$	=	0
Variable-cost variance, Grade 2:	$1,000(1.61 - 1.60)$	=	$10 U
Variable-cost variance, Grade 3:	$2,100(1.105 - 1.15)$	=	95 F
Total Variable-cost variance			$85 F

Alternatively, if the variable-cost variance in Level 3 had been split among labor, material, and variable-overhead variances, these variances could be further decomposed in the Level 4 analysis along traditional variance-analysis dimensions. That is, the labor variance is split into a usage or efficiency variance and a price (or rate) variance. The material variance can be split into a quantity and price variance. We do not have enough data from the Omar Company to perform this analysis.

The period cost variance can be decomposed along a variety of dimensions—controllable versus noncontrollable; functional categories such as plant overhead, selling, administration, and so on—depending on individual company circumstances as to which level of analysis or responsibility reporting would be most helpful.

Exhibit 9-2 summarizes the Level 0 to Level 4 decomposition of operating results for the Omar Company. The key items would appear to be a decline in overall industry sales (70 U) only partially offset by a slight increase in market share ($35 F). The selling price of grade 3 decreased ($150 U), offset somewhat by a decrease in variable costs for grade 3 ($95 F). Fixed expenses were above budgeted levels ($70 U). This is a more complete summary than our initial statement (at Level 0) that profits were $150 below the expected level.

Obviously, this process can be continued further. The market-share change could be computed by product line. The sales-mix variance could be decomposed by geographic region or type of customer. Each product-mix variance could be decomposed into subproduct grades such as color, style, or width. Sales-price variances could be split between list-price changes and discounts or special orders. The analysis stops at any level for which the next level of information either is

Actual Profit = $300
Expected Profit = 450
Profit Variance = $150 U

Level 1

	Actual	Expected	Variance
Sales Revenue	$5,810	$7,000	$190 U
Variable Expenses	4,490	4,600	110 F
Contribution Margin	$1,320	$1,400	$80 U
Period Expenses	1,020	950	70 U
Net Income	$300	$450	$150 U

Level 2

Actual Net Income $300
Flexible Budget 425
Cost/Price/Efficiency/Variance $125 U

Flexible Budget $425
Budgeted Net Income 450
Sales Activity Variance $25 U

Level 3

Sales-Price Variance = $140 U

Variable-Cost Variance = $85 F

Period Cost Variance = $70 U

Sales-Volume Variance = $35 U

Sales-Mix Variance = $10 F

Level 4

Market-Size Variance = $70 U   Market-Share Variance = $35 F

Product-Mix Variance
Grade 1 = $10 F
Grade 2 = 0
Grade 3 = 0

Product-Price Variance
Grade 1 = $ 10 F
Grade 2 = 0
Grade 3 = 150 U

Product-Cost Variance
Grade 1 = 0
Grade 2 = $10 U
Grade 3 = 95 F

Components
Traceable Fixed = $ 45 U
Selling & Administrative = 25 U

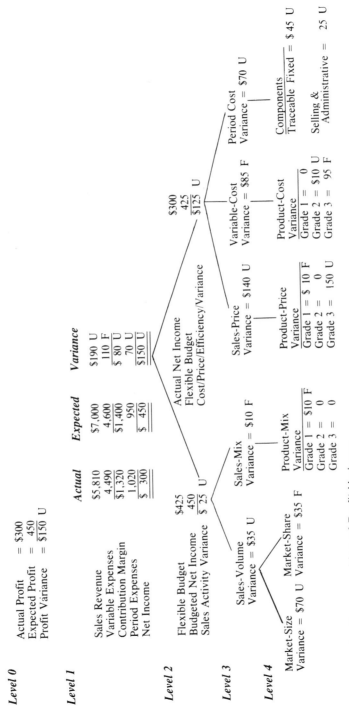

EXHIBIT 9-2. Decomposition of Profit Variance

not available or is not deemed sufficiently useful to warrant the complexity of additional computations. The guiding principle of this decomposition approach is to develop the story behind the profit variance gradually without getting into great detail or complexity too quickly. The analysis serves to illustrate where the sales-mix and sales-volume variances, introduced earlier in the chapter, fit in an overall analysis of product profitability. Of particular importance in the decomposition approach is the separation that occurs in Level 2 between the sales-activity variances and the cost/price/efficiency variances. This separation enables management to distinguish between the effects caused by changes in the physical level of activity and the effects caused by changes in pricing and operating efficiencies after controlling for the actual level of activity. An important requirement for computing and understanding both sets of variances is to have a good separation of factors that vary with the level of activity (variable costs and revenues) from factors that should be relatively independent of the level of activity (fixed costs).

SUMMARY

In this chapter we extended the price-quantity variance analysis, typically used for control of material and labor costs of manufactured goods, to analyze the sales and profit performance of a firm. A sales-quantity variance was decomposed into a sales-volume variance, analyzing the total number of units sold, and a sales-mix variance, analyzing the mix between high and low contribution margin products. The mix variance was defined so that it was positive when more of high-margin products and less of low-margin products are sold. The volume and mix variances were also defined and illustrated for input materials used in a production process.

A decomposition approach to variance analysis was introduced to organize the myriad accounting variances produced each period. The approach proceeds systematically so that an appropriate level of detail can be presented to each different management level in an organization. A key feature of this method is the separation between a sales-activity variance, representing variation in the physical level of activity of the firm, and a cost/price/efficiency variance, representing variations in financial factors (prices and costs) and operating efficiencies of the firm.

PROBLEMS

9-1.   Profit Variance Analysis

John Swann, Managing Director of Post Electric Corporation, glanced at the summary profit and loss statement for 1980, which he was holding (Table 1), and tossed it to Randy Cunningham. Swann looked out the window of his office and declared, somewhat smugly,

TABLE 1. Post Electric Corporation 1980 Operating Results (000)

	Budget	Actual
Sales	$5400	$5710
Manufacturing Costs	2000	2090
	$3400	$3620
G & A Expenses	1500	1650
Net Income Before Taxes	$1900	$1970

"As you can see Randy, we exceeded our sales goal for the year, improved our margin, and earned more profit than we had planned. Although some of our expenses seemed to grow a little faster than sales, 1980 was a pretty good year for us, don't you think?"

Randy Cunningham, a recent graduate of a highly-touted business school, was serving a training period as executive assistant to Swann. He looked over the figures and nodded his agreement. Swann continued:

"Randy, I'd like you to prepare a short report for the Board Meeting next week summarizing the key factors that account for the favorable overall profit variance of $70,000. I think you're about ready to make a presentation to the Board if you can pull together a good report. Check with the Controller's Office for any additional data you may need or want. Remember, the Board doesn't want a long complex presentation. See what you can come up with."

Randy Cunningham agreed to the assignment and gathered the data shown in Table 2. How can he present an analysis of 1980 operating results to the Board?

TABLE 2. Additional Information*

	Meters		Generators	
	Budget	Actual	Budget	Actual
Price	$30	$29	$150	$153
Manufacturing Cost	15	16	40	42
Margin	$15	$13	$110	$111
Units Sold	80,000	65,000	20,000	25,000
Industry Sales (units)	800,000	700,000	200,000	250,000

* Post's products are grouped into two main lines of business for internal reporting purposes. Each line includes many separate products which are averaged together for purposes of this problem.

9-2. Profit Variance Analysis (A. Atkinson)

Chapel Hill Foods distributes a line of frozen meats. The company's three "products" are in fact, three different packages, each of 500 pounds, of assorted cuts of beef wrapped in a manner suitable for freezing.

TABLE 1.

BUDGET

	Economy Package	Custom Package	Deluxe Package	Total
Sales-Pounds	2,000,000	3,000,000	1,000,000	6,000,000
Revenue	$4,000,000	$8,400,000	$3,500,000	$15,900,000
Variable Costs	3,000,000	6,000,000	2,500,000	11,500,000
Contribution Margin	$1,000,000	$2,400,000	$1,000,000	$ 4,400,000
Traceable Fixed Costs	500,000	800,000	200,000	1,500,000
Traceable Margin	$ 500,000	$1,600,000	$ 800,000	$ 2,900,000
Allocated Fixed Costs*	200,000	300,000	100,000	600,000
Division Income	$ 300,000	$1,300,000	$ 700,000	$ 2,300,000

ACTUAL

	Economy Package	Custom Package	Deluxe Package	Total
Sales-Pounds	2,500,000	2,500,000	500,000	5,500,000
Revenue	$5,250,000	$5,750,000	$1,400,000	$12,400,000
Variable Costs	4,000,000	5,000,000	1,200,000	10,200,000
Contribution Margin	$1,250,000	$ 750,000	$ 200,000	$ 2,200,000
Traceable Fixed Costs	550,000	700,000	200,000	1,450,000
Traceable Margin	$ 700,000	$ 50,000	$ 0	$ 750,000
Allocated Fixed Costs*	295,455	295,455	59,090	650,000
Division Income	$ 404,545	$ (245,455)	$ (59,090)	$ 100,000

* Allocated on the basis of sales in pounds.

For purposes of planning and control, the company prepares an annual budget on both a product and aggregate basis.

The company's budget and actual results, for the year just ended, appear in Table 1. Industry volume in Chapel Hill's market was forecasted as one million tons. Actual industry volume was 1.2 million tons.

Required:

Charles Krep, President of Chapel Hill Foods is very dismayed with results. Charlie grouses "we came within 8.3 percent of our beef poundage sales target but profits are only 4.3 percent of budgeted." Prepare an analysis of sales and profits.

9-3. Materials Price-Mix-Yield Variances (CMA)

The LAR Chemical Co. manufactures a wide variety of chemical compounds and liquids for industrial uses. The standard mix for producing a single batch of 500 gallons of one liquid is as follows:

Liquid Chemical	Quantity (in gallons)	Cost (per gallon)	Total Cost
Maxan	100	2.00	$200
Salex	300	.75	225
Cralyn	225	1.00	225
	625		$650

There is a 20 percent loss in liquid volume during processing due to evaporation. The finished liquid is put into 10 gallon bottles for sale. Thus, the standard material cost for a 10 gallon bottle is $13.

The actual quantities of raw materials and the respective cost of the materials placed in production during November were as follows:

Liquid Chemical	Quantity (in gallons)	Total Cost
Maxan	8,480	$17,384
Salex	25,200	17,640
Cralyn	18,540	16,686
	52,220	$51,710

A total of 4,000 bottles (40,000 gallons) were produced during November.

Required:

1. Calculate the total raw material variance for the liquid product for the month of November and then further analyze the total variance into a:
   a. material price variance.
   b. material mix variance.
   c. material yield variance.
2. Explain how LAR Chemical Co. could use each of the three material variances—price, mix, yield—to help control the cost to manufacture this liquid compound.

9-4. Sales-Profit-Cost Variance Analysis (CMA)

The Markley Division of Rosette Industries manufactures and sells patio chairs. The chairs are manufactured in two versions: a metal model, and a plastic model of a lesser quality. The company uses its own sales force to sell the chairs to retail stores and to catalog outlets. Generally, customers purchase both the metal and plastic versions.

The chairs are manufactured on two different assembly lines located in adjoining buildings. The division management and sales department occupy the third building on the property. The division management includes a division controller responsible for the divisional financial activities and the preparation of reports explaining the differences between actual and budgeted performance. The controller structures these reports such that the sales activities are distinguished from cost factors so that each can be analyzed separately.

The operating results for the first three months of the fiscal year as compared to the budget are presented in Table 1. The budget for the current year was based upon the assumption that Markley Division would maintain its present market share of the estimated total patio chair market (plastic and metal combined). A status report had been sent to corporate management toward the end of the second month indicating that divisional operating income for the first quarter would probably be about 45 percent below budget; this estimate was just about on target. The division's operating income was below budget even though industry volume for patio chairs increased by 10 percent more than was expected at the time the budget was developed. (see Table 1)

During the quarter, the Markley Division manufactured 55,000 plastic chairs and 22,500 metal chairs. The costs incurred by each assembly line is also presented as Table 2.

The standard variable manufacturing costs per unit and the budgeted monthly fixed manufacturing costs established for the current year are presented below.

TABLE 1.   Markley Division Operating Results for the First Quarter

	Actual	Budget	Favorable (unfavorable) relative to the budget
Sale in units			
Plastic model	60,000	50,000	10,000
Metal model	20,000	25,000	(5,000)
Sales revenue			
Plastic model	$630,000	$500,000	$130,000
Metal model	300,000	375,000	(75,000)
Total sales	$930,000	$875,000	$ 55,000
Less variable costs			
Manufacturing (at standard)			
Plastic model	$480,000	$400,000	$(80,000)
Metal model	200,000	250,000	50,000
Selling			
Commissions	46,500	43,750	(2,750)
Bad debt allowance	9,300	8,750	(550)
Total variable costs (except variable manufacturing variances)	$735,800	$702,500	$(33,300)
Contribution margin (except variable manufacturing variances)	$194,200	$172,500	$ 21,700
Less other costs			
Variable manufacturing costs variances from standards	$ 49,600	$ —	$(49,600)
Fixed manufacturing costs	49,200	48,000	(1,200)
Fixed selling & admin. costs	38,500	36,000	(2,500)
Corporation offices allocation	18,500	17,500	(1,000)
Total other costs	$155,800	$101,500	$(54,300)
Divisional operational income	$ 38,400	$ 71,000	$(32,600)

TABLE 2. Actual Manufacturing Costs

Raw Materials (stated in equivalent finished chairs)	Quantity	Price	Plastic Model	Metal Model
Purchases				
Plastic	60,000	$5.65	$339,000	
Metal	30,000	$6.00		$180,000
Usage				
Plastic	56,000	$5.00	280,000	
Metal	23,000	$6.00		138,000
Direct labor				
9,300 hours @ $6.00 per hour			55,800	
5,600 hours @ $8.00 per hour				44,800
Manufacturing overhead				
Variable				
Supplies			43,000	18,000
Power			50,000	15,000
Employee benefits			19,000	12,000
Fixed				
Supervision			14,000	11,000
Depreciation			12,000	9,000
Property taxes and other items			1,900	1,300

	Plastic Model	Metal Model
Raw material	$5.00	$6.00
Direct labor		
$\frac{1}{6}$ hour @ $6.00 per DLH	1.00	
$\frac{1}{4}$ hour @ $8.00 per DLH		2.00
Variable overhead		
$\frac{1}{6}$ hour @ $12.00 per DLH	2.00	
$\frac{1}{4}$ hour @ $8.00 per DLH		2.00
Standard variable manufacturing cost per unit	$8.00	$10.00
Budgeted fixed costs per month		
Supervision	$4,500	$3,500
Depreciation	4,000	3,000
Property taxes and other items	600	400
Total budgeted fixed costs for month	$9,100	$6,900

Required:

1. Analyze the causes of the $32,600 unfavorable income variance.
2. Based upon your analysis:
   a. Identify the major cause of Markley Division's unfavorable profit performance.

313

b. Did Markley's management attempt to correct this problem?

c. What other steps, if any, could Markley's management have taken to improve the division's operating income?

9-5. Mix and Yield Variances in a Decision Setting*

The Sagebrush Feed Company produces a cattle feed that can be made from various combinations of four raw materials. The assumptions and constraints on this product include:

1. Each batch of feed must contain at least 18 percent protein.
2. Each batch must contain no more than 20 percent of Raw Materials 2 and 3.
3. Other processing and input factor costs are independent of the raw materials mix.

The characteristics of the four input raw materials are:

Raw Material	Percent Protein	Standard Cost Per Ton
1	50	$45
2	10	30
3	15	25
4	35	40

At present, Sagebrush produces each ton (2000 lbs.) of feed by using 400 pounds of Raw Material 3 and 1600 pounds of Raw Material 4.

Required:

1. Verify that this mixture meets the protein constraint. Compute the standard cost per ton of feed with this mixture.
2. Raw Material prices fluctuate during the period so that the actual average prices for the four raw materials are:

Raw Material	Current Cost Per Ton
1	$45
2	25
3	28
4	32

---

* This problem is adapted from Harry Wolk and A. Douglas Hillman, "Materials Mix and Yield Variances: A Suggested Improvement," *The Accounting Review XLVII* (July 1972) 549–55.

The company, however, followed its standard practice of mixing each ton of feed with 20 percent of Raw Material 3 and 80 percent of Raw Material 4. Compute the price variance from following this plan.

3. A newly hired employee in the controller's department observed that with the current set of prices, the firm is no longer producing at minimum cost. Set up and solve (perhaps by inspection) the linear program that enables him to obtain the minimum cost mix of raw materials for each ton of feed produced.

4. Suppose the revised optimal production plan (computed in Question 3) had been implemented during the period. Compute the price, mix and yield variances from following this plan. Interpret the implications of these variances.

5. Instead of computing the standard mix and yield variances, compute the forecasting and opportunity cost variances (see Chapter 8) associated with not having switched from the prior plan in light of the revised raw material costs. Which set of variances would seem more relevant and helpful to management in understanding the lowered cost per ton of feed produced.

6. Can you think of improved methods for computing mix and yield variances when substitution is possible among input factors as specified by a well defined decision model of the production process?

9-6. *Short Term Budget and Profit Analysis in a Highly Inflationary Economy*

The Koor Company is operating in a very inflationary economy. Recently the inflation rate has been running between 10 and 12 percent per month. This high rate of inflation is accompanied with high dispersion of relative price changes; that is, some prices are going up much faster than the rate of inflation while others are lagging behind the rate of inflation. In this situation, the management of the Koor Company is finding it very difficult to develop its short term profit budget and to analyze operating performance after the fact.

The controller, Avram Dinitz, has been examining the problem and has collected the following data as of the end of October 1981:

a. Anticipated sales during December 1981 = 1000 units

b. Each unit produced requires 10 kgm of material (M) and 5 hours of labor (L).

c. The prices of these input factors are presently.

$$M: \quad 6 \text{ shekels/kgm.}$$
$$L: \quad 20 \text{ shekels/hour}$$

d. The current price of the product is 250 sh/unit

Avram is considering three possible budget assumptions for December 1981:

A1. Budget based on end of October 1981 prices

A2. Budget based on a general 10 percent increase in prices during November, but no change in relative prices.

A3. Budget based on
   a. an increase in output prices of 10%
   b. an increase in labor prices of 8%
   c. an increase in material prices of 15%

Required:

1. Prepare the three budgeted income figures for December 1981 using these three different scenarios.

2. Actual results in December 1981 were:
   a. 900 units sold at an average price of 277 Sh/unit.
   b. 9100 kgm of M were used whose cost was 60,970 Sh.
   c. 4450 hours of L were consumed at a cost of 103,240 Sh.
   Prepare the flexible budget for December 1981 based on actual sales and the budgeted price and cost data for each of the three budget assumptions (A1–A3).

3. For each of the three budgets, compute the
   a. Selling Price Variance
   b. Material Price Variance
   c. Material Quantity Variance
   d. Labor Price Variance
   e. Labor Quantity Variance
   Be sure to reconcile the actual variance (Actual Profits-Budgeted Profits) among these individual variance accounts.

4. (Ex Post Analysis). Government Statistics for December 1981 are released in January 1982. These statistics show the following increase in prices from the end of October through December:

Item	Percentage Increase
General Price Index	12%
Products similar to Koor's output	12%
Material similar to M	10%
Labor Cost similar to L	14%

Compute the ex-post budget based on these government statistics and analyze the three Price Variances (Selling, Material, and Labor) computed in Question 3 for the budget based on Assumptions A3. Each Price Variance can be decomposed into:
   a. a Relative Price Variance—the difference between the actual price faced by Koor and that which would be predicted from the government statistics; and
   b. a Forecast Variance—the difference between the ex post prediction (from the government statistics) and that forecast in budget assumptions A3.

5. Comment on the value of this extensive exercise in explaining variances in prices and costs during a highly inflationary environment. Which set of budget assumptions and variance analyses would seem most (or least) helpful?

9-7. *Extensions of Standard Cost Analysis* (Y. Ijiri)

XYZ Company produces and sells a single perishable product. Since inventories at the end of each day are disposed of at a bargain price, sales volume equals production volume. The company's daily operating cost K (production, sales, and administration) is approximated by a quadratic function

$$K = a + bx + cx^2$$

where x is daily volume of production and sales and a, b, and c are positive coefficients.

The average selling price of the product p for any day is approximated by a linear function of volume:

$$p = g - hx$$

where x is volume as before and g and h are positive coefficients.

Required:

1. Express daily profit π as a function of daily volume x and find x at which π is maximized. (Show that π is actually maximized and not minimized at the indicated volume.)

2. For the purpose of cost accounting, the company uses standard costing. Standard cost u per unit of product is

    $$u = K(\bar{x})/\bar{x} = (a + b\bar{x} + c\bar{x}^2)/\bar{x}$$

    where $\bar{x}$ is normal daily volume preselected by the company at the beginning of each month so that it will come close to average daily volume for the month. Since actual cost is not available on a daily basis, the daily profit is determined by multiplying actual volume x^a by standard cost u. If K^a is actual operating cost for the day in which actual volume was x^a, analyze the variance

    $$D = K^a - ux^a$$

    into a spending variance S and a volume variance V and derive the proper formula for each.

3. The normal volume happens to be such that the volume variance can never be favorable no matter what the actual volume may be. Derive the normal volume with such a property.

4. Derive formulas for decomposing the revenue variance, into a realization variance R, and a volume variance W.

REFERENCES

FRANK, WERNER, and RENE MANES, "A Standard Cost Application of Matrix Algebra," *The Accounting Review* XLII (July 1967), 516–25.

HASSELDINE, C. R., "Mix and Yield Variances," *The Accounting Review* XLII (July 1967), 497–515.

SHANK, JOHN, and NEIL CHURCHILL, "Variance Analysis: A Management-Oriented Approach," *The Accounting Review* LII (October 1977), 950–57.

WOLK, HARRY I., and A. DOUGLAS HILLMAN, "Materials Mix and Yield Variances," *The Accounting Review* XLVII (July 1972), 549–55.

COST-VARIANCE INVESTIGATION MODELS

Introductory cost accounting textbooks provide extensive discussion of standard cost systems and the computation of variances. The variances indicate deviation between actual results and the results that would have occurred if the standards had been met exactly. Since any standard is only an estimate about what can actually be achieved in practice, it would be unlikely for the actual results of any interesting process to exactly equal the standard or expected result. Therefore, a manager could receive a document, each reporting period, showing a variance for every material, labor, and overhead item under his responsibility for which a standard has been established.

What should a sensible manager do, then, after receiving such a report? Should he investigate every deviation? A manager's time is a scarce resource, and so is the time of subordinates. Interrupting a production process entails an additional cost. A policy of investigating every reported variance will be expensive and, almost surely, without commensurate benefits.

If, however, the manager does not investigate or follow up on reported variances, then the control function of the standard cost system is being ignored and the value of installing and maintaining the system has been overestimated. The system likely will become obsolescent once those involved realize that no one is paying attention to deviations between actual and predicted results.

Between the two extremes—of investigating every deviation that is reported and of investigating none of them—lies the optimal policy. Somehow the manager, with or without the aid of a decision support system, must selectively decide which variances are the most serious, the most significant, the most unexpected, or, in general, the ones for which an investigation will most probably yield the largest benefits. In this chapter we will discuss a variety of procedures, ranging from simple rules of thumb to complex dynamic optimization techniques, that could prove useful for a manager attempting to decide which variances should be investigated. Despite the plethora of suggestions that can be made to abet this decision, we must be sobered by the realization that, once we go beyond the simplest procedures (for example, investigate all variances larger than 10 percent of the standard), there is as yet little evidence that the procedures proposed have been implemented in actual organizations. Apparently an observation made more than a decade ago is still valid:

> In some general inquiry from some prominent corporations, I was unable to find a single use of statistical procedures for variance control. . . . Accountants have not recognized a conceptual distinction between a significant and an insignificant variance.[1]

Are accountants at fault, or are statistical techniques simply inappropriate decision aids in this area? A prominent managerial accountant expresses doubts about the techniques:

> Researchers continue to explore the possibility of finding a mathematical way of stating whether a variance between planned and actual cost is or is not significant. . . . The differences between the data on the overall costs of a department that are measured once a month are so great that few if any managers believe that statistical techniques in the latter case are worth the effort to calculate them. They prefer either to establish control limits by judgment or to run down the report item by item and determine, without any numerical calculation, whether a difference between planned and actual costs is worth investigation. . . . Attempts to be even more sophisticated and to apply Bayesian probability theory or dynamic programming to the control chart idea do not strike me as being very promising.[2]

Thus the value of the proposed models for determining which variances warrant investigation are still to be determined by actual experiment and practice.

INTRODUCTION TO THE PROBLEM

We can illustrate the relevant issues by referring to a very simple example. Suppose a cost center in the Monroe Company manufactures Gidgets that require 0.74 lb of raw material X9 for each Gidget produced. The standard of 0.74 lb includes a normal allowance for scrap, wastage, spillage, and other nonproductive uses of X9. The raw material X9 is used only to produce Gidgets. Price variances for X9 are expensed as X9 is purchased, so that it is carried in inventory at its standard cost of $0.40/lb and we need concentrate here only on the usage variance of X9 in the manufacture of Gidgets.

During March 1980, 4,320 Gidgets were manufactured by the Monroe Com-

---

[1] Koehler [1968].

[2] Anthony [1973].

pany and 3,450 lb of X9 were consumed in their manufacture. We therefore have the following usage-variance report on product X9:

Actual usage, 3,450 lb at $0.40	$1,380.00
Standard usage, $4,320 \cdot 0.74 \cdot \$0.40$	1,278.72
Usage variance for X9	$ 101.28 U

The manager who receives the X9 usage-variance report may have one or more of the following reactions:

A. "I have better ways of spending my time than worrying about monthly variances as small as $100."

B. "The variance is less than 10 percent. I'm not going to bother with it."

C. "It sure is hard to figure out how much X9 should be used to make Gidgets. Some months we're 15 percent above standard, some months we're 10 percent below. Anytime the variance is within 10 percent of standard, it should probably be considered normal fluctuation."

D. "Usually the X9 consumption is within 3 percent of standard. I'm surprised to see a variance as high as 8 percent."

E. "The industrial engineers set the X9 standard so high that it is never achieved. Sure, under ideal working conditions, we might get by with as little as 0.74 pounds per Gidget, but this standard is mostly for motivational purposes, not what can realistically be achieved in normal operations."

F. "I wonder whether to believe this variance. The inventory requisition and accounting procedures are so unreliable that the variance could have been caused by counting some of the February use of X9 in March or by not measuring the amount of usable X9 still on the shop floor that will be used for April production. I could go to the trouble of investigating this variance and then discover it was a measurement or accounting error."

G. "I'm consistently seeing unfavorable usage variances from manufacturing Gidgets. Perhaps the foreman there is not supervising his workers adequately, perhaps he's using less skilled workers than had been intended for this process, or else they're not following the procedures suggested by industrial engineers."

H. "I've been hearing rumors about a decrease in quality of the raw material X9 we've been receiving. If X9 is not up to our previous standards, it could easily lead to increased waste and scrap."

I. "If we're going to be using 8 percent more X9 than we thought to produce Gidgets, we might decide not to produce Gidgets at all. It's only marginally more profitable than some other products we could be making and perhaps we would do better, with our machines and labor, to produce some of these other products rather than Gidgets. Alternatively, we could drop it from our product line and concentrate our resources on the remaining products we're now selling. This could save us a substantial inventory and distribution expense."

J.   "Last year when we investigated how to manufacture Gidgets, we decided to use raw material X9. But X9 was only marginally better than raw material Z7. Perhaps we made the wrong input decision if we keep using 8 percent more X9 than we had anticipated."

Thus, the decision whether to be concerned with or to investigate a variance encompasses many dimensions:

1. *Materiality*. Significance in terms of overall operations of the company, division, or individual account (see A or B).
2. *Normal fluctuation*. Consistency with prior experience with the account (see C or D).
3. *Inaccurate standard*. Standard set too tight (see E) or too loose (perhaps ignoring learning-curve effects); standard changed because of external conditions (usually for a price or wage-rate standard) or change in production process (such as the introduction of different equipment or procedures).
4. *Measurement errors*. Poor record keeping or accounting practices (see F).
5. *Poor procedures*. People not attempting to achieve efficient operations (see G), or controllable factors outside the cost center causing its performance to deteriorate (see H).
6. *Decision significance*. If the variance is expected to persist, the firm might make different output (see I) or pricing decisions; or it might vary the inputs used in the production process (see J).

With so many different factors, interpretations, and consequences arising from a variance, no single model has been developed that can provide guidance along all the relevant dimensions. We know that we prefer to investigate variances caused by poor procedures (item 5 above) rather than by normal fluctuations (item 2). We will be most interested in learning when the standard is inaccurate (item 3) if the revised standard will affect some output or input decision the firm is making (item 6). If the standard can be tightened because of efficiency improvements and learning-curve effects, the expected costs in future periods will be lower. Obviously, we prefer to concentrate on accounts where deviations will have a major impact on the firm (item 1) or where we can detect a change from prior experience with high probability (item 2). Measurement errors (item 4) can contribute to what is considered normal fluctuation. An investigation undertaken to correct poor procedures (item 5) will lead to disappointment if it is discovered that the cause was poor record keeping. At that time, the cost of improving the record-keeping system must be compared to the potential benefits—fewer false-alarm investigations in the future, more reliable cost data for product decisions, and the chance for tighter control of the production process by eliminating a current source of random fluctuation. The procedures described in this chapter attack different subsets of these issues. Thus the decision as to which procedures will be most beneficial, net of the costs of implementing and maintaining them, is a managerial judgment taken in light of the dimensions that seem most critical in a particular situation.

A final consideration in the installation of a variance-investigation decision system is the effect of such a system on the manager of the department being monitored. Unlike the passive monitoring of the output of an automated production process to detect aberrant performance, a cost accounting variance system will affect the performance of a manager and his department. A manager, knowing that standards have been set and that performance will be measured relative to these standards, should be more attentive to meeting the standards so that an investigation decision is not triggered. Since the cost accounting data will be used to control performance, there is always the possibility that the manager will manipulate the data to provide a somewhat better picture of operations than actually exists. Therefore, the measurements used as an input to a variance-investigation model should be objective and perhaps subject to occasional audits to assure their validity and reliability. Also, when installing a variance investigation model, one should be aware of and sensitive to the effect of the model on the motivation of the responsible managers. These are important effects; unfortunately, however, the current state of the art of behavioral research does not permit us to offer formalized ways of incorporating them into the process of deciding which variance-investigation model should be installed.[3] The effects, therefore, must be considered on an intuitive, subjective basis, but this should not lead us to discount their importance.

MATERIALITY SIGNIFICANCE

The simplest filter rule is to choose a fixed percentage, say 10 percent, and investigate all variances that exceed the standard by this fixed percentage. For example, in the use of X9 in producing Gidgets, we would investigate whenever

---

[3] See Baiman and Demski [1980] for a formal model capturing the incentive and motivational factors associated with a variance-investigation policy.

the standard amount of 0.74 lb of X9 per Gidget varied by more than 0.074 lb. During March 1980, the average use of X9 was 3,450/4,320 = 0.8 lb/Gidget. Thus the usage was 0.06 lb/Gidget higher than the standard, which is less than the materiality amount of 0.074. Hence this usage variance would not be highlighted.

The fixed-percentage rule is extremely easy to implement once the manager, on the basis of his experience and judgment (see the remarks by Anthony quoted earlier) specifies the percentage he wishes to use. One could implement the rule by having a separate column in the variance report in which the variance as a percentage of standard is printed. The manager could then scan this column and identify all the high-percentage variances. To facilitate the scanning process, all variances larger than the specified percentage could be printed in a different color. As an executive summary for the variance report, all accounts with high-percentage variances could be printed on the first page (or pages) of the variance report, thereby relieving the manager of the burden of turning through many pages to learn about all the large deviations.

The advantage of the fixed-percentage rule is its great simplicity, intuitive appeal, and ease of implementation. It has a number of disadvantages:

1. It will not signal when an important account that historically has been controlled very closely, say within 3 percent, suddenly departs from its historical pattern but is still within the preset percentage.

2. It will frequently flag accounts where sizable fluctuation is normal from period to period. An account whose standard deviation is comparable to or larger than the preset percentage will trigger an investigation signal too often.

3. The rule may flag many small accounts that are not controlled too closely and that therefore may have large period-to-period fluctuations.

4. There is no attempt to account for investigation costs and benefits from an investigation that may vary across accounts and that make some accounts more or less worthwhile to investigate.

5. The past history (variances from previous periods) of each account is not incorporated into the fixed-percentage rule when flagging a given account. The manager would have to line up the reports from two or more months to determine whether large deviations have been typical for a given account. The past history of variances for each account is important if we believe that inefficiencies tend to persist once they have crept into the process. Such a persistent inefficiency would be signaled by a sequence of two or more large deviations. In this case, we would be more confident of our investigation's detecting a correctible practice rather than finding that a temporary situation had generated a single large cost variance.

Some of these difficulties can be overcome by allowing the manager to vary the materiality percentage by account. Thus, he might use a smaller percentage for high-dollar-volume, carefully monitored accounts and a larger percentage for low-dollar-volume, relatively minor accounts. In this way he would more quickly detect inefficiencies in key accounts and not be overburdened by seemingly large percentage deviations in insignificant accounts. The problems arising from lack of formal statistical control and from failure to balance the costs and benefits of an investigation would remain, however.

STATISTICAL SIGNIFICANCE

The next step in developing a variance-investigation model requires that a measure of expected dispersion be specified for each account. Initially, we will assume that deviations about the standard (or expected value) are normally distributed so that the standard deviation, σ, is the appropriate measure of dispersion. The typical standard cost system provides us only with an estimate of the expected value, μ, for the account (either the expected usage, the expected price or wage rate, or the expected cost of an overhead item at a given level of activity). Frequently, however, this mean estimate is obtained from an analysis of historical data from which we could also estimate the standard deviation for the account. For example, suppose the standard of 0.74 lb of X9 per Gidget was obtained from noting the previous twelve months of X9 usage. Production was approximately equal in each of the twelve months, so that we can weight each observation equally. The monthly usages, total pounds of X9 divided by number of Gidgets produced, were:

0.70, 0.73, 0.79, 0.76, 0.72, 0.72, 0.75, 0.74, 0.71, 0.75, 0.73, 0.78.

The average of these observations is 0.74, the standard we used in our analysis. But it is easy to estimate the standard deviation from

$$\hat{\sigma} = \left[\frac{\sum (x_i - \bar{x})^2}{n - 1} \right]^{1/2} = \left(\frac{\sum x_i^2 - n\bar{x}^2}{n - 1} \right)^{1/2} = 0.027$$

where $\bar{x} = 0.74$ and $n = 12$.

Thus for the X9 usage account, we would have a standard of 0.74 and an estimated standard deviation of 0.027. The March 1980 result, when we averaged 0.8 lb of X9 per Gidget, is therefore 2.2 standard deviations [$(0.8 - 0.74)/0.027 = 2.2$] from the expected value. This deviation is fairly unusual under the assumption of normally distributed deviations. The probability is less than 0.02 (2 chances in 100) of obtaining a deviation this large from a normal distribution with a mean equal to the standard. Strictly speaking, since we only have an estimate of the standard deviation (from twelve months of historical data) rather than the true standard deviation, the deviation from the mean follows a t distribution (with 11 degrees of freedom in this case) rather than a normal distribution. The t

distribution has more dispersion than the normal distribution to allow for the additional uncertainty that exists when we are using an estimate rather than the true standard deviation. The probability that a random variable having a t distribution with 11 degrees of freedom will exceed 2.2 is still quite small, equal to 0.025 (1 chance in 40). Therefore, we remain fairly confident that the March usage of X9 in producing Gidgets represents a significant departure from prior experience.

An estimate of the standard deviation of the standard for an account is also available when the standard is obtained from a regression analysis. This is most likely to happen when we develop standards for overhead accounts using historical data as the basis for analysis (see Chapters 3 and 4). For example, suppose we have the following eight observations on indirect labor expense (ILE) and direct labor-hours (DLH):

				Month				
	1	*2*	*3*	*4*	*5*	*6*	*7*	*8*
DLH	480	530	490	550	610	510	510	640
ILE	$270	310	290	300	320	290	330	370

A simple regression of indirect labor expense versus direct labor-hours yields

$$ILE = 75.1 + 0.435 \cdot DLH, \qquad R^2 = 0.66.$$
$$(1.09) \quad (3.4)$$

(The figure in parentheses is the t statistic of the coefficient.) The predictions and error from the regression are as follows:

				Month				
	1	*2*	*3*	*4*	*5*	*6*	*7*	*8*
Actual ILE	$270	310	290	300	320	290	330	370
Predicted ILE	284	306	288	314	340	297	297	354
Error	-14	4	2	-14	-20	-7	33	16

The standard error of the regression, s_e, is 19.4, and, indeed, six of the eight observations are within ± 19.4 of the predicted regression line.

The regression of indirect labor expense versus direct labor-hours can be used to compute both the predicted value and the standard error of the prediction for a new monthly observation. When we predict the value of a new observation from a regression line, remember that two factors contribute to the standard error of the forecast. One is the random distribution of observations about the regression line. This factor is represented by the standard error of the regression, 19.4 in this case. The other factor is the uncertainty about the true regression line. This uncertainty increases as the independent variable takes on values far away from the mean of the independent variables used in estimating the regression line. In our example, the average of the eight monthly DLH equals 540. The equation for the standard error of the forecast, s_f, is given by

$$s_f = s_e \left[1 + \frac{1}{n} + \frac{(x_f - \bar{x})^2}{\sum (x_i - \bar{x})^2} \right]^{1/2}, \qquad (10\text{-}1)$$

where

$\bar{x}$ = the mean of the independent variable in the estimation period,

n = the number of observations in the estimation period,

x_f = the value of the independent variable in the forecast month,

$\sum (x_i - \bar{x})^2$ = the sum of the squared deviations of the independent variables in the estimation period.

The formula for the standard error of forecast when there are multiple independent variables is more complex and is most easily expressed in matrix notation. This topic was covered in Chapter 4.

With the data from our example, we use equation (10-1) to obtain

$$s_f = 19.4 \left[1 + \frac{1}{8} + \frac{(x_f - 540)^2}{23,000} \right]^{1/2}$$

Suppose, now, that in March 1980 the Monroe Company had 500 direct labor-hours. The flexible budget for indirect labor expense (ILE) would give an expected value of

$$\text{ILE} = 75.1 + 0.435 \cdot 500 = \$292.60.$$

In addition to this estimate of the expected indirect labor expense we would also have an estimate of the standard deviation about this forecast:

$$s_f = 19.4 \left[1.125 + \frac{(500 - 540)^2}{23,000} \right]^{1/2}$$

$$= 21.2.$$

If the actual indirect labor expense in March 1980 were $300, this would be well within the normal forecast interval for this account, since it would be only $(300 - 292.60)/21.2 = 0.35$ standard deviations from the predicted value. The actual indirect labor expense in March would have to be in excess of $335 before the deviation would start to look statistically significant. The value $335 represents 2 standard deviations from the predicted value, and for a t distribution with 6 degrees of freedom (eight observations in the estimation period less 2 degrees of freedom used up to estimate the two regression coefficients), the likelihood of such a large deviation is slightly less than 0.05. Note that an observation of $335 would be more than 14 percent above the standard. Being 10 percent over standard

($322) would yield a t statistic of only 1.38, which has a probability of occurrence greater than 0.10.

Thus, whenever a standard is established from statistical analysis of historic data, one can also obtain an estimate of the standard error to be expected about this forecast. If the standard is set after an industrial engineering study, one should also attempt to obtain an estimate of the standard error from the study. The estimated standard error can then be used to determine the statistical significance of the accounting variance reported in any period. One way of displaying the statistical significance of an accounting variance would be to report, in a separate column, the t statistic associated with each accounting variance. The t statistic represents the number of standard errors by which the actual observation differs from the predicted or standard value. The manager could then scan the report, noting those accounts with large t statistics—for example, all those for which the t statistic exceeds 2 (roughly a 0.05 significance level). If one wanted to get a little fancier, the probability level associated with each t statistic (controlling for degrees of freedom) could be reported and the manager could focus on those accounts for which the probability of the observation arising from the standard distribution was less than 0.05 or 0.01. As with the rule highlighting deviations larger than a specified percentage, the cover page of the variance report could list all deviations having t statistics above a specified amount (say 2.0 or 3.0). It seems sensible to combine the fixed-percentage and the statistical-significance rules by reporting both percentage deviations and t statistics (or probability levels) for each account, allowing the manager to decide, after observing both factors, which accounts warrant investigation or closer scrutiny.

The statistical-significance rule provides useful improvements over the fixed-percentage rule. It can signal when an account that historically has fluctuated very little about its standard has drifted away from the standard. It recognizes those accounts that historically have had a fair amount of unexplained or random fluctuation from their expected value (such as the indirect labor expense account, where one-third of the variance is unexplained) and may not signal a statistically significant deviation even when the percentage deviation is fairly large. These improvements come at the cost of having to estimate a new parameter for a standard cost system, the standard error of the "standard." When statistical analysis has been used to obtain the standard in the first place, this additional estimate is not difficult to obtain. When the standard was based on personal judgment, the standard error is not directly available. But one could still try to obtain a subjective estimate of the likely fluctuation in the account.

NONNORMAL PROBABILITIES

The discussion above made extensive use of the properties of the normal distribution. We assumed a model of the form:

$$x_i = \mu + \epsilon_i, \tag{10-2}$$

where x_i = observation from given account in period i,

μ = standard for the account,

ϵ_i = random fluctuation in the account with $\epsilon_i \sim N(0, \sigma)$.

That is, we assumed that the random fluctuation in an account is normally distributed with a standard deviation, σ. After the fact, the accounting variance, e_i,

$$e_i = x_i - \mu,$$

was obtained and the t statistic computed:

$$t = \frac{e_i}{\sigma}.$$

Nothing in the technique requires that the error term, ϵ_i, be normally distributed. If, somehow, one knew the distribution for ϵ_i were lognormal, gamma, Cauchy, or any arbitrary distribution, one could still compute the probability that an accounting variance came from the specified distribution. The normal distribution is discussed because much random fluctuation in the real world is well approximated by a normal distribution. Also, the normal distribution is convenient to work with in practice because it is easy to specify (requiring only an estimate of the mean and the standard deviation), and people seem familiar with bell-shaped distributions. But certainly the statistical-significance rule can be implemented for any distribution of the error term, albeit at greater cost of specifying the appropriate distribution or computing the probability significance level.

Some researchers have suggested that, rather than make any distributional assumption at all for the error term, we could use Chebyschev's inequality to compute an upper bound on the probability of an accounting variance coming from the "standard" distribution. For Chebyschev's inequality we assume that the mean, μ, and standard deviation, σ, of a random variable are known but not the form of the distribution. The inequality gives an upper bound on the probability of the random variable being greater than a specified distance from the mean of the distribution regardless of the actual form of the distribution. Formally, if d is the distance of the random variable from the mean of the distribution, Chebyschev's inequality states that

$$\Pr(|x - \mu| \geq d) \leq \frac{\sigma^2}{d^2}. \tag{10-3a}$$

Equivalently, by dividing through by σ, we have

$$\Pr\left(\frac{|x - \mu|}{\sigma} \geq d\right) \leq \frac{1}{d^2}. \tag{10-3b}$$

For our initial example in the production of Gidgets, $\mu = 0.74$ and $\sigma = 0.027$. The new observation was 0.80. Using Chebyschev's inequality, we compute the probability of a deviation this large ($0.80 - 0.74 = 0.06$) as

$$\Pr(|x_f - 0.74| \geq 0.06) \leq (0.027/0.06)^2 = 0.20.$$

Notice this probability bound of 0.20 is much higher than the 0.025 obtained when an underlying normal distribution is assumed. This is the principal and devastating weakness of relying on Chebyschev's inequality in a practical situation. The probability bound is just much too conservative, greatly reducing the power of the statistical procedure. There is little reduction in the information required to use Chebyschev's inequality, since the mean and the standard deviation of the error term still need to be estimated. Just how one would estimate the standard deviation of a distribution without having any knowledge of the underlying distribution is never made very clear by researchers advocating this procedure. It seems more reasonable to assume a simple parametric form, such as the normal, unless one has specific knowledge to the contrary. Chebyschev's inequality is mathematically interesting, but its practical significance in this application is questionable.

CONTROL CHARTS

Testing for the statistical significance of an accounting variance is similar to testing whether a batch of produced items is within preset tolerance limits. Industrial quality control techniques have long been employed to monitor the output from a production process. Usually samples from the process are taken hourly or daily. The mean, and frequently the range or dispersion, of the sampled items are computed and plotted on a quality control chart. A widely used technique is the Shewhart or $\bar{X}$ control chart (see Exhibit 10-1). Each observation period the mean of the sampled items is plotted on the $\bar{X}$ chart. Upper and lower statistical confidence limits are placed on the chart. For example, assuming normally distributed sample means, 95 percent confidence limits are obtained by setting $k = 1.96$ in Exhibit 10-1. An observation falling outside such confidence limits (see observation 7 in Exhibit 10-1) would have less than a 5 percent probability of arising from the in-control (standard) distribution. A 99 percent confidence interval could be obtained by setting $k = 2.58$.

Some articles have appeared in the accounting literature advocating the use of $\bar{X}$ charts for monitoring accounting variances. For example, if one computed usage variances on an item-by-item basis, it would be a relatively simple matter

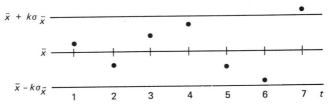

Exhibit 10-1 $\bar{X}$ Control Chart

to sample a few items each hour or each day and plot the mean and range of usage variances on control charts. But the decision to measure usage on so microscopic a basis would have to be made for purposes of production efficiency—not to satisfy the reporting or control requirements of a standard cost system. The accounting system is usually geared to a monthly or at best weekly reporting period. Therefore the traditional control-chart approach will be of limited use for a standard costing system. It is simpler to compute the significance level of an accounting variance as we described previously and present this significance level on the regular accounting report. The detailed computation of sample means and ranges would not seem relevant to the typical accounting variance system.

There is one large advantage in displaying even the monthly variances in a control-chart format. Recall that a disadvantage of the significance-level rule is its failure to incorporate prior observations in the statistical test. The graphical format of a control chart is an excellent way of communicating trends for ready interpretation by the human eye.

For example, Exhibit 10-2a plots the actual monthly cost or usage of an account relative to the standard amount, μ, and its expected standard deviation σ. No one of the observations is statistically significant (larger than 2σ from the standard, μ), but the last four observations are well above 1σ from the standard. In Exhibit 10-2b we can see a pattern of steadily increasing accounting variances without yet hitting a 2σ deviation. Both patterns indicate that a shift away from standard operations is highly likely, but no signal would be given by a mechanical 2σ statistical-significance rule applied only to the most recent observation. The control-chart presentation enables the manager to use his superior pattern-recognition ability in conjunction with the computer's superior ability to compute and display numbers. Six- or twelve-month histories of key accounts could be presented in the control-chart format to enable managers to detect emerging or consistent problems faster than they could if only one or two months of data were presented in tabular form.

The statistical-significance rules we have been describing retain some of the disadvantages noted for the fixed-percentage rule. First, the decision to investigate

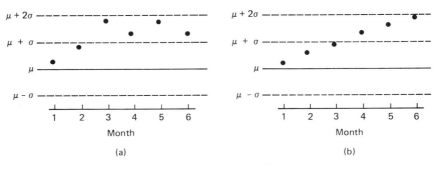

Exhibit 10-2a   Exhibit 10-2b

uses an arbitrary probability rule: Take action if the probability of an observation's arising from the historical distribution of the standard is below 0.05 or 0.01. The use of a predetermined level of statistical significance, such as 0.05 or 0.01, bears no particular relation to the cost of conducting an investigation or the benefits that might accrue from making such an investigation. The costs and benefits of investigating a large accounting variance will vary across accounts, and a complete model would incorporate these factors into the variance-investigation decision. The second limitation is that, for each account, only the most recent observation is used when computing the probability that the accounting variance came from the "standard distribution." In general, if problems or poor procedures can be expected to persist from period to period, we will feel more confident about taking action when large accounting variances have been consistently reported in the most recent periods. The simple hypothesis test on the most recent observation ignores the previous history in each account. More complex models have been developed to (1) use prior, as well as current, observations, and (2) incorporate the expected costs and benefits of an investigation.

FORMAL MODELS FOR MULTIPLE OBSERVATIONS

Specialized techniques have evolved for using the information in a series of observations to signal when a process has drifted or shifted away from a specified "in control" distribution. These techniques are fairly complex and have rarely been tested in an accounting context.[4] One control-chart technique that seems particularly applicable is the *cumulative-sum (cusum) procedure*. The standard, μ, for the process (or account) is subtracted from the current observation, x_r, and a series of partial sums formed, S_r, where

$$S_r = \sum_{i=1}^{r} (x_i - \mu). \qquad (10\text{-}4)$$

Under the null hypothesis, these partial sums should follow a random walk with zero mean. But if a shift in the mean has occurred (away from μ), the partial sums will start to develop a positive or negative drift. While an analytic test to detect a drift is not hard to develop, many writers advocate a graphical approach for the cusum technique. Successive partial sums, $S_r = S_{r-1} + x_r - \mu$, are plotted ($S_r$ on the vertical axis, r along the horizontal axis) and a V mask applied from the most recent observation (see Exhibit 10-3). If any previous cumulative sum ($S_i, i = 1, \ldots, r - 1$) is covered by the V mask, a significant shift in the mean is deemed to have occurred. Cusum charts can be made sensitive to small changes in the mean of a process, since these will cause the trajectory of cu-

---

[4] For a brief summary of these techniques, see Kaplan [1975, pp. 316–18].

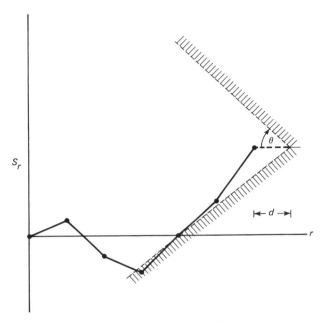

Exhibit 10-3   Cumulative-sum procedure

mulative sums to drift away from previous observations until one limb of the V mask cuts across a prior point to signal an out-of-control condition.

The two design parameters of a cusum V mask are the offset distance, d, and the angle of the mask, θ. These can be set based on (1) an assumed shift in the mean of the process of δ, (2) the average run length in control before a false investigate signal is generated, and (3) the average run length out of control (mean shift of δ) before an investigate signal is given. In practice, these parameters are frequently set by experimenting with different values for d and θ on charts derived from past data from the process being controlled until the right incidence of false and true signals is achieved.[5]

Use of either the cumulative-sum procedure or the display of successive observations in a Shewhart chart (see Exhibits 10-2) allows the manager to identify accounts where consistent departures from the standard have been occurring in recent accounting periods. By signaling a more rapid response to inefficient and correctable procedures, they could be useful supplemental decision aids to the manager in assessing the significance of variances. Offsetting this potential benefit is the cost of calculating and presenting the charts and the extra time the manager

[5] These design issues are discussed in Ewan and Kemp [1960] and Goldsmith and Whitfield [1961]; see also Taylor [1968] and Goel and Wu [1973] for determining the parameters of cumulative-sum charts based on an economic analysis of the costs and benefits from an investigation.

must spend to process these new displays. Also there could be an increased incidence of false alarms—investigations undertaken that do not uncover any correctable problems.

DECISION MODELS WITH COSTS AND BENEFITS OF INVESTIGATION

The control-chart approaches still do not formally incorporate the expected costs and benefits from a variance investigation. Extensions of the control-chart approach have been developed to set the design parameters of the chart to balance the cost of unnecessary false-alarm investigations against the cost of operating "out of control." For our purposes, it seems preferable to develop a simple single-period model using a straightforward decision-theory approach.

We start with a simple model of the process (or account) being monitored. We assume that the process is either *in control* (IC) or *out of control* (OOC). If an investigation is undertaken when the process is OOC, the cause is always found and the process can always be reset to the IC state. This assumption, which is reasonable when controlling the quality of output from a production process, captures only a portion of the issues in the accounting variance setting. It ignores the situation where the cause of the shift in the standard is not reversible because the old standard was inaccurate or there was an external or permanent change in some aspect of the process. Also, it does not capture the situation where the investigation was signaled by a measurement error somewhere in the accounting process. Finally, many accounting contexts may not be well represented by the simple in-control/out-of-control dichotomy. Realistically, the mean of the process may drift over a continuum of values, not oscillate between two distinct states. Nevertheless, even with these limitations, the situation is sufficiently rich to illustrate the basic ideas at the heart of a benefit-cost analysis of the variance-investigation decision.

There is a cost, C, to investigate the variance. This cost includes the value of the manager's or subordinate's time spent on the investigation, any cost of interrupting a production process, and any cost associated with correcting an out-of-control situation. For simplicity we assume that the cost, C, is incurred independent of the true state of the system (that is, correction costs are negligible and, on average, an investigation that discovers the process to be in control is as costly as one that finds it out of control). The assumption of a constant investigation cost is not critical since it can easily be generalized to incorporate an incremental correction cost if the process is found to be out of control.

If the process is out of control, there is a benefit, B, associated with returning the process to standard operation. Just how to measure B is not a trivial problem. At first glance one would think that B could be the sum of cost savings in the current and future periods until the process goes out of control again. But this computation does not recognize that if we don't investigate during this period, we can always investigate during the next period. Therefore the opportunity loss from not investigating now (equivalent to the benefit of investigating now) is not as large as the savings for many periods in the future. This problem is best dealt with in a multiperiod rather than a single-period model. For our purposes, let us define B to be the expected one-period benefit from operating in control rather than out of control, recognizing that this will underestimate the actual benefits.

To illustrate how the one-period benefit might be computed, recall the usage of X9 to produce Gidgets. The standard is 0.74 lb of X9 per Gidget. Past experience has indicated that when the usage of X9 goes out of control, the average amount of X9 used per Gidget is about 0.82 lb, or 0.08 lb per unit above standard. If production of 5,000 Gidgets is planned for next month, and the actual usage per Gidget has increased by 0.08 lb, the expected extra usage of X9 would be 0.08 (5,000) = 400 lb. At an average cost per pound of $0.40, this would cause an additional cost of $160. Assuming that an investigation would enable us to return the usage of X9 to its standard amount of 0.74 lb per Gidget, the expected potential one-month savings would be $160.

Assume that the cost, C, of an investigation is $30. The value, B, of an investigation is equal to $160 if the X9 process is found to be out of control. If the investigation reveals that the process is in control and that the March observation of 0.80 lb/Gidget was due to nonrecurring or random factors, then the benefit from the investigation will be zero. Thus, the critical parameter needed to make an intelligent decision at this stage is the probability that the X9 process is out of control. Let us denote this probability by P. If we knew P, we could compare the certain $30 cost of the investigation with the expected benefit:

$$
\begin{aligned}
\text{Expected Benefit} = \; & \text{Pr(out of control)} \cdot \text{Benefit from correcting an out-} \\
& \text{of-control situation} \\
& + \text{Pr(in control)} \cdot \text{Benefit from investigating an in-} \\
& \text{control situation} \\
= \; & PB + (1 - P) \cdot 0 \\
= \; & PB.
\end{aligned}
\tag{10-5}
$$

Therefore, an investigation is worthwhile, assuming expected-value maximizing, if the expected benefit exceeds the cost; that is, investigate if

$$
PB > C \quad \text{or} \quad P > \frac{C}{B}. \tag{10-6}
$$

With the X9 process for manufacturing Gidgets, we should investigate if

$$
P > \frac{30}{160} = 0.1875.
$$

How can we estimate this critical parameter, P, the probability of the X9 process being out of control? One group of authors[6] has suggested that we could work from the "standard distribution," assuming the process is in control. Recall that the distribution of the amount of X9 used per Gidget was normal with a mean of 0.74 and a standard deviation of 0.027. From this distribution we could compute the probability that an observation of 0.80 (or larger) that occurred during March could have come from this in-control or standard distribution. This probability was previously computed (using a t distribution with 11 degrees of freedom) to be about 0.025. It was suggested that P, the probability of being out of control, must be 1 minus the probability of being in control:

$$P = 1 - 0.025 = 0.975,$$

and an investigation clearly is called for.

This calculation, though deceptively intuitive, is incorrect. Formally, after an observation, x, where x is the actual usage in the most recent month ($x = 0.80$), we are interested in obtaining

$$\Pr(OOC \mid x) = P$$

The calculation we performed previously, which yields the in-control probability of 0.025, is in fact

$$0.025 = \Pr(\text{observation of } x \text{ or larger} \mid \text{in-control}) \tag{10-7}$$

$$= \Pr(\geq x \mid IC).$$

Therefore the complementary probability of 0.975 is

$$0.975 = 1 - \Pr(\geq x \mid IC) = \Pr(\leq x \mid IC),$$

and this quantity is quite different from the probability we want for our model, which is the probability of being out of control (OOC) given an observation as large as x.

The two quantities, $\Pr(OOC \mid x)$ and $\Pr(\geq x \mid IC)$, are related through the mechanism of Bayes' theorem. We need to start with a probability, P', that represents the manager's prior probability that the X9 process is out of control *before* receiving the March observation that $x = 0.80$; that is,

$$P' = \Pr(OOC).$$

To obtain the posterior probability, P, that the process is out of control, given the observation $X = 0.80$, we use the following sequence of steps:

$$
\begin{aligned}
P &= \Pr(OOC \mid x) \\
&= \frac{\Pr(OOC \cap x)}{\Pr(x)} = \frac{\Pr(x \mid OOC)\Pr(OOC)}{\Pr(x \mid OOC)\Pr(OOC) + \Pr(x \mid IC)\Pr(IC)} \\
&= \frac{\Pr(x \mid OOC)P'}{\Pr(x \mid OOC)P' + \Pr(x \mid IC)(1 - P')}.
\end{aligned}
\tag{10-8}
$$

---

[6] See Bierman, Fouraker, and Jaedicke [1961].

From equation (10-8) we see that the 0.025 figure computed earlier in equation (10-7) [$\Pr(\geq x \mid \text{IC})$] is somewhat but not exactly like one term in the denominator, $\Pr(x \mid \text{IC})$, and certainly is not a substitute for the probability, P, that we need for the expected-benefit computation. We see also that we need a new probability—the probability of obtaining an observation of x given that the X9 process is operating out of control, $\Pr(x \mid \text{OOC})$. In order, then, to use an observation, x, to compute the probability of being out of control, we need to know not only the properties of the in control distribution but also:

1. The prior probability of being out of control (P') [or in control ($1 - P'$)]; and

2. The properties of a specific out-of-control distribution [to compute $\Pr(x \mid \text{OOC})$].

Before proceeding further, we must acknowledge that we have been informal (some would say sloppy) in developing these ideas. Strictly speaking, when we are working with a continuous probability distribution such as the normal distribution, the probability of any particular observation, x, is zero. Thus, $\Pr(x \mid \text{IC}) = 0$. In order to obtain nonzero probabilities, we must compute the probability of obtaining an observation in an interval. There are two ways to deal with this problem. One is to compute the probability of obtaining an observation within a small interval of the actual observation. That is,

$$\Pr(x = 0.80 \mid \text{IC}) \cong \Pr(0.795 \leq x < 0.805 \mid \text{IC})$$

$$= \Pr[0.795 \leq x < 0.805 \mid x \sim N(0.74, 0.027)]$$

$$= F_N \left(\frac{0.805 - 0.74}{0.027} \right) - F_N \left(\frac{0.795 - 0.74}{0.027} \right)$$

$$= F_N(2.41) - F_N(2.04) = 0.992 - 0.979$$

$$= 0.013.$$

Alternatively, we can rewrite equation (10-8) by dividing numerator and denominator by $\Pr(x \mid \text{OOC})$ to yield

$$P = \frac{P'}{P' + (1 - P') \dfrac{\Pr(x \mid \text{IC})}{\Pr(x \mid \text{OOC})}} \tag{10-9}$$

From equation (10-9) we see that we are interested only in the ratio of probabilities (called the likelihood ratio):

$$\frac{\Pr(x \mid \text{IC})}{\Pr(x \mid \text{OOC})}.$$

This ratio can be obtained by simply using the ratio of the two density functions at the observation x rather than working with the cumulative distribution function, $F_N(\cdot)$. We will illustrate this point with a numerical example.

Suppose we specify that when the X9 process drifts out of control, we expect observations to come from a distribution with higher mean, say $\mu = 0.82$, but the same standard deviation as before, 0.027—that is, we expect a shift in the location of the distribution but not in its shape (or width). Following the first approach we developed above, we compute

$$\Pr(x = 0.80 \mid \text{OOC}) = \Pr[0.795 \le x < 0.805 \mid x \sim N(0.82, 0.027)]$$

$$= F_N \left(\frac{0.805 - 0.820}{0.027} \right) - F_N \left(\frac{0.795 - 0.820}{0.027} \right)$$

$$= F_N(-0.56) - F_N(-0.93)$$

$$= [1 - F_N(0.56)] - [1 - F_N(0.93)]$$

$$= F_N(0.93) - F_N(0.56)$$

$$= 0.824 - 0.712$$

$$= 0.112.$$

Thus the likelihood ratio is

$$\frac{\Pr(x \mid \text{IC})}{\Pr(x \mid \text{OOC})} = \frac{0.013}{0.112} = 0.116.$$

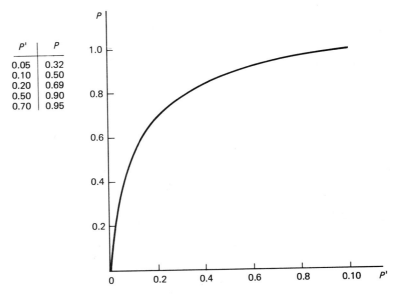

P'	P
0.05	0.32
0.10	0.50
0.20	0.69
0.50	0.90
0.70	0.95

Exhibit 10-4

The alternative computation, using the ratio of the two density functions at the actual observation, yields

$$\frac{\Pr(x \mid IC)}{\Pr(x \mid OOC)} = \frac{f_N(x = 0.80 \mid x \sim N(0.74, 0.027))}{f_N(x = 0.80 \mid x \sim N(0.82, 0.027))}$$

$$= \frac{f_N(0.06/0.027)}{f_N(-0.02/0.027)}$$

$$= \frac{f_N(2.22)}{f_N(0.74)}$$

$$= \frac{0.034}{0.303} = 0.112.$$

The two computations give similar but not identical results. The first method would come closer to the second answer were an interval smaller than 0.05 chosen around the observation. Rather than explore further this relatively minor technical issue, we will accept the results from the second computation and proceed.

Rewriting equation (10-8) or (10-9), we now have that

$$P = \Pr(OOC \mid x = 0.80)$$

$$= \frac{P'}{P' + 0.11(1 - P')}$$

$$= \frac{1}{1 + 0.11 \dfrac{1 - P'}{P'}}$$

(where P' is the prior probability that the process is out of control before we observe the outcome $x = 0.80$). Thus the posterior probability, after the observation $x = 0.80$ is reported, that the process is out of control is a function of P' (see Exhibit 10-4). If we were reasonably certain that the process was in control ($P' = 0.05$) before receiving the monthly report, the high observation of $x = 0.80$ shifts the probability of being out of control up only to one out of three. With a prior probability of being out of control of 0.5, the posterior probability rises to 0.9.

From our simple benefit-cost analysis, we agreed to investigate if the probability of being out of control was above 0.1875. With the numbers we used in this example, as long as the prior probability of being out of control, P', is greater than 0.025, an observation of 0.8 will be sufficient to trigger an investigation.

One benefit of specifying the formal cost structure and probability distributions is that the one-period model we developed here can readily be expanded to handle the multiperiod case in which both past and present observations are used to compute the current probability that the process is out of control. We will not present this method here (Kaplan [1969, 1975] describes this dynamic model with variations). But it should be easy to see in principle how the single-period model developed here is extended. Recall that the cost report changed a prior probability of being out of control, P', into a posterior probability of out of control: $P' \longrightarrow x \longrightarrow P = \Pr(OOC \mid x)$. If P is below a critical value, so that an investigation decision is not signaled, the probability P becomes the prior probability of being out of control for the next reporting period. After the next cost observation is received it is, in turn, updated in a similar fashion through Bayes' theorem to obtain the probability of being out of control. Dynamic programming optimization techniques are used to compute the critical value, at each stage, that determines when the posterior probability of being out of control is high enough to warrant an investigation.

Let us review the purpose of this extended excursion into probability theory. The standard statistical models we developed first enabled us to compute the probability that a given observation came from the standard or in-control distribution. An investigation decision was signaled when this probability fell below a specified level, say 0.05 or 0.01. The information required for this decision model was relatively simple. In addition to the standard, we needed only to specify the standard deviation of the observation from the standard. A limitation of this analysis was that the investigation's cost and expected benefits were not explicitly modeled. Instead, arbitrary probability levels were used as surrogates. In order to incorporate the costs and benefits of an investigation in our decision model, we need to specify:

1. The benefits expected from a successful investigation.
2. The cost of an investigation and whether it varies with the state of the process.
3. The probability of being out of control so that an investigation would be considered successful.

But to obtain the third item we needed to specify further:

4. A specific alternative hypothesis of being out of control.
5. The prior probability of being out of control.

Thus a formal benefit-cost analysis requires a considerable expansion of information. This information will be subjective and much more difficult to specify than just the standard itself and its standard deviation, which we needed for the traditional variance analysis and simple statistical analysis of accounting variances.

Is this increased formalization and complexity justified? Magee [1976] performed a simulation study to determine whether the benefit-cost analysis approach coupled with a dynamic optimization algorithm produces significant cost savings when compared with the simple models we introduced at the beginning of this chapter. For a reasonable variety of assumptions on the costs and benefits of an investigation and mixtures of in-control and out-of-control distributions, the simple rule of investigating all deviations more than 2σ from the expected value worked almost as well, in terms of minimizing average costs, as the more complex models.

Dittman and Prakash [1978] proposed an alternative procedure, called Markovian control, in which an investigation is signaled whenever an observation, x, exceeds a specified control limit, x^*. This method is easier to implement in practice than the policy based on the posterior probability of being out-of-control, since the Bayesian revision process is eliminated. Dittman and Prakash show how the optimal value x^* can be computed based on properties of the in-control and out-of-control cost distributions, the probability of going out of control, and the expected cost of investigation and correction. Basically, this approach is a variant of the control chart we described earlier, but where the investigation limit is determined from the relevant costs rather than from arbitrary probability levels such as 0.05 or 0.01. In another simulation study, Dittman and Prakash [1979] showed that the somewhat simpler Markovian approach could produce total costs virtually identical to the optimal, but more complex, dynamic programming approach.

SUMMARY

In practice, it seems sensible to model the variance-investigation decision in a sequential fashion. First, attempt to obtain a standard deviation for each standard, and for each observation compute the probability that it came from the in-control distribution. Depending upon the importance of an account, and the cost of an investigation, develop rough rules of thumb to determine whether an investigation is signaled by a probability level, say, of 0.10, 0.05, or 0.01. Over time, refine the probability limits signaling the investigation of an account to balance off false alarms versus the cost of not investigating out-of-control processes. For particularly important processes it may prove beneficial to introduce a benefit-cost approach as more data on the process, both in control and out of control, become available. But starting with complex models does not seem worthwhile when one considers the cost of the information requirements and processing algorithms and the small incremental benefits these models have yielded in simulation studies.

A further limitation is the assumption that an out-of-control situation, once discovered, can be reset to the standard or in-control process. In many instances the accounting variance may have been caused by a permanent change in the process—increased price of raw material or labor, or changes in the production process or in raw-material availability. In such instances the investigation, while discovering the cause of the variance, has not yielded the expected benefit, since future operations will remain at the higher cost level. This feature of the variance-investigation decision is not captured in the benefit-cost analysis done previously and may further limit its applicability. There is, however, some benefit derived from learning of permanent shifts in the production process, since planning and control may be improved in future periods. We discussed this topic in Chapter 8, when we computed the opportunity losses caused by not having accurate estimates of costs.

PROBLEMS

10-1. Use of Control Chart to Monitor Machine Hour Usage

The machining department of the Russell Company monitors closely the number of machine hours used in the production process. The department produces only one product which requires different components to be machined separately and then assembled together. During a 15-day period, industrial engineers monitored the production process to insure that standard and efficient procedures were followed. At the end of each day, the engineers counted the number of parts produced and the total number of machine hours used to produce these parts. The daily machine hours per part produced is presented below:

Day	Machine Hours per Part	Day	Machine Hours per Part
1	12.3	9	12.4
2	12.7	10	12.4
3	12.2	11	11.8
4	12.4	12	12.5
5	12.3	13	12.7
6	12.5	14	12.7
7	12.8	15	12.5
8	12.4		

Based on this data, the controller of the Russell Company wished to implement a control chart approach for monitoring machine hour usage in the machinery department.

Required:

1. Compute the parameters for a control chart with 95 percent confidence limits for the Russell Company machinery department. You may assume that departures from the mean, in the fifteen test observations, are normally distributed.

2. One day, the machinery department uses 13.0 machine hours per part produced. What is the probability (assuming normally distributed errors) that this observation arose from the in-control distribution observed by the industrial engineers during the 15-day test period? What probability of coming from the in-control distribution would be computed if the Chebyschev inequality (rather than the normality assumption) were used to

compute the probability of an observation as large as 13.0 machine hours/part.

3. Evaluate the use of a statistical control limit rule for monitoring machine hours per part versus a materiality rule that would signal deviations that are more than 10 percent from the standard.

10-2. Statistical Quality Control

The Deming Company monitors electricity usage on a weekly basis. The company uses a great deal of machinery in its production process and hence wants to be sure that electricity, whose price has more than doubled in the past five years, is used efficiently. In a study, several years ago, Deming's controller computed an index for the company's output and estimated the amount of electricity that should be used to produce a standard amount of output. This study led to a mean estimate of 32.5 kwhr per standard unit of output with an upper control limit of 33.1 kwhr/output and a lower control limit of 31.9 kwhr/output.

Recently, the controller was reviewing the reports for the past 21 weeks of electricity consumption per unit of output:

Week	Electricity (Kwhr/output)	Week	Electricity (Kwhr/output)	Week	Electricity (Kwhr/output)
1	32.9	8	33.0	15	32.6
2	31.9	9	32.8	16	32.8
3	31.5	10	32.9	17	32.5
4	31.7	11	32.8	18	31.7
5	32.4	12	32.8	19	32.7
6	32.2	13	33.0	20	31.7
7	33.0	14	32.9	21	32.2

Required:

Plot these data on the control chart. Comment on this pattern of electricity consumption and the value of the control chart approach now being used to monitor electricity consumption at the Deming Company.

10-3. Statistical Quality Control: Identifying High Cost (Mistake-Prone) Individuals Using the Poisson Distribution*

The Eazy Express Trucking Co. operates an extensive motor freight business. Drivers of trucks, in response to customers' calls, pick up shipments and bring them to a local terminal for sorting, reloading, and shipment to their final destinations. Drivers are susceptible to many types of mistakes in the long chain of operations from initial pickup to final delivery. The most common types of mistakes are listed below but many others can also occur:

---

* This example is adapted from W. Edwards Deming, "On Some Statistical Aids Toward Economic Production," *Interfaces* V (August 1975) 1–15.

Driver Mistakes

Short on pick up
Over on pick up
Failure to telephone about over, short, or damaged loads.
Incomplete bill of lading
Improperly marked cartons
Incomplete signature

Although most drivers make few mistakes, the loss to Eazy Express from the total number of mistakes made is substantial. In 1982, Eazy's drivers made a total of 617 mistakes just in the Pittsburgh area. These mistakes led to costs in excess of $50,000, or about $81 per mistake. For example the losses from Mistake No. 1, Short on Pick Up, could include:

1. Search cost of $25 on platform or on truck for the missing carton;
2. $15 to return the driver to the shipper to pick up the missing carton;
3. A handling charge of $15 to segregate the remaining cartons in the shipment until the missing carton is located, and
4. The potential liability of between $10 and $1000 equal to the shipper's carton value if the carrier can not locate the missing carton.

These out of pocket costs do not include administrative costs, delay costs, and loss of customer goodwill due to Eazy's errors.

An analysis of the Pittsburgh drivers' performance during 1982 yielded the following table:

Number of Mistakes in 1982	Number of Drivers Making This Number of Mistakes	Total Number of Mistakes
0	26	0
1	18	18
2	22	44
3	14	42
4	22	88
5	8	40
6	9	54
7	3	21
8	4	32
9	7	63
10	7	70
11	3	33
12	0	0
13	1	13
14	1	14
15	2	30
16	1	16
17	1	17
18	0	0
19	0	0
20	0	0

Number of Mistakes in 1982	Number of Drivers Making This Number of Mistakes	Total Number of Mistakes
21	0	0
22	1	22
23	0	0
24	0	0
25	0	0
Total	150	617

At present, Eazy has been sending a reprimand letter to a driver each time a mistake is noted. The letter was the same whether this mistake was the only one of the year for the driver or the fifteenth.

Roger Smith, the newly hired assistant to the controller of Eazy Express, feels that his newly acquired knowledge of probability and statistics could be used well in understanding this process. Roger believes that the number of mistakes made by a driver each year can be modeled, to a first approximation by a Poisson process. This process assumes that errors are randomly distributed among drivers, and just due to the vagaries of chance, some drivers will have more errors than the average and some fewer than the average. Roger argues, "If I toss 1,000 pennies in the air on ten separate occasions, one penny is likely to come up Heads ten times in a row and another could come up Tails ten consecutive times. This doesn't mean that these two pennies are particularly "lucky" or "unlucky." They are just following the laws of probability in which, with a large number of trials, rare events become likely to happen."

Roger estimates the mean, λ, of the Poisson process as 4.1 = 617 mistakes/ 150 drivers. Checking back in his probability text for the formula of the Poisson process, he finds that

$$\Pr\{k \text{ mistakes} \mid \lambda = 4.1\} = \frac{(4.1)^k}{k!} e^{-4.1}$$

for $k = 0, 1, 2, 3, \ldots$, and Roger produces the following table:

Number of Mistakes (k)	Pr {k mistakes}	Pr{≤k Mistakes}
0	.017	.017
1	.068	.085
2	.139	.224
3	.190	.414
4	.195	.609
5	.160	.769
6	.109	.878
7	.065	.943
8	.033	.976
9	.015	.991
10	.006	.997
11	.002	.999
12	.001	1.000
13	.000	1.000

1. How can this information help Roger analyze the performance of the 150 drivers?

2. What changes in the "investigation" or mistake-follow-up procedure could Roger recommend?

3. What additional information could be helpful before the controller considers reprimanding severely the drivers with more than twelve mistakes in a year?

10-4. Statistical Quality Control and Measurement of Performance*

John Murrin has just come back from a seminar on quality control and is anxious to implement an incentive scheme to encourage zero defects among his workforce. At present there are 50 workers on an important production line each of whom is monitored by a statistical control chart based on the expected proportion and dispersion of defective items. Murrin has proposed to award monthly both a prize and a half day off to the production worker whose output during the preceding month showed the smallest proportion of defective items.

Required:

Comment on this proposal, indicating the strengths and weaknesses of Murrin's idea.

10-5. Developing Standards and Investigation Rules from Historic Data

The controller of the Palmer Company is concerned with the ever increasing cost of natural gas used to heat the company's factories and office buildings in its central Ohio location. During the past nine weeks, the firm instituted an extensive education and awareness program of the need to conserve gas by keeping thermostats turned down to 68° and to reduce heat levels when the buildings are not being used (evenings and weekends). During this nine-week period, the consumption of natural gas was monitored for each five-day work week and the number of degree days (68°F less the mean daily temperature) for the five weekdays was also recorded as shown below.

Week	Degree Days	MCF of Gas
1	193	523.7
2	272	628.1
3	320	706.0
4	242	572.3
5	184	551.0
6	219	582.7
7	242	615.8
8	220	582.9
9	260	605.0

---

* This problem is also adapted from an example in Deming *ibid.*

The controller is pleased with the conservation efforts during this nine-week period since gas-consumption seemed to be about 10 percent below the comparable period last year when the weather was similar to this year's. He would like, however, to establish a system to keep track of weekly gas consumption, now that the conservation drive has been completed, so that he can detect if gas consumption starts to drift away from current levels.

Required:

1. Set up a specific monitoring and control system for Palmer's controller indicating how it can be used to signal unusual consumption of gas during a week.

2. In the week after the conservation program, there were a total of 195 degree days and weekly consumption of natural gas was 595 MCF. While this is slightly below the mean weekly consumption of 596.4 MCF of gas, the controller is concerned since, last week was warmer than usual and he felt that gas consumption should have been much lower than the nine-week average. Should the controller be concerned with this most recent report?

10-6. Developing a Regression Model to Predict Maintenance and Repair Costs (T. Beechy, adapted)

The Eazy Express Company is pleased with the driver evaluation system established by its newly hired assistant controller, Roger Smith (See Problem 10-3). Roger has now been assigned to develop a procedure to monitor the repair and maintenance costs of the company's fleet of trucks. The firm has evolved from a small family owned business and has never developed sophisticated methods for analyzing or controlling costs.

Repair and maintenance costs are among the most important controllable expenses for Eazy but devising standards for these costs has not been easy. These costs vary by the type and age of the truck, the number of miles driven, weather and road conditions, average length of run between stops, average speed driven, type and weight of freight hauled, etc.

Roger Smith decided that a multiple-regression model would really be nifty in this application. The model could be estimated on recent repair costs and used to establish a standard for current or future repair costs. By being able to determine if repair costs were more or less than expected as each repair or group of repairs were performed, it would be easier to determine the reason for any significant variances. For example, if in one repair facility, costs were consistently exceeding the standard, an investigation might reveal that the facility was using an unqualified or poorly trained mechanic.

Repair and maintenance costs include:

1. Preventive maintenance, performed on a regular basis after a specified number of months or miles driven since the last maintenance;

2. Occasional repairs of components (muffler, tires, battery, minor engine problems) which do not incapacitate the vehicle; and

3. Road repairs due to failure of engine, axle, brakes etc. requiring the truck to be towed back to the repair facility. Road repairs are very expensive because of the high cost of towing to a repair facility and the decreased service to the customer.

After studying the truck repair business for a month, Ralph decided to build his regression model using the following variables:

R—Repair and maintenance cost per period for each truck (the dependent variable)

M—Miles driven since the last preventive maintenance procedure

P—Dummy Variable for type of fuel used (1 = diesel; 0 − gasoline)

D—Average number of deliveries per trip

S—Dummy Variable for season (winter, spring, summer)

Using a variable for the type of fuel would enable the company to compare the average repair costs for the two types of engines. The season dummy variables enabled the model to control for the greater damage caused by winter driving and the body repair typically performed in Spring. The average number of deliveries variable controls for the wear and tear on the truck's hydraulic system caused by frequent loading and unloading.

Roger felt that if the estimated model had a high R^2, it could be depended on to establish standards for repair and maintenance costs. Also, he planned to test the statistical significance of each of the independent variables. Finally, he would compute, for each truck repair record he examined, the standard error of the forecast and only investigate those repair jobs whose costs exceeded twice the standard error of the forecast.

Required:

Comment on the use of a regression model in this context and the initial effort by Roger Smith to formulate and develop a specific model.

10-7. Determining the Critical Probability for an Investigation Decision

In a production line, daily costs fluctuate around a level of $20,000 when the assembly line is operating properly. When the assembly line is out of adjustment, excess operating costs average $2,000 per day higher. At the beginning of the week, the foreman has the option of investigating closely the operation of the assembly line and, if necessary, resetting the line to proper operation. If the line is out of adjustment at the beginning of the week it will remain out of adjustment for the entire week. Even if the line is adjusted properly at the beginning of the week, there is a chance it will drift out of adjustment sometime during the week so that the anticipated benefit from resetting an improperly operating line is about $7,500.

The investigation to determine whether the line is adjusted properly or not, costs $1,000 and the average cost to correct a line that is found to be out of adjustment is $2,000. How large does P, the probability of being out-of-adjustment, have to be before the foreman should decide to investigate?

10-8.   Deciding Whether to Investigate

The Webster Company uses a single machine to stamp out materials for its product. When properly adjusted the machine uses 32 pounds of the input material for each part produced. The material costs $400/ton. On average, material for 400 parts is stamped out each week and based on this production quantity, the standard deviation of the weekly average of material used per part is 2 pounds. When the machine is not properly adjusted the mean amount of material per part shifts upward to 36 pounds but the standard deviation around the weekly mean remains the same at 2 pounds.

The machine is scheduled to be overhauled after one more week of production. Prior to the most recent week's production, the foreman estimated that the probability that the machine was still properly adjusted was 0.8 but he has just received his weekly production report indicating that the mean amount of material used per part produced was 35. While this is within two standard deviations of the standard value (of 32 pounds), the foreman is wondering whether it is worth calling a maintenance crew in over the weekend to assure that the machine will be properly adjusted for the next week's production run. The cost of the maintenance crew adjusting the machine would be $150 independent of whether the machine was in or out of adjustment.

Required:

What would you advise the foreman to do?

10-9.   Value of Partial Information in an Investigation Decision

The Floyd Company is about to produce a 1,000 unit batch of thermatrons. Thermatron production is highly automated and when the process is operating correctly, 40 thermatrons per hour can be produced with a standard deviation around this estimate of 3 thermatrons per hour. Occasionally the thermatron process drifts out of adjustment and can only produce an average of 32 thermatrons per hour (same standard deviation as before). Once the order for the 1,000 units is initiated, it can not be interrupted except at significant cost and inconvenience.

Variable operating costs for the thermatron production line are $60 per hour. (This does not include the cost of material for thermatrons.) The cost of adjusting the line prior to the start of the production run to assure efficient operating performance is $100.

Required:

1. What is the critical probability of being out-of-adjustment such that the cost of adjustment just equals the expected excess operating costs?
2. The Floyd Company discovers it has the option of performing a test by

operating the production process for one hour at an incremental cost of $50 and observing how many thermatrons are produced. Prior to conducting the test, it believes that there is a 80 percent probability that the line will operate efficiently at the 40 thermatron per hour rate. The company decides, however, that it is worth $50 to help resolve the current uncertainty and opts for the test run which reveals that only 35 thermatrons were produced. Should the company now pay to have the line adjusted?

10-10. Decision to Investigate in Multi-Period Setting* (G. Foster)

From a cost variance analysis report for the previous period, Hobie Leland discovers that Department Y had a $4,000 unfavorable material usage variance. If the usage process is out of control, the variance will continue for this period and a subsequent two periods. The usage variance occurs continuously throughout each period. If the usage process is in control this period, it will remain in control for the subsequent two periods.

Hobie has a decision to make. If he makes an investigation, an outlay of $1,000 is required now (start of the current period). If the usage is found to be out of control, correction is made at the end of the current period (at an additional cost of $2,000) due to the length of time necessary for an investigation. Thus, any out-of-control variances will remain for at least the current period, even if an investigation is made. Hobie has a desired rate of return of 10 percent per period.

Required:

1. Outline the cash flows for the current period and the two subsequent periods for each of the two actions available to Hobie (investigate/not investigate).

2. What is the probability of the process being in control at which Hobie should be indifferent between investigating and not investigating the process?

3. In Questions 1 and 2, it is assumed that the cost to the firm of the process being out of control is the $4,000 unfavorable materials usage variance. Give three reasons why this assumption need not be valid.

4. Assume the cost of the process being out of control is now assessed to be $3,000 per period. Department Y has a $4,000 unfavorable materials usage variance. What is the expected opportunity cost of using the materials usage variance of $4,000 as the period cost of being out of control? Assume the probability of the process being out of control is .3.

5. Hobie has been using the following rule of thumb for investigating cost variances—investigate if an unfavorable variance exceeds the standard by more than 10 percent. Hobie decides that some more sophistication is necessary and adopts the 2σ rule in deciding whether to investigate a cost variance. Hobie is astounded when his friend from the "Institution of

---

* This problem appears in Charles Horngren, *Cost Accounting*, Fifth Edition (Prentice-Hall, 1982); reproduced with permission.

Cost-Benefit Analysis'' suggests that further analysis is necessary before changing his current rule of thumb to the 2σ rule. Discuss four specific factors that should be considered in the cost-benefit analysis of which cost investigation rule to adopt.

REFERENCES

ANTHONY, R. N., "Some Fruitful Directions for Research in Management Accounting," in N. Dopuch and L. Revsine, eds., *Accounting Research 1960–1970: A Critical Evaluation*. Center for International Education and Research in Accounting: University of Illinois, 1973.

BAIMAN, S., and J. DEMSKI, "Variance Analysis Procedures as Motivational Devices," *Management Science* XXVI (August 1980), 840–48.

BIERMAN, H., L. E. FOURAKER, and R. K. JAEDICKE, "A Use of Probability and Statistics in Performance Evaluation," *The Accounting Review* XXXVI (July 1961), 409–17.

DITTMAN, D. A., and P. PRAKASH, "Cost Variance Investigation—Markovian Control of Markov Processes," *Journal of Accounting Research* XVI Spring 1978, pp. 14–25.

————, and P. PRAKASH, "Cost Variance Investigation: Markovian Control Versus Optimal Control," *The Accounting Review* LIV (April 1979), 358–73.

DUNCAN, A., "The Economic Design of $\bar{x}$ Charts Used to Maintain Current Control of a Process," *Journal of the American Statistical Association* LI (June 1956), 228–42.

DYCKMAN, T. R., "The Investigation of Cost Variances," *Journal of Accounting Research* VII (Autumn 1969), 215–44.

EWAN, W. D., and K. W. KEMP, "Sampling Inspection of Continuous Processes with No Autocorrelation Between Successive Results," *Biometrika* XLVII (1960), 363–80.

GIBRA, I. N., "Economically Optimal Determination of the Parameters of $\bar{X}$-Control Charts," *Management Science* XVII (May 1971), 635–46.

GOEL, A. L., S. C. JAIN, and S. M. WU, "An Algorithm for the Determination of the Economic Design of X-Charts Based on Duncan's Model," *Journal of the American Statistical Association* LXIII (1968).

GOLDSMITH, P. L., and H. WHITFIELD, "Average Run Lengths in Cumulative Chart Quality Control Schemes," *Technometrics* III (February 1961), 11–20.

KAPLAN, R. S., "Optimal Investigation Strategies with Imperfect Information," *Journal of Accounting Research* VII Spring 1969, pp. 32–43.

————, "The Significance and Investigation of Cost Variances: Survey and Extensions," *Journal of Accounting Research* XIII Autumn 1975, pp. 311–37.

KOEHLER, R. W., "The Relevance of Probability Statistics to Accounting Variance Control," *Management Accounting* L October 1968, pp. 35–41.

MAGEE, R. P., "A Simulation Analysis of Alternative Cost Variance Investigation Models," *The Accounting Review* LI July 1976, pp. 529–44.

PAGE, E. S., "Continuous Inspection Schemes," *Biometrika* XLI (1954), 100–115.

SHEWHART, W. A., *The Economic Control of the Quality of Manufactured Profit.* New York: Macmillan, 1931.

TAYLOR, H. M., "The Economic Design of Cumulative Sum Control Charts for Variables," *Technometrics* X (August 1968), 479–88.

COST ALLOCATION:
The Case
of Service
Departments

11

BENEFITS OF SERVICE DEPARTMENT PRICING

We can usually distinguish two types of departments in organizations: those that are directly involved in producing and distributing the firm's outputs, and those whose main output is service to other departments. The latter, which we will call *service departments,* involve difficult planning and control problems since they do not produce profits directly for the firm.[1] Because their output is not sold outside the firm, their costs must be covered by the contribution margins generated by the revenue-producing departments. Managers of revenue-producing departments tend to have a scornful attitude toward service departments, viewing them as costly and inefficient units that reduce the firm's profits. But presumably service departments are just as necessary to the production of the firm's output as the final production departments.

A good cost accounting system should provide incentives for efficient performance by managers of service departments and for prudent use of service departments' outputs by the managers of revenue-producing departments. If the costs of an internal service department are not charged to user groups, a number of negative consequences can occur. First, more of the service will be demanded by user groups than is economically reasonable to supply. Without seeing the costs of using a service department, a user will attempt to use the service up to the point where the marginal benefit is zero. Naturally, this will be well beyond the optimal usage, where the marginal benefit from the service equals the marginal cost of supplying it.

A second consequence is that it will be difficult to determine whether the

---

[1] Examples of such service departments include utilities, maintenance, housekeeping, and information systems. Units such as R&D or advertising that produce companywide service may not be included in this analysis except to the extent their output is produced for specific departments or products.

service department is operating efficiently. In the absence of prices charged to profit-conscious departmental managers, the service department must be treated as a cost center. If budgeted costs are obtained from historical experience, there is no guarantee that they represent efficient operation. Also, no signals are available to determine the optimal scale or size of the service department. At times of financial stringency, the output of the service department may be restricted as a way of reducing costs. This may not be desirable if it restricts or downgrades the performance of revenue-producing departments that would be willing to pay for additional amounts of the service.

Third, if a service department's output is not priced, there is little guidance on whether the firm should continue to supply the service internally. For many service activities, firms have the option to purchase the service externally. For example, utilities, data processing, maintenance, housekeeping, consulting, industrial engineering, and security can either be supplied internally or purchased externally. Without a price system to compare relative costs, it may not be obvious when an internal service center is noncompetitive with external alternatives, because of either internal inefficiencies or an uneconomically small scale of operation.

A fourth consideration is that, in the absence of a pricing system, there is no simple way to decide on the quality of service to be provided. A service department may wish to avoid complaints from users and may obtain satisfaction by providing service of excellent quality, based on acquisition of sufficient resources to provide a Cadillac level of services. If user departments were made to see the cost of receiving this quality of service, they might opt for a Chevrolet level—functional, without frills, and less expensive. But without the incentives and signals emanating from a pricing system for the output of a service department, there is little opportunity for a user department to communicate its preferences on the price-versus-quality dimension.

By charging for the output of a service department, we can overcome these four difficulties. The department manager of a consuming department being charged for the output of a service department will (1) exercise more control over the consumption of that output in his department; (2) compare the costs of the internal service department with the costs of comparable services purchased outside the firm; and (3) attempt to communicate to the service department the quality level of services he desires, showing his willingness to pay more to receive higher quality or his willingness to accept lower quality in order to pay less. The manager of a service department whose output must be sold, rather than just allocated, to user departments is aware that his prices will be reviewed critically by profit-conscious departmental and divisional managers; hence he will be motivated to keep his costs down. The manager of a service department who must break even by charging for the output of his department may be more entrepreneurial and innovative as he attempts to provide a level and quality of service that will be demanded by user departments. He will therefore be more responsive to the demands of user groups rather than offering service on a take-it-or-leave-it basis.

Charging for the output of service departments helps the firm in internal resource-allocation decisions. For some departments (such as utilities, data processing, or departments with skilled personnel) there may be short-run capacity limits. If demand is high for the output of these service departments, it may be difficult for the firm to allocate the available supply among all the user groups. Prices, however, can be set above the actual costs of service departments so as to ration the excess demand to those user departments who most value the service. If enough user groups are willing to pay a high price for a service, the firm can use this clearing price to determine whether it pays to invest in additional (and costly) capacity for the service department. If, conversely, a service department is unable to recover its long-run marginal costs, when it prices its output to users, the firm has a good signal that the department has more capacity than is economically warranted over the long run. Service departments unable to cover even their short-run variable costs through charges to user departments should be identified for special attention. Such departments should be examined closely by top management to determine why their cost structure is so high or their output so lightly demanded.

We have been focusing on the use of prices to control the demand and supply of the output from a service department. In principle, the prices could be determined by reference to potential outside suppliers of these services. This possibility will be extensively discussed in Chapter 14 on transfer pricing. Using externally referenced prices would treat service departments as profit centers and, if carried to its logical conclusion, would allow revenue-producing centers the choice of acquiring the service either from the internal service department or from an outside supplier. Typically, however, the charges for use of service departments are based on the budgeted or actual costs of these departments. We will follow a cost-based pricing scheme for service departments throughout this chapter, and defer the consideration of a market-referenced pricing system to Chapter 14. Most of the benefits of a service department pricing system can be achieved even when prices are based on the costs of the service department.

A cost-based pricing system has the advantage of allowing service department costs to be included in final-product costing and pricing decisions. As a minimal requirement, the variable cost of providing service needs to be allocated to revenue-producing departments and subsequently to the actual goods and services sold by the departments, if we want to account for all the variable costs of producing these goods and services. In order to do a product-line profitability analysis, we should include not just the direct costs incurred in the production departments but the costs incurred in service departments that support the production departments. The escapable fixed- and variable-cost components of service departments should be included in any cost-volume-profit analysis of the firm's goods and services. If service department costs are not included in final-product costs, we will overstate profit margins and distort the relative profitability of products that use differing amounts of the output of service departments. Firms that price part or all of their output on a cost-plus basis will certainly want to include service department costs in the computed cost of their output.

Financial reporting requirements provide a final reason for allocating service department costs to producing departments and subsequently to final goods and services. Generally accepted accounting principles require that the full costs of production be allocated to products sold and placed in inventory during a period. The cost of providing service to the revenue-producing departments is part of the total cost to produce these products.

ALLOCATING SERVICE DEPARTMENT COSTS

Service department costs are allocated to other departments based on some measure of usage of the service department's output. Thus for each service department we need to choose a measure of activity that serves as a surrogate for usage. Ideally we can choose a direct measure of output of that service department—for example, kilowatt-hours or pounds of steam from a utility department, CPU hours from a data processing department, or purchase orders filled for a purchasing department. For some departments we will have to settle for input measures (hours of maintenance supplied rather than improvement in equipment performance), whereas for other departments we may have to use a surrogate but not very accurate measure for allocating out costs (such as square footage for housekeeping and security, number of employees for the personnel department, total direct costs for a controller's department). We settle for these surrogate measures because the cost of obtaining direct bases for allocation (for example, monitoring the amount of time the housekeeping staff spends in each department) greatly exceeds any potential benefit from using these direct measures. If a service department provides a variety of different kinds of services, it may be desirable to have multiple measures of activity to reflect these different types of activities. In any case we presume that, after careful thought and deliberation, the firm is able to decide on a reasonable set of measures to use as the basis for allocating service department costs.

Even with a good set of activity measures for each service department, pitfalls await the unwary analyst when allocating service department costs. To illustrate these pitfalls, let us look at an example.

The Maxwell Company has a utility department that provides its three operating departments with power. The three operating departments have the following standard and actual demand for power:

| | Operating Department | | | |
	1	2	3	Total
Practical capacity (kW-hr)	70,000	100,000	30,000	200,000
Normal activity (kW-hr)	60,000	85,000	25,000	170,000
Actual activity in January (kW-hr actually used)	60,000	50,000	27,000	137,000
Standard kW-hr allowed for output actually produced in January	55,000	50,000	28,000	133,000

At the normal activity level of 170,000 kilowatt-hours (kW-hr) the utility department's standard cost is $8,500. Power costs are budgeted to the operating departments at a rate of $0.05/kW-hr to fully recover the utility department's standard cost at normal activity levels. The actual charges to the operating department, however, are done at the end of each month based on the actual cost of the utility department and the actual number of hours used by each operating department. During January the utility department incurred costs of $8,220. For fluctuations up to 25 percent on either side of the normal activity level the variable cost of the utility department is $0.02/kW-hr.

As a first pass at analyzing the cost of power to the three operating departments we can compute the variance between actual and budgeted costs for the month of January. During this month, power is billed at a rate of $0.06/kW-hr, a figure obtained by dividing the $8,220 actual cost by the actual number of kilowatt-hours, 137,000. For the three departments we have the following variance report:

	1	*2*	*3*	*Total*
Actual costs (actual kW-hr · 0.06)	$3,600	$3,000	$1,620	$8,220
Budgeted costs (allowed standard kW-hr · 0.05)	2,750	2,500	1,400	6,650
Variance	$ 850 (U)	$ 500 (U)	$ 220 (U)	$1,570 (U)

where (U) represents an unfavorable variance. Clearly something is wrong with this allocation scheme. Department 3 has used more than the normal number of kilowatt-hours (which should produce a favorable variance because variable costs are well below full costs) and has actually used less than the standard number of kilowatt-hours for the output it produced—yet it shows an unfavorable variance on power costs.

A clearer picture emerges when the total variance is decomposed into a price variance and a usage (or quantity) variance:

	1	*2*	*3*	*Total*
Price variance: Actual kW-hr · (actual rate − budgeted rate)	$600 (U)	$500 (U)	$270 (U)	$1,370 (U)
Usage Variance: (Actual kW-hr − allowed standard kW-hr) · 0.05/kW-hr	250 (U)	0	50 (F)	200 (U)
	$850 (U)	$500 (U)	$220 (U)	$1,570 (U)

We now see that most of the unfavorable variance is caused by the $0.01 increase in the rate per kilowatt-hour charged for power. The manager of Department 3 is being penalized for two factors not ordinarily under his control: (1) the total amount of power consumed by the other two departments, and (2) the unit price and efficiency of the utility department. These two uncontrollable factors produce the $270 unfavorable price variance shown for Department 3. Note that if Department 2 had used its normal amount of 85,000 kW-hr, instead of the 50,000 kW-hr it actually used, the cost per kilowatt-hour would have declined significantly for all departments. The fixed costs of the utility department would have been spread over many more actual hours of service. In effect, by working many fewer hours than normal, Department 2 has generated an unfavorable price variance for itself and for the other two departments.

Also contributing to the unfavorable price variance are inefficiencies in the utility department. With a variable cost saving of $0.02/kW-hr, the reduction in actual number of kilowatt-hours demanded should have reduced costs by

$$(\text{Normal kW-hr} - \text{Actual kW-hr}) \cdot \text{Variable Cost/kW-hr}$$

$$= (170,000 - 137,000) \cdot 0.02$$

$$= \$660.$$

The actual reduction in costs was $8,500 - $8,220 = $280. Thus, there is a spending or efficiency variance of $660 - $280 = $380 in the utility department, which is being passed on to the operating departments through a higher average hourly rate. The present charging scheme, therefore, is undesirable, because a manager's performance is affected by activities and inefficiencies in departments over which he has no control. An additional undesirable factor is that the operating departments are being charged on an average- rather than marginal-cost basis. Thus their managers might be turning down profitable opportunities that they might have accepted if power cost them $0.02 to $0.03/kW-hr rather than the current budgeted figure of $0.05/kW-hr.

An improved system for allocating service department costs would have the following characteristics:

1. The level of activity and inefficiency in any single operating department should not affect the evaluation of other operating departments.

2. Efficiencies or inefficiencies in the service department should be reflected in the evaluation of the service department but not in the evaluation of any operating department.

3. The evaluation of the service department should not be affected by factors beyond its control, such as unanticipated fluctuations in the quantity of service demanded of it.

4. The operating departments should be encouraged to expand the use of the service department as long as the incremental benefits to them exceed the company's marginal cost of supplying the service.

5. The long-run costs of the service department should be paid by the users of its service. If a service department is being used to

capacity under the pricing system, this can be viewed as a reliable signal to expand its capacity. If operating departments balk at paying long-run costs, the service activity can be contracted over time or perhaps made more efficient.

One relatively simple scheme achieves most, if not all, of these benefits. We consider a scheme in which

1. Each department is charged on the basis of budgeted service department costs, not actual costs.
2. Charges are separated into fixed and variable costs. Under this scheme, each operating department would be charged $0.02/kW-hr actually used. The $0.02 figure is the budgeted variable cost of the service department.

The fixed costs of the service department can be estimated as

$$\$8,500 - \$0.02(170,000) = \$5,100.$$

The allocation of this $5,100 to the operating departments is rather arbitrary but probably useful. It alerts the managers of these departments to the cost of supplying capacity in the power department. It is a reservation price to have access to the relatively low-cost (2¢/kW-hr) power on a variable-cost basis. It can also be considered the long-run component of marginal cost. Two reasonable possibilities for allocating the fixed-cost component are (1) proportional to practical capacity and (2) proportional to normal activity levels:

	Department			
	1	*2*	*3*	*Total*
Practical capacity	70K	100K	30K	200K
Percent of total	35%	50%	15%	100%
Allocated fixed costs	$1,785	$2,550	$765	$5,100
Normal activity level	60K	85K	25K	170K
Percent of total	35.3%	50%	14.7%	100%
Allocated fixed cost	$1,800	$2,550	$750	$5,100

In this example there is very little difference between the two allocation bases.

Under the proposed scheme, and allocating fixed costs based on normal activity levels, the power department costs charged to the three operating departments in January are:

$$
\begin{array}{rl}
1: & \$1,800 + 60,000(\$0.02) = \$3,000 \\
2: & 2,550 + 50,000(\$0.02) = 3,550 \\
3: & \underline{750 + 27,000(\$0.02) = 1,290} \\
\text{Total:} & \$5,100 + 137,000(\$0.02) = \$7,840
\end{array}
$$

The only variance recognized in the operating departments arises from using a nonstandard amount of power for the amount of output produced. In Department 1, 60,000 kW-hr were used instead of the standard allowance of 55,000 kW-hr. This generates an unfavorable usage variance of $(5,000)(0.02) = \$100$. Department 2 shows a favorable usage variance of $20, since it used 1,000 fewer hours than the standard allowance (1,000 hours at $0.02 = \$20$). The utility department shows an unfavorable spending (or efficiency) variance of

$$\text{Actual Costs} - \left(\begin{array}{c} \text{Budgeted Costs at} \\ \text{Actual Volume} \end{array} \right) = \$8,220 - \$7,840 = \$380.$$

Notice that this method eliminates the influence of rate fluctuations and usage by other departments from the evaluation of services consumed by an individual department. The managers in each operating department will be motivated to use the output from the service department for applications in which the benefit exceeds the $0.02/kW-hr short-run variable cost. But the operating managers will still see some of the capacity or longer-run costs of operating the service department through the allocated fixed-cost charge. The manager of the service department will be evaluated on a flexible budget, hence his performance will not be affected by fluctuations in demand for his service. Any inefficiencies in the service department will be reflected in a spending variance for the service department and not passed on as higher charges to the operating departments.

INTERACTIONS AMONG SERVICE DEPARTMENTS

The procedure developed in the previous section is easily extended to allocate the costs of multiple service departments to multiple production departments as long as there are no interactions among the service departments. With no interactions, each service department can develop its fixed and variable costs and allocate them to the various production departments it services. The manager of each production department would then absorb, for each service department that it uses, a fixed monthly charge plus a variable charge for each unit of service it demands.

It would be unusual, however, for multiple service departments to have no interaction among themselves. In general, service departments provide service to other service departments as well as to revenue-producing or production departments. For example, a personnel department hires and oversees people for all departments in the organization; a utility department provides heat and light to all departments (including itself), a data processing department provides computer services and output to many service departments, a housekeeping department cleans all facilities, and a maintenance department repairs machinery throughout a facility. With such interactions, an analysis that charges all the costs of each service department directly to production departments will not give an accurate picture of cost dependency.

At first glance, it would seem simple to allocate the costs of each service department to all departments that use its output, both production and other service departments. But one soon realizes that once we begin this process, it is not clear what "the costs" of a service department are. Besides the traceable costs incurred, each service department will start to accumulate charges from other service departments from which it receives services, and these must be reallocated back to its user departments. Once started, the allocation and reallocation process can cycle for a long time before a stable solution is reached.

To avoid this cycling of cost reallocations, introductory cost accounting texts tend to ignore the reallocation process and just allocate service department costs to production departments, ignoring the interaction among service departments. The first refinement to this simplistic approach attempts to rank service departments by the amount of service received from other service departments. The first-ranked service department is the one that provides the most service to all the other service departments and receives the least in return. The second-ranked department receives the next least amount of service from the remaining service departments, and so forth. If we are lucky, we can perhaps find a ranking of the n service departments, call them $S_1, S_2, \ldots, S_n$, such that

S_1 supplies service to $S_2, S_3, \ldots, S_n$ but receives none from them,

S_2 supplies service to $S_3, \ldots, S_n$ but receives none from them,

S_i supplies service to $S_{i+1}, S_{i+2}, \ldots, S_n$ but receives none from $S_{i+1}, \ldots, S_n$,

S_n supplies service only to production departments but not to any service department.

If we can obtain such an ordering, the service department allocation problem is easily solved. First, we allocate S_1's costs to $S_2, \ldots, S_n$ and all production departments served by S_1; second, we allocate S_2's cost, including the allocated cost from S_1, to $S_3, \ldots, S_n$ and all production departments served by S_2; and, in general, we allocate S_i's costs, including the allocations it received from S_1, $\ldots, S_{i-1}$, to $S_{i+1}, \ldots, S_n$ and production departments. When such an ordering is possible, the cycling situation previously described will not occur. Once a service department's costs are allocated, it never receives a new allocation from another service department. In general, however, there will not be an ordering of service departments that eliminates the cycling problem.

We illustrate these ideas with an example. The Wilson Company has two production departments, fabrication and assembly, and two major service departments, material handling and power generation. The costs and outputs of the service departments in a typical period are tabulated below:

	Material Handling	Power Generation	Fabrication	Assembly
Traceable costs	$10,000	$4,000	—	—
Pounds of material used	—	20	50	30
Power used, kW-hr	50	—	40	10

Allocation Method 1—Direct Apportionment

The simplest method allocates the costs of the two service departments directly to the production departments, ignoring service department interactions. With this scheme we obtain the following allocations:

$$\text{Fabrication:} \quad \tfrac{5}{8}(10,000) + \tfrac{4}{5}(4,000) = \$\ 9,450$$
$$\text{Assembly:} \quad \tfrac{3}{8}(10,000) + \tfrac{1}{5}(4,000) = \underline{\$\ 4,550}$$
$$\$14,000$$

Allocation Method 2—Sequential

Each service department in the Wilson Company provides some service to the other service department. Therefore, there is no natural order for sequentially allocating the service department costs. Let us perform the sequential allocation in each of the two possible orders and see whether the order makes any difference.

	Material Handling	Power Generation	Fabrication	Assembly
I. *Allocate material handling first*				
Overhead costs before allocation	$10,000	$4,000		
Material handling (0.2,0.5,0.3)	(10,000)	2,000	$5,000	$3,000
Power generation (0.8, 0.2)		(6,000)	4,800	1,200
Reallocated Costs			$9,800	$4,200
II. *Allocate power generation first*				
Overhead costs	$10,000	$4,000		
Power generation (0.5,0.4,0.1)	2,000	(4,000)	$1,600	$ 400
Material handling (0.625, 0.375)	(12,000)		7,500	4,500
Reallocated Costs			$9,100	$4,900

The three possible allocations may be summarized as follows:

	Fabrication	Assembly
Direct apportionment	$9,450	$4,550
Sequential—material handling first	9,800	4,200
Sequential—power generation first	9,100	4,900

Thus the allocation of service costs varies considerably, depending on which method is selected and, for the sequential method, which order is selected for the two service departments. Of course, for many actual situations the difference between the two methods or among various orderings of service departments in the sequential method may not be substantial. Nevertheless, one wants to be able to handle situations in which there are significant differences among the various possible allocation schemes as occurred for the Wilson Company, above.

RECIPROCAL ALLOCATION METHOD

The direct apportionment and sequential procedures are heuristic methods developed before the widespread use of computers in business and before there was much mathematical sophistication among accountants. Students even of high school algebra should recognize that the cycling problem of reallocating costs from one service department to the next is a special case of a simultaneous equation system. If we could just write down the series of equations describing the interactions among service departments, we would be able to solve these equations directly to obtain the reallocations without having to make arbitrary assumptions about the sequence in which service department costs are to be allocated. If there are more than two or three service departments, it becomes convenient to use linear algebra to represent the system of equations and to rely on computer-based routines to invert a matrix to solve the equations.

For a general treatment, assume there are m service departments and n production departments. Let

a_{ij} = proportion of the jth service department's output provided to the ith service department $(i, j = 1, \ldots, m)$.

c_{kj} = proportion of the jth service department's output provided to the kth production department $(k = 1, \ldots, n; j = 1, \ldots, m)$.

b_j = traceable cost of the jth service department.

It must be true that for each service department j,

$$\sum_{i=1}^{m} a_{ij} + \sum_{k=1}^{n} c_{kj} = 1.$$

Referring back to the Wilson Company, we can label Material Handling as service department 1, Power Generation as service department 2, Fabrication as production department 1, and Assembly as production department 2. Then $a_{12} = 0.50$, since 50 percent of the output of service department 2 (Power) goes to service department 1 (Material Handling). Continuing in this manner, we obtain

$$a_{12} = 0.50, \qquad a_{21} = 0.20,$$

$$c_{11} = 0.5, \qquad c_{21} = 0.3, \qquad c_{12} = 0.4, \qquad c_{22} = 0.1,$$

$$b_1 = \$10,000, \qquad b_2 = \$4,000.$$

Using the notation above, the term a_{jj} represents the percentage of service that a service department provides to itself. For example, a personnel department has to hire and supervise its own personnel; a utility department has to provide heat, light, and power to its own facilities; a data processing department requires extensive computing for its own operations; and a controller's department needs to plan and control its own budget. There are two possibilities for handling these self-service costs. One is to ignore the amount of service a department provides to itself and allocate costs based on service it provides to production and other service departments. This is the common practice. The other possibility is to incorporate the self-service cost explicitly into the analysis, recognizing that if the output of a service department is to be expanded for external use, it may require even further output to provide additional levels of service to itself. Note that it is not obvious how to deal with this self-service cost when using the sequential method. A department will continually be allocating costs to itself, and its costs will never fully be reallocated to production and other service departments. Fortunately, the proposed reciprocal allocation procedure will yield the identical allocation of service department costs to production departments independent of whether self-service costs are ignored or explicitly recognized. Thus one can either include or exclude these costs without affecting the final allocation.

With the reciprocal allocation method, we define a new variable, x_j, equal to the reallocated cost of service department j:

$$x_j = b_j + \sum_{i=1}^{m} a_{ji} x_i, \qquad j = 1, 2, \ldots, m. \tag{11-1}$$

The reallocated cost, x_j, includes not only b_j, the traceable costs of department j, but also an allocation of costs from the other service departments (the allocation from service department i is given by $a_{ji} x_i$). Therefore, the x_j's sum to more than the traceable costs of the service departments:

$$\sum_j x_j > \sum_j b_j.$$

At first this appears to be a strange property, but the sum of the final allocation of service department costs to production departments will just equal the sum of all service department costs ($\sum b_j$), so that we will not be overcharging for service department costs. An interpretation of the variable x_j, which explains why it sums to more than traceable service department costs, will be presented later.

The system of equations given by (11-1) has m equations (one for each service department) and m unknowns ($x_1, x_2, \ldots, x_m$). Therefore we can use simultaneous-equation techniques to solve for the quantities $x_1, x_2, \ldots, x_m$.

Once we have solved for ($x_1, x_2, \ldots, x_m$), we can define z_k to be the allocation of service department costs to production departments k. Using the reallocated service department costs, x_j, we obtain the allocation to production departments as

$$z_k = \sum_{j=1}^{m} c_{kj} x_j. \tag{11-2}$$

While not obvious, it does work out that the sum of allocated costs to production departments equals the sum of traceable service department costs:

$$\sum_{k=1}^{n} z_k = \sum_{j=1}^{m} b_j. \tag{11-3}$$

Applying this method to the Wilson Company, we first obtain the equations for the reallocated service department costs [the equivalent of equations (11-1)]:

$$x_1 = 10,000 + 0.5x_2,$$

$$x_2 = 4,000 + 0.2x_1.$$

Solving these two simultaneous equations[2] yields

$$x_1 = \frac{120,000}{9} = 13,333,$$

$$x_2 = \frac{60,000}{9} = 6,667.$$

Allocating these costs to the two production departments using equations (11-2), we obtain for fabrication

$$z_1 = c_{11}x_1 + c_{12}x_2 = 0.5(13,333) + 0.4(6,667)$$

$$= 9,333,$$

and for assembly

$$z_2 = c_{21}x_1 + c_{22}x_2 = 0.3(13,333) + 0.1(6,667)$$

$$= 4,667.$$

Notice that this allocation is different from the three allocations obtained using the direct apportionment and sequential methods. As a useful check on both our definitions of the a_{ij} and c_{kj} and the correctness of the computations, we should verify that equation (11-3) is satisfied:

$$z_1 + z_2 = 9,333 + 4,667 = 14,000,$$

and $14,000 is the sum of the traceable costs of the two service departments. If equation (11-3) is not satisfied by the final allocation, an error was made somewhere in the calculations.

---

[2] These equations can be rewritten as

$$x_1 - 0.5x_2 = 10,000,$$

$$-0.2x_1 + x_2 = 4,000.$$

Multiplying the first equation by 2 and adding the two equations together permits one to solve for x_1.

If there are more than two service departments, it becomes tedious to do the required calculations to obtain the reallocated service department costs, x_j. It is useful to formulate the reciprocal allocation problem in matrix format. Computerized matrix inversion and multiplication routines can then be used to solve the system of equations and obtain the final allocations.

Define $A = \{a_{ij}\}$, an $m \times m$ matrix representing the interservice department allocations:

$$A = \begin{bmatrix} a_{11} & a_{12} & \cdots & a_{1m} \\ a_{21} & a_{22} & \cdots & a_{2m} \\ \vdots & & & \\ a_{m1} & & \cdots & a_{mm} \end{bmatrix}.$$

Similarly define $C = \{c_{kj}\}$ an $n \times m$ matrix of service department to production department allocation proportions. The traceable costs of service departments are represented in an $m \times 1$ column vector, b, whose jth component is b_j, the costs of service department j. The $m \times 1$ vector, x, represents the reallocated service costs, and the final allocations of service costs to production departments are represented by the $n \times 1$ vector, z.

With this notation, we can write the system of equations (11-1) in matrix format as

$$x = b + Ax. \tag{11-4}$$

Solving this equation system for x, using matrix operations,

$$(I - A)x = b, \tag{11-5}$$
$$x = (I - A)^{-1}b,$$

where I is the $m \times m$ identity matrix (1's on the main diagonal, 0's in all off-diagonal places). To obtain the allocations from service departments to production departments:

$$z = Cx = C(I - A)^{-1}b. \tag{11-6}$$

Applying the matrix representation to the Wilson Company, we first obtain the following matrices:

$$A = \begin{bmatrix} 0 & 0.5 \\ 0.2 & 0 \end{bmatrix}, \quad C = \begin{bmatrix} 0.5 & 0.4 \\ 0.3 & 0.1 \end{bmatrix}, \quad b = \begin{bmatrix} 10{,}000 \\ 4{,}000 \end{bmatrix}.$$

The matrix $I - A$ is obtained by

$$I - A = \begin{bmatrix} 1 & 0 \\ 0 & 1 \end{bmatrix} - \begin{bmatrix} 0 & 0.5 \\ 0.2 & 0 \end{bmatrix} = \begin{bmatrix} 1 & -0.5 \\ -0.2 & 1 \end{bmatrix}.$$

We can now solve for the reallocated service department cost vector, x:

$$x = (I - A)^{-1}b = \begin{bmatrix} 1 & -0.5 \\ -0.2 & 1 \end{bmatrix}^{-1} \begin{bmatrix} 10,000 \\ 4,000 \end{bmatrix}$$

$$= \frac{1}{0.9} \begin{bmatrix} 1 & 0.5 \\ 0.2 & 1 \end{bmatrix} \begin{bmatrix} 10,000 \\ 4,000 \end{bmatrix}$$

$$= \frac{1}{0.9} \begin{bmatrix} 12,000 \\ 6,000 \end{bmatrix}$$

$$= \begin{bmatrix} 13,333 \\ 6,667 \end{bmatrix} .$$

Naturally this agrees with the allocation we computed before. The only difficult step in the above procedure is inverting the matrix $(I - A)$. For 2×2 or even 3×3 matrices, we can do the inversion by hand. But once we get beyond this size, it will be much easier if a computer can be found to do the required inversion. Inverting matrices is one of the most useful arithmetic computations done by computers.

The final allocation of service department costs to producing departments is easily obtained from

$$z = Cx = \begin{bmatrix} 0.5 & 0.4 \\ 0.3 & 0.1 \end{bmatrix} \begin{bmatrix} 13,333 \\ 6,667 \end{bmatrix} = \begin{bmatrix} 9,333 \\ 4,667 \end{bmatrix} .$$

FIXED AND VARIABLE COSTS IN RECIPROCAL ALLOCATION MODELS

We have been concentrating on the allocation of costs of interacting service departments without being concerned with the uses of this allocation for decision or control purposes. An even stronger need for the simultaneous-equation or matrix method arises when the total costs of interacting service departments vary with the output they provide. In this case, only by using the matrix method of allocation can we compute the marginal cost of providing service from each service department to obtain a figure that can be compared with the cost of obtaining this service externally rather than internally.

Again we should try to separate the costs of service departments into fixed and variable components. We can allocate the fixed component using the technique described in the previous section to obtain the reservation or capacity cost to be charged to each producing department. The variable component can be allocated separately to obtain a unit price for incremental use of a service department by a production or other service department. To illustrate these issues, let us look at an example.

The Prairie State Paper Company located a plant near one of its forests. At the time of construction there were no utility companies available to provide this plant with water, power, or fuel. Therefore, the original facilities included (1) a water plant, which pumped water from a nearby lake and filtered it; (2) a coal-fired boiler room, which produced steam used in part for the manufacturing process and in part for producing electricity; and (3) an electric plant.

An analysis of these activities revealed that water was used 60 percent for the production of steam and 40 percent in manufacturing. Steam produced was used 50 percent for the production of electric power and 50 percent for manufacturing. Twenty percent of the electric power was used by the water plant and 80 percent went to manufacturing.

For the year 1980 the following costs were charged to these departments:

	Variable	*Fixed*	*Total*
Water plant	$ 4,000	$16,000	$20,000
Steam room	36,000	24,000	60,000
Electric plant	12,000	18,000	30,000
			$110,000

A new power company has offered to sell electricity to Prairie State for 4 cents a kilowatt-hour. In 1980 the electric plant generated 600,000 kilowatt-hours. The manager of the electric plant has advised that the offer be rejected, since (he says) "our variable costs were only 2 cents per kilowatt-hour in 1980."

At a minimum we wish to compute the variable cost of producing electricity. This variable cost will include not only variable costs incurred within the electric plant but also a portion of the variable costs incurred in the water plant and steam room. The electric plant cannot operate without the output of the steam room, which in turn requires service from the water plant. Since the water plant also needs electricity, we have completed a cycle, and we must resort to the simultaneous-equation approach for computing the cost of operating the electric plant.

Labeling the water department, steam room, and electric plant as service departments 1, 2, and 3, respectively, we have that

$$a_{13} = 0.2 \quad \text{[20\% of the electric plant (department 3) is used by the water plant (department 1)]},$$

$$a_{21} = 0.6$$

$$a_{32} = 0.5.$$

Therefore the A matrix is

$$A = \begin{bmatrix} 0 & 0 & 0.2 \\ 0.6 & 0 & 0 \\ 0 & 0.5 & 0 \end{bmatrix}$$

and

$$I - A = \begin{bmatrix} 1 & 0 & -0.2 \\ -0.6 & 1 & 0 \\ 0 & -0.5 & 1 \end{bmatrix}$$

The vector of traceable variable costs is

$$b = \begin{bmatrix} 4,000 \\ 36,000 \\ 12,000 \end{bmatrix},$$

so that the vector of reallocated service department costs, x, is

$$x = (I - A)^{-1}b$$

$$= \frac{1}{0.94} \begin{bmatrix} 1.0 & 0.1 & 0.2 \\ 0.6 & 1.0 & 0.12 \\ 0.3 & 0.5 & 1.0 \end{bmatrix} \begin{bmatrix} 4,000 \\ 36,000 \\ 12,000 \end{bmatrix}$$

$$= \frac{1}{0.94} \begin{bmatrix} 10,000 \\ 39,840 \\ 31,200 \end{bmatrix} = \begin{bmatrix} 10,638 \\ 42,383 \\ 33,191 \end{bmatrix}.$$

In this problem there is only one production department, so that the allocation of service department costs to production departments is trivial: all service costs must be allocated out to the single production department. But in order to respond to the outside offer from the power company, we need to know the variable cost per kilowatt-hour of generating electricity internally. The reallocated cost of the electric plant, x_3, is equal to $33,191 (see above). This quantity is also equal to the variable cost of generating the total output of the electric plant for external users. (This is not an obvious result but it can be formally proven—see Kaplan [1973].) From the problem statement, we learn that in 1980 the electric plant generated 600,000 kW-hr of electricity. Therefore, the internal cost of generating electricity is

$$\frac{\$33,191}{600,000} = \$0.0553/\text{kW-hr}.$$

We can obtain this figure by an alternative computation. The production department consumes 80 percent of the output of the electric plant. Thus, it would receive a variable-cost allocation of

$$0.8(33,191) = \$26,553$$

for its consumption of 480,000 kW-hr. This yields a variable cost to the production department of $0.0553/kW-hr.

A final computation confirms this figure. We would like to know how much variable cost can be saved by eliminating the internal electric plant. If the electric plant is eliminated, the steam room can be operated at 50 percent of its previous level (since it no longer needs to supply the 50 percent of its output to the internal electric plant). With the steam room operating at 50 percent of its previous level, the demands on the water department are less. Since 60 percent of its output goes to the steam room, a 50 percent reduction in steam output reduces the demand on the water department by 30 percent. Thus, by shutting down the internal electric plant, we can save the following variable costs:

Electric plant:	100% of $12,000	$12,000
Steam room:	50% of 36,000	18,000
Water plant:	30% of 4,000	1,200
Total savings:		$31,200

If electricity were to be supplied externally, we would need the 480,000 kW-hr for the production department. At 1980 output levels, the water department received 120,000 kW-hr (20 percent of 600,000 kW-hr). Working at 70 percent of this level, it would need only

$$0.70(120,000) = 84,000 \text{ kW-hr.}$$

Therefore, we would need to purchase $480,000 + 84,000 = 564,000$ kW-hr of electricity externally. A more direct but nonintuitive method for computing the demand for an external service department to replace an internal service department is available from the $(I - A)^{-1}$ matrix. The main diagonal terms of this matrix represent the number of units of internally generated service that could be replaced by a single unit of externally generated service. For Prairie State, these main diagonal terms are $1/0.94 = 1.0638$. Dividing the 600,000 kW-hr output of the electricity plant by 1.0638 (or, equivalently, multiplying it by 0.94) gives the 564,000 kW-hr requirement for externally purchased electricity in one simple and direct computation.

We break even if the cost of the 564,000 kW-hr from external sources just equals the $31,200 savings from shutting down the internal electric plant. Thus the breakeven price is

$$\frac{\$31,200}{564,000 \text{ kW-hr}} = 0.0553/\text{kW-hr},$$

and this must agree with the variable cost of supplying electricity internally.

Therefore, we can conclude that the variable cost of internally supplied electricity is 5.53¢/kW-hr and the company would benefit from purchasing electricity from the power plant at a cost of 4¢/kW-hr. We would make this decision even if we would still incur the fixed costs allocated to the electric plant. In general, we can obtain the variable cost of each service department by dividing each component of the x vector of variable costs,

$$x = \begin{bmatrix} \$10,638 \\ 42,383 \\ 33,191 \end{bmatrix},$$

by the physical output of each service department. If the water department's output in 1980 was 4 million gallons, the variable cost of the water department is

$$\frac{\$10,638}{4,000,000} = \$2.66/1,000 \text{ gal.}$$

Self-Service Costs

In the development above we twice referred to quantities derived from the inverse matrix, $(I - A)^{-1}$. First, we interpreted the x vector obtained by post-multiplying this inverse matrix by the vector of traceable variable costs,

$$x = (I - A)^{-1}b,$$

as the variable cost of generating the total output of each service department for external consumption. Therefore, the variable cost of generating one unit of service from each service department could be obtained by dividing each component of x by the output of the corresponding service department. Second, the main-diagonal terms of the inverse matrix were interpreted as the number of units of internally generated service that could be replaced by a *single* unit of externally generated service (1.0638 for each Prairie State service department; in general, the main-diagonal terms will be different for each service department). Thus, the components of the $(I - A)^{-1}$ matrix do have direct economic significance.

Earlier, we mentioned briefly the issue of self-service costs ($a_{jj} > 0$)—the percentage of service that a service department provides to itself. We indicated that the allocation of service department costs to production departments is unaffected by whether the service department costs are included or ignored in the analysis. But the inverse matrix $(I - A)^{-1}$ is affected by the inclusion of self-service costs. Therefore for the two applications above, which use terms from the inverse matrix, it is important that self-service costs be explicitly recognized and included in the analysis. The intuitive reason is that when we are considering the replacement of an internal service department or computing the cost of providing a unit of service to an external user, a service department that must consume some of its own output is more expensive than one that can provide all its output to other users. The higher cost of a service department that has a significant self-service term is reflected in the $(I - A)^{-1}$ matrix when self-service percentages (a_{jj}) are included in the original allocation matrix, A.

Fixed Costs

The fixed costs can be allocated using the same method by substituting the fixed costs into the b vector in equations (11-5) and (11-6):

$$x_f = (I - A)^{-1}b_f$$

$$= \frac{1}{0.94} \begin{bmatrix} 1.0 & 0.1 & 0.2 \\ 0.6 & 1.0 & 0.12 \\ 0.3 & 0.5 & 1.0 \end{bmatrix} \begin{bmatrix} 16,000 \\ 24,000 \\ 18,000 \end{bmatrix} = \frac{1}{0.94} \begin{bmatrix} 22,000 \\ 35,760 \\ 34,800 \end{bmatrix} = \begin{bmatrix} 23,404 \\ 38,043 \\ 37,021 \end{bmatrix}.$$

The fixed-cost allocation from each of the three service departments to the production department is given by

$$z_f = Cx_f$$

$$= [0.4 \quad 0.5 \quad 0.8] \begin{bmatrix} 23,404 \\ 38,043 \\ 37,021 \end{bmatrix} = 9,362 + 19,022 + 29,617 = \$58,000.$$

In this case, of course, the allocation of fixed costs to production departments is trivial, since there is only one production department. In general, the fixed costs of the interacting service departments will be allocated to the various production departments by this technique. While not of direct decision significance, an allocation of fixed costs does signal to users information about the long-run marginal cost (including capacity costs) of providing the internally generated service.

SUMMARY

There are many advantages to allocating the cost of service departments to production and revenue-producing departments. This cost allocation sets up an internal market for the supply and demand of internally produced services. By charging for service departments' output, we can

- Ration demand from user departments
- Provide signals on service department efficiency
- Facilitate comparison with externally supplied service
- Provide opportunity for price-quality trade-offs
- Provide incentives to service department managers for efficient operation and to satisfy the demands of users
- Include service department costs in cost-volume-profit analyses
- Allocate service department costs between cost of goods sold and inventory.

When charging for service department costs, a user department's charges should not be affected by activity levels in other user departments or by inefficiencies in the service department. Also, fluctuations in demand by user departments should be charged on a marginal-cost basis. A reasonable procedure for accomplishing these goals charges user departments a fixed or reservation price each month plus an incremental cost per unit based on the budgeted variable cost of the service department. Inefficiencies in the service department will be treated as a spending variance from the service department's flexible budget.

A special problem arises when service departments provide service to each other as well as to production departments. In this case, the costs of the interacting service departments can be allocated using a simultaneous-equation (or matrix) technique. The simultaneous-equation approach is essential when attempting to decide whether to replace an internal service department by purchasing the service externally.

PROBLEMS

11-1. Allocating Central Service Department Costs

"I can't believe it. We just went through a study showing how my department could save money by using the central data processing facility. But the first month using this facility shows that my costs are up more than 20 percent." Don Thompson, the general manager of the Delta Division of ABC Products, had just received his monthly bill from the Data Processing Service Division and he was obviously upset.

Prior to converting to the central facility, the Delta Division had used outside vendors for its data processing services, at a cost of $15,000 per month. An internal task force, investigating the use of outside services that were also available internally, had found that all the data processing needs of the Delta Division could be handled internally. At present, there was time available at the central computing facility and the services required by Delta could be supplied at an incremental cost of $10,000. After some assurance that his division's data processing services could be supplied at this lower incremental cost, Don Thompson agreed to convert from external to internal supply of services.

After receiving a monthly bill for more than $18,000 from the Data Processing Division, Thompson demanded an explanation. Phil Johnson, the manager of Data Processing, provided the following data. Table 1 shows the allocation of the monthly data processing costs of $120,000 to the three other divisions of ABC Products, prior to handling Delta's requirements:

TABLE 1.

Division	CPU Minutes	Percentage	Allocated Costs
Able	6,000	50%	$60,000
Baker	4,000	33%	40,000
Carter	2,000	17%	20,000
	12,000	100%	$120,000

As Johnson explained, "We have to charge out the costs of our division in some equitable manner. We've decided that an allocation based on CPU minutes used is as good as any." Johnson then showed (see Table 2) how the allocation to Delta was derived based on incremental costs of $10,000 and the 2,000 CPU minutes required to provide the data processing services to Delta:

TABLE 2.

Division	CPU Minutes	Percentage	Allocated Costs
Able	6,000	42.9%	$55,700
Baker	4,000	28.6%	37,100
Carter	2,000	14.3%	18,600
Delta	2,000	14.3%	18,600
	14,000	100%	$130,000

Required:

1. Comment on the method used by Johnson to charge for the use of data processing services in ABC Products. Why does this method cause Delta's charges to increase from $15,000 to $18,600 per month?
2. Suggest alternative methods for charging for the use of this internal service department that would provide better incentives for use of this department.

11-2. Allocating Service Department Costs—Fixed and Variable; Actual and Budgeted

"I get overcharged by the printing department each month," declared Bud Perles, the manager of the Greene Company's advertising department. "Even though my usage is down during the month, the total amount I have to pay keeps going up. The work done by our printing department is certainly high quality but if these charges keep escalating, I'm going to start taking my business to outside printers."

The printing department of the Greene Company provides services to many departments throughout the company. The cost budget for the printing department at a normal volume of 800 service hours, as well as the actual expenses for September (when 700 hours were actually used) appears below:

	Budget at 800 hours		Actual in September
	Amount	Fixed (F) or Variable (V)	
Labor	$10,000	V	$ 9,000
Supervision	2,000	F	2,000
Indirect Labor	3,000	V	2,800
Supplies	11,000	V	10,500
Depreciation	6,000	F	6,200
Rent	4,000	F	4,500
Total	$36,000		$35,000

Depreciation charged each month is a fixed percentage of the original cost of equipment installed in the printing department. The rental charge is an allocated share of total monthly building costs. The allocation is proportional to the space occupied by each department.

The cost of the printing department is charged to other users on the basis of average *actual* departmental costs during the month multiplied by the number of printing hours used during the month.

The advertising department of the Greene Company is a heavy user of the printing department's services. Normally the department uses 100 hours each month from the printing department but during September it used 95 hours. The quote at the beginning of the problem was made when Bud Perles received his bill for September usage from the printing department.

Required:

1. Compute the budgeted charge to the advertising department at normal volume. Also compute what the budgeted charge would be if the advertising department uses 95 hours in a month (assume that total demand for the printing department remains constant at the budgeted 800 hours).

2. Compute the actual charge from the printing department to the advertising department during September.

3. Analyze the difference between what advertising might have expected to pay at its normal volume of 100 hours, from what it actually had to pay for the 95 hours it used during September. Indicate who is responsible for various differences between budgeted and actual costs.

4. Comment on any changes you would recommend in charging for the services of the printing department.

5. Alice Deming, the manager of the printing department, responds to Perles' criticism. "We do the best we can in controlling our costs but it has been difficult because the number of hours we've been working has decreased over the past several years. At the same time, however, we've had to acquire more expensive and sophisticated printing equipment to handle the requests being made by the advertising department. That department has been a heavy user of these machines which the other departments in the company hardly use. If anything, we should charge the advertising department more for our services." How did this situation develop and should a change in the pricing method for the printing department's services be made in light of this new information?

11-3. Allocating Fixed Costs of Central Facility (A. Atkinson)

Squirrel Hill Distributors is a decentralized firm specializing in the distribution of consumer products. The firm is divided into three operating divisions along the major product lines: Tru-Fit Hardware Supplies, Mudd Beauty Products, and Atomo Lighting Fixtures.

Three years ago the company acquired a huge, highly automated regional warehouse. This effort was undertaken as a company project since no single division had the size to take advantage of the economies of scale attainable by using such a warehouse. At the time of purchase the three divisions agreed to "share costs on the basis of usage."

The past three years have witnessed large changes in the divisions. Tru-fit Hardware Division has nearly doubled its volume of operations while the Atomo Lighting Fixtures Division has suffered serious sales set-backs.

Against this background a meeting took place between the corporate controller and the three divisional controllers. The meeting had been requested by the controller, Art Green, of the Tru-Fit Hardware Division who was upset about the rapidly increasing warehouse costs being allocated to his division. Green commented "this business of allocating total warehouse costs to divisions on the basis of actual usage has been prejudicial to our division." Further, Green proposed "that in the future fixed cost (capital costs) be allocated on the basis of planned usage and *standard* variable cost on the basis of actual usage." Ralph White, the Atomo controller objected saying "what if our usage continues to fall? We will end up subsidizing the capital charges associated with the facilities which Tru-Fit uses."

Required:

1. Comment on this controversy. Do you believe that White's point is valid? If not, why? If so, what would you do to resolve this impasse?

2. Assume that all the facts are the same as before with one exception. In this case the above discussion ends with the following comment from Reg Brown, controller of the Mudd Division. "I'm sick of having to fight about these unreasonable cost allocations all the time. There is an organized market for warehouse space out there which would cost us less than what we pay now. We are taking our business outside."

   How, if at all, would this alter your response?

11-4. Charging for Use of a Central Computer Facility (M. Jensen)

In December 1980, the General Student Corporation of America purchased a Comprox Sigma 1102 electronic data processing machine. The machine was bought primarily for Department A, which began using about half of its capacity.

After the machine was installed, four other departments (B, C, D, and E) decided they, too, would like to use it. They claimed, however, that they should pay for the direct costs of use only, and that the total overhead should be carried by Department A. This arrangement would be fair, they claimed, because the purchase of the Sigma 1102 could be justified on the basis of its use in Department A alone. Moreover, the opportunity cost of letting other departments use the machine would be nil,[1] because if the machine were not used, it would just stand idle. Renting the machine to outsiders on a part-time basis was not considered appropriate.

The arrangement proposed by the four departments was put into force, to everyone's satisfaction. By January 1981, the machine time was fully booked. At that point a sixth department, F, also found ways to use the machine. The controller decided that machine time should be used where its benefits were the greatest. To accomplish this, a new system was devised, whereby each department would have to pay a share of the overhead, the cost being divided in proportion to the time used.

---

[1] This assumption is made only to simplify the analysis of this problem. In general, this is an inaccurate characterization of this technology.

This new system reduced the hourly charges to Department A, which maintained its usage at about half of the time available. Department B took one quarter of the machine time, but the other departments decided the system was too costly and took their work off the machine. The machine, therefore, remained idle one-fourth of the time.

Required:

Comment on the two methods used to charge for machine time. If you believe both methods are undesirable, propose an alternative scheme and specifically identify the advantages your proposal has in charging for machine time.

11-5. Reciprocal Cost Allocations (A. Atkinson)

Carnegie Industries manufactures a line of quality speakers. The main production departments are shipping, assembly, and fabrication. These departments are provided with services from centrally maintained facilities: computer, heating/conditioning, and power.

The company is organized on a profit-center basis with the service departments treated as cost centers. Consequently, each period the costs of computing, heating, and power must be allocated to the production departments.

The company follows the practice of allocating budgeted fixed costs on the basis of planned usage and standard variable costs on the basis of actual usage.

The distribution of actual units of service provided last week is:

	Computer	Heating	Power	Shipping	Assembly	Fabri-cation	Total Units
Computer	500	1,000	2,000	2,000	2,500	2,000	10,000
Heating	3,000	2,000	4,000	5,000	3,000	3,000	20,000
Power	750	750	250	750	1,000	1,500	5,000

These service levels corresponded to the amount of planned usage. This week's cost were as follows:

	Standard Variable Cost	Budgeted Fixed Cost
Computer	$30,000	$ 50,000
Heating	$60,000	$100,000
Power	$40,000	$ 80,000

Required:

1. Allocate fixed costs using the reciprocal allocation method.
2. Allocate variable costs using the reciprocal allocation method.

3. What is the variable cost per unit of service provided by the computer facility?

4. Suppose that one-half of the fixed power costs can be avoided if the power unit is shut down.
   a. How many units of power would have to be purchased externally?
   b. What is the maximum price the company would be willing to pay for one unit of service supplied externally?

11-6. Reciprocal Service Costs (R. Manes)

The following exhibit and table describe the flow of production of services and final products in a system of reciprocal services.

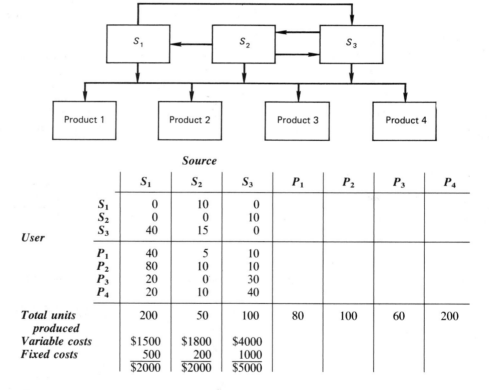

Source

	S_1	S_2	S_3	P_1	P_2	P_3	P_4
S_1	0	10	0				
S_2	0	0	10				
S_3	40	15	0				
P_1	40	5	10				
P_2	80	10	10				
P_3	20	0	30				
P_4	20	10	40				
Total units produced	200	50	100	80	100	60	200
Variable costs	$1500	$1800	$4000				
Fixed costs	500	200	1000				
	$2000	$2000	$5000				

User labels the left group of rows.

Required:

1. Calculate the reciprocal variable costs of S_1, S_2, S_3; the reciprocal full costs of S_1, S_2, S_3.

2. Calculate service charges to P_1, P_2, P_3, P_4 on a variable and on a full cost basis.

3. If budgeted demands for products are changed to $P_1 = 100$, $P_2 = 100$, $P_3 = 80$ and $P_4 = 150$, how much output from S_1, S_2, and S_3 should you budget for?

11-7. Incremental Costs in a Reciprocal Cost System (R. Manes)

The Darwin Co. has two main products, S & T, each of which is produced in a separate division. In order to produce S & T, the Darwin Co. has two Service Departments, A and B, which supply intermediate goods and services both to the S & T divisions and to themselves. For the sake of discussion, let A be a material handling service and B a power generator.

The budget for work to be done by the firm in a coming period is tabulated as follows:

TABLE 1.

	Production Schedule			
	Source A	Source B	Source S	Source T
User of Output				
A (Material Handling)	0	30	0	0
B (Power)	20	0	0	0
Division S	30	35	0	0
Division T	40	55	0	0
Outside Markets	0	0	60	100
Total (in units of goods & services)	90	120	60	100
	A	B		
Costs of Service Dept.				
1. Variable Labor, Overhead & Material Costs	$7,200	$4,800		
2. Supervision and other out-of-pocket fixed costs	6,000	7,000		
3. Depreciation	4,800	8,200		
	$18,000*	$20,000**		

* Plus share of Dept. B's power costs.
** Plus share of Dept. A's Material Handling Cost.

Depreciation expenses are straight line depreciation of generating equipment in the fifteenth year of an estimated 20-year life, that is to say it is relatively old equipment (although well maintained).

Required:

1. Using the reciprocal allocation method, what are the variable costs of Service Departments A and B allocated to Products S and T?
2. Choose a basis for allocating the fixed costs of the service departments and determine the fixed cost allocation to the two products.
3. Suppose that economic conditions change so that product sales are now

expected to be $S = 80$ and $T = 90$. Recalculate Table 1, the production schedule, and the service department budget.

4. What are the new sets of allocated variable and fixed service department costs?

5. The local utility company offers to sell unlimited amounts of B to Darwin at $130 per unit. Should Darwin accept this offer?

11-8.   Service Cost Allocation: Step Method and Simultaneous* (Edward Deakin)

The annual costs of hospital care under the Medicare program exceed $20 billion per year. In the Medicare legislation, Congress mandated that reimbursement to hospitals would be limited to the costs of treating Medicare patients. Ideally, neither the patients nor the hospitals would bear the costs of the Medicare patients nor would the government bear costs of non-Medicare patients. Given the large sums involved, it is not surprising that cost reimbursement specialists, computer programs, publications, and other products and services have arisen to provide hospital administrators with the assistance needed to obtain an appropriate reimbursement for Medicare patient services.

Hospital departments may be divided into two categories: (1) revenue-producing departments and (2) non-revenue producing departments. This classification seems mundane, but is useful since the traditional accounting concepts associated with "service department cost allocation," while appropriate in this context, lead to a great deal of confusion in terminology because all of the hospital's departments are considered to be rendering services.

Costs of revenue-producing departments are charged to Medicare and non-Medicare patients on the basis of actual usage of the departments. These costs are relatively simple to apportion. The costs of non-revenue producing departments are somewhat more difficult to apportion. The approach to finding the appropriate distribution of these costs begins with the establishment of a reasonable basis for allocating non-revenue producing department costs to revenue producing departments. Statistical measures of the relationships between departments must be ascertained. The cost allocation bases listed in Table 1 (page 382) have been established by Medicare regulations as acceptable for cost reimbursement purposes. The regulated order of allocation must be used for Medicare reimbursement even though the general rule would call for another order.

A hospital may then use either a simultaneous solution method to the cost allocation problem or they may use the "step-down" or step method. If the step-down method is used, the order of departments for allocation is the same order as that by which the departments are listed in Table 1. Thus, depreciation of buildings is allocated before depreciation of movable equipment. Cost centers must be established for each of these non-revenue producing costs that are relevant to a particular hospital's operations.

Patient's Hospital is a small, Midwestern hospital. In the past year, the hospital reported the following departmental costs:

Non-revenue producing

Laundry & linen	$ 250,000
Depreciation—Buildings	830,000
Employee Health & Welfare	375,000
Maintenance of personnel	210,000
Central supply	745,000

Revenue producing

Operating room	$1,450,000
Radiology	160,000
Laboratory	125,000
Patient rooms	2,800,000

Percentage usage of services by one department from another department were as follows

From	Laundry & Linen	Depreciation Buildings	Employee Health & Welfare	Maintenance of Personnel	Central Supply
Laundry & linen	—	0.05	0.10	0	0
Depreciation—Buildings	0.10	—	0	0.10	0
Employee Health & Welfare	0.15	0	—	0.05	0.03
Maintenance of personnel	0	0	0	—	0.12
Central supply	0.10	0	0	0.08	—

From	Operating Rooms	Radiology	Laboratory	Patient Rooms
Laundry & linen	0.30	0.10	0.05	0.40
Depreciation—Buildings	0.05	0.02	0.02	0.71
Employee Health & Welfare	0.25	0.05	0.04	0.43
Maintenance of personnel	0.36	0.10	0.08	0.34
Central supply	0.09	0.04	0.03	0.66

The proportional usage of revenue producing department services by Medicare and other patients was as follows:

	Medicare	Other
Operating rooms	25%	75%
Radiology	20%	80%
Laboratory	28%	72%
Patient rooms	36%	64%

Nonrevenue Cost Center	Basis for Allocation
Depreciation—buildings	Square feet in each department
Depreciation—movable equipment	Dollar value of equipment in each department
Employee health & welfare	Gross salaries in each department
Administrative & general	Accumulated costs by department
Maintenance & repairs	Square feet in each department
Operation of plant	Square feet in each department
Laundry & linen service	Pounds used in each department
Housekeeping	Hours of service to each department
Dietary	Meals served in each department
Maintenance of personnel	Number of departmental employees housed
Nursing administration	Hours of supervision in each department
Central supply	Costs of requisitions processed
Pharmacy	Costs of drug orders processed
Medical records	Hours worked for each department
Social service	Hours worked for each department
Nursing school	Assigned time by department
Intern/resident service	Assigned time by department

Required:

1. Determine the amount of the reimbursement claim for Medicare services using the step down method of allocation.
2. With the assistance of a computer, determine the claim for Medicare services using the simultaneous solution method.

11-9. Allocating Costs in a Joint Venture* (Ed Deakin)

Eastern Refineries, Ltd.

In 1966 American Oil Corporation and United Petroleum (two large integrated petroleum companies) entered into an agreement to construct and operate a petroleum fuels refinery in the Far East. A corporation named Eastern Refineries Limited was formed to operate the refinery. At the time the agreement was drawn up, American provided 70 percent of the capital while United provided 30 percent.

The sponsoring companies received capital stock in Eastern in proportion to the capital provided by them.

The Refinery

A refinery processes crude oil through various heat, pressure, and chemical operations to extract as much gasoline from the crude as possible. Other products such as sulphur, kerosene, distillate fuels, and asphalt are produced as byproducts.

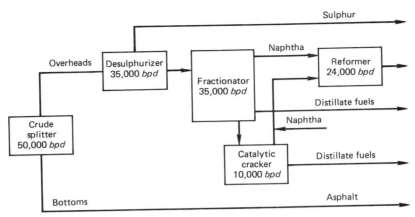

Exhibit 1   Flow of Product Through the Eastern Fuels Refinery

A certain quantity of fuel extracted from the crude is used to provide the heat necessary to operate the refinery as well as to provide heat and power for the refinery administrative and service support functions.

The original Eastern fuels refinery consisted of five principal processing units as diagrammed in Exhibit 1. Crude oil was shipped to the refinery and piped to the crude splitter. This unit separates the crude oil into two products: "Overheads" which consist of the lighter fractions from the crude, and "Bottoms" which contain the heavier fractions. Bottoms have relatively little energy content and are, therefore, usually sold as asphalt with very little further processing.

The overheads contain naphtha, a very light fraction; fuel oil, an intermediate product, and sulphur. Some overheads are immediately usable as refinery outputs. Others must flow through the remaining system. Sulphur is removed before the overheads are processed into finished products. A desulphurization unit extracts the sulphur from the overheads. The remaining overhead flow is then distilled in the fractionator. The products with the lower boiling point (i.e., the lighter fractions) vaporize as the temperature in the fractionator equals the boiling point of the respective fraction. The vaporized fractions are then cooled and return to their liquid state.

Naphtha, one of the lighter fractions, is used to make gasoline. With the use of heat and pressure in the reformer unit, naphtha is converted into gasoline. The remaining fractions are then directed to the catalytic cracker. This unit employs chemical and heat processes to convert some of the heavier materials from the fractionator into the more valuable naphthas. The naphthas from the catalytic cracker are then processed through the reformer in the same manner as the naphthas from the fractionator. The remaining output from the catalytic cracker is sold as distillate fuel products such as kerosene, jet fuel, and heating oil.

Refinery Investment Costs

The costs to construct the initial refinery totalled $60 million. These initial costs were related to different units and support functions as follows:

Unit	Investment Cost ($000)
Crude Splitter	$10,000
Desulphurizer	6,000
Fractionator	13,000
Catalytic Cracker	15,000
Reformer	9,000
Administrative, support and other	7,000
TOTAL	$60,000

The sponsoring companies entered into a contract for the processing of crude oil through the refinery. Each sponsor was permitted to utilize the refinery capacity to process crude oil in the same ratio as its equity investment. Thus, American was permitted to process 35,000 barrels per day (70 percent of 50,000 bpd capacity). The refinery does not take title to the crude it processes, but rather acts as a processing service which receives the crude, processes it and delivers the end products to each processor. To recover its costs, the refinery charges a processing fee to each of the sponsors. The processing fee consists of a variable charge based on the crude oil actually processed during a period plus a fixed charge based on the sponsor's share of refinery capacity.

Certain operating and cost data related to refinery processing during the years 1980 and 1981 are shown in Table 1.

Expansion Proposal

American had been utilizing close to its share of capacity for several years. Indeed, to supply all of its customers in the market area served by this refinery, it was necessary to import finished distillate fuels from other, distant refining facilities. On occasion, to supply its customers, the company was required to purchase distillate fuels on the spot market.

As a result of market conditions, company management proposed that parts of the Eastern refinery be expanded. The expansion would provide additional distillate fuels for American's local needs and, in addition, would provide naphthas which could be transported to another American refinery for further processing. There would be a net reduction in the company's transportation costs as a result of the savings in distillate fuels transportation. As a result of this, and by eliminating the need to make spot market purchases, American management estimated it could obtain net after tax cash savings of $2,500,000 in each of the estimated twenty years' life of the refinery expansion. The return on investment for the project was quite high because the project could utilize the tankage, wharf and piping systems that were already in place at the refinery site.

According to the agreement between the sponsors of Eastern, any sponsor could request that the refinery company construct an expansion or modification to increase the maximum capacity of the refinery. If one of the sponsors proposed an expansion, it had to advise the other sponsor of the nature of the project, the estimated investment costs of the project together with an estimate of the fixed costs that would arise from the expansion. The other sponsor could elect to join in the

TABLE 1. **Summary Operating and Cost Data**
(000 omitted)

	1981	1980
Crude processed (barrels):		
American	12,700	12,775
United	4,100	4,050
Total	16,800	16,825
Variable Costs:		
American	$3,061	$2,965
United	1,008	954
Total	$4,069	$3,919
Fixed Costs:		
American	$6,510	$6,447
United	2,790	2,763
Total	$9,300	9,210
Products Delivered:		
American		
Gasoline (bbls)	6,126	6,103
Distillate Fuels (bbls)	2,780	2,759
Sulphur (tons)	16	16
Asphalt (bbls)	417	408
United		
Gasoline (bbls)	2,362	2,376
Distillate Fuels (bbls)	591	597
Sulphur (tons)	7	8
Asphalt (bbls)	134	136

project or could decline. If this sponsor declined participation the expansion could still be conducted, but all of the investment costs would then be charged to the sponsor that proposed the expansion.

The agreement between the sponsors further provided that any such expansion would become a part of the refinery but that the sponsor who financed the expansion would receive the exclusive right to use the expansion. In addition, appropriate adjustments were to be made to the accounting procedures to reflect the existence of the expansion and to make certain that neither party was adversely affected by the expansion. The definition of "appropriate adjustments" was not specified in the agreement.

In 1980, American submitted a proposal to expand the crude splitter, desulphurizer and fractionator. Summary data concerning the estimated incremental costs, investment required and capacity expansions for the units are shown in Table 2. Information concerning American's estimated cash savings from the project were not disclosed because those data are proprietary.

After reviewing the proposal, United notified Eastern that it did not wish to participate. United objected to Eastern's construction of the proposed expansion on the grounds that it would suffer a reduced ability to compete with American should American obtain the proposed additional ability to produce distillate fuels.

American agreed to finance all of the costs of the expansion and to pay the

TABLE 2. **Proposal for Expansion Units to be expanded:**
Crude splitter
Desulphurizer
Fractionator

	Expansion Details (dollars in thousands)		
	Crude Splitter	**Desulphurizer**	**Fractionator**
Incremental Capacity	30,000 bpd	10,000 bpd	10,000 bpd
Projected Costs of Investment	$4,000	$800	$2,200
Projected Incremental Fixed Costs (Per Year)	$ 300	$100	$ 150

fixed costs of the expansion. The expansion was constructed for the investment costs shown in Table 2. The new units were placed in service at the start of 1982.

At the end of 1982, a report of operating and cost data was prepared. This report is reproduced in Table 3. The fixed costs included $9,500,000 attributed to the original refinery plus $560,000 considered related to the expansion.

TABLE 3. **Summary operating and cost data**
(000 omitted)

	1982
Crude processed (barrels):	
American	23,750
United	3,840
Total	27,590
Variable Costs:	
American	$5,556
United	1,150
Total	$6,705
Fixed Costs:	
American	$7,210
United	2,850
Total	$10,060
Products delivered:	
American:	
Gasoline (barrels)	6,128
Distillate (barrels)	6,320
Sulphur (tons)	25
Asphalt (barrels)	830
Naphthas (barrels)	3,975
United:	
Gasoline (barrels)	2,337
Distillate (barrels)	610
Sulphur (tons)	7
Asphalt (barrels)	133

Upon receipt of this statement, United immediately objected to the allocation of fixed costs. In a memorandum to the Board of Directors of the refinery, United management stated:

> As you know, we objected to the expansion of this refinery because we believed such an expansion was not in the best interest of the refinery and would be harmful to our competitive position in the local market.
>
> Our agreement calls for the allocation of fixed costs on the basis of the maximum capacity of the Eastern refinery. Whereas we previously had 30 percent of that maximum capacity and paid 30 percent of the fixed costs, we now only have 18.75 percent of that capacity. However, you have charged us 28.3 percent of the total fixed costs. Our share of the fixed costs should not exceed 18.75 percent and we request an immediate adjustment to our account.
>
> We note that under your allocation scheme our fixed costs per barrel amounted to $.74 this year but the fixed costs allocated to American only amounted to $.30. This disparity clearly demonstrates that your method of allocation is incorrect.
>
> Finally, it is apparent that the wharf and related facilities which we helped construct is being utilized to a much greater extent now that American is processing a greater share of the refinery throughput. We believe that American should be required to reimburse us for the difference between our 30 percent investment in the wharf and our usage which this year only amounted to 13.9 percent.
>
> We trust this matter can be resolved promptly at the next meeting of the Board.

The Chairman of the Board of Eastern has directed this memorandum to the Controller's Office with the following comment:

> The points raised in this letter will be discussed at next week's meeting of the Board. It is imperative that we straighten this out at once. The points appear logical, and I hope that any error in your office can be corrected.
>
> What is the amount by which they appear to have been overcharged? How would their method affect the economic viability of the expansion? What accounting principles did you use in arriving at your method of allocation?

Required:

The controller has asked you to prepare a draft of a response to the Chairman of the Board together with any supporting schedules or documents that would be required. Your response should address each of the points raised in the letter from United.

REFERENCES

CHURCHILL, N., "Linear Algebra and Cost Allocations: Some Examples," *The Accounting Review* XXXIX (October 1964), 894–904.

CAPETTINI, R., and SALAMON, G., "Internal versus External Acquisition of Services when Reciprocal Services Exist," *The Accounting Review* LII (July 1977), 690–96.

IJIRI, Y., "An Application of Input-Output Analysis to Some Problems in Cost Accounting," *Management Accounting* (April 1968) pp. 49–61.

KAPLAN, R., "Variable and Self Service Costs in Reciprocal Allocation Models," *The Accounting Review* XLVIII (October 1973), 738–48.

LIVINGSTON, J. L., "Matrix Algebra and Cost Allocation," *The Accounting Review* XLIII (July 1968), 503–508.

WILLIAMS, T. H., and GRIFFIN, C. H., "Matrix Theory and Cost Allocation," *The Accounting Review* XXXIX (July 1964), 671–78.

COST ALLOCATION:
Joint and By-Product Costs

Joint products arise whenever a single resource produces a diverse set of useful outputs. One of the classic problems in accounting is to allocate the cost of the single resource to the different products that are derived from it. Just why accountants should be concerned with different methods for allocating joint costs is not altogether clear. The initial motivation for devising joint cost allocation schemes probably arose because of the need, in both financial and tax reporting, to trace all product-related costs to finished goods. This enabled these costs to be allocated between cost of goods sold and items still remaining in inventory. An additional incentive for allocating joint costs arises for firms in regulated industries in which prices are derived from the ''costs'' (however determined) of the goods or services sold. For example, a telephone company may have to allocate the costs of a common switching facility to all the types of communications using this facility (local calls, long distance calls, digital data, and so on), since the prices of each of these services must be related to the ''costs'' of supplying the service.

A popular and easily recognizable example of the joint-product situation occurs when a cow is slaughtered. From this single resource (the cow) comes meat that is processed into different grades of steak, roasts, and hamburg, hides that can be used for leather, and relatively worthless by-products such as bones, fat, or inedible organs. The joint costing problem is the attempt to allocate the cost of the cow to all the outputs produced from it. It is easy to think of many such joint-product situations. Petroleum is processed in a refinery to produce intermediate products such as naphtha or benzene, which are combined with other additives to produce final products such as gasoline, home heating oil, and jet fuel. Mined ore produces traces of many different types of metals, and cut logs produce lumber of varying grades as well as veneer that can be glued together to produce plywood.

Other accounting problems are merely different versions of costing joint products. Factory and general administrative overhead can be considered the cost of providing the capability to produce the final goods of the firm. The joint costing problem here is to allocate the cost of the fixed overhead to the many final goods produced each period. Thus overhead allocation is a special version of the joint cost problem. In an example drawn from financial reporting, depreciation is the process of allocating the cost of a durable asset to the different periods over which it produces services. In this case, the outputs obtained from the single resource are the different time periods during which we obtain services from the durable (but finite-lived) asset. Thus, with depreciation, the common asset cost is allocated across periods rather than across products.

Clearly the allocation of joint costs gets the accountant involved in some of the more arbitrary and difficult-to-defend decisions associated with the profession. By the very nature of the problem, it is usually hard to defend any particular allocation. Some allocations, however, are worse than others, particularly if the resulting product costs are used as the basis for decisions. The major defense for any joint cost allocation is an appeal to inventory valuation for financial reporting, regulatory, or income tax requirements. In decisions such as how much of a product to produce, most joint cost allocations will lead to more trouble than benefit. It is typical, for such decisions, to have to undo any joint cost allocations before performing the analysis. It is possible, if one is careful, to obtain joint costs that are consistent with a decision model of the firm and that permit some apparent decentralization of decision making. We present such an analysis later in this chapter.

A SIMPLE JOINT COSTING EXAMPLE: MADISON COMPANY

We present a typical joint costing situation to illustrate standard alternatives offered for allocating joint costs. Consider the Madison Products Company. It produces three chemical products, Able, Baker, and Cane, from a single product

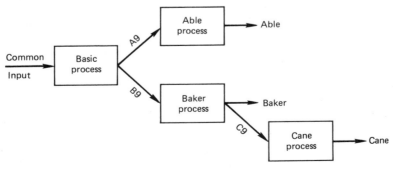

Exhibit 12-1 Madison Products Company Chemical Process

(see Exhibit 12-1). Raw materials are processed in a common facility to produce two intermediate products, A9 and B9, in fixed proportions. There is no market for these two intermediate products. A9 is processed further to yield the Able product. B9 is converted into Baker by a separate finishing process. The Baker finishing process produces both Baker and a waste material, C9, which has no market value. The Madison Company can convert C9, after additional processing, into a salable by-product, Cane. The company can sell as much Cane as it can produce at a price of $0.30/lb.

At normal operations, 600,000 lb of the common input material are purchased and processed each month. This amount yields fixed quantities of Able, Baker, and Cane as shown below with approximate market prices:

Product	Quantity (lb)	Market Price Per Pound	Market Value
Able	400,000	$0.485	$194,000
Baker	100,000	0.90	90,000
Cane	10,000	0.30	3,000

At these normal volumes, materials and processing costs are as follows:

| | Basic Process | Separate Finishing Processes | | |
		Able	Baker	Cane
Materials	$ 64,000	$22,000	$ 3,000	$ 200
Labor	30,000	45,000	18,000	1,100
Variable overhead	6,000	10,000	5,000	100
Fixed overhead	10,000	5,000	1,000	600
Total	$110,000	$82,000	$27,000	$2,000

Selling and administrative costs are entirely fixed and cannot be traced to any of the three products. Output can fluctuate by as much as 25 percent of normal volume in either direction without affecting the above cost structure. Fixed costs and per unit costs of materials, labor, and variable overhead will remain constant within this fluctuation in output.

TYPICAL TREATMENT OF BY-PRODUCT COSTS

For the Madison Company, the joint cost to be allocated is the $110,000 cost of the basic process. Before we discuss the allocation of this cost to the products, a decision on the treatment of the Cane product should be made. Cane is a relatively low-value by-product of the Baker process. Its revenue of $3,000 barely covers its additional processing cost of $2,000 and is an insignificant contributor to company profits relative to Baker, the main output of the Baker process. This is a typical example of a by-product, one that has very minor sales value compared with the major products of a company. Other examples of by-products include sawdust from a lumber mill, remnants from clothing and carpet manufacture, and minor chemicals from gasoline production. The distinction between a joint product and a by-product can be fuzzy. For many companies, what was initially a by-product eventually becomes an important contributor to company profits. For example, in the production of photographic film, it was discovered that some previously discarded intermediate products could be processed into vitamins. This developed into an entirely new line of business for film companies.

The typical accounting treatment of by-products subtracts the net realizable value, the gross revenues less additional processing costs of the by-product, from the cost of the major product (in this case, Baker). For Madison, the $2,000 finishing cost of Cane is subtracted from its gross revenues of $3,000 to obtain a net realizable value of $1,000. This $1,000 quantity is subtracted from other costs attributed to Baker, the main output from the Baker process.

For the by-product itself, the standard procedure computes the unit cost as equal to the selling price, so that the product appears to just break even. Thus Cane would have a standard cost of $0.30/lb. At this cost, the standard volume overrecovers the finishing cost by the $1,000 allocated back to reduce the cost of Baker.

If the waste material, C9, could not be processed further into a salable product, it would be discarded or scrapped. In this case, any cost of disposal would be added back to the cost of producing Baker. The accounting treatment is therefore the same whether a minor output from a process is called scrap or a by-product. The net realizable value (revenues less additional processing or disposal costs) is subtracted from the cost of main products. Net realizable value can be negative if disposal costs are expensive, particularly when companies are prevented by environmental restrictions from dumping unwanted chemicals into sewage systems or nearby bodies of water.

TRADITIONAL JOINT COST ALLOCATION METHODS

Physical-Units Basis

A common method for allocating joint cost is proportional to some physical measure of the output. For the Madison Company, the natural physical measure is pounds of output. With this measure, Able, which is 80 percent of the weight (of the two main products), would receive 80 percent of the $110,000 joint cost or $88,000. Baker would receive an allocation of $22,000, equal to 20 percent of the joint cost. With the physical-units basis, we would obtain the following product costs:

	Able	*Baker*
Number of pounds produced	400,000	100,000
Joint cost	$88,000	$22,000
Joint cost per pound	$ 0.22	$ 0.22
Separate finishing cost	$82,000	$27,000
By-product contribution		(1,000)
Net finishing cost	$82,000	$26,000
Net finishing cost per pound	$ 0.205	$ 0.26
Total cost per pound	$ 0.425	$ 0.48

Under the physical-units basis of allocation, Able is a barely profitable product. With a current selling price of $0.485 per pound and a manufacturing cost of $0.425/lb, Able has only a contribution margin of $0.06 per pound to cover administrative overhead, selling expenses, and profit contribution. Baker, in contrast, appears to be a highly profitable product with a contribution margin of $0.42/lb, nearly 90 percent of manufacturing cost.

The physical-units basis is easy to apply. Beyond this, it is hard to find much else good to say about the method. The allocation may bear no relation to the revenue-producing power of the individual products and, if followed unthinkingly, may lead to poor decisions. For example, a firm may decide to abandon or cut back certain products because their profitability may be too low when joint costs are allocated on a physical-units basis. As an extreme example, consider the use of the physical-units basis for allocating the cost of cattle to various cuts of beef on the basis of weight. Bones, fat, and discarded hooves would bear heavy costs, whereas filet and tenderloin would bear very low costs. It is hard to see what benefit is obtained from showing huge profits on filet and huge losses on shank bones. While this example may seem fanciful, a newspaper article on the rising prices of meat described a "meat information program" sponsored by a local supermarket chain:

> Consumers learned through these programs that a side of beef weighing 320 pounds has bone and waste amounting to 33 percent or 105 pounds. They also learned that a supermarket sells about 28 percent of each side of beef BELOW COST. [Capitals in original]

Before one admires the generosity and public-spiritedness of the local supermarket for selling so much of its product below cost, one should attempt to discover how this supermarket computes the cost of a particular cut of beef. Undoubtedly, the physical-unit basis is being used.

For a more serious application, it is common in the petroleum industry to allocate the joint cost of crude oil, its transportation, and its refining to the various refinery output products based on BTU (energy) content. This is perhaps a more reasonable basis than weight but still is arbitrary and misleading. Some products may have low market value relative to BTU content and may appear marginally profitable or even unprofitable. This could discourage further exploitation of these products because of the high cost allocated to them, whereas if lower costs were allocated, new and profitable applications might be found. Thus, a physical-units allocation basis runs the risk of distorting the profitability of joint products and, if taken seriously by management, could contribute to poor decisions.

Net-Realizable-Value Method

The net realizable value of a product is the selling price less the costs, after the split-off point, of completion and sale. The net-realizable-value method allocates the joint costs proportional to the net realizable values of the joint products. This method is illustrated below for the Madison Company's two main products.

	Able	Baker	Total
Gross revenues	$194,000	$90,000	$284,000
Finishing costs	(82,000)	(27,000)	(109,000)
By-product contribution		1,000	1,000
Net realizable value	$112,000	$64,000	$176,000
Proportion of total net realizable value	7/11	4/11	1
Allocation of common cost	$ 70,000	$40,000	$110,000
Number of pounds	400,000	100,000	
Joint cost per pound	$ 0.175	$ 0.40	
Finishing cost per pound	0.205	0.26	
Total cost per pound	$ 0.38	$ 0.66	

We can see that with the net-realizable-value method, the joint cost per unit of Able is $0.175/lb—a significant reduction from the allocated joint cost of $0.22/lb when joint costs are allocated proportional to weight. The net realizable value per pound is $112,000/400,000 = $0.28 for Able and $64,000/100,000 = $0.64 for Baker. We see that the ratio of joint cost per pound for the two products (0.175/0.40 = 0.4375) equals the ratio of net realizable value per pound (0.28/0.64). This is the essential characteristic of the net-realizable-value method. By allocating joint costs proportional to net realizable value, we hope to avoid distorting the relative profitability of products. Of course, this is not strictly true. It would still be possible for the joint cost allocation using the net-realizable-value method to cause a profitable product to appear only marginally profitable or even unprofitable.

Variations of the Net-Realizable-Value Method

The computations are simpler if market prices exist for all the intermediate products immediately after the split-off point. In this case, the firm has the option of either selling each intermediate product or processing it further. Joint costs can be allocated proportional to the selling price of these intermediate products without regard to further processing. In the Madison Company the intermediate products, A9 and B9, do not have market prices, so this option is not available. The allocations computed based on market prices immediately after split-off will differ from those computed on a net-realizable-value basis. It is difficult if not impossible to argue that the relative-sales-value method immediately after split-off is either better than or worse than the net-realizable-value method. One would have to determine within the context of a decision or control problem which method yielded a preferable outcome. In general, neither allocation method would be suitable for direct use in a decision context.

The net-realizable-value method can become complicated if an intermediate product goes through several further processing stages, each of which produces a new intermediate product that can either be sold immediately or processed further. In this case, one needs to construct the actual decisions the firm will make concerning how much of the product is sold at each stage and how much is processed further. Eventually, when the final processing stage is reached, the revenues from all products sold to external sources are added together and the sum of all processing costs is accumulated and subtracted from the gross revenues to yield the net realizable value of the initial intermediate product. This can be a tedious computation (even more so if some of the subsequent processing stages introduce new joint-product situations, a not unlikely occurrence) and could argue for use of the relative-sales-value method immediately after split-off on simplicity grounds alone.

DECISION MAKING WITH JOINT PRODUCTS

The various procedures just described do arrive at unambiguous allocations of joint costs to final products. The allocations, however, differ for each method. Apart from rejecting occasional nonsensical allocations that arise with use of the physical-units method, there is little basis for choosing among various allocation schemes. This should indicate that one should not put too much faith in the outcome of any particular allocation for decision or control purposes. In particular, a fully allocated product cost is often used for pricing purposes (see the discussion of cost-plus pricing in Chapter 7). Unfortunately, the joint cost allocation cannot be used logically for pricing decisions. Either the net-realizable-value or relative-sales-value method requires the price to be known before the joint cost allocation is made. Subsequent use of the joint cost allocation for a pricing decision would involve us in circular reasoning. Unlike the case for interacting service departments, such a reasoning circle cannot be broken by use of simultaneous-equation techniques. Thus, one cannot use joint costs as an input or a justification for pricing decisions.

The joint cost is not even helpful in product-mix or expansion decisions. Suppose a new customer came to the Madison Company with an offer to purchase 10,000 lb of Baker per month at a price of $0.70/lb. This is above the standard cost of $0.66/lb computed under the net-realizable-value method and the cost of $0.48/lb from the physical-units method. This sale would not affect the market price ($0.90) to the other customers, who are in a completely different industry. Should the Madison Company accept this offer? Based on the fully allocated joint cost, it looks like a good deal, especially since the fully allocated cost includes significant components of fixed cost, which will not increase if the new customer's order is accepted. Nevertheless, the only way to be completely sure is to perform the analysis on an incremental-benefit, incremental-cost basis.

Unless we are sure that we can sell as much Able as we produce, we cannot analyze the potential sale of an additional 10,000 lb of Baker by comparing revenues and costs of Baker by itself. For in order to increase the production of Baker by 10 percent (from 100,000 to 110,000 lb per month) we will need to acquire 10 percent more of the common input materials and operate the basic process at a 10 percent higher level of activity. This is the essential nature of the joint process. If we wish to obtain an additional 10,000 lb of Baker, we must also obtain enough of the intermediate product, A9, to produce up to 40,000 lb of Able.

The incremental revenues from the additional sale of Baker are easy to compute. At a price of $0.70/lb, Madison Company will gross $7,000. In addition, Madison will obtain an additional 1,000 lb of Cane, which it can sell for $300. Thus, gross revenues total $7,300 without selling any additional amounts of Able.

The incremental costs include:

Variable costs, Basic process:	0.10 (100,000)	$10,000
Variable costs, Baker process:	0.10 (26,000)	2,600
Variable costs, Cane process:	0.10 (1,400)	140
Total incremental costs		$12,740

Because of the $10,000 variable cost from the basic process, the additional revenue from the sale of Baker can not cover, by itself, the increase in total costs of the firm. Madison will need to process and sell additional amounts of Able if the incremental order is to be profitable.

Producing an additional 40,000 lb of Able will increase the cost of the Able process by $0.10(77,000) = $7,700$. Therefore the total contribution margin required from sales of these 40,000 lb must cover:

Excess of variable costs over revenues from sale of Baker, $12,740 − 7,300	$ 5,440
Variable costs, Able process	7,700
	$13,140

If a separate market can be found for an additional 40,000 lb of Able produced each month, a selling price of $13,140/40,000 lb = $0.3285/lb will enable Madison to break even on the entire incremental order. Thus the decision to accept the outside offer for an additional 10,000 lb of Baker per month depends upon whether

Madison can sell an additional 40,000 lb of Able each month at a price in excess of $0.33/lb without affecting the price to any existing customers.

Alternatively, we could examine the overall demand curve for Able to determine how much Madison could afford to drop the average price to all customers of Able in order to expand demand for this product by 10 percent. At present sales levels, Madison grosses $194,000 from sale of Able. It needs to gross an additional $13,140 to cover additional processing costs for 40,000 lb more of Able and unrecovered basic process costs. Therefore, the minimum average price must exceed

$$\frac{\$194,000 + \$13,140}{440,000} = \$0.47/\text{lb}.$$

before Madison will increase its profits. If the 10 percent increase in supply of Able decreases the overall market price by more than 4 percent, Madison will be worse off.

At this stage, the response to the new customer is clear. Unless Madison is willing to buy into a new market by accepting losses on this new contract, the decision to accept depends upon whether Madison can either:

- Sell an additional 40,000 lb of Able each month to a new set of customers at a price of at least $0.33/lb, without lowering the price to any existing customers; or
- Sell an additional 40,000 lb of Able each month by dropping the price to all customers by no more than $0.02/lb.

If neither of these outcomes is likely, the profit-maximizing decision is to refuse the offer.

Note that the standard costs obtained with the net-realizable-value method were of no help in this analysis. Even though the selling price for the new order exceeded the fully allocated cost of Baker, the order would not be profitable without increased sales of Able. The joint cost allocation offers us no help in making this decision.

Other types of decisions also arise with joint products. A firm may need to decide whether to sell an intermediate product or process it further to produce a different product. In such problems, the decision whether to sell as is or process further does not depend on a particular joint cost allocation to the intermediate product. The decision should be made based on incremental revenues and incremental costs, as illustrated for the Madison Company. Exceptions occur only if the firm is selling on a cost-plus contract, is in an industry with price regulation, or is under government surveillance that requires the firm to cost-justify its pricing decisions. In such circumstances, typified by noncompetitive market conditions, costs do matter, and decisions might sensibly be affected by how joint costs are allocated. Of course, when operating in such nonmarket environments, the firm might still attempt to perform a profit-maximizing analysis, compare incremental benefits with incremental costs, and then choose a joint cost allocation method that justifies the decision it wishes to make.

A NONLINEAR PROGRAMMING MODEL FOR JOINT COST ALLOCATION[1]

We have stressed that traditional joint cost allocations are not useful for product-mix and output decisions. If enough information exists about the cost and demand functions for the joint products, however, it is possible to obtain simultaneously the optimal price-output decision *and* a joint cost allocation that is consistent with this decision. In order to obtain this desirable situation, we must be willing to abandon traditional joint cost allocation methods and use nonlinear programming techniques. Even if a company does not use this mathematical programming approach, it is useful to understand the approach because it does give insight into the essential nature of the joint-product situation. As a side benefit, it provides an operational distinction between joint products and by-products, a distinction that is unclear without resort to the mathematical approach.

Consider a simple joint-product situation in which for each unit of a common raw material, we obtain two units of output product 1 and one unit of output product 2. Both products are sold in markets in which the amounts of the products we attempt to sell will influence the price. Letting p_i denote the price of product i $(i = 1, 2)$ and x_i the amount of product i produced and sold, we assume the following specific output-price demand functions:

$$x_1 = \frac{49 - p_1}{2},$$

$$x_2 = 15 - p_2. \tag{12-1}$$

We can obtain unlimited amounts of the common raw material at a price of \$3 per unit. Variable processing costs of the raw material equal \$2 per unit processed. The problem is to decide how much of the raw material to acquire and process, and the output and price of the two joint products.

Let z be the amount of raw material to be acquired and processed. Given this quantity z, we can produce up to $2z$ units of product 1 and z units of product 2. If we sell x_1 units of product 1 and x_2 units of product 2, our gross revenues will be

$$x_1 p_1(x_1) + x_2 p_2(x_2) \tag{12-2}$$

[where we write $p_1(x_1)$ to show explicitly that the price of product 1 is a function of the amount to be sold.] Solving the assumed-demand equations (12-1) in terms

---

[1] This section requires knowledge of Lagrange multipliers and nonlinear programming theory, including Kuhn-Tucker conditions.

of p_i and substituting into the gross-revenue equation (12-2), we obtain the gross revenues as an explicit function of output:

$$x_1(49 - 2x_1) + x_2(15 - x_2) = 49x_1 - 2x_1{}^2 + 15x_2 - x_2{}^2. \qquad (12\text{-}3)$$

Thus the decision problem for the firm is to maximize contribution margin (gross revenues less variable processing costs) subject to availability and non-negativity constraints:

$$\text{Maximize:} \quad 49x_1 - 2x_1{}^2 + 15x_2 - x_2{}^2 - 5z$$

$$\text{Subject to:} \quad x_1 \leq 2z, \qquad\qquad (12\text{-}4)$$

$$x_2 \leq z,$$

$$x_1, x_2, z \geq 0.$$

This is a nonlinear programming program with two inequality constraints. In general, computer algorithms must be used to obtain the solution to such problems. When linear demand functions are assumed, as in this problem, the objective function involves just linear and squared values of the decision variables. This is a special case of the nonlinear programming problem, called a quadratic programming problem. Quadratic programming algorithms are widely available and obtain solutions faster than general nonlinear programming algorithms.

For small problems, such as this, we can try to obtain a solution to the firm's problem using Lagrange multipliers. With each inequality constraint in (12-4) we associate a nonnegative Lagrange multiplier, λ_i:

$$x_1 \leq 2z \quad (\lambda_1),$$

$$x_2 \leq z \quad (\lambda_2).$$

If the constraint on product 1 is binding (that is, $x_1 = 2z$), λ_1 will be strictly greater than 0 (unless there is a trivial boundary solution with both $x_1 = 2z$ and $\lambda_1 = 0$). If the constraint is not binding ($x_1 < 2z$), λ_1 must equal 0. Thus, the λ_i's play very similar roles to the dual variables of a linear programming model.

From the theory of nonlinear programming, we learn that the optimal solution to the maximization problem (12-4) must also be a local maximum for the following problem, which uses the Lagrange or dual variables:

$$\text{Maximize:} \quad L = 49x_1 - 2x_1{}^2 + 15x_2 - x_2{}^2 - 5z$$

$$+ \lambda_1(2z - x_1) + \lambda_2(z - x_2) \qquad (12\text{-}5)$$

$$\text{Subject to:} \quad x_1, x_2, z, \lambda_1, \lambda_2 \geq 0.$$

We attempt to solve (12-5) by computing the necessary first-order conditions (ignoring the nonnegativity constraints) and finding the solution consistent with the nonnegativity conditions. Taking first partial derivatives and setting them equal to zero (a necessary condition for a maximum),[2] we obtain:

$$\frac{\partial L}{\partial x_1} = 49 - 4x_1 - \lambda_1 = 0,$$

$$\frac{\partial L}{\partial x_2} = 15 - 2x_2 - \lambda_2 = 0,$$

$$\frac{\partial L}{\partial z} = -5 + 2\lambda_1 + \lambda_2 = 0, \qquad (12\text{-}6)$$

$$\frac{\partial L}{\partial \lambda_1} = 2z - x_1 = 0,$$

$$\frac{\partial L}{\partial \lambda_2} = z - x_2 = 0.$$

The system of equations (12-6) has five linear equations with five unknowns. Thus we can obtain a unique solution to these equations.

One way to proceed is to let $x_1 = 2z$ and $x_2 = z$ [from the fourth and fifth equations in (12-6)] and substitute in the first two equations:

$$\lambda_1 = 49 - 8z,$$

$$\lambda_2 = 15 - 2z,$$

or

$$-\lambda_1 + 4\lambda_2 = 11.$$

Also, from the third equation,

$$2\lambda_1 + \lambda_2 = 5,$$

so that

$$8\lambda_2 + \lambda_2 = 22 + 5 = 27.$$

Hence

$$\lambda_2 = 3,$$

$$\lambda_1 = 1,$$

$$z = \frac{15 - \lambda_2}{2} = 6,$$

$$x_2 = 6,$$

$$x_1 = 12.$$

---

[2] Setting the first derivatives equal to zero is correct if we assume all variables (x_1, x_2, z, λ_1, λ_2) are strictly greater than zero. More precisely we should write the first equation, for example, in (12-6), as $(49 - 4x_1 - \lambda_1) \leq 0$ with equality if $x_1 > 0$.

With $x_1 = 12$, then p_1 must equal 25, and with $x_2 = 6$, p_2 must equal 9.[3]

As a check on our computations, we can compute the marginal revenue of the two products and verify that the sum of the two marginal revenues equals the marginal cost of processing the common input material.

The marginal revenue of the two products is

$$MR_1 = \frac{\partial(p_1 x_1)}{\partial x_1} = \frac{\partial}{\partial x_1}(49x_1 - 2x_1^2) = 49 - 4x_1,$$

$$MR_2 = \frac{\partial(p_2 x_2)}{\partial x_2} = \frac{\partial}{\partial x_2}(15x_2 - x_2^2) = 15 - 2x_2.$$

At the optimum values ($x_1 = 12$, $x_2 = 6$) the two marginal revenues are

$$MR_1 = 49 - 4(12) = 1,$$

$$MR_2 = 15 - 2(6) = 3.$$

Since each unit of input material produces two units of product 1 and one unit of product 2, the marginal revenue obtained by processing an additional unit of raw material equals $2 \cdot MR_1 + 1 \cdot MR_2 = 5$. Naturally this equals the marginal cost of acquiring and processing one unit of the common input material.

The procedure above yields the optimal output of the two joint products and, via the demand equations, the optimal price. What insights, however, does this procedure offer for allocating joint costs? The key relationship is the third equation of (12-6):

$$\frac{\partial L}{\partial z} = -5 + 2\lambda_1 + \lambda_2 = 0.$$

At the optimum,

$$2\lambda_1 + \lambda_2 = 5,$$

and 5 is the joint cost to be allocated to the two products. This equation suggests the following joint cost allocation to the two products:

λ_1 to each of the two units of product 1 and λ_2 to product 2.

In general, λ_i is the joint cost allocation to product i. With the optimal values of $\lambda_1 = 1$ and $\lambda_2 = 3$, the joint cost allocation is $2 to the two units of product 1 and $3 to one unit of product 2. While it is obvious that an allocation of $2 to the

---

[3] For completeness, we need to point out that this solution is a local but not global maximum of (12-5). It is, however, a saddle point to (12-5)—that is,

$$\min_{\lambda_1, \lambda_2} \max_{x_1, x_2, z} L(x_1, x_2, z, \lambda_1, \lambda_2) = 49x_1 - 2x_1^2 + \dots,$$

and this guarantees that the solution maximizes the original problem (12-4). The details of these technical issues would require an exploration into the duality theory of nonlinear programming, which, while interesting, is not crucial to becoming a good cost accountant.

two units of product 1 and $3 to product 2 does allocate the $5 joint cost of the common material and process, it is not so obvious what properties such an allocation has. Why have we gone through such a long process to obtain this particular allocation?

DECISION SIGNIFICANCE OF THE JOINT COST ALLOCATION

It turns out that the joint cost allocation derived from the nonlinear programming model is consistent with the underlying output decision of the firm and can be used as a basis for decentralized and incremental decisions. In principle, with this joint cost allocation the output-pricing decisions for the two products could be decentralized without regard to the common material and process that actually link the two products. Consider product 1. With a joint cost allocation of $1 per unit, the separate optimization problem for this product is

$$\max (p_1 - 1)x_1 = (49 - 2x_1 - 1)x_1$$
$$= 48x_1 - 2x_1^2.$$

The maximum is obtained by setting the first derivative equal to zero:

$$48 - 4x_1 = 0$$

or

$$x_1 = 12,$$

which agrees with the optimum obtained from solving the joint maximization problem. Similarly the optimal output for product 2, with an allocated joint cost of $3 per unit, is

$$\max (15 - x_2 - 3)x_2 = (12x_2 - x_2^2),$$
$$\frac{d}{dx_2}(\cdot) = 12 - 2x_2 = 0$$

or

$$x_2 = 6.$$

Therefore, the allocated joint costs are consistent with the decisions of the firm. By allocating a joint cost of $1 to each unit of product 1 (or, equivalently, $2 for the two units of product 1) and $3 to each unit of product 2, the output and pricing decisions for these two joint products can actually be decentralized to separate product managers. The profit-maximizing decisions of the two independent product managers will be consistent with the global maximizing decision of the firm. Further, each will demand the same amount of the common raw material and processing, so that the two product output decisions, though reached separately, will be consistent with each other.

A second property of this allocation is that the joint costs provide guidance for incremental decisions on expanding output. For example, if an order for one additional unit of product 1 is offered at a price of $2, we can accept this order, since the marginal revenue of $2 exceeds the allocated joint cost of $1. To see this, consider what happens if we produce one more unit of product 1. We need to order and process 0.5 unit of raw material, which costs $0.5(5) = 2.50. At first, this already looks unprofitable, since we receive only $2 for the last unit of product 1.[4] But we also obtain 0.5 more unit of product 2 from the joint process. Previously the total revenues from selling six units of product 2 were

$$x_2 p_2 = 6(15 - 6) = 54.$$

The revenues from selling 6.5 units of product 2 are $6.5(15 - 6.5) = 55.25$. Therefore, total incremental revenues to the firm are $2 from sale of product 1, $1.25 from selling 0.5 more unit of product 2, less the joint processing costs of $2.50. The net result is an increase in contribution margin of $0.75.[5]

A similar analysis reveals that if we could sell one more unit of product 2 at a price in excess of its allocated joint cost of $3 (say $4 or even $3.50), the firm's contribution margin would increase. This analysis is in sharp contrast to that for the Madison Company, where the joint cost allocation provided no guidance for incremental decision making. When confronted with an opportunity for additional sales in the Madison Company, we had to do an extended analysis before obtaining the conditions for profitability.

An alternative to considering the private sale of products 1 or 2 for prices in excess of the joint cost allocation is deciding whether to process either of these products further. Perhaps new products could be developed that use one or both of the two joint products. In determining the profitability of such new applications for the joint products, it would be desirable to have a measure of the opportunity cost of using them. The joint cost allocation from the dual variables provides just

---

[4] It may also seem unprofitable because the current price for product 1 is $25. But in order to sell one more unit of product 1 in the outside market, we must lower the price to all customers to $23. Thus, in order to sell one more unit in the external market we lose $2 per unit for the 12 units we are now selling and only gain $23 from the sale of one more unit. We therefore lose $1 from attempting to sell one more unit of product 1. We are better off if we can find a new customer that we can sell to at a price of $2 as long as we can maintain the current $25 price to existing customers and do not violate any price-discrimination statutes. This is a nonintuitive result but valid if one believes that the demand curve $x_1 = (49 - p_1)/2$ accurately represents the external market.

[5] Actually if we re-solve the nonlinear programming problem, we can increase the contribution margin by $0.78 by producing and selling 6.44 units of product 2 and 11.88 units of product 1 in the market, and selling the last unit of product 1 for $2. Thus this is a slight improvement from the indicated solution of selling 6.50 units of product 2 and 12 units of product 1 to the outside market.

such a measure. If new products can be found that are profitable using small amounts of product 1 at a cost of $1 per unit or product 2 at a cost of $3 per unit, the new products will be profitable for the firm to market.

The joint cost allocation derived from the nonlinear programming model also facilitates the decision on when to purchase additional amounts of an intermediate or final product. The joint cost of $1 per unit of product 1 tells us that we would be willing to pay up to $1 for an additional unit of product 1 from an outside supplier. Similarly, we would be willing to pay up to $3 for an additional unit of product 2.

A LIMITATION OF THE JOINT COST ALLOCATION PROCEDURE

One problem arising from using the Lagrange multipliers to allocate the joint costs is that the decision-relevant information from the multipliers is valid only for small changes from the previous equilibrium (or maximizing) values. As we expand or contract the amount of any product we produce or sell, the Lagrange multiplier and therefore the joint cost allocation will change continuously. In the example where we could sell one extra unit of product 1 for $2, which is $1 more than its allocated cost, we should have expected an incremental revenue of the $1. In fact the incremental revenue was only $0.75. Strictly speaking, the multiplier value is valid only for very small changes from the maximizing values. That is, if we could sell 0.01 extra units of product 1, at a price of $2 per unit, for total revenues of $0.01 \cdot 2 = \$0.02$, then the net incremental revenues would be close to the predicted value of $0.01 \cdot 1 = \$0.01$. (In fact the actual net incremental revenues turn out to be $0.009975.) As we attempt to expand the output of product 1, its allocated joint cost increases so that the net contribution margin continually shrinks from the $1 it has at the initial optimal level of 12 units. As the output of product 1 expands to 13 units (because of the incremental sale), its joint cost allocation increases. Therefore, the overall net revenues from expanding sales by one unit are less than the $1 predicted from the excess of selling price over allocated joint cost. Thus, the joint cost allocation provides initial guidance for product expansion or acquisition decisions, but if output will be significantly different from the initial optimum, we should still perform an incremental-revenue, incremental-cost analysis to verify that net contribution margin will increase.

COMPARISON WITH NET-REALIZABLE- VALUE METHOD

It is interesting to contrast the joint cost allocation from the mathematical programming approach with that obtained from the net-realizable-value method. At the optimum output of $x_1 = 12$, $x_2 = 6$, the prices for the two products are p_1

$= 25$ and $p_2 = 9$. Since no further processing is required, the net-realizable-value and the relative-sales-value methods yield identical allocations. Recalling that we obtain two units of product 1 for each unit of product 2, the net-realizable-value allocation to product 1 is $2 \cdot 25/(2 \cdot 25 + 9) = 0.85$ of the joint cost of $5 per unit. Similarly, the allocation to product 2 is 0.15 of the joint cost. Therefore, the per-unit joint cost of product 1 is $(0.85)(5)/2 = \$2.125$ and the allocated joint cost to product 2 is $0.75 per unit. These allocations, based on average rather than marginal profitability, are quite different from the $1 and $3 unit allocations we obtained previously. Unlike these previous allocations, the net-realizable-value allocations of $2.125 and $0.75 per unit offer no apparent insight. We have already seen that it would be profitable to sell one more unit of product 1 at a price of $2, a finding not suggested by a net-realizable-value allocation of cost to product 1 of $2.125. Thus, even though, strictly speaking, the Lagrange multiplier allocation is valid only for small changes about the optimum, it at least provides some guidance for local decision making. The net realizable value allocation provides no such insights.

IDENTIFYING BY-PRODUCTS WITH THE MATHEMATICAL PROGRAMMING METHOD

Suppose there is a decrease in demand for product 1. Analytically we consider a downward shift in the demand curve to

$$x_1 = \frac{31 - p_1}{2} .$$

Forming the Lagrangian, we attempt to solve

$$\max L = x_1(31 - 2x_1) + x_2(15 - x_2) - 5z + \lambda_1(2z - x_1) + \lambda_2(z - x_2).$$

The first-order conditions are

$$\frac{\partial L}{\partial x_1} = 31 - 4x_1 - \lambda_1 = 0,$$

$$\frac{\partial L}{\partial x_2} = 15 - 2x_2 - \lambda_2 = 0,$$

$$\frac{\partial L}{\partial z} = -5 + 2\lambda_1 + \lambda_2 = 0, \qquad\qquad (12\text{-}7)$$

$$\frac{\partial L}{\partial \lambda_1} = 2z - x_1 = 0,$$

$$\frac{\partial L}{\partial \lambda_2} = z - x_2 = 0.$$

If we proceed as before, we could set $x_1 = 2z$, $x_2 = z$, and $\lambda_2 = 5 - \lambda_1$ and substitute into the first two equations in (12-7) to obtain

$$31 - 8z - \lambda_1 = 0$$

and

$$10 - 2z + 2\lambda_1 = 0.$$

Adding one-half the second equation to the first equation yields

$$36 - 9z = 0$$

or

$$z = 4.$$

Therefore $x_1 = 2z = 8$ and $x_2 = 4$. But at an output of $x_1 = 8$, the marginal revenue from x_1 is

$$MR_1 = 31 - 4x_1 = 31 - 32 = -1.$$

Thus, we are actually losing money from selling the last unit of product one.

This paradoxical result is resolved once we notice that with the proposed solution of $z = 4$, $x_1 = 8$, $x_2 = 4$, the Lagrange multipliers are

$$\lambda_1 = 31 - 4x_1 = -1,$$

$$\lambda_2 = 15 - 2x_2 = 7.$$

(As before, these correspond to the marginal revenues of the two products.) We have obtained an incorrect solution by ignoring the nonnegativity constraint on λ_1.

It is clear that we will do better by selling less of product 1 than may actually be produced. Since the marginal revenue of product 1 after the downward shift in demand,

$$MR_1 = 31 - 4x_1,$$

is zero at $x_1 = 7.75$, we would never wish to sell more than 7.75 units of product 1 even if more is produced (assuming we can dispose of extra units of product 1 without cost). Therefore, we should look for a solution to the first-order conditions in which $\lambda_1 = 0$ and $x_1 < 2z$.[6]

---

[6] Because we are dealing with an inequality rather than an equality constraint (that is, $x_1 < 2z$), the correct first-order condition is actually $\lambda_1(2z - x_1) = 0$. If $\lambda_1 > 0$, then x_1 must equal $2z$, as we assumed previously. But if $\lambda_1 = 0$, x_1 can be less than $2z$ and still satisfy the necessary first-order condition for a maximum. The condition $\lambda_1(2z - x_1) = 0$ comes from the Kuhn-Tucker conditions for maximizing a nonlinear function subject to inequality constraints. The Lagrangian approach is appropriate for equality rather than inequality constraints (see also footnote 2 of this chapter).

Returning to the first-order equations (12-7) with $\lambda_1 = 0$ and $x_1 < 2z$, we obtain

$$31 - 4x_1 = 0,$$

$$15 - 2x_2 - \lambda_2 = 0,$$

$$-5 + \lambda_2 = 0,$$

$$z - x_2 = 0,$$

which are easily solved to yield

$$x_1 = 7.75, \quad x_2 = 5, \quad z = 5, \quad \lambda_1 = 0, \quad \lambda_2 = 5.$$

In this case we discard 2.25 units from the ten units of product 1 that are actually produced by the joint process. The profit-maximizing solution is to sell only 7.75 units at a price of $31 - 2(7.75) = \$15.50$ for total revenues of $120.13. (Attempting to sell all ten units would require a price of $11 and would only yield $110 in total revenues.) Thus product 1 is truly a by-product, since we are discarding some of it rather than attempting to sell it externally. Note that the dual variable, λ_1, of this product is zero. Thus the nonlinear programming approach provides a direct and operational method for identifying by-products. By-products are products whose associated dual or Lagrange variable equals zero.

Naturally, if we could price-discriminate and find customers for product 1 at any positive price, without disturbing the price to our main customers who are paying $15.50 per unit for product 1, we could increase our profits by selling to them. But this policy of attempting to sell product 1 to private customers becomes obvious once we interpret the dual or Lagrange variables as the allocated joint cost: 0 to product 1 and $5 to product 2. Because more product 1 is produced than can profitably be sold, it bears none of the joint cost. Product 2 must bear the full cost of the joint process since the joint process is operated, for the last units, only to produce product 2. Therefore, this product must be profitable enough to bear the full cost of the joint process. Naturally at the optimal value of $x_2 = 5$ this is true. The marginal revenue of product 2 is

$$MR_2 = 15 - 2x_2.$$

At $x_2 = 5$, its marginal revenue is equal to 5, which just covers the full $5 cost of the joint process.

EXTENSIONS AND LIMITATIONS

The dual-variable allocation method has been illustrated on a very simple two-product unconstrained-production example with linear demand functions. There is little difficulty in extending the analysis to multiple products, constrained production, and more complex revenue functions including product interdependencies. The resulting nonlinear programming problem will become more difficult to solve, but once solved, the dual variables on the product-availability constraints (for example, $x_1 \leq 2z$, $x_2 \leq z$) will be nonnegative and sum to the per-unit cost of the joint process. Hence they can be interpreted as the allocation of the cost of the joint process and be used for decentralization or local decision making, as we have illustrated.

A crucial assumption is that the per-unit cost of operating the joint process must be constant. If the unit cost of acquiring the common input material or operating the joint process is not constant over the expected range of operation, then the dual variables will sum just to the marginal cost of operating the joint process. For a nonlinear function, the marginal cost and the average cost will differ. This may occur, for example, when the cost of the joint process has fixed and variable components. In this case we should use the proposed method to allocate the variable joint process cost to the output products and allocate the fixed cost on some other basis. This would be not unlike the procedure we proposed for allocating fixed and variable service department costs in Chapter 11.

Another crucial assumption is that the common raw material not have binding constraints on its supply or that the common input process not be a constraining resource. If, in formulating the firm's maximization problem, the variable representing the level of operation of the common process (labeled z in our numerical example) appears in a constraint other than those defining the fixed-proportion outputs of the joint process (for example, $x_1 - 2z \leq 0$), we will lose the property that the dual variables will sum to the per-unit cost of the joint process.

If we have upper bounds on raw-material availability or on the processing capacity of the initial joint process, additional constraints will need to be included in the maximizing model [see (12-4)]. Consider our numerical example when we need to add a third constraint to represent the maximum activity level of the joint process:

$$z \leq Z_u.$$

Then a third dual variable, λ_3, would be defined for this inequality. The associated necessary first-order condition for an optimum would become

$$2\lambda_1 + \lambda_2 - \lambda_3 = 5,$$

and we would have lost the property that the sum of the dual variables, of the constraints defining the fixed-proportion yields of the output products from the joint process, equals the per-unit joint process cost of $5. Thus the dual-variable allocation technique depends critically on not having factors, other than demand, that will limit the operation of the common input process. There is no problem with constraints on production or sale of the output products, but constraints on the input material or input process destroy the property that the dual variables on the yield constraints will sum to the per-unit cost of the input process. In this case, we cannot interpret the dual variables as an allocation of the joint cost. The dual variables are still useful, however, in providing guidance for the local decisions we considered: opportunity cost of the output product for further processing into a new product, maximum amount we would be willing to pay for the output product from an outside supplier, and the minimum price we would accept for a special private order for the output product.

SUMMARY

Joint costs arise in many situations. Accountants have devised a variety of schemes to allocate these costs to the products derived from the common resource and joint process. These schemes include allocating the joint costs proportional to (1) a physical measure such as weight, volume, or energy content; (2) the net realizable value of the finished products; and (3) the market value of the products immediately after the split-off point.

The initial motivation for allocating joint costs probably arose from the demands of financial and tax reporting to trace all product related costs to finished goods. In this way, incurred costs could be allocated between inventory and cost of goods sold. But attempts to use these allocated joint costs for product related decisions or to evaluate the profitability of the finished goods are likely to yield misleading conclusions. Decision making with joint products is complicated requiring a careful specification of the sales and further production opportunities for each of the joint products. The allocation of joint costs by any of the above methods will not be helpful when making these decisions.

An exception to the decision irrelevance of allocated joint costs occurs if the allocation is derived from an explicit mathematical model of the sales and production opportunities for the joint products. In the special case where (1) we can estimate a demand function for the finished products and (2) the production of the common input process is unconstrained, then the dual (or Lagrange) variables from a nonlinear programming (NLP) formulation can be used to allocate joint costs to the finished products. The NLP allocation can be a guide to decision making when we are considering small changes from the optimal solution, such as selling additional amounts to a new customer or processing any of the products further to produce a new product.

The NLP allocation also provides a clear distinction between joint products and by-products. By-products are those products that are not finished and sold up to the maximum availability. As a result, they bear none of the joint costs.

PROBLEMS

12-1. Joint Cost Allocations and Processing a Product Further

The Spencer Company processes a basic chemical through a manufacturing process which yields three intermediate substances. Each of these three substances is processed further into final products designated Product A, Product B, and Product C. At present, 1,000,000 pounds of the basic chemical are processed each year into 500,000 pounds of A, 300,000 pounds of B, and 200,000 pounds of C. The manufacturing process always produces these three outputs in fixed proportions (10 pounds of chemical will produce 5 pounds of A, 3 pounds of B, and 2 pounds of C. The budgeted product-line income statement for next year is:

TABLE 1. **Product Line Income Statement**

	A	B	C	Total
Pounds Produced	500K	300K	200K	1,000K
Selling Price/pound	$1.20	$ .70	$1.50	
Revenues	$600K	$210K	$300K	$1,110
Manufacturing Process Cost	$250K	$150K	$100K	$500K
Incremental Costs of Further Processing (all variable)	$120K	90K	100K	310K
Net Income	$230	$(30K)	$100K	$300K
(Cost per pound	$0.74	$0.80	$1.00)	

Required:

1. What technique is being used to allocate the cost of the initial manufacturing process?

2. The Treasurer of the Spencer Company points out that Product B should not be processed and sold since it shows a loss of $.10 per pound. Do you agree? Be sure to give your reasons.

3. A recently hired analyst from the controller's department recalls that the Net Realizable Value Method can be used to allocate joint costs and that this method provides costs indicative of the relative revenue generating capability of products. Prepare a budgeted product-line income statement for the three products using the Net Realizable Value Method for allocating the $500K manufacturing cost.

4. Product C can be processed further to yield a new product, called Product D, that sells for $2.40 per pound. From 200,000 pounds of Product C, we can obtain 150,000 pounds of Product D at an additional processing cost of $75,000. The Marketing Manager advocates promoting Product D because of its higher margin. Should the Spencer Company shift its activities from selling Product C to selling Product D? How does the cost of $1.00 per pound of C in Table 1, or the cost you derived in Question 3, help you in this analysis?

5. The Spencer Company has an opportunity for a special order next year for Product A. The order will be for 200,000 pounds of A at a price of $1.10 per pound. Since this is above the cost of producing Product A (see Table 1), management will likely accept the order. Do you agree? Briefly give your reasons and analysis.

6. (Ignore Previous Parts of Problem.)

    Suppose that each product line in its uncompleted state (after the joint manufacturing process) can be either sold immediately after split-off or processed further. Each product requires a different amount of processing time on a common resource to obtain the finished form. Details are shown below:

	Product Lines		
	A	B	C
Pounds produced	500K	300K	200K
Selling Price per unit of Unfinished Product	$0.40	$0.30	$0.60
Unit Cost of Further Processing (all variable)	$0.24	$0.30	$0.50
Rate of Processing	10 lbs/hour	100 lbs/hour	5 lbs/hour
Selling Price per unit of Finished Product	$1.20	$0.70	$1.50

To produce all three finished products will require 93,000 hours of resource time:

Product	Pounds	Processing Rate per hour	Total Hours Required
A	500K	10 lbs.	50K
B	300K	100 lbs.	3K
C	200K	5 lbs.	40K
			93K

If less than 93,000 hours of resource time are available, how should the Spencer Company decide on which products to finish and which to sell in the unfinished state? Be as specific as you can using the data provided.

12-2. Joint Cost Allocations and Product Decisions

The Thompson Company processes 10 pounds of Material X in Department 1 to yield 4 pounds of Product A and 2 pounds of Product B. Product A can either be sold at the split-off point as A* or processed further in Department 2 and sold as

A'. Similarly, Product B can either be sold at the split-off point as B* or processed further in Department 3 and sold as B'.

Product X costs $2 per pound. The costs of operating Departments 1, 2, and 3 are:

	Department		
	1	*2*	*3*
Fixed Costs	$80,000/month	—	—
Variable Costs	$1/lb. of X	$6/lb. of A	$4/lb. of B

Also: **Selling Price**

A*	$8/lb.
A'	15/lb.
B*	7/lb.
B'	10/lb.

At present, only 80,000 pounds of Material X are available each month; all of this is processed in Department 1. All of intermediate Products A and B are processed further and sold as A' and B'. A product-line profit analysis appears below:

	Profit Statement	
	A'	*B'*
Selling Price	$15	$10
Processing Costs	6	4
	$ 9	$ 6
Joint Costs	7.5	5
Profit/lb.	$ 1.5	$ 1.0

Required:

1. What method is being used to allocate the cost of acquiring and processing Material X?

2. What is the monthly profit being earned by Thompson? Is Thompson earning the maximum possible profit from its operations?

3. Product A' can be processed further to yield a new product, called Product C that sells for $25 per pound. From 32,000 pounds of A' we can obtain 20,000 pounds of C with incremental processing costs of $40,000. The Marketing Manager advocates promoting product C because of its higher price. Should Thompson shift its activities from selling product A' to selling product C?

4. (Ignore the option in (3) above) Suppose that Departments 1, 2, and 3 require processing time on a common resource. The resource is such that the following production rates are achievable: 20 lbs. of X per hour, 8 lbs. of A per hour, 10 lbs. of B per hour. Only one product at a time can be processed on this resource and a maximum of 6,000 hours of resource

time are available each month. Show how the Thompson Company can determine a product mix that would maximize its profits.

12-3. *Joint Cost Processes and Linear Programming* (A. Atkinson)

Dartmouth Chemical manufactures chemicals used in the resource extraction industry. The production operation consists of two main processes as follows:

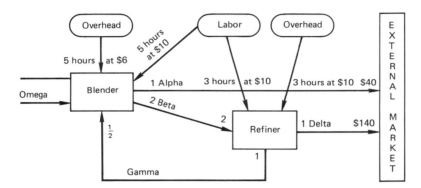

In the blender, $\frac{1}{2}$ gallon of gamma, 2 gallons of omega at $12 per gallon are combined with 5 labor hours at $10 per hour, and 5 overhead hours at $6 per hour to produce 1 gallon of alpha and 2 gallons of beta.

Alpha is sold in the external market for $40 per gallon.

Beta is used internally in the refiner to produce Delta and Gamma. In the refiner 2 gallons of Beta, 3 labor hours at $10 per hour, and 3 hours of overhead at $10 per hour are combined to produce 1 gallon of Delta and 1 gallon of Gamma.

Delta is sold in the external market for $140 per gallon.

There is no external market for Gamma or Beta.

Since the chemicals are unstable and cannot be stored for any prolonged period, in the past excess stocks of Gamma and Beta have been dumped, surreptitiously, in a local swamp.

Elmo Slack, the factory analyst, recently developed the following analysis to model the firm's operations.

Notation

x_1 units of activity of blender

x_2 units of activity of refiner

x_3 units of Alpha produced and sold

x_4 units of Delta produced and sold

Costs

The out-of-pocket cost per unit of activity of x_1:

Cost of Omega:	2 gallons at $12 =	$24
Labor:	5 hours at $10 =	50
Overhead:	5 hours at $ 6 =	30
		$104

The out-of-pocket cost per unit of activity of x_2:

Labor:	3 hours at $10	$30
Overhead:	3 hours at $10	30
		$60

Objective Function

$$\text{Max } - 104x_1 - 60x_2 + 40x_3 + 140x_4$$

Constraints

				Associated Dual Variable
a.	Alpha:		$x_1 \geq x_3$	
		OR	$-x_1 + x_3 \leq 0$	(y_1)
b.	Beta:		$2x_1 \geq 2x_2$	
		OR	$-2x_1 + 2x_2 \leq 0$	(y_2)
c.	Delta:		$x_2 \geq x_4$	
		OR	$-x_2 + x_4 \leq 0$	(y_3)
d.	Gamma		$x_2 \geq \frac{1}{2}x_1$	
		OR	$.5x_1 - x_2 \leq 0$	(y_4)

In addition, it was discovered that a maximum of 368 labor hours are available per period.

e. Labor $5x_1 + 3x_2 \leq 368 \ (y_5)$

Elmo solved the linear program and obtained the following optimal solution.

$$x_1 = 46 \qquad y_1 = 40$$

$$x_2 = 46 \qquad y_2 = 37$$

$$x_3 = 46 \qquad y_3 = 140$$

$$x_4 = 46 \qquad y_4 = 0$$

$$y_5 = 2$$

Excess Gamma = 23.

1. Explain the meaning of this solution. If there are any interrelationships among the marginal values explain them. Are there any accounting applications suggested by these relationships?

2. Charlie Nelson, the company president, reports that local citizen groups are getting suspicious about the firm's disposal operations and are prepared "to make trouble for Dartmouth Chemical."

   The company has only two alternatives for disposal:

   a. A contractor has been found who can reclaim Gamma for use as a weed killer. This contractor will take, if paid $6 per gallon, all the Gamma that Dartmouth Chemical wishes to dispose of.

   b. Use 1 gallon of Gamma, 1 gallon of Alpha, 1 gallon of Beta, 1 hour in the refiner process, and 1 labor hour to produce 3 gallons of a new product which will sell for $30 per gallon.

   What is the cost to the firm of producing three gallons of the new product? Should three gallons of the new product be produced? In responding to this question, use the data to illustrate the concept of opportunity cost.

12-4. *Comprehensive Problem on Joint Product Costs, Optimal Production, and Variance Analysis* (R. Hilton)

Palymar Processing Company

The Palymar Processing Company began operations on January 1, 1982 to produce three industrial chemical products called gluon (G), hadron (H) and meson (M). Hadron and meson are joint products of a single process which uses a chemical called DBT. The processes are shown schematically below:

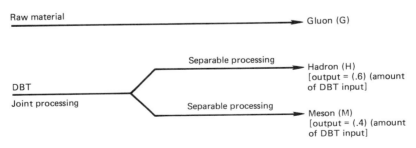

As indicated above, every gallon of DBT entered into the joint process results in .6 gallons of hadron and .4 gallons of meson. Palymar's standards as of January 1, 1982 are as follows:

Direct Materials

Raw material for gluon	$ 5/gallon of gluon
DBT	$14/gallon of DBT

Direct Labor: Standard rate: $10/hour

Standard quantity per gallon of gluon	0.2 hours
Standard quantity per gallon of DBT in the joint process	0.3 hours
Standard quantity per gallon of hadron in its separable process	0.1 hours
Standard quantity per gallon of meson in its separable process	0.2 hours

Variable Overhead: Standard rate: $10/direct labor hour

Since 1982 is the first year of its operations, Palymar has made a policy decision to produce at least 10,000 gallons of each of its three products. This decision was made in order to enable Palymar to establish all three of its products in the market. The only other constraint which Palymar faces is the limited supply of labor for its operation. The company anticipates 14,000 hours of labor for the year 1982. Company officials anticipate that all of the company's output in 1982 will be sold. Estimated prices are as follows:

Gluon	$13/gallon
Hadron	$32/gallon
Meson	$24/gallon

Palymar anticipates fixed costs in 1982 of $20,000. All of this cost is a cash outflow in 1982.

Required:

1. Palymar's production manager has been asked to determine the firm's optimal production plan for the year in accordance with the constraints, standards and other estimates given above. In so doing, he found it useful to answer the following questions:
   a. What is the contribution margin per gallon of gluon?
   b. What is the contribution margin per gallon of DBT entered into the joint process?
2. What is Palymar's optimal constrained production plan?
3. Actual production and sales for 1982 were as follows:

Gluon	12,000 gallons
Hadron	16,500 gallons
Meson	11,000 gallons

Prepare a flexible budget for Palymar for 1982, including direct materials, direct labor, variable overhead and fixed overhead.
4. Two departures from standard performance were noted during 1982. Due to unavoidable supply interruptions, the raw material for gluon actually

cost $6/gallon instead of the estimated $5/gallon. The labor required to produce gluon averaged .15 hours/gallon instead of the standard 0.2 hours/gallon. Compute the following variances from the traditional variance analysis. Indicate whether each variance is favorable or unfavorable.
   a.   Material price variance:
   b.   Variable overhead efficiency variance:
   c.   Interpret the variable overhead efficiency variance:

5.   Using the ex-post variance analysis scheme of Chapter 8, compute the following:
   a.   Ex-post contribution margin per gallon of gluon:
   b.   Ex-post contribution margin per gallon of DBT entered into the joint process:
   c.   Ex-post optimal production plan:

6.   Using the Chapter 8 ex-post variance analysis scheme, compute the relevant forecasting and opportunity loss variances. Interpret each variance for management.

7.   Palymar allocates joint product costs on the basis of net realizable value. What is the final full product cost (i.e., traceable plus allocated cost) for hadron and meson on a per unit basis?

8.   Suppose Palymar has an opportunity to process meson further into a chemical compound called M70. The additional processing would require a fixed set-up cost of $1,000. The additional variable processing cost would be $7/gallon of M70. Palymar can sell M70 for $35/gallon. A fee of $3/gallon sold must be paid to the inventor of the M70 process. No additional labor time is required to produce M70 instead of meson. Should Palymar sell its product as meson or M70?

12-5.   *Joint Cost Production when Intermediate Joint Products may be Sold or Purchased in the Market Place* (R. Manes)

A producer of joint products may sell some or all of a semi-processed joint product in the open market or may supplement its supply of the intermediate joint product for purposes of further processing by purchasing the semi-processed product on the open market.

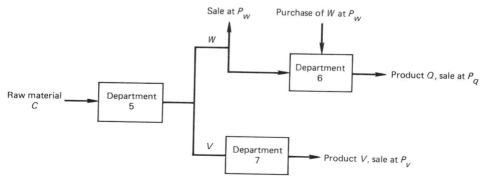

Part A

Two units of C produce 1 unit each of W and V. W can be sold as is or further refined to produce Q, 2 units of W being required to produce 1 unit of Q. Demand functions for Q and V are $P_Q = (20 - Q)$ and $P_V = (20 - V/4)$ respectively. On the other hand, W can be sold for 5 without further processing. Raw material C costs 4, further processing of V and of Q costs 3 and 1 respectively.

Required:

1. Compute the optimum production schedule of V, W and Q together with prices of V and Q. How much of the joint cost of C will be charged to V and to Q per unit of these products?

Part B

Part A is unchanged except that demand for Product Q has grown so that $P_Q = 60 - Q$.

Required:

2. Same as Question 1 in Part A.

Part C

(Purchase of additional amounts of W to meet demand for Q)

What is the solution to Part B, if unlimited amounts of W can be bought as well as sold at 5 per unit?

12-6. *Use of Linear Programming to Determine when to Process an Intermediate Product Further* (R. Manes)

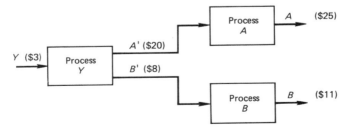

The Hartley Company processes a Raw Material Y into two unrefined (intermediate) Products A' and B'. These two intermediate products can be sold in the market, for $20 and $8 respectively, after incurring incremental costs after split-off of $8 and

$4 respectively, for collecting, packaging and delivering the unrefined Products, A'
and B'. The Hartley Company also has the option of processing A' and B' further
into refined Products A and B. In this case it saves $1 of delivery charges associated
with intermediate Products A' and B', but it incurs an additional $4 and $2 per unit
respectively for processing Products A' and B' into A and B respectively.

Other Production and Marketing Conditions

1.   The Raw Material Y costs $3 per unit. One unit of Y produces 3 units of
A' and 2 units of B'.

2.   All the processing of Product Y and to refine Products A' and B' into
Products A and B requires the same equipment. The processing time per unit of each
product is:

Process	Hours per Unit
Y	2.0
A	2.5
B	0.5

Available equipment time is limited to 100,000 hours per period.

3.   Raw Material Y can be purchased up to a maximum amount of 16,000
units per period.

4.   Maximum sales per period are:

Product	Max. Sales
A'	50,000
B'	8,000
B	10,000

Required:

1.   Solve the problem to find the optimal production and sales schedule.
    Interpret the solution.

2.   In the solution to Question 1, how would profit be affected if Hartley had
    1,000 hours of extra equipment time per period? How would profit be
    affected if Hartley could sell another 100 units of product B?

12-7.   Joint Costs and Nonlinear Optimization (R. Manes)

Part A: Two Prime Products (an interior solution)

A raw material C, purchased and processed at a cost of $12.00 per pound,
produces two important joint products, A & B. Facts about the processing and sale
of A & B are summarized below:

Demand Data:	Product A	Product B
Price	P_A	P_B
Quantity demanded per period	Q_A	Q_B
Price as a function of Quantity	$(200 - Q_A)$	$(150 - 0.4Q_B)$
Output of Joint Products from 10 lbs. of C	3 lb.	5 lb.
Direct, Traceable Cost of Processing A & B beyond split-off point	$20/lb.	$10/lb.

Required:

1. Calculate optimal quantities and prices of A & B, the optimal quantity of C, and the resulting profit.
2. Calculate and interpret the joint cost allocation of C per unit of A & B as suggested in the chapter.
3. Compare the joint cost allocation of Question 2 to a net realizable sales value allocation of the cost of C.
4. Is either A or B a byproduct as defined in the chapter?

Part B: A Boundary Solution (Prime Products & By Products)

A very similar problem with a different outcome is developed by Professor Bierman. One unit of raw material, R, can be used to produce one unit of A and one unit of B. Costs associated with the processing of one unit of R to split-off are:

Cost of purchasing one unit of R	$20
Cost of processing R to split-off	7
Direct, separable cost of further	
processing of A	5
processing of B	3
Demand for A: $Q_A =$	$100 - 2P_A$
Demand for B: $Q_B =$	$20 - 0.5 P_B$

Required:

1. Calculate quantities and prices of A and B and the quantity of R which will yield maximum profit.
2. Interpret the allocation of joint costs for this problem.

Part C: Disposal of Joint Products and Environmental Policy Impacts

Consider the situation in which all or part of the production of a joint product must be disposed of, either because of inadequate demand or because the joint product is a noxious effluent. Part B above provides an example of a joint product for which there is inadequate demand. Recalculate the solution to that problem on the assumption that there is a cost of $1 per unit for any output not ultimately sold—

i.e., production destroyed or otherwise disposed of. Compare your answer to the solution in Part B where there is no such tax.

Part D: Joint Cost and Production Under a Capacity Constraint

Assume now that the joint processing of Raw Material C produces one unit of A and one unit of B, neither of which requires further processing. Cost of $C = 2$. The demand functions for A and B are:

$$Q_A = 4.8 - .4P_A$$

$$Q_B = 5 - .5P_B$$

Required:

1. Find the optimal solution for this situation.
2. Assume now that, because of limited physical facilities or a shortage of C, that a maximum of 2 units of C can be processed. Recalculate the optimal solution and interpret the new Lagrange multipliers. Repeat this calculation if 2.1 units of C are available.

12-8.   *The Williamson Chocolate Company, Ltd.** (David Solomons)

The Williamson Chocolate Co., Ltd., which has its headquarters and principal factory in Leicester, England, has been engaged in the production of chocolate and cocoa products since the beginning of this century. Subsidiary companies have been established in Canada, Australia, and South Africa, and each of the subsidiaries manufactures the more important of the company's products and markets them in its home market.

The Australian company is located in Melbourne, where all of its manufacturing activities take place, and warehouses for local distribution are also maintained in Sydney, Adelaide, and Perth. The main output at the factory is chocolate in bars. Cocoa beans, the principal raw material for the manufacture of chocolate, are imported from abroad. As a rule, the beans are cleaned, roasted, ground, and then passed through a press. In the press, cocoa butter is separated from cocoa powder. The cocoa butter leaves the press in liquid form because of the heat that is generated during the press operation. The cocoa butter is then stored in large tanks, ready for use in the current production of chocolate.

The Melbourne factory was a net user of cocoa butter, that is, its chocolate production called for more cocoa butter than could be obtained from the pressing of cocoa beans for powder manufacture. This extra cocoa butter could have been imported but it was subject to a heavy import duty, and the local management believed that it was cheaper to import beans and extract the cocoa butter from them. As a result of implementing this policy the factory found itself with a steadily mounting stock of cocoa powder.

---

* Reproduced with permission.

The following figures show how the stock of cocoa powder (in pounds) increased during the period 1968–70:

1968:

Stock at January 1, 1968		30,500
Output of press		416,975
		447,475
Less: Usage in 1968		324,500
Stock at December 31, 1968		122,975
1969:		
Output of press		638,750
		761,725
Less: Usage in 1969	506,420	
Sales in 1969	35,500	541,920
Stock at December 11, 1969		219,805
1970:		
Output of press		792,125
		1,011,930
Less: Usage in 1970	641,600	
Sales in 1970	43,385	684,985
Stock of cocoa powder, December 31, 1970		326,945

These large stocks of cocoa powder held at the factory caused a serious storage problem, and the local management made continuous efforts to find profitable outlets for the excess cocoa powder. However, the sale of this powder on the Australian market raised a question as to its proper valuation. In accordance with accounting instructions issued by the head office in London some time before the last war, the cost of the cocoa beans purchased together with the labor and overhead costs of the pressing process had to be allocated between the cocoa butter and the cocoa cake on the basis of the fat content remaining in these two products after the pressing operations. This gave a cost for cocoa powder of about $0.23 a pound or about 50 percent above its current market price at the end of 1970. The company was therefore unable to dispose of its excess stock of cocoa cake without incurring a considerable loss. For balance sheet purposes, however, the company made a provision in its accounts in order to bring the book value of its stock of cocoa down to the market value.

During 1971, cocoa prices fell further and the subsidiary was unable to sell any large quantities of its excess stocks, because its costs were too high. There was practically no internal market for cocoa powder. It did succeed however, in exchanging 13,000 pounds of powder against 2,000 pounds of cocoa butter with another manufacturer.

In the middle of 1971, Mr. Cannon, the marketing manager, brought forward a scheme to market a new cocoa preparation for making a hot chocolate drink. The marketing prospects seemed good as long as the selling price could be kept low enough. This new product offered a promising means of disposing of the excess stocks of cocoa powder but only if they were costed out at substantially less than the cost allocated to them in the books.

The production manager, Mr. Parker, supported this proposal with enthusiasm. He had repeatedly drawn the attention of the subsidiary's managing director, Mr.

Woodstock, to the storage problem created by the cocoa stocks, and he welcomed the possibility which now opened up of dealing with this problem once for all. Besides, he said, he had never been able to see the logic of basing the cost of cocoa powder on its fat content. It was its flavor which was important, and fat content had little to do with flavor.

Both Cannon and Parker were surprised to find that Mr. Woodstock was not unreservedly enthusiastic about Cannon's proposal. He pointed out that if cocoa powder were charged to the new product at present cost levels, the product would never show a profit; and without a drop in the price of cocoa beans greater than anyone could at present foresee, the only way to reduce the cost of cocoa powder would be to change the basis of cost allocation between cocoa powder and cocoa butter. This could not be done without permission from London and he was by no means certain that such permission would be given unless some basis of cost allocation which was clearly better than the present one could be proposed. It was all very well to attack the present basis of allocation, as Mr. Parker had done. But unless he or somebody else could suggest a better one, why should London agree to a change?

Mr. Woodstock went on to point out that there was another aspect of the matter which made him reluctant to approach London. If the allocation of costs to cocoa powder were reduced, with a consequent increase in the cost of cocoa butter, the calculation which had been supplied to London in 1967 to support the expenditure of $40,000 on a new cocoa press would be completely undermined. Only on the basis of the present cost of producing cocoa butter as compared with the cost of importing it could investment in the press be justified. If more cost were to be allocated to cocoa butter, it might be shown that it ought to be imported after all, and the investment in the press would be shown to have been misguided.

What should Mr. Woodstock tell London? Should he recommend a change in the allocation method?

12-9. *Effect of Joint Cost on Product Profitability and Capital Budgeting Analysis** (John Shank)

Ajax Petroleum

Bill MacGregor was still puzzled as he thought about the financial report lying on his desk (see Table 1). The report summarized the key financial statistics for a capital expenditure project which one of MacGregor's subordinates was recommending. MacGregor was the general manager for Ajax Petroleum's Middletown, Ohio, refinery. Although he was a chemical engineer by training, his policy was to rely on the people reporting to him for recommendations about the technical side of the business. He strongly objected to second-guessing his managers on things for which they were responsible.

* This case was prepared by Professor John K. Shank with the cooperation of a major oil company. All data in the case are generally realistic as of April, 1980, but proprietary information has been disguised. This case appears in John Shank, *Contemporary Managerial Accounting* (Prentice-Hall, 1981). Reproduced with permission.

TABLE 1. **Memorandum**

March 17, 1980

TO: W. MacGregor
FROM: B. Anderson, Economic Analyst
RE: The Solvent Decarbonizing Unit Proposal

Here is the information you requested concerning the economics of the SDU project. I have the backup file if you want to dig deeper.

1) Investment cost	$30,000,000	(delivered and installed)
Less Investment Tax Credit	3,000,000	(10% of cost)
Net Investment	$27,000,000	
2) Annual Operating Costs (three-shift basis)	$ 3,300,000	(Labor, maintenance, insurance, property taxes, supplies)

Per barrel of Cracking Stock Produced

3) Fuel	$	2.90 bbl. (See Note 1 below)
4) Feedstock Cost	$	32.30/bbl. (See Note 2 below)
5) Value of Cracking Stock Produced	$	37.50/bbl. (See Note 3 below)

6) Thruput is 9,000 bbls. per day (assuming an average of 90% utilization of theoretical capacity on a 365-day/year basis). One bbl. of resid will produce one bbl. of cracking stock.

7) Economic life is 20 years. (This is also the depreciable life for tax purposes. The current tax rate is 46%.) Use straight-line depreciation for simplicity and to be conservative.

8) Inflation in costs and prices is ignored. This would tend to offset for a project like this one.

Project Profitability

Payback = 9.10 years
Net Present Value (at 20% after taxes) = negative $12.6 million
Economic Rate of Return = 9%
Profitability Index = .72
Return on Capital Employed = 19.8%

Note 1   The SDU runs on fuel gas,[a] to which Ajax currently assigns a cost of $29.00 per equivalent bbl. It takes .10 bbl. of fuel gas to produce a barrel of thruput at the SDU. Thus, fuel gas costs $2.90 per barrel of thruput.

Note 2   Feedstock for the SDU is No. 6 oil. The cost of No. 6 is computed by assigning crude oil cost and crude-still operating costs to the set of outputs at the crude still, based on relative production volumes for each product. With crude running $29.00 average for the refinery, this equates currently to about $32.30/bbl. for resid.

Note 3   Gasoline is currently selling for about $39/bbl. at the refinery. The cost is about $1.50/bbl. at the cat cracker to convert feedstock into gasoline. Thus, the net realizable value of thruput at the SDU which feels the cat cracker is $37.50/bbl. ($39 minus $1.50).

---

[a] "Fuel gas" is generated at the crude still in a gaseous state as one of the products when a barrel of crude is "cracked." It is not feasible to convert the fuel gas into a salable end product, but it can be used as fuel to power the various production units in the refinery. The DOE-approved guidelines for measuring the allowable cost of gasoline for price control purposes charge fuel gas for a proportionate share of the average cost of crude oil but not for any portion of the operating costs of the crude still. Currently, about 5% of the equivalent volumetric production at the crude still is fuel gas. With crude cost at $30.45 for the incremental barrel and $29.00 on average, Ajax followed the DOE-approved approach and costed fuel gas at $29.00 per equivalent barrel.

John Patterson, general superintendent for the catalytic cracking unit ("cat cracker") was pushing strongly for MacGregor's approval of a proposal to install a solvent-decarbonizing unit (SDU) in the refinery at a cost of roughly $30,000,000. The function of an SDU is to clean and purify residual fuel oil so that it can serve as raw material ("feedstock") for the cat cracker. The cat cracker would then convert this feedstock into gasoline. Residual or No. 6 oil is one of the outputs when crude oil is refined. However, it represents, literally, what is left after the desirable end products are extracted from the barrel of crude. As the dregs, "resid" is dirty, smelly, and so viscous that it will not even flow at room temperature. It was considered in Ajax to be more a nuisance than anything else. However, there is an established nationwide market for resid, at a low enough price, with uses ranging from heating apartment buildings to generating electricity to powering other equipment designed to run on low-grade fuels. John Patterson was convinced that converting resid into more gasoline was a great idea, particularly since gasoline prices at the refinery were stable at $39/bbl. while resid prices were very volatile, having been as low as $18/bbl. in recent weeks. There was sufficient excess capacity at the cat cracker to process the extra feedstock, and no alternative external source of additional feedstock was available.

MacGregor had been intrigued by Patterson's idea because he was no great fan of No. 6 oil either. Because of wide seasonal swings in demand and supply and a relatively thin market, residual prices were notoriously volatile and unpredictable. MacGregor knew that the current price was about $25/bbl., but it had been as low as $18/bbl. and as high as $35/bbl. in recent months. Patterson had also told MacGregor that many of Ajax' competitors already had SDUs in their refineries and that there was always a waiting list for installation of an SDU, so they must be a good investment. MacGregor wasn't particularly impressed by these arguments, however, because he knew that the major oil companies often differed on strategic issues. Just because Ashland and Marathon were deemphasizing heavy oil (No. 6) to yield more light oil (gasoline) from the barrel of crude did not mean Ajax should automatically follow along. In fact, this might make the heavy-oil business a lot better for the remaining suppliers. MacGregor had heard that Exxon, for one, still considered heavy oil to be a viable item in the product line. Also, MacGregor knew that the Ajax marketing department might not agree with deemphasizing resid since there were residual oil sales managers in each sales district and many long-standing customer relationships involved, including many electric utilities in the politically sensitive northeast. MacGregor did know, however, that the additional gasoline could easily be sold in the wholesale market. Long-run prospects for gasoline demand were less certain.

MacGregor had told Patterson that the key in selling the SDU idea would be return on investment. He told Patterson to work with the economic analysis department to pull together the numbers for the SDU proposal. If it was such a good idea the numbers would show it and MacGregor could then recommend the project to the corporate capital expenditures committee. The corporate "hurdle rate" for new investment proposals was currently 20%, after taxes. Patterson had eagerly accepted this idea, noting that an acquaintance of his at Ashland Oil had called the SDU in his refinery one of the more profitable investments he had seen in 20 years in the business. When MacGregor received the financial summary report, he was puzzled because the numbers for the SDU project just didn't look that good.

When MacGregor showed the report to Patterson, the latter accused the "bean counters" of trying to scuttle the project with "funny numbers." He took exception to two items in the report, the cost of $29.00/bbl. for fuel gas and the cost of $32.30/bbl. for residual oil. He said that fuel gas was really free because there wasn't anything else to do with it except use it as fuel. He argued that since the refinery gets it automatically when a barrel of crude is processed and it has no sales value, it should be considered as free. In fact, he said, fuel gas should show a negative cost since it costs money for equipment to flare it off if it isn't used. He should be encouraged to use it up, he said, to save this cost and to save the hassle with EPA about the air pollution when fuel gas is flared. He was even more unhappy with the reported cost of $32.30/bbl. for resid. He said it was absolutely crazy to show resid at a higher cost than crude itself when, in fact, resid is what's left after you take all the desired products out of the crude. Why should resid show a higher value than raw crude when it was dramatically less desirable to customers? Raw crude itself, although dangerous to handle because of static electricity buildup, is a substitute product for resid in nearly all applications. Patterson had said that he had never been much interested in cost calculations because he figured that the accountants were accurate, but if this report was an example of how they think, Ajax was in trouble. MacGregor had agreed that Patterson's points seemed to make sense.

MacGregor had subsequently called in Ben Anderson to discuss Patterson's objections to the cost calculations in Anderson's report. Anderson had assured MacGregor that he had no desire to scuttle Patterson's idea. In fact, he said, the analysis in the report was slanted in favor of the proposal and he had even felt guilty about leaning over backward to make the project look good. The problem with the report, he said, was that fuel gas should be costed at $32.30/bbl. rather than $29.00. It is true, he continued, that fuel gas shows an actual cost of $29.00 per equivalent barrel under Ajax' cost accounting system and that this is the cost approved by DOE for determining gasoline "ceiling" prices. However, he said, actual historical cost was not relevant for the proposed new capital investment. Anderson noted that about one-half of the refinery's current fuel needs were being met by fuel gas and the other half by residual oil. The SDU project would not increase the amount of fuel gas generated at the crude still, but it would consume as fuel some of the fuel gas already being generated. The net result for the refinery as a whole would be to increase the consumption of resid used as fuel by an amount equal to the fuel needs of the SDU. Since resid costs $32.30/bbl., fuel cost for the SDU project should be $32.30. Anderson called this the "opportunity-cost" concept, as opposed to actual historical cost.

Regarding the question of what No. 6 costs, Anderson said he sympathized with Patterson but that the $32.30 was a factual number. In fact, he said, the refinery *does* produce a set of products at the crude still, *including* residual oil, and these products *must each* carry a share of the costs incurred in producing them. A barrel of residual oil thus costs whatever a barrel of crude oil costs, plus some share of the operating costs at the crude still. These crude-still operating costs, he said, could be allocated based on value of products produced, volume of products produced, total energy value (BTUs) of products produced, or some other basis. But under any allocation scheme, outputs from the crude still will cost more than crude oil. Anderson concluded by saying that with fuel gas and resid at $32.30, the SDU actually would be even less profitable than as shown in Table 1 and that the project just couldn't be justified on economic grounds. But, since most companies use historical costs rather than opportunity costs in their accounting systems, he (Anderson) could "bend" as far as the analysis in the report, as an accommodation to Patterson. The meet had ended with MacGregor agreeing that Anderson's points seemed to make sense.

MacGregor's background included very little training in cost accounting. He had always considered this area as a technical specialty for which general managers could hire the expertise they needed. He was, however, feeling very frustrated about which cost numbers to believe for the solvent decarbonizing project. He also felt a little foolish for agreeing with both Patterson and Anderson when they talked to him.

He asked his plant controller, Fred Morton, to have lunch with him one day to look at Ben Anderson's report and comment on John Patterson's objections to it. Morton said the basic issue was what cost to show for No. 6 oil in the calculations. He said that Anderson was currently using the cost numbers generated by Ajax' cost accounting system. Resid was considered to be one of the joint set of products produced in the refinery and, accordingly, was assigned a cost of $32.30/bbl. (as compared to middle distillate at $32.90 and gasoline at $34.80). He agreed that the *particular* allocation scheme (weight, volume, heat value, etc.) was essentially arbitrary, but he emphasized that charging a share of refining cost to resid makes it more costly.

He said that one way to show significantly lower cost on resid would be to consider it a "by-product" rather than a "joint product." A by-product has the following characteristics:

1. It is not a desired output from the production process; it just happens to be created in the process of making the desired products.
2. It is low in sales value relative to the main products.
3. It is produced in relatively small quantities.

A clear example of the distinction between a by-product and a joint product is pigs feet versus bacon to a hog butcher. Morton went on to say that normal cost accounting procedure shows a zero cost for by-products. They are just sold for whatever the market will bring, and the sales revenue is netted back against the costs which must be assigned to the desired products. For the refinery, this would mean allocating the sum of crude cost plus crude-still operating costs minus resid sales revenue to gasoline and middle distillate (jet fuel, diesel fuel, and home heating oil), with resid showing a zero cost for accounting purposes. He noted that several of the major oil companies follow this approach, although several others use the same approach as Ajax.

Under the by-product approach, resid would be valued in the capital expenditure analysis at whatever you could sell it for if you didn't convert it to cracking stock or use it as refinery fuel. With gasoline selling for $39/bbl., he thought resid would average around $20 over its price cycles. However, he added that the long-run average price of resid would certainly be heavily influenced by regulatory pressures to stop utilities from burning resid and by trends in gasoline consumption. The average price by 1985 could be as low as $17/bbl. or as high as $25/bbl., even if crude prices didn't change. Morton said this is what Anderson termed the opportunity-cost approach, as opposed to the historical-cost approach. He concluded by saying that this same idea applies to the fuel gas item. The reported cost incurred is $29/bbl. and the opportunity cost will average around $20/bbl. (the revenue forgone by not selling a barrel of resid).

MacGregor went back to Anderson the next day and asked him to refigure the SDU project showing both the joint product costing and by-product costing approaches for resid and both recorded cost and opportunity cost approaches for fuel gas. Anderson said that would be no problem and agreed to get the information to MacGregor by the next day. MacGregor wondered how much impact these accounting questions would have on the profitability of the SDU project. He couldn't imagine that bookkeeping issues would be that important to the overall analysis. He was anxious to see Anderson's revised report.

Required:

1. Using the same format as in Table 1, recalculate the economic return for the project, using both joint product costing ($32.30) and by-product costing ($20.00) for resid and using DOE costing ($29.00) and opportunity costing for fuel gas ($20.00 or $32.30, depending on the assumed cost of resid). All the basic data will be the same as in Table 1 except for the cost of fuel gas and resid.

2. What do you believe is the best accounting method for fuel gas and residual oil? Why? Which set of accounting numbers produces the most meaningful economic return calculations?

3. Is the proposed solvent decarbonizing unit profitable enough to justify the investment?

4. As MacGregor, would you recommend the SDU project to headquarters? What economic analysis would you present to support your recommendation? What qualitative (versus quantitative) factors influence your decision?

REFERENCES

BIERMAN, HAROLD, "Inventory Valuation: The Use of Market Prices," *The Accounting Review* XLII (October 1967), 731–37.

HARTLEY, RONALD V., "Decision Making When Joint Products Are Involved," *The Accounting Review* XLVI (October 1971), 746–55.

JENSEN, DANIEL L., "The Role of Cost in Pricing Joint Products: A Case of Production in Fixed Proportions," *The Accounting Review* XLIX (July 1974), 465–76.

LITTLECHILD, S. C., "Marginal Cost Pricing with Joint Costs," *Economic Journal* LXXX (June 1970), 323–34.

MANES, RENE, and VERNON L. SMITH, "Economic Joint Cost Theory and Accounting Practice," *The Accounting Review* XL (January 1965), 31–35.

THOMAS, ARTHUR L., "On Joint Cost Allocations," *Costs and Management,* September–October 1974.

TURVEY, RALPH, "Marginal Cost," *Economic Journal,* LXXIX (June 1969), 282–99.

WEIL, ROMAN L., "Allocating Joint Costs," *American Economic Review* LVIII (December 1968), 1342–45.

13

DECENTRALIZATION

CENTRALIZATION AND DECENTRALIZATION

Earlier chapters of this book focused on particular issues: cost estimation and classification, product-mix and profitability analysis, pricing and inventory decisions, profit and cost control, service department usage, and joint-product analysis. For each issue we isolated the essential information relevant to the decision or analysis. This approach is helpful for understanding decision making in small relatively simple organizations and in local decision-making units within large organizations. But in the very large multiproduct, multilocation, hierarchical entities typical of our modern business enterprises, a broader set of information and cost accounting issues arise. Questions of who in the organization will have the authority and responsibility to make particular decisions and how such a decision maker will be evaluated and rewarded require answers from a broader perspective than we have taken in previous chapters. In this and the chapters that follow we will introduce the notion of decentralized operations: their benefits, costs, and special problems that arise in the management and evaluation of decentralized organizational units.

A large corporation contains many diverse production and marketing activities that interact with each other but still may be operated separately. The output products of one activity may be the inputs to another, making it important that the volume of these two activities (such as component production and assembly, or production and marketing) be balanced. Some commodities may have to be purchased from external vendors, stored at various sites, transported among and within plants, and assigned to the activities that use these commodities. Some activities produce finished goods that need to be transported, stored, and sold by the other activities. This coordination is needed not only at a single point in time but continually—over many time periods—as the diverse activities respond to changes in the marketplace. Further, in addition to the production and marketing activities of acquiring the inputs to the production process, performing the actual manufacture and assembly, and marketing the product to the customers, a whole range of support and service activities must be coordinated to supplement the production and marketing activities. Functions such as personnel, information systems, finance, legal, research and development, utilities, maintenance, and engineering must be made part of the firm's overall planning and control process.

One approach to managing the diverse and complex activities of a large organization has been to stress central control. With this view, organizations are characterized by vertical, hierarchical relations; control is exercised by orders from above, executed in detail by those below. Interacting activities are coordinated by plans set at higher levels. Accounting systems and periodic reports provide the central management with all the information needed to formulate plans and to detect any departures from centrally determined policies.

In practice, of course, no central management can possibly know everything about an organization's many activities. Therefore, central management cannot make all the decisions for lower-level managers. For this and other reasons, many decisions must be made at the lower or local levels of any organization. The challenge in organizational and informational design is to balance the benefits and costs of decentralized decision making that arise from a firm's particular resources, constraints, and opportunities.

That a certain amount of decentralized decision making is necessary within a firm should not be surprising. A modern corporation, after all, is an economy in miniature (some of our largest corporations actually produce more goods and services than many economies around the world). A large corporation has internal capital and labor markets—or at least mechanisms for allocating capital and labor within the firm. It has unemployment problems, suffers from cyclic fluctuations, and must be concerned with its supply of money. The firm employs planners, forecasters, and stabilizers. The actions of one organizational unit can affect many other organizational units, so that externalities among organizational units are abundant.

Most of us accept the idea that central direction and resource allocation in an economy lead to inefficiencies and provide insufficient incentives for response to consumer preferences and the continually changing demands of the marketplace. If one believes that information and computational complexities make it desirable to have dispersed resource allocation and decision making in an economy, one should also believe that a certain degree of decentralization is desirable for large organizational units within an economy. The problem is that prices, which play such a vital role in a capitalist economy, are not as readily available within the firm to guide local decision making. There are not enough homogeneous economic agents within a firm to simulate a full market system. Therefore, a firm uses a collection of nonmarket mechanisms (such as contracts, incentives, standards, penalties, and reporting) that facilitate resource allocation and decision making in the presence of information constraints that prevent markets from operating well. The focus of this and the next four chapters is the design and evaluation of these nonmarket institutional arrangements within the firm.

The introductory remarks provide some general motivation for the demand for decentralized decision making. Let us look more closely now at the specific incentives for firms to decentralize.

Information Specialization

Perhaps the strongest factor leading to decentralization is the difficulty if not impossibility of sharing all local information with the central management. Local managers, through observation and experience, get information on such matters as local market opportunities, production possibilities and constraints, morale and capabilities of their labor force, and quality and reliability of local suppliers. It would be extremely difficult, costly, and time consuming for local managers to communicate all the relevant information they possess to a central management. Many of these observations would be difficult to quantify or even verbalize. Language limits people's ability to articulate their knowledge and intuition, whether using words, numbers, or graphics, in ways that will be understood by others. Managers will find, despite their best efforts, that their information is not sufficiently well formulated to communicate their intuition, judgment, and "gut feelings" about relevant local information. Thus, an extremely important force toward decentralization is the desire to place decision making where the relevant information is acquired, stored, accessed, and processed.

Timeliness of Response

A second rationale for decentralization is to take advantage of the responsiveness of local managers in making and implementing decisions. By allowing some degree of local decision making, the decentralized unit can respond to unexpected conditions faster than if all actions had to be approved by a central management group. Centralized decision making introduces delays during (1) transmission of the decision-relevant information from the local to central unit, (2) deliberations of the central decision-making unit, and (3) transmission of the recommended decision from the central unit back to the local unit where it will be implemented.

Conservation of Central Management Time

Presumably, the time of the central management group is one of the firm's scarcest resources. The vast numbers of local decisions called for would overwhelm even the most talented and resourceful group of top executives. The law of comparative advantage is operative within firms. Even though, for any particular local decision, a top executive may make a somewhat better local decision (once all the relevant situation-specific factors are explained to him) than the less-experienced or less-talented local manager, it is not necessarily optimal for the top executive to make all local decisions. For if he confines his attentions to making slightly superior day-to-day operating decisions, he may be ignoring the strategic decisions that in the intermediate to long run are far more vital to the firm's success. Therefore, it is preferable to confine central management attention to policy and strategic decisions and allow local managers to make the necessary operating decisions consistent with the broader objectives established by top management.

Computational Complexity

Even if it were decided to centralize all decision making, it may not be possible to compute globally optimal decisions. With exceedingly complex operations characterized by extensive interactions and discontinuities in scale, it may be virtually impossible to solve reasonably sized resource allocation problems centrally. There are limits to the complexity of problems that can be solved by human decision makers (a situation referred to as bounded rationality), and even computer-based algorithms cannot optimize very large systems, especially systems with nonlinearities and discrete (integer) variables. When the environment is also characterized by uncertainty, the simplifications and heuristics required for centrally determined decisions could easily lead to decisions inferior to those that would be reached at decentralized levels. Again, the analogy between a centralized firm and a socialist economy is instructive; socialist economies have found it impossible to make all major resource-allocation and production decisions centrally. General directions and guidelines are provided to local plant mangers, who still retain some discretion for decisions on resource acquisition, product mix, and distribution. These decisions are guided by incentive plans and a limited use of the price system.

Training for Local Managers

If all significant decision making were done centrally, local managers would be mainly implementing the centrally determined plans. The managers would acquire experience in motivating employees and meeting production or distribution schedules but would not receive training in decision making. How, then, would the next generation of central management acquire the requisite experience to become good resource allocators and strategic decision makers? And on what evidence could we determine who, among the many local managers, would be best qualified for advancement to the higher decision-making levels? Some degree of local decision making is desirable to (1) provide training for future general managers and (2) indicate which managers seem best qualified for advancement to higher levels of decision making.

Motivation for Local Managers

Finally, good managers are ambitious and take pride in their work. If their role is restricted to carrying out instructions determined at higher levels, they may lose interest in their assignments and cease applying all their talents to their assignment. Also, the firm may find it difficult to attract creative and energetic people to serve merely as decision implementers. Managers will become more motivated and interested in their assignments when they are permitted more discretion in performing their tasks. Allowing for decision making at a local level will encourage managers to be entrepreneurial and strategic in their actions. The challenge, of course, is to design incentive systems so that such entrepreneurial and strategic activities at a local level are consistent with overall corporate goals and objectives.

The arguments for decentralization seem compelling. The outcome or payoff of any reasonably sized organization depends upon many interrelated decisions about decentralized or local activities. Different members in the organization have different bodies of knowledge and abilities to act. It is impossible for any individual or central group to possess all the relevant information, experience, time, and computational power to determine the detailed operating plans for the organization. Accepting this argument, however, still leaves us with the extremely difficult problem of how to decentralize decision making. Present practice provides evidence on five types of decentralized organizational units. These units differ depending on the degree of authority and responsibility given to the local manager.

ORGANIZATION OF DECENTRALIZED UNITS

All units in an organization acquire inputs and produce outputs, either goods or services. Units differ, however, in the ease with which the outputs can be measured and in the discretion that the local manager is given for acquiring inputs and choosing the type and mix of outputs. These considerations make different types of decentralized units appropriate depending upon the difficulty of measuring outputs and the discretion or responsibility given to the local manager. We shall briefly review five principal types:

1. Standard cost centers
2. Revenue centers
3. Discretionary expense centers
4. Profit centers
5. Investment centers.

Profit centers and investment centers are treated in more depth in the subsequent two chapters.

Standard Cost Centers

Standard cost centers can be established whenever there is a well-defined and measurable output together with a known requirement on the amount of inputs required to produce each unit of output. Usually, we think of standard cost centers as arising in manufacturing operations where, for each type of output product, a standard amount and standard price of input materials, labor, and overhead can be specified. Standard cost centers, however, can occur for any repetitive operation for which we can measure the physical amount of output and specify a desirable production function relating inputs to outputs. Thus, even in service industries such as fast-food franchises, banking, or health care, we can establish standard cost centers based on the number of hamburgers and milk shakes sold, on the number of checks processed, or on the number of patient tests or radiological procedures performed.

In general, managers of standard cost centers are not held responsible for variations in activity levels in their centers. They are held responsible for the *efficiency* with which they meet externally determined demands as long as the demands are within the capacity of the cost center. Efficiency is measured as the amount of inputs used in order to produce the demanded level of outputs. This implies that if a full-cost scheme is being used, the managers are not responsible for underabsorbed overhead due to volume variances. They are, however, responsible for controlling the fixed costs in the center.

Managers of standard cost centers do not determine the price of their outputs, so they are not responsible for revenue or profit. Nevertheless, if the output does not meet the specified quality standards or is not produced on schedule, the cost center will adversely affect the performance of other units in the organization. Therefore, it is necessary to specify quality and timeliness standards for any standard cost center and to require the manager to produce according to these standards.

For a standard cost center, then, *efficiency* is evaluated by the relation between inputs and outputs and *effectiveness* is evaluated by whether the center achieved the desired production schedule at specified levels of quality and timeliness.

Standard cost centers and the detailed analysis of variances from standards are discussed extensively in other cost accounting textbooks (for example, Horngren [1982, chaps. 6, 7, and 8]) so that further discussion is not required here. For our paradigm, standard cost centers are justified when we can measure the output objectively, including quality and timeliness as well as physical units, and when we have a well-specified relationship between outputs and inputs. The product (or output) must be standard enough that the manufacturing unit need not make decisions on price, output quantity, or product mix; these decisions can be made centrally or delegated to a marketing unit. Also, decisions on plant equipment and technology for the standard cost center will usually be made centrally, not at the discretion of the cost center manager.

Revenue Centers

Revenue centers exist in order to organize marketing activities. Typically, a revenue center acquires finished goods from a manufacturing division and is responsible for selling and distributing these goods. If the revenue center has discretion for setting the selling price, then it can be made responsible for the gross revenues it generates. If pricing policy is determined outside the revenue center (say, at the corporate level), then the manager of the revenue center is held responsible for the physical volume and mix of sales. The profit and sales-mix variance analysis method described in Chapter 9 should be very useful in evaluating the performance of a revenue center. The decomposition of profit variance described in that chapter enables us to decompose a sales-activity variance into effects caused by changes in overall market size, market share, and product mix.

When a performance measure is chosen for a revenue center, some notion of the marginal cost of each product should be included so that the center is motivated to maximize contribution margin rather than just sales revenue. If evaluated solely on sales revenue, managers may be motivated to cut prices to increase total sales, spend excessive amounts on advertising and promotion, or promote low-profit products. Each of these actions could increase total sales revenue but decrease overall corporate profitability.

Discretionary Expense Centers

Discretionary expense centers are appropriate for units that produce outputs that are not measurable in financial terms or for units where there is no strong relation between resources expended (inputs) and results achieved (outputs). Examples of discretionary expense centers are general and administrative departments (controller, industrial relations, human resources, accounting, legal), the research and development departments, and some marketing activities such as advertising, promotion, and warehousing. The output of G&A departments is difficult to measure, whereas for R&D and marketing functions, there is no strong relation between inputs and outputs. For the R&D and marketing functions we can determine whether the responsible departments are being effective. That is, we can see whether they are meeting the company's goals in terms of new products and improved technologies (for R&D) and sales volume or market penetration (for marketing). Because of the weak relationship between inputs and outputs in these departments, however, we are unable to determine whether they are operating efficiently—that is, producing the actual amount of output with the minimally required inputs. For the G&A departments it is just about impossible to measure output, so that neither effectiveness nor efficiency can be determined.

Given the difficulty of measuring the efficiency of discretionary expense centers, there is a natural tendency for their managers to desire a very high quality (Cadillac) department even though a somewhat lower quality (Chevrolet) department would provide almost the same service at significantly lower costs. Accentuating this tendency, the white-collar professionals who typically staff these centers prefer to have the best people in their discipline associated with them so that they can take pride in the quality of their department. Thus it becomes very difficult for a central management to determine appropriate budget, quality, and service levels for discretionary expense centers.

One solution is to look at industry practice to see whether the company's expenditures on a given function are in line with those of other companies. (A cynic could deride this guideline as the blind following the blind.) We frequently see a company's R&D budget, for example, expressed as a percentage of sales. Even though there is no plausible reason why a company's R&D expenditures should be causally related to its sales, such a percentage rule facilitates intercompany comparisons.

Basically, determining the budget for a discretionary expense center requires the judgment of informed professionals. The central management needs to trust and work closely with the managers of discretionary expense centers to determine the appropriate budget level. The managers of such centers are in the best position to predict the consequences of changing the budget by ± 10 or ± 20 percent. After finding out which activities would be augmented or reduced by changes, central management can then decide on the budget and hence on the quality or intensity of effort for the next period. Discretionary expense centers are an excellent example of where there is likely to be great information asymmetry between a local unit manager and central management.

Once the budget has been determined, there is no great benefit from pressuring the local manager to bring actual costs in under budget. It is not necessarily favorable nor a sign of efficiency for actual spending to be below budgeted levels. Here is a major difference between a discretionary expense center and a standard cost center. For a standard cost center we have good measures of output quantity and quality, so that producing a given amount of output for less than budgeted costs is a favorable indication. For a discretionary expense center, a favorable cost variance may only mean that the center is operating at a lower level of quality or service than was intended when the budget was established. Similarly, cost overruns in a discretionary expense center may be caused by favorable circumstances, such as a new-product breakthrough that justifies higher development expenditures or an improved marketing climate in which increased advertising and distribution expenditures may yield great returns.

Nobody ever said that managing and evaluating a discretionary expense center is easy. The lack of measurable outputs or strong relationships between inputs and outputs makes it difficult to use traditional financial control techniques for evaluating the operation of these centers. Although the existence of budgeted and actual expenses for these centers may give an illusion of precision, such data may not yield much insight into whether the centers are operating effectively or efficiently. Ultimately, the control of discretionary expense centers requires the informed judgment of knowledgeable professionals on the level and quality of service the centers are producing.

Profit Centers

The three types of centers described above have limited decentralization of decisions. Managers of standard cost centers may acquire and manage inputs at their discretion, but the outputs from these centers are determined and distributed by other units. Revenue centers distribute and sell products but have no control over their manufacture. Discretionary expense centers produce a service or staff function for the organizations.

A significant increase in managerial discretion occurs when managers of local units are given responsibility for both production and sales. In this situation, they can make decisions on which products to manufacture, how to produce them, the quality level, the price, and the selling and distribution system. The managers must make product-mix decisions and determine how production resources are to be allocated among the various products. They are then in a position to optimize the performance of their centers by making trade-offs among price, volume, quality, and costs.

If the managers do not have responsibility or authority for determining the level of investment in assets in their centers, then profit is the single best performance measure for the centers. Profit, properly measured, is a comprehensive measure of the ability of managers to create value from the resources at their disposal and the input factors they acquire. Such units, where the managers have almost complete operational decision-making responsibility and are evaluated by a profit measure, are called *profit centers*. The importance of profit centers and the difficulties associated with measuring profit in them justify an extensive discussion, which is presented in Chapter 14.

Investment Centers

When local managers have all the responsibilities described above for profit centers and also have responsibility and authority for working capital and physical assets, then a performance measure based on the level of physical and financial assets employed in the center is preferred. *Investment centers* are generalizations of profit centers in which profitability is related to the assets used to generate the profit. Return on investment (ROI) and residual income are typical investment-center performance measures; these measures are discussed in Chapter 15.

In each of the five types of decentralized centers, the center's manager has some discretion in directing its activities. In order to guide the manager's decisions and evaluate his or her performance and that of the center, we require a performance measure. Specification of the local performance measure is perhaps the most difficult problem in decentralizing decision making and responsibility. Through this measure the organization communicates how it wishes the local manager to behave and how this behavior will be judged and evaluated. Central management needs to determine rules, measures, and rewards for local decision making that are compatible with overall corporate goals. These guidelines and incentives must facilitate the coordination of individual or divisional goals with the corporate goals and attempt to minimize added informational and dysfunctional costs. Clearly, this is not an easy task.

In a centralized decision-making environment, the local managers follow detailed operating rules that instruct them how to act. The decisions are determined centrally and implemented locally. Any failure to perform in a centralized system is relatively obvious because job descriptions and tasks are well specified.

In decentralized operations the operating rules are much less specific, hence performance evaluation is more difficult. We can think of the operating rules as consisting of two parts: constraints and objectives. First, the bounds of permissive or admissible behavior are specified, and the action alternatives of the managers are limited; for example, illegal behavior is proscribed, and managers may be instructed to use certain suppliers, meet certain quality standards, meet the demands of particular customers, and refrain from disposing of certain assets.

Once their range of action alternatives is specified, the local managers must also be given a well-specified reward or incentive function that they are expected to maximize. Thus, managers may be instructed to maximize divisional income, return on investment, or residual income. Managers in a sales division may be instructed to maximize sales revenues, or managers in a production division to minimize costs while satisfying an externally derived demand for the product. The specification of the local reward or incentive function is both extremely important and extremely difficult. It is important because this function will be used to measure the local managers' performance. Therefore, they will probably act to optimize this measure, perhaps at the expense of the goals of the corporation or other divisions. For example, the sales manager of a revenue center may try to maximize total revenue rather than total contribution margin. The expectation that managers will attempt to optimize this local measure to the exclusion of all other goals or measures is what makes the appropriate specification of a single local reward measure so difficult.

To gain a better understanding of this problem, we analyze the dysfunctional aspects associated with developing a measure of performance for a decentralized operation.

Problems of Goal Congruence

The measure of performance of a decentralized unit is a new piece of information to be developed by the firm. Costs are incurred to acquire the necessary data and to compute the actual performance measure. But the consequences of developing the local performance measure go far beyond the cost of data acquisition and computation. Ideally, the local performance measure should be consistent with overall corporate goals. But it is just about impossible in complex and uncertain environments for any single performance measure to achieve perfect goal congruence between a decentralized unit and the overall corporation. The measure of performance tends to become an end to itself, more important than the economic performance that it attempts to represent. In a revenue center, for example, salesmen may be motivated to sell only high-priced items in an attempt to maximize revenues rather than contribution margin. Any single measure may be manipulated to benefit the decentralized unit at the expense of the corporation.

This fundamental problem arises because, unlike the situation in the physical sciences, the act of measurement in the social sciences and in management changes the event and the observer.[1] Measurement is neither neutral nor objective. The measure chosen for evaluating performance acquires value and importance by the fact of being selected for attention. People within the system change their behavior as a function of the measure chosen to summarize the economic performance of their organizational unit.

A second problem arises because most measures of performance are based on internal achievement rather than external opportunities. A unit may be perceived as having performed well because it exceeded last year's measure of performance or the budgeted measure. But the current good performance may have been caused by an unexpected expansion of demand in the industry, in which all the companies in the industry participated. When viewed against overall industry performance, the decentralized unit may not have maintained its market share or relative profitability. In this case, the performance will not look as favorable against an external reference base as it does against the more typically measured internal criterion.

A third limitation on a single performance measure is its lack of attention to future economic consequences of current activities. Typical performance meas-

---

[1] Strictly speaking, the Heisenberg uncertainty principle establishes that even in the physical sciences the act of measurement affects the phenomenon being measured. But such effects show up at the subatomic level of observation and do not affect everyday measurements of speed, weight, and dimensions of physical objects.

ures focus on short-term operating results and ignore longer-term effects that are harder to measure. These longer-term effects usually arise from expenditures on intangibles—research and development, advertising and promotion, plant design, maintenance, human resource development, quality control. Because the benefits from such expenditures on intangibles are measured with difficulty and subjectivity we tend to ignore the benefits and concentrate on aspects of performance that we can measure more easily. As a result, an incentive is created for managers to spend less on intangibles and maintenance than would be desirable for long-term corporate goals. Such expenditures would reduce the current performance measure, while the adverse effects of neglecting them would not show up until later, perhaps much later when the current managers are in entirely different positions in the organization.

Similarly, transactions in a period have characteristics and longer-term consequences that are difficult to measure objectively. The quality of the product, the morale of the employees, and the output of professional services (legal, R&D, controller's office), for example, are important characteristics affecting the long-term performance of the organizational unit that are not easily captured in a short-term performance measure. Undesirable consequences will occur if too much burden is placed on a single measure of performance that ignores longer-term, less objectively measured consequences of current-period decisions.

Problems of Externalities

Interactions among organizational units introduce a second set of problems when local units are optimizing their own performance measures. When such interactions exist, the actions of an individual unit affect not only its own measure of performance but also the measures of other units. For example, when goods or services are transferred from one unit to another, it will usually be necessary to price these goods or services in order to recognize revenue for the supplying unit and an input-factor cost to the purchasing unit. This *transfer pricing* is one of the most difficult problems in the organizational design of a decentralized firm, and it is discussed extensively in the next chapter.

Even assuming that the transfer-pricing problem can be solved in a satisfactory manner, there are many problematic nonprice aspects of transactions among organizational units. The quality of a product or service and the timeliness of the transfer will affect the operation of the unit receiving the good or service, but the financial impact of varying quality or delivery times will be difficult to quantify. In principle, a price system could be established as a function of delivery delay (or product quality), but such a system would be extremely complex. It would be difficult to develop and to maintain. It would also introduce uncertainty to both units about the price of the transfer, since some delay might be caused by random, unexpected factors. Both units might then change their operations to minimize the effect of this inherent uncertainty. This change in operation could reduce overall output, thereby affecting the firm adversely.

The performance of other decentralized units may affect the performance measure of an individual unit, too. For example, the efficiency of a manufacturing plant may be affected by the quantity of output demanded from it, which is determined in part by the activities of a sales division. Under simple conditions of certainty, it can be argued that the performance measure of the manufacturing plant should not be affected by the activities of the selling division; effects due to variations in activity level should be the responsibility of the sales division, not the manufacturing unit. But once we recognize conditions of uncertainty and private information, it is no longer obvious that the manufacturing plant's performance measure should be made independent of sales activity. We argued earlier that there are nonprice characteristics of transactions from one unit to another, especially quality and timeliness. Therefore, the performance of the manufacturing division could affect the performance of the sales division in ways that are difficult to capture in a price system (because of uncertainty, lack of observability, and so on). One remedy would be for part of the performance measure of the manufacturing division to depend on the level of sales. More generally, the performance measure of individual local units could include a component reflecting the performance of other organizational units and, perhaps, the overall corporation. This would provide an incentive for managers of individual units to cooperate, avoid unnecessary frictions, and emphasize a corporate rather than a local viewpoint when managing their operations. We will return to this point in Chapter 17 when we discuss incentive contracts.

Problems of Risk Sharing[2]

We have been implicitly assuming that the managers of decentralized units care about the measure of performance of their units. Various mechanisms exist to create this motivation. Promotion chances and esteem of colleagues, for example, lead managers to prefer favorable performance measures for their units. A more explicit mechanism exists when a manager's compensation is in part determined by the performance measure. While this arrangement may seem intuitively like a good idea, it introduces additional consequences if managers are risk averse (as most people are). For if managers' compensation depends on the realization of partially random outcomes, not completely under their control, risk-averse managers may take actions that are not optimal for the firm as a whole.

The firm, or its owners, is likely to be less risk averse to a local project than any individual manager. The firm consists of a collection of imperfectly correlated projects, so that some of the project-specific risk at the local level will be diversified away at the firm level. Also, the stockholders of the firm achieve further reduction in project-specific risk by investing in a diversified portfolio of firms. The compensation and reputation of local managers, however, is strongly affected by the outcome of projects under their responsibility. These managers will find it difficult to diversify away from this project-specific risk to any substantial

---

[2] This section assumes that the reader has a working knowledge of the use of utility functions to represent a decision maker's attitude toward risk.

degree. The effect of risk aversion on a manager's decision is illustrated in an example in the appendix to this chapter.

The conflict between incentives and risk aversion is the essential dilemma of decentralization in an uncertain environment. We wish to decentralize to take advantage of the unique or private information of local managers. In order to motivate local managers to acquire this special knowledge and to exert maximal efforts to make their units profitable, we provide an incentive payment based on a measure of performance, such as profit. But when the managers' compensation is a function of the performance measure, which in turn is influenced by the realization of a noncontrollable random variable, uncertainty is introduced into their compensation schedules. This uncertainty causes managers to prefer a different level of output and lower expected profits than a risk-neutral firm or set of owners would prefer.

If central management had all the relevant information about each unit's decision problem, it could tell the local managers precisely how to act. The lack of this information, in general, forces the firm to a second-best solution in which some expected profits are foregone because of local managers' risk aversion in order to exploit the local managers' specialized knowledge and experience. This topic of optimal incentive contracts and risk sharing is being given a great deal of attention by researchers in economics, accounting, and finance; we will cover it in more detail in Chapter 17.

It is interesting that traditional cost accounting procedures, such as flexible budgeting and budgets in general, can be viewed as attempts to reduce the riskiness of local performance measures. By comparing managers' performance to predetermined standards or budgets, we are measuring their relative, rather than absolute, performances. Some factors not under the managers' control are thereby excluded from their performance measures. For example, the manager of a standard cost center, evaluated with a flexible budget, is not held responsible for the (uncertain) quantity demanded from the center by the sales division. With an annual budgeting cycle, the sales manager in a revenue center may be shielded from a sales decline caused by a forecasted decline in general economic activity. More generally, the distinction between a forecasting variance and an opportunity-cost variance, as developed extensively in Chapter 8, can be seen as an additional step that could be taken to shield a manager from the consequences of a random, uncontrollable change in the environment. In these cases the firm attempts to absorb some of the risk of the decentralized unit and thereby minimize the dysfunctional aspects of risk-averse behavior of local managers. But the use of budgets and forecasts in performance evaluation raises another set of problems—those of obtaining the requisite information.

Problems of Obtaining Information for Standards and Budgets

Standards and budgets occupy a prominent place in the literature of cost accounting, management control, and organization theory. Standard-setting and budgeting activities are so pervasive in management teaching and and practice that we tend to accept them without considering the fundamental forces that make these activities desirable. In an ideal world of certainty, costless information, and unbounded computational capability, a central decision maker can make globally optimal decisions and can direct subordinates (local managers) to implement centrally determined plans. In this setting there would seem to be little role for budgets. Such an ideal world, however, is not a good representation of the environment faced by firms. As a consequence, local managers are given degrees of decision-making authority. In order to motivate them to make decisions that are in the firm's best interests, profit-sharing incentive contracts may be instituted. But we have seen that simple profit-sharing contracts introduce uncertainty into the managers' compensation function, and that managers take actions (such as lowering output levels) to compensate for this uncertainty. This risk-avoiding behavior is not generally desirable from the viewpoint of the firm as a whole or its stockholders.

Articles published in recent years[3] have demonstrated that simple profit-sharing plans, as described in the previous section and illustrated in the appendix, are not optimal compensation contracts under conditions of uncertainty and costly or incomplete observability. Under these conditions it can be shown that contracts based on budgets or standards are superior to linear profit-sharing plans. Budget-based plans can be characterized by a penalty or at least an absence of additional compensation if performance is below a specified standard, and by the award of additional compensation if performance exceeds the standard. Thus, we are now beginning to understand that budgets and standards are useful mechanisms under conditions of uncertainty and limited observability, the same conditions that provide incentives for decentralization.

The critical problem is how to obtain information for determining budgets and standards. Much discussion is available on the role of budgets in organizations, participative budgeting, and the budgetary process (see, for example, Chaps. 5 and 10) in Horngren [1982] and all the references given in the footnotes to those chapters). Most writers advocate that managers participate in the budgetary process by providing estimates as to what results are attainable. For most companies, the budgetary process starts with preliminary budgets developed by local managers. This participation may be fine where the objective of the budgetary process is to provide the firm with information about the detailed plans of its diverse operating units and to enable the firm to coordinate these activities. But an entirely different set of issues arises if the budgets are also used to evaluate the performance of the local managers. In this case, the local managers are not just providing information that central management can use for planning and coordinating overall firm activities; they are also providing information that will affect their future compensation and promotion potential. One would be naive to think that managers are unaware of the implications to their future rewards of the information they provide to central management.

Therefore, an inherent problem in the use of budgets to control and evaluate

---

[3] See Harris and Raviv [1978], Demski and Feltham [1978], and Atkinson [1978].

the performance of managers in a decentralized environment is that of obtaining unbiased information from these managers. Local managers possess valuable, perhaps unique, information about their local environment but may not convey it truthfully. We are not suggesting that managers are evil or indifferent to the overall performance of the firm. We are suggesting that when managers will be evaluated and promoted based on comparing their performance to some standard, we should not expect managers to act contrary to their own self-interest when they are asked to provide information on the appropriate level of the standard. On occasion, this self-interest may motivate them to engage in strategic manipulation of information and misrepresentation of intentions.[4] For example, a sales manager may provide a low sales forecast so that this forecast, when used as a sales quota, may be met easily. Because of inherent uncertainty and the costliness of observation, it will generally be very difficult to detect whether an outcome different from what was predicted was due to prior misrepresentation of information or an unusually good or bad outcome.

Again, research is actively in progress to investigate "truth-inducing" incentive contracts, but this research is still preliminary. At present, we should recognize that budgets are useful devices to motivate the performance of local managers, but we lack the means to prevent local managers from acting in their self-interest by being somewhat less than candid in revealing their valuable private information for the budgetary process. The local managers' selective or distorted information disclosure is an additional cost of decentralization.

The Agency Problem

A further problem arises in decentralization if a local manager with discretionary spending authority consumes an excessive amount of perquisites. For example, the manager may decide to improve his local working environment by acquiring large, expensively decorated office space, by hiring an unnecessarily large number of administrative assistants and support personnel, and by purchasing the latest and fanciest office equipment. These expenditures will reduce the manager's performance measure, but the manager may prefer the direct consumption of these perquisites to the perhaps small increase in pecuniary compensation that could be earned by foregoing these expenditures.

An *agency problem* exists whenever an economic agent (in this case, the local manager), who is hired to perform a certain task, can take actions that make the agent better off at the expense of the employer (such as central management and the stockholders). The agency problem arises because of local or private information; the employer finds it too costly to monitor all the manager's actions. Therefore, decentralized operations will incur an additional cost because of the overconsumption of nonpecuniary perquisites, relative to the optimal (full-infor-

---

[4] See Williamson, Wachter, and Harris [1975, pp. 256–260].

mation) trade-off between direct financial compensation for the local manager and improved working environment.

A subtle form of the agency problem arises in discretionary expense centers. In our earlier discussion we pointed out the tendency for such centers to be overstaffed and to deliver a higher quality of service than the firm would prefer to pay were the central management group fully informed on the price/quality trade-off. This occurs because many managers engage in an activity, called empire building, that attempts to increase the size of the organization they are managing. The nonpecuniary rewards of empire building include the increased power and prestige associated with managing a larger organization. These nonpecuniary factors can even become pecuniary if the managers' compensation or promotion probability is made an increasing function of the size of the units they are managing.

Agency costs refer generically to the increase in costs caused by the actions of local managers when optimizing their own welfare at the expense of the employer; in the case of empire building, the firm has a larger support staff than it would otherwise select. Agency costs exist because it is too expensive or even not possible for the firm's central management to acquire the same information possessed by local managers (such as the managers of discretionary expense centers) and to monitor all the actions these managers take.[5]

LOCAL PERFORMANCE MEASURES: A SUMMARY

In summary, some degree of decentralization seems essential for most enterprises so that they can take advantage of specialized information and action capabilities. Significant problems arise, however, when local managers are given discretion in decision making. These include:

1. Maximizing of local performance measures at the expense of the firm's global and long-range interests.
2. Interactions, frictions, and competition among decentralized units.
3. Risk-avoiding behavior by local managers.
4. Strategic misrepresentation of information by local managers.
5. Agency costs, including overconsumption of perquisites and empire building.

If these problems are not recognized and mitigated, the costs of decentralization may outweigh the benefits. It will be impossible to eliminate all of these five problems. Awareness of these problems, however, and alertness to any evidence of these behavior patterns in the actions of individual managers, should

---

[5] See Jensen and Meckling [1976] for an extensive formulation of the agency problem.

help central management limit the damage that could be caused by a too loosely controlled decentralized operation. The challenge is to devise the right combination of delegation of effort and decision making, observation of effort (perhaps with conditional variance investigations as discussed in Chapter 10), and reward or incentive schemes. At present this combination must be determined subjectively, on the basis of judgment and experience, rather than scientifically.

THE ROLE OF INSURANCE

We have seen that uncertainty, in the form of noncontrollable random outcomes, makes it difficult to develop local performance measures for the managers of decentralized units. Uncertainty leads managers to engage in risk-avoiding behavior that may not be optimal for the overall firm. It also hinders contractual arrangements between units that interact with each other and leads to a demand for subjective information to develop budgets for performance appraisal.

An insightful reader may wonder whether some form of insurance contract cannot be developed to reduce the adverse effects of uncertainty. After all, on a personal level we purchase insurance to limit the negative financial consequences from uncertain events such as death, illness, or accidents. Why cannot such arrangements be developed for commercial transactions within a firm? If local managers could purchase insurance to compensate themselves (or their divisions) from the adverse consequences of uncertainty, deleterious risk-avoiding behavior could be eliminated.

Unfortunately, there is probably good reason why insurance against uncertain events is not readily available for local managers. Two factors, moral hazard and adverse selection, make it difficult to offer reasonably priced insurance in this situation. *Moral hazard* refers to the difficulty of distinguishing between genuine risks (such as delays caused by exogenous random events) and failures to take the best action to avoid the event being insured against. Once the insured manager is protected from the negative consequences of events such as sales declines, delivery delays, or uncertain product quality, the manager's incentive to exert a maximum effort to overcome normal commercial difficulties is greatly reduced. But we do not want the manager, because he is "insured" against these events, to accept such commercial difficulties passively. We want him to do whatever he can to reach his sales target, expedite delivery, or improve product quality.

Moral hazard arises in personal insurance when people with automobile insurance drive less carefully or when people with full medical insurance coverage forego health-building activities or demand excessive amounts of medical care. Because of moral hazard, the insurer must insure not only against random factors causing losses but also against the expected reduction in effort to avoid the insured event by the insured manager. Moral hazard occurs whenever the individual or unit has some degree of control over the event being insured against and the insurer finds it costly and difficult to observe the actions of the insured.

The second factor limiting the role of insurance in reducing uncertainty within the firm is *adverse selection*. In general, the insured knows its own risks better than the insurer. The insurer may set rates on an overall fair actuarial basis after observing many similar events. High-risk units will find it profitable to purchase this insurance while low-risk units will find the insurance too expensive. The actual experience for the insurer will therefore have a higher incidence of claims than had been expected when rates were initially set. When rates are raised to reflect the higher-than-expected losses, more lower-risk units will withdraw from the insurance contract. Thus, because of the inequality of information between the insured and the insurer, there will be many units whose risks are inadequately covered. Both moral hazard and adverse selection are caused by *limited observability* (also referred to as *private* or *asymmetric information*).

Since limited observability will be characteristic of most activities within a firm, it is unlikely that insurance arrangements can be developed to eliminate the unfavorable consequences of uncertainty. Devices such as flexible budgets and annual budgeted performance can be viewed as limited forms of insurance to shield managers from some uncontrollable factors, but a significant degree of uncertainty in evaluating managerial performance is unavoidable if incentives for excellent performance are to be part of the managers' compensation arrangement.

SUMMARY

The complex environment in which business is conducted today makes it impossible for any reasonably sized firm (say, with annual sales in excess of $10 million) to be controlled centrally. Some degree of decentralization seems essential to capture the benefits of the specialized information and flexibility of response possessed by local managers. Decentralization also conserves the scarce time of the top executives and frees them from making complex, interdependent resource-allocation decisions. Providing local managers with discretion in managing their operations has the additional benefits of developing their capabilities as general managers and making their daily job a little more interesting.

Decentralization can take many forms. Repetitive processes producing well-specified and easily measured outputs can be managed as standard cost centers, where the manager is responsible for meeting externally generated demands according to a cost-minimizing, efficient standard. Marketing departments can be organized as revenue centers with the objective of meeting targeted goals in sales revenue, market share, or contribution margin. Some functions for which the output is not easily measurable or where the outputs are not causally and deterministically related to the inputs expended cannot be controlled by the use of traditional techniques such as standard costs or budgets. These functions are usually organized as discretionary expense centers in which the level of expenditures and the number of personnel are determined by negotiation with the central management to determine appropriate levels of quality and service. Much greater decentralization can occur when an operating unit is given responsibility both for acquiring inputs and for selling or distributing its outputs. Such units are organized as profit or investment centers.

While decentralization seems essential for organizing complex operations, it introduces many problems of its own. Local managers are evaluated with a performance measure that captures some but not all of the economic consequences of their decisions. Therefore, the managers may engage in dysfunctional behavior, failing to internalize the effects of their decisions on other organizational units or on the future of the entire firm. Conflicts between decentralized units can arise over the transfer of goods. With decentralization, the evaluation and compensation of local managers will usually depend on the performance measures of their divisions. Since the performance measures will be affected by random uncontrollable factors, local managers will take risk-avoiding actions to shield themselves from some of the randomness in their environment. This will typically cause them to take actions that are less risky than would be preferable for the firm as a whole.

One mechanism for reducing the adverse consequences of risk-avoiding local manager behavior is to introduce budgets and standards into the evaluation process. Obtaining unbiased information from managers for the budget-setting process, however, is not easy. The managers know that the information they are providing will later be used to evaluate their performances. Therefore, they are likely to respond to budget requests selectively and with some distortions.

All these problems are inherent costs of decentralization. We would prefer to have easy solutions to them, but the current state of the art does not provide any. The best we can do at this stage is to understand the costs as well as the benefits of decentralization, keeping alert to situations where narrow-minded local optimizing performance or misrepresentation of local information is significantly impairing the overall well-being of the firm.

APPENDIX

EFFECT OF RISK AVERSION ON A
MANAGER'S DECISION

A local manager produces a product that has a quadratic cost function. The product is sold in a perfectly competitive market but with uncertain price; that is, after the production decision is undertaken, the market price is revealed and the manager can sell whatever has been produced without affecting this market price (think of a farmer producing a crop to be sold in a highly competitive spot market immediately upon harvest). We assume the manager is paid according to a simple linear sharing rule consisting of a base wage plus a share of any profits or losses.

We have the following notation:

$$\tilde{a} = \text{random price of the commodity,}$$

$$b_0 + b_1q + b_2q^2 = \text{total cost of producting } q \text{ units of the commodity (with } b_0, \\ b_1, b_2 > 0),$$

$$w = \text{wage rate of manager,}$$

$$U(\cdot) = \text{utility function for wealth of manager, assumed to be in-} \\ \text{creasing and concave to represent the risk aversion of the} \\ \text{manager; that is, } U'(\cdot) > 0 \text{ and } U''(\cdot) < 0.$$

The manager's problem is to choose output, q, to maximize

$$EU\{w + k[\tilde{a}q - (b_0 + b_1q + b_2q^2)]\}.$$

This is a highly simplified utility function for the manager. In general, we would need to insure that w is high enough to attract managers to the position and where they are exposed to some risk. Also, since the manager may experience some disutility from working hard to maximize the performance measure, the profit-sharing parameter, k, would have to be large enough to compensate the manager for the disutility of effort. In this simple example, however, we just need k to be positive (but perhaps quite small) in order to provide an incentive for good decision making.

Before solving the problem for the risk-averse manager, consider the situation from the point of view of a risk-neutral manager (or owner) with $U(x) = x$ (linear utility). The risk-neutral manager will choose q to maximize expected profits:

$$\max E\{w + k[\tilde{a}q - (b_0 + b_1q + b_2q^2)]\}$$
$$= w + k[qE(a) - (b_0 + b_1q + b_2q^2)].$$

Computing the first derivative with respect to q and setting it equal to zero (to obtain the maximum; the second-order condition is easily verified since $b_2 > 0$), we have

$$k[E(a) - b_1 - 2b_2q] = 0$$

or

$$q^* = \frac{E(a) - b_1}{2b_2}$$

as the optimal output for the risk-neutral manager.

Returning to our more normal risk-averse manager, the first-order condition yields

$$\frac{dEU(\cdot)}{dq} = E(U'\{w + k[\bar{a}q - (b_0 + b_1q + b_2q^2)]\}$$

$$\times \, k[\bar{a} - b_1 - 2b_2q]) = 0$$

or

$$EU'(\cdot)(\bar{a} - b_1 - 2b_2q) = 0,$$

$$q = \frac{1}{2b_2}\left\{\frac{E[\bar{a}U'(\cdot)]}{EU'(\cdot)} - b_1\right\}.$$

Using the identity $E(XY) = E(X)E(Y) + \text{Cov}(XY)$, we obtain

$$q = \frac{1}{2b_2}\left\{\frac{E(\bar{a})E[U'(\cdot)]}{EU'(\cdot)} + \frac{\text{Cov}\,[\bar{a},\,U'(\cdot)]}{EU'(\cdot)} - b_1\right\}$$

or

$$q = \frac{1}{2b_2}\left\{E(\bar{a}) - b_1 + \frac{\text{Cov}\,[\bar{a},\,U'(\cdot)]}{EU'(\cdot)}\right\}.$$

The first two terms in this expression equal the optimal output for the risk-neutral manager. By the concavity of $U(\cdot)$ we can show that $\text{Cov}\,[\bar{a},\,U'(\cdot)]$ is negative, so that the output quantity for the risk-averse manager is less than that for the risk-neutral manager. This is a common occurrence; in most situations risk aversion leads to lower output and lower expected profits. The optimal output is independent of the manager's wage, w, and the profit-sharing parameter, k, because of our simplifying assumptions, mentioned earlier, of no disutility to the manager's effort and no recognition of what the manager could earn in another position.

PROBLEMS

13-1. *Decentralizing Decision-Making in a Large Organization*

"We just could not react fast enough within the corporate structure," said Charles F. McErlean, Executive Vice-President and Chief Operating Officer of United Airlines.* Mr. McErlean was describing the motivation for decentralizing United Airlines' management structure. United, the largest airline in the U.S., had just split its route structure into three semiautonomous regions: Western, Central, and Eastern. The three regional divisions would compete with other airlines for passengers and with each other for earnings performance. In addition, 1,700 cost centers were

* "How United Airlines pulled out of its dive," *Business Week* (June 29, 1974) pp. 66–70.

identified and their individual managers made responsible for productivity and cost control.

Edward Carlson, the CEO of United Airlines, claimed "our people out in the field really know their own immediate operations so much better than we do at headquarters. We can provide over-all direction, but they can better make most of the routine decisions." These daily decisions included marketing programs, advertising levels and copy, service levels between cities in the region, type of in-flight meals served, and personnel staffing requirements.

The separation of United into three regional divisions created some surprises. The Central and Western regions discovered that their main competition came from other regional airlines (such as Continental and Western) rather than United's traditional transcontinental rivals American Airlines and TWA. Also, regional managers looked much harder at aircraft allocation decisions. The Denver regional manager revealed, "I wanted very much to put a 747 on the Denver-Hawaii trip but I knew there would be $350,000 in expenses for ground equipment charged to my income statement before the first planeload left. I decided to postpone a 747 flight for at least a year." Before the implementation of decentralized operations, the decision as to which routes would receive the latest aircraft were made centrally, based on proposals prepared and submitted by marketing managers around the country.

The new operating system was not without its costs. There was the expected confusion and disruption caused by an almost overnight switch from a highly centralized company, with nine executives making all important decisions, to a divisional and decentralized mode of operation. McErlean admitted, "It took a year for all the problems to work themselves out." The firm also greatly expanded its information and reporting system. The 1700 cost centers, which formerly operated with quarterly reports, had to institute a monthly reporting cycle and, in some cases, weekly or even daily summary of operations.

Required:

1. Comment, using the framework introduced in this chapter, on the motivation for decentralization at United Airlines. How would decentralization improve the performance and profitability of the airline? Is it possible to decentralize virtually all of the operating decisions for United Airlines?

2. What costs or difficulties were introduced by decentralizing decision-making at United Airlines? Why was there an increase in the information collected and analyzed by United's managers?

13-2. Emphasis on Short Term Performance

A recent article* criticized business schools and their graduates. "A lot of what is preached at business schools today is absolute rot," claimed a New York financial consultant; ". . . Business schools teach that business is nothing but the numbers—and the numbers only for the next quarter."

The over-emphasis on short term performance measures was echoed by other critics, "There has been too much emphasis on short-term profit, not enough on

---

* "The Money Chase," TIME (May 4, 1981) pp. 58–65.

long-range planning, too much on financial maneuvering, not enough on the technology of producing goods; too much on readily available markets, not enough on international development."

One U.S. expert on productivity added, "Our managers still earn generally high marks for their skill in improving short-term efficiency, but their counterparts in Europe and Japan have started to question America's entrepreneurial imagination and willingness to make risky, long-term investments."

Finally, even foreign executives criticized the U.S. system, "The misguided emphasis on short-term profit seems to blind U.S. managers to the need for more research and development; moreover, they appear unable to develop strategies for dealing with long-range problems of chronic inflation and soaring energy costs. Also the quality of U.S. manufactured goods is declining because managers have cared less about what they produce than about selling it."

Required:

1. Are business schools, in general, and cost accounting/management control courses, in particular to blame for the alleged preoccupation of recent business school graduates with measurable short term performance?

   What conditions provide the environment for short term rather than long term optimizing behavior?

2. What forces provide explanations for the accusations that U.S. managers are more concerned with short term "safe" strategies rather than longer-term risky, entrepreneurial strategies?

3. What are the implications of these charges for the design of management control systems in decentralized organizations?

13-3.   *Externalities and Variance Analysis* (A. Atkinson)

Comox Corporation manufactures and distributes a line of high-quality men's shirts. The company is organized on a responsibility center basis. Purchasing, Cutting, Assembly, and Marketing are four of the departments in this firm.

The company follows the procedure of isolating variances and assigning the variances to departments. The corporate controller, Ralph Smart, has provided the following data regarding standards per unit.

Sales Price			$30
Costs			
Material:			
1 yard @ $10.00		$10	
Labor:			
Cutting—$\frac{1}{2}$ hour @ $8	$4		
Assembly—$\frac{1}{2}$ hour @ $12	6	10	
Overhead:			
Variable—$2 per direct labor hour	$2		
Fixed—Allocated as $1 per D.L.H.	1	3	
Selling:			
Variable—4% of selling price	$1		
Fixed—Allocated as 100% of variable	1	2	25
Profit Per Unit			$ 5

During the past period, actual results are as follows:

Sales (Actual 50,000 planned 70,000)	$1,250,000
Costs—	
Material 60,000 yards @ $8	480,000
Labor—30,000 hours @ $8	
—28,000 hours @ $12	576,000
Overhead: variable: 58,000 hours @ $2.20	127,600
fixed actual	70,000
Selling: variable: 1,250,000 × .05	62,500
fixed actual	70,000
Net Income (Loss)	($ 136,100)

A conventional variance analysis produced the following:

Materials Usage (10,000 × 10)	$100,000	U
Materials Price (60,000 × 2)	120,000	F
Labor Usage (5,000 × 8 + 3,000 × 12)	76,000	U
Overhead Efficiency (8,000 × 2)	16,000	U
Overhead Spending (58,000 × .2)	11,600	U
Selling—Variable Cost (1,250,000 × .01)	12,500	U
Selling—Price (50,000 × 5)	250,000	U
	($346,100)	U

Ralph proposed allocating these variances as follows:

Purchasing		$120,000	F
Cutting	Material	100,000	U
	Labor	40,000	U
	Overhead—E	10,000	U
	—S	6,000	U
Assembly	Labor	36,000	U
	Overhead—E	6,000	U
	—S	5,600	U
Marketing	Cost	12,500	U
	Price	250,000	U
		$346,100	U

The proposal created an uproar in the normally peaceful firm. Joe Green, Manager of the Cutting Division, argued that the unfavorable variances experienced in his department were due to inferior materials acquired by the Purchasing Department. These inferior materials caused excessive rework and usage and created production delays. In addition, Joe argued that the entire favorable purchase price variance should not be allocated to Purchasing. The joint variance of $20,000 [(60,000 − 50,000) × (10 − 8)] should be assigned to Cutting and Assembly.

Frank Brown, the Manager of the Assembly Division, argued that the unfavorable variances in his department were due to low-grade material and also due to scheduling inefficiences caused by delays in the Cutting Department.

Red Jones, Manager of the Marketing Division, added, "I don't care who is blamed, but the production delays this year caused us to lose at least 20,000 units of sales and has alienated customers. This may have an adverse effect on future sales. We have had to cut prices just to prevent a landslide.''

Required:

Comment on how responsibility for these variances should be assigned and propose a specific allocation for the variances.

13-4. *Divisional Profit Maximizing and Externalities* (A. Atkinson)

Monroeville Chemicals manufactures two specialty chemicals, Alpha and Beta, which are widely-used industrial solvents.

For control purposes, the company is organized on a profit center basis into two divisions: the Alpha Division and the Beta Division. Each Division Manager receives a bonus based on the profits of his/her division.

In the Alpha Division 1,000 gallons of Gamma, an externally purchased solvent, are combined with 20 process hours, $1,000 of materials, and 50 direct labor hours to produce 1,000 gallons of Alpha.

In the Beta Division 1,000 gallons of Gamma are combined with 10 process hours, $1,500 of materials, and 40 direct labor hours to produce 1,000 gallons of Beta.

Direct labor costs the firm $15 per hour and each process-hour costs $1,000. Gamma costs $5.00 per gallon.

Resource availabilities are as follows:

Maximum process hours, Alpha Division:	12,000
Maximum direct labor hours, Alpha Division:	40,000
Maximum process hours, Beta Division:	7,000
Maximum direct labor hours, Beta Division:	24,000
Maximum Gamma:	1,000,000 gallons

There is unlimited demand for both Alpha and Beta which can be sold for $30 and $20 per gallon respectively.

Required:

1. What is the optimal production plan from the point of view of the Alpha Division? How many gallons of Gamma will be used?

2. What is the optimal production plan from the point of view of the Beta Division? How many gallons of Gamma will be used?

3. What is the optimal production plan from the point of view of the firm? How many gallons of Gamma will be used? What is the marginal value of Gamma to the firm?

4. What problems arise if the Alpha and Beta Divisions are allowed to pursue their profit-maximizing plans (computed in Questions 1 and 2) independently? How can a centralized purchasing division of Monroeville Chemicals alleviate these problems? What problems would arise from centralized resource acquisition and allocation?

13-5. Bargaining Strategies in a Decentralized Organization (A. Atkinson)

Maccan Motors is an automobile dealership which, for organizational purposes, is divided into three departmental profit centers: New Car Sales, Used Car Sales, and Service. The manager of each department has been instructed to attempt to maximize the profits of his department. Unfortunately, the three departments frequently interact since the Service Department does dealer preparation and warranty work for new cars, and repairs used cars to get them ready for sale. Also, most of Maccan's used car supply arises from trade-ins on new car purchases.

Each year the Managers of the three service departments negotiate transfer prices on all commodity transfers which take place within the firm. This year the stumbling block to harmonious intra-firm relations is the price at which shop labor is to be charged out to the Used Car Department.

Ralph Smart, the owner and President of Maccan Motors, has a strictly "hands-off" policy regarding divisional inter-relationships and refuses to get involved in the squabbles which often arise. Ralph says "The boys sort these things out themselves and this is consistent with the spirit of decentralization."

The acrimony between Al Green, the Manager of the Service Department, and Joe Brown, the Manager of the Used Car Department is especially strong this year. In fact, the men are not speaking to each other and are sending their representatives to the final negotiation sessions.

Each manager has two bargaining strategies: cooperative and noncooperative. The potential divisional profits for this area of the business are as follows:

Bargaining Strategy Used Car	Bargaining Strategy Service Dept.	Payoff Used Car	Payoff Service Dept.
Cooperative	Cooperative	$500,000	$400,000
Cooperative	Non-cooperative	100,000	600,000
Non-cooperative	Cooperative	700,000	100,000
Non-cooperative	Non-cooperative	200,000	200,000

Each manager has decided to instruct his representative on the bargaining strategy to use. The representative will then enter negotiations and implement the strategy without further communication.

Hint: Students wishing to peruse background material for this problem are directed to a discussion of the prisoner's dilemma in any game theory text.

Required:

1. What is Al's optimal strategy?
2. What is Joe's optimal strategy?
3. From the point of view of Ralph, what are the optimal strategies?
4. Bearing in mind Ralph's preference for non-interference, what solution do you propose for the issue raised in Question 3?
5. (Independent of Questions 1–4) What overall guidance would you provide to Ralph Smart on how interactions should be handled among service

departments. For example, how should the value of a used car obtained in a trade-in be determined; how should the charge for required repairs to used cars be determined? What benefits or problems arise from Ralph's philosophy of complete decentralization of decisions to the three departments?

13-6. Monitoring Local Performance v. Choosing a Local Performance Measure (A. Atkinson)

Cumberland Fast Foods runs a chain of fast food restaurants.

All operating procedures are dictated by the Head Office and communicated to the individual restaurants via operations manuals. Restaurants are run by individual managers according to these central office directives. The restaurant operations are supervised by Head Office inspectors who monitor local operations and bring them into line with corporate policy.

Recently concern has been expressed about this style of operation. The manager, Ralph Smart, of the Southampton Restaurant complains that Head Office directives are not uniformly suitable for all restaurants. Ralph believes that individual managers should be free to respond to the local situation as required.

On the basis of past experience, the corporate controller predicts the Southampton annual profit is:

$$R = 100,000 + 15,000t + 4,500t^2$$

where t is the number of visits of the inspector per year. The cost function for the inspector who visits Ralph's restaurant is:

$$C = 20,000 + 10,000t + 5,000t^2$$

Ralph expects that if he is allowed to run the Southampton Restaurant with a free hand (i.e., no inspectors) that he could generate a profit of $100,000 per year. Ralph indicates that this would call for enhanced effort on his behalf and he would expect to be compensated with his current salary plus 10 percent of the increase in divisional profits which result from his restaurant.

Required:

Should Ralph be allowed independence in running the Southampton Restaurant?

13-7. Decentralization, Information Specialization, and Information Costs (A. Atkinson)

Marner Company manufactures and distributes a specialized novelty item. The company operates in two distinct marketing regions: East and West. In the conservative East region, demand may be either 200 or 300. In the frontier West region demand is more volatile and may be 100 or 400.

The product's wholesale price is $100. All products are manufactured at a central facility. The company's total manufacturing cost (*TMC*) function has been estimated using curve fitting as

$$TMC = (7/15,000)X^3 - (74/150)X^2 + (208\ 2/3)X - 8,400$$

where X is total output. All distribution costs are paid by middlemen.

Demand is distributed according to the following table of *joint* probabilities.

		Demand West	
		100	400
Demand East	200	.25	.15
	300	.15	.45

All production which is not sold is disposed at zero salvage value.

Traditionally, Marner Company has been managed as a highly centralized operation with all decisions made at the Head Office on the basis of the above information.

J. Felski, President of Marner, is now considering four additional organizational possibilities:

1. *Centralized—Full Information*

   Under this option an agent would be sent into each marketing region. The agents, because of their market proximity, would be able to ascertain the actual periodic demand in each market and report that information to Head Office before a production decision was made.

2. *Centralized—East Information*

   Under this option an agent would be sent into the East market only. The agent would observe actual demand and report that demand to Head Office before a production decision was made.

3. *Centralized—West Information*

   Under this option an agent would be sent into the West market only. The agent would observe actual demand and report that demand to Head Office before a production decision was made.

4. *Decentralized*

   Under this option an agent would be sent into each market, observe demand, and then, independently of the agent in the other market, make a production decision.

It costs $3,000 to send an agent into a market. In addition, for each communication received at Head Office, there is an out-of-pocket cost of $500 to evaluate the message and compute strategies.

Required:

1. If Marner is an expected profit maximizer, what is the optimal organization structure and what are the optimal operating rules within that structure?

2. Suppose the cost of observation and communication are variable. Develop

a decision rule for Mr. Felski to choose an optimal structure based on values of observation (O) and communication (C).

13-8. Adverse Selection Problem (A. Atkinson)

Able Cain the owner/operator of Butler Farms is making his plans for the forthcoming harvest.

Butler Farms grows strawberries, and each summer Cain must hire workers to harvest the crop.

There are two types of workers: high productivity and low productivity. Each type of worker knows his or her productivity but the worker productivity is unknown to Able at the time the worker is hired.

When the worker is hired, he or she makes a commitment to work for two weeks. The individual worker's output depends upon two things: the worker type and harvesting conditions. Harvesting conditions depend upon the crop, the weather and the location of berries on the bushes.

Harvesting Conditions

		Good	Poor
Worker Type	High	3	2
	Low	2	1

The table gives output, for the two week period, in standard containers, under the four possible situations.

Cain is on excellent terms with the union which demands two things:

a.   all workers are offered the same contract

b.   contracts must be signed at the start of the season.

Cain is risk neutral in evaluating decisions. Farm workers tend to be highly risk averse. All farm workers have the opportunity of alternative employment, requiring similar effort, which promises a fixed wage for the two week period of $600.

All individuals agree on the following probabilities

$$P_r \text{ (harvesting condition Good)} = 0.6$$

$$P_r \text{ (worker type High)} = 0.5$$

Required:

1.   Comment on the type of contract which should be offered to the prospective farm worker if output can be observed.

2.   Assume the same data as before except that each worker can produce 1, 2, or 3 containers of output but with varying probability depending on type and weather conditions. Probabilities are as follows:

	Output		
	1	*2*	*3*
High Skill Worker, Good Conditions	0.1	0.1	0.8
Low Skill Worker, Good Conditions	0.1	0.7	0.2
High Skill Worker, Poor Conditions	0.2	0.6	0.2
Low Skill Worker, Poor Conditions	0.7	0.2	0.1

How does this change your response to Question 1?

13-9. *Decentralization: Cost and Profit Centers**

Western Pants, Inc., is one of America's oldest clothing firms. Founded in the mid-nineteenth century, the firm weathered lean years and depression largely as the result of the market durability of its dominant, and at times only, product—blue denim jeans. Until as recently as 1950, the firm had never seriously marketed other products or even additional types of trousers. A significant change in marketing strategy in the 1950s altered that course, which had been revered for 100 years by Western's management. Aggressive new management decided at that time that Western's well-established name could and should be used to market other lines of pants. Initial offerings in a men's casual trouser were well received. Production in different patterns of this basic style continued, and stylish, tailored variations of the same casual motif were introduced almost yearly.

Alert planning in the early 1960s enabled Western to become the first pants manufacturer to establish itself in the revolutionary "wash and wear" field. Further refinement of this process broadened the weave and fabric types that could be tailored into fashionable trousers and still survive enough machine washings and dryings to satisfy Western's rigid quality-control standards.

With the advent of "mod" clothing and the generally casual yet stylish garb that became acceptable attire at semiformal affairs, pants became fashion items, rather than the mere clothing staples they had been in years past. Western quickly gained a foothold in the bell-bottom and flare market, and from there grew with the "leg look" to its present position as the free world's largest clothing manufacturer.

Today Western, in addition to its still remarkably popular blue denim jeans, offers a complete line of casual trousers, an extensive array of "dress and fashion jeans" for both men and boys, and a complete line of pants for women. Last year the firm sold approximately 30 million pairs of pants.

Production

For the last twenty years, Western Pants has been in a somewhat unusual and enviable market position. In each of those years it has sold virtually all its production and often had to begin rationing its wares to established customers or refusing orders from new customers as early as six months prior to the close of the production year. Whereas most business ventures face limited demand and, in the long run, excess production, Western, whose sales have doubled each five years during that twenty-

---

* This case was developed by Charles Horngren and appears in C. Horngren, *Cost Accounting*, 5th ed. (Englewood Cliffs, N.J.: Prentice-Hall, 1982). Reproduced with permission.

year period, has had to face excess and growing demand with limited—although rapidly growing—production.

The firm has developed 25 plants in its 150-year history. These production units vary somewhat in output capacity, but the average is roughly 20,000 pairs of trousers per week. With the exception of two or three plants that usually produce only the blue denim jeans during the entire production year, Western's plants produce various pants types for all of Western's departments.

The firm has for some years augmented its own productive capacity by contractual agreements with independent manufacturers of pants. At the present time, there are nearly 20 such contractors producing all lines of Western's pants (including the blue jeans). Last year contractors produced about one-third of the total volume in units sold by Western.

Tom Wicks, the Western vice-president for production and operations, commented on the firm's use of contractors. "The majority of these outfits have been with us for some time—five years or more. Five or ten of them have served Western efficiently and reliably for over 30 years. There are, of course, a lot of recent additions. We've been trying to beef up our output, because sales have been growing so rapidly. It's tough to tell a store like Macy's halfway through the year that you can't fill all their orders. In our eagerness to get the pants made, we understandably hook up with some independents who don't know what they're doing and are forced to fold their operations after a year or so because their costs are too high. Usually we can tell from an independent's experience and per-unit contract price whether or not he's going to be able to make it in pants production.

"Contract agreements with independents are made by me and my staff. The word has been around for some years that we need more production, so we haven't found it necessary to solicit contractors. Negotiations usually start either when an interested independent comes to us, or when a salesman or product manager interests an independent and brings him in. These product managers are always looking for ways to increase production! Negotiations don't necessarily take very long. There are some incidentals that have to be worked out, but the real issue is the price per unit the independent requires us to pay him. The ceiling we are willing to pay for each type of pants is pretty well established by now. If a contractor impresses us as both reliable and capable of turning out quality pants, we will pay him that ceiling. If we aren't sure, we might bid a little below that ceiling for the first year or two, until he has proven himself. Nonetheless, I'm only talking here about a few cents at most. We don't want to squeeze a new contractor's margins so much that we are responsible for forcing him out of business. It is most definitely to our advantage if the independent continues to turn out quality pants for us indefinitely. Initial contracts are for two years. The time spans lengthen as our relationship with the independent matures."

Mr. Wicks noted that the start-up time for a new contractor can often be as short as one year. The failure rate of the tailoring industry is quite high; hence, new entrepreneurs can often walk in and assume control of existing facilities.

The Control System

"We treat all our plants pretty much as cost centers [See Exhibit 1]," Mr. Wicks continued. "Of course, we exercise no control whatever over the contractors. We just pay them the agreed price per pair of pants. Our own operations at each

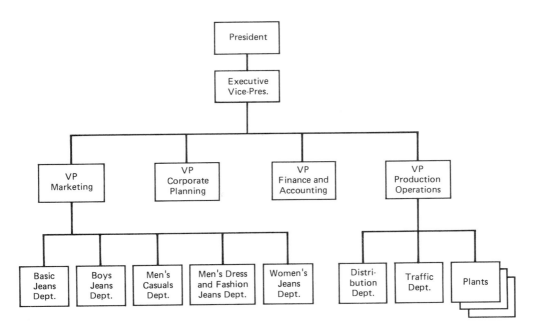

Exhibit 1   Organization Chart Western Pants Inc.

plant have been examined thoroughly by industrial engineers. You know, time-motion studies and all. We've updated this information consistently for over ten years. I'm quite proud of the way we've been able to tie our standard hours down. We've even been able over the years to develop learning curves that tell us how long it will take production of a given type of pants to reach the standard allowed hours per unit after initial start-up or a product switchover. We even know the rate at which total production time per unit reaches standard for every basic style of pants that Western makes!

"We use this information for budgeting a plant's costs. The marketing staff figures out how many pants of each type it wants produced each year and passes that information onto us. We divvy the total production up among plants pretty much by eyeballing the total amounts for each type of pants. We like to put one plant to work for a whole year on one type of pants, if that's possible. It saves time losses from start-ups and changeovers. We can sell all we make, you know, so we like to keep plants working at peak efficiency. Unfortunately, marketing always manages to come up with a lot of midyear changes, so this objective winds up like a lot of other good intentions in life. You know what they say about the road to Hell! Anyhow, it's still a game plan we like to stick to, and two or three plants making the basic blue jeans accomplish it every year.

"The budgeting operation begins with me and my staff determining what a plant's quota for each month should be for one year ahead of time. We do this mostly by looking at what past performance at a plant has been. Of course, we add a little to this. We expect people to improve around here. These yearly budgets are updated at the end of each month in the light of the previous month's production.

Budget figures, incidentally, are in units of production. If a plant manager beats this budget figure, we feel he's done well. If he can't meet the quota, his people haven't been working at what the engineers feel is a very reasonable level of speed and efficiency. Or possibly absenteeism, a big problem in all our plants, has been excessively high. Or turnover, another big problem, has been unacceptably high. At any rate, when the quota hasn't been made, we want to know why, and we want to get the problem corrected as quickly as possible.

"Given the number of pants that a plant actually produces in a month, we can determine, by using the standards I was boasting about earlier, the number of labor hours each operation should have accumulated during the month. We measure this figure against the hours we actually paid for to determine how a plant performed as a cost center. As you might guess, we don't like to see unfavorable variances here any more than in a plant manager's performance against quota.

"We watch the plant performance figures monthly. If a plant manager meets his quota and his cost variances are OK, we let him know that we are pleased. I almost always call them myself and relay my satisfaction, or, if they haven't done well, my concern. I think this kind of prompt feedback is important.

"We also look for other things in evaluating a plant manager. Have his community relations been good? Are his people happy? The family that owns almost all of Western's stock is very concerned about that."

A Christmas bonus constitutes the meat of Western's reward system. Mr. Wicks and his two chief assistants subjectively rate a plant manager's performance for the year on a one-to-five scale. Western's top management at the close of each year determines a bonus base by evaluating the firm's overall performance and profits for the year. That bonus base has recently been as high as $3,000. The performance rating for each member of Western's management cadre is multiplied by this bonus base to determine a given manager's bonus.

Western's management group includes many finance and marketing specialists. The casewriter noted that these personnel, who are located at the corporate headquarters, were consistently awarded higher ratings by their supervisors than were plant managers. This difference consistently approached a full point. Last year the average rating in the corporate headquarters was 3.85; the average for plant managers was 2.92.

Evaluation of the System

Mia Packard, a recent valedictorian of a business school, gave some informed opinions regarding Western's production operation and its management control procedures.

"Mr. Wicks is one of the nicest men I've ever met, and a very intelligent businessman. But I really don't think that the system he uses to evaluate his plant managers is good for the firm as a whole. I made a plant visit not long ago as part of my company orientation program, and I accidentally discovered that the plant manager 'hoarded' some of the pants produced over quota in good months to protect himself against future production deficiencies. That plant manager was really upset that I stumbled onto his storehouse. He insisted that all the other managers did the same thing and begged me not to tell Mr. Wicks. This seems like precisely the wrong kind of behavior in a firm that usually has to turn away orders! Yet I believe the quota system that is one of Western's tools for evaluating plant performance encourages this type of behavior. I don't think I could prove this, but I suspect that most plant managers aren't really pushing for maximum production. If they do increase output, their quotas are going to go up, and yet they won't receive any immediate monetary rewards to compensate for the increase in their responsibilities or requirements. If I were a plant manager, I wouldn't want my production exceeding quota until the end of the year.

"Also, Mr. Wicks came up to the vice-presidency through the ranks. He was a plant manager himself once—a very good plant manager. But he has a tendency to feel that everyone should run a plant the way he did. For example, in Mr. Wicks' plant there were eleven workers for every supervisor or member of the office and administrative staff. Since then, Mr. Wicks has elevated this supervision ratio of 11:1 to some sort of sacred index of leadership efficiency. All plant managers shoot for it, and as a result, usually understaff their offices. As a result, we can't get timely and accurate reports from plants. There simply aren't enough people in the offices out there to generate the information we desperately need *when we need it!*

"Another thing—some of the plants have been built in the last five years or so and have much newer equipment, yet there's no difference in the standard hours determined in these plants than the older ones. This puts the managers of older plants at a terrific disadvantage. Their sewing machines break down more often, require maintenance, and probably aren't as easy to work with."

Required:

Evaluate the management control system used for Western's plants. What changes should be given serious consideration?

13-10. Cost and Profit Centers*

Laitier S.A.

"It is terribly frustrating to be evaluated as a profit center when I do not have complete control over revenues," said Henri Goudal, Managing Director of Laitier S.A. "The Export Division is responsible for over 75 percent of our total sales. They determine the price, the destination and the quantity of most of the milk we sell. We have no direct authority over that department, yet we are held responsible when sales are poor. If they do not perform up to expectations, then we cannot meet the budgeted profit target for which we are held responsible by headquarters."

Company Background

Laitier S.A. was a Belgian-based subsidiary of Universal Brands, a widely diversified U.S. food manufacturer. Of Laitier's fiscal 1975 sales of 2,300 million Belgian francs, 2,140 million (93 percent) were milk products, 90 million (4 percent)

* Copyright © 1975 by the President and Fellows of Harvard College. Reproduced by Permission. This case was prepared by William A. Sahlman under the supervision of Professor M. Edgar Barrett.

were metal cans, and 70.0 million (3 percent) were pet food products. Laitier had two milk processing plants in Belgium, one making evaporated milk and the other condensed (sweetened) milk. These plants supplied products for export to more than 80 countries spread throughout Eastern Europe, Africa, the Pacific Basin and Central and South America. No milk products were sold within Belgium.

Laitier also had a can manufacturing plant in Belgium. Half of the output of that plant was used internally, and half was sold to outside customers, including Universal's German subsidiary. Finally, Laitier was in the process of introducing a line of Denmark-manufactured pet food products into the Belgian market.

Approximately 76 percent of Laitier's total milk production in terms of volume (72 percent of milk product revenues) was evaporated milk. The remaining 24 percent (28 percent) was condensed milk. Both products were sold to two different categories of outlets. The first category was foreign governments who purchased large quantities of milk for distribution to the poor. The second category for Laitier was the more traditional retail-oriented distribution network. That is, Laitier's products were sold to local distributing agents in each country who would in turn sell the milk to retail outlets.

Sales destined for retail distribution were handled by Universal's Export Division, a separate company from Laitier. Both companies were located in Brussels, Belgium. The Export Division was headed by a General Manager who reported directly to the Vice-President of Marketing at Universal Headquarters in Chicago. The General Manager of the Export Division had no formal reporting relationship with the Managing Director of Laitier, though it was necessary to coordinate the activities of the two groups. Well over 75 percent of Laitier's unit production (and of milk product revenues) was channelled through the Export Division. The Export Division also handled export sales for other European Universal subsidiaries.[1]

The remainder of Laitier's milk production was sold by an internal marketing group (See Exhibit 1). Generally, these sales were made directly to foreign governments which distributed the milk to the poor. This business was done on a bid basis, with Laitier submitting a bid directly to the foreign government, usually on a large quantity of milk. Laitier was also directly in charge of one or two markets in which the milk was intended for retail distribution. However, sales to these markets were small in relation to total sales.

The Production Process

The production process at Laitier was relatively simple. Laitier did not own any dairy farms. The company purchased milk from farmers in the area around the processing plant. There were no formal contracts between Laitier and the farmers, though the company had established a very strong, long-term relationship with its milk suppliers. As a result, Laitier felt that it had a moral if not a legal commitment to purchase all the milk produced by these farmers.

The raw milk was processed by Laitier at one of its two plants, one for

[1] As a separate company, the Export Division was not actually required to handle the milk products of Laitier. They could handle the milk from whichever Universal subsidiary had the lowest overall cost and wished to sell through them.

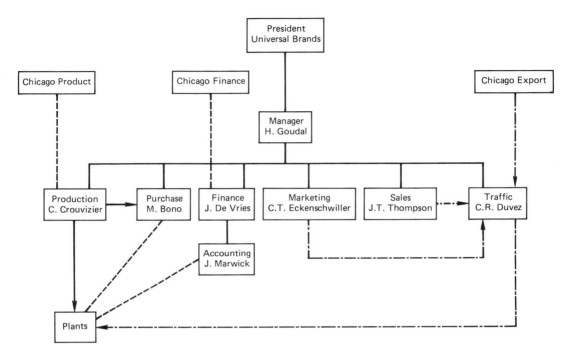

Exhibit 1   Laitier S.A.

evaporated milk and the other for condensed milk.[2] Within these two broad product categories, several variations were possible. Laitier had three standard levels of fat content milk, which it could produce according to market needs. Laitier could also produce several different standard sugar content levels in its condensed milk.

The processed milk was put into a number of standard containers. Laitier used six different sizes of tin cans and three different sizes of paper cartons. Beginning in 1972, Laitier produced its own cans, supplying approximately one-half its can needs from this source. Cartons were purchased from outside sources.

Because Laitier's products were sold in a very large number of countries, labelling created some difficulties. Laitier purchased labels from a local printer who could react quickly to their needs. Labels were printed directly on the cartons by the carton manufacturer, who also could provide the necessary flexibility to Laitier.

Once packaged, the milk was prepared for shipping by Laitier. Depending upon the final destination, the milk had different packaging requirements. Laitier was responsible for arranging for all transportation of its products, including those sold through the Export Division, to the port of final destination.

---

[2] Laitier always had the option of turning the raw milk it purchased into a less processed product such as butter. Laitier might make this kind of intermediate conversion if it believed it had an excess supply of milk or could make larger profit in the butter than on evaporated or condensed milk.

Raw Milk: Intervention Prices and Restitutions

Because raw milk was such an important cost component for Laitier, the process by which milk prices were set was of crucial importance. The price Laitier paid for raw milk was determined during periodic negotiations between all the milk users and the farmers in the region around each plant. The Belgium Government did not directly control raw milk prices. However, the European Economic Community did influence the level of prices through a system of EEC "intervention prices" for intermediate milk products (e.g., butter or powdered milk). Essentially, the EEC Agricultural Committee set a price for powdered milk, for example, which gave the farmer the option of selling his milk in unprocessed form or converting his raw milk to powdered milk and selling it directly to the EEC at the intervention price.[3,4] Because the farmer always had the option to sell to the EEC, he would not accept too low a price for his milk from processors like Laitier.

The system of intervention prices designed by the EEC was intended to maintain income stability for the farmers. However, the resulting raw milk prices were higher than those in New Zealand or in the United States, both of which were larger exporters of processed milk. In order to make EEC produced milk products competitive in the world market, the EEC had to subsidize exports through a system of restitutions. A restitution was a rebate given to processors like Laitier when they delivered their products outside the EEC. The level of restitutions was set by the EEC Agricultural Committee in Brussels and could amount to as much as one-third of the raw milk cost (See Exhibit 2). Even after restitutions, raw milk could represent as much as 50 percent of Laitier's manufacturing cost. When the intervention price levels were changed, the restitutions generally were also changed. However, there was always considerable uncertainty about the extent to which higher raw milk costs would be offset by increased restitutions.

Because the levels of intervention prices and restitutions were sensitive political issues within the EEC, planning at companies like Laitier was very difficult. To facilitate planning for milk processors, the EEC allowed exporters to "pre-fix" a restitution for the next six months. To illustrate, Laitier could tell the EEC it intended to export a certain amount of evaporated milk in the next six months. The EEC would then guarantee a restitution for that period for that quantity of exports. Unfortunately, if the intervention price increased during the six months, then Laitier was faced with higher milk costs with no relief from an increased subsidy. Also, if Laitier did not export the quantity of milk products it originally estimated with the EEC, then it was penalized, and actually had to pay a fine to the EEC. Laitier, of course, always had the option of not pre-fixing the restitution if it believed that the intervention price would increase in the near future. The hope was that the restitution would also increase, thus protecting Laitier from the higher milk costs.

In order for Laitier to determine its restitution policy and its milk and other raw materials needs, it was very important to obtain accurate forecasts of milk

---

[3] Laitier also had the option of converting some of its raw milk supply into powdered milk, for example, if it believed this was a more profitable alternative than processing the milk.

[4] In the last few years, the EEC had accumulated a surplus supply of powdered milk amounting to 1 million tons. This milk was to be distributed as development aid.

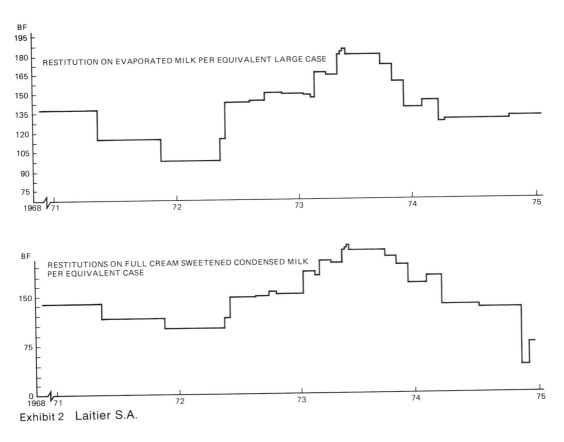

BF

RESTITUTION ON EVAPORATED MILK PER EQUIVALENT LARGE CASE

BF

RESTITUTIONS ON FULL CREAM SWEETENED CONDENSED MILK
PER EQUIVALENT CASE

Exhibit 2   Laitier S.A.

product sales. As noted previously, Laitier depended on the Export Division for the sales of over 75 percent of its milk production. Thus, Laitier had to rely on sales estimates from the Export Division to do its planning.

The process by which sales estimates were made at Laitier involved two iterative steps. First, Laitier provided unit manufacturing cost estimates to the Export Division. A distinction was made between fixed and variable costs in order to allow the marketing people to base their pricing decisions on the contribution margin of each product (See Table 1). The Traffic Department within Laitier also provided estimates of shipping costs to each of the export markets.[5] The Export Division then provided sales price and volume estimates by product line for each market to Laitier. The process involved a certain degree of negotiation between the Export Division and Laitier, though it was difficult for Laitier to question the accuracy of the Export Division's forecasts.

The internal marketing group at Laitier also had to estimate sales of milk products generated internally. These estimates—when combined with those gen-

---

[5] Transportation costs could be as high as 30% of the cost of the finished product.

TABLE 1. Laitier S.A.—Belgium Monthly Export Cost Estimates[2]

Date: August 10, 1975	Local Currency—BFr.[3] Evaporated Milk—9.0% Butter Fat		Local Currency—BFr.[3] Condensed (Sweetened) Milk	
	Large Cases	Small Cases	8% Butter Fat	Skim
Line				
1. Cases Available				
August				
September				
October				
November				
2. Milk cost	427.50	354.82	364.52	213.14
2a. Sugar	—	—	146.61	144.45
3. Packaging Material	107.80	115.81	96.71	93.02
4. TOTAL MATERIAL COST	535.30	470.63	607.84	450.61
5. Miscellaneous[1]	27.41	24.95	36.65	30.65
6. Restitution	148.76	123.05	123.35	26.95
7. TOTAL OUT OF POCKET COST	413.95	372.53	521.14	454.31

[1] Fuel, power, freight and interest expense, among others.

[2] All figures have been disguised.

[3] At time of case, one U.S. dollar was equal to approximately 39 Belgian Francs.

erated by the Export Division—formed the basis for production, purchasing and restitution policy at Laitier.

Budgeting and Performance Evaluation

The process of forecasting revenues, costs and therefore profits was formalized in Laitier's budgeting system. In August of each year, Laitier submitted to corporate headquarters a complete budget package for the next two fiscal years as well as a profit estimate for the third year.[6] The top management of Laitier made an oral presentation of Laitier's budget to Universal's management.[7] The final budget was arrived at through a process of negotiation between Laitier, the Export Division and Universal's management.

In addition to the initial budget, every month Laitier prepared a revised forecast of the current fiscal year. Every three months, a new budget for the current fiscal year was prepared. Finally, in February of each year, Laitier also submitted a revised budget for the next fiscal year (in addition to the revised budget for the rest of the current fiscal year).

---

[6] Laitier operated on an October 1 to September 30 fiscal year.

[7] Beginning in 1975, the Export Division manager was scheduled to be present at the budget presentation to Universal management.

These budgets formed the basis for performance evaluation of Laitier during the year. Universal required two different types of reports from Laitier. First, every month Laitier had to submit a brief (5–6 page) summary of its operations. Second, each quarter Laitier had to submit a series of reporting forms. The first group of forms showed the most recent budget (a complete income statement) for the next fiscal year, the revised forecast and the original budget for the current fiscal year, and the actual results for the previous fiscal year. These reports were also broken out by major product group. That is, detailed sales, costs and operating profit before tax estimates for such product groups as evaporated milk, condensed milk, pet food and cans would be shown (See Table 2).

A second series of forms showed the marketing expenses in aggregate and for each major product line. Marketing expenses included advertising, promotion, selling, distribution, commissions, and market research expenses. A third series of forms was devoted to non-operating income and expenses and to such miscellaneous items as tax computation, foreign exchange transactions and inventories.

A fourth series of forms was devoted to a detailed explanation of each item in the total company and individual product line profit and loss budgets. Laitier was required to make and analyze three comparisons. First, the most recent budget for the next fiscal year was compared to the revised budget for the current fiscal year. Each significant change from one year to the next had to be explained (See Table 3). The second required comparison was between the most recent revised budget for the current fiscal year and the original budget for the same year. Finally the most recent revised current year budget was compared with the actual prior year results.

A final series of reports was devoted to presenting and analyzing the most recent detailed manufacturing and packing cost budget for each product sold within each major product line. As with the profit and loss budgets, Laitier was required to make a series of comparisons of each significant cost item with prior budgets and with actual results from the previous year.

In summary, Laitier was responsible for preparing the initial budget and sub-

TABLE 2.   Laitier S.A. Statement of Profit and Loss[1]

		Fiscal 1976		Revised Fiscal 1975		Actual Fiscal 1974	
		PRODUCT—EVAPORATED EXPORT[2]					
1	*Net Sales in Cases*	2,422,000	Per Unit	2,262,060	Per Unit	2,006,973	Per Unit
2	Gross Sales Less Returns	1,666,505	688.07	1,453,312	642.49	1,170,161	583.04
3	Distribution Expenses	260,728	107.65	212,153	93.79	137,239	68.38
4	Trade Payments	7,823	3.23	6,628	2.93	9,272	4.62
5	Taxes and Duties						
6	Net Sales	1,397,954	577.19	1,234,531	545.77	1,023,650	510.04
7	Cost of Sales	1,258,471	519.60	1,084,742	479.55	971,158	453.99
8	Gross Profit	139,483	57.59	149,790	66.22	112,492	56.06
9	Selling Expenses	48,852	20.17	40,264	17.80	30,286	15.09
10	General Expenses	24,995	10.32	18,616	8.23	16,076	8.01
11	Operating Profit	65,636	27.10	90,910	40.19	66,130	32.96

TABLE 2. (Continued)

	PRODUCT—CONDENSED EXPORT [2]					
12	Net Sales in Cases	452,300	Per Unit	511,792	Per Unit	482,804	Per Unit

13	Gross Sales Less Returns	380,340	841.46	381,701	745.51	328,025	679.14
14	Distribution Expenses	32,924	72.84	25,231	49.28	17,180	35.57
15	Trade Payments	556	1.23	394	0.77	816	1.69
16	Taxes and Duties						
17	Net Sales	346,860	767.39	356,076	695.46	310,029	641.88
18	Cost of Sales	324,441	717.79	331,791	648.03	278,338	576.27
19	Gross Profit	22,419	49.60	24,285	47.43	31,691	65.61
20	Selling Expenses	9,257	20.48	6,164	12.04	5,356	11.09
21	General Expenses	6,197	13.71	6,103	11.92	4,907	10.16
22	Operating Profit	6,965	15.41	12,018	24.49	21,428	44.36

	PRODUCT—EVAPORATED OWN TRADE [2]					
1	Net Sales in Cases	427,000	Per Unit	374,040	Per Unit	196,781	Per Unit

2	Gross Sales Less Returns	269,411	630.94	223,529	597.67	98,811	501.58
3	Distribution Expenses	26,961	63.14	23,270	62.22	4.399	22.33
4	Trade Payments	3,484	8.16	3,856	10.31	2,488	12.63
5	Taxes and Duties						
6	Net Sales	238,966	559.64	196,403	525.14	91,924	466.62
7	Cost of Sales	225,486	528.07	181,715	485.87	91,711	465.54
8	Gross Profit	13,480	31.57	14,688	39.27	213	1.08
9	Selling Expenses	2,434	5.70	1,952	5.22	1,062	5.39
10	General Expenses	4,274	10.01	3,403	9.10	1,426	7.24
11	Operating Profit	6,772	15.86	9,332	24.95	(2,275)	(11.55)

	PRODUCT—CONDENSED OWN TRADE [2]					
12	Net Sales in Cases	320,000	Per Unit	320,256	Per Unit	361,453	Per Unit

13	Gross Sales Less Returns	279,910	874.72	240,486	751.52	255,844	708.71
14	Distribution Expenses	19,466	60.83	13,059	40.81	8,949	24.79
15	Trade Payments	1,331	4.16	2,557	7.99	2,170	6.01
16	Taxes and Duties						
17	Net Sales	259,113	809.73	224,870	702.72	244,725	677.91
18	Cost of Sales	230,877	721.49	210,678	658.37	213,647	591.82
19	Gross Profit	28,236	88.24	14,192	44.35	31,078	86.09
20	Selling Expenses	1,872	5.85	2,266	7.08	2,058	5.70
21	General Expenses	4,483	14.01	3,648	11.40	3,892	10.78
22	Operating Profit	21,881	68.38	8,278	25.87	25,128	69.61

[1] All figures in this Table have been disguised.
[2] "Export" sales were those handled directly by the Export Division. "Own Trade" sales were those handled by Laitier's marketing group.

TABLE 3. **Laitier S.A. Profit & Loss Budget & Fiscal 1975 & 1976**[1]

Detailed P & L Budget Commentary
FISCAL 1976 VERSUS REVISED FISCAL 1975[2]
Evaporated (Exports)

Line No.

1 Fiscal 1976 shows a sales volume increase of 159,940 cases. Most significant changes:
  Decrease: Jamaica 117,000, Chad 34,000, Botswana 63,500
  Increase: Nigeria 257,000, Turkey 46,440, Okinawa 26,000, Angola 20,390, Rhodesia
  24,610

2 Total *Gross Sales* per unit for fiscal 1976 is BFr. 45.58 higher, viz.

  Gross sales—Excl. restitutions

  (a result of increased selling prices)   67.38

  Export restitutions (reduced)   (21.80)

  The calculations included the last known restitution rates and are those
  effective as from March 26, 1975.

3 *Distribution expenses* per unit for fiscal 1976 is BFr. 13.86 higher.
  This can be attributed to the ever increasing freight rates since October 1974.

Condensed (Exports)

12 Fiscal 1976 sales volume is 59,492 cases lower.
  Increase: Taiwan 68,241
  Decrease: Trinidad 98,133, Botswana 29,600

13 Total *Gross Sales* per unit for fiscal 1976 is BFr. 95.95 higher, viz.

  Gross sales (excl. restitutions)

  The calculations included the last known restitution rates and are those effective as
  from March 26, 1975.

  The apparently high increase of gross sales per unit in fiscal 1976 is mainly due to
  the impact of the Bangladesh tender (100,000) in fiscal 1975 at the low selling price
  $8.04 = BFr. 313.56

  When omitting such Bangladesh sales the increase per unit mainly caused by the fact
  that in fiscal 1975 the restitutions on the above mentioned Bangladesh sales were
  "pre-fixed" at a high rate of BFr. 199.60

14 *Distribution expenses* per unit for fiscal 1976 is BFr. 23.56 higher.

  When omitting the Bangladesh business (fob deliveries) the increase per unit for
  fiscal 1976 will only amount to BFr. 1.47

  Such relatively minor increase in 1976 can be attributed to a higher incidence of fob
  shipments.

20 *Selling expenses* per unit for fiscal 1976 is BFr. 8.44 higher.

  The aparently lower expense per unit for fiscal 1975 is mainly caused by the impact
  of the Bangladesh sales at a low BFr. 1.85 commission per unit on 100,000 cases.

  When omitting the impact of the Bangladesh comissions the increase in selling expenses would be some BFr. 2.77 only and this can be explained by commissions on
  the higher average gross selling price per unit in fiscal 1976.

Evaporated—Own Trade

1 Sales volume in fiscal 1976 increased by 52,960 cases mainly due to:
  Increase: Bulgaria 10,760, Venezuela 69,000
  Decrease: Tunisia 26,800

2 Total *Gross Sales* per unit in fiscal 1976 is BFr. 33.27 higher, due to an increase in
  selling price per unit of BFr. 42.39 and a reduction in restitution rates of BFr. 9.12

  The calculations include the last known restitution rates and are those in effect from
  March 26, 1975.

TABLE 3.   (Continued)

Condensed—Own Trade

12   *Sales volume* in fiscal 1976 decreased by 256 cases mainly due to increased sales to Venezuela of 13,100 cases and reduced sales to Bulgaria of 11,000 cases and to Angola of 1,744 cases.

13   Total *Gross Sales* per unit for fiscal 1976 is BFr. 123.20 higher due to increased unit selling prices by BFr. 141.99 and to reduced restitution rates by BFr. 18.79

14   *Distribution expenses* increases by BFr. 20.02 per case in 1976 due to increased freight rates.

---

[1] All of the locations and figures in this Table have been disguised.
[2] Similar forms were also used to compare Revised 1975 with Actual 1974 and Revised 1975 with Original Budget 1975.

sequent revisions thereof. The Export Division supplied volume and price estimates for each market it controlled, and Laitier did the same for its own markets. In addition, Laitier supplied all the transportation and production cost forecasts. Laitier was also responsible for preparing the reporting forms for submission to Universal. The comparative analysis required on those forms was done by Laitier. The Export Division was asked by Laitier to explain any significant volume or price variations from budget, and their explanations were included in Laitier's reporting forms.

Laitier was evaluated by Universal as a profit center, just as were each of Universal's other foreign subsidiaries. The Export Division was also treated by Universal as a profit center. Henri Goudal, Managing Director of Laitier was evaluated by Universal on his performance relative to the budgets negotiated by Universal and Laitier. These budgets (and Laitier's reported results) covered the entire Laitier operation. Thus, the full financial impact of the sales handled for Laitier by the Export Division were included. The Export Division also received credit for these sales and their resultant contribution to profit.

The Informal Discussion

In early September, 1975 Mr. Henri Goudal and the Finance Manager of Laitier, Mr. Jan de Vries, discussed Universal's performance evaluation of Laitier with the casewriters. The conversation began when a casewriter asked Mr. Goudal for his opinion about the treatment of Laitier as a profit center. The following is a paraphrased summary of that discussion.

Goudal: Conceptually, I believe treating a subsidiary as a profit center is a very useful way to motivate managers. The problem arises, however, that, as presently organized, Laitier is not completely in control of its profits. This makes it difficult to view us as one might view some other subsidiary. For example, the other Universal subsidiaries in Europe do the bulk of their business in their domestic markets. They only export what they cannot use domestically.

Unfortunately, Laitier has not been able to operate in the Belgian market, primarily because it is incredibly price competitive. We cannot make an adequate return on our investment by selling milk products domestically. As a result, we are very much dependent on the Export Division for our sales.

However, as I said before, I have no direct authority over that department. They are responsible only to the Vice-President of Marketing back in Chicago.

De Vries: I agree with Henri. In the processed milk business, the revenues are the crucial determinants of profitability. Many of our costs are either fixed or extremely difficult to control. For example, our labor costs are only controllable in the long-run. We cannot fire people as one can in the U.S.

We can only decrease our labor force through attrition, and even that is sometimes difficult. Also, because the union we deal with bargains at the national level with all milk processors, we have very little impact on the cost of labor.

Similarly, the cost of milk, which represents a very large proportion of our total manufacturing cost, cannot really be controlled by Laitier.

The EEC basically determines our cost both by setting the intervention price and by fixing restitutions. All we can try to do is to predict EEC policy. We certainly cannot control it.

The point is that revenues are the primary factor in the profitability of our milk business. If revenues are bad, then so are our profits.

Casewriter: How does your relationship with the Export Division affect the budgeting process?

De Vries: We supply the Export Division with an estimate of our production and shipping costs. They, in turn, give us their volume and price forecasts. The problem is that it is very difficult for us to assess the reasonableness of their predictions. In the past, we have discovered that they have almost always been too optimistic. Our response to that problem has been to put reserves into our profit and loss forecast. If we didn't put in reserves, we would not be able to meet our profit target.

Goudal: One response on our part to the overall problem of not fully controlling our own destiny has been to try to exercise more control over our profits. Introducing the pet food line is an example. We wanted both to diversify away from milk products and to be solely responsible for one business venture. Our can plant provides the same diversification benefits and gives us a lower packaging cost in our milk business. We also make a very respectable profit on our external sales of cans. We have hired an extra marketing fellow here at Laitier to investigate other diversification possibilities.

REFERENCES

ANTHONY, ROBERT N., and JOHN DEARDEN, *Management Control Systems: Text and Cases,* 4th ed. Homewood, Ill.: Irwin, 1980.

ARROW, KENNETH, "Control in Large Organizations," *Management Science* X (April 1964), 397–408.

ATKINSON, ANTHONY A., "Standard Setting in an Agency," *Management Science* XXIV (1978), 1351–61.

DEMSKI, JOEL, and GERALD FELTHAM, "Economic Incentives in Budgetary Control Systems," *The Accounting Review* III (April 1978), 336–59.

DRUCKER, PETER, "Controls, Control and Management," chap. 31 in *An Introductory View of Management.* New York: Harper & Row, 1979.

HARRIS, MILTON, and ARTUR RAVIV, "Some Results on Incentive Contracts with Applications to Education and Employment, Health Insurance and Law Enforcement," *American Economic Review* LXVIII (March 1978), pp. 20–30.

HORNGREN, CHARLES T., *Cost Accounting: A Managerial Emphasis,* 5th ed. Englewood Cliffs, N.J.: Prentice-Hall, 1982.

JENSEN, MICHAEL C., and WILLIAM H. MECKLING, "Theory of the Firm, Managerial Behavior, Agency Costs and Ownership Structure," *Journal of Financial Economics,* October 1976, 305–60.

SPENCE, A. M., "The Economics of Internal Organization: An Introduction," *Bell Journal of Economics* VII (Spring 1976), 163–72.

VANCIL, RICHARD F., *Decentralization: Managerial Ambiguity by Design.* Homewood, Ill.: Dow Jones-Irwin, 1978.

WILLIAMSON, O. E., M. L. WACHTER, and J. F. HARRIS, "Understanding the Employment Relation: The Analysis of Idiosyncratic Exchange," *Bell Journal of Economics* VI (Spring 1975), 250–78.

PROFIT CENTERS AND TRANSFER PRICING

PROFIT AS A PERFORMANCE MEASURE

Profit is the most widely used measure of performance for a business firm. It is therefore not surprising that profit centers are extremely common in large decentralized organizations. Evaluating the performance of decentralized units with the same measure with which the firm as a whole is evaluated facilitates goal congruence between decentralized units and the firm.

There are many definitions of a profit center. At a purely descriptive level, one could define a profit center as any organizational unit for which some measure of profit is determined periodically.[1] But this definition fails to capture the purpose behind the organization of profit centers: to encourage local decision making and initiative. Merely assigning prices to the output of a unit, or attributing costs to the input materials to a unit, does not make that unit autonomous or independent. For our purposes, then, a *profit center* is a unit for which the manager has the authority to make decisions on sources of supply and choice of markets. In general, a profit center will be selling a majority of its output to outside customers and is free to choose sources of supply for a majority of its materials, goods, and services. With this definition, it is unlikely that manufacturing or marketing divisions will be profit centers, even though some firms may evaluate these units using a profit figure.

Many managers of profit centers are evaluated not just on profit but on the level of profit related to the fixed investment for their units. In this case we refer to the unit as an *investment center*. Return on investment and residual income are typical performance measures for investment centers. In this chapter we will restrict our attention purely to profit measurement, deferring discussion of investment centers and their performance measures to Chapter 15. A profit center

---

[1] See Vancil [1978, p. 146].

(as opposed to an investment center) is an appropriate structure for an organizational unit if the plant and equipment are stable from year to year and are not controllable by the profit-center manager. For example, if all major capital-expenditure decisions are made at the top management level, then the local profit-center manager is not controlling the level of investment and should not be held accountable for the past decisions on plant and equipment.

As discussed in Chapter 13, no single performance measure, such as profit, can capture all the economic consequences of the activities of a decentralized unit in a given period. Certainly, there is room for nonmonetary measures to supplement the profit measures of business segments. We will discuss some possible nonmonetary measures at the end of this chapter. But despite the known weaknesses of financial numbers for performance measurement, they are vital in any effective management control system for a decentralized firm. The financial accounting process provides a formal discipline for the production and collection of data. The discipline comes from the necessity for systematically accounting for all cash transactions. It is the only detailed and inflexible set of rules that the organization imposes on itself. No transaction involving the disbursement or receipt of cash will go unrecorded. Since almost any activity of the firm will ultimately trigger a cash transaction, the accounting system is comprehensive and pervasive. It is also mandatory, in order to meet financial reporting and tax requirements. For all these reasons, business organizations will continue to rely on financial measures of performance, of which profit is the most common and comprehensive.

Problems encountered in measuring profit include (1) choosing a profit index, including the allocation of costs and revenues to the center, (2) pricing the transfer of goods between profit centers. We will deal with these problems in the remainder of the chapter.

CHOOSING A PROFIT INDEX

Consider the following data from a division of the Easler Corporation:

Revenue from division sales	$15,000
Variable cost of goods sold and variable overhead	10,000
Fixed division overhead ($800 controllable, $1,200 noncontrollable)	2,000
Allocated G & A expenses of corporation	1,000

We can construct a structured divisional income statement as follows:

Revenues	$15,000
Variable costs	10,000
(1) Variable contribution margin	$ 5,000
Controllable fixed costs	800
(2) Controllable contribution	$ 4,200
Noncontrollable fixed costs	1,200
(3) Divisional contribution	$ 3,000
Allocated corporate expenses	1,000
(4) Divisional profit before taxes	$ 2,000

We have a choice of at least the four indicated measures to evaluate the division's performance.

Variable Contribution Margin

The division variable contribution margin of $5,000 is important for understanding the cost-volume-profit relationship within the division, but it is not as useful for performance evaluation. The division manager has control over at least some of the fixed costs and has the option of trading off between fixed and variable costs. Therefore, the performance of the division manager should include, as a minimum, controllable fixed costs.

Controllable Contribution

The controllable contribution of $4,200 is the total division revenues less all costs that are directly traceable to the division and controllable by the division manager. It includes fixed costs that may arise from the use of indirect labor, indirect materials, and utilities. The division manager has the option of reducing these fixed costs, since they are fixed only with respect to changes in activity levels. They can be reduced if the division manager wishes to operate a "leaner" organization.

Controllable contribution is perhaps the best performance measure of the division manager, since it reflects the manager's ability to use effectively the resources under his control and authority. An important limitation of this measure is the difficulty of distinguishing between controllable and noncontrollable fixed costs. For example, depreciation, insurance, and property taxes on fixed assets would be controllable if the division manager had the authority to dispose of these assets but would be noncontrollable if he did not have this discretion. Also salary levels of employees and supervisors may be set centrally, but the division manager may have the discretion of how many workers and supervisors to employ at the division.

Divisional Contribution

The divisional contribution of $3,000 represents the contribution the division is making to corporate profit and overhead. It evaluates more the performance of the division than the performance of the division manager. Some of the division overhead, such as the costs of the fixed assets, may result from past investment decisions made by top management. Also, the salaries of the divisional executives may be set by central management. The divisional contribution is clearly an important figure for evaluating the division's profitability, but unless the division manager is given great authority to restructure the investments or key personnel of the division, these costs are not controllable and hence they may not be relevant in evaluating the manager's performance.

Divisional Profit Before Taxes

Many companies allocate all central general and administrative expenses to their divisions. The motivation, apparently, is to alert division managers to the level of these common costs and indicate that the company as a whole is not profitable unless the revenue-producing divisions generate enough contribution margin to cover a "fair share" of central G & A costs. While it is true that profits generated by divisions must exceed centrally incurred costs before the company is profitable, there seems to be little gain from including these costs when evaluating the performance of a division or a division manager.

First, these costs are not controllable at the divisional level. Therefore, an unfavorable profit variance caused by an unexpectedly large corporate expense allocation cannot be attributed to divisional managers who have no control over expenditures on corporate staff functions.

Second, the basis for allocating corporate expenses to divisions is usually arbitrary, bearing no causal relation to the way in which divisional activities influence the level of these corporate expenses. Common allocation bases include percentage of sales, assets, or space occupied by each division. This procedure introduces an additional noncontrollable component to these allocated costs. For if the level of the allocation base (such as sales or assets) changes in other divisions, the percentage of costs allocated to a division will change even with no change in its own activity level. This effect is easily illustrated with an example.

Suppose $200,000 of corporate expenses will be allocated to three divisions proportional to their sales level as shown below:

	Expected Sales	*Percentage*	*Allocated Expenses*
Division 1	$2,000,000	40%	$ 80,000
Division 2	500,000	10	20,000
Division 3	2,500,000	50	100,000
	$5,000,000	100%	$200,000

If actual sales of Divisions 2 and 3 are below the anticipated levels, the actual allocation could be:

	Actual Sales	*Percentage*	*Allocated Expenses*
Division 1	$2,000,000	50%	$100,000
Division 2	300,000	7.5	15,000
Division 3	1,700,000	42.5	85,000
	$4,000,000	100%	$200,000

Division 1's actual sales equaled expected sales, and actual corporate expenses equaled the expected expenses of $200,000. Yet Division 1's share of corporate expenses increased from $80,000 to $100,000 because of the decline in sales of the other two divisions. Thus, under this scheme, Division 1 is being penalized for events outside its control (assuming that the activities of Division 1 did not contribute to the sales decline in the other two divisions).

If central management wishes to have divisions be profitable enough to cover not only their own operations but corporate expenses too, it is probably better to establish a profit standard, well above breakeven, that the divisions are expected to achieve. The division managers can then concentrate on increasing revenues and reducing costs that are under their control and not be concerned with analyzing costs that they cannot control and that are allocated arbitrarily.

There are two counterarguments to the proposal that noncontrollable corporate expenses not be allocated to divisions. The first is that divisions should be charged for *increments* in central corporate expenses caused by divisional activities. These incremental expenses would not sum to total corporate expenses, so that an unallocated portion of expense would still remain. But, to the extent that expenses could be traced to divisional activities, the allocation would absorb part of these corporate expenses and would properly be allocated back as the costs of providing services to the divisions. These costs should be part of the variable overhead costs of the divisions.

The second argument is that by allocating central overhead costs to divisions, the division managers are made more aware of these costs, so that they will exert pressure to keep down the costs of central staff departments. Recall, in the previous chapter, our discussion of discretionary expense centers, where we indicated the difficulty of deciding on appropriate budgets for these activities. There are strong tendencies for the costs of these centers to steadily increase through empire building, so that some counterpressure from operating managers may be useful in containing expansions of corporate staff. If the division managers are not made aware of these costs through some allocation process, they will not be as motivated to contain expansion of corporate staff functions. There is anecdotal evidence of division managers causing top management to sell the corporate airplane because the division managers were unwilling to bear the cost of centrally controlled aviation activities on their own income statements. Thus, if central management is willing to let division managers participate in decisions on the levels of corporate staff activities, a case can be made for allocating these expenses back to the divisions. But if the division managers have no control over these costs, our previous arguments against allocating them should prevail.

COMMON REVENUES

Occasionally a conflict may arise on the allocation of revenues between profit centers. This can occur if the salesmen for one division promote the sale of products made by other divisions when calling on customers. If a division receives no credit for selling the products of other divisions, there is little motivation for attempting to make such sales. A similar problem arises when branch banks are evaluated as profit centers. A customer may establish an account near her residence but conduct the majority of banking transactions with a branch near her place of work. Conflict between the branches could occur if all the revenues from time and savings deposits are credited to the home branch and the costs of supplying banking services are charged to the branch near the business location. In such instances, it seems reasonable to construct a fee schedule that would provide some compensation from the product division to a salesman from another division who makes a sale (such as a finder's fee) and from the home bank to the service bank for providing banking services. Such arrangements are complicated, and they illustrate the problems that arise from decentralized profit-directed operations.

TRANSFER PRICING

We have already noted some of the difficulties that arise when decentralized organizational units have to interact with each other. Nowhere is there greater potential for conflict in such interactions than when goods produced in one unit are transferred to a second unit. If both units are organized as profit centers, a price must be placed on such transfers; this price represents a revenue to the producing division and a cost to the purchasing division. Therefore, the transfer price affects the profitability of both divisions, so that the managers of both divisions have a keen interest in how this price is determined.

The transfer price serves two roles, which, unfortunately, may conflict. First, as a price, it is a guide to local decision making; it helps the producing division decide how much of the product it wishes to deliver and, for the purchasing division, how much of the product to acquire. Second, the prices and subsequent profit measurement help the top management to evaluate the profit centers as separate entities. But a set of transfer prices providing motivations that produce maximum profits to the firm may cause one division to operate at a loss. Conversely, a set of transfer prices that may be satisfactory for evaluating divisional performance may lead the divisions to make suboptimal decisions. This conflict between decision making and evaluation of performance is the essence of the transfer-pricing conundrum. A further conflict occurs if managers emphasize short-term performance in their transfer-price negotiations at the expense of long-run profitability of their division and the firm (recall the discussion on short- versus long-run performance in Chapter 13).

Market Prices

Under a restrictive set of conditions, which occasionally are realized in practice, the choice of a transfer price is clear. If a highly competitive market for the intermediate product exists, then the market price (less certain adjustments) is recommended as the correct transfer price. The conditions of a highly competitive market imply that the producing division can sell as much of the product as it wishes to outside customers and the purchasing division can acquire as much as it wishes from outside suppliers without affecting the price.

If the purchasing division cannot make a long-run profit at the outside market price, then the company is better off to not produce the product internally and go to the external market for its supply. Similarly, if the purchasing division cannot make a long-run profit when it must acquire the product at the external price, the division should cease acquiring and processing this product and should allow the producing division to sell all its output to the external market. With a competitive market for the intermediate product, the market price provides an excellent basis for allowing the decisions of the producing and purchasing divisions to be independent of each other.[2]

Some modifications to the pure market-price rule facilitate its use in practice. The company will usually benefit if the transaction occurs internally rather than having a producing division sell a certain amount externally while the purchasing division is acquiring the same amount from its own outside suppliers. To encourage internal rather than external transfers, a discount off market price is offered to reflect savings on selling and collection expenses and delivery, service, or warranty terms associated with external sales. This discount will encourage an internal transfer, all other factors being held equal.

Sometimes it is important for product quality that the transaction occur internally rather than externally. In this case, the market price may be adjusted to reflect the extra cost required to meet a more stringent quality standard or special features available only from internal manufacture. The challenge is to keep an accumulation of such special charges from driving the price far above the prices of comparable products available externally. A profit-conscious manager of the purchasing division will usually provide the necessary discipline.

Additional problems arise from the conflict between short-run and long-run

---

[2] This argument has been articulated on an intuitive basis. More formal arguments exist to establish the validity of the market price as an optimal transfer price under competitive conditions (see Hirshleifer [1956 and 1957] and Appendix A to Chapter VI in Solomons [1965].

considerations. An external supplier may quote a low price in an attempt to buy into the business, with the expectation of raising prices later. The company ordinarily should not switch its source of supply from an internal division to an outside company unless it is confident that the outside company will maintain the quoted price for a substantial period. A similar conflict arises when the price for the intermediate product or service is quoted on both a long-term-contract and a spot-market basis. As more of these complicating factors intrude on the price-setting process, they begin to violate our basic assumption of a perfectly competitive market for the intermediate product. When the market is not perfectly competitive, as it usually is not for most manufactured goods, the transfer-price problem gets much more complicated.

The Case for Marginal-Cost Transfer Prices

Consider an extreme case in which there is no market for the intermediate product; all transfers must be made internally. To see the complex issues that arise in this situation, we look at an example.[3]

Division A of the Nicosia Corporation is the only producer of an intermediate product used by Division B for conversion into a salable final product. Division A has fixed costs of $500 per day. Its variable costs are $0.10 per unit. Division B incurs additional costs in converting the intermediate product into salable form. It can process up to 1,000 units a day at a fixed cost of $1,250 a day. Thereafter, it incurs costs of $0.25 per unit processed per day. Division B faces a nonlinear demand curve for the final product. Its revenue forecast as a function of the number of units sold per day is shown below.

Sales in Units	Net Revenue Per Thousand Units
1,000	$1,750
2,000	1,350
3,000	1,100
4,000	925
5,000	800
6,000	666

Currently B is purchasing 2,000 units per day from A. Division A has computed that at this level of output its fixed costs are $0.25 per unit and its variable costs $0.10 per unit. It wants a markup over costs of $0.05 per unit and thereby establishes a price of $0.40 per unit for the intermediate product.

B's decision to acquire 2,000 units per day from A at this price of $0.40/unit is perfectly rational, as the analysis in Table 14-1 makes clear: Division B's profit

---

[3] This example is adapted from Solomons [1965, pp. 167–171].

TABLE 14-1. Calculation of Division B Profit (Loss) at Various Output Levels

Division B's Output (Units) (1)	B's Own Processing Costs (2)	Cost of Product from A at $0.40 (3)	B's Total Costs (4) = (2) + (3)	B's Revenue Per 1,000 Units (5)	B's Total Revenue (6) = (1) · (5)/1,000	B's Profit (Loss) (7) = (6) − (4)
1,000	$1,250	$ 400	$1,650	$1,750	1,750	$ 150
2,000	1,500	800	2,300	1,350	2,700	400
3,000	1,750	1,200	2,950	1,100	3,300	350
4,000	2,000	1,600	3,600	925	3,700	100
5,000	2,250	2,000	4,250	800	4,000	(250)
6,000	2,500	2,400	4,900	666	4,000	(900)

TABLE 14-2. Calculation of Combined Profit for Divisions A and B

Output (Units) (1)	Division A Costs (2)	Division B Costs (3)	Total Costs (4) = (2) + (3)	Total Revenues[a] (5)	Profit (Loss) (6) = (5) − (4)
1,000	$ 600	$1,250	$1,850	$1,750	$(100)
2,000	700	1,500	2,200	2,700	$ 500
3,000	800	1,750	2,550	3,300	750
4,000	900	2,000	2,900	3,700	800
5,000	1000	2,250	3,250	4,000	750
6,000	1100	2,500	3,600	4,000	400

[a] See column (6) in Table 14-1.

is maximized at $400 per day when it sets output at 2,000 units per day. Division A is making a profit of $100 per day at this output level (2,000 units at $0.40 less $500 fixed costs and $200 variable costs), so that the combined profits of the two divisions are $500 per day.

It may seem from this calculation that both divisions are operating reasonably well as decentralized profit centers. But this satisfaction is readily dispelled once we contemplate combining the two divisions and operating them to maximize total profits. In this case the marginal and total revenue for the combined division are the same as before [columns (5) and (6) in Table 14-1] but the total costs are obtained from adding together the costs of Divisions A and B at each output level. This calculation is performed in Table 14-2.

We see that total profits for the combined divisions are maximized at an output level of 4,000 units. Doubling output from the current level of 2,000 units increases profits from $500 per day to $800 per day. Therefore, decentralization has caused these two divisions of the Nicosia Company to operate at too low an output level and to forego $300 per day in profits. In general, the nature of a suboptimization in the transfer-pricing problem is that less is produced and transferred than is optimal for overall firm profitability.

A natural question at this point is whether a transfer price exists that would motivate the two managers to reach the profit-maximizing solution of an output of 4,000 units per day. Clearly, a transfer price of $0.40 was too high, since it led Division B to demand too little of the intermediate product from A. The general and theoretically correct answer to this transfer-pricing question is that the intermediate product should be transferred at the *marginal cost* of the producing division.[4] In this case the marginal cost is the variable cost of $0.10 per unit. The proof that this transfer price motivates the correct solution is illustrated in Table 14-3. We see that with a transfer price of $0.10 per unit, B's profit is maximized at an output of 4,000 units, which we already know is the globally optimal solution.

---

[4] Again, the proof of this proposition can be found in Hirschleifer [1956 and 1957] and Appendix A to Chapter VI of Solomons [1965].

TABLE 14-3. Calculation of B's Profit at a Transfer Price of $0.10

Division B's Output (Units) (1)	B's Own Processing Costs (2)	Cost of Product from A at $0.10 (3)	B's Total Costs (4) = (2) + (3)	B's Total Revenues (5)	B's Profit (Loss) (6) = (5) − (4)
1,000	$1,250	$100	$1,350	$1,750	$ 400
2,000	1,500	200	1,700	2,700	1,000
3,000	1,750	300	2,050	3,300	1,250
4,000	2,000	400	2,400	3,700	1,300
5,000	2,250	500	2,750	4,000	1,250
6,000	2,500	600	3,100	4,000	900

This latest calculation vividly illustrates the conflicts between the role of a transfer price to motivate optimal local decision making and its role to evaluate divisional performance. The transfer price of $0.10 per unit that motivates the optimizing behavior causes Division A to show a loss of $500 (from its unrecovered fixed costs) while Division B shows a profit of $1,300. While this produces a combined profit of $800, the manager of Division A will not be happy with the allocation of this profit between the two divisions. On the other hand, without imposing a marginal-cost rule, Division A has quoted a "cost-plus" price of $0.40 per unit, leading to a suboptimizing output level of 2,000 units but a more equal sharing of the total profit of $500 between A ($100) and B ($400).[5]

We have now considered two polar cases: transfers in which a competitive market exists for the intermediate product, and transfers in which there is no market at all for the product. In the first case, the market price was the appropriate transfer price, in the second, the product's marginal cost was the transfer price that motivated optimal decision making within the firm. Despite their apparent dissimilarities, these both are actually special cases of the general rule for determining an optimal transfer price. The unifying concept for obtaining an appropriate transfer price is to recognize the *opportunity cost* to the company as a whole for making the transfer. For the Nicosia company, the opportunity cost is measured by what is foregone by the supplying division when it produces the last unit of the intermediate good *and* transfers it to the buying division. The only opportunity cost of a transfer from Division A (the supplying division) to Division B is the out-of-pocket variable cost of $0.10 per unit. This represents the incremental cost that Division A incurs for producing additional units of the intermediate product.

---

[5] If this were the only product produced by A, then we could simply budget a $500 loss for A and direct it to transfer 4,000 units to B. But the transfer-price problem usually arises when only a few out of many products are involved in an internal transfer. In these cases, it is not convenient to budget losses and specify output for a few out of hundreds of different products and transactions. But if most of a producing division's output must be sold to other internal divisions, and little opportunity exists for a producing division to sell its output externally, then we should control the producing division as a standard cost center, pricing its output at standard cost, and avoiding all these transfer-pricing problems.

It may not be obvious how the opportunity-cost rule leads to transfers at market price when a competitive market exists for the intermediate product. But when a competitive market exists, the opportunity cost of the producing division (A) is no longer the out-of-pocket cost of production. The opportunity cost of an internal transfer is the loss of a potential sale to an external customer.

To see this, let us modify our example to allow for an outside market price of $0.40 per unit for the intermediate product. Is an internal transfer price of $0.10 still appropriate? At a transfer price of $0.40 per unit, we know that Division B will demand 2,000 units per day and earn a profit of $400. But Division A can now sell 4,000 units (say 2,000 units to B and 2,000 units externally) at a price of $0.40 per unit and earn $700 ($1,600 − $500 fixed costs − $400 variable costs) for a combined profit of $1,100 for the two divisions.[6] Thus, when a competitive market price exists, the opportunity cost of the transfer becomes the market price (less associated selling and distribution expenses), and this transfer price leads to a globally optimal solution, since either division can transact with external firms to sell excess production or acquire additional amounts of the intermediate product.

The Case Against Marginal-Cost Transfers

The incremental-cost rule for internal transfers (when no intermediate market exists) may be theoretically desirable, but hardly any companies follow this guideline. This suggests that the rule has defects that we have not made explicit. One problem, already mentioned, is that the supplying division will typically record a loss while large profits are allocated to the acquiring division selling the product in final form. In this case we are forcing the supplying division to operate at a loss and thereby reducing its autonomy. If the transferred product represents a small fraction of the total output of the supplying division, this may be only a minor annoyance. If, however, the great majority of the supplying division's output must be transferred internally, and no external reference prices for these products exist, then it is probably best to recognize that it is a fiction to treat the supplying division as a profit center. The division should either be controlled as a standard cost center or combined into a larger profit center with a division that processes the bulk of its output.

A second problem with incremental-cost transfers occurs if the marginal cost is not constant over the range of output. In this case, the supplying division must supply a marginal-cost schedule to the acquiring division. The situation gets even more complex if there is more than one purchasing division, so that the level of output is jointly determined by the separate decisions of each purchasing division. This would require an iterative solution, as the supplying division varied its marginal cost according to the shifting demands of the purchasing divisions,

---

[6] In fact, in this situation Division A should produce as much of the product as it can or until its incremental costs rise to the market price of $0.40 per unit.

or else a combined decision among all divisions involved. (This situation is illustrated in a problem at the end of the chapter.)

The marginal-cost rule also starts to break down when the supplying division is operating near a capacity constraint. In this case the opportunity cost shifts suddenly from the variable cost, when operating below capacity, to the profits foregone when the supplying division can no longer meet all the demands for the product. When demand is at or above the capacity of the supplying division, incremental costs are well below the opportunity costs of production and provide poor guidance for resource-allocation decisions. It is tempting to try a mathematical programming solution whenever capacity constraints arise, especially when the dual or shadow prices from such an approach seem to represent appropriate opportunity costs (or transfer prices) for the scarce resources. We will discuss programming approaches to the transfer-pricing problem later in the chapter, where we will show that they are not a panacea to this problem.

Marginal-cost transfer prices also provide an incentive for the manager of the supplying division to misrepresent the cost function of producing the intermediate product. If the transfer is to occur at marginal cost, and if the manager of the producing division is evaluated on the basis of the profits of this division, it is in the best (short-run) interest of the manager to overstate the marginal cost of production and thereby obtain a higher transfer price. All the deterministic models used to prove the optimality of the marginal-cost procedure assume that the cost function is known or that the manager will truthfully report it when asked. But there are strong incentives for the manager to misrepresent the marginal-cost function, since this will increase the transfer price and thereby increase divisional profits.

For example, in our two-division example of the Nicosia Company, the manager of Division A may claim that all costs are variable and that at the previous output level of 2,000 units the incremental costs are $0.35 per unit. (Recall that the actual costs of Division A at this output level are $700, of which $500 were fixed.) At this price, a computation similar to that performed in Table 14-1 reveals that Division B would earn maximum profits of $500 at a volume of either 2,000 units or 3,000 units. Assuming B decided to order 3,000 units, Division A would earn revenues of $1,050 and incur fixed costs of $500 and variable costs of $300, for a profit of $250. The manager of Division A is much happier at this transfer price of $0.35, since the division now shows a profit of $250 as opposed to the $400 loss reported at the marginal-cost transfer price of $0.10 per unit. The firm as a whole suffers, since it earns only $750 in profit per day ($250 for A, $500 for B) at an output level of 3,000 units as opposed to the maximum profit of $800 that could be earned at an output level of 4,000 units. Of course the Division A manager may have to explain how a profit of $250 was earned when transfers were supposedly made at incremental cost. An appeal to cost-saving efficiencies or reduced incremental costs when increasing output from 2,000 to 3,000 units per day might serve to counter this accusation.

This incentive for misrepresenting local information was mentioned in Chapter 13. When managers are asked to provide information for decision making that will also be used to evaluate managerial performance, we should expect some "strategic manipulation of information." The distorted information will improve the local performance measure but at the expense of overall firm profits. Thus marginal-cost transfers (1) conflict with the divisional autonomy of profit centers, (2) are difficult to implement if the marginal cost varies over the range of demanded output, especially if there is more than one purchasing division, (3) may be indeterminate as the supplying division reaches capacity, and (4) provide incentives for the supplying division to misrepresent its cost function.

Incremental Cost Plus Fixed Fee

One variation of the marginal-cost transfer-price scheme that has some desirable properties is to price all transfers at incremental cost but charge the purchasing division a fixed fee for the privilege of obtaining these transfers at incremental cost. Under this scheme, the purchasing division pays incremental cost for additional units, so that when it chooses an output level to maximize profits, by equating marginal cost to marginal revenue, it is seeing the appropriate marginal costs of the producing division. The producing division has the opportunity to cover its fixed costs and earn a profit through the fixed fee charged each period. The fixed fee represents a reservation price that the purchasing division is paying for the privilege of acquiring the intermediate product at marginal cost. The fee can be established on the basis of budgeted fixed costs plus a percentage return on the capital invested in the product line.

The purchasing division can evaluate the total cost of acquiring the intermediate product internally by adding the fixed fee plus incremental costs and dividing this sum by estimated volume. This amount can be compared to the acquisition cost of a comparable product from outside suppliers; if it is too high, the company has a signal that the fixed fee is excessive or that the producing division is not as efficient as outside suppliers.[7]

This approach, of a budgeted fixed fee to cover period costs and a return on capital, plus incremental cost per unit for each unit transferred is exactly analogous to the proposal made in Chapter 11 for charging for the cost of service departments. It leads to efficient resource allocation among divisions while still letting purchasing divisions see the full cost of obtaining goods or services from other divisions. The system begins to break down if the supplying division is operating at or above capacity so that variable costs no longer represent the opportunity costs of additional transfers.

There may also be difficulties if the demand for the final product contracts. The producing division is assured of recovery of its costs plus a nice profit margin. But the purchasing division, while making money on each unit sold on an incre-

---

[7] Again we are talking about a system for a distinct minority of a division's products. If almost all a division's products are transferred internally, it should be reorganized as a standard cost center. The lack of an active intermediate market for a division's output eliminates one necessary condition for organizing a profit center.

mental basis, may lose money because of the fixed fee it must pay to the producing division. The purchasing division, in this situation, is absorbing all the uncertainties caused by fluctuations in the marketplace. The case can be made that both divisions are involved in the production of the final product and therefore that both should share in profit fluctuations caused by variations in market demand.

Finally, whenever a transfer price is determined by requesting one division to reveal its cost structure, an incentive for misrepresentation emerges. Therefore, even with a fixed-fee-plus-incremental-cost transfer price, the manager of the producing division may find it advantageous to manipulate these figures to maximize the reported profitability of the division at the expense of distorting the optimal firmwide decision.

Full Costs

Perhaps the least satisfactory transfer price is a mechanical full-cost pricing scheme. We have already seen, from the Nicosia Company example, that such a scheme distorts decision making. Nor is it a good guide for evaluating divisional performance. It provides the wrong incentives for the supplying division by allowing it to accumulate all costs and add markups to generate profits. Efficiency is certainly not rewarded nor inefficiency penalized on a full cost-plus transfer-pricing scheme. Perhaps the only argument in its favor is simplicity. This point was stressed in Chapter 7 when we discussed full-cost pricing for external customers.

As a simple illustration of the perverse effects of a full-cost transfer-pricing scheme, consider the practice of a very large industrial company (for which we shall preserve anonymity) that allocates all corporate G&A expenses to its operating divisions and imposes a transfer price based on cost plus profit markup for all internal transfers. Assume it is manufacturing a product that must be processed through three divisions before final sale. The company allocates $12,000 of general and administrative expenses to the three divisions manufacturing this product. Transfers between each division are done at full cost plus 20 percent markup, which is also the procedure used to price the final product.

Suppose that the G&A expenses are allocated equally to each division, $4,000 each. The first division takes the $4,000 allocation, marks it up by 20 percent, and transfers these costs on to the second division (along with all other product-related costs). The second division now has not just its own $4,000 G&A expense allocation for the product but also the $4,800 from the first division ($4,000 + 20 percent markup). Division 2 takes the $8,800 G&A allocation, marks it up by 20 percent, and transfers a total of $10,560 to Division 3. The third division accumulates its own $4,000 allocation with the $10,560, adds the 20 percent markup to this sum of $14,560, and obtains a total of $17,472 of corporate G&A that must be added to the final price of the product. Thus, the $12,000 of G&A has been increased not by a standard 20 percent markup but by a 46 percent markup [(17,472 − 12,000)/12,000)] because of the escalating effect as the product passes from one division to the next. When last heard from, the company was calling in a consultant to determine how competitors were able to price their products so much lower and why the company was steadily losing market share in its product lines. Poorly conceived transfer-pricing policies can be highly dysfunctional.

Negotiated Market-Based Price

Lacking a perfectly competitive market for the intermediate product and being aware of the limitations of cost-based pricing rules, perhaps the most practical method for establishing a transfer price is through negotiation between the managers of the two divisions. The negotiating process typically begins when the producing division provides a price quotation plus all relevant delivery conditions (timeliness, quality, and so on). The purchasing division may:

1. Accept the deal.
2. Bargain to obtain a lower price or better conditions.
3. Obtain outside bids and negotiate with external suppliers.
4. Reject the bid and either purchase outside or not purchase at all.

In a different sequence, the purchasing division may make an offer to the producing division for a portion of its current output or an increment to current output. The producing division can then bargain with the purchasing division over terms, talk to its existing customers, or decide not to accept the purchasing division's offer.

In either case, a negotiated transfer price requires that the managers of both divisions are free to accept or reject a price at any stage of the negotiation. Otherwise we would have a dictated rather than a negotiated price.

The conditions under which a negotiated transfer price will be successful include:

1. Some form of outside market for the intermediate product. This avoids a bilateral monopoly situation in which the final price could vary over too large a range, depending on the strength and skill of each negotiator.
2. Sharing of all market information among the negotiators. This should enable the negotiated price to be close to the opportunity cost of one or preferably both divisions.
3. Freedom to buy or sell outside. This provides the necessary discipline to the bargaining process.
4. Support and occasional involvement of top management. The parties must be urged to settle most disputes by themselves, otherwise the benefits of decentralization will be lost. Top management must be available to mediate the occasional unresolvable dispute or to

intervene when it sees that the bargaining process is clearly leading to suboptimal decisions. But such involvement must be done with restraint and tact if it is not to undermine the negotiating process.

The limitations of a negotiated-price system are that:

1. It is time consuming for the managers involved.
2. It leads to conflict between divisions.
3. It makes the measurement of divisional profitability sensitive to the negotiating skills of managers.
4. It requires the time of top management to oversee the negotiating process and to mediate disputes.
5. It may lead to a suboptimal (too low) level of output if the negotiated price is above the opportunity cost of supplying the transferred goods.

The negotiated-price system depends also on the willingness of external suppliers or purchasers to supply legitimate bids to the company. If, each time these external bids are solicited, the transfer price is determined so that all transfers are eventually made internally, the external bidders will soon tire of participating in this exercise. Therefore some amount of external purchase or sale should be a realistic expectation in order to keep the faith among these outside participants and thereby assure a continuing source of legitimate external prices. Despite these limitations, a negotiated-transfer-price system is widely used and has many benefits to recommend it.

Pricing and output decisions are complex; they require subjective judgments about alternative opportunities and the importance of maintaining current pricing policies. We organize decentralized operations and profit centers because we wish to take advantage of the divisional managers' special knowledge of local conditions. This requires that, insofar as possible, we allow them to make local decisions and hold them responsible not for the optimality of each decision (an impossibility under conditions of uncertainty and private information) but for overall divisional performance. Negotiated-price systems seem to offer desirable mechanisms for permitting local managers to exploit the specialized information they possess about local opportunities.

Transfer Prices from Mathematical Programming Models

The opportunity cost of transfers goes up significantly when a division is operating at one or more capacity constraints. In this case, additional production and transfer of a product requires not only the incremental variable resources required for that product (labor, material, variable overhead) but also the reduced production of some other product. Therefore the opportunity cost is the sum of incremental variable resources plus foregone profit opportunities. We solved such problems in Chapter 5 when discussing the use of mathematical programming models to handle multiple-product, multiple-resource cost-volume-profit problems. In that analysis, however, we assumed that all production and sales occurred within a single organizational unit. How can we handle a capacity-constrained production problem when there is a transfer of intermediate products between divisions?

This issue can be illustrated by a simple numerical example.[8] Division B sells two products, B_1 and B_2, made of three materials (A_1, A_2, A_3) produced by Division A. Division A has no outside market for these three materials. The required amounts (per unit of B_1 and B_2) of Division A's materials, the variable costs, and A's maximum productive capacity are shown below:

	A_1	A_2	A_3
Variable cost/lb	$1.00	$0.50	$0.75
Quantity used (lb)			
per unit of: B_1	2	0.5	1
B_2	2	2	3
Processing capacity (lb/week) in			
Division A	4,000	3,000	4,800

The prices and variable processing costs for products B_1 and B_2 are:

	B_1	B_2
Price	$8.00	$14.00
Processing cost in Division B	$2.00	$ 1.75

We can formulate the global optimization problem as a linear programming model. Let y_1 and y_2 be the amounts of B_1 and B_2 produced, respectively, and let x_1, x_2, x_3 be the amounts of A_1, A_2, A_3 produced. Then, the firm's problem can be represented as:

Maximize: $(8 - 2)y_1 + (14 - 1.75)y_2 - 1x_1 - 0.5x_2 - 0.75x_3$

$$
\begin{aligned}
\text{Subject to:} \quad & 2y_1 + 2y_2 - x_1 && \leq 0 \\
& 0.5y_1 + 2y_2 - x_2 && \leq 0 \\
& y_1 + 3y_2 - x_3 && \leq 0 \\
& x_1 && \leq 4{,}000 \\
& x_2 && \leq 3{,}000 \\
& x_3 && \leq 4{,}800 \\
& y_1, y_2, x_1, x_2, x_3 \geq 0.
\end{aligned}
$$

---

[8] This example is adapted from Solomons [1965, pp. 188–191].

The first three inequalities derive the demand for each of the three Division A products in terms of the amount of the two Division B products to be produced; for example, the first inequality indicates that the demand for product A_1 is 2 lb for each unit of B_1 produced plus 2 lb for each unit of B_2. The last three inequalities represent the capacity constraints on the production of A_1, A_2, and A_3, respectively.

The optimal solution for this problem is

$$y_1^* = 666.67, \qquad x_1^* = 4,000,$$

$$y_2^* = 1,333.33, \qquad x_2^* = 3,000,$$

$$x_3^* = 4,666.67,$$

yielding a profit of $11,333.

Of more relevance to the discussion in this chapter, however, are the shadow prices obtained from the dual solution to the linear programming problem. Recall that we obtain a shadow price or dual variable for each constraint in the maximizing problem and that these shadow prices represent the value of an additional unit of resource for each constraint—that is, how much the objective function (profits in this case) would increase if we could increment the right-hand side of each constraint by one unit. Letting $w_1, w_2, \ldots, w_6$ represent the dual variables for the six constraints, the values of these variables at the optimal solution are:

$$w_1^* = 1.833, \qquad w_4^* = 0.833,$$

$$w_2^* = 3.167, \qquad w_5^* = 2.667,$$

$$w_3^* = 0.75, \qquad w_6^* = 0.$$

The interpretation of w_4^*, w_5^*, and w_6^*, is relatively straightforward. At present the output of products B_1 and B_2 is constrained by the capacity constraints on products A_1 and A_2. A_3 is not being produced to capacity; its dual variable (w_6) therefore equals zero. If an additional unit of A_1 could be produced, profits would increase by $0.833. This also represents the opportunity cost of transferring the last unit of A_1 to Division B. Therefore, a transfer price for product A_1 based on opportunity cost would add $0.833 (the imputed cost of using the last unit of capacity for producing A_1) to the variable cost of $1.00 to obtain a price of $1.833. A similar computation yields a transfer price of $3.167 for product A_2. Product A_3 is not being produced to capacity, so its opportunity cost of production is just the variable cost of $0.75.

Note that these three transfer processes are precisely the shadow prices (w_1^*, w_2^*, w_3^*) for the first three constraints. These constraints are written so that the shadow price represents the value of having an additional unit of each of the three products transferred from Division A to Division B. Therefore, these shadow prices do represent the imputed value for each of the three input products.

Can these transfer prices, imputed from the mathematical programming model of production and sales opportunities, be used as a basis for decentralized decision making? Unfortunately, they cannot—for a number of reasons.

First, in the linear programming framework illustrated here, all the profits are imputed to the scarce (limiting) resources. In this case the scarce resources are the capacity constraints in Division A, so that all profits are imputed to Division A and none to B. To see this, note that if the three input products are transferred to B at prices of (1.833, 3.167, 0.75) and B sells the optimal amount of the two final products (667 B_1 and 1,333 B_2), the profits to Division B are 0, since

$$667(6) + 1,333(12.25) - 1.833(4,000) - 3.167(3,000) - 0.75(4,667) = 0.$$

All profits are "earned" in the division that has the capacity constraints, Division A. With the imputed transfer prices, Division A profits are $11,333:

$$4,000(1.833 - 1.00) + 3,000(3.167 - 0.50) + 4,667(0.75 - 0.75) = 11,333.$$

This reverses the allocation of profits from the marginal-cost transfer-pricing rule discussed earlier in this chapter, where the producing division could not even cover its fixed costs (when marginal cost was constant) and all profits were earned by the selling division. A system that bases transfer prices on the dual values of a mathematical programming solution rewards divisions that have scarce resources and penalizes divisions with adequate or surplus capacity. This induces a strange set of incentives, encouraging each division to limit capacity so that any profits will be imputed to use of its resources.

A second limitation is that, at least in a linear context, the use of dual values for local decision problems will lead to multiple optimal solutions, only one of which corresponds to the globally optimal solution. In our simple example, the maximum profit for Division B is zero. But it can obtain this profit level either by doing nothing ($y_1 = y_2 = 0$) or by following the optimal solution ($y_1 = 667$; $y_2 = 1,333$). For Division A, its local maximizing problem with transfer prices of (1.833, 3.167, 0.75) is:

Maximize: $(1.833 - 1.00)x_1 + (3.167 - 0.50)x_2 + (0.75 - 0.75)x_3$

Subject to: x_1 $\leq 4,000,$

                                      x_2 $\leq 3,000,$

                                                  $x_3 \leq 4,800,$

                                          $x_1, x_2, x_3 \geq 0.$

Division A can earn its maximum profits of $11,333 either by the optimal solution of (4,000, 3,000, 4,667) or by not producing product A_3 at all [say a production plan of (4,000, 3,000, 0)], since Division A earns no profits from the production and transfer of A_3. Thus, the transfer prices from the linear programming solution do not provide reliable guidance for local decision making.[9] Therefore, apart from generating the globally optimal solution, the linear programming formulation is not very helpful as a guide to decentralization, since it does not provide a good basis for evaluating the performance of the two divisions nor does it facilitate local decision making.

A third problem is that the linear programming formulation requires the communication of a great deal of local information to the staff department that formulates and solves the model. Once the local managers learn that the linear programming approach imputes profits to the divisions with the scarce resources, one can hardly expect them to communicate candidly about the productive capacities in their divisions.

In situations where capacity constraints exist or where divisions are competing for the use of common resources, it is tempting to turn to a mathematical programming formulation to allocate the scarce resources for the most profitable uses. If truthful information can be obtained to solve the mathematical programming problem, then a profit-maximizing use of the scarce resources may be obtained. Such a solution, however, can not be used to allocate profits among divisions without encouraging dysfunctional behavior or the strategic manipulation of information by local managers. Once the firm uses a mathematical programming formulation, it must recognize that it is imposing a centrally determined solution and undermining decentralization. It would be counterproductive to attempt to simulate decentralized decision making by using the dual values from the programming solution as transfer prices.

Summary of Transfer Pricing

We have covered much ground in our discussion of transfer pricing. We have obtained some results under fairly restrictive conditions, and we have learned of some pitfalls from using transfer prices inappropriately. Accounting and economic researchers now realize that under conditions that make decentralization worthwhile—that is, an uncertain environment with private information possessed by local managers—we do not know a great deal about optimal transfer-pricing policies. Research, though, is actively in progress, and future editions of this text may have more to say on this subject.

---

[9] The existence of alternative optima in the local maximizing problems is caused by our having a linear programming example. In the nonlinear case, the prices imputed by the dual prices would direct the two divisions to obtain the globally optimum solution even while solving their local problems separately (see Charnes and Kortanek [1968]). This result is analogous to the use of dual variables to allocate the common costs in a joint costing situation when there is a nonlinear revenue function (see discussion in Chapter 12).

We can summarize our current recommendations as follows:

1. Where a competitive market exists for the intermediate product, the market price, less selling, distribution, and collection expenses for outside customers, represents an excellent transfer price.

2. Where an outside market exists for the intermediate product but is not perfectly competitive, a negotiated-transfer-price system will probably work best. At least occasional transactions with outside suppliers and customers must occur if both divisions are to have credibility in the negotiating process and if reliable quotes from external firms are to be obtained.

3. When no external market exists for the intermediate product, transfers should occur at the incremental cost of production. This will facilitate the decision making of the purchasing division. A periodic fixed fee should also be paid to enable the producing division to recover budgeted fixed costs and the cost of invested capital. The fixed fee also forces the purchasing division to recognize the full cost of producing the intermediate product internally. If the market for the final product is weak, the portion of the fixed fee representing a return on investment (the accounting profit) to the producing division may be lowered, so that the selling division does not absorb all the fluctuations due to market uncertainty.

    If a significant fraction of a producing division's output does not have an external market reference, so that the fixed-fee-plus-incremental-cost rule must be implemented for most of its transfers, this division should probably not be organized as a profit center. It should either be combined with the division that purchases most of the output (if such a division exists) or else restructured as a manufacturing cost center and evaluated using flexible budgets and standard costs.

4. When no outside market price exists, and the producing division is operating at capacity constraints, some amount of central intervention may be required to rationalize the use of scarce resources for the overall benefit of the firm. Assuming truthful information can be obtained from the divisional managers on production and sales possibilities, a mathematical programming formulation can provide the optimal production and sales schedule. It would be inadvisable to use the results of this centrally determined plan to allocate profits among divisions or to evaluate divisional performance.

5. We find it difficult to discover circumstances in which a transfer price based on fully allocated costs per unit or full cost plus markup has desirable properties. Perhaps its only recommendation is sim-

plicity and ease of computation. It does not facilitate local decision making, nor does it provide a reasonable basis for evaluating divisional performance.

TRANSFER PRICING—A SURVEY

As a refreshing conclusion to this extensive, normative, and theoretical discussion on transfer pricing, let us look at the real world to see what transfer-pricing policies are actually being used by companies with decentralized operations. Umapathy (1978) reports the results of a survey of 291 responding companies who claimed to have at least two profit centers in their organization. Most were medium to large companies (90 percent had 1974 sales in excess of $100 million; 27 percent had sales in excess of $1 billion). Of these 291 companies, 249 (or 85 percent) reported that goods were transferred among profit centers. The median amount of such transfers was 5 percent of total cost of corporate sales (8 percent for those that reported at least some transfers), and less than one-fourth of all responding companies reported internal transfers in excess of 15 percent of sales. Two-thirds of the companies handle transfers of goods as a purchase and a sale (including a profit in the transfer price), and one-third of the companies transfer goods at cost. Table 14-4 summarizes the transfer-pricing policies of these companies.

In light of our previous analysis it is encouraging to see that 53 percent of companies use a market-price or negotiated-market-price scheme. (With our classification scheme, the 28 companies listed under the market-price category as using a competitor's price might be included in the negotiated-price category.)

TABLE 14-4.   **Transfer-Pricing Policies of Decentralized Firms (from Exhibit B-10 of Umapathy [1978])**

Transfer-Price Method		*Number of Companies*	*Percentage*
Variable cost		11	4.6
Full cost		61	25.5
Cost plus		40	16.7
Markup on cost	26		
Return on sales	7		
Return on investment	7		
Negotiated price		53	22.2
Market price		74	31.0
Competitor's price	28		
List or bid price	46		
Total		239	100.0

It is discouraging to find that one-fourth of the companies use a full-cost scheme and an additional one-sixth use full cost plus markup. Thus 42 percent of companies use a scheme for which we have no theoretical justification other than simplicity and objectivity.

The survey did not report whether any of the cost or cost-plus companies used a combination of incremental cost plus fixed fee to obtain the cost-based transfer price. The percentage of such firms is likely to be quite low. Only 5 percent of firms transferred at variable cost, and most of these were in the smallest companies (sales less than $200 million). No follow-up was conducted to determine whether the controllers of the variable-cost firms had ever read Hirschleifer or Solomons, the most prominent advocates of incremental-cost transfer pricing.

The survey raises the disturbing question as to why 42 percent of companies use a full-cost-based transfer-pricing rule. Perhaps the volume of interdivisional transactions is considered small enough that a simple and objective rule is preferable to more theoretically valid but more complex transfer-price rules. Alternatively, the full-cost rule may be useful as a defense of transfer prices to income tax or tariff regulators. The prevalence of cost-based pricing in these companies justifies our discussion of cost-plus practice in this chapter and in Chapter 7 on external pricing decisions.

NONPROFIT MEASURES OF PERFORMANCE

By now, the limitations of profit as the sole measure of performance for divisional managers should be disturbingly obvious. There are not, however, any obvious candidates to replace profit. We have identified a number of problems with profit measurement, but probably the most serious concern with a narrowly focused attention on periodic profit reports is that managers will take actions that sacrifice long-term profitability for short-term reported profits. We have noted a number of ways in which this could occur, such as lowering of quality controls, inadequate maintenance, insufficient funding for R&D and employee training, and lack of attention to customer relations and employee morale.

To balance off an exclusive concentration on reported accounting profits, some companies have developed performance appraisal systems in which profitability is only one component. For example, a divisional manager may be given objectives to meet in human resources, distribution, technology, product quality, or new products, depending upon which of these key areas are most crucial to the long-run success of the division and which are susceptible to the greatest improvement. The manager would then be evaluated on whether targeted objectives were achieved in these key areas. At first glance this seems like an intrusion into the decision-making authority of a divisional manager in a profit center, and it probably is. But the intrusion may be necessary because of inadequate measurement of the long-term consequences of the manager's current actions. Because of limited observability of the division manager's actions and the cost of measuring the present value of all the relevant assets in a division (including customer goodwill, equipment availability and condition, quality of work force, product quality), it is likely that the optimal contract between the division manager and the corporation is a function of variables in addition to reported accounting profit. The focus on key areas with long-term benefit to the corporation may be seen as a means of insuring that short-term profit maximizing is not the only objective of the divisional manager.

An evaluation program developed by General Electric, based on eight key result areas, is a good example of the use of multiple factors to evaluate divisional performance.[10] While somewhat dated, the multiple-factor GF system is still representative of attempts by today's companies to evaluate profit-center managers on factors other than annual reported profit. The eight key result areas are:

1. *Profitability*. The first and most important index of performance, of course, is still profitability. General Electric uses the residual-income measure of profitability, a measure that will be discussed extensively in the next chapter.

2. *Productivity*. This variable represents the ratio of output to input. We are most familiar with labor productivity, measured by the amount of output per unit of labor input, but any input factor or combination of input factors can be used to measure productivity. For example, the rapid rise in the price of energy during the 1970s has made the calculation of energy productivity—amount of output per unit of energy supplied—a worthwhile measure to watch carefully and improve. Many problems arise in constructing productivity indices, including controlling for relative price-level changes and aggregating diverse physical output and inputs; extensive discussions of these issues can be found in the literature on productivity measurement.

3. *Market position*. General Electric measures this variable as market share in the appropriately defined market category. The company must decide on what comprises the product line and what comprises the market—for example, directly competing (identical) products or indirectly competing products (substitutes); geographic boundaries of the market; population of companies considered (including foreign imports); wholesale or retail sales.

4. *Product leadership*. A divisional panel appraises each of the division's main products to assess (a) the percentage of products superior, equal, and inferior to those of competitors, (b) where the product was developed in the company, and (c) whether General

---

[10] This system is described in Jerome [1961] and Lewis [1955] and is summarized in Chapter VIII of Solomons [1965].

Electric or a competitor introduced the product and subsequent improvements.

5. *Personnel development.* Three measures were developed to evaluate the output of employee development programs: (a) the ratio of people promoted to the number considered promotable, also the number of people promotable to total number employed; (b) the proportion of employees whose performance is considered to be (1) improving, (2) unchanged, and (3) deteriorating; and (c) the percentages of employees who are satisfied or dissatisfied with their career development.

6. *Employee attitudes.* This area is measured by periodic surveys of employee attitudes toward factors such as job satisfaction, pay policies, and promotion chances. The percentage of favorable responses is noted and compared with previous results. More objective measures are also collected on turnover rates, absenteeism, tardiness, number of grievances filed, and accidents.

7. *Public responsibility.* This area is less well specified than the previous six. An attempt is made to insure compliance with antitrust regulations and avoid conflicts of interest. Surveys of suppliers, customers, and the local community were to be conducted to assess the impact of a division on external constituencies.

8. *Balance between short- and long-range goals.* This factor indicates that, ideally, in each of the seven previous key result areas there are both short- and long-run components. The outcomes in each of the seven areas, therefore, are evaluated in terms of both their short-term and long-term consequences. It is not entirely obvious what role this factor was expected to play, since each of factors 2 through 7 can be viewed as directing managers' attention to the long-term consequences of current actions—consequences that may not have an immediate impact on current profitability.

Whenever a manager or division is evaluated on more than one dimension, the problem of weighting the various dimensions into an overall measure arises. It is probably best not to have an explicit formula that would encourage managers to trade off performance along one dimension against performance on another. The existence of multiple performance factors should signal the manager that each is considered important and that poor performance in any one could cause a negative performance review. Thus the manager is dissuaded from neglecting any of the measured factors. If a direct conflict between two factors does arise, the manager admittedly faces a serious dilemma. In the 1960s, for example, despite the existence of a multiple-measurement performance-review system (including one factor on public responsibility), several G.E. executives admitted to participation in an attempt at price fixing. The executives claimed they were motivated by the perceived pressure to produce short-term profits. Thus, management must remain constantly vigilant to ensure that long-run profitability is not sacrificed by actions that maximize short-term reported profits.

PROBLEMS

14-1. Cost Allocations and Measurement of Division Profitability

The Young Corporation has three operating divisions. The managers of these divisions are evaluated on their divisional Net Income Before Taxes, a figure which includes an allocation of corporate overhead proportional to the sales of each division. The operating statement for the first quarter of 1982 appears below:

	Division			
	A	B	C	Total
Net Sales (000)	$2,000	$1,200	$1,600	$4,800
Cost of Sales	1,050	540	640	2,230
Division Overhead	250	125	160	535
Division Contribution	700	535	800	2,035
Corporate Overhead	400	240	320	960
Net Income Before Taxes	$ 300	$ 295	$ 480	$1,075

The manager of Division A is unhappy that his profitability is about the same as Division B and much less than Division C's, even though his sales are much higher than either of these other two divisions. The manager knows that he is carrying one line of products with very low profitability. He was going to replace this line of business as soon as more profitable product opportunities became available, but has retained it until now since the line was still marginally profitable and used facilities that would otherwise be idle. The manager now realizes, however, that the sales from this product line are attracting a fair amount of corporate overhead because of the allocation procedure and maybe the line is already unprofitable for him.

This low margin line of products had the following characteristics for the quarter:

Net Sales (000)	$800
Cost of Sales	600
Escapable Divisional Overhead	100
Contribution	$100

Thus the product line accounted for 40 percent of divisional sales but less than 15 percent of divisional profit.

1. Prepare the operating statement for the Young Corporation for the second quarter of 1982 assuming that sales and operating results are identical to the first quarter except that the manager of Division A drops the low margin product line entirely from his product group. Is the Division A manager better off from this action? Is the Young Corporation better off from this action?

2. Suggest improvements to the Young Corporation's divisional reporting and evaluation system that will improve local incentives for decision-making that is in the best interests of the firm.

14-2. Transfer Pricing Dispute*

A transportation equipment manufacturer is heavily decentralized. Each division head has full authority on all decisions regarding sales to internal or external customers. Division P has always acquired a certain equipment component from Division S. However, when informed that Division S was increasing its unit price to $220, Division P's management decided to purchase the component from outside suppliers at a price of $200.

Division S had recently acquired some specialized equipment that was used primarily to make this component. The manager cited the resulting high depreciation charges as the justification for the price boost. He asked the president of the company to instruct Division P to buy from S at the $220 price. He supplied the following:

P's annual purchases of component	2000 units
S's variable costs per unit	$ 190
S's fixed costs per unit	$ 20

Suppose there are no alternative uses of the S facilities.

Required:

1. Will the company as a whole benefit if P buys from the outside suppliers for $200 per unit?

2. Suppose the selling price of outsiders drops another $15 to $185. Should P purchase from outsiders?

3. Suppose (disregarding Question 2 above) that S could modify the component at an additional variable cost of $10 per unit and sell the 2000 units to other customers for $225. Would the entire company then benefit if P purchased the 2000 components from outsiders at $200 per unit?

4. Suppose the internal facilities could be assigned to other production operations which would otherwise require additional annual outlays of $29,000. Should P purchase from outsiders at $200 per unit?

---

* Problem adapted from one in Charles Hongren, *Cost Accounting*, 5th ed. (Englewood Cliffs, N.J.: Prentice-Hall, 1982).

14-3. Effects of a Cost-Plus Transfer Price

The Conpont Corporation has decentralized its manufacturing and marketing activities. Each function is now organized as a profit center. The output of a manufacturing division is transferred to the marketing division at standard cost plus a 20 percent markup. For one of the company's largest volume products, the following flexible budget has been computed at typical output levels:

	Output (units)		
	40,000	50,000	60,000
Overhead			
Indirect Materials	$ 80,000	$100,000	$120,000
Indirect Labor	150,000	162,000	174,000
Equipment Rentals +			
Depreciation	200,000	200,000	250,000
Utilities, Taxes, + Misc.	140,000	145,000	150,000
Total Overhead	$570,000	$607,000	$694,000
Direct Materials	320,000	400,000	480,000
Direct Labor	160,000	200,000	240,000
Total Budgeted Costs	$1,050,000	$1,207,000	$1,414,000

The standard cost per unit is calculated at an annual volume of 50,000 units but the forecasted volume level for the next year is 45,000 units.

Required:

1. At what price is this product transferred from the manufacturing to the marketing division?

2. The marketing division has uncovered an opportunity to sell 15,000 additional units to a new customer at a price of $22 per unit. This is a special one year contract that will not affect the pricing for current or potential customers. The manager of the marketing division has asked the manufacturing manager to supply these units at a transfer price of $20 per unit. The manufacturing manager has emphatically declined this offer, "How can I transfer these items below my cost? Not only will I not make my standard mark-up on each unit, I'll lose money on every item I produce at this transfer price. I'm willing to be reasonable since business is slower than usual, but this offer is ridiculous." Analyze the situation in an attempt to mediate this dispute.

14-4. Transfer Pricing in Imperfect Market: One Supplying Division, Two Purchasing Divisions*

Division A produces a chemical Calmite, that is processed further and sold by two other divisions (B and C) of the company. Division A's nonlinear cost structure for producing Calmite is given below:

---

* Problem adapted from example in Chapter VI of David Solomons, *Divisonal Performance: Measurement and Control* (Homewood, Ill.: Irwin, 1965)

Pounds of Calmite Produced	Division A's Total Cost
4,000	$2,000
5,000	2,100
6,000	2,250
7,000	2,425
8,000	2,625
9,000	2,925
10,000	3,325

For simplicity, you may assume that the marginal cost is constant between the production levels specified above.

Divisions B and C both face markets in which their output affects the selling price of their final product. The demand in these markets, plus the cost structure of the two finishing divisions, are well summarized by the following tables showing each division's net revenues (total revenues less finishing costs in each division):

DIVISION B

Pounds of Calmite Processed	Revenues-Net of Finishing Costs
1,000	$600
2,000	900
3,000	1,100
4,000	1,200

DIVISION C

Pounds of Calmite Processed	Revenues-Net of Finishing Costs
2,000	$1,200
3,000	1,800
4,000	2,100
5,000	2,300
6,000	2,400

Required:

1. From the point of view of the firm, what is the optimal output of Calmite for Division A and how much of this should be transferred to Division B and Division C?

2. What transfer price will motivate Division A to produce this output and also motivate Divisions B and C to demand the appropriate quantities? How would you describe the rule used to generate this transfer price?

3. How would the above analysis be affected if Division A can also sell Calmite in an imperfect external market?

4. In practice, how could a firm determine and implement a transfer price that leads to optimal production and transfers in a situation with a sup-

plying division, more than one purchasing division, and nonlinear cost and revenue functions, as described above?

14-5. Transfer Pricing with Imperfect Market for the Intermediate Product: The Linear Case (A. Atkinson)

Penn Hills Computers manufactures small control units used in process control equipment. In the Manufacturing Division, two basic products are constructed: a Machine Control Unit (MCU) and a Process Control Unit (PCU). A Machine Control Unit can either be sold in an external market, or transferred to the Assembly Division where it will be made part of a Precision Control Device that sells for $270. The Process Control Units are sold externally to other manufacturers at a price of $120 per unit. The firm has a contractual obligation to deliver at least 80 PCU's and can sell up to 120 more to its external customers at this price.

The Manufacturing Division has the following cost structure:

	MCU	PCU
Direct Materials	$50	$20
Direct Labor	40	20
Overhead	90	60
Total	$180	$100

Labor costs are $20 per hour and overhead is charged at $30/machine hour. The overhead charge includes an allocation of the Manufacturing Division's fixed overhead of $10,000 to the 1,000 hours of available machine time.

At present, the price of the MCU in the external market is $215, but this price had been below $200 recently. The internal price for transferring MCU's from the Manufacturing to the Assembly Division has been set at $198 based on a 10 percent markup over costs.

The cost structure for the Assembly Division for producing the Precision Control Device is:

Transfer Price of MCU	$198
Direct Materials	5
Direct Labor	30
Overhead	30
	$263

The overhead rate is $20/Direct Labor Hour of which 50 percent is variable. The hourly labor cost in the Assembly Division is identical to the Manufacturing Division's since they share the same labor pool.

At present, neither division manager is happy with the current transfer price. Walter Patterson, the Assembly Division manager, complains that at the $198 transfer price, he earns less than a 3 percent profit margin over costs, whereas the Manufacturing Division is allowed a 10 percent markup over costs. Linda Martin, the Manufacturing Division manager, however, is upset about the transfer price being well below the price at which she can sell the MCU's in the external market. At present, she is being asked to produce and transfer 240 MCUs to the Assembly Division. This doesn't leave much machine time to produce MCUs for the external market especially when at least 80 PCUs must also be manufactured on the same equipment to meet already contracted sales.

At present the Manufacturing Division has been scheduled to produce 125 PCUs and 250 MCUs of which 240 MCUs are to be transferred internally and 10 will be sold externally. The budgeted profit for this plan is:

$$
\begin{aligned}
125 \text{ PCUs @ \$20} \quad (\$120-100) &= \$2,500 \\
240 \text{ MCUs @ \$18} \quad (\$198-180) &= 4,320 \\
10 \text{ MCUs @ \$35} \quad (\$215-180) &= \underline{350} \\
\text{Total Manufacturing Division} & \\
\text{Profit} \quad\quad\quad\quad\quad\quad\quad & \$7,170
\end{aligned}
$$

Linda Martin argues that she could increase her profits by selling all of her output externally and that it is silly for the firm to force internal transfers when there are more profitable external opportunities available.

Walter Patterson is upset about the proposed shift in Linda's sales plans. He reminds her that when the external price of the MCUs was below $200, she was glad to have a secure internal market for these units at the $198 transfer price. Walter continues, "One can hardly run a business on a sensible long term basis if the supplying division shifts its output between internal and external customers based on short term shifts in prices. How can I plan my production levels and schedule my labor force if there are dramatic swings in the output I am supposed to produce. Also, since I can hardly make money, even at the $198 transfer price, perhaps we should just stop making the PCD entirely."

Required:

1. Analyze the problems that have arisen from the transfer price of $198.
2. Given the current pricing structure, what production plan maximizes Linda Martin's profits in the Manufacturing Division?
3. Given the current pricing structure, what production plan maximizes the profits of Penn Hills Computer (the sum of the profits in the Manufacturing and Assembly Divisions)?
4. What transfer price will motivate the two divisional managers to seek the company wide profit-maximizing plan?
5. How does your answer to the above questions change if we introduce the additional information that there is a constraint that no more than 1,000 Direct Labor Hours can be used by the two divisions, combined?

14-6. Transfer Pricing with Imperfect Market for the Intermediate Product: The Nonlinear Case (A. Atkinson)

Penn Hills Computers (see Problem 14-5) has discovered that the demand, q, in the external market for the Machine Control Unit (MCU) can be characterized by a linear demand function:

$$
p = 1650 - 5q
$$

where p is the market price for MCU's.

You can assume that Penn Hills is the only supplier of MCU's to this market. Assume that the cost structure of the Manufacturing and Assembly Divisions remains the same as described in Problem 14-5. Also the price of the PCU is $120 per unit; a minimum of 80 and a maximum of 200 PCUs are sold at this price. The price of the PCD is $270. Finally, a maximum of 1,000 machine hours are available to the Manufacturing Division. (Labor supply is unlimited at the $20/DLH rate).

Required:

1. What is the optimal production plan for the firm?
2. What transfer price is consistent with motivating this optimal production plan by the Manufacturing and Assembly Divisions?
3. As a practical matter, how could a firm discover the optimal transfer price?

14-7. Using Linear Programming to Compute Transfer Prices

The Graves Corporation has two divisions that process raw materials into intermediate and final products. Division X manufactures two chemicals, $X1$ and $X2$. Product $X1$ cannot be sold externally. It can, however, be processed further by Division Y into a salable product, $Y1$. Division Y also manufactures a second chemical $Y2$. Characteristics of these four products are given, below:

	Product			
	X1	*X2*	*Y1*	*Y2*
Selling Price/ton	$0	$16	$22	$11
Variable Cost/ton	4	8	9	6
Processing Time/ton	3 hours	6 hours	4 hours	5 hours
Labor Time/ton	4 hours	4 hours	3 hours	2 hours

Division X has 48(000) hours of processing time and 36(000) hours of labor time available to it each period. Division Y's available processing and labor times are 28(000) and 14(000) hours respectively. One ton of $X1$ is required to manufacture each ton of $Y1$.

Divisions X and Y are treated as profit centers and the transfer price of $X1$ has become a source of considerable controversy. The present practice is to transfer at $6 per ton representing a 50 percent markup over variable cost. The manager of Division Y is willing to pay this price but the manager of Division X has been balking and threatens to curtail production of $X1$, shifting all of his productive resources to the manufacture of product $X2$. You have been asked to examine this situation and recommend a course of action to the company controller.

Required:

1. Show why the manager of Division X is unhappy with producing $X1$ at the current transfer price of $6 per ton. Also show why the manager of Division Y is willing to pay $6 per ton for $X1$, as long as he is assured an adequate supply of this intermediate product.

2. What production quantities of the four products maximize the contribution margin for the Graves Corporation as a whole? What is this maximum contribution margin?

3. From a linear programming formulation of the production possibilities of the firm, obtain a transfer price from the dual variable of the constraint representing the transfer of Product $X1$ to produce $Y1$ (i.e., $-X1 + Y1 \leq 0$).

4. What problems arise from use of this transfer price? (*Hint*: Among other factors, look at alternative solutions to the local optimizing problems of Divisions X and Y).

14-8. Transfer Pricing with no External Market: Incentive for Misrepresenting Cost Functions (A. Atkinson)

Orleans Products produces and distributes the "Jungle" a child's combination swing and climbing set. The manufacturing division's total production cost function (in dollars) is:

$$TPC(X) = 10X + .01X^2$$

where X is the number of units produced.

After the "Jungle" is produced by the manufacturing division, it is transferred to the marketing division. The marketing division reports that the revenue for the "Jungle" (in dollars) is:

$$R = (217 - Q)Q$$

where Q is units sold.

The marketing division's costs are strictly variable and equal to $5 per unit sold. The company's market is stable so the firm has a policy of carrying no inventories.

Required:

1. From the point of view of the *company*, what is the optimal production and sales quantity?

2. What is the transfer price associated with this quantity? What are the firm and division profits? Explain the properties of this price.

3. Suppose that the manufacturing division misrepresents its cost function by reporting its cost curve as;

$$TPC(X) = 20X + .01X^2$$

a. What quantity will be produced and sold?
b. What will be the transfer price?
c. What will be firm and division profits?
d. Is the manufacturing division motivated to lie about its manufacturing cost function?
e. What is the effect on the firm of lying?

14-9. Transfer Pricing with No External Market: Problems of Suboptimization from Bargaining Procedures (A. Atkinson)

Arnprior Electronics manufactures and distributes a thermostat which is used in home heating systems. For organizational control purposes the company has been divided into two divisions: manufacturing and marketing. The cost function of the manufacturing division is

$$(5 + .05x)x$$

where x equals the number of units manufactured.

The net revenue function of the marketing division (i.e., revenue less marketing cost) is

$$(50 - .1x)x$$

where x equals the number of units sold.

Required:

1. What is the optimal production level from the point of view of the firm? What are the firm and division profits?
2. If the manufacturing division is allowed to determine the transfer price, what production quantity will result? What are the firm and division profits?
3. If the marketing division is allowed to determine the transfer price, what production quantity will result? What are the firm and division profits?
4. Comment on the likely consequences of allowing divisions to bargain over a transfer price.

14-10. Transfer Price System for a Commercial Bank*

Allegheny Bank is a full-service commercial financial institution with extensive retail branch banks and a large corporate lending business. Recently, Allegheny Bank decided to institute an internal pricing system for its basic product: money. Previously, the bank had evaluated each of its units with different costs for money, based on how each unit raised money and loaned it out. For example, a retail branch raised money from demand and time deposits (or, in everyday language, checking accounts and savings accounts) and loaned money for real estate mortgages, automobile financing, personal and student loans, and local small business loans. The profit of a branch was computed as the interest income from all its lending activities less the interest cost on time deposits, the cost of servicing demand deposits, and direct operating and administrative expenses. A commercial lending division's profit was computed as the interest from loans outstanding less the bank's average cost of capital and less the operating and administrative expenses of the lending division.

---

* This is a considerably simplified version of the systems actually installed in many commercial banks. Among many features omitted from the description are the complications introduced by reserve requirements and compensating balances.

In recent years, interest rates had risen well above the rate the bank was permitted to pay on passbook accounts. Non-bank financial instruments such as money market funds were being offered to the public draining off funds formerly kept in checking and savings accounts. As a result, Allegheny found that the rate of growth of its customers demand and time deposits was not keeping pace with the banks' increased lending activity. The bank was relying more and more on "high cost" money obtained from issuing its own certificates of deposits that had to be sold at money-market interest rates in competition with U.S. Treasury Bills and other banks' C.D.'s. The top management of the bank was concerned that the effective interest rate its lending officers were offering to customers did not fully reflect the cost of this high-cost money.

Under Allegheny Bank's new transfer price policy, a short-term cost-of-funds rate called the interunit interest rate is computed for all bank operations. This rate is determined from market interest rates. Specifically, the interunit interest rate is computed each month based on the daily average of the interest rate on short term Certificate of Deposits that are actively traded in money markets. Beyond this, rates for longer-term loans (automobiles, housing) are computed based on the cost of long term funds at the time each long term loan is booked. The cost of long term funds is approximated by the premium (or discount) over the short term rate on intermediate and long-term U.S. government bonds.

For purposes of understanding the transfer price system, we can simplify the bank's structure into three types of units: retail branch, commercial lending, and money management. The retail branch receives credit for all its demand and time deposits based on the difference between its cost for these funds and the interunit interest rate. The cost of funds for any loan made by the retail branch is also computed from the interunit interest rate. Real estate and other longer term loans are charged for the cost of longer term funds, as explained above. Note that under this system, a retail branch could operate profitably even if it made no loans at all.

A commercial lending department's profit is computed as the excess of the yields on its loans over the interunit interest rate, less operating and administrative expenses. The only difference in the computation under the new scheme is that all commercial loans are charged at the marginal cost of short-term funds (the C.D. rate) rather than the average cost of funds, as before.

The money management division handles the bank's maturity, liquidity, and money-buying decisions. It will buy, at fair market value (i.e., the interunit interest rate) all the deposits generated by the retail branch units. It will sell all funds (also at market interest rates) to divisions making loans. Thus, the money management division becomes the conduit by which funds generated at one location can be put to work funding loans made by other units. The money management division will actively trade in money market instruments—federal funds, certificates of deposit, commercial paper—and keep an investment securities portfolio for yield and liquidity. It will forecast the demand for and supply of money and the term structure of interest rates as it determines the average maturity of the banks' investment securities. The money management division will show a profit if, through its transacting with different financial instruments and different maturities, it obtains funds at a lower average cost than the short term C.D. rate.

In the process of instituting the new system many questions have arisen from bank personnel. These include:

1. A branch manager: "I have lots of cheap demand and savings money in my own office. Why do I have to sell these to the money manager? Why can't I simply fund my own loans?

2. Another branch manager: "With the new system, all my loans are losing money. What am I supposed to do—shut down my operation?

3. A commercial lending officer: "I don't agree with your choice of a 3 month rate for commercial loans. I would have purchased longer term funds at a lower rate than those 3 month C.D.'s."

4. A second commercial lending officer: "I made a three year fixed rate loan to a good customer that was profitable at the time it was booked. This year with the increase in interest rates, this loan is now showing a substantial loss."

Required:

Evaluate the desirability of Allegheny Bank's decision to implement the market-based transfer price system for money. What are the advantages of the new system and what are the disadvantages? How would you respond to the four questions or complaints raised by the bank officers?

14-11. Transfer Pricing Among Related Businesses

Kirkpatrick Associates, Incorporated*

Mr. Richard (Rick) Kirkpatrick, Sr. started Columbus Realty, Inc., a real estate firm about 40 years ago. His personality and honesty made this undertaking a success. When his eldest son, John Kirkpatrick, graduated with an engineering degree, Kirkpatrick, Sr. incorporated K & S Construction Company and put John in charge. 40 percent of the stock was given to John, and 60 percent was deposited with Kirkpatrick Associates, Incorporated which Kirkpatrick, Sr. controlled, 100 percent. Having intimate knowledge of the housing market, Kirkpatrick, Sr. suggested, and John agreed, that the construction company should concentrate on custom designed and built houses in the price range of $100,000 to $200,000. John Kirkpatrick's technical knowledge and imagination made the construction company a success.

Kirkpatrick, Sr.'s second son, Court, received a degree in architecture but upon graduation was not ready to enter employment. Upon the suggestion of several friends and the family, Court Kirkpatrick continued with his education and pursued an M.B.A. degree. During this study, and because of a special project he was assigned, he became interested in the development of living complexes around shopping centers. In this project, both the living complex and the shopping center were designed with a continental motif. Further research convinced him that this project would not only be feasible, but also very profitable. He discussed his idea and all the information he had gathered with his father, who agreed that this kind of design seemed to be the upcoming style. Upon Court's graduation, the Columbus Rental

---

* Copyright 1976 by Professor Felix P. Kollaritsch. Reproduced with permission.

Company was incorporated with the same stock arrangement as with the K & S Construction Company.

Court bought land and proceeded with the design and building of a shopping center and several apartment buildings around this shopping center. This undertaking was an instant success, too. The shopping center has an extraordinary 100 percent lease commitment, and some prospects on a waiting list. The apartments have an 85 percent occupancy rate. This complex has been and still is the "in thing" in this community. Mostly young upper middle class people are living there.

Up until several years ago, Court had to maintain a large maintenance crew whose task was to keep up both the shopping center and the apartment buildings. However, when the youngest of the children, Richard Kirkpatrick, Jr., graduated, this function was separated from his brother's company, and the Columbus Remodeling Company was incorporated. Stock arrangements were the same as for the other companies. Rick, Jr. was put in charge of this company. Over the years, the various family members have retired from active participation in the day-to-day activities of the companies. Each still sets overall policies and objectives for the entities, but leaves the daily operations to the general managers. Each general manager shares in the profit of his company. Although there still exists very close cooperation among these companies, they have grown to be rather independent of each other. If one inside company wants any service from the other, these services are priced the same as to outsiders. Managers of each feel they are competitive and offer the best service for the lowest cost. For instance, the Columbus Remodeling Company does all the maintenance for the Columbus Rental Company. However, to keep this contract, Columbus Remodeling must be competitive with other maintenance companies.

These arrangements have generally been successful although occasional complaints have been raised. Recently, however, the complaints have become more vocal. To some degree they were due to poor general economic conditions. Last year was a depression year and, although the Kirkpatrick complex fared better than the average real estate company, the general managers experienced a considerable cut in their profit participation, and are now very conscious of any dealing which would reduce their profits.

During the last year, the Kirkpatrick family came up with another innovation in the real estate business—the "house trade-in". The Construction Company will construct a house for a buyer with the understanding that his old residence be taken in as a trade, providing it is located in Columbus. In many instances, this practice would avoid downpayments for the buyer, as well as the inconveniences of selling the house.

The value of the trade-in is established by the real estate company and the Remodeling Company. The Remodeling Company will determine what should be done to the house and give an estimate for necessary repair work. The real estate company will make suggestions as to certain remodeling needs which make a house more valuable and salable. The Remodeling Company will also give firm estimates on these suggestions. The real estate company will then give the construction company a realistic market value of the house.

The value of the renovated house, less the renovation costs, is used internally by the construction company to determine its profit on a sale and trade-in. Externally, the construction company will quote the buyer the renovated house value as the trade-in value, but also will increase its normal price for a given house for the costs of the remodeling. The reason for this valuation is that the buyer may see the asking price for his old house in a sales advertisement and may feel cheated if the price is more than he received. Very likely, he may not be aware of the total renovation costs.

Until the house is sold, the construction company has title to the house. It is responsible for any house repairs and remodeling, and for any interest, taxes, insurance, or other costs. The real estate company will list and sell the house, collecting a 6 percent commission from the buyer. This plan has been successful and has made the name of Kirkpatrick a household word in the real estate business throughout the state. However, the plan is not without drawbacks. The following transaction is an example, and your advice is solicited.

The K & S Construction Company sold a newly constructed house to Mr. Baxter as follows:

Price of New House	$200,000
Trade-In from Old House	50,000
Cash (from mortgage)	$150,000
Value Received	
Cash	$150,000
Trade-In	40,000
Total	$190,000
Cost of Building New House	160,000
Profit	$ 30,000

The trade-in value was established as follows: the fair market value of the house, if fixed-up, was determined as $50,000 by the real estate company. The renovation needs were jointly determined by the manager of the real estate company and by the manager of the remodeling company. These needs were costed by the manager of the remodeling company as $10,000.

Two days after the deal was closed, a heavy rain occurred, and it was discovered that the roof must be replaced and the basement water-sealed. The costs for these repairs were established at $4,000 and $2,000.

The managers of the real estate and construction companies think that these repairs should be priced at $3,000, only, since the remodeling company has a 50 percent variable cost factor. The remodeling company's manager says that under no condition will he make the repairs for a price other than that quoted. He claims to have enough outside business to keep him occupied during the present high season. He might consider doing it for a somewhat lesser price during the off-season, which will begin in seven months. But his delay would mean not selling the house for at least a full year. Also, predictions for next year's prices for houses are impossible to make.

To complicate matters further, the manager of the rental company stated that he would like to acquire the house, since it is located within the general territorial boundaries which he would like, eventually, to incorporate. Furthermore, some of the people in the continental complex would prefer houses to apartments, if they were available. He is unwilling to pay more than $50,000 and the commission. He estimates rental income to be $500 per month, with an estimated 80 percent occupancy. Real estate taxes are $951 per year, maintenance is estimated to be about $500 per year, and allocated management expenses, $500 per year. Management expenses are fixed and would not change with the acquisition of this house. Income tax rate is 50 percent. Land value is estimated at $8,000. Life of the building is 30 years.

Required:

1. Determine the profit of the K & S Construction Company for this sale.
2. What should the charge be for fixing up the house?
3. Who should be charged with the fixing up costs? Why? Are there any changes in procedures you would suggest?
4. If the house is to be sold to outsiders, what alternatives are open to the company?
5. If the house is sold to the rental company, what is its price?
6. Should the house be rented or sold?

14-12. Transfer Pricing in a Multi-National Corporation*

Del Norte Paper Company (A)

"If I had purchased the kraft linerboard for the African box sale from one of our mills, I would have paid $360 per ton, $140 per ton higher than the price I actually paid by purchasing the linerboard in the spot market," said Frank Duffy, Managing Director of Del Norte Paper's Italian subsidiary (DNP-Italia). "I can't possibly make a profit for Del Norte if I have to pay so much for my principal raw material."

Del Norte Paper Company was a large, fully-integrated paper manufacturer. 1974 sales were about $2.8 billion, making Del Norte Paper one of the 75 largest industrial companies in the United States. The company's product line ranged from raw pulp to a large variety of converted paper products, including corrugated boxes.

DNP-Italia purchased kraft linerboard from outside suppliers and converted it into corrugated boxes. These boxes were sold primarily within Italy, though occasional sales were made outside of Italy. DNP-Italia had 6 plants, each of which represented a separate profit center.

The African Bid

In mid-1975, an African firm asked a number of paper companies to submit bids on a large quantity of corrugated boxes. In total, 22 companies submitted bids, including DNP-Italia and another Del Norte subsidiary, DNP-Deutschland. The bids were said to have ranged from approximately $340 per ton to over $550 per ton, with most of them within 5 percent of $400 per ton. Del Norte-Italia won the contract by submitting the lowest bid from a firm viewed as being capable of meeting the customer's desired delivery and quality standards.

* Copyright © 1976 by the President and Fellows of Harvard College. Reproduced by permission. This case was prepared by William Sahlman under the supervision of M. Edgar Barrett.

The price quoted by DNP-Italia had been substantially below that quoted by DNP-Deutschland. The primary difference between the two bids was the raw material (kraft linerboard) cost calculation embedded in each. DNP-Deutschland had formed its estimate using a per ton price for kraft linerboard of $360 while DNP-Italia had used $220. The $360/ton figure was the price (inclusive of freight) quoted for export by a Del Norte Paper mill located in the Eastern United States. The $220 figure was the price for kraft linerboard of comparable quality in the European "Spot" market.

There were basically two reasons why the Del Norte Paper mill price was so much higher than the European spot price. First, Del Norte Paper was a member of the Kraft Export Association (KEA), a group of kraft linerboard manufacturers which was responsible for setting and stabilizing linerboard prices for the export market. The Del Norte Paper Company mill could not, as a member of the KEA, offer a lower price to its own converting plant than to any other external customer.

The second reason for the large price differential was the extremely weak economic conditions present in mid-1975. The paper and container industries were suffering from a worldwide slump. As a result of this slump, many non-KEA producers of kraft linerboard were selling their product at very low prices. This was the exact opposite situation as had existed in 1973, a year in which there was a worldwide paper and container economic boom, when the spot price for kraft linerboard had actually exceeded by a small amount the KEA set price.

Del Norte's Transfer Pricing System

Prices on domestic (U.S.) intra-company sales of linerboard at Del Norte Paper were set at the "market" level. That is, the transfer price was the price at which the linerboard could be bought or sold in the market place. However, on international intra-company sales, the product price was set at a level determined by the Kraft Export Association. The KEA price could vary according to market conditions, but tended to fluctuate less than the so-called spot price. Officials of Del Norte Paper in San Francisco estimated that, even if all foreign subsidiary managers agreed to take all of the KEA priced, Del Norte Paper linerboard available, some 60 to 65% of their linerboard would have to come from other sources.[1]

When a Del Norte Paper converting plant located in the United States purchased its linerboard from a company mill, the profit made by the mill on the transaction was included as part of one of the reported profit figures of the converting plant. The method employed for allocating the profit was rather complex. At the time of preparing the annual budget, the converting plant made a commitment to purchase a specific amount of kraft linerboard from a specific mill. The income statement of the converting plant was then credited with the actual mill profit resulting from delivery of actual orders placed against the commitment.

The figure used for the "mill profit" was determined by taking the mill profit applicable to the specific shipment after a full allocation of both fixed and variable costs and amending it for two specific items. First, any manufacturing variances

---

[1] This 60 to 65 percent was basically in grade lines not produced by DNP mills in the United States. In addition, it generally consisted of lower quality material than was normally found in the American market.

were added to or subtracted from the mill profit. Second, in the event that the converting plant did not take as much of the mill's production as expected, the proportional cost of the resulting mill down time was charged to the converting plant.

In Del Norte's international operations, the profit allocation process was similar. The foreign converting plant entered into a commitment for its U.S. produced requirements. The "mill profit," as defined above, was credited to the converting plant and its manager. However, in contrast to domestic operations, the set of financial statements in which this amount was credited was not made freely available to the foreign subsidiary's managing director and other management personnel. The reason for this was to maintain a legal, arms-length business relationship. Such statements of "integrated profit" were, however, available upon request to the managing director of each foreign subsidiary.

The African Sale

The bid submitted by DNP-Italia to the African customer was $400 per ton of corrugated boxes. DNP-Italia's direct costs (variable costs) were approximately $325 per ton of which 72% or $235[2] represented the cost of kraft linerboard.

The bid submitted by DNP-Deutschland was $550 per ton of corrugated boxes. DNP-Deutschland's direct costs on the transaction were approximately $460 of which $385 represented the cost of kraft linerboard.

The average Del Norte Paper mill had a direct cost per ton of linerboard of $190.[3] Thus, the contribution per ton at the mill was approximately $170, given the KEA selling prices of $360 per ton. The $170 contribution figure minus the actual freight costs from the U.S. to Germany (approximately $45 per ton) and the allocated overhead at the mill level would have been credited to the DNP-Deutschland converting mill had Germany won the contract.

An Informal Discussion

Late one afternoon in July 1975, Frank Duffy, Managing Director of DNP-Italia held a discussion with John Powell, General Manager—International Operations of Del Norte Paper's Container Division. The specific topic of the discussion was the African container sale, but the conversation also touched on the transfer pricing system used by Del Norte Paper.

Duffy: John, you know I would prefer to buy all my linerboard from a Del Norte Paper mill, but I just cannot compete if I have to pay $360 per ton. The price competition in the box market has been absolutely fierce this year. If I paid that much for linerboard, I would have to price my corrugated boxes below cost in order to win any contracts. If I am supposed to be a profit center, you can't expect me to report

---

[2] Editor's Note: This figure represents the linerboard cost per ton of corrugated box sold. The actual cost per ton of linerboard used was $220.

[3] The direct cost figure of $190 per ton at the linerboard mill included the cost of raw wood going into the mill. Approximately 30% to 40% of the raw wood used by the mill was purchased from the Del Norte Paper Company Woodlands Division at a market determined transfer price.

a loss on every sale I make—which is exactly what I would do using $360 per ton linerboard.

Powell: But you would get credited with the mill profit in the transaction—you wouldn't have to report a loss.

Duffy: Maybe on your books I wouldn't show a loss, but on my books I sure would. We never see that profit here in Italy. The transaction is noted in some secret little book back in San Francisco. How am I supposed to convince my plant managers and sales people they are being credited with the mill profit when they never see it?

Furthermore, from a financial point of view, the transfer pricing system doesn't make sense. Even if the mill profit were put directly into our profit and loss statement, our cash flow would not benefit. As you know, John, this is a completely self-financed operation in Italy. If I have to borrow more money than I need to, then I incur extra interest costs. There is no offsetting credit for these expenses.

Powell: I sympathize with you, Frank, but we also have a responsibility to keep our mills operating. Further, by not purchasing Del Norte Paper linerboard when times are bad, you run the risk of not being able to buy linerboard from our U.S. mills when there is a shortage like there was two years ago. As you know, we're moving increasingly toward long-term commitments for delivery by our kraft linerboard mills. You also don't help maintain the pricing stability we've been working so hard to establish through the KEA.

Duffy: I appreciate the problem, but I also have the responsibility to keep my plants running. Unlike the U.S., I can't fire any of my laborers in Italy—the unions just won't allow it. Any orders I can get to keep those laborers busy is pure contribution to me.

Powell: I still think you're making a mistake by not purchasing Del Norte Paper linerboard. However, we're not going to resolve the issue today. If it were not for this damn recession, the problem probably wouldn't even exist. If it's O.K. with you, Frank, I'd like to have a chance to give the problem some more thought.

Required:

Analyze the Del Norte transfer pricing situation.

REFERENCES

ABDEL-KHALIK, RASHAD, and EWARD J. LUSK, "Transfer Pricing—A Synthesis," *The Accounting Review* XLIX (January 1974), 8–23.

CHARNES, A., and K. O. KORTANEK, "On the Status of Separability and Non-Separability in Decentralization Theory," *Management Science* XV (October 1968), B12.

GOULD, JOHN R., "Internal Pricing in Firms When There are Costs of Using an Outside Market," *Journal of Business* XXXVII (January 1964), 61–67.

HIRSCHLEIFER, JACK, "On the Economics of Transfer Pricing," *Journal of Business* XXIX (July 1956), 172–84.

————, "Economics of the Divisionalized Firm," *Journal of Business* XXX (April 1957), 96–108.

JEROME, WILLIAM TRAVERS III, *Executive Control—The Catalyst.* New York: Wiley, 1961, pp. 217–37.

LEWIS, ROBERT W., "Measuring, Reporting and Appraising Results of Operations with Reference to Goals, Plans and Budgets," *Planning, Managing and Measuring the Business.* New York: Controllers Institute Research Foundation, 1955.

MANES, RENE, "Birch Paper Company Revisited: An Exercise in Transfer Pricing," *The Accounting Review* XLV (July 1970), 565–72.

RONEN, J., and G. McKINNEY III, "Transfer Pricing for Divisional Autonomy," *Journal of Accounting Reseach* VIII (Spring 1970), 99–113.

SOLOMONS, DAVID, *Divisional Performance: Measurement and Control.* Homewood, Ill.: Irwin, 1965.

UMAPATHY, SRINIVASAN, "Transfers Between Profit Centers," Sec. B in Part Two of Vancil, *Decentralization* (1978).

VANCIL, RICHARD F., *Decentralization: Managerial Ambiguity by Design.* Homewood, Ill.: Dow Jones-Irwin, 1978.

INVESTMENT CENTERS:
Return on Investment and Residual Income

15

Investment centers are decentralized units or divisions for which the manager has maximum discretion in determining not only short-term operating decisions on product mix, pricing, and production methods but also the level and type of investment. An investment center extends the profit-center concept in that the measured profit is compared with the center's assets or investment base. What we are calling an investment center is commonly described also as a profit center, since a profitability measure is being developed for the center. We prefer to distinguish between the two terms so that we can talk about the particular problems in measuring profits, which are common to both types of centers, separately from those involved in measuring assets and relating profits to assets employed. In a survey of 620 industrial companies[1] (drawn from the *Fortune 1000* in 1976), only 26 reported that they used neither profit nor investment centers. Of the remaining 594 companies, 135 had only profit centers and 459 had at least two investment centers. Thus, the investment-center form of organization is used extensively by large industrial corporations in the United States.

The concept   relating profits to assets employed seems intuitive and obvious. It is only when we do so that we can determine whether the profits are generating a sufficiently high return on the capital invested in the division. Capital is always a scarce resource, and it is important that an evaluation be made of the returns that a division and the overall company are earning on invested capital. Most companies have elaborate systems for authorizing capital expenditures. Without some form of measurement of the ex post returns to capital, however, there will be little incentive for accurate estimates of cash flows during the capital budgeting process. Measurement of investment-center performance can be viewed

---

[1] Reece and Cool [1978].

as the evaluation of an aggregation of past and present capital projects as opposed to the evaluation of each project individually. Such a measurement also provides an incentive for division managers to monitor capital investments carefully while managing their operations. The managers will also be motivated to watch the levels of inventory and receivables, since these accounts will almost always be included in their investment base.

Despite the intuitive appeal of investment centers, many conceptual and measurement problems arise in the construction of a particular measure. In this chapter we will illustrate these problems, so that the reader can be aware of the more obvious pitfalls and limitations in measuring investment-center performance. No measurement will be perfect, and simplicity and practicality will lead many companies to use a less than theoretically ideal measure. Nevertheless, a knowledge of the properties of various measures will permit an intelligent interpretation of the system that any particular company uses. Among the issues we will be discussing in this chapter are:

1. Choice of an appropriate measure: return on investment, residual income, cash recovery rate.
2. Choice of depreciation method.
3. Measurement of assets: historical cost-net or book value, current cost.
4. Selection of assets to include in the investment base.

RETURN ON INVESTMENT

The most common measure of evaluation for an investment center is the accounting *return on investment* (*ROI*). This is defined as the division's net income before taxes (NIBT) divided by some measure of assets employed in the division. Consider a division with assets of $90,000 and net income before taxes of $20,000. Its ROI is 22.2 percent:

$$\text{ROI} = \frac{\text{NIBT}}{\text{Assets}} = \frac{20{,}000}{90{,}000} = 0.222.$$

There are many positive aspects of the ROI computation. It is generally an objective measure based on accounting data already collected. It facilitates a comparison among divisions of different sizes and in different lines of business. It is a common measure, since it is analogous to a cost of capital for which external referents exist in capital markets. Divisions with a 5 percent ROI are earning below what is available from far less risky investments, whereas divisions with a ROI in excess of 25 percent appear, at first glance, to be highly profitable (assuming, say, that the cost of capital is between 10 and 20 percent). Since analysts, external to the company, compute an ROI for the firm as a whole in evaluating corporate profitability, the use of this measure for evaluating divisional performance encourages goal congruence between the division and the firm.

Actions that the division takes to increase its ROI will often (but not always) increase the overall ROI of the corporation. Most important, perhaps, the measure focuses the division manager's attention on the assets employed in the division and motivates the manager to invest in assets only to the extent that an adequate return can be earned on them. If a manager is evaluated only on the level of profits, without regard to the assets employed, the temptation is to expand assets (for example, by increasing inventories or extending receivables) as long as any incremental profit can be earned on the expanded assets. Such actions, however, will lower the divisional ROI and hence will not be taken if an ROI performance measure is being used.

Defects of the ROI measure are well known.[2] Actions that increase the divisional ROI may make the division worse off and, conversely, actions that decrease divisional ROI may increase the economic wealth of the division. For example, assume the cost of capital to the division mentioned above (with the ROI of 22.2 percent) is 15 percent. Suppose the division sees an opportunity requiring a new investment of $15,000 that will earn $3,000 per year. The return on this investment is 20 percent, well above the cost of capital. But the new ROI for the division will be

$$ROI = \frac{20,000 + 3,000}{90,000 + 15,000} = \frac{23,000}{105,000} = 21.9 \text{ percent,}$$

a decrease from the previous level of 22.2 percent. Therefore, the division manager is tempted to refuse this investment, since even though it returns in excess of the cost of capital (it generates $750 per year in new cash flow after paying the investment financing cost), it lowers the divisional ROI. Conversely, if the division has an asset carried at a $20,000 cost that is earning $3,600 per year (an 18 percent return), the division can increase its ROI by disposing of this asset even though it is earning above the cost of capital:

$$ROI = \frac{20,000 - 3,600}{90,000 - 20,000} = \frac{16,400}{70,000} = 23.4 \text{ percent.}$$

A similar problem arises when two divisions with different investment bases are compared. For example, a second division with assets of $50,000 and net income of $12,500 will show an ROI of 25 percent. It might appear that this second division is more profitable, since its ROI of 25 percent exceeds the 22.2 percent ROI of the first division. But on closer inspection we see that the first division has $40,000 more in assets, on which its incremental earnings are $7,500 (from $20,000 − $12,500). Therefore, its incremental ROI is 7,500/40,000 or 18.75 per-

---

[2] See, for example, Dearden [1969] and Chapter III in Solomons [1965]. These ROI defects are added to all the previously discussed problems when short-term profit (the numerator in ROI) is used as a measure of performance.

cent, well above the cost of capital of 15 percent. Hence the first division is more profitable, after subtracting capital costs, than the second division.

This problem is caused by evaluating divisional performance with a ratio (ROI). A manager attempting to maximize a ratio can either increase the numerator or decrease the denominator. Unfortunately, it may prove easier to maximize the ROI ratio by decreasing the denominator, through shrinking or containing investment—actions that may not be in the best interests of the firm—and foregoing investment in many successful projects that can earn in excess of the divisional cost of capital but yield returns below the current average ROI of the division. In general, any project or asset whose return is below the average ROI of the division will be a candidate for disposal or will not be recommended for funding, since its inclusion in the investment base will lower the division's ROI.

RESIDUAL INCOME

To eliminate the problems associated with using a ratio to measure and evaluate performance, many companies have adopted the *residual income* (*RI*) approach, first popularized by the General Electric Company. When computing residual income, an explicit cost of capital must be specified and multiplied by the investment base to obtain a capital charge. This charge is subtracted from net income before taxes, and the remainder is called the residual income—the income earned after charging for the cost of capital. For our two divisions, the RI computation is presented in Table 15-1. This computation shows that Division 1 is indeed more profitable than Division 2, since its residual income is higher. The RI difference of $1,500 is precisely due to the return in excess of the cost of capital of 0.0375 (obtained from 0.1875 − 0.15) applied to the incremental investment of $40,000 [since 0.0375(40,000) = 1,500] in Division 1.

Also, if Division 1 takes its 20 percent project opportunity ($15,000 investment, $3,000 annual return), its RI will increase, whereas if it disposes of the $20,000 asset earning $3,600 per year, its RI will decrease (see Table 15-2).

The RI measure will always increase when we add investments earning above the cost of capital or eliminate investments earning below the cost of capital. Therefore there is goal congruence between the evaluation of the division and

TABLE 15-1. **Residual-Income Computation**

	Division 1	Division 2
Invested capital	$90,000	$50,000
NIBT	$20,000	$12,500
Capital charge (15% of invested capital)	13,500	7,500
Residual income	$ 6,500	$ 5,000

TABLE 15-2.   **Options for Division 1**

	Now	*Option 1 (New $15,000 Investment)*	*Option 2 (Dispose of $20,000 asset)*
Invested capital	$90,000	$105,000	$70,000
NIBT	$20,000	$ 23,000	$16,400
Capital charge	13,500	15,750	10,500
Residual income	$ 6,500	$ 7,250	$ 5,900

actions that maximize the economic wealth of the division and the firm. The firm will always prefer the division to have a higher rather than a lower residual income. In this regard, RI offers significant advantages over the ROI measure, since we have already noted examples where actions that increased the ROI made the firm worse off. The RI measure is also more flexible, since a different percentage can be applied to investments of different risks. Modern finance theory[3] recommends that the cost of capital reflect a risk premium for the systematic risk of the assets. Therefore, the cost of capital for divisions in different lines of business may differ, and even assets within the same division (compare cash or short-term receivables with long-lived specialized fixed assets) may be in different risk classes. In principle, an RI evaluation permits the recognition of differing risk-adjusted capital costs, whereas the simple ROI evaluation does not.

Residual income is a less convenient measure than ROI, however, because it is an absolute number, not deflated by the size of the division. It is easier for a much larger division to earn a given amount of residual income than a smaller division. For example, consider two divisions, one with $1 million in assets and the second with $10 million in assets; both have a cost of capital of 15 percent. In order to earn residual income of $100,000, the first division would need to earn net income of $250,000 (a 25 percent ROI) whereas the second division would have to earn $1,600,000 (only a 16 percent ROI). For this reason, most companies using an RI evaluation will not simply direct managers to maximize residual income. Rather they will set targeted or budgeted levels of RI, appropriate for the asset structure of each division, and evaluate divisional managers by comparing actual to budgeted RI.

An alternative and less satisfactory approach reports residual income as a percentage of investment. This method is less satisfactory, since it reintroduces the problem we had with the ROI measure that was eliminated by using residual income. That is, actions that increase the residual-income percentage of investment are not always in the best interests of the firm. If the small $1 million division mentioned above with $250,000 in net income found an investment opportunity costing $200,000 and earning $40,000 per year, its residual income would increase

---

[3] See, for example, Chapter 8 in Van Horne [1980].

from \$100,000 to \$110,000, indicating that this was a favorable investment. But its residual income as a percentage of investment would decline from

$$\frac{100,000}{1,000,000} = 10 \text{ percent} \quad \text{to} \quad \frac{110,000}{1,200,000} = 9.2 \text{ percent}.$$

Therefore, this measure is not congruent with the economic wealth of the firm.

The Reece-Cool [1978] survey of investment centers found that 65 percent used return on investment exclusively, only 2 percent used residual income exclusively, and 28 percent used both ROI and RI (5 percent used some other method, not specified). A study conducted more than ten years earlier had found a higher percentage of investment centers using residual income[4] (6 percent used RI exclusively and 42 percent used both RI and ROI). Thus, in spite of theoretical reasons for preferring RI, there is no discernible trend away from ROI to RI. It is not clear why we continue to see companies using ROI, despite its known disadvantages, unless:

1. The dysfunctional behavior motivated by use of this measure is not a material problem in actual practice.
2. The extensive use of ROI by financial analysts causes the company to wish its divisions to make this ratio as large as possible.
3. Companies are unwilling to specify the cost of capital required for the RI calculation.
4. Managers prefer profitability measured as a percentage rate, as in ROI, to compare with other financial measures such as inflation rates, interest rates, and the profitability rates of other industries, companies, or divisions.

The discussion, so far, has focused on properties distinguishing the ROI measure from the RI. With both measures, however, there remain significant problems of interpretation and measurement that we have not addressed. We have been deliberately vague in specifying how investment and net income in a division are measured and in interpreting the accounting rate of return as if it were analogous to the cost of capital. In fact, each of these issues requires greater elaboration in order to understand the properties of investment center measures of performance.

ACCOUNTING VERSUS TRUE RATE OF RETURN

The accounting rate of return—net income before taxes divided by investment—is a popular measure because it has been interpreted as representing the true underlying economic rate of return for investments in the division. Unfortunately,

---

[4] See Mauriel and Anthony [1966].

except in very special circumstances, the accounting ROI will not equal the underlying yield of the assets in the division. To demonstrate this clearly, let us elaborate on our numerical example.

Recall our division with $90,000 in assets and annual net income of $20,000. This division actually consists of five identical assets of different ages. Each asset costs $30,000 and generates a net cash flow (revenues less variable costs and traceable fixed cash costs) of $10,000 per year for five years. After five years of operation the asset is worthless and is scrapped for zero salvage value. The division has reached a steady state in which each year a five-year-old asset is scrapped and a new one purchased. The division operates in an idealized world where there is no inflation and no relative price changes. (We will deal with inflation subsequently.) To keep the analysis simple, we will ignore tax effects. Also, for simplicity, we will assume that all cash flows and investment occur at a single point in time, on the last day of the year.

For financial reporting purposes the company uses straight-line depreciation. With five assets, each generating a depreciation charge of $6,000 per year ($30,000 divided by five years), the total depreciation charge is $30,000 per year. Therefore the net income is the $50,000 net cash flow less $30,000 depreciation, or $20,000. The appropriate measure of investment for the year is $90,000, derived as follows:

Age of Asset (Years)	Book Value
0	$30,000
1	24,000
2	18,000
3	12,000
4	6,000
	$90,000

As previously noted, the accounting ROI of this division is 20K/90K or 22.2 percent.

In fact, however, each asset is generating a return of about 20 percent. The sequence of cash flows of an initial $30,000 outlay followed by five annual net cash flows of $10,000 has about zero present value for a discount rate of 20 percent.[5]

Even in this simple example the accounting rate of return of 22.2 percent does not equal the actual rate of return of slightly less than 20 percent. Therefore, it is inappropriate to impute the actual yield of assets in a division or company from the accounting ROI. The difference in the two yields is caused by using straight-line depreciation for the accounting measure. In order for the accounting ROI to equal the actual yield, we must use a depreciation method derived from the decline in the present value of the asset.

---

[5] As we see from Table 15-3, the yield is slightly below 20 percent (actually it is 19.86 percent). In order to keep the numbers simple, we will ignore the error of less than 1 percent caused by this approximation.

TABLE 15-3.

Year	Cash Inflow	Present-Value Factor at 20%	Discounted Cash Flow
1	$10,000	0.8333	8,333.33
2	10,000	0.6944	6,944.44
3	10,000	0.5787	5,787.04
4	10,000	0.4823	4,822.53
5	10,000	0.4019	4,018.78
	$50,000	2.9906	29,906.12

PRESENT-VALUE DEPRECIATION METHOD[6]

The present-value depreciation method is derived directly from the cash-flow schedule used to justify the acquisition of the asset. In this way we can obtain a periodic ROI performance measure such that, when actual cash flows equal forecasted cash flows, then each year's ROI figure will equal the yield (internal rate of return) of the asset. The anomalous case noted above, where we obtain an accounting ROI different from the actual yield of the project even though actual cash flows equal expected cash flows, is due solely to the inappropriate use of the straight-line depreciation method for internal evaluation purposes. When the depreciation method used for external reporting (such as straight-line, sum-of-years'-digits, declining-balance) is applied to internal performance evaluation, then a deviation between the true rate of return and the measured rate of return is introduced.

The present-value depreciation method is derived from the discounted-cash-flow approach. Depreciation is computed as the loss over time of the present value of the asset. At the beginning of our asset's five-year life, we anticipate five years of $10,000 annual cash flows from it. After one year has passed, we have four years of cash flow remaining. Therefore, after one year, we have lost one year of cash flow, a loss that we will notice five years in the future. Because, after the first year, the cash flow is lost five years in future, the depreciation or decline in present value of the asset is initially relatively low. From the data in Table 15-3, the loss of a $10,000 cash flow five years in the future causes a decline of $4,019 in the value of the asset. The decline in present value (depreciation) increases each year, since the loss of one annual cash flow comes closer to the time at which the present value is computed. At the start of the fifth and final year there is still one more $10,000 cash flow, whose present value (at 20 percent) equals $8,333. At the end of the fifth year the asset is worthless. The present-

---

[6] This section deals with an unorthodox method for depreciating assets for internal reporting purposes. At first reading, it can be skipped without loss of continuity.

value depreciation charge in year 5 is $8,333, more than twice the first year's charge.

When an asset yields level cash flows over its useful life, as in our simple example, the present-value depreciation method is identical to the annuity depreciation method. A depreciation schedule derived from the annuity method can be constructed for any asset and will have the following properties:

1. The depreciation charges over the life of the asset, n, will sum to the original cost of the asset.

2. The depreciation charge will increase at a compound rate of r percent per year. (This constant growth rate arises from the assumption of level cash flows each year.)

If r is the internal rate of return of the asset and there are level cash flows each of the n years, then we can show that the accounting rate of return with annuity depreciation will equal the internal rate of return each year. The formula for computing the annuity depreciation rate in each year $i(i = 1, 2, \ldots, n)$ is

$$\left(\begin{array}{c}\text{Annuity depreciation} \\ \text{rate in year } i\end{array}\right) = \frac{r(1 + r)^{i-1}}{(1 + r)^n - 1}$$

$$= \frac{\left(\dfrac{1}{1 + r}\right)^{n-i+1}}{a_{\overline{r}\rceil n}},$$

where $a_{\overline{r}\rceil n}$ represents the present value at an interest rate r of paying $1 per year for n years:[7]

$$a_{\overline{r}\rceil n} = \frac{1 - (1 + r)^{-n}}{r}.$$

With $r = 0.1986$ and $n = 5$, the depreciation rates for each of the five years of our asset are:

Year	Depreciation Rate	Depreciation Rate × 30,000
1	0.1348	4,044
2	0.1615	4,845
3	0.1936	5,808
4	0.2320	6,960
5	0.2781	8,343
	1.0000	30,000

[7] Note that if $r = 0$, then $a_{\overline{r}\rceil n} = n$, and the annuity depreciation rate is a constant $1/n$ each year. Therefore, straight-line depreciation can be viewed as a special case of annuity depreciation with an assumed interest rate of 0.

Age of Asset (Years)	Accumulated Depreciation	Book Value
0	0	30,000
1	4,044	25,956
2	8,889	21,111
3	14,697	15,303
4	21,657	8,343
	49,287	100,713

The accounting ROI is now computed as

$$\text{ROI} = \frac{50,000 - 30,000}{100,713} = 19.86 \text{ percent,}$$

which is exactly the true rate of return. Therefore, in this simple case, any divergence between the accounting ROI and the true rate of return is caused by using the straight-line depreciation method rather than the annuity method with the correct interest rate.

In theory, one could know the expected cash flow from each asset and compute from these flows the present-value depreciation schedule. In the special case where the cash flows are expected to be uniform over the life of the asset, we simplify by using the annuity depreciation method. This is not likely to be a practical procedure, however, for all of a company's depreciable assets. As a result, most companies use a method (straight-line depreciation) that assumes a zero rate of return (see footnote 7). A company could try an alternative procedure by assuming level cash flows and using an interest rate, r, based on a cost of capital for all the assets in the division. Assuming an interest rate equal to a cost of capital is certainly no less arbitrary than assuming a zero interest rate. The computation of depreciation and ROI for our five-asset division, using a 15 percent interest rate for annuity depreciation, is shown in Table 15-4. The accounting rate of return is computed as

$$\text{ROI} = \frac{20,000}{98,316} = 20.3 \text{ percent.}$$

This is a slight overestimate of the true rate of return but is much closer than the 22.2 percent ROI computed assuming zero cost of capital (that is, using the straight-line depreciation method).

The perverse incentives associated with using straight-line depreciation in conjunction with an ROI evaluation criterion can be vividly illustrated. Observe what happens if the manager decides to stop investing in a new asset each year to replace the five-year-old asset just scrapped (see Table 15-5). The ROI steadily increases because the book value of the assets decreases faster than the net income falls. Note, however, that the manager of this division should hope for a promotion or transfer sometime before the end of the fourth year after adopting this policy. After that time the division will be rather short of operating assets.

TABLE 15-4. Depreciation Schedule—Annuity Method at 15 Percent

Age of Asset	Depreciation Rate	Depreciation	Book Value at Start of Year[8]
0	0.1483	4,449	30,000
1	0.1706	5,118	25,551
2	0.1961	5,883	20,433
3	0.2256	6,768	14,550
4	0.2594	7,782	7,782
	1.000	30,000	98,316

With annuity depreciation at the 15 percent cost of capital, the apparent gains from following the above policy are greatly reduced (see Table 15-6). There is a slight increase in the annual ROI's but certainly much less than in the straight-line depreciation case. If the actual rate of return (19.86 percent) had been used to compute the annuity depreciation, there would have been no upward drift at all and therefore no incentive to deplete the assets of the division.

Because of the bias against new investment when using straight-line depreciation and an ROI performance measure, a number of companies measure assets at their gross book value rather than net book value. In the Reece-Cool [1978] survey, 85 percent of companies used net book value while 14 percent used gross book value. When assets are measured at gross book value, the incentive to avoid investing in new assets is eliminated. In fact a new incentive—to replace existing assets with new assets—is created, since the measured increase in investment is only the difference between the historical cost of the existing asset and the purchase cost of the new asset. This is well below the actual net outlay for the new asset as measured by the purchase cost less trade-in or salvage value of the existing asset. A case can be made for valuing assets at gross book value, but

TABLE 15-5. ROI by Years, No Asset Replacement, Straight-Line Depreciation

	Year				
	0	1	2	3	4
Net cash flow	50,000	40,000	30,000	20,000	10,000
Depreciation	30,000	24,000	18,000	12,000	6,000
NIBT	20,000	16,000	12,000	8,000	4,000
Investment	90,000	60,000	36,000	18,000	6,000
ROI	22.2%	26.7%	33.3%	44.4%	66.7%

---

[8] The book value at the end of each year is the start-of-year book value less depreciation in that year. Thus, during the last year, the depreciation charge of 7,782 is sufficient to write down the start-of-year book value of 7,782 to 0 by the end of the asset's life.

TABLE 15-6. ROI by Years, No Asset Replacement—Annuity Depreciation at 15 Percent

	Year				
	0	*1*	*2*	*3*	*4*
Net cash flow	50,000	40,000	30,000	20,000	10,000
Depreciation	30,000	25,551	20,433	14,550	7,782
NIBT	20,000	14,449	9,567	5,450	2,218
Investment	98,316	68,316	42,765	22,332	7,782
ROI	20.3%	21.2%	22.4%	24.4%	28.5%

then one should not subtract depreciation when computing the return or income from the asset. We will discuss this proposition at the end of the chapter in the context of a cash-flow accounting system. For now, the use of gross book value is perhaps an overreaction to problems caused by use of net book value and straight-line depreciation to compute the ROI. While eliminating some distortions, it introduces new problems of its own. A better compromise would use a form of the present-value depreciation method to minimize the more obvious incentives for disinvestment caused by the ROI computation with straight-line depreciation.

The limitations of the straight-line depreciation method are also apparent when the residual-income method is used, though the effects are less perverse than for the ROI measure. In the steady state, our five-asset division would show the following residual-income computation with a 15 percent cost of capital:

Investment	$90,000
Net cash flow	50,000
Depreciation	30,000
Net income	20,000
Capital charge at 15%	13,500
Residual income	$ 6,500

There is a slight incentive to disinvest, as shown by Table 15-7, which computes the residual income as the retired asset is not replaced each year. The RI increases initially but, unlike the ROI measure, it eventually declines as the asset base shrinks and earnings decline. This is another demonstration of the preferability of the RI method.

Nevertheless, incorporating a present-value depreciation method with the residual-income computation produces even more satisfying results. If the capital charge for the residual-income method equals the asset's economic rate of return, then the residual income of the asset in each year of its life will be zero. This is a sensible result, since the economic (or internal) rate of return is that interest rate for which the net present value of cash flows equals zero. The RI measure with present-value depreciation is able to convert this result into an analogous periodic performance measure, for which the return in excess of the internal rate

		Year			
	0	*1*	*2*	*3*	*4*
Investment	$90,000	$60,000	$36,000	$18,000	$ 6,000
Net cash flow	50,000	40,000	30,000	20,000	10,000
Depreciation	30,000	24,000	18,000	12,000	6,000
Net income	20,000	16,000	12,000	8,000	4,000
Capital charge at 15%	13,500	9,000	5,400	2,700	900
Residual income	$ 6,500	$ 7,000	$ 6,600	$ 5,300	$ 3,100

of return equals zero each period. In practice, however, the residual-income capital charge may be below the internal rate of return of many assets, so that these assets will show a positive residual income each year.

It would seem that the present-value depreciation method offers significant advantages over the straight-line method for evaluating the performance of investment centers. Yet just as the users of residual income rather than ROI are a distinct minority, the users of the present-value or annuity depreciation methods represent a tiny, perhaps invisible minority. The Reece-Cool [1978] survey reports that only 7 percent of 351 profit centers use a depreciation method different from that used for external reporting. Since the present-value method is not approved as part of GAAP, this 7 percent must represent an upper bound of the number of companies that could possibly be using this procedure. It appears that:

1. Companies are very unwilling to use a depreciation method for internal performance evaluation different from that used for external reporting.

2. Companies are unaware of or unconvinced by the arguments promoting the benefits of the present-value depreciation method for evaluating investment centers.

3. The consequences of using the straight-line or accelerated depreciation methods are not material enough to cause them to use a less familiar and seemingly more complex depreciation method.

4. The annuity depreciation method yields its desired properties only when cash flows are assumed to be uniform over the life of the project. If investments have higher cash flows in earlier years than in later years, then straight-line depreciation may be a better approximation to the decline in the present value of the asset over time.

5. Finally, the annuity, or any present-value, depreciation method requires a shift in thinking by management. Ordinarily, a depre-

ciation schedule is computed first and profit determined as a residual (after depreciation). With the annuity or present-value depreciation method, profit must first be forecasted by management and then depreciation determined (as a residual) based on the forecast of future cash flows. This shift in thinking may be too radical for many managers to accept.

PRICE-LEVEL CHANGES

Up to this point in the chapter we have discussed ROI and RI measures assuming a stable price level; there have been no changes in the prices of the assets or the net cash flows of the firm. The reason is not that zero price-level changes are representative of any known country or industry, but that we wanted to identify the assumptions and limitations of traditional investment-center performance measures without simultaneously treating the changing-price-level problem. Price-level changes introduce entirely new distortions into ROI and RI measures.

The principal distortion occurs because revenues and cash costs are measured in current-year dollars, whereas the investment base and depreciation charges are measured by the historic dollars used to acquire the assets. Depreciation based on historic cost underestimates what the depreciation charge would be based on either restated or current-dollar cost. This causes the income of the firm to be overstated. At the same time, the investment of the firm is understated, because most of the firm's assets were acquired in previous years at lower price levels than those currently prevailing. The combination of overstated net income and understated investment causes the ROI ratio or RI measure to be much higher than if inflation had not occurred. The increased ROI or RI is not a signal of higher profitability; it is due solely to a failure to adjust for the money illusion caused by inflation. We add together 1970 dollars and 1980 dollars as if they were the same units, when in fact they are as different as dollars and deutschmarks.

This effect is easy to illustrate. Consider our five-asset division and allow the price level of our basic five-year asset to increase by 10 percent per year for four years, a rate that corresponds to the actual inflation rate in the economy. Assume, however, that the division is not able to raise prices fast enough to keep pace with either its asset costs or its variable input costs, so that net cash flow increases by only 6 percent per year during this four-year inflationary period. After four years the net cash flow of the division will be

$$\$50,000 \cdot (1.06)^4 = \$63,124.$$

The investment and associated depreciation charges[9] for the assets acquired in each of the past years are shown in Table 15-8.

The ROI and RI of the division are now easily calculated as follows:

---

[9] For simplicity, we will illustrate our examples with the popular if problem-plagued straight-line depreciation method. Similar effects occur with present-value depreciation.

TABLE 15-8. Investment and Depreciation: 10 Percent Annual Inflation

Age of Asset (Years) (1)	Asset Cost (2) = $30,000 \cdot (1.1)^{4-(1)}$	Annual Depreciation (3) = (2)/5	Net Book Value, End of Year 4 (4) = (2) − (1) · (3)
0	$30,000 \cdot (1.1)^4 =$ 43,923	$ 8,785	$ 43,923
1	$30,000 \cdot (1.1)^3 =$ 39,930	7,986	31,944
2	$30,000 \cdot (1.1)^2 =$ 36,300	7,260	21,780
3	$30,000 \cdot (1.1)^1 =$ 33,000	6,600	13,200
4	$30,000$ = 30,000	6,000	6,000
	183,153	$36,631	$116,847

Investment	$116,847
Net cash flows	63,124
Depreciation	36,631
Net income	26,493
Capital charge at 15%	17,527
Residual income	$ 8,966

$$\text{ROI} = \frac{26,493}{116,847} = 22.7 \text{ percent.}$$

After four years of a general 10 percent yearly inflation, during which the division is able to increase its net cash flows by only 6 percent per year, the division is able to show an ROI slightly above its preinflation figure. Its new residual income of $8,966 is also higher than the preinflation RI of $6,500. The division could easily be deluded into thinking that despite its inability to pass on cost increases to the marketplace, it is still coping rather well during this difficult inflationary period. Such reasoning, however, will eventually be shown to be fallacious. The apparent increases in both ROI and RI are due solely to the failure to restate historic costs in units of either current cost or current purchasing power. Were the inflation rate to be stopped suddenly at the end of year 4, the firm would maintain its current net operating cash flows, replace its older assets at the higher price level, and eventually see the consequences of its failure to keep pace with inflation:

Investment[10]	$131,769
Net cash flows	63,124
Depreciation: 5 · 8,784.60	43,923
Net income	19,201
Capital charge at 15%	19,765
Residual income	(564)

$$\text{ROI} = \frac{19,201}{131,769} = 14.6 \text{ percent.}$$

The residual income is now negative, and the postinflation ROI of 14.6 percent is well below the preinflationary value. The postinflationary figures of both ROI

---

[10] Investment, at net book value, equals $43,923 \cdot (1 + \frac{4}{5} + \frac{3}{5} + \frac{2}{5} + \frac{1}{5}) = \$131,769.$

and RI are now below the misleadingly high figures reported at the end of the inflation cycle when the firm had yet to replace its older assets.

The message from this example is simple and direct. During inflationary periods, the use of historical cost to compute depreciation expense and measure the investment base causes the reported ROI or RI of a division to be deceptively high. It is easy for a division or company to look highly profitable with these measures when price-level changes are occurring. Firms may be misled into thinking that asset returns are much better than they actually are. Reality starts to sink in when older assets are replaced at the currently high price level. Firms occasionally report that the current return on investment is adequate but not sufficient to justify new investment. Such firms are, in all likelihood, being victimized by monetary illusion caused by inflation. Properly measured, if returns on investment are satisfactory, the returns to new investment should also be satisfactory. But when the adequate or satisfactory returns are caused by under-depreciation of older assets and the failure to restate investment in terms of current cost or current dollars, firms will discover that new investment at the current price level yields less-than-satisfactory returns.

Note that divisions with newer assets will tend to show lower ROI and RI measures than equally profitable divisions whose assets were acquired at lower price levels (ignoring the effects of productivity or quality improvements embedded in the newer assets). Unless some provision is made to neutralize such inflationary biases, managers will be reluctant to make new investments because of the negative impact on their ROI and RI. Conversely, managers will tend to delay the replacement of low-(historical)-cost aged assets because of the misleading high ROI or RI earned from these assets.

Our having identified the problem does not imply that there is an obvious solution. The problem of adjusting internal performance reports to neutralize the effect of inflation is identical to the problem of inflation-adjusting corporate financial statements for shareholders and other external users. Since hundreds of books and articles have been written on this latter subject without any noticeable consensus emerging, and many authoritative figures are still confused on the difference between movements in the general price level and changes in relative prices, it is unlikely that a few paragraphs in one chapter of a book will provide a definitive and universally accepted set of recommendations. With this disclaimer we can offer the following observations.

The simplest and most straightforward method to adjust for inflation, as defined by a general change in the price level, is to apply a general price index such as the Consumer Price Index (CPI) or the Gross National Product (GNP) Implicit Price Deflator to older assets so that their historic cost will be measured in units of current dollars.[11] With this method, the historic cost of each asset is

---

[11] The GNP deflator is a much broader and probably a better index of changes in the general price level. The CPI index is distorted by inappropriate measurement of housing costs and too-infrequent revisions to reflect substitution effects. These distortions became painfully obvious during 1979 and 1980.

multiplied by the ratio of the current year's price index to the value of the index in the year the asset was purchased. This will enable all assets to be measured and depreciated using the same units—units that represent the current year's purchasing power. This simple adjustment will alleviate much of the inflationary bias from ROI and RI measures.[12]

Many authors and business people, however, are not enthusiastic about using this general-price-level adjustment. They seem concerned that the restated cost may not approximate the current cost of assets and hence may give an unrealistic measure of how the ROI or RI would change were older assets to be replaced by newer assets at current prices. This argument is unresolvable on theoretical grounds, since it involves personal value judgments as to what a divisional ROI is supposed to measure. The GPL historic-cost advocates emphasize measurement of historic performance, including perhaps the purchase of assets at higher or lower relative prices than today's assets, once general-price-level adjustments are removed. Advocates of current-replacement-cost or current-market-value measures place more emphasis on predicting current and future performance. They claim that replacement cost or market value provides a better estimate of the current investment base of the division. If reliable market prices of assets could be obtained, the return from continuing to operate these assets could be compared with the return from alternative investment opportunities. Also, the effect of holding gains and losses could be isolated so that the operating or sustainable income from current assets could be computed.[13] Therefore, these advocates prefer to adjust the historic cost of assets to some measure of current cost or current value.

The simplest way to perform the adjustment to current cost is to use an index specific to each asset class. Thousands of indices for specific classes of assets are produced by the government and trade associations. A problem with almost all these specific indices is that they are not adjusted for technological change. Therefore, many specific price indices have increased not only because of genuine increases in costs to obtain the same basic asset but also because the newer assets are better than the older assets; they may have greater capabilities, lower labor or energy costs, finer tolerances, and so on. One must be careful that the restatement of older assets with a specific price index does not overcompensate for price-level changes and value the asset well above what a newer but comparable asset would cost. Measurements of current market value can be

---

[12] The reader can verify that by price-level adjusting the investment and depreciation figures in Table 15-9, the ROI, after four years of 10 percent annual inflation, would drop from the inflation-distorted figure of 22.7 percent to the postinflation level of 14.6 percent. This adjustment would clearly indicate to management that the failure to increase net cash flows to keep pace with inflation had lowered the division's return on investment.

[13] *Holding gains* occur when the value or replacement cost of assets increases faster than the general price level. *Holding losses* occur when assets decrease in value or increase less than the general price level. *Operating* or *sustainable income* is net income less all holding gains. These are not trivial concepts. The interested reader can consult Vancil and Weil [1976] for an excellent collection of articles on this subject.

obtained by independent appraisals or by making comparisons to the selling prices of recently traded comparable assets.

In making these adjustments, it is important to use an objective method, such as indexing. Recall that our objective is to measure, evaluate, and motivate the performance of the managers of investment centers. Once the method of measurement has been determined, managers will attempt to make their performance measure look as good as possible. If asset and income measures are subjective, requiring estimates from the general manager or the divisional controller, these individuals may maximize the performance measure not just by producing more output for sale at higher prices and lower costs but also by influencing the asset and income measures. Thus, these measures need a certain "hardness"[14] to be able to resist the pressures that will be brought to bear on them by the individuals whose performance is being measured. Forecasts of discounted cash flows and estimates of current market values are required for many special decisions, such as capital acquisition or abandonment. But they provide a vulnerable basis for establishing a management control and performance evaluation system that must function continually and reliably.

To summarize this section, inflation adjustments must be made to prevent enormous distortions in the evaluation of investment-center performance. Inflation adjustments are needed for depreciation and cost of goods sold when computing the net income (or return) figure and for the inventory and fixed capital included in the investment base. Index methods, either general or specific, will provide a good basis for adjusting for price-level changes while maintaining the objectivity and freedom from manipulation necessary for a system of measuring the performance of rational persons. Index methods also are the least expensive way of adjusting the historic cost of assets to current-year dollars.

One final issue is the effect of inflation on the cost of capital. During a period of anticipated inflation, investors and creditors will demand a higher rate of return for their invested capital to compensate them for the cheaper dollars they will receive in the future. The cost of capital, therefore, is a function of anticipated inflation, so that companies should not use a fixed target rate for divisional ROI or to compute capital charges for an RI measure. Adjustments of the corporate or divisional cost of capital as a function of anticipated inflation should already be occurring as part of the capital-budgeting process. The current cost of capital can be derived from data on market interest rates and expected rates of return in equity markets.[15] Such rates will already have the market's best estimates of inflationary expectations imbedded in them. Hence, as long as capital costs are derived from market measures, inflationary expectations will be incorporated and

---

[14] This concept of "hardness" of measurement is developed well by Ijiri [1975 and 1981], the most articulate advocate for general-price-level, historic-cost measurement.

[15] Measuring the cost of capital is a complex and controversial process. It would take us too far afield to develop the relevant concepts. Chapters 3, 7, and especially 8 in Van Horne [1980] provide an excellent introduction to this subject.

no further adjustments need be performed. Firms will use incorrect costs of capital only if a fixed rate has been established as company policy and left unchanged independent of market conditions, or if the cost of capital is based on historic financing costs such as the coupon rate on debt issued several years earlier.

We conclude this section by observing that of 472 investment centers surveyed in Reece-Cool [1978], only ten (2 percent) indicated that they used replacement costs to value plant and equipment. There was no suggestion that any companies used general-price-level adjustments for their costs. Again, one can interpret this finding only by recognizing that a desire to have divisional evaluation measures coincide with shareholder reporting must be extremely strong in almost all companies. One cannot be sanguine about the immateriality of the inflation bias on ROI and RI measures or the ability of top managers to heuristically control for the effects of inflation on these investment-center performance measures. Perhaps the resistance to adopt inflation-adjusted performance measures reflects the lack of attention to this subject in accounting and business education programs in the days when most of today's top executives received their formal education. A more cynical viewpoint would suggest that bonus systems for corporate and divisional executives are based on income reported using historic-cost measures. Managers may be reluctant to adopt inflation adjustments for divisional performance evaluation for fear that such adjustments would reveal how much of current corporate profitability, from which bonuses are computed, is caused by using nonadjusted historical-cost numbers.

CAPITALIZING VERSUS EXPENSING

For certain expenditures, especially on intangibles, there is discretion as to whether these expenditures should be expensed in the period in which they are incurred or capitalized and amortized over the future periods when their benefits are expected to be realized. The Financial Accounting Standards Board has been discouraging the capitalization of most intangible expenditures (see, for example, Statement 2 on Research and Development Expenditures), but internal performance evaluation need not be bound by regulations established for external reporting. In a steady-state situation, where roughly equal expenditures on intangibles are made each year, there is no effect on net income, since the sum of amortization expenses of current and past expenditures will equal the current year's expenditures. But the failure to capitalize expenditures with expected future benefits will penalize earnings in the short run, until the steady state is reached, and overstate the ROI and RI in the steady state since the expenditures on intangibles will not be included in the measured investment base.

We can illustrate these distortions by allowing our five-asset division to engage in a promotional activity each year. This activity costs $3,000 but produces incremental cash flows of $1,000 for each of the next five years. (Note that this activity is analogous to purchasing an additional 10 percent of one of our basic assets.) If this expenditure is expensed as incurred, we will observe the following sequence of net-income measures:

	Year					
	0	*1*	*2*	*3*	*4*	*5*
Net cash flows	$47,000	$48,000	$49,000	$50,000	$51,000	$52,000
Depreciation	30,000	30,000	30,000	30,000	30,000	30,000
Net income	$17,000	$18,000	$19,000	$20,000	$21,000	$22,000

Initially, the $3,000 expenditure reduces net income with no compensating benefit. By year 5, the annual $3,000 expenditure is more than offset by the five $1,000 increments in cash flows from the expenditures in the previous five years, and overall the net income has increased by $2,000 from these cumulative expenditures.

If the annual $3,000 expenditure had been capitalized and amortized over five years, the sequence of net-income figures would be:

	Year					
	0	*1*	*2*	*3*	*4*	*5*
Net cash flow	$50,000	$51,000	$52,000	$53,000	$54,000	$55,000
Depreciation and amortization	30,000	30,600	31,200	31,800	32,400	33,000
Net income	$20,000	$20,400	$20,800	$21,200	$21,600	$22,000

Thus, both methods eventually reach the same net-income figure in the steady state, but the capitalization/amortization alternative has a more gradual transition.

When used to evaluate investment-center performance, however, the two methods yield quite different measures. Under the expensing alternative, the ROI in year 5 (at steady-state conditions) is

$$\frac{22,000}{90,000} = 24.4 \text{ percent}$$

and the RI is

$$22,000 - 13,500 = \$8,500.$$

With the capitalization/amortization alternative, the investment base increases by $9,000 to $99,000 so that the ROI is 22,000/99,000 = 22.2 percent and the RI is 22,000 − 14,850 = $7,150. The performance measures for the capitalization/ amortization alternative are consistent with the measures we derived previously (ROI is the same, and the RI is 10 percent higher because of the effective 10 percent increase in our asset).

We conclude from this little exercise that divisions that treat expenditures with future-period benefits as current-period expenses will

1. Show depressed profits until a steady-state level of such expenditures is reached, or any time an unusually large expenditure is made in a year, and
2. Report a higher ROI and RI than is actually being earned in the steady state because of the failure to properly classify such expenditures as investments.

Divisions with a high proportion of expenditures on intangibles will therefore tend to show higher ROI's than, say, manufacturing divisions where most expenditures with future-period benefits tend to be tangible; one can see and touch what one acquired for these expenditures. This is why marketing divisions with heavy advertising and promotional expenditures, or divisions with large numbers of professional employees (whose human capital is not recorded on the balance sheet), will show unusually high ROI performance measures. These divisions are not as profitable as they would appear. Their currently high profitability (as measured by ROI) occurs because profitability in earlier years was understated, as all expenditures on intangibles were expensed as incurred. In the current years the firms are enjoying the benefits from these previous investments in intangibles, but the current benefits are not being related to the intangible investment base developed in previous years. Thus these divisions' ROI appears to be higher because they have many assets that are not being counted as part of their investment base.

IDENTIFICATION OF ASSETS IN THE INVESTMENT BASE

Controllable Versus Noncontrollable Investment

In determining which assets to include in a division's asset base, we must decide whether the primary purpose is to measure the performance of the division or that of the divisional manager. If the purpose is to evaluate the divisional manager, then only those assets that are directly traceable to the division and controlled by the divisional manager should be included in the asset base. Corporate assets used by the central administration or assets controlled at the central level, such as cash, are examples of assets that are neither directly traceable nor controllable at the divisional level and that should be excluded from an evaluation of the divisional manager.

With this approach, the divisional manager would be held responsible for divisional property, plant and equipment, and inventories.[16] If the manager has

---

[16] Inventories should be valued at FIFO or average cost even when the company uses LIFO for financial and tax reporting. LIFO valuation would grossly underestimate the investment in inventories.

control over sales terms and credit policy, then divisional receivables should also be included. This assumes that corporate records are kept so that the receivables traceable to each division's sales activities can be identified. Typically, cash will be controlled at the corporate level, but any cash balances held and managed at the divisional level could be included in the investment base. If the division manager can control the payment terms to suppliers, then accounts payable may be subtracted from the investment base. This will encourage the manager to seek out the most favorable credit terms for purchases.

We can refer to this narrowly defined investment as *controllable divisional investment*. It is analogous to the recommended use of controllable contribution as the appropriate income measure for evaluating managerial performance (see the discussion at the beginning of Chapter 14).These definitions, which exclude common corporate expenses, corporate investment, and, in general, expenses and assets not under the control of the division manager, attempt to base managerial performance measures on actions over which the manager has both responsibility and authority.

Central management, however, may also be interested in evaluating a division's economic performance and in comparing it to that of comparable firms in the same industry. For this situation, an evaluation based solely on controllable investment overstates the division's actual profitability. The overstatement occurs because no division could operate without the services represented by corporate assets (such as buildings and furnishings for senior executives and corporate staff departments, and cash and marketable securities managed at the corporate level). Such assets will be included in the investment base of nondiversified firms in the same industry as the decentralized division, and the managers of the nondiversified firm will attempt to earn a competitive return on these assets, too.

Therefore, many decentralized firms allocate investments in cash, marketable securities, and corporate assets to divisions when computing investment-center performance measures. As discussed elsewhere in this book, such allocations of noncontrollable investments will be mostly arbitrary, based on measures such as sales, square feet occupied, and personnel employed. Even though the divisional manager cannot be held responsible for the allocated values of such assets, their inclusion in the division's investment base serves to signal the divisional manager that, overall, investments in the division must earn somewhat above the cost of capital to provide a return on these common or corporate assets. This does not imply that the cost of capital be raised arbitrarily so that investments just returning the marginal cost of capital would be rejected. The hope is that enough investments are returning above the cost of capital to cover the investment in common assets.[17]

Some firms exclude idle assets from the division's investment base. Again, the critical question is one of controllability. If central management does not

---

[17] A more extensive discussion of controllable versus noncontrollable assets in the investment base appears in Chapter 5 of Solomons [1965], esp. pp. 128–131, 143–148.

permit the division manager to dispose of idle or surplus assets, then these assets are not controllable at the divisional level and should not be included in the division's investment base. If the assets are thus excluded, then the central management should take possession of them and have the right to transfer them to other divisions where they may be needed. If the central management sees no other use for currently idle assets, then they can remain in the division's investment base and the decision left at the local level whether to retain or dispose of them.

One relatively minor issue is whether to use start-of-period, average, or end-of-period values. Since income will usually be earned and measured continuously through the period, it is probably best to use the average level of assets during the period. For a quarterly, semiannual, or annual review, this could be accomplished by averaging the assets at the end of each month. If a residual-income measure is used, a monthly cost of capital could be computed and multiplied by the end-of-month (or average of start and end-of-month) values of the assets to obtain the monthly capital charge.[18]

Leased Assets

One ploy that a clever manager of an investment center might adopt is to lease assets instead of purchasing them. We have already noted the pervasive tendency for divisional accounting procedures to be driven by the procedures for external reporting. The limited capitalization of leases that existed before FAS 13, therefore, provided an incentive for managers to acquire assets through leases, since they would not appear in the division's investment base. The flexible conditions in FAS 13 (plus all subsequent modifications and interpretations) still enable managers to structure many leases so that the assets need not be capitalized for financial reporting purposes and hence will likely be excluded from the divisional investment base.

The incentive for leasing instead of purchasing assets can easily be illustrated in the context of our five-asset division. Suppose that, at the end of a year, instead of purchasing a new asset to replace the one just retired, the divisional manager finds a supplier willing to provide the asset on a five-year lease. The supplier has the same 15 percent cost of capital as the division and computes the equivalent annual lease payment using the five-year 15 percent annuity factor, $a_{\overline{0.15}|5} = 3.3522$, as

$$\text{annual lease payment} = \frac{\$30,000}{3.3522} = \$8,950.$$

After one year with the leased asset, the division has the same physical assets

---

[18] In the simple numerical example we have been using throughout this chapter, we have used the start-of-year (SOY) value, because all cash flows were assumed to occur on the last day of the year. In effect, the SOY investment worked throughout the year to produce the end-of-year cash flows.

and revenues but an extra cash expense of $8,950, a decrease in recorded investment of $30,000, and a decrease in (straight-line) depreciation expense of $6,000. The computation of the ROI and RI for the first several years is shown in Table 15-9.

The ROI of the division increases dramatically as leased assets are substituted for purchased assets. Eventually, when all the assets are leased, the division will show an infinite ROI, since it will be earning net income of $5,250 with no recorded assets. The RI also increases initially but eventually declines. These fluctuations in ROI and RI are purely an artifact of excluding leased assets from the investment base. The size of the division and its profitability are identical to the situation in which all five assets were purchased and owned by the division. Regardless of what the company does for financial reporting purposes, there seems to be no reason for it to exclude leased assets from the divisional investment base. This exclusion provides an incentive for a division to substitute leased assets for purchased assets even when there is no apparent economic advantage for such a substitution; that is, the equivalent purchase price and cost of capital are identical in the two situations.

To remedy this situation, leased assets should be included in the investment base at their fair market value. If an independent estimate of the cost of the asset is not available, then the leased asset can be valued at the discounted present value of the lease payments.[19] Once on the books, the firm has two options on how to treat the annual lease payment. It would be incorrect to charge the full $8,950 lease payment as an expense of the period, since much of this payment represents a financing cost and financing costs are not charged to specific assets in an ROI or RI computation.[20] The preferable method would be to have the depreciation schedule follow the amortization of the debt as represented by the capitalized lease payments. The amortization and depreciation schedule appears below:

Year	Debt—Start of Year	Lease Payment	Effective Interest Expense	Debt Amortization (Depreciation Expense)
1	$30,000	$8,950	$4,500	$4,450
2	25,550	8,950	3,833	5,117
3	20,443	8,950	3,065	5,885
4	14,548	8,950	2,182	6,768
5	7,780	8,950	1,167	7,783[a]

[a] Rounding error caused by using annual lease payment of $8,950 instead of $8,949.50.

---

[19] This sounds simpler than it actually is. Considerable controversy still exists as to the appropriate discount rate for evaluating the leasing option. Tax effects that we are ignoring here become important. See Chapter 19 in Van Horne [1980].

[20] Otherwise we would be double-counting interest expense—once as a subtraction from operating cash flows and a second time as the capital charge in computing RI. This is the same reason why interest costs are not subtracted when performing a discounted cash flow analysis for evaluating a proposed capital acquisition.

TABLE 15-9. **Effect of Substituting Leased Assets for Owned
Assets**

	Year			
	0	*1*	*2*	*3*
Investment	$90,000	$60,000	$36,000	$18,000
Net cash flows	$50,000	$41,050	$32,100	$23,150
Depreciation	30,000	24,000	18,000	12,000
Net income	$20,000	$17,050	$14,100	$11,150
Capital charge	13,500	9,000	5,400	2,700
Residual income	$ 6,500	$ 8,050	$ 8,700	$ 8,450
ROI	22.2%	28.4%	39.2%	61.9%

Only the depreciation expense, shown in the last column, would be charged as an expense to the division. The astute reader will have observed that this depreciation schedule corresponds exactly (apart from trivial rounding errors) to that computed by the annuity depreciation method (see Table 15-4), thereby providing additional support to the use of the annuity method for ROI and RI computations.

Most companies, however, will depreciate capitalized leased assets using the traditional straight-line method. In this case the depreciation expense will be $6,000 per year (just as for owned assets) and the annual depreciation charge will have no particular relationship with the annual $8,950 lease payment. As we have already seen, the straight-line depreciation method distorts the ROI and RI computation, but at least the firm will be consistent in distorting owned and leased assets in the same manner.

Survey Results

In the Reece-Cool [1978] survey, one-third of the firms reported that capitalized leases were included in an investment center's asset base even though the leases were not capitalized for external reporting. Thus, two-thirds of the companies provide an incentive for divisions to lease rather than purchase assets, since the income from the leased assets will be included in the divisional return but the investment in leased assets will be excluded from the investment base. Table 15-10 presents the percentage of companies that include a given category of assets in the investment center's asset base. It is not obvious why inventories, land, building, and equipment were excluded from any of the investment centers. Perhaps there were no assets in these categories for the companies who did not include them in the asset base. Only a minority of companies included common or shared assets, indicating a greater emphasis on evaluating the division *manager's* performance rather than the division's *economic* performance.

TABLE 15-10.   Assets Included in Investment Base

Asset Category	Percentage of 459 Companies
Cash	63
Receivables	94
Inventories	95
Other current assets	76
Land and buildings (used only by investment center)	94
Land and buildings (prorated, when used by more than one investment center)	45
Equipment (used only by investment center)	83
Equipment (prorated when used by more than one investment center)	41
Common (corporate) assets—prorated	16

CASH FLOW ACCOUNTING

In a recent series of articles, Ijiri[21] has noted the paradox between the way investment decisions are made and the way in which the results of these decisions are evaluated. In investment decisions, the primary focus is on cash flows. Investment evaluation measures, including discounted present value, internal rate of return (IRR), and the payback period, are computed using cash flows. In performance evaluation, however, the emphasis shifts to earnings or earning-based measures such as ROI or RI. As we have seen, there frequently is no direct connection between the investment evaluation measure of a project and its subsequent evaluation through an earnings-based measure. The extensive use of straight-line depreciation for performance evaluation, a method which has no direct counterpart in project evaluation, is the most obvious example of the inconsistency between the two types of measurement.

Ijiri argues that to make project and performance evaluation more congruent, either investment decisions should be based on net-income measures or performance evaluation should be based on cash flows. While some authors advocate and some companies practice investment analysis based on earnings rather than cash flow, there seems to be little economic justification for this practice.[22] Earnings are only a surrogate to help predict the current and future cash flows of the firm. It would seem preferable to develop performance measures based on cash flows

[21] Ijiri [1978, 1980].

[22] Again, corporate concern with the earnings implication of a proposed investment project may be explained by the use of management compensation and incentive contracts based on reported income. In addition, lending agreements may be conditioned on reported earnings so that management will need to monitor compliance with debt covenants.

rather than turn the process on its head by using earnings-based measures to evaluate investment projects.

Ijiri has proposed the use of the *cash recovery rate (CRR)* for periodic performance measurement. The cash recovery rate is defined simply as

$$\text{CRR} = \frac{\text{cash flow from operations}}{\text{gross assets}},$$

where cash flow from operations also includes the proceeds from disposal of long-term assets and changes in net working capital, and gross assets is the average value of the historical (undepreciated) cost of all assets in operation. This measure is analogous to using gross book value in computing the ROI measure but differs by excluding depreciation and any other accounting accruals that would be used to compute net income. For our simple five-asset division the cash recovery rate is

$$\text{CRR} = \frac{\$50,000}{\$150,000} = 33.3 \text{ percent.}$$

The CRR is the reciprocal of the payback period if projects have uniform cash flows (three years for our simple asset). For long-lived assets ($n \geq 15$ years) the CRR provides a reasonable approximation to the internal rate of return. An advantage of the CRR is that assumptions about the average life of projects can be added after the measure is computed. They are not needed to compute the measure, in contrast to the ROI or RI measures, where depreciation expense must be estimated before net income can be obtained. If we make an assumption about the average life of projects, n, and that cash flows are uniform each year, then the internal rate of return of the projects, r, can be estimated from the CRR by solving

$$\frac{r}{1 - (1 + r)^{-n}} = \text{CRR}$$

for r. The term on the left of the equation is the reciprocal of the annuity factor at r percent for n years. To solve for the IRR we search for a value of r for which

$$a_{\overline{r}|n} = \frac{1}{\text{CRR}}.$$

In our example, with CRR = 0.333, $a_{\overline{r}|5}$ equals 3 when $r = 20$ percent, confirming that the IRR of our five-year project is about 20 percent. In general, there will be a different IRR computed for each assumed average life, permitting the analyst to perform sensitivity analysis as a function of average project lives.

Despite or perhaps because of the absence of all accounting accruals, Ijiri has found that the cash recovery rate for many corporations is remarkably stable from year to year, suggesting that the average profitability of corporate projects can be measured through the CRR. One problem with the measure is that it is a ratio and therefore has many of the problems we discussed when using the ROI to measure divisional performance. Managers being evaluated by the CRR might turn down investments returning above the cost of capital but whose adoption would lower the average CRR for the division. Therefore, a residual cash flow measure, analogous to the RI measure, might provide a better basis for the maximizing behavior of division managers. Residual cash flow is the remainder after the cost of capital is multiplied by gross investment and subtracted from the cash flows.

SUMMARY

Investment centers are decentralized units or divisions for which the manager has maximum discretion in determining not only short-term operating decisions on product mix, pricing, and production methods but also the level and type of investment in the center. The profitability of such units is best evaluated by relating the income or cash flows generated to the level of investment employed. The most common measure used to evaluate investment-center performance is the accounting return on investment (ROI), but this measure suffers from many defects. A primary problem is the incentive provided to managers, when attempting to maximize the ROI, to reject investments that will earn below the average ROI but above the divisional cost of capital. This particular problem can be avoided by shifting to the residual income (RI) measure. RI is obtained after a capital charge (obtained from multiplying the cost of capital by the average investment) is subtracted from divisional net income.

Both the ROI and RI measures can be distorted by the use of straight-line depreciation, a method that has no analog with the cash flow analysis used to evaluate projects and to compute their internal rate of return (IRR). If cash flows are assumed to be uniform, the annuity depreciation method provides a greater correlation between periodic performance measures and summary measures, such as the IRR, of projects in the investment center. The ROI and RI performance measures are also greatly distorted if investment and depreciation expense are not adjusted for the effects of price-level changes after the assets were acquired. A too-liberal expensing policy of investments in intangible assets and the exclusion of leased assets from the investment base also cause traditional investment-center performance measures to be overstated.

All of these accounting problems are symptomatic of the desire of corporations to use practices adopted or required for external financial reporting for internal evaluation purposes too. The external constituency is extremely important for corporations, and it may seem sensible to evaluate internal managers with the same practices used by outsiders to evaluate the corporation's performance. But the process of establishing financial reporting standards occurs in a highly charged political environment, is subject to much debate, delay, and compromise, and frequently may not provide desirable practices or incentives for managers of investment centers within the firm. The firm has the option of determining asset-valuation methods, depreciation methods, expense/capitalization policy, and treatment of leased assets in a manner consistent with desired economic consequences rather than simply using the particular practices currently being used for financial reporting. Such modifications, however, also require a change in the way management bonus and incentive contracts are computed so that performance measures will be congruent with compensation incentives.

One way to avoid many of these complex accounting issues is to move to a simpler performance measure, based solely on cash flows, for evaluating investment-center performance. The challenge is to obtain a cash flow performance measure that does not distort optimal decision making by divisional managers and that is congruent with the goal of long-term profitability of the firm.

APPENDIX: ANNUITY DEPRECIATION AND RESIDUAL INCOME

In this chapter we indicated that for assets with level cash flows over their useful lives, the present-value depreciation method reduces to the annuity depreciation method. We also suggested that, for level-cash-flow assets for which the rate of return is not known, the annuity depreciation method with an interest rate equal to the cost of capital enables the accounting ROI to yield a better approximation to the asset's actual rate of return than the straight-line depreciation method. We can extend this suggestion to demonstrate an interesting result when the same interest rate is used both for annuity depreciation and for the capital charge with the residual-income method.

Consider an asset with level cash flows over its useful life. We are able to show that for such an asset, and using the same interest rate for the annuity depreciation method and the residual-income capital charge, we can estimate the actual rate of return of the asset from the residual-income figure. First, we demonstrate that the sum of the annuity depreciation expense and the residual-income capital charge is a constant for each year of the asset's life. We can show this easily by using one of our five-year assets, used as the basic example throughout the chapter.

Year	Book Value, Start of Year	Capital Charge at 15%	Annuity Depreciation Expense at 15%	Capital Charge + Depreciation
1	$30,000	$4,500	$4,449.5	$8,949.5
2	25,550.5	3,832.6	5,116.9	8,949.5
3	20,433.6	3,065.0	5,884.5	8,949.5
4	14,549.2	2,182.4	6,767.1	8,949.5
5	7,782.1	1,167.3	7,782.2	8,949.5

Since residual income equals net cash flows less depreciation and the capital charges, we see that if the asset has level cash flows, the residual income is a constant for each year of the asset's life. Thus we see again that the annuity depreciation method eliminates the incentive to avoid investing in new assets or to scrap assets prematurely, since the performance measure does not vary over the asset's life as it does with straight-line depreciation.

The residual-income figure, with annuity depreciation and level cash flows, has an even more interesting property that enables us to estimate the internal rate of return. If we let RI be the annual residual income and A the original cost of the asset, then we can derive the following relationship:

$$\frac{1}{a_{i\rceil n}} = \frac{RI}{A} + \frac{1}{a_{r\rceil n}},$$

where $a_{r,n}$ is the annuity factor representing the present value at r percent of receiving \$1 at the end of n consecutive years, r is the interest rate used to compute the capital charge and annuity depreciation schedule, and i is the actual rate of return for the asset assuming level cash flows for n years. Therefore, we can estimate the true rate of return from this formula once we know the residual income and the asset's original cost. In our numerical example we have annual cash flows of \$10,000 per year, so RI $= 1,050.5$. Also, for $r = 15$ percent, $a_{\overline{0.15}\rceil 5} = 3.3522$, so that

$$\frac{1}{a_{i\rceil n}} = \frac{1,050.5}{30,000} + \frac{1}{3.3522} = 0.3333.$$

A value of $a_{i\rceil n} = 3.000$ implies a value of i equal to 19.86 percent, which we know to be the correct value. This relationship also holds for a collection of assets having identical lives and uniform cash flows. We can therefore use the residual-income measure to derive the effective yield from any collection of identical-lived level-cash-flow assets.

PROBLEMS

15-1. ROI and Divisional Performance

The Solomons Company uses ROI to measure the performance of its operating divisions. A summary of the annual reports from two divisions is shown below. The company's cost of capital is 12 percent.

	Division A	Division B
Capital Invested	\$2400	\$4000
Net Income	\$ 480	\$ 720
ROI	20%	18%

Required:

1. Which division is more profitable?
2. At what cost of capital would both divisions be considered equally profitable?
3. What performance measurement procedure would more clearly show the relative profitability of the two divisions?
4. Suppose the manager of Division A were offered a one year project that would increase his investment base (for that year) by $1,000 and show a profit of $150. Would the manager accept this project if he were evaluated on his divisional ROI? Should he accept this project?

15-2. ROI and Residual Income: Straight-Line and Annuity Depreciation Methods

The Dearden Company is contemplating an investment of $100,000 that is expected to produce annual savings (after tax) of $15,000 per year for the next ten years. This produces an internal after-tax rate-of-return of 8 percent which equals the company's required return. [The manager of the company is evaluated by the company's accounting ROI. Net income is measured as net cash savings less depreciation, and investment is measured as the average of the start-of-year and the end-of-year book values.] Straight-line depreciation is used for financial statements and for computing the ROI measure.

Required:

1. Compute the Average Investment, Net Income, and ROI for each of the ten years of the project's life. Why does the annual ROI fluctuate over the project's life? What motivation or incentive effect will this fluctuation likely have on the manager's willingness to accept the new investment?
2. Perform the same computations as before except using the annuity depreciation method, with an annual interest rate of 8 percent, to compute net income and the book value of investment.
3. Compute the residual income each year with an 8 percent cost of capital and the annuity depreciation schedule. Interpret your results.
4. Which depreciation method provides better local managerial incentives for new investment?

15-3. ROI for Measuring Divisional Performance (CMA)

The Texon Co., is organized into autonomous divisions along regional market lines. Each division manager is responsible for sales, cost of operations, acquisition and financing of divisional assets, and working-capital management.

The vice-president of general operations for the company will retire in September 1982. A review of the performance, attitudes, and skills of several management employees has been undertaken. Interviews with qualified outside candidates also have been held. The selection committee has narrowed the choice to the managers of Divisions A and F.

Both candidates were appointed division managers in late 1978. The manager of Division A had been the assistant manager of that division for the prior five years. The manager of Division F had served as assistant division manager of Division B before being appointed to his present post. He took over Division F, newly formed in 1977, when its first manager left to join a competitor. The financial results of their performance in the past three years are reported below:

	Division A			Division F		
	1979	1980	1981	1979	1980	1981
Estimated industry sales			*(000 omitted)*			
—market area	$10,000	$12,000	$13,000	$5,000	$6,000	$6,500
Division sales	$ 1,000	$ 1,100	$ 1,210	$ 450	$ 600	$ 750
Variable costs	$ 300	$ 320	$ 345	$ 135	$ 175	$ 210
Discretionary costs	400	405	420	170	200	230
Committed costs	275	325	350	140	200	250
Total costs	$ 975	$ 1,050	$ 1,115	$ 445	$ 575	$ 690
Net income	$ 25	$ 50	$ 95	$ 5	$ 25	$ 60
Assets employed	$ 330	$ 340	$ 360	$ 170	$ 240	$ 300
Liabilities	103	105	115	47	100	130
Net investment	227	235	245	123	140	170
Return on investment	11%	21%	39%	4%	18%	35%

Required:

1. Texon Co. measures the performance of the divisions and the division managers on the basis of their return on investment (ROI). Is this an appropriate measurement for the division managers? What additional measure(s) could be used for performance evaluation?
2. On the basis of the information given, which manager would you recommend for vice-president of general operations?

15-4. Evaluating Divisional Performance (CMA)

Darmen Corporation is one of the major producers of prefabricated houses in the home building industry. The corporation consists of two divisions:

(1) Bell Division, which acquires the raw materials to manufacture the basic house components and assembles them into kits, and
(2) the Cornish Division, which takes the kits and constructs the homes for final home buyers. The corporation is decentralized and the management of each division is measured by its income and return on investment.

Bell Division assembles seven separate house kits using raw materials purchased at the prevailing market prices. The seven kits are sold to Cornish for prices ranging from $45,000 to $98,000. The prices are set by corporate management of

Darmen using prices paid by Cornish when it buys comparable units from outside sources. The smaller kits with the lower prices have become a larger portion of the units sold because the final house buyer is faced with prices which are increasing more rapidly than personal income. The kits are manufactured and assembled in a new plant just purchased by Bell this year. The division had been located in a leased plant for the past four years.

All kits are assembled upon receipt of an order from the Cornish Division. When the kit is completely assembled, it is loaded immediately on a Cornish truck. Thus, Bell Division has no finished goods inventory.

Bell Division
Performance Report
For the Year Ended December 31, 1980

	1980	1979	Increase or (decrease) from 1979 Amount	Percent Change
Summary data				
Net income ($000 omitted)	$ 34,222	$ 31,573	$ 2,649	8.4
Return on investment	37%	43%	(6)%	(14.0)
Kits shipped (units)	2,000	2,100	(100)	(4.8)
Production data (in units)				
Kits started	2,400	1,600	800	50.0
Kits shipped	2,000	2,100	(100)	(4.8)
Kits in process at year-end	700	300	400	133.3
Increase (decrease) in kits in process at year end	400	(500)	—	—
Financial data ($000 omitted)				
Sales	$138,000	162,800	$(24,800)	(15.2)
Production costs of units sold				
Raw material	$ 32,000	$ 40,000	$ (8,000)	(20.0)
Labor	41,700	53,000	(11,300)	(21.3)
Factory overhead	29,000	37,000	(8,000)	(21.6)
Cost of units sold	$102,700	$130,000	$(27,300)	(21.0)
Other costs				
Corporate charges for				
Personnel services	$ 228	$ 210	$ 18	8.6
Accounting services	425	440	(15)	(3.4)
Financing costs	300	525	(225)	42.9
Total other costs	$ 953	$ 1,175	$ (222)	(18.9)
Adjustments to income				
Unreimbursed fire loss	—	$ 52	$ (52)	(100.0)
Raw material losses due to improper storage	$ 125	—	125	—
Total adjustments	$ 125	$ 52	$ 73	(140.0)
Total deductions	$103,778	$131,227	$(27,449)	(20.9)
Division income	$ 34,222	$ 31,573	$ 2,649	8.4
Division investment	$ 92,000	$ 73,000	$ 19,000	26.0
Return on investment	37%	43%	(6)%	(14.0)

The Bell Division's accounts and reports are prepared on an actual cost basis. There is no budget and standards have not been developed for any product. A factory overhead rate is calculated at the beginning of each year. The rate is designed to charge all overhead to the product each year. Any under- or over-applied overhead is allocated to the cost of goods sold account and work in process inventories.

Bell Division's annual report is presented below. This report forms the basis of the evaluation of the division and its management by the corporation management. Additional information regarding corporate and division practices is as follows:

- The corporation office does all the personnel and accounting work for each division.
- The corporate personnel costs are allocated on the basis of number of employees in the division.
- The accounting costs are allocated to the division on the basis of total costs excluding corporate charges.
- The division administration costs are included in factory overhead.
- The financing charges include a corporate imputed interest charge on division assets and any divisional lease payments.
- The division investment for the return on investment calculation includes division inventory and plant and equipment at gross book value.

Required:

1. Discuss the value of the annual report presented for the Bell Division in evaluating the division and its management in terms of:
   a. The accounting techniques employed in the measurement of division activities.
   b. The manner of presentation.
   c. The effectiveness with which it discloses differences and similarities between years.
   Use the information in the problem to illustrate your discussion.
2. Present specific recommendations you would make to the management of Darmen Corporation which would improve its accounting and financial reporting system.

15-5. Effect of Depreciation on ROI Computations

The Streetorn Corporation is contemplating the purchase of a new piece of equipment. The equipment has an expected life of five years and is expected to produce the following after-tax cash flow savings for the following five years:

Year	After-Tax Cash Flow Savings
1	$50,000
2	46,000
3	42,000
4	36,000
5	30,000

The asset will cost $138,300 and thus has an after tax yield of 16 percent which is above the company's after-tax cost of capital of 15 percent. The declining pattern of annual cash flow savings is caused by higher maintenance costs as the equipment ages, as well as the reduction in tax benefits from use of the Sum-of-Years Digit's Method for depreciation. For example, the gross cash flow savings in Year 3 (before depreciation and before taxes) is $51,560. The net after-tax cash flow savings is obtained by the following computation:

Gross Cash Flow Savings	$51,560
Depreciation (138,300)(3/15)	27,660
Taxable Income	23,900
Taxes (@ 40%)	9,560
Net Income After Taxes	14,340
+ Depreciation	27,660
After-Tax Cash Flow Savings	$42,000

Optional: Compute the Gross Cash Flow Savings for Years 1–5.

The president's bonus is based on the company's Return-on-Investment (Net Income After Taxes/Investment at Start-of-Year). The company prides itself on its conservative accounting policies and therefore uses the same depreciation method for financial reporting as it does for its tax return. The controller of Streetorn has prepared the following table to show the president the annual ROI from the new piece of equipment:

	(1)	(2)	(3)	(4) = (2) − (3)	(5) = (4)/(1)
		Net Cash			
	Book Value	Flow After	SYD	Net Income	
Year	Start-of-year	Taxes	Depreciation	After Taxes	ROI
1	$138,300	$50,000	$46,100	$ 3,900	2.8%
2	92,200	46,000	36,880	9,120	9.9%
3	55,320	42,000	27,660	14,340	25.9%
4	27,660	36,000	18,440	17,560	63.5%
5	9,220	30,000	9,220	20,780	225.4%
Average	$ 64,540	$40,800	$27,660	$13,140	20.4%
(5 years)					

The president is astonished by this table. He says, "Something's very wrong here. According to your cash-flow analysis, this piece of equipment has a 16 percent after tax yield. Yet our financial statements show a different yield each year and the low ROI in the first two years is going to keep me out of bonus money. Sure the equipment shows a fantastic ROI in its last two years, but I may not be with the company by then. I need results right away, not four years from now!"

The controller decides that the trouble may be with the firm's conservative accounting practices. Perhaps, if the firm used straight-line depreciation for financial reporting, like most of the other firms in the industry, the numbers would look better. He proceeds to produce the following table:

Year	Book Value Start-of-Year	Net Cash Flow After Taxes	Straight-Line Depreciation	Net Income After Taxes	ROI
1	$138,300	$50,000	$27,660	$22,340	16.2%
2	110,640	46,000	27,660	18,340	16.6%
3	82,980	42,000	27,660	14,340	17.3%
4	55,320	36,000	27,660	8,340	15.1%
5	27,660	30,000	27,660	2,340	8.5%
Average	$ 82,980	$40,800	$27,660	$13,140	15.8%

The president is much happier with this presentation especially since now the asset shows good returns in the earlier years. But he is still puzzled as to why an asset with a yield of 16 percent doesn't show a 16 percent ROI each year.

Required:

1. Verify that this piece of equipment does have a 16 percent yield.

2. Show, using the present value depreciation method, how the equipment can have a 16 percent ROI for each of the five years of the asset's life.

3. Why did the ROI using the straight-line depreciation method approximate the actual yield reasonably well (for at least the first four years of the asset's life)?

15-6. Performance Evaluation and Present Value Depreciation* (G. Foster)

I. Hobie Leland, Jr. has just been appointed divisional manager for the Goal Congruence Corporation. He must choose between adopting one (or neither) of two projects, both of which are in mining ventures. The cash inflows and outflows of the two projects are predicted to be:

	Project A	Project B
Cash outflow at Start of Period 1	$15,000	$15,000
Net Cash Inflows at End of Period 1	$ 6,000	$ 5,000
" " " 2	$ 6,000	$ 5,000
" " " 3	$ 6,000	$ 5,000
" " " 4	$ 3,000	$ 5,000
" " " 5	$ 2,000	$ 5,000

Hobie's contract with Goal Congruence specifies his bonus to be 10 percent of annual residual income (if positive) of the division. Depletion (depreciation) of the mine is based on the straight-line method, assuming a life of five years and no salvage

---

* This problem appeared originally in Charles Horngren, *Cost Accounting*, 5th ed. (Englewood Cliffs, N.J.: Prentice-Hall, 1982).

value. The capital charge for assets employed in the division is calculated as 10 percent of the opening book value of the mine ($15,000 − accumulated depletion) for each period. All analysis is performed on a before-tax basis.

Required:

1. Which project has the greater net present value (before considering any bonus to Hobie) at a cost of capital of 10 percent?

2. Hobie decides to choose the project that maximizes the net present value of his bonuses and he uses a 20 percent discount rate in determining the net present value of the bonuses. Which project will he choose?

3. When it came time to submit capital budgeting proposals to the head office, Hobie made the mistake of sending in his working papers rather than his formal proposal. The working papers were received at the head office by Delilah Jones, assistant to the president of Goal Congruence, who was very upset at the contents of the working papers. She showed them to the president accompanied with a suggestion—change the depletion rate on the mine from straight-line to sum-of-the-years'-digits method. The new depletion rate would be implemented prior to Hobie taking a final decision between the two projects. How much is Delilah's suggestion worth to Goal Congruence?

II.   The president of Goal Congruence is a realist. He knows that Hobie will not always make the convenient mistake of mailing his working papers rather than formal proposals. Moreover, he views Delilah's suggestion as, at best, providing an interim solution. He seeks your advice on what problems may arise with the existing performance measurement and incentive system used for Hobie.

Required:

1. What are the problems you would mention in a report to the president of Goal Congruence?

2. What proposals would you make to help reduce these problems?

III.   The president of Goal Congruence learns about the present value depreciation method. However, the president is confused on how this method works when the project's internal rate of return exceeds the cost of capital. Delilah suggests he consider two alternatives:

1. Use the internal rate of return to compute the depletion on the mine. The divisional net income would be calculated as:

Cash Inflow	x
− Depletion	x
= Divisional Net Income	x

2. Increase the "cost" of the investment to the present value of the cash inflows using the cost of capital (10 percent). Then use (a) the revised

"cost" figure as the opening investment base for year one and (b) the cost of capital in computing the "depletion" on the mine. In the year the project is adopted, the excess net present value is credited to the divisional net income. Thus, the divisional net income would be calculated as:

Cash Inflow	x
− Depletion	x
+ Excess N.P.V. of Newly Adopted Projects	x
= Divisional Net Income	x

Hobie's bonus would be calculated as 10% of divisional net income under either (1) or (2).

Required:

1. Illustrate how each alternative present value depletion method would work for Goal Congruence. Would either alternative overcome some (or all) of the problems mentioned in II(1)?
2. What problems may exist in implementing either version of the present value depletion method?

15-7. Effects of Inflation on ROI

The Carter Company uses the ROI criterion to evaluate the performance of its divisions. The company prides itself on the formal capital budgeting procedures it uses for approving new investments, and the subsequent control procedures it has implemented to measure the performance of these new investments. Recently, however, the ROI measure has been producing performance statistics quite at variance with the criterion used to screen the investments. The company believes that recent high inflation rates may be contributing to the erratic performance evaluation measures. The problem is well illustrated by comparing the performance of two divisions.

Division Y made a major investment ten years ago. This investment cost $3,000,000, had an expected life of fifteen years, and annual after-tax cash flows of $525,000. The rate-of-return of slightly more than 15 percent was above the Carter Company's cost of capital. During the past ten years, the price level had risen by 67 percent, and the after-tax cash flows from the investment had increased to an annual level of $800,000. The ROI for Division Y for the most recent year was computed as:

Investment Book Value (Start-of-year)	$1,200,000
Investment Book Value (End-of-year)	1,000,000
Average Investment	$1,100,000
Net Cash Flow	$ 800,000
Depreciation	200,000
Net Income	$ 600,000
ROI - Division Y	54.5%

Division Z, in a different region than Division Y, made a major investment of a very similar type just two years ago. Because of the increase in construction and equipment costs, the investment now had cost $4,500,000. The expected life of this investment was ten years, and the annual after-tax cash flow was $900,000. This investment also had a yield slightly in excess of 15 percent so that the performance measure of Division Z was expected to be similar to that of Division Y. In fact, Division Z's investment appeared to be much less profitable than Division Y's and did not even reach the expected 15 percent ROI cut-off figure. The most recent year's data show:

Investment Book Value (Start-of-year)	$4,050,000
Investment Book Value (End-of-year)	3,600,000
Average Investment	$3,825,000
Net Cash Flow	$1,000,000
Depreciation	450,000
Net Income	$ 550,000
ROI - Division Z	14.4%

The price index was 120 ten years ago when Division Y's investment was made. Two years ago, when Division Z made its investment, the index was 180, and in the most recent year, for which the above data were prepared, the index averaged 200.

Required:

Analyze this situation explaining why two divisions with such similar investments (15 percent after-tax returns from the discounted cash flow analysis) are showing such disparate ROI's.

15-8. ROI and Leasing

The Malone Division of the Stoudt Corporation is organized as an investment center. Because of excellent operating results, the divisional manager, Terry Trocano, has been given considerable freedom in investment decisions. Terry knows that the top management of the Stoudt Corporation measures the performance of the operating divisions using an ROI criterion and that it is important for her to maintain a divisional ROI of 20 percent before taxes and 14 percent after taxes. Her annual bonus depends upon achieving these targeted levels and her compensation can increase considerably if she is able to obtain even higher ROI's.

Terry Trocano has just completed a five year forecast of annual operating performance for the Malone Division. The best estimate is that the current net investment level of $20,000,000 will be maintained over this period (that is, new investment will about equal the depreciation charge each year) and that the Net Income Before Taxes will be $4,000,000 and Net Income After Taxes will be $2,800,000 each year.

While Terry is pleased that her forecasted results indicate that she will achieve both the before and after tax ROI targets, she is actively looking for projects that will enable her to exceed the targeted rates.

A new investment proposal has recently emerged that seems particularly promising. The project requires an initial investment of $15,000,000 and will generate annual before-tax cash flows of $6,000,000 for five years. The discounted cash flow analysis indicates that the project has a before-tax yield in excess of 28 percent and an after-tax yield of more than 19 percent. (The Stoudt Corporation has a marginal tax rate of 40 percent and uses sum-of-years digits depreciation for computing taxable income). Since both of these yields are well in excess of the company's targeted ROI, the proposed project seems like an excellent investment.

Before making a final decision on the $15,000,000 investment, Terry has asked the divisional controller to forecast the first year's operating results for the Malone Division, including the income generated by the new project. She is surprised when she receives the following pro forma results:

Before Tax Analysis (000)

	Net Income from Existing Projects	$ 4,000
	Cash Flow- New Project	6,000
Less:	Depreciation (straight-line, 5 year life)	(3,000)
	Net Income	$ 7,000
	Investment—Existing Projects	$20,000
	—New Project	15,000
	Total Investment	$35,000
	ROI	20%

After Tax Analysis (000)

Net Income After Taxes—Existing Projects	$ 2,800
Net Income Before Tax—New Project	3,000
Taxes on New Project[a]	
(Sum-of-Years-Digits Depreciation)	(400)
Net Income After Taxes	$ 5,400
Total Investment	35,000
ROI	15.4%

[a] The company uses actual tax expense, based on the accelerated depreciation schedule, in allocating tax expense to divisions.

The project doesn't hurt the measured performance of the Malone Division but it certainly doesn't show the large increase in divisional ROI that Terry had hoped for.

The controller proposes an alternative scheme for undertaking the investment. He has learned that another company is willing to acquire the buildings and equipment for the new project and lease these to the Malone Division at an annual rental payment of $5,200,000 for five years. The terms of the lease can be structured so that it is considered an operating lease and hence will not be capitalized on the Stoudt Corporation's financial statements. The controller has prepared the following pro forma analysis of the lease option.

Before Tax Analysis (000)

Net Income from Existing Projects	$ 4,000
Cash Flow—New Project	6,000
Less: Lease Payment	(5,200)
Net Income	$ 4,800
Investment—Existing Projects	20,000
ROI	24%

After Tax Analysis (000)

Net Income After Taxes—Existing Projects	2,800
Income from New Project—Net of Lease	
Payment	800
Taxes—New Project	(320)
Net Income After Taxes	3,280
Investment	20,000
ROI	16.4%

The lease option seems much more attractive to Terry Trocano since it generates a significant increase in both before and after-tax ROI for her division. She submits the proposed new project, with a recommendation to lease the new facilities, to the central administration staff expecting a routine approval for this attractive investment opportunity.

Required:

Assume that you are the newly hired assistant to the head of the corporate finance division and have been asked to review the project proposal from the Malone Division.

1. Verify that the proposed project will yield the forecasted returns (28 + percent before tax, 19 + percent after tax).

2. Compute the before and after tax ROI for the Malone Division for each of the next five years for both the purchase and the lease options. The investment base for each year is the book value (using straight-line depreciation) of investment at the start of the year.

3. At the company's after-tax cost of capital of 14 percent, is it better to purchase or lease the asset? (You may assume that the company is not able to use the investment tax credit.)

4. Why does the leasing option generate higher ROI measures than the purchase option?

5. Suggest an alternative scheme that will reduce the incentive to lease rather than purchase assets. Demonstrate how your scheme will work were the Malone Division to enter into the five year lease with annual payments of $5,200,000 per year.

15-9. Corporate Recovery Rate

Yuji Ijiri[*] has defined the Corporate Recovery Rate (CRR) as:

$$CRR = \frac{\text{Cash Recoveries}}{\text{Gross Assets}}$$

where Cash Recoveries = Funds from Operations
+ Proceeds from Disposal of Long-Term Assets
+ Decrease in Total Current Assets
+ Interest Expense

---

[*] Yuji Ijiri, "Recovery Rate and Cash Flow Accounting," *Financial Executive* (March 1980) pp. 54–60.

and Gross Assets   = Total Assets + Accumulated Depreciation
                       (averaged between beginning and ending
                       balances)

Excerpts from the 1979 and 1980 Goodyear Annual Reports are reproduced below:

	(000,000)		
	1980	*1979*	*1978*
Current Assets	$2,856	$2,875	$2,881
Property Plant, and Other Assets	2,512	2,496	2,350
Accumulated Depreciation	2,493	2,375	2,247
Funds from Operations	460	427	439
Property and Plant Disposals	24	29	10
Interest Expense	227	204	182
Net Income	231	146	226
Shareholders' Equity	2,303	2,163	2,108

Required:

1. Compute the Corporate Recovery Rate and the Return on Shareholders' Equity for 1979 and 1980.
2. What differences exist between these two measures? What adjustments would need to be made to the CRR to make it more comparable to an ROI figure?
3. Assume that Goodyear's assets have a 15-year life on average. What is the internal rate of return consistent with the average of the Cash Recovery Rates computed for 1979 and 1980?

15-10. *Convergence of Cash Recovery Rates*

Yuji Ijiri* has shown that the Corporate Recovery Rates of selected U.S. corporations show a remarkable stability from year-to-year (see Table below)

	Corporate Recovery Rates							
	1972	*1973*	*1974*	*1975*	*1976*	*1977*	*1978*	*Average*
Alcoa	8.2%	7.8%	9.2%	6.4%	8.4%	8.4%	10.4%	8.4%
American Can	6.5	8.0	8.5	8.1	8.4	8.6	8.1	8.0
Bethelehem Steel	6.3	7.2	9.0	8.1	7.2	2.4	8.4	6.9
DuPont	10.8	12.7	10.2	9.1	11.3	11.9	12.7	11.2
General Electric	9.9	10.1	10.4	10.8	10.7	10.5	11.2	10.5
General Foods	12.1	10.8	10.7	11.3	11.2	11.7	9.8	11.1
General Motors	14.6	15.2	9.9	12.0	16.1	15.8	16.7	14.3

---

* Yuji Ijiri, "Recovery Rate and Cash Flow Accounting," *op. cit.* and "Convergence of Cash Recovery Rates," in Y. Ijiri and A. B. Whinston (eds.) *Quantitative Planning and Control* (Academic Press, 1979), pp. 259–267.

Corporate Recovery Rates

	1972	1973	1974	1975	1976	1977	1978	Average
Goodyear	8.4	8.1	7.8	7.1	7.3	8.7	8.7	8.0
Gulf Oil	10.7	13.3	12.9	10.5	11.5	8.9	9.8	11.1
IBM	18.2	19.0	18.8	18.3	18.7	19.5	19.9	18.9
RCA	14.0	13.9	12.0	10.3	13.7	15.1	15.6	13.5
U.S. Steel	4.3	6.3	9.5	7.4	6.4	4.8	5.0	6.2
Westinghouse	7.7	8.1	6.4	6.7	6.9	6.6	7.3	7.1

At first glance, the stability in recovery rates seems surprising since a corporation invests in a variety of projects, each having a different cash recovery pattern and different economic life. But for mature corporations, it may be reasonable to assume that the mix of projects and the aggregate cash flow pattern is fairly stable over time. In this case, corporate investments may be regarded as repeated investments in a given composite project with a given cash flow pattern over its life. While new projects may continually be added to this "composite project," their impact may be relatively minor, especially in the short run.

To show how repeated investments of cash recoveries in the same composite project eventually lead to a convergence of the corporate recovery rate, consider the following project. A firm invests $1 million at the end of Year 0 in a project that returns in cash 60 percent of the initial investment one year later, and 72 percent of the investment two years later. At the end of Year 1, the firm recovers $0.6 million in cash which is immediately reinvested in the same project. At the end of Year 2, the firm recovers $.72 million from the year 0 investment and $.36 million from the Year 1 investment (see Table below)

Recoveries and (Reinvestments)

		0	1	2	3
Year	0	(1)	0.6	0.72	
	1		(0.6)	0.36	.432
	2			(1.08)	·
	·				·
	·				·
	·				
Recoveries			0.6	1.08	
Investments			1.0	1.60	
Corporate Recovery Rate			.6	.675	

Required:

Extend the above table until you can obtain an approximation to the figure to which the Corporate Recovery Rate is converging. Show that this figure, called the Capital Recovery Factor (CRF), equals

$$\text{CRF} = r/[1 - (1 + r)^{-n}]$$

where r is the internal rate of return of the project and n is the project's life.

REFERENCES

DEARDEN, JOHN, "Problem in Decentralized Profit Responsibility," *Harvard Business Review* XXXVIII (May–June 1960).

————, "The Case Against ROI Control," *Harvard Business Review* XLVII (May–June 1969), 124–35.

IJIRI, YUJI, *Theory of Accounting Measurement,* Studies in Accounting Research No. 10. Sarasota, Fla.: American Accounting Association, 1975.

————, "Cash-Flow Accounting and Its Structure," *Journal of Accounting, Auditing and Finance* I (Summer 1978), 331–48.

————, "Recovery Rate and Cash Flow Accounting," *Financial Executive* XLVII (March 1980), 54–60.

————, "Historical Cost Accounting and its Rationality," Research Monograph No. 1, Canadian Certified General Accountants' Research Foundation, 1981.

LOOMIS, CAROL J., "How G E Manages Inflation," *Fortune* CIII (May 4, 1981), 121–24.

MAURIEL, JOHN J., and ROBERT N. ANTHONY, "Misevaluation of Investment Center Performance," *Harvard Business Review* XLIV (March–April 1966), 98–105.

REECE, JAMES S., and WILLIAM R. COOL, "Measuring Investment Center Performance," *Harvard Business Review* LVI (May–June 1978).

SOLOMON, EZRA, "Alternative Rate of Return Concepts and Their Implications for Utility Regulation," *Bell Journal of Economics and Management Science* I (Spring 1970), 65–81.

SOLOMONS, DAVID, *Divisional Performance Measurement and Control.* Homewood, Ill.: Irwin, 1965.

VAN HORNE, JAMES C., *Financial Management and Policy,* 5th ed. Englewood Cliffs, N.J.: Prentice Hall, 1980.

VANCIL, RICHARD, and ROMAN L. WEIL, *Replacement Cost Accounting: Readings on Concepts, Uses and Methods.* Glen Ridge, N.J.: Thomas Horton and Daughters, 1976.

EXECUTIVE CONTRACTS AND BONUS PLANS

16

A crucial ingredient in the motivation of the top executives of a corporation is the nature of their compensation contract, particularly incentive and bonus plans. One can not talk about decentralization without an explicit treatment of how the top divisional managers are rewarded (or penalized). Almost all highly decentralized firms have incentive compensation contracts for their top management group (usually less than 1% of all employees) to encourage profit maximizing decisions at the divisional and corporate levels, and to stimulate individuals to higher levels of performance.

One of the most enthusiastic advocates of incentive compensation plans for top management was Alfred Sloan who helped institute the General Motors Bonus Plan in 1918.[1] The objective of the plan was to increase the commonality of interests between the senior managers and the stockholders of the firm by awarding the annual bonus based on each manager's contributions to the overall success of the corporation. General Motors had decentralized its operating decisions and before instituting the bonus plan, the key executives had little incentive to think of the overall welfare of the organization. Rather, they tended to focus narrowly on their own division's profitability, occasionally at the expense of the overall corporation's welfare. After the bonus plan was installed, the senior executives were more sensitive to how their individual efforts affected the welfare of the entire organization. Sloan noted that the plan was successful in molding top level executives into a cooperative constructive group but without destroying individual ambition and initiative.

The General Motors bonus plan was structured so that rewards were increased more than proportionately to salary as executives were promoted to higher positions. Therefore, there was a great incentive for mangers to first become eligible for bonus awards and then to continue to perform in an outstanding fashion so that they could be promoted to even higher ranks. Apart from the

---

[1] The General Motors Bonus Plan is described in Chapter 22 of Sloan [1962].

direct financial reward from the plan, it seemed to provide an intangible incentive just by the recognition that the executive had made a significant personal contribution to the success of General Motors. One executive claimed that the ego satisfaction from receiving the award was prized just as much as the actual monetary compensation.

The enthusiasm of Alfred Sloan and the General Motors Corporation for executive incentive plans is now widespread. More than 90 percent of the top managers of decentralized profit centers in large corporations are eligible for an annual bonus. The median bonus is about 25 percent of annual salary.[2] The form of the bonus plan varies across corporations. Payments can be made in cash, in the stock of the company, in stock options, and more recently, in performance shares, stock appreciation rights, or participating units. The bonus can be made contingent on corporate results (as in General Motors) or on divisional profits. It can be based on annual performance or on performance over a 4–6 year period. It can be paid out immediately, deferred, or spread over a 3–5 year period.

There is no single bonus incentive plan that will dominate all other plans for all companies. Incentive plans will vary as a function of the degree of decentralization, the time horizon for critical decisions of the firms, the degree of interaction among divisions, the amount of uncertainty faced by the firm, the nature of its business activities, and the structure of the industry. In addition, many plans, alleged to provide incentives to managers, have as their greatest benefit the reduction of taxes of the manager and the firm.[3] At present, both contemporary practice and the theory of incentive contracts are evolving rapidly. In this chapter, we will survey existing practice and comment on the properties, strengths, and weaknesses of different incentive schemes. In the next chapter, we will introduce the emerging literature in optimal contracting and describe some preliminary results for constructing optimal incentive contracts between owners and chief executives, and between a central management group and its divisional executives.

INCENTIVE COMPENSATION AND THE PRINCIPAL-AGENT RELATIONSHIP[4]

Before starting our survey of incentive compensation arrangements, we must introduce the principal-agent paradigm. It is impossible to analyze incentive compensation plans without some knowledge of the theory of agency relationships.

---

[2] See, for example, the survey reported by Kamm in Section F, Part II, of Vancil [1978].

[3] The tax consequences of different kinds of management compensation managements are analyzed in Miller and Scholes [1980]. They attempt to distinguish those schemes that are motivated primarily by tax considerations from those that appear to have incentive properties.

[4] This literature which has an extensive history, was synthesized in Jensen-Meckling [1976]. See also Zimmerman [1979] for a particular application to cost accounting issues.

Although principal-agent theory is intuitively plausible, the importance of having a formal theory was not recognized until the 1970s. Extensive research is now being conducted in this rapidly developing field, which has implications not only for management control and executive compensation systems but, more broadly, for the theory of finance and the economic theory of the firm.

An agency relationship exists whenever one party (the principal) hires another party (the agent) to perform some service; this service requires the principal to delegate some decision-making authority to the agent. For our purposes, two types of principal-agent relationship arise in management control systems. First, there is the arrangement in which a firm's owners or shareholders, as the *principal* (perhaps acting through the Board of Directors), hire the Chief Executive Officer (or, more broadly, the top management group) to be their *agent* in managing the firm in their best interests. Second, there is the arrangement in which the firm's top management group acts as the *principal* and hires divisional managers as *agents* to manage the decentralized units of the organization.

We adopt the assumption that all individuals—principals and agents—are rational utility maximizers who care not only about financial compensation and wealth but also about perquisites of the job (such as attractive working conditions and flexibility in hours worked). They prefer leisure to hard or routine work. Agents therefore may not always act in the best interests of the principal. The agency relationship requires a specification of incentive, monitoring, and bonding relationships to minimize the net costs of the divergence of interests between the principal and the agent.

For example, if the top executives of the company are compensated only by a straight salary, they may not be motivated to take actions that maximize the value of the firm to the shareholders. They will "overconsume" nonpecuniary items such as attractive working conditions and company perquisites. If the ownership group knew what actions were optimal for the firm and could costlessly observe the actions of the top managers, they could direct the managers to implement these optimal actions with the threat of withholding compensation if these actions were not carried out effectively and efficiently. But because a dispersed ownership group will probably have inadequate information and will find monitoring costly, it is unlikely either to know what the optimal decisions should be or to be able to direct and monitor the actions of the top executives. In order, therefore, to encourage the top executives to take actions that are in the firm's best interests, the owners introduce an incentive compensation plan that enables the top executives to share in the firm's increased wealth. These plans can take the form of stock options or bonuses based on reported performance.

Incentive compensation plans are designed to create a complete commonality of interest between the principal (owners) and the agents (managers). But because of differences in risk attitudes, the existence of private information (managers knowing more than the owners about the environment and their actions), and limited or costly observability, there will always be some divergence of interest between the principal and the agent. The principal attempts to limit divergence from his interests by establishing appropriate incentives for the agents and by incurring monitoring costs designed to limit actions that increase the agents' welfare at the expense of the principal. Audited financial statements are an excellent example of a costly monitor of managerial behavior. They generate an accountability report from the agent (managers) to the principal (shareholders and creditors).[5] Even with costly incentive and monitoring arrangements, however, the agent's decisions will still diverge from those that would maximize the principal's welfare. For example, audited financial statements provide a less-than-complete summary of the manager's decisions and actions. This remaining divergence is referred to as the "residual loss" in the agency relationship. Thus agency costs in the owner-manager relationship are the sum of the costs of the incentive compensation plan, the costs of monitoring the managers' actions, and the remaining costs of actions taken by managers that diverge from the preferences of the owners.

To see how agency costs affect the compensation managements of top executives, let us informally trace through a simple scenario. We have already noted that because of the private information of managers and costly observation of managers' actions, owners may provide an incentive compensation scheme for the top executives. The objective of such a plan is to obtain a greater commonality of interests between owners and managers. One obvious incentive scheme is to provide managers with a stock option or stock bonus plan, since actions that the managers take to increase stock prices should benefit the owners in a direct and obvious manner. Although certainly popular, this incentive scheme is not used by all companies with publicly traded stock. As good scientists, we must try to understand why such an incentive arrangement may not always be optimal.[6]

What factors limit the desirability of stock ownership plans for top executives? First, there is a problem of risk aversion. The highly paid top executives of the firm already have most of their wealth, in the form of human capital (as measured by the discounted present value of their expected compensation), directly tied to the firm's well-being. If the firm were to do poorly, their managerial reputation could suffer, limiting their outside job offers and slowing the rate of compensation increases within the firm. If a significant part of their nonhuman-capital wealth were also invested in shares of the firm's stock, they could suffer a significant decline in their financial wealth at the same time that bad outcomes were affecting their human-capital wealth.

In order to avoid this calamitous situation, the executives will attempt to

---

[5] In addition, the agent can expend resources (such as bonding costs) to guarantee that certain actions will not be taken or that the principal will be compensated if such actions are taken (see Jensen-Meckling [1976]). These bonding costs seem less relevant than the costs of incentive and monitoring contracts for executive bonus plans.

[6] It will not suffice to claim that companies not using stock incentive plans are acting irrationally. Irrational behavior could explain any social phenomenon and hence explain (or predict) no behavior. Our job as social scientists is to find universal, generalizable laws of behavior, not a series of ad hoc alibis.

avoid risky investments and risky decisions, even those with high expected returns, since their risk aversion causes them to value the potential gains far less than the penalties from possible losses. Therefore, stock ownership by top executives reinforces risk-avoiding behavior—avoidance of risks that the owners would prefer the executives to take. The owners will have less risk-averse attitudes since (1) their human capital may be independent of the firm's outcomes, and (2) they can diversify their wealth through ownership of many different firms. Firm managers already have more of their wealth, (in the form of nondiversifiable and nontradable human capital[7]) tied up in the firm than they would probably prefer. Additional stock ownership in the same firm increases their specific risk even further.

A second problem with executive stock ownership is that there is no direct causal relationship between executive actions and stock market performance. Many noncontrollable random events, such as general business conditions, governmental actions, unexpected material, energy, or labor shortages, and international developments, may overwhelm the best (or worst) efforts of management. If the stock price unexpectedly rises because of these noncontrollable events, the executives obtain a windfall gain at the expense of the original set of owners. Conversely, if the stock price plunges, the executives suffer a significant loss in expected income or wealth. The uncertainty of the stock market, therefore, introduces an additional component of noncontrollable risk into the executives' compensation schedule and does not provide reliable feedback on the quality of decisions and extent of effort exerted by these executives.

In an attempt to obtain a performance measure under greater executive control than stock prices, owners may develop a measure based on an internal evaluation of the economic well-being of the firm. The stock market provides one estimate of the economic value of the firm's assets, but it has the problems described above. Appraising the value of the firm's assets provides another estimate, but this measure may be very costly to obtain each year and could be a source of controversy because of its subjectiveness. Therefore, it may not provide a good basis for contracting between owners and managers. An incentive contract could, however, be based on data that are already prepared and audited for external parties, namely the historical-cost-based financial statements. Performance goals can be set based on earning per share or return on shareholders' investment. These figures are more under management's control than stock prices and, at least in the long run, should correlate with the economic welfare of the firm. In fact, many incentive compensation plans do depend directly on earnings per share (EPS) and accounting return on equity (ROE).

The agency cost associated with use of accounting-based measures for ex-

---

[7] Human capital cannot be easily traded because of laws against slavery as well as the moral-hazard problem; once you sell shares in your human capital, you no longer capture the gains from hard work and good decision making. Therefore, you would have a much lower incentive to work hard and to make good decisions.

ecutive compensation schemes arises from the imperfect association between accounting income and the economic well-being of the firm. Executives can take many actions that increase reported income—and hence increase their income from incentive compensation plans—but decrease the firm's value from the owners' point of view. How else can we explain the persistence of so many United States corporations in remaining on FIFO for inventory valuation rather than switching to LIFO? For most companies, LIFO saves taxes and increases the cash flows to the firm but reports lower income and hence lowers earnings-based performance measures. Executives have many other opportunities to increase reported earnings via actions that do not benefit the firm and that may, in some cases, actually decrease the value of the firm. These actions include (1) repurchasing debt or preferred stock selling at a discount, (2) switching to straight-line depreciation or the flow-through method for the investment credit for financial reporting, (3) purchasing other companies under terms that permit use of pooling-of-interest method, (4) selling off assets whose market value is well in excess of book value, and (5) increasing the leverage of the firm by issuing debt and acquiring assets whose returns exceed the after-tax debt cost but are below the risk-adjusted cost of capital.

Conversely, executives could decline investments that would increase the long-run value of the firm but penalize short-run earnings. For example, profitable capital investments with heavy initial start-up costs might not be undertaken, and research and development expenditures could be underfunded because of the longer-term risky nature of the rewards from such expenditures. Also factors such as foreign currency fluctuations under FAS 8 can affect earnings per share in the short run. One can imagine the hostility felt toward the FAS 8 by executives falling short of an earnings-based performance measure because of an unexpected currency translation adjustment. In general, any financial reporting initiative will be viewed skeptically by executives under an earnings-based incentive scheme.

Thus accounting-based performance measures may be more desirable than stock incentives because they relate to activities that are more under the control of top executives. Their disadvantage, however, is that they may be too controllable by executives who can manipulate the measures in ways that are not beneficial to the owners. One very important mechanism for reducing this agency cost is the board of directors, who must approve virtually all the actions that could increase an accounting-based performance measure without increasing the economic value of the firm. An effective board of directors, looking out for the best interests of the firm's owners, can play an extremely important role in reducing the agency cost of the contractual relationship between owners and managers. For example, the board could define earnings for computation of executive bonuses to exclude expenditures on long-term intangibles (R&D, maintenance, quality control, personnel development) so that executives would not be motivated to underinvest in these important areas. Similarly, the board could undo accounting policies that increase reported income but do not benefit the company directly (holding gains reported under FIFO, flow-through of the investment tax credit, unadjusted historic cost, straight-line depreciation). In this way, the managers would be rewarded for behavior related to the long-run profitability of the firm.

Having completed this introduction to agency cost in the contractual relationship between owners and managers, we are ready for our survey of contemporary executive compensation schemes.

FORMS OF BONUS AND INCENTIVE CONTRACTS

Cash or Stock Awards

The simplest reward system is a current bonus in either cash or stock. Current bonuses generally are a function of both individual performance and corporate profits. Typical formulas (to be discussed later in more detail) are a fixed percentage of corporate profits or a percentage of profits in excess of a specified return on stockholders' equity. Current bonuses are equivalent to salaries in their tax consequences to the firm and its executives. The principal difference between salary and a current bonus is that bonuses may be cut or eliminated during a year of poor economic performance but salaries are rarely cut. The advantage of a stock award is that it creates a closer affinity of interests between the top management group and the shareholders. A disadvantage is that the executive will need to find cash or financing to pay taxes on the stock award if the shares are not sold immediately. Also, significant stock ownership by managers may lead to risk-averse behavior, as mentioned in our principal-agent discussion.

Deferred Bonus and Compensation

In some companies bonuses are not paid until the executives retire. The main objective of the deferral is to have the executives receive the income when they are in a lower tax bracket. As long as the deferred compensation is "unfunded" and based solely on the unsecured credit of the employer, current taxes can be avoided. The overall tax benefit of deferred compensation to the company and the executive combined is worthwhile only if the executive's original tax bracket on interest income exceeds the corporate tax rate.[8] In 1980, top executives needed a salary in excess of about $50,000 for their marginal tax to be in excess of the 46 percent corporate tax rate.

Some plans defer the bonus over a period of three to five years after it is earned. Receipt is contingent on the employee's continuing to work for the company. Such plans are referred to as "golden handcuffs" because they make it

---

[8] See Miller and Scholes [1980].

very expensive for key executives to leave a company. These plans are especially useful in high-technology companies, where it is important to prevent the loss of senior executives who could transfer the latest technology to a rival.

Stock Options

A *stock option* is a financial arrangement in which executives are given the right to purchase company stock at a future date, at a price established when the option was granted (usually the current market price or 95 percent of the market price). The assumption behind stock options is that executives will be motivated to strive for the firm's long-term performance, rather than short-term profits, in the hope that the stock price will increase significantly. Of perhaps greater importance is the fact that an option has no downside loss (since the executive does not actually own the stock) and unlimited upside potential. Therefore, executives may be encouraged to reduce the risk-averse behavior that would otherwise accompany their ownership of stock and to undertake riskier projects with higher payoffs. After the 1976 Tax Reform Act, the only permissible stock option plans are nonqualified options in which any gains are considered as earned income and are therefore ineligible for favorable capital gains treatment. For the firms, the difference between the stock price and the exercise (option) price is considered deductible compensation expense. Stock options have no apparent net tax advantage to the executive and the company. Therefore, the presumption is that incentive effects must explain their existence. Stock options may reduce the risk-averse behavior otherwise associated with direct ownership of stock. But they share the disadvantage that events not directly under managerial control may have a more significant impact on share prices.[9] For example, disappointing stock market performance during the 1970s led companies to devise other schemes to reward the managers of growing and profitable companies, since many stock option plans turned out to provide little additional compensation. Still, more than half of all large American corporations have nonqualified stock option plans.

Performance Shares

First adopted by CBS in 1971, and spreading to many other companies, performance shares are shares of company stock awarded to executives who achieve a predetermined performance objective *and* remain with the company. The specified performance goals—whether corporate, divisional, or individual—are usually linked to a companywide performance measure. The most common measure is cumulative growth in earnings per share (EPS) over a period of four to six years. A typical range for cumulative EPS growth is between 9 and 15 percent per year. Executives generally receive no additional reward for exceeding

---

[9] Both these points—risk aversion and noncontrollable events—were discussed earlier as factors limiting the desirability of stock compensation for managers.

the EPS growth objective but may receive a fraction of the awarded shares if the objective is partially met.

Performance shares have several desirable features. First, by focusing on a four- to six-year horizon, they encourage longer-term decision making than does an annual cash bonus plan. Second, because the shares are awarded as a bonus, the executive is not faced with the financing problems of buying stock under an option plan and then paying taxes on the difference between exercise and market price. (With performance shares, however, the current market value of the stock received is taxable to the executive as earned income. Some companies therefore provide a cash bonus with the performance shares to ease the financing burden of the tax liability.) Third, performance shares, unlike stock options, provide the executive with a definite award. This award is contingent on achieving a specified internal objective, an objective that is presumably under greater executive control than the stock price. But the executive retains an interest in the stock price because the ultimate value of the award is a direct function of the future stock price.

A disadvantage of performance shares is their reliance on a measure such as earnings per share. As noted earlier (in our discussion of the principal-agent relationship), a variety of executive actions can increase EPS without benefiting the shareholders.

Stock Appreciation Rights and Phantom Stock

Stock appreciation rights (SAR) are deferred cash payments based on the increase of the stock price from the time of award to the time of payment. SAR's are frequently used in conjunction with stock option plans to provide a means for executives to purchase stock earned under stock option plans. Increasingly, however, executives offered a choice are opting to take all cash and acquire no stock. *Phantom stock* plans are awards in units of number of shares of stock. After qualifying for receipt of the vested units, the executive receives in cash the number of units multiplied by the *current* market price of the stock. Both SAR's and phantom stock are essentially deferred cash bonuses but with the value of the bonus a function of the future stock price. Thus, they have both the strengths and the weaknesses that result when compensation is a function of share price.

Participating Units

Participating unit plans are similar to SAR's except that payment is keyed to operating results rather than stock price. Commonly used operating measures include pretax income, return on investment, sales and backlog, or a combination of these. The units awarded can vary continuously with the measure of operating results. Participating units are most useful for a organization with little or no publicly traded stock or for a specialized division in a company whose fortunes are not closely linked to overall results. Participating units permit the greatest flexibility in relating executive incentives to long-term performance measures internal to the organization. They are not affected by stock market fluctuations. This is an advantage in reducing some noncontrollable uncertainty in the executive's compensation function but a disadvantage because of the divergence of interests created between executives and shareholders. Participating unit plans require a careful and operational specification of the long-term operating results desired for the firm and the way in which incentive compensation will vary with partial or complete attainment of these operating results.

EVALUATION OF ACCOUNTING-BASED INCENTIVE COMPENSATION SCHEMES

Within the broad framework of incentive schemes, ranging from the annual cash bonus to more recent and sophisticated schemes such as performance shares, many crucial design issues can determine whether the incentive plan provides the appropriate motivation at minimum cost to the firm's owners. The two most crucial questions are (1) how the total size of the bonus pool is determined each year and (2) how the bonus pool is allocated to the corporate and divisional executives.

Establishing the Size of the Bonus Pool

The simplest rule for determining the magnitude of executive bonuses is to compute the bonus pool as a fixed percentage of profits. This rule, however, will award bonuses even with very low profits, when the firm is earning a low return on invested capital. Consequently, this rule is not often implemented.

A fairly common procedure is to compute the bonus pool as a percentage of profits after a prespecified return on invested capital or shareholders' equity has been earned. For example, the Goodyear Tire & Rubber Company, in its annual report (1979), describes how the amount in its profit-sharing plan for officers and key personnel is determined each year:

> Under the present formula of the Plan, the company's consolidated net income after tax (adjusted) for any year must exceed 5% of the average amount of the consolidated book value of its capital stock before any amount become available for distribution to participants. Ten per cent of the excess of adjusted net income [is distributed, subject to the approval and discretion of outside members of the Board of Directors in cash and stock].

The Koppers Company's incentive plan for 80 key employees indicates:

> There shall be credited to the incentive fund an amount not to exceed 5% of the company's total income before any provision for incentive payments, interest, income taxes and extraordinary items, after deducting 13% of invested capital. (from the 1979 Annual Report).

And, Alfred Sloan's favorite, the General Motors Bonus Plan:

> The Corporation maintains a reserve for purpose of the Bonus Plan to which may be credited each year an amount which the independent public accountants of the corporation determine to be 8% of the net earnings which exceed 7% but not 15% of net capital, plus 5% of the net earnings which exceed 15% of net income, but not in excess of the amount paid out as dividends on the common stock during the year. (from the 1979 Annual Report)

A variety of issues arise in these formulas. First is the definition of the investment base. Goodyear uses shareholders' equity, whereas Koppers and General Motors use invested capital (generally computed as shareholders' equity plus long-term debt). The use of shareholders' equity provides an incentive to increase leverage as long as the net cash flows from the asset acquired exceed the after-tax borrowing cost plus straight-line depreciation. By including long-term debt in the investment base, as Koppers and General Motors do, we eliminate the bias to increase debt. A more comprehensive approach might include all interest-bearing debt, short and long term, in invested capital.

A second problem arises if only shareholders' equity is used for computing bonus payments. Several years of losses may reduce the shareholders' equity to a low level and make future bonuses very easy to earn, even though total return on assets is still not at highly profitable levels.

As an aside, it is interesting to speculate whether one of the forces giving rise to the "big bath" approach to determining earnings is related to incentive compensation schemes. Under the big-bath philosophy, corporations with disappointing (or even negative) earnings in a year will decide to write off a variety of dubious assets that had been capitalized over the years. The idea seems to be to concentrate all the bad news in a single year (who cares how negative a price-earnings ratio gets?) and clean up the books for future profitability. Such an action becomes easy to explain if the managers reason:

1. "With earnings this low, we're not going to earn a bonus this year anyway. Let's clean off these accruals so that we won't have to keep amortizing them against earnings in future years."
2. "A good healthy loss reduces shareholders' equity and will make future bonuses a little easier to earn and a little larger."

This interpretation is speculative and deserves research before we decide it helps explain the occasional big baths in earnings reports.

TABLE 16-1. Price-Level Adjustment of Koppers Company Shareholders' Equity (Millions of Dollars)

Year	Shareholders' Equity	Change in Shareholders' Equity	GNP Deflator	Adjusted Change in Shareholders' Equity (1979 $)
1969	$188.5	$188.5	86.7	$359.8
1970	210.7	22.2	91.4	40.2
1971	221.1	10.4	96.0	17.9
1972	238.1	17.0	100.0	28.1
1973	259.0	20.9	105.8	32.7
1974	297.1	38.1	116.0	54.4
1975	353.1	56.0	127.2	72.9
1976	410.2	57.1	133.8	70.6
1977	454.8	44.6	141.6	52.1
1978	504.7	49.9	152.1	54.3
1979	590.2	85.5	165.5	85.5
		$590.2		$868.5

A third and more serious problem with the use of shareholders' equity, either by itself or as part of total invested capital, is the failure to adjust for price-level changes. Shareholders' equity represents the capital contributed each year in the firm's history through retained earnings and sales of stock. This capital has been contributed at dramatically different price levels, yet it is added together as if it had all been contributed in the most recent year. To illustrate this problem, consider the changes in the shareholders' equity figure for the Koppers Company between 1969 and 1979 (Table 16-1). For simplicity we will assume the 1969 figure represents contributions made at the 1969 price level, even though we know that it does not and that it grossly underestimates the shareholders' equity in 1969, as measured in 1969 dollars.[10] We will use the Gross National Product Deflator to adjust the annual increases in shareholders' equity to avoid the measurement problems caused by the more widely used but overstated Consumer Price Index.

Assume that the bonus payment is 5 percent of net income before taxes, interest, and incentive payments, and after deducting 13 percent of the average sum of shareholders' equity and long-term debt for the year. In 1978, long-term debt (in millions) was $233.6, and in 1979 it was $224.2. The 1979 net income before taxes, interest, and incentive payments was $157.3. Based on the reported financial data, the approximate[11] incentive payment of $2.8 is computed as follows:

---

[10] Without this simplifying assumption, we would have to go back in history to the start of the company and price-level-adjust each year's figures. Our point is illustrated well enough by adjusting only the data since 1969.

[11] This is a rough approximation, since the precise definition of invested capital is not provided in the Koppers annual report. Also, we have ignored the simultaneity problem: the 1979 equity figure appears after the 1979 incentive payment has been subtracted.

Average invested capital 1979:

$$\tfrac{1}{2}(504.7 + 590.2) + \tfrac{1}{2}(233.6 + 224.2) = \$776.35.$$

13% Average invested capital:

$$0.13(776.35) = \$100.9.$$

5% Net income in excess of invested capital:

$$0.05(157.3 - 100.9) = \$2.8.$$

Using the price-level adjusted stockholders' equity data, we have:

Average invested capital 1979 (measured in $1979):

$$\tfrac{1}{2}(783.0 + 868.5) + \tfrac{1}{2}(233.6 + 224.2) = \$1054.65.$$

13% Average invested capital:

$$0.13(1,054.65) = \$137.1.$$

5% Net income in excess of invested capital:

$$0.05(157.3 - 137.1) = \$1.0.$$

This simple adjustment, without even compensating for the underdepreciation in the net income figure or for the loss in purchasing power for capital contributed before 1969, reduces the bonus payment by almost 65 percent. For many companies, a simple price-level adjustment on shareholders' equity would likely completely eliminate what had been a lucrative bonus and incentive payment. This example reinforces a point made in the preceding chapter. During periods of inflation, it is easy for division and corporate managers to show quite reasonable returns on investment or returns on equity. It is a lot harder to demonstrate good performance once inflationary biases are removed from the reported financial results.

Thus, the failure to restate shareholders' equity for price-level changes makes the bonus pool larger than it should be, if the goal is to reward the earning of income in excess of a specified return on invested capital. Of course, an additional problem is caused by using a specified percentage return that was established when the inflation rate was less than 3 percent per year, which will be below the competitive return required by investors when the inflation rate is 10 percent per year or higher. Investors will wish to receive a real, risk-adjusted rate of return plus a return based on expected inflation. Therefore, the minimal return on invested capital that the firm should earn, before it feels that executives have earned a bonus, should vary with the anticipated inflation rate. This will signal to executives that a 7 percent return (recall the GM plan), which may have been adequate when the inflation rate was essentially zero, is certainly not good performance when the inflation rate and short-term interest rates exceed 10 percent.

A third method for establishing the bonus pool (in addition to a fixed percentage of profits, or a percentage of income in excess of a specified return on invested capital) would base performance on profit improvement. With this procedure, bonuses would be awarded for annual increases in profits. Apart from increases in profits caused by accounting manipulations, as we discussed earlier in considering the principal-agent relationship, this procedure may reward or penalize executives for events beyond their control. General business conditions or specific industry factors could cause earnings to expand or contract for reasons not controllable by company executives. This could mean "windfall" gains or losses for these executives in their incentive plans. One way to reduce the impact of noncontrollable factors is to compare a company's performance to that of other firms in the same industry. In this way, the executives of a company whose earnings increased 15 percent, while the industry average earnings increased 25 percent, would not be rewarded for a good absolute but poor relative performance.

Increasingly, firms have become more diversified, so that it may not always be easy to define the "industry" the firm is in or to identify comparable dominant-product firms in the same industry. In this case, even a comparison to a national average of corporate earnings or to a three-digit or two-digit Standard Industrial Classification (SIC) aggregation of companies[12] would provide a better comparison of relative firm performance than simple, absolute year-to-year comparisons of the firm with itself.

Finally, one can always attempt to evaluate managerial performance against a profit plan or budget and avoid all the problems that arise when using mechanical formulas for profitability. If the board of directors could obtain forecasts that truly represented what profits were achievable, given (1) anticipated business conditions, (2) high-quality managerial decision making, and (3) the best administrative efforts of the managers, then achievement of the profit plan would provide an excellent basis for incentive compensation. The problem, of course, with any incentive plan based on budgeted performance is to obtain information that is not biased or distorted in order to influence the ease of achieving the targeted plan. In the next chapter we will suggest schemes to motivate truthful forecasting. Without such schemes, however, budget-based incentive schemes will be subject to the problem of strategic manipulation of information (see the discussion in Chapter 13), which makes it difficult to implement these plans in practice despite their many desirable properties.

Allocation of Bonus Pool to Managers

Once the size of the entire bonus pool is determined, there remains the question of how to divide it among the executives of the corporation. It seems common to limit those participating in the bonus pool to the top 0.5 percent of salaried employees, so that only the most senior executives participate in the

---

[12] The Department of Commerce and Labor collect and classify a variety of corporate data, including profits, according to industrial (SIC) codes.

incentive plan. The simplest procedure awards the bonus pool proportional to the salary of the eligible executives. This rule is reasonable if the annual salary reflects the contribution to divisional or overall corporate performance, but it does not provide the flexibility for rewarding exceptional performance by a manager during the year. Also it may provide a bonus to a manager whose performance has not been particularly noteworthy recently.

In general, the bonus system will be more effective as an incentive and reward if the bonus allocation is reviewed by top management and the board of directors. This will enable the bonus award to also be a function of longer range, less quantifiable performance criteria and thereby relieve the pressure on exclusive use of a short-term accounting-based measure of performance. The board of directors is in the best position to tie incentive payments to the establishment and implementation of plans for long-term profitability. For example, the board can use non-accounting-based measures of strategic performance, such as those we discussed at the end of Chapter 14 in the context of the General Electric plan. Review by the board also permits an evaluation of relative performance, comparing results to industry performance when awarding incentive payments.

An important consideration in the allocation of a bonus pool is whether awards to divisional managers should reflect divisional or just corporate performance. The remarks by Sloan quoted at the beginning of the chapter advocate a flexible bonus payment based on individual performance for achieving overall corporate goals. The GM plan attempted to minimize actions by divisional managers that increased division profits but had adverse consequences for the overall corporation.

It is difficult to generalize, but awards based on overall corporate, rather than divisional, performance would seem to work best for dominant-product firms—that is, vertically integrated firms producing a single major product (such as automobiles, tires, or steel) and where a high degree of interaction or coordination among divisions is required for the firm to function effectively. Awards based on divisional performance seem most appropriate when the firm is highly decentralized with little interaction among its divisions, which are organized as profit or investment centers. For example, firms that can be characterized as conglomerates, venture capitalists, or holding companies for diverse operating units can use incentive plans based primarily on divisional performance. For firms somewhere in the middle of the continuum between dominant-product and highly diversified firms, a combination of corporate and divisional performance may provide the right mixture of incentives for optimizing local performance while still looking out for overall corporate goals.

SUMMARY

Incentive plans provide strong motivation for the top corporate executives to perform well along specified measures of performance. Formula-based plans reduce uncertainty and ambiguity about how performance will be evaluated, but it is extremely difficult to devise mechanistic formulas that will not lead to dys-functional behavior. Limitations of accounting-based formulas, such as the failure to control for changes in price levels, can lead to the awarding of large bonuses even when the firm is earning less than a competitive return on capital. It would seem indispensable for the board of directors, particularly an independent com-pensation committee consisting solely of outside directors, to play an active role in awarding incentive payments. Such a committee could control for:

1. Increases or decreases in profits caused by accounting conventions rather than operating performance.
2. Increases in profits caused by the failure to adjust for price-level changes.
3. Increases in profits not commensurate with performance of similar companies in the same industry.
4. Increases in profits caused by concentration on short-term rather than long-term performance measures.
5. Actions that maximize divisional performance measures at the ex-pense of overall corporate welfare.

The board, at its discretion, can restate corporate earnings to exclude ex-penditures on intangibles (R&D, maintenance, and so on), exclude special non-recurring items, eliminate the effects of special tax features, adjust depreciation expense (perhaps to the annuity method) to encourage new investment, and per-form similar adjustments so that executives are motivated to strive for the firm's long-range profitability.

PROBLEMS

16-1. Executive Compensation Plan

Fortune Magazine (July 27, 1981) reported on the new Chief Executive Officer of AM International (formerly Addressograph-Multigraph), Richard B. Black, char-acterizing him as a turnaround specialist. Black recently announced huge write-offs, partly in connection with discontinued products. These resulted in an $82.8 million loss on revenues of $206 million in the quarter ending April 30, 1981. The article states that "Black has ample incentive to improve the bottom line. On top of a $300,000 annual paycheck, he gets a $1000 bonus for every penny increase in earnings per share up to $1, and more for every subsequent penny, up to a maximum of $550,000."

The Wall Street Journal (November 20, 1980) reported similarly on the value of compensation plans for chief executives:

"Performance plans, which pay executives cash or stock bonuses based on a company's growth statistics, are increasingly replacing stock options as companies revamp their executive-incentive programs. Among the nation's largest 100 companies, 41 have adopted 'performance-share' or 'performance-unit' plans to reward executives for meeting growth targets up to six years away.

Performance shares or units aren't tied to the stock market. Instead, success is measured by earnings per share, return on assets, return on shareholders' equity, increases in capital spending, or some other measure. Some companies use a single guideline, others a combination.

Honeywell, for example uses growth in earnings per share as its performance guideline. The company has two overlapping four-year performance periods, one beginning in 1978 and the other in 1980. If the company achieves a cumulative average growth of 13 percent in annual earnings per share, executives will earn 100 percent of their performance shares. The maximum allowable is 130 percent, which would require a 17 percent growth rate; below 9 percent they get nothing."

Since Honeywell's earnings rose more than 50 percent in the first two years of the plan, executives were already starting to receive payments ($1.6 million in 1979 alone to 41 participating executives).

Champion International Corp. adopted a performance plan that compares the company's earnings per share growth with 15 competitors in the forest-products industry. If Champion's four year EPS growth exceeds the industry average, twelve senior executives receive an award of 25 percent of their total regular bonuses during the four year term.

Criticisms of performance shares also exist. Union Carbide scrapped its program because EPS growth was affected more by external events (such as inflation, energy price escalation, price controls) than by the actions of executives. Also, performance awards can sometimes prove embarrassing as when the chairman of International Harvester was forgiven a $1.8 million loan because 1979 performance exceeded goals set in 1977, but the company then showed a large loss for fiscal year 1980.

Required:

Comment on the motivation for establishing incentive plans for the senior executives of large companies. What are the strengths and weaknesses of performance share plans, in general, and the specific plans described for AM International, Honeywell, and Champion International?

16-2. *Incentives and Decision Making* (A. Atkinson)

Wilkinsburg Metal Works (WMW) specializes in custom metal work. For this reason the company uses many different types of machines which are repaired and replaced at regular intervals.

The factory manager, Ralph Smart, recently authorized the purchase from

Grinding Machine Systems of a $1,000,000 automated grinding machine system. This system has just been installed. At the projected level of operations this machine is expected to last for ten years and have annual operating costs of $500,000. The machine is assumed to be worthless at the end of its life.

Ralph is concerned by a recent development. The Revolutionary Machine Corporation has just announced the availability of a new machine which performs the same tasks as the machine just installed in WMW. The new machine would cost $1,500,000, last for ten years and have annual operating costs of $200,000. This new machine has rendered WMW's current machine obsolete and net of salvage, its current value is $200,000. The new machine would be worthless in ten years.

Ralph is currently paid a salary of $60,000 and receives a bonus of one half of one percent of corporate net income. Ralph estimates that he will remain with WMW for "about two more years." At that time he expects to achieve a promotion and raise by moving to another company.

In the questions which follow ignore income taxes and assume that the company's required return is 14 percent. The company uses the straight-line method to compute depreciation.

Required:

1. What is the best decision from the point of view of the company?
2. What is Ralph's preferred decision?
3. What motivation problems are caused by using short-run financial measures of performance as reward devices?
4. How might the inconsistencies raised in Questions 1 and 2 and the problems raised in 3 be mitigated?

16-3. Incentive Program for Improving Productivity (CMA)

Rimald Corporation is a large decentralized organization with six subsidiary companies operating as individual businesses each having independent manufacturing and marketing operations. Subsidiary performance is measured by return on total assets employed less current liabilities.

The Mospace subsidiary manufactures and markets products for the automotive and aerospace industries. It has accounted for 60 percent of Rimald's total sales for the past four years. Unfortunately Mospace's profits and return on investment have declined in the last four years. Mospace was responsible for about 40 percent of Rimald's total net income before taxes in 1978 which is considerably lower than in prior years. The decreasing contribution to total corporation profits is causing concern throughout Mospace.

One sales manager commented, "The increases in sales prices, of about 15 percent over the four years are inadequate to keep pace with increasing manufacturing costs—especially direct labor costs. The hourly wage rates and employee benefit costs have increased, and the number of workers seems to have increased even though our production levels have not changed during the past four years. We need some kind of incentive program to control labor costs in order to improve profitability."

After further thought the sales manager proposed an incentive program keyed to labor costs. The incentive program would be based on the reduction in the labor cost ratio (LCR). The LCR would be computed by dividing the cost of labor, including benefits, by the "added value" of Mospace products. The "added value" would be determined by subtracting all costs except labor and benefits from sales. The incentive features of the program are:

- The improvement in the LCR over the prior year ratio multiplied by the labor cost of the prior year will be defined as the gross savings to be shared equally between management employees and the subsidiary.
- The management employees' share will be divided equally among the 25 employees which are affected.
- A report of the results and payments will be made no later than the second month following the end of the year.

Mospace management accumulated financial data for the last four fiscal years so that the sales manager's proposal can be evaluated.

Mospace Subsidiary
(000 omitted)

	1978	1977	1976	1975
Sales	$21,500	$20,675	$19,500	$18,750
Expenses				
Raw material	10,360	9,855	8,875	8,450
Labor cost[1]	7,061	6,649	6,171	5,760
All other expenses	1,900	1,920	1,875	1,850
Total	$19,321	$18,424	$16,921	$16,060
Net income before taxes	$ 2,179	$ 2,251	$ 2,579	$ 2,690
Other data				
Volume data				
Pounds of raw material (000 omitted)	3,700	3,650	3,550	3,500
Labor hours (000 omitted)	614	610	605	600
Unit data				
Average cost per pound of raw material	$ 2.80	$ 2.70	$ 2.50	$ 2.41
Average labor rate per hour[1]	$11.50	$10.90	$10.20	$ 9.60

[1] Includes employee benefit costs.

Required:

1. How effective would the participation provisions (e.g., share equally with the subsidiary, share equally with other management employees, and the annual payment of share) be in the motivation of managers? Explain your answer.

2. The incentive program, based upon the improvement in the LCR, is designed to motivate managers to be more effective in the control of labor cost.

    a. Does the formula measure only the effect of changes in labor cost?

    b. Are the factors which affect the changes in the LCR within the control of the subsidiary management?

3. Did the sales manager identify the primary cause of Mospace's profit decline?

16-4. General Motors Incentive Program

The following footnote appeared as part of the 1978 General Motors' annual financial statements:

Note 3 Incentive Program

"The Incentive Program consists of the General Motors Bonus Plan, first approved by stockholders in 1918. The Incentive Program was last approved by stockholders at the 1977 Annual Meeting. . . .

The Corporation maintains a reserve for purposes of the Bonus Plan to which may be credited each year an amount which the independent public accountants of the Corporation determine to be 8 percent of the net earnings which exceed 7 percent but not 15 percent of net capital, plus 5 percent of the net earnings which exceed 15 percent of net capital, but not in excess of the amounts paid out as dividends on the common stock during the year. . . .

For the year 1978, the Bonus and Salary Committee directed a credit to the Reserve for the Bonus Plan of $168.4 million (the maximum permitted under the Bonus Plan formula. .) as set forth in the following table":

Net Capital (000,000)	
Stockholders' equity and long term debt (at 12/31/77)	$16,478.4
Computation of Net Earnings (000,000)	
Net Income for 1978	$ 3,508.0
Add provision for Bonus Plan	168.4
Add interest and discount on long term debt	55.2
Deduct loss of prior bonus awards	(1.8)
Net Income for Bonus Plan computations	3,729.8

The stockholders' equity at December 31, 1977 was $15,766.9:

Preferred Stock	$283.6
Common Stock	479.5
Capital Surplus	772.1
Retained Earnings	$14,231.7
Stockholders' Equity	$15,766.9

Most of the increase in Stockholders' Equity arose from additions to retained earnings since the end of World War II as shown by the following table:

	Addition to Retained Earnings	Change in Stockholders' Equity	Gross National Product Deflator (1977 = 100)
1977	$1379.8	$1381.7	141.70
76	1299.4	1302.8	133.71
75	551.8	551.8	127.15
74	(36.1)	(36.2)	116.02
73	883.9	883.9	105.80
72	876.8	862.0	100
71	950.3	951.4	96.02
70	(374.9)	(374.1)	91.36
1969	470.3	471.1	86.72
68	491.5	495.6	82.57
67	530.0	535.1	79.02
66	482.4	488.8	76.76
65	615.9	638.3	74.32
64	455.5	478.0	72.71
63	443.1	470.0	71.59
62	595.7	625.3	70.55
61	172.5	211.0	69.28
60	381.9	443.7	68.67
1959	298.3	354.2	67.52
58	61.8	111.7	66.06
57	275.2	323.5	65.02
56	281.6	326.5	62.90
55	584.3	916.0	60.98
54	356.5	356.6	59.69
53	236.4	255.3	58.88
52	196.8	196.8	58.00
51	143.0	143.0	57.27
50	295.0	295.0	53.64
1949	292.1	292.2	52.59
48	229.7	229.6	53.13
47	142.9	142.9	49.70

Stockholders' Equity: Dec. 31, 1946   1427.7

Required:

1. Show how the Bonus Plan provision of $168.4 million is computed from the 1978 net income and capital figures.

2. Assume that the Stockholders' Equity at the end of 1946 was contributed at the 1947 price level. Price level adjust the S/H equity position plus the additions to Stockholders' Equity each year since 1946 to obtain the capital contributed by General Motors shareholders as measured in 1977 dollars.

   How would the use of a "constant dollar" Stockholders' Equity figure affect the bonus computed in 1978?

3. General Motors reported that its 1978 Net Income, adjusted for price level changes in cost of goods sold and depreciation, and measured in 1967 dollars was $1384.5. The GNP Deflator for 1978 was 152.05. What was

General Motors price level adjusted 1978 income as measured in 1978 dollars?

4. Perform the bonus computation using constant (1978) dollar income and stockholders' equity.

5. Comment on the use of the same interest rates (7 percent and 15 percent of net capital) in the GM Bonus Formula, independent of the rate of inflation.

16-5.   Devising a Bonus Plan for a Purchasing Manager* (G. Foster)

OUTBACK ARTIFACTS

South Pacific Imports is a U.S. importer of distinctive cultural items from Australia, New Guinea, and other countries of the South Pacific area, with headquarters in San Francisco. It has seven wholly-owned subsidiaries, each of which specializes in cultural items from individual sub-regions of the South Pacific. The major part of South Pacific's business is as a wholesale supplier to speciality stores in North America. It also operates two retail outlets of its own in California (in San Francisco and Los Angeles). South Pacific's operations are managed on a divisionalized basis. Each subsidiary submits budgets to South Pacific for the forthcoming period, which after negotiation become the standard for subsequent performance evaluation. At the end of each period, a "management by exception" approach to evaluating the performance of each subsidiary and its management team is adopted. South Pacific has grown rapidly in the past few years and has recently appointed a full-time Controller who reports directly to the President. One reason for this rapid growth has been its reputation for concern with the quality of its merchandise, its emphasis on maintaining a varied stock, and the close attention paid to customer requirements.

Inventory Decisions at Outback Artifacts

Outback Artifacts is one of the seven subsidiaries of South Pacific Imports. One of its main lines of business is importing hand-carved boomerangs. It also imports such items as bark paintings and didgeridoo's. The purchasing department at Outback is organized as a cost center, while the sales department is organized as a profit center. The purchasing department is headed by Hobie Leland, Jr. Hobie purchases boomerangs from an Alice Springs supplier named Bill King Enterprises, one of three major Australian exporters of hand-carved boomerangs. Outback is the sole North-American agent for Bill King Enterprises.

Up to this period, Hobie has been using the following model in deciding the economic order quantity for each order of boomerangs:

$$q = \sqrt{\frac{2 \cdot C_p \cdot D}{C_s}}$$

---

* © 1980 by the Board of Trustees of the Leland Stanford Junior University (reproduced with permission).

where

q = economic order quantity,
C_p = incremental acquisition cost per order,
D = total demand for the period, and
C_s = incremental holding cost per unit of average inventory.

Prior to the start of this period, the Alice Springs supplier had always quoted Outback a fixed unit price (regardless of units purchased) for orders made at least one month in advance of the shipping deadline. For orders made on shorter notice, the price quoted was based on "demand and supply considerations as determined by Bill King Enterprises." On his last visit to Alice Springs, Hobie managed to convince Bill King that it was in his best interest to adopt a differential pricing structure (based on size of the order) for long-term contracts.

The demand for next period was estimated by the sales manager of Outback to be 10,000 boomerangs. Next period's contract with Bill King Enterprises called for an annual retainer of $A18,000 and an additional payment of $A3,600 per order to cover packaging and handling costs. This contract was negotiated by Hobie on his last visit to Alice Springs. The annual retainer was up significantly from the $A10,000 paid during the prior period. Each order took approximately three months from the time it was packaged in Alice Springs to its arrival at the Port of San Francisco. Payment to Bill King Enterprises was due in Australian dollars 30 days after the order arrived in San Francisco.

Hobie's compensation package comprised a fixed salary of $U.S.20,000 plus a bonus designed to encourage him to seek out cost-effective sources of supply. The bonus was calculated as:

$$20\% \times \left[\begin{array}{l} \text{Standard Unit Purchase Price} \\ -\text{ Actual Unit Purchase Price} \end{array}\right] \begin{array}{l} \text{Actual} \\ \times \text{ Units} \\ \text{Purchased} \end{array}$$

The "bonus" system only came into effect when the standard price exceeded the actual price. The standard unit purchase price was calculated as standard purchase price (in the currency of the supplying country) × the exchange rate at the time the standard was set. The actual unit purchase price was calculated as actual purchase price × the exchange rate at the time of payment. The standard purchase price was set by the general manager of Outback prior to the start of each period after discussions with Hobie Leland.

The standard unit purchase price for the next period was set at $U.S.104 ($A92.00 × the exchange rate of $A1 = $U.S. 1.130). Shortly after the period had started, Hobie received the new price schedule from Bill King Enterprises. It provided for a $A0.90 discount per unit for purchases in lots of 10,000 boomerangs. The unit purchase price for lots less than 10,000 units was $A90.00 per boomerang. Processing cost of Outback Artifacts for each order was estimated to be $U.S.6,000. (This $U.S.6,000 was in addition to the above payments to the Alice Springs supplier.) When each order arrived from Australia, the boomerangs were placed into storage (accomplished at the rate of 30 per hour). Similarly, when each sale was made, the boomerangs had to be taken out of storage (also at a rate of 30 per hour). The average cost per hour of labor was estimated at $U.S.30. The company required a before-tax rate of return of 10% per period on its investment.

When Hobie received details of the new price schedule, he was delighted. He quickly decided to place one order of 10,000 units for the period.

Evaluating Hobie's Decision

Around the time of Hobie's decision to purchase in lots of 10,000 units, the Controller of South Pacific received a letter from a former employee of Outback Artifacts. The letter presented some allegations and some basic data concerning Hobie's purchasing decisions. The Controller was concerned with the allegations in the letter and sent his assistant, Delilah Jones, to visit Outback Artifacts. He stressed that she was not on a witch-hunt. Rather her concern was to determine if the existing compensation package to Hobie was in need of modification. One week later, Delilah and the Controller arranged to discuss her preliminary findings. She mentioned the following problem areas with the existing bonus system:

myopic focus on purchase price,

bonus works only one way—incentives lacking when purchase price was greater than standard,

responsibility factors ignored—other departments may affect the purchase price Hobie obtained,

"qualitative aspects" of Hobie's performance ignored, and

no ex post revision of standards.

Delilah said that further analysis would probably reveal other problem areas, and that each item in the problem area list was not of equal importance.

To illustrate the dollar magnitude of several of these problem areas, Delilah presented an analysis of Hobie's decision to buy in lots of 10,000 units. (See Exhibit 1.) In making the calculations in Exhibit 1, Delilah used the current exchange rate of \$A1 = \$U.S. 1.111. She noted that a major portion of Hobie's bonus was due to a favorable change in the Australian—U.S. exchange rate. This she found to be incongruous, given that Hobie had no ability to control movements in foreign exchange rates.

The Controller prided himself on his analytical abilities and thought that the inventory decision model used by Hobie was "simplistic." In his M.B.A. production management class, the simple EOQ model Hobie used was covered in only the first of six sessions on inventory management models. It was a single-period model and it assumed that demand was known with certainty—both rather unrealistic assumptions. He also noted that it did not take into account the possibility of stock-outs occurring and stated that models had been proposed in the literature for explicitly considering such costs when deciding on the economic order quantity.

The normal delivery time for orders from Outback Artifacts warehouse was four weeks. However, Bill King guaranteed that it could process rush orders within one week. Thus, Outback could minimize possible stock-outs by using airfreight. Delilah reported that possible stock-outs had been a problem for two months of the prior year, when there was a strike by wharf workers in Australia. In the end, Outback had to have Qantas fly in a small order of boomerangs for some of their important customers. She stated that Outbacks' airfreight bill for this small order averaged \$U.S.6.00 per boomerang. Also, Bill King had to be paid an extra \$A10.00 per boomerang due to "supply shortages" at Alice Springs at that time. (These extra costs were added to the actual unit purchase price when calculating Hobie's bonus and when transferring goods between the purchasing and sales departments of Outback Artifacts.)

By the end of the meeting, the Controller had decided that changes were in order for the purchasing division of Outback Artifacts. He sent the President of South Pacific a copy of Delilah's analysis and his recommendation that the existing performance evaluation-incentive system be re-evaluated. The President accepted the recommendation and assigned the problem to Delilah. Her task was to design a performance evaluation-incentive system that could be used (a) to measure the important aspects of Hobie's performance as a purchasing officer, and (b) to provide incentives to Hobie such that the decisions he made were those that were in the best interests of Outback Artifacts. He noted that the system she designed had to be operational, although she should not feel constrained to working within the existing reporting system

Required:

1. Describe the problem areas with the existing performance evaluation-incentive system for Hobie. Do not restrict yourself to those areas you think are easily amenable to solution. Which problem areas do you think are the most critical?

2. Outline (in detail) the performance evaluation-incentive system you would propose Outback Artifacts adopt.

3. Document which of the problem areas cited in Question 1 are addressed by your proposed system. Which problem areas cited in (1) are not as yet addressed in your proposed system? Describe the difficulties in designing an operational system to address these "as yet non-addressed" problems.

Exhibit 1   Delilah's Evaluation of Hobie's Decision

1. With the EOQ model Hobie used, he should have purchased in lots of 4,450 units:

$$q = \sqrt{\frac{2 \cdot C_p \cdot D}{C_s}}$$

$C_p = \$4,000 + \$6,000 = \$10,000$

$D = 10,000$ units

$C_s = 10\% \times (\$100 + 1/30 \times \$30) = \$10.10$

$$q = \sqrt{\frac{2 \times 10,000 \times 10,000}{10.10}} = 4,450$$

The cost of this order size is estimated to be \$44,945:

$$TC = \frac{C_s \cdot q}{2} + \frac{C_p \cdot D}{q}$$

$$= \frac{10.10 \times 4,450}{2} + \frac{10,000 \times 10,000}{4,450}$$

$$= \$44,945$$

2. Given that Hobie purchases in one lot of size 10,000 boomerangs, the cost is estimated to be $60,000:

$$C_p = \$10,000$$

$$D = 10,000 \text{ units}$$

$$C_s = 10\% \times (\$99 + 1/30 \times \$30) = \$10$$

$$TC = \frac{10 \times 10,000}{2} + \frac{10,000 \times 10,000}{10,000} = \$60,000$$

3. The "opportunity cost" of Hobie's decision to Outback Artifacts is estimated to be $7,055:

Policy in 1

Purchase Cost	=	$ 1,000,000
+ Inventory Cost	=	44,945
+ Bonus to Hobie	=	8,000
		$ 1,052,945

Policy in 2

Purchase Cost	=	$ 990,000
+ Inventory Cost	=	60,000
+ Bonus to Hobie	=	10,000
		$ 1,060,000

Note: All calculations are in $ U.S. dollars. Amounts expressed in $ A dollars have been multiplied by 1.111 and then rounded to the nearest $U.S. dollar.

Exhibit 2 $A—$U.S. Exchange Rate Movements

The following year-end exchange rates were taken from *The Wall Street Journal*:

Year	Exchange Rate
1970	$A1.00 = $U.S. 1.117
1971	" = $U.S. 1.195
1972	" = $U.S. 1.280
1973	" = $U.S. 1.495
1974	" = $U.S. 1.324
1975	" = $U.S. 1.260
1976	" = $U.S. 1.093
1977	" = $U.S. 1.141
1978	" = $U.S. 1.151
1979	" = $U.S. 1.108

16-6. McDonald's Corporation: Designing an Incentive System*

Designing an equitable compensation system is not an easy task for the top management of any company, as the attention the subject has received in these pages and elsewhere makes clear. But the difficulties of designing a compensation program for managers in a service business are particularly severe. When a company's product—be it flying lessons, cleaner offices, waffles, or Caribbean cruises—is manufactured and consumed almost simultaneously, there is no second chance to sell or perform.

Although bank tellers, chambermaids, and short-order cooks may have little in common, they are all at the forefront of their employers' public images. How they perceive and perform their jobs can promote or undermine the success of their organizations, and their proper and effective management keeps many a banker, innkeeper, and restaurateur on his toes.

The problems of motivation and reward in service-oriented companies are increasingly important as the provision of service assumes an ever-growing role in our economy. In this article we show how one such company—perhaps the world's largest and most successful food-service organization—is grappling with these problems and how other executives concerned with similar compensation issues view the plans the company has devised.

"We consider our first-line management to be the managers of our company-owned units," a senior executive of McDonald's Corporation told us. "And they do a tremendous job for us. Somehow we have to design a compensation system that will reward them for the hard work they do and still motivate them to continue putting in the extra effort that has made McDonald's a household name. We've tried various compensation programs, but none has proved to be totally successful."

The company's concern was not academic. At the time of the 1972 compensation system evaluation—the take-off point for this case—McDonald's and its subsidiaries operated, licensed, and serviced 2,127 fast-service restaurants throughout the United States and Canada, and a few in other countries. About 25 percent of the units were company owned and operated. (The ratio has now risen to about 30 percent.) By 1977, the company has estimated, the system will have some 4,000 units, and company-owned outlets will number more than 1,000.

The average volume of a company-owned unit in 1971 was $540,000. The company expected sales to rise to about $600,000 by the end of 1972.

Pervasive throughout McDonald's operations has been a success formula often stated by the founder, Chairman Ray Kroc: quality, service, and cleanliness ("QSC" in the corporate shorthand). Accordingly, McDonald's maintains a year-round training program at all levels of operations, such as at the world's only Hamburger University, at Elk Grove, Illinois. At this $2 million facility licensees as well as managers of company-owned restaurants must take an intensive course on McDonald's operational policies; refresher courses are also available. In 1973 some 1,200 persons were graduated from Hamburger U.

Below the managerial level, most jobs are quite simple and can be easily taught

* Case originally prepared for classroom use by Charles Horngren based on W. E. Sasser and S. H. Pettway, "Case of Big Mac's Pay Plans," *Harvard Business Review* (July-August, 1974) (reproduced with permission of *Harvard Business Review* and Charles Horngren).

to new employees within hours, with the aid of operating manuals and in-store visual material supplied by the corporate training staff.

Initial efforts

Between 1963 and 1972 McDonald's tried several compensation systems in an effort to encourage superior performance by managers of its company-owned outlets. But, as noted, none of the plans left front-line or top management entirely satisfied.

In 1963 a restaurant manager's bonus was merely a function of his sales increase over the previous year. The managers complained that volume frequently varied independently of their control, and so they jockeyed for assignments to units with the most potential for revenue growth. Equally detrimental to corporate health was the lack of recognition offered the cost-conscious manager. In 1964 the plan was abandoned.

For the next three years the company had no formal incentive system in effect and awarded bonuses purely on the basis of subjective evaluations. Many managers felt that their regional superiors were not adequately recognizing and rewarding their performance. In 1967 this informal plan was abandoned.

McDonald's then made its first attempt to provide a comprehensive and equitable compensation program. The company tied the base salaries of each unit's manager and first assistant manager to their ability to meet the QSC standards. It made the quarterly bonus payments depend on a profit contribution defined as "the difference between sales volume and those costs over which unit management normally exercises direct or indirect control through managerial judgment, decision, and action." The list of controllable costs on which unit management was being judged appeared to be reasonable and complete.

But the plan proved unpopular with those on the front line because it mainly rewarded high volume. Since a restaurant's profit contribution depended considerably more on increased revenues than on cost control, superior management and cost control did not always gain a commensurate bonus. The result was a wide disparity in bonuses; while the median was $2,000, they ranged from $700 to $8,000. In 1971 this plan was also abandoned.

The 1972 plan

In the 1972 compensation package for line managers, McDonald's tried to satisfy the complaints and at the same time to maintain harmony between managerial incentives and corporate goals. The unit manager's annual compensation consisted of his base salary and a quarterly bonus that rewarded his ability to meet predetermined objectives in the areas of labor costs, food and paper costs, QSC, and volume projections.

1.   *The fixed salary*: After surveying each market in which it owned restaurants, McDonald's established three salary ranges according to prevailing labor rates and other economic factors. Range I, the highest, usually applied to very large metropolitan areas; Range II applied to somewhat smaller areas where industrial and rural influences on the labor market were about equal; and Range III applied to small metropolitan markets with little industrial influence. In addition, annual merit in-

creases were awarded within each range according to whether an employee was judged superior, satisfactory, or still in the new employee bracket. In 1972 the base salary schedule began at $6,800 for a trainee in Range III and rose to $15,000 for a consistently outstanding manager in Range I.

2.   *The bonus*: Meeting the optimum labor crew expenses—figured according to projected sales volume and labor crew needs for each month of the quarter—entitled the manager to a bonus of 5 percent of his base salary.

Together the area supervisor and the unit manager determined the food and paper cost objective based on current wholesale prices, product mix, and other operating factors peculiar to the unit. By meeting the objective to which he had agreed previously, the manager earned another 5 percent bonus.

Below is an excerpt from the monthly management visitation report by which each store's QSC was—and still is—rated. Based on the average score for the quarter, units were designated "A," "B," or "C." Managers of "A" stores received a bonus of 10 percent of base salary, "B" store managers 5 percent and "C" store managers no bonus.

In addition, the manager received a bonus of 2.5 percent of the increase over the previous year's sales, up to 10 percent of his base salary. If unit volume was significantly affected by operating circumstances beyond his control, the regional manager could grant him a semiannual payout of 5 percent of his base salary.

Therefore, the maximum annual incentive bonus to an "A" store manager who met all his objectives was 20 percent of his base salary plus an additional 10 percent of his salary because of the volume gain at his restaurant. (His first assistant was entitled to a bonus of approximately 60 percent as much.)

Bonuses for meeting cost objectives were paid quarterly, while those for meeting the QSC standards and volume increases were paid semi-annually.

Still another try

While the 1972 compensation system eliminated many shortcomings of previous programs, unit managers now protested that it was much too complicated. Moreover, complaints about undue subjectivity and dependence on volume patterns were heard anew. McDonald's top management went back to the chalkboards and calculators and came up with four alternative plans.

Plan A: The unit manager's base salary would be determined initially according to the range system described earlier. Thereafter he would be rated monthly by the regional operations staff on six factors: quality, service, cleanliness, training ability, volume, and profit. Each factor would be rated 0 for unsatisfactory, 1 for satisfactory, and 2 for outstanding. A manager whose semiannual total is 12 would earn a bonus of 40 percent of his base salary for half a year, a score of 11 would warrant a 35 percent bonus, and so on. At the end of the year his two semiannual scores would be averaged and he would receive a salary increase of 12 percent for a score of 12, 11 percent for a score of 11, and so on, down to a point where the manager presumably would be encouraged to seek his fortune with a competitor.

Plan B: After receiving the base salary suggested by the range system in his first year as manager, the person would be placed on a draw against commission. The draw would be his salary as before; the commission would be a bonus of 10 percent of any sales gain plus 20 percent of the profit (provided that gross profit amounted to at least 10 percent of the gross take). For example, if sales increased by $50,000 this year to $550,000 and profit were 12 percent (or $66,000), the manager's total compensation package would be 10 percent × $50,000 plus 20 percent × $66,000 = $18,200.

A variation of this plan being considered would incorporate a sliding scale— that is, 10 percent of the sales increase at units with sales up to $500,000, plus 20 percent of the profit; 7 percent of the sales increase at units with sales up to $700,000, plus 17 percent of the profit; and 7 percent of the sales gain at units with sales exceeding $700,000, plus 15 percent of the profit.

Plan C: Similar to Plan B in its draw against commission, the so-called "supermanager" program would base total compensation solely on sales volume. For units having volumes of $500,000 and less, salaries were set at different levels—for example, $10,500 for unit sales of $300,000, $11,500 for sales of $400,000, and $12,500 for $500,000.

Any volume exceeding $500,000 would be multiplied by the factor of 2 percent and added to the base of $12,500. For example, the manager of a $750,000 unit would earn $12,500 plus $5,000. Managers of new stores and of stores considered to be in inferior locations would be paid at the $12,500 base rate for the first 12 months of their stay.

Plan D: Based on the size of the management team and the volume of the store, a predetermined lump sum would be allocated for management salaries. Individual performance as evaluated by the regional operations staff would determine the percentage of the total allocation to be received by each team member. The total amounts that would be available are shown in Table 1.

As this article was being written, McDonald's was still wrestling with these alternatives. A senior officer of the company summarized his feelings about the compensation dilemma in this way:

> "When this company began, it was a fight for survival. Just meeting the payroll was an accomplishment. Later, as we become better known and began to grow, we could concentrate on perfecting our operations. We started the first comprehensive training program for fast-food service in the industry.
>
> "Now is the first time we've been able to look carefully at an area that we really should have considered years ago—our compensation programs and

TABLE 1.   **Total Compensation Available by Unit According to Size of Management Team**

Sales	2 Persons	3 Persons	4 Persons	5 Persons
$ 0– 300,000	$ 19,500	$ 28,500		
301,000– 400,000	20,000	30,000		
401,000– 500,000	22,500	32,500	$ 45,000	
501,000– 600,000		33,000	48,000	$ 60,000
601,000– 700,000		35,000	49,000	63,000
701,000– 800,000			52,000	64,000
801,000– 900,000			54,000	67,500
901,000–1,000,000			55,000	70,000

how they affect our people. We know we have a real opportunity here but quite frankly we're not sure how to proceed. When you're growing internally at a 30 percent annual rate plus acquiring licenses, the issue of management training in the company stores becomes acute, particularly when so much training must be on the job.

"In short, we're faced with a situation where our unit managers are putting great pressure on us to simplify and improve their compensation system. At the same time we have to design a system somehow that's equitable across the board and encourages the manager to give close attention to training his subordinates."

MANAGEMENT VISITATION REPORT

Store Address: _____
            NUMBER   STREET   CITY   STATE
This store is in the _____TV market. This report was completed by _____at __
a.m./p.m. on _____197__ and the day of the week was _____. There were
            MONTH   DATE
_____cars on the lot, and _____customers in line waiting to be served and _____
persons seated in the dining area. The person totally in charge of the store during this visit is __
and his title is _____. The manager of this store is _____;
the supervisor is _____; and the operator is _____. When
completed this report was reviewed with _____on _____.
                                                                    DATE

SCORE: Outside (Sec. I) _____out of 30.   Inside (Sec. II) _____out of 35.
Food (Sec. IV) _____out of 35.   Overall _____out of 100
              (MAXIMUM SCORE PER QUESTION IS 5.)

Question No.	SECTION I (Outside)	Item Score
1.	Is area within one block of the store free of all litter?	
2.	Are flags being displayed properly and are they in good condition? Are entrance and exit and road signs in excellent condition?	
3.	Are waste receptacles in an excellent state of repair and clean? Is trash being emptied as necessary?	
4.	Is the parking lot and landscaping as clean, litter-free, and well picked up as you could reasonably expect for this business period? Do these areas reflect an excellent maintenance program? Is traffic pattern well controlled?	
5.	Do the sidewalks surrounding the building and the exterior of the building reflect an excellent maintenance program? Were these areas being maintained properly during this visit?	
6.	Were all inside and outside lights which should have been on, on, and were windows clean?	
	SECTION TOTAL	

Question No.	SECTION II (Inside Store Pre-Purchase of Food)	Item Score
7.	Was the restroom properly maintained? Was the inside lobby and dining area properly maintained?	
8.	Does P. O. P. in the store present a unified theme?	
9.	Is menu board in excellent repair and clean? Are napkins and straws available near all registers?	
10.	Is the general appearance of all stations good? Is all stainless steel properly maintained?	
11.	Is there an adequate number of crew and management people working for this business period and are they positioned properly?	
12.	Are all crew members: wearing proper McDonald's uniforms, properly groomed, and does their general conduct present a good image?	
13.	Are all counter persons using the Six Step Method and does their serving time per customer meet McDonald's standards?	
	SECTION TOTAL	

Question No.	SECTION IV (After Food Order)	Item Score
14.	Was the sub total, tax, and total charged to you exactly correct and did you receive the correct change?	
15.	Was your order placed properly in the proper size bag, on the correct tray, and did the total packaging appear neat? Was the bag double folded?	
16.	Was the Production Caller controlling production properly?	
17.	Did sandwiches appear neat and do they reflect that the prescribed operational procedures were used when preparing the food?	
18.	Were all sandwiches hot and tasty?	
19.	Were your fries a full portion, hot, and did they meet finish fry standards?	
20.	Did all soft drinks, shakes, or coffee meet McDonald's standards?	
	SECTION TOTAL	

Required:

1. What factors should *McDonald's* consider when designing a compensation plan for its first line managers?

2. Assume you are a first-line manager. Outline your views on the 1972 plan and Plans A-D. Which plan would you prefer *McDonald's* adopt and why?

3. Assume you are the senior officer charged with making recommendations on a compensation plan. Which plan would you recommend *McDonald's* adopt and why?

16-7. Effect of Incentive System on Decision Making*

WAYSIDE INNS, INC.

It was May 11, 1977 and Kevin Gray was conducting a routine quarterly inspection of the Memphis Airport Wayside Inn. The property was one of those that fell under his jurisdiction as Regional General Manager for Wayside Inns, Inc. During his inspection tour Gray was called aside by the Inn's Manager, Layne Rembert, who indicated some concern about a proposed expansion of his motel.

"I'm a little worried, Kevin, about that plan to bring 40 more rooms on stream by the end of the next fiscal year."

"Why all the concern, Layne? You're turning away a significant number of customers and, by all indications, the market will be growing considerably."

"Well, I've just spoken with Ed Keider. He's certain that the 80 room expansion at the central Toledo property has lowered his return on investment. I'd really like to chat with you about what effects the planned expansion will have on my incentive compensation and how my income for the year would be affected."

The Company

Wayside Inns, Inc., located in Kansas City, Missouri, was formed in 1965 as the successor corporation to United Motel Enterprises, a company that operated several franchised motels under licensing agreements from two national motel chains. Due to the complicated and restrictive contract covenants, United was unable to expand the scope of either of its two motel operations through geographical dispersion.

The successor corporation was formed to own, operate, and license a chain of motels under the name "Wayside Inns," as well as to continue to operate the present franchises held by United. Management felt that the strategy of developing their own motel chain would afford them greater flexibility and would allow them to more easily attain the long-term growth strategies. Another major reason for the move was that the new corporate strategy would allow management to pursue the implementation of a comprehensive marketing plan which they had been slowly developing over the last seven years.

The company's fundamental strategy was to cater to those business travellers who were generally not interested in elaborate settings. There were no common areas such as lobbies, convention rooms, bars, or restaurants. The chain emphasized instead clean rooms, dependable service, and rates that generally were 15 to 20 percent lower than other national motel chains. A free standing restaurant was always located on the motel's property—in some cases it was operated by Wayside. In general, however, concessionary leases were granted to regional restaurant chains.

---

* This case was prepared by Charles T. Sharpless under the supervision of Professor M. Edgar Barrett. Copyright © 1978 by M. Edgar Barrett (reproduced with permission).

Wayside's management made it a point to locate their properties near Interstate Highways or major arteries convenient to commercial districts, airports, and industrial or shopping facilities. In a given city, one would often find Wayside Inns at various strategic locations. This strategy was founded on the belief that it was preferable to have a total of 600 rooms in five or six locations within one city rather than one one large hotel with 600 rooms. This strategy resulted in the clustering of hotels in those cities that could support the market. Once several hotels had been built in a particular city, management would seek new properties in regions commercially linked to that city.

Wayside was well aware that its aggressive strategy was successful only to the extent that unit managers followed corporate policies to the letter. In order to insure an aggressive spirit among the unit managers a multifaceted compensation plan was developed. The plan was composed of four elements, but was basically tied to profitability. A base salary was calculated which was loosely tied to years of service, dollar volume of sales, and adherence to corporate goals. An incentive bonus was calculated on sales volume increases. An additional incentive bonus was calculated using the Inn's return on investment. Fringe benefits were the final element and were a significant factor in the package. (See Table 1). Generally, base salaries ranged from $11,000 to $14,000 and total compensation was in the neighborhood of $16,000 to $20,000. The Unit Managers always lived on the premises and their wives usually played a role in managing the Inn. As a result, the average couple were in their late 40's or beyond. Many did not have previous motel experience.

The firm had grown substantially since its inception and the prospects for future growth were favorable. The company's expansion strategy had evolved into a three-tiered attack. Most importantly, management actively pursued the construction of new motels seeking an ever-widening geographical distribution. Secondly, 76 to 116 room properties were expanded if analysis demonstrated that they were operating near or at full capacity. Thirdly, old properties that became a financial burden or did not contribute the required rate of return were sold. Wayside Inns were usually constructed in one of three sizes: 76 rooms, 116 rooms, or 156 rooms.

Wayside Inns was a public corporation listed on the American Stock Exchange. It had 1,542,850 shares outstanding, with an average float of 400,000 shares. The common stock price had appreciated considerably and analysts felt that investor interest was due to a number of factors but was primarily linked to its innovative marketing strategy. Wayside's average occupancy rate on established properties was 10 to 20 percent higher than competitive motels. Its specifically targeted market segment (the business traveller) was generally unaffected by seasonal or environmental factors. Additional company strengths, considered significant by service industry analysts, were an aggressive management, reduction of construction costs and completion times due to standardization, and efficient quality control of present properties.

The Memphis Airport Wayside Inn

The Wayside Inn at Memphis Airport was one of the mid-sized units in the chain—one of the original 116 room properties. It was located at the intersection of Brooks Road and Airways Road, approximately 5 miles from the center of the city.

TABLE 1.
WAYSIDE INNS, INC.
Unit Managers Compensation Package

Base Salary

Base salary ranges are calculated on the basis of years of service and relative sales volume for a particular Inn. Salaries are subject to annual review and the amount of adjustment will largely depend upon the recommendation of the Regional General Manager. Every attempt will be made to keep salary levels consistent with competitive chains

Sales Volume Incentive

Every Unit Manager, having earned a profit before taxes, will receive a bonus equal to 1 percent of any revenue increase over the previous year's level. In the event of a revenue decrease, there will be no bonus and the following year's bonus will be calculated using the revenue of the year preceding the decline as a base figure.

Return on Investment Bonus

Investment will be defined as current assets, fixed assets, other assets, and any deferred expenses. Return is defined as profit before interest expense and taxes.

The formula for the bonus calculation will be:

$$ROI \times PF = ROI \text{ Bonus}$$

$$\text{where ROI} = \frac{EBIT}{Investment} \text{ and PF = Performance Factor}$$

The Performance Factor is used to differentiate between the larger and smaller investments and to offset the inherent complexities of managing the larger properties.

Size of Investment ($)	Value of P.F. ($)*
0–500,000	10,000
500,000–1,000,000	18,000
1,000,000–1,500,000	25,000
1,500,000–2,000,000	31,000
2,000,000–up	35,000

Fringe Benefits

Each Unit Manager shall receive an apartment (2 bedrooms, full kitchen, and den) on the premises, a company car for sales calls, laundry service, and local phone service at no expense.

---

* The Regional General Manager has the discretion to reduce or increase the value of the PF for a particular property upon Central Headquarter's approval.

The motel opened on February 9, 1969 and had developed a very good following in the succeeding years. While the occupancy rate had averaged near 43 percent for the first year, it had increased steadily over the years. By 1976, it operated at near full capacity for five nights a week. The Inn depended on salesmen and commercial travelers for approximately 80% of its revenue.

The property had been originally purchased in 1967 for $150,450. Construction costs for the motel had amounted to approximately $615,345 and furnishings, hardware, software, and office equipment had been purchased for $175,775.

Wayside Inns had contributed an initial equity capitalization of $50,000. The parent had also loaned $175,000 to the subsidiary which was secured by promissory notes. A national insurance company granted a mortgage of $631,550 on the land and physical plant. Finally, $275,795 had been received from Memphis Interstate

Bank to finance equipment and supply purchases and to provide the necessary working capital. (See Tables 2 and 3 for operating data and Tables 4 and 5 for financial statements).

There were approximately 10 competitive motels, which were franchises of the major national chains, within a two mile radius of the Memphis Airport Inn. There also existed a number of independent motels within the area. However, they were generally of the budget type and did not offer the quality on which Wayside based its reputation. Recent surveys conducted by the Memphis Chamber of Commerce indicated that average occupancy rates hovered near 72 percent and that the average room sold for $17.25. Expansion plans by the major chains were expected to account for an additional 800 rooms across the whole city in the following 18 months.

The Proposed Expansion

Wayside's Project Development staff had arrived at a projected schedule of costs that would be associated with the completion of a 40 room expansion. Cost

TABLE 2.
MEMPHIS AIRPORT WAYSIDE INN
Selected Operating Statistics
(for the periods January 1 to December 31)

Occupancy Report	1976	1975	1974	1973	1972
Room Nights Available	41,975	41,975	41,975	41,975	41,975
Occupied Room Nights	36,634	35,595	33,454	32,613	31,522
Occupancy Rate (%)	87.3	84.8	79.7	77.7	75.1
Room Revenue ($)	613,619	560,621	510,173	472,888	446,036
Average Room Rate ($)	16.75	15.75	15.25	14.50	14.15
Weekly Occupancy (%)					
Monday	99	99	95	94	92
Tuesday	99	99	94	92	91
Wednesday	99	98	96	94	89
Thursday	99	97	92	87	86
Friday	91	87	72	70	65
Saturday	61	55	51	50	48
Sunday	63	59	58	57	55
Turnaway* Tally					
Monday	26.1	22.8	15.1	10.1	11.5
Tuesday	27.7	21.0	19.3	16.0	12.1
Wednesday	38.2	33.2	26.9	19.5	13.3
Thursday	43.9	36.3	31.4	20.4	16.6
Friday	22.6	15.8	10.9	5.2	2.4
Saturday	9.6	5.7	2.8	0.2	0.6
Sunday	8.5	6.4	3.0	1.3	0.5

* A Turnaway is considered a customer who either calls the motel, requests a room in person, or calls Central Reservation Service and is told there are no vacancies. See Table 3 for further data.

TABLE 3.
MEMPHIS AIRPORT WAYSIDE INN
Daily "Turnaway" Statistics for 1976

Week	Sun.	Mon.	Tues.	Wed.	Thurs.	Fri.	Sat.
1	0	25	26	36	45	0	0
2	0	23	21	24	25	0	0
3	0	10	11	17	23	3	0
4	0	20	21	16	46	5	0
5	0	16	17	25	38	0	0
6	0	20	15	38	43	7	0
7	0	25	32	45	25	0	0
8	0	10	12	42	46	10	0
9	0	21	14	40	71	12	0
10	0	23	28	39	23	15	0
11	0	19	25	41	45	16	0
12	0	25	30	43	39	20	0
13	0	46	42	24	45	21	0
14	0	28	25	58	40	30	0
15	0	35	14	61	63	32	0
16	0	24	22	25	45	43	4
17	0	13	46	26	49	15	11
18	0	25	29	13	45	12	2
19	0	43	40	61	71	10	15
20	0	22	55	62	68	45	23
21	20	42	36	67	55	46	36
22	22	39	35	50	47	39	33
23	23	22	33	38	35	38	32
24	24	28	25	25	41	17	0
25	10	29	24	15	41	25	10
26	0	24	20	39	35	18	6
27	0	30	18	25	24	42	38
28	25	29	15	35	35	45	27
29	29	26	66	41	82	11	12
30	15	25	50	62	65	18	9
31	13	42	43	47	48	16	5
32	17	31	25	35	50	17	15
33	18	32	16	28	32	18	12
34	12	15	22	23	28	20	14
35	10	14	25	27	26	21	23
36	6	17	24	61	67	15	12
37	19	56	27	43	40	15	16
38	18	55	71	39	42	20	18
39	14	16	35	46	41	23	17
40	5	12	20	48	47	27	6
41	16	23	15	45	53	29	5
42	7	25	18	42	43	31	4
43	0	18	20	41	39	43	4
44	0	19	21	48	53	46	11
45	0	29	23	19	47	47	4
46	0	31	24	25	29	41	16
47	0	20	26	31	33	52	12

TABLE 3. (Continued)

Week	Sun.	Mon.	Tues.	Wed.	Thurs.	Fri.	Sat.
48	10	22	16	49	52	26	10
49	15	24	18	40	38	20	8
50	16	21	19	31	41	10	4
51	43	37	45	47	37	15	2
52	35	31	40	38	42	6	20
Total	442	1,357	1,440	1,986	2,283	1,175	498

adjustments would be necessary depending on the particular city and conditions. However, variances were not expected to be significant.

Engineering and legal fees were expected to be somewhere in the neighborhood of $12,250. Environmental Impact Studies to comply with Federal regulations and the local building permits were estimated to cost $8,500. Construction costs for the expansion and adjoining parking facility were expected to be near $730,000. Such an expansion was expected to generate additional annual, non-direct operating costs of $31,300 (largely for personnel, utilities, and maintenance). Direct room expenses were expected to remain at an average of 23 percent of room revenue. Management and reservation fees paid to the parent were based on a formula of 5 percent of room revenue plus $24 per room per year.

TABLE 4.
MEMPHIS AIRPORT WAYSIDE INN
Income Statement
(for the years ended December 31)

	1975	1976
Revenues:		
Room Revenue	$560,621	$613,619
Restaurant Rental	19,432	21,536
Other	10,532	12,675
Total Revenues	590,585	$647,920
Operating Costs and Expenses		
Room	$126,476	$144,875
Selling and Administrative	136,511	144,691
Depreciation and Amortization	37,642	46,752
Utilities	23,610	25,473
Maintenance and Repairs	32,672	30,498
Management and Reservations Fees	30,815	33,464
Operating Income	$202,859	$222,167
Interest Expense	106,513	95,278
Profit Before Taxes	$ 96,346	$126,889
Federal Taxes	32,746	47,406
Net Earnings	$ 63,600	$ 79,483

TABLE 5.
MEMPHIS WAYSIDE INN
Balance Sheets

Assets	1975	1976
Current Assets:		
Cash	$ 16,059	$ 15,545
Trade receivables	54,721	63,820
Merchandise	15,617	17,821
Prepaid Expenses:		
Insurance	3,098	2,778
Mortgage	5,673	5,242
Linens	1,550	1,675
Total Current Assets:	$ 96,718	$ 106,881
Fixed Assets:		
Land	$ 150,450	$ 150,450
Building, Equipment, Furniture, & Fixtures	925,160	961,215
Less: Accumulated Depreciation	(183,375)	(229,127)
Total Fixed Assets:	$ 892,235	$ 882,538
Other Assets:		
Franchise	$ 8,000	$ 7,000
Supplies	19,671	19,286
Total Other Assets:	$ 27,671	$ 26,826
	$1,016,624	$1,016,245
Liabilities		
Current Liabilities:	$ 45,671	$ 47,583
Accounts Payable	15,629	21,472
Taxes Payable	38,978	38,611
Accrued Expenses	$ 100,278	$ 107,666
Total Current Liabilities:		
Long-Term Liabilities:		
Mortgage Payable	$ 454,716	$ 429,454
Notes Payable	206,000	169,000
Notes Payable to Parent	90,000	65,000
Total Long-Term Liabilities:	$ 750,716	$ 663,454
Net Worth:		
Capital Stock	$ 50,000	$ 50,000
Retained Earnings	115,630	195,125
Total Net Worth:	$ 165,630	$ 245,125
Total Liabilities:		
	$1,016,624	$1,016,245

Performance Evaluation

After dinner that evening, Kevin Gray decided to review his file on Layne Rembert's compensation package and on his related performance evaluation. He checked his records to determine what Rembert's total compensation had been for 1976. He then performed a rough calculation of what it would be for 1977 if the additional 40 rooms were to have been available during all of this time period (See Table 6).

Over the past few years, Gray had also developed a twenty-point performance evaluation report which he used to base his decisions on salary increases (See Table 7). This system was derived from one he had witnessed when he had been previously employed by a national food service organization. While the report had been de-

TABLE 6.
Effect of Proposed Expansion on Rembert's Income

Total Compensation for 1976	
Base Salary	$12,500
Sales Volume Incentive	
$(647,920 - 590,585) \times .01$	
$57,335 \times .01 =$	573
Return on Investment Bonus	
$\dfrac{222,167}{1,016,245} \times 25,000$	
$.2186 \times 25,000 =$	5,465
Total Compensation	$18,538
Projected Compensation after Expansion	
Base Salary	$12,500
Sales Volume Incentive	
$(834,079 - 647,920) \times .01$	
$186,159 \times .01 =$	1,862
Return on Investment Bonus	
$\dfrac{311,039}{1,785,245} \times 32,000$	
$.1742 \times 32,000 =$	5,574
Total Compensation	$19,936

Projected Income Statement (As Calculated by Gray)

Revenue	
Room Revenue	$790,332
Restaurant Rental	27,047
Other	16,700
Total Revenues	$834,079
Operating Costs and Expenses	
Room	$181,776
Operating Expenses	231,888
Depreciation and Amortization	66,115
Management and Reservation Fees	43,261
Operating Income	$311,039

Remarks

Room Revenue projected as 47,184 occupied room nights at an average price of $16.75. This figure is attributed slightly to annual growth but largely to turnaways accomodated.
Investment is figured loosely and may vary in actuality, but variance will not significantly affect ROI.

TABLE 7.
PERFORMANCE EVALUATION REPORT

Motel Environment	1 Poor	2 Average	3 Good	4 Superior	
Exterior Appearance	___	___	___	___	× .2 = ___
Interior Appearance	___	___	___	___	× .5 = ___
Maintenance Work	___	___	___	___	× .3 = ___
Room Spot Check	___	___	___	___	× .5 = ___
Personnel Attitude	___	___	___	___	× .3 = ___
Managerial Factors					
Accurate Reports	___	___	___	___	× .3 = ___
Reservation Control	___	___	___	___	× .2 = ___
Accounts Receivable	___	___	___	___	× .2 = ___
Payroll	___	___	___	___	× .3 = ___
Controllable Costs	___	___	___	___	× .5 = ___
Occupancy Rate	___	___	___	___	× .5 = ___
Other Factors					
Cooperation with RGM	___	___	___	___	× .3 = ___
Sales Calls	___	___	___	___	× .3 = ___
Personnel Turnover	___	___	___	___	× .3 = ___
Complaints	___	___	___	___	× .3 = ___
Total	___	___	___	___	___

RANKING

20.0–17.8	Excellent
17.7–15.0	Good
14.9–11.0	Must Improve
10.0– 5.0	Very Poor

veloped primarily for his own use in helping to determine who should receive merit increases in salary, Gray placed a great deal of weight on his report. In fact, he was entertaining the notion of recommending that it be instituted companywide. He made no bones about letting unit managers know that he looked for other things than pure return on investment. He felt that there were a number of variables that could seriously affect profitability over which the unit manager had no control. In addition, he believed an efficient operation was to a large extent contingent on customer satisfaction.

REFERENCES

BAKER, JOHN C., "Are Corporate Executives Overpaid?" *Harvard Business Review* LV (July–August 1977), 51–56.

CAREY, JAMES F., "Successors to the Qualified Stock Option," *Harvard Business Review* LVI (January–February 1978), 140–46.

DEARDEN, JOHN, "How to Make Incentive Plans Work," *Harvard Business Review* L (July–August 1972), 117–24.

FOOTE, GEORGE H., "Performance Shares Revitalize Executive Stock Plans," *Harvard Business Review* LI (November–December 1973), 121–30.

GREENLAW, PAUL S., and WILLIAM D. BIGGS, "Individual Incentive Systems," chap. 10 in *Modern Personnel Management*. Philadelphia: Saunders, 1979.

JENSEN, MICHAEL C., and WILLIAM H. MECKLING, "Theory of the Firm: Managerial Behavior, Agency Costs, and Capital Structure," *Journal of Financial Economics* III (October 1976), 305–60.

MILLER, MERTON H., and MYRON S. SCHOLES, "Executive Compensation, Taxes, and Incentives," Graduate School of Business, University of Chicago Working Paper No. 42 (January 1980).

PATTON, ARCH, "Why Incentive Plans Fail," *Harvard Business Review* L (May–June 1972), 58–66.

RAPAPORT, ALFRED, "Executive Incentives vs. Corporate Growth," *Harvard Business Review* LVI (July–August 1978), 81–88.

SALTER, MALCOLM, "Tailor Incentive Compensation to Strategy," *Harvard Business Review* LI (March–April 1973), 94–102.

SLOAN, ALFRED, *My Years With General Motors*. New York: Doubleday, 1964.

STATA, RAY, and MODESTO A. MAIDIQUE, "Bonus System for Balanced Strategy," *Harvard Business Review* LVIII (November–December 1980), 156–63.

VANCIL, RICHARD F., *Decentralization: Managerial Ambiguity by Design*. Homewood, Ill.: Dow Jones-Irwin, 1978.

ZIMMERMAN, JEROLD L., "The Costs and Benefits of Cost Allocations," *The Accounting Review* LIV (July 1979), 504–21.

FORMAL MODELS IN BUDGETING AND INCENTIVE CONTRACTS

17

THE PRINCIPAL-AGENT PARADIGM REVISITED: A FORMAL APPROACH

Contemporary research in economics, finance, and accounting has developed interesting insights about the nature of incentive contracts and risk sharing under conditions of uncertainty. This analysis requires a formal specification of the economic agents' preferences and risk attitudes (as modeled by a utility function for wealth) and beliefs (as modeled by the agents' subjective probability distributions for random outcomes) as well as possible states of the world, actions, and outcome functions. The results to date have been obtained in highly simplified settings so that it could be misleading to extrapolate them to the far more complex situations of large divisionalized firms. Nevertheless, the research represents the first formal attempt to capture the effects of uncertainty, risk aversion, and delegated responsibility in decentralized settings. It therefore provides a valuable discipline by establishing a conceptual framework for thinking about issues in devising performance measures and incentive contracts.[1]

Most of the results can be described in terms of two economic agents. The first agent, indexed by a subscript $i = 0$, can be called the *owner* or the *principal*. The second agent, indexed by the subscript $i = 1$, is called the *manager* or the *agent* (of the principal). As mentioned before, the principal can be the stockholders, who hire a chief executive (the agent) to run the firm. Alternatively, the principal can be the central management group, who hire division managers (the agents) to operate the decentralized divisions.

The principal's utility function over monetary rewards is represented by $u_0(\cdot)$ and that of the agent is $u_1(\cdot)$, where u_0 and u_1 have the usual properties of risk-averse utility functions [$u_i'(\cdot) > 0$, $u_i''(\cdot) < 0$]. The agent can choose actions

---

[1] An excellent survey of this literature, which influenced the organization of material in this chapter, appears in Jennergren [1980].

from a set A, with the particular action chosen denoted by a (a member of the set A). The payoff to the firm if action a is taken and a (random) state of the world θ occurs is $x = p(\theta, a)$. The principal's beliefs about the likelihood of the random-state occurrence θ is given by the probability function $h_0(\theta)$. The agent's beliefs are represented by the probability function $h_1(\theta)$. For simplicity, it is generally assumed that the realization θ is independent of the agent's action, a. We can think of θ as the random level of sales in a period and the agent's action a as the amount of the product ordered or produced by the agent. The payoff, x, would depend jointly on θ, the level of demand, and a, how much of the product was produced and available for sale.

The crucial ingredient of the principal-agent setting is the fee paid by the principal to the agent for making and implementing the decision. This fee is denoted by $f(x, \theta, a)$, since the fee can depend on the payoff x, on the state of the world θ, and on the agent's action a, if these are observable by the principal. The fee can be based only on items that are observable by both the principal and the agent. In general, observability is a critical concept in determining efficient incentive contracts.

With this notation we can formulate the agent's and principal's problems. Given a specific fee schedule $f(x, \theta, a)$, the agent will choose an action a in A to maximize

$$\sum_{\theta} u_1[f(x, \theta, a)]h_1(\theta). \tag{17-1}$$

The principal will want to choose the fee schedule f to maximize

$$\sum_{\theta} u_0[x - f(x, \theta, a)]h_0(\theta). \tag{17-2}$$

The principal, knowing that the agent will maximize expression (17-1), wants to select a fee schedule f such that a large value of expression (17-2) occurs when the agent chooses a to maximize (17-1).[2] The fee schedule must provide a minimum level of expected utility to the agent [as computed by (17-1)] in order to motivate the agent to work for the principal rather than work in alternative, perhaps less risky, managerial positions.

Incentive problems arise because of differences in beliefs and risk attitudes between the principal and agent, as well as different observability situations; in some settings the principal may be unable to observe the agent's actions, or able to observe them only imperfectly or at some cost.

AN EXAMPLE

We can illustrate this situation with a simple example. Consider a firm with only a one-period life selling a product. The product sells for $2 per unit and costs

---

[2] This formulation assumes that the principal knows the agent's utility function and probability function.

$1 per unit to manufacture. Demand for the product is uncertain; the owner and the manager agree that demand is uniformly distributed between 100 and 200 units. The decision on how much to produce must be made before the actual demand for the period is known. If demand is less than the amount produced, excess items are scrapped as worthless. If demand exceeds production, the opportunity cost is the foregone contribution of $1; there is no customer goodwill loss. Both the owner and the manager have identical risk-averse utility functions:

$$u_0(x) = u_1(x) = \sqrt{x}.$$

With our notation, the random-state variable θ equals the demand for product, and the action variable a represents the amount produced by the manager. The payoff function, $x = p(\theta, a)$, is therefore

$$x(\theta, a) = \begin{cases} 2\theta - a, & \theta \le a, \\ a, & \theta \ge a. \end{cases}$$

In a risk-neutral environment the decision makers would choose to maximize the expected payoff $Ex(\theta, a)$, defined as

$$Ex(\theta, a) = \frac{1}{100} \left[\int_{100}^{a} (2\theta - a)\, d\theta + \int_{a}^{200} a\, d\theta \right] \tag{17-3}$$

$$= -100 + 3a - \frac{a^2}{100}.$$

By differentiating this expression with respect to a and setting the derivative equal to zero to obtain the maximum, we learn that $a = 150$ maximizes expected profits.[3] At this production level, substitution back into equation (17-3) yields maximum expected profits of $125.

The owner, knowing that the manager is risk averse and cannot be held responsible for the actual realization of the random demand, decides initially to offer the manager a payment based on expected (not actual) profits. The owner proposes a contract of 20 percent of the profits expected from the manager's production decision. In this situation the manager faces no uncertainty (as long as actual costs equal the expected costs of $1 per unit and the actual production quantity equals the planned production quantity), so the manager wishes to choose a to make the expected profits as large as possible. As we have already seen, the manager should choose $a = 150$, yielding expected profits of $125. This produces a payment of 20 percent of $125, or $25, to the manager. Formally, the fee contract is defined as

$$f(x, \theta, a) = 0.20 Ex(\theta, a)$$

$$= 0.20 \left(-100 + 3a - \frac{a^2}{100} \right)$$

---

[3] Recall the discussion of the newsboy problem in Chapter 6 where we showed that the solution is the critical fractile, which in this case turns out to be the median, of the demand distribution.

and
$$f(x, \theta, 150) = 25.$$

In this case the fee depends only on the action a, which is under the control of the manager, and not on the random-state occurrence θ or the uncertain actual payoff $x(\theta, a)$. The manager's utility for this contract is
$$Eu_1[f(x, \theta, a)] = u_1(25) = \sqrt{25} = 5.$$

The owner, on the other hand, is absorbing all the risk from the random outcome. The owner's expected utility [from equation (17-2)] is computed based on the owner's knowledge of the manager's utility-maximizing decision. That is, given the manager's contract of 20 percent of expected profits, the owner correctly anticipates the manager's decision of $a = 150$ and the subsequent payment of \$25 and can compute his own expected utility as

$$
\begin{aligned}
Eu &= \frac{1}{100} \left[\int_{100}^{150} (2\theta - 150 - 25)^{1/2} \, d\theta + \int_{150}^{200} (150 - 25)^{1/2} d\theta \right] \\
&= \frac{1}{100} [\tfrac{1}{3}(125)^{3/2} - \tfrac{1}{3}(25)^{3/2} + 50(125)^{1/2}] \\
&= 9.832.
\end{aligned}
$$

A student of the benefits of risk sharing, however, points out to the owner that the above contract may not be optimal, since the owner, who is as risk averse as the manager, is absorbing all the risk from the random outcome. The owner, somewhat indignant, replies that he is a fastidious follower of good cost accounting practice and he has been taught not to have a manager's performance affected by events beyond the manager's control. The student responds that in most economic situations there is a price for everything, and for a small increase in expected profits the manager can be induced to absorb some of the risk, leaving both the manager and the owner better off. The owner is still skeptical but is willing to listen to any proposal that might make him better off. The student proposes a new fee schedule for the manager based on actual rather than expected profit. Because the payoff to the manager could now be uncertain, the percentage of profit should be raised from 20 to 21 percent to compensate the manager for the increased uncertainty.

The student shows the owner that with the newly proposed contract,
$$f(x, \theta, a) = 0.21x(\theta, a),$$

the manager's expected utility will be given by

$$
\begin{aligned}
Eu_1[f(x, \theta, a)] &= \frac{1}{100} \left[\int_{100}^{a} [0.21(2\theta - a)]^{1/2} \, d\theta + \int_{a}^{200} (0.21a)^{1/2} \, d\theta \right] \\
&= \frac{(0.21)^{1/2}}{100} \left[-\frac{2}{3}(a)^{3/2} + 200a^{1/2} - \frac{1}{3}(200 - a)^{3/2} \right].
\end{aligned}
\tag{17-4}
$$

In order to find the action that maximizes the manager's expected utility, the above expression is differentiated with respect to a and the derivative set equal to zero:

$$\frac{d\,Eu_1}{da} = 0 = \frac{(0.21)^{1/2}}{100}\left[-a^{1/2} + 100a^{-1/2} + \frac{1}{2}(200 - a)^{1/2}\right].$$

By a process of trial and error, the maximizing value of a is determined to be 144.7.

The owner smirks and declares, "Just as I thought! As soon as the manager's payoff is made to depend on a risky outcome, he becomes more conservative and chooses an action that lowers output. At a production level of 144.7, the total expected profit [see equation (17-3)] is only \$124.7, below the 125 attainable when 150 units are produced." The student responds by showing the owner the computation of the expected utility for both the manager and the owner under the new contract. For the manager, by substituting $a = 144.7$ into equation (17-4), we obtain

$$Eu_1 = (0.21)^{1/2}(11.0834) = 5.079.$$

The expected utility for the owner requires evaluating the identical integral in equation (17-4) but with the owner capturing 79 percent of the expected utility (rather than the manager's 21 percent). Therefore:

$$Eu_0 = (0.79)^{1/2}(11.0834) = 9.851.$$

The student thus is able to show that both the manager's and the owner's expected utility increase when they share the noncontrollable risk.

RISK SHARING AND CONTROLLABILITY

This little example is typical of a broader class of principal-agent situations. Whenever the principal and the agent have identical probability beliefs and utility functions in the same class, where the class is of the exponential, logarithmic, or power function type (with the same power as in our example, when the power was equal to ½ for both the owner and the manager), then it can be demonstrated that an optimal contract includes a sharing of actual profits between the principal and the agent.[4] With such a sharing, however, we have introduced a noncontrollable outcome into the agent's (or manager's) compensation schedule, thereby apparently violating one of the cherished dictums of cost accounting—the dictum that a manager's performance is best evaluated on those aspects of performance

---

[4] This important result was developed by Wilson [1968] and Ross [1973].

controllable by the manager.[5] This arrangement also seems to violate the principles we discussed in Chapter 13 of devising ways to shield managers from noncontrollable risky outcomes, so that they will not be too conservative in their decision making. Thus, the example demonstrates how a formal approach to modeling uncertainty can lead to nonintuitive conclusions.

The example, however, is misleading because of its overly simplified context and its failure to capture the essence of interesting managerial situations. If we review the motives for decentralization of decision making discussed in Chapter 13—information specialization, timeliness of response, conservation of central management time, computational complexity, and training and incentives for local managers—we notice that none of these factors is represented in the above example. Both the owner and the manager have access to the same information and both can compute the optimal solution. The only useful role that the manager is playing in this model is to share some of the owner's risk. Unless one believes that an important function for managers of firms is to share the risks of the owners or the central management group, then the reason for including noncontrollable random outcomes in the managers' incentive function disappears. In practice, capital markets provide a myriad of economic agents to offer risk-sharing arrangements for the owners of firms. Managers will typically be hired, not because of their desirable risk-sharing abilities, but because they have specialized information, are good at making and implementing decisions, and have the capability for advancement to higher-level managerial positions and responsibility. Only when the problem situation has been reduced to two economic actors, the principal and the agent, does the agent need to perform in the dual roles of decision maker and risk sharer. Therefore, the nonintuitive result, that the manager's compensation should be a function of a noncontrollable outcome, occurs only because of a highly simplified representation of the environment in which a manager makes decisions.

In more realistic situations, where many more individuals are available in the economy, the decision-making and risk-sharing arrangements can be split among different economic agents. When these more realistic situations are modeled, we may not require the managers to share the risk of the owners or the central management group. Our problem will probably be the opposite one: how to shield the managers from the negative consequences of random outcomes from their own decisions. Thus, the example is useful in illustrating how current researchers are modeling incentive contracts under uncertainty. But it is misleading if interpreted naively or literally to mean that a manager's compensation should be based on noncontrollable factors, unless one believes that an important aim in decentralization is to share risk with lower-level managers. Perhaps the main message from this simple example is that senior management should be aware of the risk attitudes of operating managers when designing incentive systems.

---

[5] The optimality of including a noncontrollable outcome in the manager's incentive function was pointed out by Demski [1976].

A more general formulation of the principal-agent situation allows for the agent's having a disutility for work or effort. In this setting, the action *a* represents not a decision to be implemented but an effort level chosen by the agent. The higher the effort level, the greater the expected payoff to the firm. But the agent's utility decreases with the effort level, since the agent is assumed to value leisure (or lack of effort) as well as monetary outcomes. Formally, the agent's utility function has two arguments, wealth and effort, and, holding wealth levels constant, the agent prefers less effort to more effort.[6] Again, we should be cautioned that results obtained in this setting should be viewed with some care, since the effort level *a* is a very rough, perhaps inaccurate, representation of a chief executive's or divisional manager's activities. The model is more representative of a sharecropping setting in which there is a direct return from the amount of effort exerted by the hired worker and where the worker prefers leisure to hard agricultural work.

In general, the payoff to the activities of managers and executives has more to do with the quality than the quantity of their decisions. The increase in expected payoff and decrease in utility associated with increases in effort may be more relevant for workers in a production setting than for managers in a decision-making or leadership process. Nevertheless, the paradigm has yielded some interesting findings and suggests the possible direction of future research. For example, rather than interpret *a* literally as effort, we could let *a* represent the manager's reducing his use of nonpecuniary factors, such as office space, high-quality furnishings, and staff support. With this interpretation the principal's problem is to devise an incentive scheme to deter the manager's overconsumption of these nonpecuniary and nonproductive factors.

The key issue in this abstract setting, where the agent but not the principal has a disutility for effort, is the moral-hazard problem in which the agent is motivated to provide less effort than is optimal from the principal's viewpoint. Low payoffs can be due either to bad realizations of the random-state outcome, θ, or to a low level of effort chosen by the agent. If the principal can observe only the payoff *x* but not the action (effort level) chosen by the agent, then the agent can always attempt to explain away bad outcomes by claiming they were due to unfortunate states of the world. Therefore, it becomes important for the principal to obtain some information about the agent's effort level.

If the principal can observe the agent's effort levels, then the principal will attempt to devise a forcing contract in which (1) the agent receives appropriate compensation (such as computed in the previous example) if the proper effort

---

[6] Algebraically, the agent has a utility function $u_1(f, a)$, with f being the fee earned by the agent, and $\partial u_1/\partial a < 0$. Also, the payoff function $x = p(\theta, a)$ is such that $\partial x/\partial a > 0$.

level was selected, but (2) the agent receives nothing (or, more desirable, a severe penalty) if the proper effort level was not selected.

If the principal can observe only the outcome, and not the effort level, then (except for two special cases) a less desirable contract depending only on the payoff must be used. In this less desirable contract the agent bears more of the risk than would be optimal if the effort level could be observed, but the agent never bears all the risk of the random outcome. One of the exceptions to this rule occurs if the agent happens to be risk neutral. Then the optimal contract is for the agent to "rent the firm from the principal" by paying the principal a fixed fee and receiving the actual outcome less this fixed fee for his own compensation. Restating this result formally, if the agent is risk neutral ($\partial^2 u_1/\partial f^2 = 0$), then the optimal fee schedule is of the form $f(x, \theta, a) = x - k$, where k is the (constant) rental fee paid to the principal.

The other exception to the suboptimality of contracts not dependent on the agent's effort occurs if the principal can observe the realization of the state variable, θ. In this case the optimal contract will be a fee schedule depending only on x and θ, and this contract dominates any contract that also includes the agent's effort, a.

We have considered the polar cases (1) where the principal can observe the effort level a costlessly and perfectly (the pure risk-sharing arrangement) and (2) where the principal does not observe the effort level at all (fee schedule based solely on the random outcome). In the intermediate case, where the principal obtains an imperfect signal about the agent's effort (say, from the cost accounting system), a fee schedule based on this imperfect signal will introduce a new source of risk into the agent's compensation function. Nevertheless, it can be shown that any informative signal about the agent's effort level, even if it is not a perfect indicator, will have a net positive value in obtaining an efficient contract between the principal and the agent, as long as the signal can be obtained without cost. If it is costly to acquire the imperfect signal, then the net increase in the utility of the principal and agent when using a contract based on this signal must be compared with the cost of the signal.[7]

As previously mentioned, this research may be most relevant in settings where the agent is supplying a quantity of work, such as in a production setting, rather than in the unstructured, decision-making environment of chief executives and general managers of divisions. The research may also be appropriate for insurance situations where the effort level a denotes the activities exerted by the insured to avoid the event being insured against (staying in good health, driving carefully, eliminating fire and safety hazards, and so on). Demski and Feltham [1978] have adapted this paradigm to the cost accounting setting where standards are set for workers by their managers. They demonstrate that incentive contracts

---

[7] This is only a greatly condensed summary of some highly significant but abstract research. The details can be found in Harris and Raviv [1978 and 1979], Holmstrom [1979], and Shavell [1979].

based on attaining these predetermined standards (or budgets) are preferable to simple wage contracts or wage-plus-linear-profit-sharing contracts. Thus, for the first time, researchers have been able to devise an analytic model for which the desirability of standards or budget-based contracts can be derived and demonstrated, rather than asserted. Similarly, Atkinson [1978] has shown the desirability of a contract based on comparison of actual profits to budgeted or expected profits in a principal-agent situation where the agent is known to have "better" information about the random-state variable, θ. These results are obtained in highly simplified settings, but they do offer the promise that further research may provide a more solid conceptual basis for many cost accounting and management control procedures that are now advocated on an intuitive, judgmental basis.

INCENTIVES FOR TRUTHFUL REVELATION OF BUDGETS AND FORECASTS

The demonstration of the desirability of budget-based contracts for performance evaluation again brings up the role of budgets and standards in the planning and control of the activities of the firm. Budgets have long been advocated for carrying out a variety of functions for the firm: planning, evaluating performance, coordinating activities, implementing plans, communicating, motivating, and authorizing actions (see Horngren [1982, chaps. 5–7]). In our discussion of management control systems, we have observed that by evaluating performance against a budget, managers can be shielded from some of the effects of random, noncontrollable factors. The formal results of Demski and Feltham [1978] and Atkinson [1978] provide further evidence of the value of budget-based performance measures.

Despite these advantages, the problem remains of how to establish budgets that can both facilitate the planning process (including coordinating the activities of diverse but interacting organizational units) and permit a realistic appraisal of managerial performance. As we have often noted, once managers learn that information being provided for planning, decision making, and coordination will also be used to evaluate their performance, an incentive is created for them to distort or bias the information in ways that will make their performance measure more favorable. One possibility for reducing the managerial distortion of budgets and forecasts is to evaluate managers on their forecasting ability as well as their actual performance. This may be especially important for an organizational unit, such as a revenue center, that is responsible for achieving a high level of sales. So many important decisions throughout the firm depend on the sales forecast that managers should have an incentive to reveal their best estimate of sales. An analogous situation occurs in a socialist economy where the output of many manufacturing facilities has to be coordinated. A knowledge of the expected output of each facility is virtually indispensable for rational resource allocation and distribution in the economy.

The central planners of the Soviet Union have devised and apparently implemented a system of bonuses that rewards both accurate forecasts and outstanding performance.[8] Independently, essentially identical schemes have been advocated for eliciting accurate forecasts in a sales organization and for a budget forecasting system.[9] The proposed schemes provide disincentives for the manager to set output targets so low that the budget is easily achieved. Also, they attempt to reduce the incentive for managers, after achieving the budgeted performance, to minimize extra performance in order to avoid affecting future-period budgets.

With the forecast incentive scheme, the top management establishes a basic bonus pool, B_0, and specifies three positive parameters: α, β, and γ. The manager declares a targeted or budgeted output level $\hat{y}$ and this increases the bonus pool by $\beta\hat{y}$. Therefore, an incentive is created to declare a higher rather than a lower budgeted output level. If the actual output level, y, exceeds the budgeted level, $\hat{y}$, an additional bonus of $\alpha(y - \hat{y})$ is paid. This insures that there is an incentive for exceeding budgeted performance. But α is set less than β, so that if output is going to be high, it is better to declare this in the budget than to realize it by exceeding the budget. If the actual output level, y, is less than budget, a penalty of $\gamma(\hat{y} - y)$ is subtracted from the bonus. In this case γ is set larger than β, so that there is no benefit in inflating the budget, only to be disappointed later.

Formally, if B is the actual bonus paid to the manager, this plan can be described by

$$B = \begin{cases} B_0 + \beta\hat{y} + \alpha(y - \hat{y}) & \text{for } y \geq \hat{y}, \\ B_0 + \beta\hat{y} - \gamma(\hat{y} - y) & \text{for } y < \hat{y}, \end{cases} \qquad (17\text{-}5)$$

with $0 < \alpha < \beta < \gamma$. A rule of thumb is that β should be at least 30 percent larger than α and that γ should be at least 30 percent larger than β. As an example of how this incentive scheme operates, Table 17-1 displays the bonus, B, as a function of $\hat{y}$ and y when $B_0 = 70$, $\alpha = 0.2$, $\beta = 0.3$, and $\gamma = 0.5$.

For any given value of actual output, y, in Table 17-1 (reading along a row), the highest bonus is achieved when the forecast, $\hat{y}$, equals y. That is, the largest bonuses appear along the main diagonal. Therefore, if the manager knows for certain what the actual output will be, he can maximize his bonus by issuing a forecast equal to this actual amount. Any other forecast will decrease the bonus below the maximum achievable level. Looking down a column reveals that once a forecast $\hat{y}$ is issued, the manager will always prefer more output to less output. This provides an incentive for the manager to produce the maximum output regardless of the forecast. Also, the parameters have been established so that not achieving the forecasted output is penalized more heavily than output in excess of the forecast is rewarded. In general, the parameters can be set so that excess

---

[8] This system is described in Weitzman [1976]. Extensions have appeared in Snowberger [1977] and Weitzman [1980]. Criticisms of the Soviet incentive system are presented in Loeb and Magat [1978].

[9] See Gonik [1978] and Ijiri, Kinard, and Putney [1968], respectively.

TABLE 17-1. **Truth-Inducing Budget-Based Contract**

$$B = \begin{cases} 70 + 0.3\hat{y} + 0.2(y - \hat{y}) & \text{for } y \geq \hat{y} \\ 70 + 0.3\hat{y} + 0.5(\hat{y} - y) & \text{for } y < \hat{y} \end{cases}$$

		\multicolumn{8}{c}{*Budgeted Output, $\hat{y}$*}						
		50	*60*	*70*	*80*	*90*	*100*	*110*	*120*
	50	85	83	81	79	77	75	73	71
	60	87	88	86	84	82	80	78	76
	70	89	90	91	89	87	85	83	81
Actual Output, y	*80*	91	92	93	94	92	90	88	86
	90	93	94	95	96	97	95	93	91
	100	95	96	97	98	99	100	98	96
	110	97	98	99	100	101	102	103	101
	120	99	100	101	102	103	104	105	106

and insufficient production are treated symmetrically, or even to provide greater reward for exceeding the budget than for underproducing.

In summary, the bonus forecasting incentive system given by equations (17-5) and illustrated in Table 17-1 produces the desirable incentives of rewarding accurate forecasts and encouraging greater rather than lesser output. The parameters α, β, and γ are set based on the relative values of accurate forecasts, the benefits of output in excess of the forecast, and the costs of not achieving the forecasted output level.

LIMITATIONS OF THE TRUTH-INDUCING BUDGET SCHEME

The forecasting incentive scheme provides an attractive but not perfect mechanism for eliciting realistic forecasts. It is a costly mechanism, since real resources are being transferred on the basis of a forecast, $\hat{y}$, rather than actual output. This cost seems necessary and even desirable if resource allocation and coordination decisions are to be based on budgeted output levels. The scheme has some other major limitations. First, there still are multiperiod gaming effects that are not captured in the simple one-period incentive scheme. For example, the manager may believe that the bonus pool in the subsequent period is a function of the budgeted and actual output levels in the current period—for example, $B_1 = B_0 + f(\hat{y}, y)$. This *ratchet effect* (see Weitzman [1980]) is a well-known budgeting procedure, particularly in governmental organizations. If the ratchet effect is a plausible assumption, the manager when determining what the current forecast and actual output should be will try to solve a multiperiod optimization problem, based on expectations of how current forecasts and actual output will affect future bonus pools. If this occurs, the nice one-period properties described above (for example, optimal forecast equals expected output) will not be valid.

A second problem is that under conditions of uncertainty, conditions not formally treated with our simple formulation, the piecewise linear sharing rules, given by equations (17-5), will not be an optimal sharing of risk between the manager and the central management group. This may not be a critical objection, since the role of the manager in sharing the risk of the firm is still speculative.

More important is the third limitation: if real resources are to be transferred among divisions (or among firms in the economy) based on the forecasts, there is still an incentive to misrepresent forecasts. When headquarters allocates resources to divisions based on forecasts, divisions may be motivated to conceal certain production or profit opportunities (see Loeb and Magat [1978] and Jennergren [1980, pp. 193–97]). Thus, despite the intuitive attraction of the proposed forecasting incentive scheme, implementation difficulties keep it from being a perfect solution to the problem of eliciting truthful forecasts from knowledgeable subordinates.

TRUTH-INDUCING SCHEMES
FOR RESOURCE ALLOCATION DECISIONS

Some research has been carried out to devise truth-inducing incentive mechanisms when two or more divisions are competing for common scarce resources of the firm. One class of performance measures have been shown to have desirable properties in motivating truthful reporting by divisional managers.[10] For specificity, we will illustrate such measures in the context of a linear programming example, but the procedure can be implemented for any resource-allocation decision where decentralized divisions are competing for or sharing common resources.

Consider a firm with n divisions, each with a linear technology and selling products in perfectly competitive markets. The short-term product-mix production problem can be described by

$$\text{Maximize:} \qquad \sum_i m_i x_i$$

$$\text{Subject to:} \qquad B_i x_i \le b_i,$$

$$\sum_i C_i x_i \le c, \qquad \text{(17-6)}$$

$$x_i \ge 0,$$

---

[10] This class of performance measures was derived by Groves [1973] and is also featured in Loeb and Magat [1978] and Groves and Loeb [1979].

where m_i = the vector of contribution margins for products in division i,

   x_i = the vector of outputs from division i,

   b_i = the vector of capacity resources unique to division i,

   c = a vector of availability of common resources, used by more than one division.

The constraints $C_1 x_1 + C_2 x_2 + \cdots + C_n x_n \le c$ express the joint usage of the common resources by the n divisions. These resources are already owned by the firm, so that there is no acquisition cost involved here, just an allocation decision. While the central management would like to be able to solve (17-6) to obtain a global maximum, it does not have information about the local production and sales opportunities (that is, b_i, m_i, B_i, or C_i) for any of the divisions. We wish to devise a procedure in which each division can bid for an quantity of the common resources. The firm receives bids or claims for these common resources from all the divisions and must eventually decide on their allocation to the divisions.

The truth-inducing scheme requires the divisions to first solve their individual problems:[11]

$$\text{Maximize:} \quad m_i x_i$$

$$\text{Subject to:} \quad B_i x_i \le b_i, \tag{17-7}$$

$$C_i x_i \le c_i,$$

$$x_i \ge 0,$$

for different levels of the common resources, c_i. This produces a divisional profit function $\pi_i^F(c_i)$, where the superscript F denotes a forecasted profit level. Each division then reports its profit function to central headquarters, which then solves the nonlinear resource-allocation problem:

$$\text{Maximize:} \quad \sum_i \pi_i^F(c_i)$$

$$\text{Subject to:} \quad \sum c_i = c, \tag{17-8}$$

$$c_i \ge 0,$$

to obtain the optimal allocation vectors c_1^*, c_2^*, . . . , c_n^*. Division i is then allocated an amount c_i^* of the common resources and attempts (we hope) to maximize its contribution margin, given this allocation of common resources, by re-solving the problem (17-7) with $c_i = c_i^*$. The incentive design problem is how to select a performance measure so that:

---

[11] For this discussion we assume that there is no uncertainty at divisional level about production and sales possibilities. Central management knows only the level of common resources, c. No division has or needs knowledge about the production and sales possibilities of the other divisions.

1. Each division is motivated to report the true profit function $\pi_i^F(c_i)$ at the first stage.

2. Each division strives to maximize its total contribution margin after the allocation c_i^* has been given to it.

The *Groves mechanism* (named after its founder and expositor) computes a performance measure for division i based on the *actual* realized profits in division i plus the *forecasted* profits of the *other* divisions at their actual allocated resource levels. Formally, letting G_i be the Groves measure for division i, we compute

$$G_i = \pi_i^A(c_i^*) + \sum_{j \neq i} \pi_j^F(c_j^*) - K_i, \qquad (17\text{-}9)$$

where $\pi_i^A(c_i^*)$ = the actual profit for division i, with resource allocation c_i^*,

   $\pi_j^F(c_j^*)$ = the *reported* profit function from division j (from the first stage of the process) computed at the actual resource-allocation level of c_j^* for division j, and

   K_i = a constant for division i, independent of its forecast or actual profits.

We will not work through the proof, but it can be shown that if divisions attempt to maximize their Groves measures, then:

1. Each division will attempt to maximize its realized or actual profits, since G_i is strictly increasing in the division's profits.

2. Each division is best off sending an accurate forecast function, $\pi_i^F(c_i)$, independent of what any other division sends or how it believes any other division is computing its forecast function.

3. Each division's performance measure will be independent of the realized (actual) profits or operating efficiency of the other divisions.

Thus, this measure seems to have the desirable properties we would prefer to see in a performance measure.

The Groves mechanism achieves its desirable properties by using a combination of realized division profits [the first term in (17-9)] and a profit-sharing scheme based on expected corporate profits [the second term in (17-9)]. If the division reward were based solely on realized division profits (the first term), the division managers would be motivated to distort the communicated information about the value of allocating the common resources to the division. Eliminating this tendency is the second term in the reward function, which provides a measure of the opportunity cost of the communicated information from all the divisions. This term represents the sum of the profit expectations of all the other divisions conditioned on an optimal centrally determined resource-allocation decision and the prior information of the central agent. Because the reward function for each division represents overall corporate profits, the incentive for divisional honesty in communicating its opportunity set dominates the incentive for nontruthful reporting, and all divisions report truthfully. Finally, there is no need for each division to be concerned, ex post, about efficiency or forecasting variances in other divisions, since such variances are allocated solely to the responsible division [through the first term in (17-9)].

There is still an element of noncontrollability, since the evaluation of a division depends on forecasts produced by other divisions, but this seems inevitable because of the divisional interactions through the common resources. The noncontrollable aspect may even be desirable in this setting, since it highlights the interdependence among the operating divisions and, therefore, the need for the divisions to work together for their overall benefit.

The constant term K_i in (17-9) does not affect the incentive properties of the Groves measure, since neither the division's profit forecast nor its actual realized profit influences the value of K_i. The measure can be varied to affect the interpretation of the performance measure and the separation between managerial and divisional performance (see Groves and Loeb [1979]). A particularly interesting interpretation of K_i occurs when it is defined as

$$K_i = \text{Maximum:} \quad \sum_{j \neq i} \pi_i^F(c_i)$$

$$\text{Subject to:} \quad \sum_{j \neq i} c_j \leq c, \tag{17-10}$$

$$c_j \geq 0.$$

This is a modified version of the firm's problem (17-8), but excluding division i. With this interpretation, K_i is the maximum profit of the firm without division i (and its unique resources, b_i). The Groves measure for division i, with K_i defined by equations (17-10), then represents the overall profits of the firm less the maximum obtainable without division i—in effect, the opportunity cost of abandoning division i.

One shortcoming of the Groves mechanism is that it does not incorporate the compensation of the divisional managers when solving the global or divisional maximizing problem. That is, it assumes that managers will act to maximize the performance measure of their division, but will not be rewarded for achieving the maximizing profit plan. No resources are committed to provide an incentive for truthful reporting or optimal resource allocation by divisional managers. This may limit the usefulness of the mechanism in actual applications. Also, the information-gathering and computational process required for the Groves mechanism is cumbersome and costly, further limiting the immediate practicality of this procedure.

We have introduced formal models for incentives and truth-inducing mechanisms. The research is abstract and is performed in highly simplified settings. At this stage, it would be premature to advocate major changes in a firm's management control system based on these research findings. But our study of these models should increase our sensitivity to the critical issues that arise with uncertainty and private information. These issues include the value of risk sharing, the importance of observability in specifying incentive contracts, and the difficulty of obtaining truthful information for planning and decision making when that information will also be used to evaluate managerial performance and allocate resources within the firm.

PROBLEMS

17-1. Risk Sharing and Efficient Contracts*

The manager of a maintenance company must supply all the maintenance requested by its only customer. The fee for this service is a fixed retainer of $10 plus a price of $2 per unit of demanded maintenance. The manager can acquire maintenance capacity in advance at a cost of $1 per maintenance unit. If more maintenance is demanded in a period than the firm's capacity, the manager must subcontract with another maintenance company, at a cost of $2 per maintenance unit, to meet this demand (in effect he breaks even on this excess demand).

The net cash flow to the maintenance firm, therefore is:

$$x = \begin{cases} 10 + 2s - a & \text{for } s \le a \\ 10 + a & \text{for } s > a \end{cases}$$

where s is the amount of service (maintenance) demanded and a is the amount of maintenance capacity acquired by the firm.

The manager believes that the demand, s, for maintenance is uniformly distributed over the interval $[0, 10]$.

The manager of the maintenance firm is risk averse and has a power utility function of the form:

$$U_m(x) = x^{1/2}$$

where x is the net cash flow to the manager.

The manager is evaluated by a flexible budget based on the expected cash flows to the firm given the decision taken on how much maintenance capacity he

---

* This problem is adapted from Demski, Joel, "Evaluation Based on Controllable Performance," *Journal of Accounting Research* XIV (Autumn 1976) pp. 230–45.

decides to acquire. In particular, his compensation is 40 percent of the expected cash flow.

Required:

1. a. Compute the action, a, that maximizes the expected utility for the manager. (Hint: Show that the manager wishes to maximize:

$$\frac{1}{10}\left[\int_0^a (10 + 2s - a)ds + \int_a^{10} (10 + a)ds \right]$$

    b. What is the expected utility of the manager from following this action?
    c. Suppose the owner is risk-neutral. What is the owner's expected return after compensating the manager according to the above plan?
    d. Suppose the owner is risk-averse with the same utility function as the manager ($U_0(x) = x^{1/2}$). What is the owner's expected utility from the above arrangement?

2. Consider an alternative contract in which the manager's compensation is changed to 42 percent of actual cash flow.

    a. Show that the manager now wishes to choose a to maximize:

$$\frac{1}{10}\left\{ \int_0^a [.42(10 + 2s - a)]^{1/2}\, ds + \int_a^{10} [.42(10 + a)]^{1/2}\, ds \right\}$$

    b. What value of a maximizes this expression (try to obtain an approximate figure)?
    c. What are the manager's and owner's expected utility from this arrangement?

3. Given that the manager is risk-averse, why is it optimal to have an arrangement in which he is subject to some non-controllable risk? (Note that under the second arrangement, the manager's compensation varies with the random and non-controllable level of maintenance demanded.)

17-2. *Optimal Risk Sharing Between Owner and Manager*

Hank Raiffa, the owner of Risky Widgets, Inc. has an opportunity for a new product introduction but he is busy on all his other projects, and needs to hire a manager to organize and supervise the new venture. Fixed costs that must be committed to the product are $10,000, and this amount must be spent before demand is known. The selling price of the product is $12 and the variable cost per unit is $6. Hank figures that demand will either be 1,000, 2,000, or 3,000 units and these will occur with probability .2, .5, and .3 respectively. Production can be organized to satisfy demand so that there is no inventory problem; the only risk is committing the $10,000 up front and then only being able to sell 1,000 units.

While the project looks good on an expected value basis, Hank has some aversion to risky outcomes. His utility function for income, x, from this project is given by:

$$u_0(x) = 1 - e^{-x/3000}$$

Hank has found a manager for the project, Ronald Meyer, who would be willing to oversee the venture for a fixed fee of $119. Hank would like to share some of the risk of the project with Ron but he has learned that Ron is even more risk averse than he is. Meyer's utility function for income from this project is given by:

$$u_1(x) = 1 - e^{-x/1000}$$

Required:

1. Would Hank undertake this project by himself if he had the time to organize and supervise it?
2. Would he be willing to hire Ron Meyer at a fixed fee of $119 to run the project?
3. Hank's first thought on risk sharing is to offer a 50-50 split with Ron; that is, they each share equally in the gains or losses. Is this a good arrangement between Hank and Ron?
4. Show that Ron is essentially indifferent among the following compensation arrangements
   a. Fixed fee of $119
   b. Pay Hank $52 but receive 10% of the profits or losses
   c. Receive 25% of the profit or losses
   d. Receive a fixed fee of $630 and share 50% in the profits or losses
5. Which of these four compensation arrangements is best for Hank?
6. Comment on the role of risk-sharing in determining the desirability of a risky investment.

17-3. Optimal Contracting and Risk Sharing (A. Atkinson)

Ezra Jones, owner of the Pembrooke Novelty Company is planning for his semi-retirement from his firm. Ezra has decided to hire a manager to run the firm. The manager will be paid a competitive salary of $300,000 per year. In addition, Ezra indicates that he will offer the manager 10 percent of the firm's net income "to provide a motivation for the manager to work hard when I'm not around".

The company manufactures a small plastic ornament distributed widely through a network of chain stores. The company's market can be viewed as competitive but at the time the production decision is made the price to be received for output is uncertain. The firm's cost function is:

$$C(q) = 2,000,000 + 5q + .00001q^2$$

where q is the number of units produced.

The price to be received for output can be described as normally distributed with a mean of $20 and a standard deviation of $2.

Ezra is an expected value decision-maker. The manager's utility function is independent of his effort level and can be described as:

$$U(\pi_m) = -e^{[-\pi_m/10,000]}$$

where π_m is the manager's end of period wealth.

1. What level of output would the manager choose with the indicated compensation package? Assume that the 10% share of net income motivates him to provide a high level of effort.

   HINT: $\dfrac{1}{\sqrt{2\pi s^2}} \displaystyle\int_{-\infty}^{+\infty} exp - \left[\dfrac{p^2}{2s^2} - 2bp \right] dp = exp\, [2b^2s^2]$

2. What level of output would Ezra prefer?
3. Can you propose a better contract than what Ezra is considering?

17-4. Effect of Profit Sharing Parameter on the Selection of a Risky Project*

Jane Atkins is choosing among three risky projects for the next year. The three opportunities are characterized by the following expected returns and variances:

Project	A	B	C
Expected Return	20	15	30
Variance of Return	8	5	20

Jane's annual compensation, w, consists of a fixed salary, a, plus a share of the return from the risky project. Formally this function is given by

$$w = a + b(y - 15)$$

where y is the return from the risky project, and b is a positive constant, less than 1, representing a share in the profit (or shortfall) in excess of the minimum desired return of 15.

Jane is risk averse and her preference for wealth can be characterized by a mean-variance utility function: $U(w) = E(w) - 2\,\text{Var}\,(w)$

Required:

1. Compute Jane's utility for the compensation from each of the three projects.
2. Central management prefers that Project A be selected and wants to set the parameters (a and b) of Jane's compensation function so that she will select this project. For what values of a and b will Project A be Jane's most preferred alternative?
3. Suppose that Jane is compensated on a straight salary basis but she wishes to make her decision as if she were the top management of the firm; that is, she acts as if $w = y$. Which project would she select and is this the project actually preferred by top management?

---

* This example is adapted from Hiro Itami, "Evaluation Measures and Goal Congruence Under Uncertainty," *Journal of Accounting Research* XIII (Spring 1975) pp. 73–96.

17-5. Risk Sharing and the Value of Budget-Based Contracts* (A. Atkinson)

Nepean Electronics manufactures and distributes silicon chips used in the manufacture of electronic control devices and electronic games. The company sells its output to wholesale specialists.

The company's annual production cost function, $C(q)$, is given by

$$C(q) = 500,000 - 9q + (3.75 \times 10^{-6})q^2 + (5 \times 10^{-13})q^3$$

where q is the number of chips produced annually.

While the firm is confident about its knowledge of production costs, it is much less certain about the final market for the chips. The market is competitive but the price fluctuates considerably.

The price per chip is estimated as (approximately) normally distributed with a mean of $12.00 and a standard deviation of $2.00.

Elmo Rich, the owner of Nepean Electronics is considering some alternative ways of compensating Roger Smith, the general manager of the company. Elmo has decided that the compensation contract will have the form:

$$\pi_m = w + k\pi_F$$

where π_m is Roger's compensation
       w is Roger's fixed wage
       k is a profit share $0 < k < 1$
       π_F is a measure related to the company's actual return

Elmo is an expected value decision-maker. Roger is risk averse and has a utility function which can be described by:

$$U(\pi_m) = -1000e^{[\pi_m/1000]}$$

Required:

1. What is the optimal level of production from Rich's point of view?
2. Suppose that the parameter π_F in Roger's compensation function is set equal to the company's profit. For any level (q) of output chosen, what risk does Roger face? Use variability of return to approximate risk.
3. In general, how would Roger respond to the risk computed in Question 2? Would production be higher or lower than the amount for Question 1?
4. Suppose now that Elmo's and Roger's beliefs about the distribution of price are not necessarily equal. Elmo sets a budgeted (or target) output, (q_B), based on his beliefs. Roger's compensation is based on this budgeted output and is given by:

$$\pi_m = w + k\{(pq - C(q)) - (pq_B - C(q_B))\}$$

In other words, Roger gets a wage and a share of the accounting variance

---

* This problem is adapted from A. Atkinson, "Standard Setting in an Agency," *Management Science* XXIV (September 1978) pp. 1351–61.

between actual and planned profits. (Note that w and k may differ with π_m redefined in this manner but ignore this complication). What risk does Roger face under this mechanism? Comment on the potential of a budget to alter a manager's risk.

5. For the problem discussed in Question 4, it can be shown that Roger's expected utility is

$$EU_m(\pi_m) =$$

$$-aexp\left\{ -\frac{1}{a}[w + k[(\bar{p}q - C(q)) - (\bar{p}q_B - C(q_B))] - \frac{k^2(q - q_B)^2\sigma_p^2}{2a}\right\}$$

where, in this case $a = 1000$, $\sigma_p^2 = 2$ and $\bar{p} = 12$.

From this equation, find the formula that yields Roger's optimal quantity choice. If Roger and Elmo have the same beliefs of the expected price, $\bar{p}$, will Roger choose a lower or higher quantity than Elmo would like? How is Roger's choice of q affected by increases in

a. q_B
b. k
c. σ_p^2

6. Recall that, under the assumptions of the problem, Elmo would choose q_B as follows

$$\bar{p}_B = C'(q_B)$$

where $\bar{p}_B$ is Elmo's expected price.

With this equation and the equation in Question 5, complete the following table assuming that $k = 0.1$ and that both Elmo and Roger know the cost function.

$\bar{p}_B$	$\bar{p}$	q_B	q	q_m	q_0
10	12				
12	12				
14	12				

The variables q_B and q are defined above, q_m is the quantity that Roger would choose if $q_B = 0$ (i.e., if straight profit sharing was used), and q_0 is the quantity that Elmo would choose if he had Roger's beliefs. Comment on any relationships *which appear to exist* in this table.

17-6. Design of Optimal Incentive Contract when Employee is Work Averse (A. Atkinson)

Don Quack, the owner of North York Company, is pondering the employment contract currently in effect between himself and his sole employee, Arthur Milton.

Arthur utilizes his unique engineering/craftsman/selling skills to manufacture the "Quacker," a novelty toy. This toy is the company's sole product. The firm's total output, X, is a function of Arthur's level of effort, a, and a combination of outside, uncertain events, θ, over which no one has any control ($X = X(a, \theta)$).

Don and Arthur have studied the production function and found that it has the form:

$$X = a + \theta$$

where θ is thought to take on values lying between zero and b.

Don evaluates decisions on the basis of expected value and Arthur is admittedly effort averse. That is, Arthur suffers utility loss (or discomfort) when exerting effort.

This admission has prompted Don to offer Arthur a share in output "to motivate Art to provide higher effort." After a certain amount of haggling, Art has agreed to provide 100 units of effort in exchange for a salary of $1,000 and 10 percent of the value of the output.

The business is such that output, (X), is trivially and costlessly observed but neither θ nor a can be observed by Don at any cost. Although the matter has not been discussed, if Arthur is caught supplying less than 100 units of a he will face immediate dismissal from the firm. This will result in irreparable damage, so Art will avoid putting himself in danger of dismissal at any cost.

Required:

1. Do you think that this contract will achieve its intention of motivating "more effort" from Arthur? Consider both the situation when Arthur is risk neutral and risk averse. Can you think of a better contract?

2. How does the situation change if X is of the form $X = a\theta$?

17-7. Choice of Performance Measurement System in Principal-Agent Setting* (G. Foster)

EUREKA GOLD RUSH

Hobie Leland, Jr. has acquired ownership of the Eureka Gold Rush Syndicate. Gold has been found on its lease, and production has commenced. Kodiak is in charge of operations and must decide about the timing of sale of the 100 units of gold that will be produced in the first period. Two options are possible: sell 75 units in Period 1 and 25 units in Period 2 (a_1), Or sell 25 units in Period 1 and 75 units in Period 2 (a_2). Eureka can sell gold at $150 per unit in period 1. There is uncertainty about the period 2 price. It will be either $200 ($s_1$) or $130 ($s_2$). Kodiak assesses that $\phi(s_1) = .2$ and $\phi(s_2) = .8$. The production cost is $50 per unit. Kodiak shares his probability assessments with Hobie.

Under his employment agreement, Kodiak's salary is 10 percent of income (if positive), payable at the end of each year. There is, however, some ambiguity about how to recognize income for a gold producing company. The two alternatives that could be used are:

> *Sale Basis* (η_1): Recognize income only when the gold is sold; any unsold gold produced in Period 1 is shown as inventory at the production cost of $50 a unit.
>
> *Production Basis* (η_2): Recognize income when the gold is produced; any unsold gold produced in Period 1 is valued at $150 a unit. If the selling price of gold in Period 2 differs from $150, the price variation is included in Period 2 income as a holding gain or loss.

Hobie would prefer that the option chosen by Kodiak maximize the present value of the income of Eureka Gold Rush. In making this calculation, he considers that income should be recognized on a sale basis. However, he is not sure whether this income concept should be used to measure Kodiak's performance. Hobie has the same risk neutral attitude as Kodiak (they both maximize the expected monetary payoff with payoffs expressed as present values). However, Hobie assesses that $\phi(s_1) = .8$ and $\phi(s_2) = .2$. Kodiak will choose the alternative which maximizes the expected present value of his salary. Both he and Hobie use a 10% discount rate. Assume the sales are made and salaries are paid at the *end* of each period.

Required:

1. What income concept should Hobie use to measure Kodiak's performance?
2. How much would Hobie pay to control the choice between a_1 and a_2 if
   a. η_1 is used to measure Kodiak's performance?
   b. η_2 is used to measure Kodiak's performance?
3. If Hobie considers that income should be recognized on a production basis, what income concept should he use to measure Kodiak's performance?
4. Why, in general, would Hobie delegate the action choice to Kodiak, when conflicts in their action preferences may arise?
5. What steps might Hobie take to reduce the likelihood of conflicts arising in his and Kodiak's action preferences?

Note: The following income figures are given to ease your computational burden.

Sale Basis (η_1)

	Period 1	Period 2
(a_1, s_1)	7,500	3,750
(a_1, s_2)	7,500	2,000
(a_2, s_1)	2,500	11,250
(a_2, s_2)	2,500	6,000

Production Basis (η_2)

	Period 1	Period 2
(a_1, s_1)	10,000	1,250
(a_1, s_2)	10,000	-500
(a_2, s_1)	10,000	3,750
(a_2, s_2)	10,000	$-1,500$

17-8. Effect of Observability on the Form of Optimal Contracts (A. Atkinson)

Ralph Smart of Swissvale Investments is considering an investment in a farming venture in the country of Markovia.

The plan is to grow and harvest Gronk, a revolutionary natural food highly prized by distance runners for its sustenance attributes. The climatic conditions and soil of southwestern Markovia are unique and are the only known conditions under which Gronk can be produced.

Gronk growing technology is well understood. Gronk production depends upon weather conditions and the effort of the farmer in the growing season and hence is subject to uncertainty.

Markovia is a new and remote country which is virtually inaccessible to outsiders. Although Markovia has a well established legal system, commercial development is backward.

Moral Hazard, a Markovian farmer and promoter has invited Ralph, and other investors, to invest in Gronk farming. Moral would farm the Gronk and supervise the distribution of the proceeds to investors.

Ralph, and all other potential investors, are risk neutral. Moral is risk averse.

Required:

1. If no other information is available, what is Ralph's optimal course of action?
2. Suppose that Ralph discovers that Markovia has a well established and reputable public accounting profession. How, if at all, would this effect your response to Question 1.
3. What further information, if any, might Ralph seek beyond the information which might be supplied by a public accountant?

17-9. Incentives for Distorting Information (A. Atkinson)

Wren Jenner Construction specializes in remodeling existing buildings and constructing office buildings, private homes, and apartment buildings. For incentive purposes the company is organized on a profit center basis with four profit-centers.

The critical resource of the firm is its carpenters. Since there is a shortage of carpenters in the area served by Wren Jenner, the company has a policy of hiring all carpenters at the corporate level and then assigning carpenters to one of the four profit-centers. The union rate for carpenters is $18.00 per hour and at this price the managers of the four profit-centers have a joint demand for carpenters which is far in excess of the available supply.

Given this situation, the company is faced with the problem of how to ration the available supply. The operation of each of the profit-centers is subject to some uncertainty so that ex-ante managerial claims regarding carpenter productivity are difficult to evaluate ex post. Consequently, the controller is reluctant to base allocations on a priori assertions by the divisional managers.

To simplify the discussion, assume there are two divisions. In Division 1, the return (p_1) received per carpenter hour (q_1) is:

$$p_1 = 500 - .2q_1.$$

For division 2, the return is:

$$p_2 = 200 - .1q_2.$$

Suppose that the controller successively announces prices and the division managers respond with demand at that price. The controller seeks to equate demand and the supply of carpenter hours which is 1,800. Divisions will be assessed a charge against profits which is equal to the bid amount. All managers are risk neutral.

Required:

1. Suppose both divisions respond honestly to the controller's price bids:
   a. What price will clear this market?
   b. How many carpenter hours will be allocated to each division?
   c. What will be the profit reported by each division?
2. Suppose that the manager of Division 1 intends to respond honestly to the controller's bids. The manager of Division 2 knows this and also knows Division 1's return function.
   Show that there is an incentive for the manager of Division 2 to be dishonest.
   (HINT: How would managers behave to have a transfer price of $0?)
3. Can you suggest a method for solving the problem raised in Question 2?
4. Under what circumstances will the solution proposed in Question 3 not have the desired motivational consequences?

17-10. Soviet Incentive System: Extensions and Problems (A. Atkinson)

Boris O'Grodnik is the foreman of Carleton Place Farms. Carleton Place Farms is organized on a profit center basis with a sub-foreman in charge of each of the divisions. These semi-autonomous divisions are: dairy, cash crops, chicken, and marketing. Boris' main responsibility is to coordinate the interactions between the four divisions.

The major coordination involves preparing the marketing department to handle the outputs of the three producing divisions. This involves obtaining production forecasts from the divisions and basing marketing plans upon these forecasts.

In the past there have been problems with the forecasts. Boris suspects that forecasts have been biased because the forecasts are issued before quotas and bonus schedules are set: the implication is that the sub-foreman wants to keep expectations of output low in order to maximize the likelihood of beating the quota and earning a bonus.

While pondering this problem Boris receives a letter from his distant cousin, Nikolai in "the old country" (Russia). Nikolai reports that a new Soviet Incentive model recently installed in his factory is supposed to have good results in improving management forecasts.

Consider each question separately.

1. In a firm with a one period life and a risk neutral manager, explain how the Soviet Incentive System can motivate accurate managerial forecasts.

2. Assume that the manager's beliefs are represented by a cumulative distribution function for output (y) given by $F(y)$. Show that a risk neutral manager will declare an output $\hat{y}$ such that $1 - F(\hat{y}) = (\gamma - \beta)/(\gamma - \alpha)$ where α, β, γ are the parameters of the incentive system plan (see text).

3. How do the incentive properties which you mentioned in Question 1 change if the firm has more than one planning period?

4. How do the incentive properties which you mentioned in Question 1 change if the firm has a risk averse manager?

5. Suppose that Boris installs this system with the understanding that planned *amounts* of output will be used to determine resource allocations within Carleton Place Farms. How would this affect the incentive properties which you mentioned in Question 1?

6. Suppose that Boris installs this system with the understanding that he may alter divisional planned amounts of output in order to balance divisional operations. How would this affect the incentive properties which you mentioned in Question 1?

17-11. Groves Mechanism: Applications and Limitations
(A. Atkinson)

John Theodore, President of Garden Grove Nursery plans the weekly operation of the firm. The crucial weekly operating decision is the allocation of the firm's ten gardeners to the firm's two operating divisions *Commercial* and *Nursery*. No other gardeners are available.

The *Commercial* division solicits contracts for landscaping and garden maintenance. It is widely known that the return here is fixed and contracts reflect market conditions. Ralph Jones, the manager of this division, knows that this division can keep all ten of the firm's ten gardeners fully occupied at a net profit to the firm of $50 per gardener hour.

The *Nursery* division, John Theodore's original operation, consists of a greenhouse operation that prepares plants and shrubs for the commercial market. The return here is uncertain and depends on volatile market conditions. Elmo Slack, the manager of this division believes that, in the current market, the distribution of net profit per gardener hour is uniform over the interval $40 to $55. These beliefs are held privately by Elmo and are not known to the other members of the senior management team at Garden Grove.

Required:

Consider each question separately.

1. Suppose that Elmo's compensation is a function of the reported weekly profits of the Nursery Division. Suppose further that John Theodore allocates gardeners to divisions on the basis of the expected returns esti-

mated by the division managers. If Elmo is an expected value decision-maker, show that this organization structure will motivate Elmo to lie about his division's expected return per gardener hour.

2. Suppose now that Elmo's compensation is a function of the reported weekly profits of Garden Grove Nursery. If Elmo is an expected value decision-maker, is there any motivation for Elmo to lie about his division's expected return per gardener hour? Explain the dysfunctional consequences of this reward mechanism if the divisional return can be influenced by managerial competence.

3. Suppose that John Theodore has decided to use the Groves mechanism to allocate the gardeners to the two divisions in his firm. For Garden Grove Nursery the Groves measure for the Nursery division would have the form:

$$G_N = \pi_N^A(x_N) + \pi_C^F(x_C) - K_N$$

where $\pi_N^A(x_N)$ = Actual weekly profits for the nursery division with x_N gardeners allocated to this division,

$\pi_C^F(x_C)$ = forecasted weekly profits for the commercial division with x_C gardeners allocated to this division, and

K_N = a constant independent of the nursery division's forecasted or actual profits.

How would use of the Groves measure improve the information elicited from Elmo Slack and the manager of the Commercial division?

4. Suppose further that Theodore wishes to make G_N relevant to Elmo by incorporating it into Elmo's compensation function. Elmo's compensation will be computed as:

$$y_E = W_E + k\, G_N$$

where y_E = Elmo's total compensation,

W_E = Elmo's fixed wage,

k = a fixed positive constant

G_N = the Groves measure for the nursery division.

Note that EG_N represents apart from the scalar K_N, *expected* corporate profits so that Elmo's expected return is a wage plus a share of expected corporate profits. Assume that Elmo could earn \$500 per week in a comparable job outside the firm. Show that a compensation policy based on y_E is unlikely to be optimal. Is G_N a reasonable basis to use for compensating divisional managers?

5. Return to the original data of this problem but assume now that the net profit per gardener in the commercial division is only \$47 per hour. Elmo has the same beliefs as before but is risk-averse. Elmo's utility for his compensation (y_E) is given by:

$$U(y_E) = -exp\,[-y_E/500]$$

where $y_E = \$500 + 0.1G_N$.

K_N is set equal to the profit of the firm if the nursery division received no gardeners; that is, K_N = ($47/hour)(10 gardeners)(40 hours/week) = 18,800.

Suppose John Theodore is risk neutral. What is the optimal allocation of gardeners from John's point of view? Show that Elmo will lie about his beliefs in this case and that all gardeners will be allocated to the commercial division. What are the implications of this result?

6. Assume the same data as question 5 with the following exception. Elmo's utility function is

$$U(y_E, x_N) = E(y_E) - 0.1x_N$$

where x_N is the number of gardeners assigned to the Nursery Division. In other words, Elmo is risk-neutral but suffers a loss of well-being (or utility) when he is assigned workers to supervise.

Show that, in this case Elmo will lie about his prospects and all gardeners will be assigned to the Commercial Division. What are the implications of this result?

REFERENCES

ATKINSON, ANTHONY A., "Standard Setting in an Agency," *Management Science*, XXIV (September 1978), 1351–61.

DEMSKI, JOEL, "Uncertainty and Evaluation Based on Controllable Performance," *Journal of Accounting Research* X (Autumn 1976), 230–45.

————, and GERALD A. FELTHAM, "Economic Incentives in Budgetary Control Systems," *The Accounting Review* LIII (April 1978), 336–59.

GONIK, JACOB, "Tie Salesmen's Bonuses to Their Forecasts," *Harvard Business Review* LVI (May–June 1978).

GROVES, THEODORE, "Incentives in Teams," *Econometrica* XLI (July 1973), 617–31.

———— and MARTIN LOEB, "Incentives in a Divisionalized Firm," *Management Science* XXV (March 1979), 221–30.

HARRIS, MILTON, and ARTUR RAVIV, "Some Results on Incentive Contracts with Applications to Education and Employment, Health Insurance, and Law Enforcement," *American Economic Review* LXVIII (March 1978), 20–30.

———— and ————, "Optimal Incentive Contracts with Imperfect Information," *Journal of Economic Theory* XX (April 1979), 231–59.

HOLMSTROM, BENGT, "Moral Hazard and Observability," *Bell Journal of Economics* X (Spring 1979), 74–91.

HORNGREN, CHARLES, *Cost Accounting: A Managerial Emphasis*, Fifth Edition (Englewood Cliffs, N.J.: Prentice-Hall) 1982.

IJIRI, YUJI, J. C. KINARD, and F. B. PUTNEY, "An Integrated Evaluation System for Budget Forecasting and Operating Performance with a Classified Budgeting Bibliography," *Journal of Accounting Research* VI (Spring 1968), 1–28.

JENNERGREN, L. PETER, "On the Design of Incentives in Business Firms—A Survey of Some Research," *Management Science* XXV (February 1980), 180–200.

LOEB, MARTIN, and WESLEY A. MAGAT, "Soviet Success Indicators and the Evaluation of Divisional Management," *Journal of Accounting Research* XVI (Spring 1978), 103–21.

ROSS, STEPHEN, "The Economic Theory of Agency: The Principal's Problem," *American Economic Review* LXIII (March 1973), 134–39.

SHAVELL, STEPHEN, "Risk Sharing and Incentives in the Principal and Agent Relationship," *Bell Journal of Economics* X (Spring 1979), 55–73.

SNOWBERGER, VINSON, "The New Soviet Incentive Model: Comment," *Bell Journal of Economics* VIII (Autumn 1977), 591–600.

WEITZMAN, MARTIN L., "The New Soviet Incentive Model," *Bell Journal of Economics* VII (Spring 1976), 251–57.

————, "The 'Ratchet Principle' and Performance Incentives," *Bell Journal of Economics* XI (Spring 1980), 302–08.

WILSON, ROBERT, "The Theory of Syndicates," *Econometrica* XXXVI (January 1968), 119–32.

APPENDIX TABLES

AREAS UNDER THE NORMAL CURVE

Each entry in this table is the proportion of the total area under a normal curve which lies under the segment between the mean and x/σ or z standard deviations from the mean. Example: $x = X - \mu = 31$ and $\sigma = 20$, so $z = x/\sigma = 1.55$. Then the required area is .4394. The area in the tail beyond the point $x = 31$ is then $.5000 - .4394 = .0606$.

Z/σ	.00	.01	.02	.03	.04	.05	.06	.07	.08	.09
0.0	.0000	.0040	.0080	.0120	.0160	.0199	.0239	.0279	.0319	.0359
0.1	.0398	.0438	.0478	.0517	.0557	.0596	.0636	.0675	.0714	.0753
0.2	.0793	.0832	.0871	.0910	.0948	.0987	.1026	.1064	.1103	.1141
0.3	.1179	.1217	.1255	.1293	.1331	.1368	.1406	.1443	.1480	.1517
0.4	.1554	.1591	.1628	.1664	.1700	.1736	.1772	.1808	.1844	.1879
0.5	.1915	.1950	.1985	.2019	.2054	.2088	.2123	.2157	.2190	.2224
0.6	.2257	.2291	.2324	.2357	.2389	.2422	.2454	.2486	.2518	.2549
0.7	.2580	.2612	.2642	.2673	.2704	.2734	.2764	.2794	.2823	.2852
0.8	.2881	.2910	.2939	.2967	.2995	.3023	.3051	.3078	.3106	.3133
0.9	.3159	.3186	.3212	.3238	.3264	.3289	.3315	.3340	.3365	.3389
1.0	.3413	.3438	.3461	.3485	.3508	.3531	.3554	.3577	.3599	.3621
1.1	.3643	.3665	.3686	.3708	.3729	.3749	.3770	.3790	.3810	.3830
1.2	.3849	.3869	.3888	.3907	.3925	.3944	.3962	.3980	.3997	.4015
1.3	.4032	.4049	.4066	.4082	.4099	.4115	.4131	.4147	.4162	.4177
1.4	.4192	.4207	.4222	.4236	.4251	.4265	.4279	.4292	.4306	.4319
1.5	.4332	.4345	.4357	.4370	.4382	.4394	.4406	.4418	.4429	.4441
1.6	.4452	.4463	.4474	.4484	.4495	.4505	.4515	.4525	.4535	.4545
1.7	.4554	.4564	.4573	.4582	.4591	.4599	.4608	.4616	.4625	.4633
1.8	.4641	.4649	.4656	.4664	.4671	.4678	.4686	.4693	.4699	.4706
1.9	.4713	.4719	.4726	.4732	.4738	.4744	.4750	.4756	.4761	.4767
2.0	.4772	.4778	.4783	.4788	.4793	.4798	.4803	.4808	.4812	.4817
2.1	.4821	.4826	.4830	.4834	.4838	.4842	.4846	.4850	.4854	.4857
2.2	.4861	.4864	.4868	.4871	.4875	.4878	.4881	.4884	.4887	.4890
2.3	.4893	.4896	.4898	.4901	.4904	.4906	.4909	.4911	.4913	.4916
2.4	.4918	.4920	.4922	.4925	.4927	.4929	.4931	.4932	.4934	.4936
2.5	.4938	.4940	.4941	.4943	.4945	.4946	.4948	.4949	.4951	.4952
2.6	.4953	.4955	.4956	.4957	.4959	.4960	.4961	.4962	.4963	.4964
2.7	.4965	.4966	.4967	.4968	.4969	.4970	.4971	.4972	.4973	.4974
2.8	.4974	.4975	.4976	.4977	.4977	.4978	.4979	.4979	.4980	.4981
2.9	.4981	.4982	.4982	.4983	.4984	.4984	.4985	.4985	.4986	.4986
3.0	.49875	.4987	.4987	.4988	.4988	.4989	.4989	.4989	.4990	.4990
3.1	.49903	.4991	.4991	.4991	.4992	.4992	.4992	.4992	.4993	.4993
3.2	.4993	.4993	.4994	.4994	.4994	.4994	.4994	.4995	.4995	.4995
3.3	.4995	.4995	.4995	.4996	.4996	.4996	.4996	.4996	.4996	.4997
3.4	.4997	.4997	.4997	.4997	.4997	.4997	.4997	.4997	.4998	.4998
3.5	.4998	.4998	.4998	.4998	.4998	.4998	.4998	.4998	.4998	.4998
3.6	.4998	.4998	.4999	.4999	.4999	.4999	.4999	.4999	.4999	.4999
3.7	.4999	.4999	.4999	.4999	.4999	.4999	.4999	.4999	.4999	.4999
3.8	.4999	.4999	.4999	.4999	.4999	.4999	.4999	.5000	.5000	.5000
3.9	.5 000	.5000	.5000	.5000	.5000	.5000	.5000	.5000	.5000	.5000

Source: Frederick E. Croxton and Dudley J. Cowden, *Practical Business Statistics* (2d ed.; New York: Prentice-Hall, Inc., 1948), p. 511. Reprinted by permission of the publisher.

VALUES OF t

The values in the table represent the point in the upper (right-hand) tail of the t-distribution with n degrees of freedom. For example, with 10 degrees of freedom, .05 of the area under the t-distribution is beyond the point t = 1.812. For a two-tailed test, double the value of α in each column; that is, .05 of the area falls outside the interval t = ± 2.228.

n	$\alpha = .10$	$\alpha = .05$	$\alpha = .025$	$\alpha = .01$	$\alpha = .005$
1	3.078	6.314	12.706	31.821	63.657
2	1.886	2.920	4.303	6.965	9.925
3	1.638	2.353	3.182	4.541	5.841
4	1.533	2.132	2.776	3.747	4.604
5	1.476	2.015	2.571	3.365	4.032
6	1.440	1.943	2.447	3.143	3.707
7	1.415	1.895	2.365	2.998	3.499
8	1.397	1.860	2.306	2.896	3.355
9	1.383	1.833	2.262	2.821	3.250
10	1.372	1.812	2.228	2.764	3.169
11	1.363	1.796	2.201	2.718	3.106
12	1.356	1.782	2.179	2.681	3.055
13	1.350	1.771	2.160	2.650	3.012
14	1.345	1.761	2.145	2.624	2.977
15	1.341	1.753	2.131	2.602	2.947
16	1.337	1.746	2.120	2.583	2.921
17	1.333	1.740	2.110	2.567	2.898
18	1.330	1.734	2.101	2.552	2.878
19	1.328	1.729	2.093	2.539	2.861
20	1.325	1.725	2.086	2.528	2.845
21	1.323	1.721	2.080	2.518	2.831
22	1.321	1.717	2.074	2.508	2.819
23	1.319	1.714	2.069	2.500	2.807
24	1.318	1.711	2.064	2.492	2.797
25	1.316	1.708	2.060	2.485	2.787
26	1.315	1.706	2.056	2.479	2.779
27	1.314	1.703	2.052	2.473	2.771
28	1.313	1.701	2.048	2.467	2.763
29	1.311	1.699	2.045	2.462	2.756
inf.	1.282	1.645	1.960	2.326	2.576

* This table is abridged from Table IV of R. A. Fisher, *Statistical Methods for Research Workers*, published by Oliver and Boyd, Ltd., Edinburgh, by permission of the author and publishers.

UNIT NORMAL LOSS FUNCTION

The value $L_N(D)$ is the expected opportunity loss (or EVPI) for a linear loss function with slope one and a unit normal distribution. The value D represents the relative position of the breakeven point.

When using $L_N(D)$ for a general normal distribution, the value D represents the absolute deviation of the breakeven point K from the mean M_0, expressed in standard deviation, S_0, units. That is,

$$D = \left| \frac{K - M_0}{S_0} \right|.$$

D	.00	.01	.02	.03	.04	.05	.06	.07	.08	.09
.0	.3989	.3940	.3890	.3841	.3793	.3744	.3697	.3649	.3602	.3556
.1	.3509	.3464	.3418	.3373	.3328	.3284	.3240	.3197	.3154	.3111
.2	.3069	.3027	.2986	.2944	.2904	.2863	.2824	.2784	.2745	.2706
.3	.2668	.2630	.2592	.2555	.2518	.2481	.2445	.2409	.2374	.2339
.4	.2304	.2270	.2236	.2203	.2169	.2137	.2104	.2072	.2040	.2009
.5	.1978	.1947	.1917	.1887	.1857	.1828	.1799	.1771	.1742	.1714
.6	.1687	.1659	.1633	.1606	.1580	.1554	.1528	.1503	.1478	.1453
.7	.1429	.1405	.1381	.1358	.1334	.1312	.1289	.1267	.1245	.1223
.8	.1202	.1181	.1160	.1140	.1120	.1100	.1080	.1061	.1042	.1023
.9	.1004	.09860	.09680	.09503	.09328	.09156	.08986	.08819	.08654	.08491
1.0	.08332	.08174	.08019	.07868	.07716	.07568	.07422	.07279	.07138	.06999
1.1	.06862	.06727	.06595	.06465	.06336	.06210	.06086	.05964	.05844	.05726
1.2	.05610	.05496	.05384	.05274	.05165	.05059	.04954	.04851	.04750	.04650
1.3	.04553	.04457	.04363	.04270	.04179	.04090	.04002	.03916	.03831	.03748
1.4	.03667	.03587	.03508	.03431	.03356	.03281	.03208	.03137	.03067	.02998
1.5	.02931	.02865	.02880	.02736	.02674	.02612	.02552	.02494	.02436	.02380
1.6	.02324	.02270	.02217	.02165	.02114	.02064	.02015	.01967	.01920	.01874
1.7	.01829	.01785	.01742	.01699	.01658	.01617	.01578	.01539	.01501	.01464
1.8	.01428	.01392	.01357	.01323	.01290	.01257	.01226	.01195	.01164	.01134
1.9	.01105	.01077	.01049	.01022	$.0^2 9957$	$.0^2 9698$	$.0^2 9445$	$.0^2 9198$	$.0^2 8957$	$.0^2 8721$
2.0	$.0^2 8491$	$.0^2 8266$	$.0^2 8046$	$.0^2 7832$	$.0^2 7623$	$.0^2 7418$	$.0^2 7219$	$.0^2 7024$	$.0^2 6835$	$.0^2 6649$
2.1	$.0^2 6468$	$.0^2 6292$	$.0^2 6120$	$.0^2 5952$	$.0^2 5788$	$.0^2 5628$	$.0^2 5472$	$.0^2 5320$	$.0^2 5172$	$.0^2 5028$
2.2	$.0^2 4887$	$.0^2 4750$	$.0^2 4616$	$.0^2 4486$	$.0^2 4358$	$.0^2 4235$	$.0^2 4114$	$.0^2 3996$	$.0^2 3882$	$.0^2 3770$
2.3	$.0^2 3662$	$.0^2 3556$	$.0^2 3453$	$.0^2 3352$	$.0^2 3255$	$.0^2 3159$	$.0^2 3067$	$.0^2 2977$	$.0^2 2889$	$.0^2 2804$
2.4	$.0^2 2720$	$.0^2 2640$	$.0^2 2561$	$.0^2 2484$	$.0^2 2410$	$.0^2 2337$	$.0^2 2267$	$.0^2 2199$	$.0^2 2132$	$.0^2 2067$
2.5	$.0^2 2005$	$.0^2 1943$	$.0^2 1883$	$.0^2 1825$	$.0^2 1769$	$.0^2 1715$	$.0^2 1662$	$.0^2 1610$	$.0^2 1560$	$.0^2 1511$
3.0	$.0^3 3822$	$.0^3 3689$	$.0^3 3560$	$.0^3 3436$	$.0^3 3316$	$.0^3 3199$	$.0^3 3087$	$.0^3 2978$	$.0^3 2873$	$.0^3 2771$
3.5	$.0^4 5848$	$.0^4 5620$	$.0^4 5400$	$.0^4 5188$	$.0^4 4984$	$.0^4 4788$	$.0^4 4599$	$.0^4 4417$	$.0^4 4242$	$.0^4 4073$
4.0	$.0^5 7145$	$.0^5 6835$	$.0^5 6538$	$.0^5 6253$	$.0^5 5980$	$.0^5 5718$	$.0^5 5468$	$.0^5 5227$	$.0^5 4997$	$.0^5 4777$

Reproduced with permission from Robert Schlaifer, *Introduction to Statistics for Business Decisions* (New York: McGraw-Hill, 1961), pp. 370–71.

AUTHOR INDEX

SUBJECT INDEX